Statistics Without Maths for Psychology

Visit the *Statistics Without Maths for Psychology, third edition*
Companion Website at **www.booksites.net/dancey** to find
valuable **student** learning material including:

- Multiple choice questions to help test your learning
- SPSS dataset files
- Study guide
- Links to relevant sites on the web

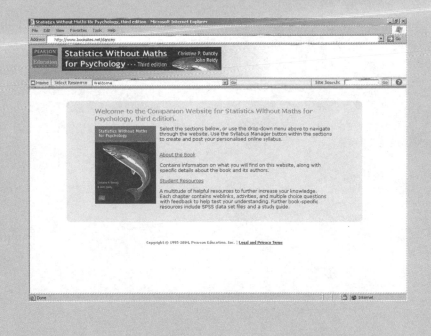

PEARSON
Education

We work with leading authors to develop the
strongest educational materials in Psychology,
bringing cutting-edge thinking and best
learning practice to a global market.

Under a range of well-known imprints, including
Prentice Hall, we craft high quality print and
electronic publications which help readers to understand
and apply their content, whether studying or at work.

To find out more about the complete range of our
publishing, please visit us on the World Wide Web at:
www.pearsoned.co.uk

Statistics Without Maths for Psychology

Using SPSS for Windows™

Third Edition

Christine P. Dancey *University of East London*

John Reidy *Sheffield Hallam University*

Harlow, England • London • New York • Boston • San Francisco • Toronto
Sydney • Tokyo • Singapore • Hong Kong • Seoul • Taipei • New Delhi
Cape Town • Madrid • Mexico City • Amsterdam • Munich • Paris • Milan

Pearson Education Limited
Edinburgh Gate
Harlow
Essex CM20 2JE
England

and Associated Companies throughout the world

Visit us on the World Wide Web at:
www.pearsoned.co.uk

First published 1999
Second edition published 2002
Third edition published 2004

© Pearson Education Limited 2004

ISBN 0 131 24941 X

British Library Cataloguing-in-Publication Data
A catalogue record for this book is available from the British Library

Library of Congress Cataloging-in-Publication Data
Dancey, Christine P.
   Statistics without maths for psychology : using SPSS for Windows / Christine P. Dancey, John Riedy. – 3rd ed.
        p. cm.
   Includes bibliographical references and index.
   ISBN 0-13-124941-X (pbk.)
     1. Psychology–Statistical methods.   2 SPSS for Windows.   3. Psychology–Statistical methods–Computer programs. I. Reidy, John. II. Title.

   BF39.D26 2004
   150′.7′27–dc22

                                                                                  2004044550

10 9 8 7 6 5 4 3 2
08 07 06 05 04

Typeset in 10/12pt Times by 35
Printed by Ashford Colour Press Ltd., Gosport

The publisher's policy is to use paper manufactured from sustainable forests.

Contents

3 Probability, sampling and distributions

4 Hypothesis testing and statistical significance

5 Correlational analysis: Pearson's *r* — 163

Chapter overview — 163

6 Analyses of differences between two conditions: the t-test — 206

Chapter overview — 206

10 Analysis of variance with more than one IV — 321

Chapter overview — 321

11 Regression analysis — 374

Chapter overview — 374

15 Non-parametric statistics 523

Chapter overview 523

Companion Website resources
Visit the Companion Website at **www.booksites.net/dancey**

For students
- Multiple choice questions to help test your learning
- SPSS dataset files
- Study guide
- Links to relevant sites on the web

Also: This website has a Syllabus and Profile Manager, online help, search functions, and email results functions.

Preface to first edition

We wrote this book primarily for our students, most of whom disliked mathematics, and could not understand why they had to learn mathematical formulae when their computer software performed the calculations for them. They were not convinced by the argument that working through calculations gave them an understanding of the test – neither were we. We wanted them to have a conceptual understanding of statistics, and to *enjoy* data analysis. Over the past decade we have had to adapt our teaching to large groups of students, many of whom have no formal training in mathematics. We found it was difficult to recommend some of the traditional statistics textbooks – either they were full of mathematical formulae, and perceived by the students as dull or boring, or they were simple, statistical cookbook recipes, which showed them how to perform calculations, but gave them no real understanding of what the statistics meant. We therefore decided to write this book, which seeks to give students a conceptual understanding of statistics while avoiding the distraction of formulae and calculations.

Another problem we found with recommending statistics textbooks was the over-reliance on the probability value in the interpretation of results. We found it difficult to convince them to take effect size, and confidence intervals, into consideration when the textbooks that were available made no mention of the debates around hypothesis testing, but simply instructed students to say $p < 0.05$ is significant and $p < 0.05$ is not significant! We hope in writing this book that students will become more aware of such issues.

We also wanted to show students how to incorporate the results of their analysis into laboratory reports, and how to interpret results sections of journal articles. Until recently, statistics books ignored this aspect of data analysis. Of course, we realise that the way we have written our example 'results sections' will be different from the way that other psychologists would write them. Students can use these sections to gain confidence in writing their own results, and hopefully they will build on them, as they progress through their course.

We have tried to simplify complex, sometimes very complex, concepts. In simplifying, there is a trade-off in accuracy. We were aware of this when writing the book, and have tried to be as accurate as possible, while giving the simplest explanation. We are also aware that some students do not use SPSS for their data analysis. SPSS, however, is the most commonly used statistical package for the social sciences, and this is why the text is tied so closely to SPSS. Students not using this package should find the book useful anyway.

We hope that students who read the book will not only learn from it, but will also enjoy our explanations and examples.

Preface to second edition

Since we wrote the first edition of *Statistics Without Maths for Psychology* we have been given extensive feedback on both the content and the style and layout of the book. We revised and rewrote substantial sections of this text as a result of this feedback. We have simplified and clarified some of the material, and added new material also. A new chapter introducing factor analysis (PCA) has been added, and the non-parametric statistics have been given a separate chapter to themselves. Revising the book also gave us an opportunity to correct some of the typos that had crept into the first edition! This edition has been updated for use with SPSSFW version 10. We hope you enjoy this edition of *Statistics Without Maths for Psychology*.

The data sets used by the authors within *Statistics Without Maths for Psychology* can be accessed at www.booksites.net/dancey.

Preface to third edition

Since writing the second edition of *Statistics Without Maths for Psychology* we have been given more useful feedback from a number of anonymous and not so anonymous reviewers. Much of this feedback has been very positive indeed and this has helped confirm our belief that this is a book with a very wide appeal. Of course, books which aim for simplicity cannot please everyone – even where feedback was less than positive, this has still proved useful as it is through such critical evaluation that we been able to update and clarify explanations of some of the more difficult concepts. We would like to thank all these reviewers for their comments as we feel that the book has benefited from such close scrutiny from the people who teach statistics. Suggestions by some reviewers were to increase mathematical accuracy. We have taken up their suggestions where possible, but in some cases taking their advice would have led to lengthy and complex explanations that would, we think, have detracted from the text. In some cases we have given references to other sources, in others we have added footnotes. It always has to be remembered that some mathematical accuracy may be lost when giving conceptual explanations and in simplifying difficult material. We hope we have struck a reasonable balance. In addition to clearer explanations in the sections where reviewers have asked for greater clarity, we have included updated examples from the psychological literature along with more multiple choice questions at the end of each chapter. Also, this edition has been updated for use with SPSSFW versions 11 and 12, although it is still appropriate for use if you are using version 10. We hope you find this third edition of *Statistics Without Maths for Psychology* useful and that it enhances your enjoyment of statistics and research in psychology.

Acknowledgements

We would like to acknowledge the valuable contributions made to the two previous editions of *Statistics Without Maths for Psychology* by the Open University Psychology course team, and in particular by Martin Le Voi and Jarrod Hollis. Thanks are also due to Elizabeth Attree, Lisa Heavey, Joan Painter, Mary Fox and Katja Lippert. We are grateful to John Todman for information on pretest–posttest designs, and to Barbara Alexander for providing us with the original data used in Chapter 12.

In addition to the above, we would like to thank the following people for their contributions to the third edition of the book: Aiden P., Brian Everitt, Dr Chong Ho (Alex) Yu, and the anonymous reviewers who took their time to provide us with useful feedback.

Christine P. Dancey
John Reidy

Publisher's Acknowledgements

We are grateful to the following for permission to reproduce copyright material:

SPSS for use of the Screen Images © SPSS Inc. SPSS is a registered trademark and the other product names are trademarks of SPSS Inc; Table on p. 210 from *Statistical Power for Behavioural Sciences*, 2nd edition, Cohen, J. (1988), reproduced by permission of Lawrence Erlbaum Associates, Inc., Publishers; Table 6.4 from the *Journal of Health Psychology*, vol. 1(1), Ketterer, M.W. *et al.* 'Denial of depression as an independent correlate of coronary artery disease', © Sage Publications 1996, reprinted by permission; Table 7.1 from the *Journal of Reproductive and Infant Psychology*, 18(2), pp. 153–62, Maclean *et al.* (2000), with permission from Taylor & Francis Ltd.; Table 8.9 from the *British Journal of Medical Psychology*, vol. 69(2), pp. 101–15, Bish, A. *et al.* (1996) 'The role of coping strategies in protecting individuals against long-term tranquilizer use', with permission from The British Psychological Society and S. Golombok (author); Table 9.6 reprinted from *General Hospital Psychiatry*, 19, pp. 62–4, Sullivan *et al.*, 'Eating attitudes and the irritable bowel syndrome' © 1997, with permission from Elsevier; Table 9.9 from the *British Journal of Psychology*, 87, pp. 653–62, Kebbell, M.R. *et al.* (1996) 'The influence of item difficulty on the relationship between eyewitness confidence and accuracy', with permission from The British Psychological Society and M.R. Kebbell; Table 11.3 from *Psychology and Health*, vol. 12, no. 12, pp. 265–275, Emery *et al.* (1997) with permission from Taylor & Francis Ltd.; Table on p. 431 reprinted from the *Journal of Psychosomatic Research*, 45(2), pp. 171–8, Tang *et al.* © 1998 Elsevier, Inc.; Table 15.4 from *Psychology, Health and Medicine*, vol. 7, no. 1, pp. 99–112, Sherr *et al.* (1996) with permission from Taylor & Francis Ltd.; Table 15.7 from the *Journal of Health Psychology*, vol. 1(4), Treloan *et al.* 'An academic detailing intervention to decrease exposure to HIV infection among health-care workers', © Sage Publications 1996, reprinted by permission; Blackwell Publishing Ltd for the poem "The problem, the implications" by Robert Rosenthal from the article 'Cumulating Psychology: an appreciation of Donald T. Campell' published in *Psychological Science 2*, 1991; and Guardian Services Limited for extract from 'Labour Website Spin Like Orwell's 1984' by David Walker published in the *Guardian* 8th October 2002 © The Guardian.

In some instances we have been unable to trace the owners of copyright material, and we would appreciate any information that would enable us to do so.

Guided Tour of the book and website

Chapter overviews list what you should have achieved or understood by the end of the chapter.

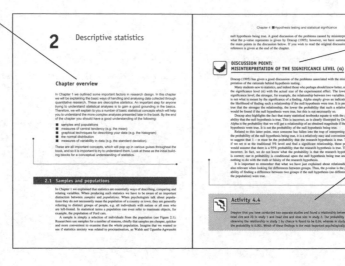

Discussion points stop to explore different ideas or theories in more detail.

Activity boxes provide additional opportunities for you to test your understanding of the theories and ideas being discussed.

Example boxes highlight further the key ideas that are discussed to aid understanding.

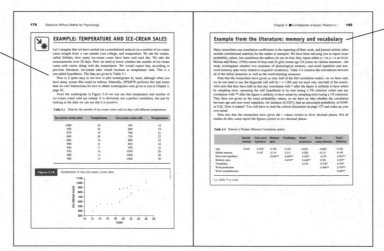

Examples from the literature expand on theories by outlining other areas of research and opinion.

Caution boxes throughout the text warn you of possible problems or issues for consideration.

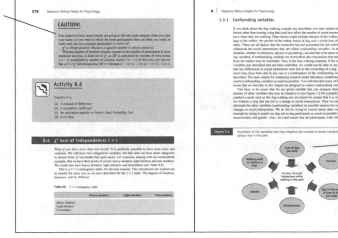

Diagrams and pictures help you to understand (and remember) the text.

Annotated screenshots are useful visual aids illustrating practical examples.

End of chapter **summaries** enable you to recap and review the main points of the chapter.

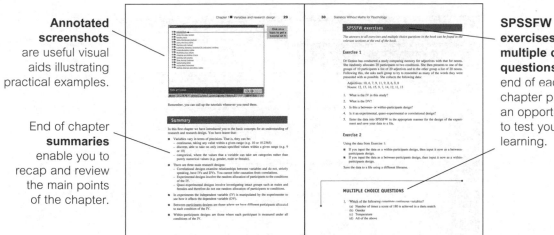

SPSSFW exercises and multiple choice questions at the end of each chapter provide an opportunity to test your learning.

References
provide a guide
to further
reading.

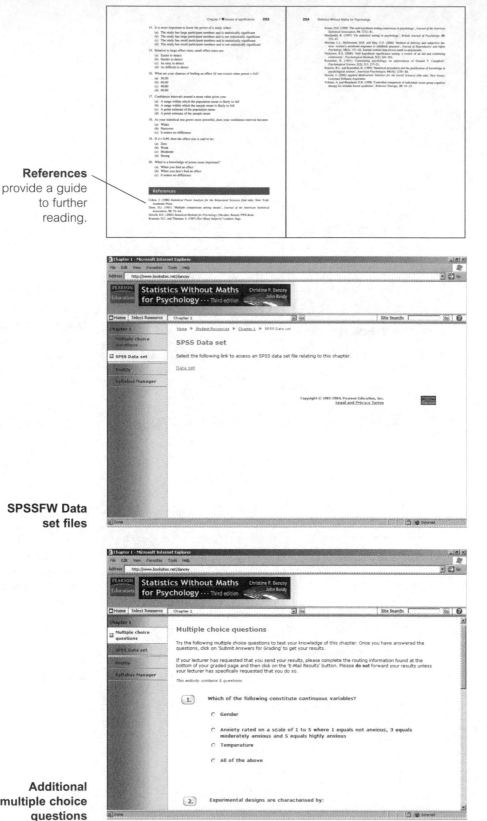

**SPSSFW Data
set files**

**Additional
multiple choice
questions**

1 Variables and research design

Chapter overview

In trying to explain how to use and understand statistics it is perhaps best to start by outlining the principal factors in designing research. We will therefore describe the most important aspects of research design with a view to explaining how they influence the use of statistics. In this chapter, therefore, we aim to teach you about the following:

■ variables: continuous, discrete and categorical
■ independent and dependent variables
■ correlational, experimental and quasi-experimental designs
■ between-participant and within-participant designs.

1.1 Why teach statistics without mathematical formulae?

Statistics as a topic tends to strike fear into the hearts and minds of most social science students and a good many lecturers too. Understanding statistical concepts should, however, be no more difficult than understanding any other theoretical concept (for example, the concept of intelligence). In fact, one would think that understanding a very concrete concept such as the arithmetical mean would be a good deal easier than understanding a rather vague psychological concept such as 'an attitude'. Yet, every year, it seems that the majority of students, who apparently grasp many non-statistical concepts with consummate ease, struggle to understand statistics. Our view is that most people are fearful of statistics because the concepts are lost in the mathematical formulae. We therefore seek to explain statistics in a conceptual way without confusing students with unnecessary mathematical formulae – that is, unnecessary in these days of statistical computer packages. If students wish to learn these formulae to enhance their knowledge, what better platform to have than a conceptual understanding of statistics?

Statistics tend to have a bad reputation, as the quote from Disraeli illustrates: 'There are three sorts of lies: lies, damned lies and statistics.' It is not the statistics that are at fault, however, but rather the way they are used. After all, we do not usually blame the gun for killing someone but the person who pulled the trigger. All too often, particularly in politics, statistics are quoted out of context. This problem is clearly illustrated in the following extract taken from an article published in the *Guardian* in 2002:

Labour website spin 'like Orwell's 1984'
By David Walker

The Labour party has 'systematically manipulated' data on its website to show improvements in health, schooling and other services, according to an unpublished study. Starting in the run-up to last year's election and continuing since, Labour has guided the public to misleading statistics for crime and unemployment as well as spending on schools and hospitals.

Figures have been 'mangled' to give a better impression of Labour's performance at the local level.

In a research paper circulating among academics, after being presented at a recent Political Studies Association conference, four distinguished geographers take apart the website's figures for local areas. Led by professors Danny Dorling of Leeds University and Ron Johnston of Bristol University, the team argue that Labour has consistently adjusted and manipulated data without acknowledging it.

'Rather than appearing to be a necessary series of occasional white lies, it is beginning to look as if the provision of this distorted picture is a longer term party strategy,' the paper says.

Labour's webmasters are compared to Winston Smith, the character in George Orwell's novel 1984, who spent his time in the Ministry of Plenty rewriting history. No individual figure is untrue 'in the strict sense of the word. It is just that the way in which the statistics have been put together – mixing and matching years and areas to present the best possible picture of improvement – is disingenuous overall.'

By typing in a postcode, visitors to Labour's site can access apparently detailed information about where they live. But some of the figures presented refer to the UK or England as a whole, some to entire regions, some to council areas, but very few to the specific area let alone the street where people live.

Website visitors are told of increases in nurses, without being told the figures relate to NHS regions rather than individual hospitals. Literacy and numeracy improvements are stated, without the public being told they refer to entire local education authority areas – which can contain up to 20 parliamentary constituencies. Crime figures on the website are not specific to postcodes but to police force areas, some very large, or even to England and Wales as a whole.

(Extract from the *Guardian*, 8 October 2002)[1]

The study referred to in this report was in fact published in 2002 in *The Political Quarterly* (Dorling *et al.*, 2002).

This article clearly illustrates the importance of viewing statistics in the correct context. If we say to you, for example, that the average (mean) height of the adult male is 5 ft 8 in (173 cm), this may be meaningful for British men but not necessarily for men from African pygmy tribes where the average height can be as low as 4 ft 9 in (145 cm).

1.2 Variables

We have explained a very important aspect of statistics: that they are only meaningful in a context. But what is it that statistics actually do? Essentially, statistics give us information about factors that we can measure. In research the things that we measure are called *variables*.

---

[1] See page 34.

Variables are the main focus of research in science. A variable is simply something that can vary, that is, can take on many different values or categories. Examples of variables are gender, typing speed, top speed of a car, number of reported symptoms of an illness, temperature, attendances at rock festivals (e.g. Ozzfest), level of anxiety, number of goals scored in football matches, intelligence, number of social encounters while walking your dog, amount of violence on television, occupation and favourite colours. These are all things that we can measure and record and that vary from one situation or person to another.

But why are we interested in variables? We are generally interested in variables because we want to understand why they vary as they do. In order to achieve such understanding we need to be able to measure and record the changes in these variables in any given situation.

1.2.1 Characteristics of variables

You will notice from the examples of variables above that they have different characteristics. Whereas you can measure temperature in terms of Fahrenheit or Celsius and put a number to it, you cannot meaningfully do this for type of occupation. This represents one important characteristic of variables, that is, how precisely they can be measured. At the most precise end of the scale variables are said to be *continuous*, that is, they can take *any* value within a given range. Or more accurately, the variable itself doesn't change in discrete jumps. A good example of a continuous variable is temperature. This is because you could measure the temperature as, say, 40 °C or you could measure it more accurately as, say, 40.2558 °C. Another less obvious example is the measurement of the amount of violence on television. We could measure this in terms of the amount of time that violence appears on screen per day. If measured in this way, in terms of time the variable could take on any value in terms of seconds or parts of seconds, e.g. 1000 s or 1000.1235672 s per day. The only limitation in the precision of measurement of such variables is the accuracy of the measuring instrument. With continuous variables there is an assumption that the underlying variable itself is continuous, even if the way in which we measure it is not. Of the examples given earlier whereas temperature, level of anxiety, top speed of a car, typing speed, and intelligence could be regarded as continuous the rest could not (see Table 1.1).

Table 1.1 Examples of continuous, discrete and categorical variables

Continuous	Discrete	Categorical
■ Temperature	■ Number of reported symptoms of an illness	■ Gender
■ A car's top speed	■ Number of cars owned	■ Occupation
■ Typing speed	■ Number of goals scored in a football match	■ Favourite colour
■ Intelligence	■ Number of social encounters while walking your dog	■ Type of fast food restaurant
■ Level of anxiety	■ Attendances at heavy rock festivals	
	■ Number of children in a family	

A variable could also be *discrete*, that is, it can take on only certain discrete values within the range. An example of such a variable is the reported number of symptoms of an illness that a person has. These can only be recorded in terms of presence or absence of symptoms and therefore in terms of whole symptoms present. Another example would be if we chose to measure the amount of violence on television in terms of the number of violent incidents per week. In such a case we could only report number of discrete violent incidents. We could not use it to measure in terms of fractions of a violent incident: therefore violence on television measured this way is termed a discrete variable. Of the examples given earlier the most obvious discrete variables are number of reported symptoms of an illness, number of social encounters while walking your dog, attendance at a rock festival, number of cars owned, number of children per family and number of goals scored in a game of football.

One problem that arises when thinking about continuous and discrete variables is confusing the underlying variable with how it is measured. A variable may in theory be continuous, but the way we measure it will always be discrete, no matter how accurate we do so. We could measure anxiety (a theoretically continuous variable) using a questionnaire (e.g. the State-Trait Anxiety Inventory, Spielberger *et al.*, 1983) where the total score on the questionnaire gives an indication of a person's level of anxiety. Total scores on this questionnaire can only increase in whole units, say from 38 to 39 or from 61 to 62. Thus, the way we have measured anxiety is discrete whereas the underlying variable is assumed to be continuous.

Additionally, often when analysing discrete variables they are treated as if they were continuous. Many of the statistical tests that we use assume that we have continuous variables. Often when a discrete variable can take on many different values within a range (e.g. attendances at heavy rock festivals) they can reasonably be treated as if they were continuous for the sake of statistical testing.

Another type of variable is a *categorical* variable. This is where the values that the variables can take are categories. A good example is gender, which has only two values that it can take: male or female. Categorical variables can also sometimes have many possible values, as in type of occupation (e.g. judges, teachers, miners, grocers, civil servants). When dealing with categorical data we have an infinite number of variables that we might wish to investigate. We could, if we wished to, categorise people on the basis of whether or not they ate chocolate sponge with tomato ketchup at 6.30 this morning, or perhaps (a little more bizarre) whether or not they supported Manchester United Football Club. The only obvious examples of categorical variables given in our list of variables described at the beginning of this section are occupation, gender and favourite colour.

Try to ensure that you understand the different types of variables that you are measuring as this is important when deciding how to analyse data.

1.2.2 Dichotomising continuous and discrete variables

It is often the case that researchers convert continuous or discrete variables into categorical variables. For example, we might wish to compare the spatial ability of tall and short people. We could do this by comparing people who are over 6 ft 4 in (193 cm) with those under 4 ft 10 in (147 cm) on a spatial ability test. Thus, we have chosen points on the continuous scale (height) and decided to compare those participants who score above and below these points (see Figure 1.1).

| **Figure 1.1** | Illustration of the conversion of continuous variables into categorical variables |

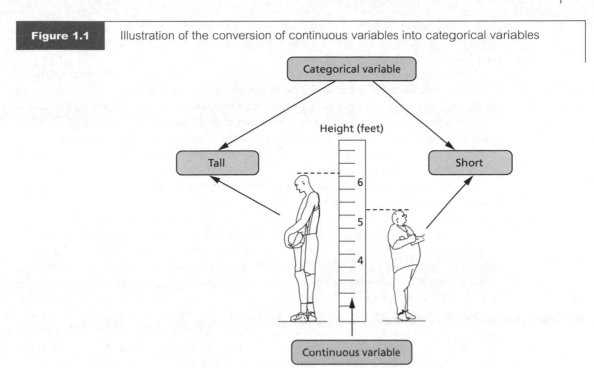

Another example might be to compare the memory ability of anxious and non-anxious individuals. We could measure anxiety levels using a questionnaire; this is a continuous variable measured on a discrete scale. For example, the Hospital Anxiety and Depression Scale has an anxiety scale that ranges from 0 to 21. To convert this to a categorical variable we would simply compare those who score above a certain value (say, 11) with those who score below this value.

This dichotomising (dividing into two categories) of continuous and discrete variables is quite common in psychology as it enables us to find out if there are differences between groups who may be at the extremes of the continuous or discrete variables, e.g. tall and short people. We do not, however, recommend such a practice as it reduces the sensitivity of your statistical analyses. There is a good discussion of such problems in Streiner (2002) and also in Maxwell and Delaney (1993). We mention this here only so that you are aware that it happens in the research literature and so that you will understand what the researchers have done.

DISCUSSION POINT:
DICHOTOMISING CONTINUOUS VARIABLES

Why do researchers dichotomise variables? Streiner (2002) highlights the point that many decisions in psychology, psychiatry and medicine are binary decisions. Binary decisions are those where there are two choices, such as whether or not a person has a mental disorder, whether or not a person has a specific disease, whether a person should be hospitalised or whether a person should be released from hospital. It is often argued that because clinicians have to make such binary decisions it is legitimate to investigate variables in a binary way. Such reasoning is used to support the widespread practice of dichotomising continuous variables.

Streiner argues that we do not have to view the sorts of decisions that clinicians make as binary. He suggests that it would be better to think of mental illness, for example, as being on a continuum: the more symptoms you have the more affected you are. We should then measure such constructs on continua rather than dichotomising them. That is, rather than using questionnaires to categorise individuals we could use the questionnaires to get a measure of where they fall on a continuum. Such information can then be utilised in our decisions for treating individuals, etc.

An example may illustrate dichotomisation better. We suggested earlier that we could categorise individuals as anxious or non-anxious on the basis of their scores on a questionnaire. Researchers investigating anxiety regularly utilise questionnaires in this way. Those participants who score high on the questionnaire are classed as high in anxiety whereas those who have low scores are classed as low in anxiety. The 'median-split' method is often used in this regard, where those participants who score above the median are categorised as anxious and those who score below the median as non-anxious (e.g. Egloff and Hock, 2003).

Streiner argues that the practice of dichotomising continuous variables tends to lead to research that is low in power (we cover power further in Chapters 4 and 7). The reason for this is that it results in us losing a lot of information about participants. For example, suppose two individuals score 20 and 38 on an anxiety inventory and that when we come to classify them they are both classed as low in anxiety (they both fall below the median). In any subsequent analyses based upon this categorisation both of these participants are treated as being identical in terms of their anxiety levels, i.e. they are both non-anxious. According to our questionnaire, however, there is a very large difference between them in terms of their actual anxiety levels. Treating these two individuals as the same in terms of anxiety level does not seem to make sense. It would be much more sensible to try to include their actual anxiety scores in any statistical analyses that we conduct.

Additionally, we may find that there is a larger difference in terms of anxiety between the two participants classed as non-anxious than there is between two participants where one is classed as anxious and one is not. For example, suppose our median was 39, all those scoring above 39 are classed as anxious and those who score below 39 are non-anxious. We can see here the non-anxious person who has a score so 38 has much more in common with an anxious person whose score is 41 than they do with another non-anxious person whose has a score of 20. Yet in any subsequent analyses the participants with scores of 20 and 38 are classified as identical in terms of anxiety and these are classed as equally different from the person who has a score of 41. This just does not make any sense.

Streiner also highlights research that has shown that analyses using dichotomous variables are about 67% as efficient as analyses using the original continuous/discrete measures. This is an incredible loss of sensitivity in the study. It means that you are only two-thirds as likely to detect relationships among variables if you dichotomise continuous variables. This is a serious handicap to conducting research. Moreover, loss of power is not the only problem that arises when dichotomising variables. Maxwell and Delaney (1993) have shown that such a practice can actually lead to spurious findings arising from statistical analyses.

Therefore, we advise you against dichotomising continuous variables.

Activity 1.1

Which of the following are continuous, which are discrete and which are categorical?

■ Wind speed
■ Types of degree offered by a university
■ Level of extraversion
■ Makes of car
■ Football teams
■ Number of chess pieces 'captured' in a chess game
■ Weight of giant pandas
■ Number of paintings hanging in art galleries

The correct answers can be found at the end of the book.

1.3 Research designs

There are a number of different statistical techniques that we use to analyse the data we have collected in research. We will be introducing you to some of the most widely used techniques in this book. Many of these techniques have complex mathematical formulae used to calculate the statistics involved; we will not be teaching these formulae, however, preferring to help you understand the techniques from a conceptual point of view.

One of the biggest factors in determining which statistical tests you can use to analyse your data is the way you have designed your study. There are several ways to design a study and the way you do so can have a great influence on the sorts of statistical procedures that are available to you. Sometimes researchers wish to look for differences between two groups of participants on a particular variable and at other times they might want to see if two variables are related in some way. An example of looking for differences between groups might be the research reported by McNicholas and Collis (2000). In this study they compared the number of social encounters that people had while walking a dog with social encounters without a dog. They found that walking with a dog increased the number of social encounters. An example of research looking for relationships would be the research reported by Walsh and Ugumba-Agwunobi (2002). In this study, amongst other things, they investigated the relationship between statistics anxiety and procrastination. They found that there were relationships between various components of statistics anxiety (e.g. fear of statistics teachers) and procrastination. The statistical tests that we would use in these examples are called *difference tests* and *correlational tests* respectively. The way you design your study will influence which of these sorts of tests you can use. In the following sections we will take you through several ways of designing studies and indicate which sorts of tests are available to the researcher conducting such studies.

1.3.1 Confounding variables

If you think about the dog-walking example just described, you may realise that there are factors other than owning a dog that could also affect the number of social encounters people have when they are walking. Other factors might include shyness of the walker, attractiveness of the walker, the gender of the walker, breed of dog and a whole host of other variables. These are all factors that the researcher has not accounted for but which may have influenced the social interactions; they are called *confounding variables*. In any research situation, whether in chemistry, physics or psychology, account has to be taken of confounding variables. If confounding variables are overlooked, the conclusions that may be drawn from the studies may be unreliable. Thus, in the dog-walking example, if the confounding variables just described had not been controlled, we would not be able to say for certain that any differences in social interactions were due to the ownership of a dog. The differences may have been due to any one or a combination of the confounding variables just described. The main reason for conducting research under laboratory conditions is to try to control confounding variables as much as possible. You will find that many of the research issues that we describe in this chapter are designed to reduce confounding variables.

You have to be aware that for any given variable that you measure there will be a number of other variables that may be related to it (see Figure 1.2 for example). When we conduct a study such as the dog-walking one we cannot be certain that it is walking with (or without) a dog that has led to a change in social interactions. Thus we need to try to eliminate the other variables (confounding variables) as possible reasons for our observed changes in social interactions. We do this by trying to control these other variables, for example by trying to match our dog and no dog participants as much as possible on shyness, attractiveness and gender. Also, we could ensure that all participants walk with the same

| Figure 1.2 | Illustration of the variables that may influence the number of social interactions a person has in the park |

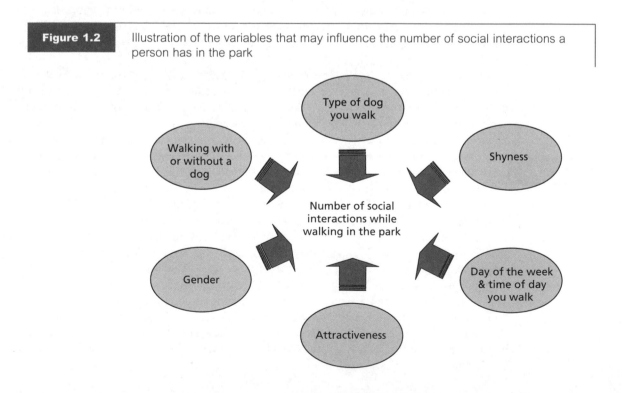

type of dog and that they do their walks at the same time and same day of the week. Once we have controlled these other variables then we may be more confident in our conclusions that walking with a dog influences the number of social interactions a person will have.

1.3.2 Correlational designs

We stated earlier that the major goal of science is to understand variables. More specifically we wish to understand how and why certain variables are related to each other. Perhaps the simplest way to examine such relationships between variables is by use of correlational designs. In such a design we measure the variables of interest and then see how each variable changes in relation to the changes in the other variables. An example might help to illustrate this. Earlier in this section we briefly described the study by by Walsh and Ugumba-Agwunobi (2002) investigating the relationship between statistics anxiety and procrastination. In this study the researchers measured statistics anxiety with the Statistics Anxiety Ratings Scale (STAR – Cruise *et al.*, 1985) and procrastination with the Aitken's Procrastination Inventory (Aitken, 1982). The STARS measures six components of statistics anxiety including fear of statistics teachers, computational self-concept, test and class anxiety, fear of asking questions, interpretation anxiety and worth of statistics. They conducted correlational analyses and found that there were relationships between procrastination and three components of statistics anxiety (the fear of statistics teachers, fear of asking for help and interpretation anxiety). The researchers concluded that fear of statistics and procrastination were *correlated*. That is, as one of the variables changed, so did the other one; the two variables were said to *co-vary*. You should note that the terms 'related', 'correlated' and 'co-varied' are often used interchangeably.

Another excellent example of research conducted using correlational designs is that into the relationship between smoking and cancer. It has generally been found that, as smoking increases, so does the incidence of cancer. Therefore there is a relationship between number of cigarettes smoked and the chances of getting cancer.

If you have used a correlational design then the sorts of statistical techniques you will probably use will be the Pearson product moment correlation coefficient, or perhaps Spearman's rho correlation coefficient. These are covered later in Chapters 5 and 15 respectively.

| Figure 1.3 | Relationship between statistics anxiety and procrastination |

1.3.3 Causation

The issue of causation is a tricky one in science and even more so when we use correlational designs. One of the important aims of science is to establish what causes things to happen. In all branches of science researchers are trying to discover causal relationships between variables. For example, Newton produced an elegant theory to explain what causes apples to fall to the ground: he established a causal relationship between the falling apple and gravity. In much research in psychology we are also trying to establish such causal relationships. When we use correlational designs, however, it is difficult to establish whether a change in one variable causes a change in another variable. The reason for this is that in such designs we are simply observing and recording changes in variables and trying to establish whether they co-vary in some meaningful way. Because we are merely observing how variables change, it is difficult (though not impossible) to establish the causal relationships among them. To be able to do this more easily we need to be able to manipulate one variable (change it systematically) and then see what effect this has on the other variables. We will discuss this approach further in the next section.

One of the golden rules of correlational designs is that *we cannot infer causation from correlations*. The smoking industry has used this weakness of correlations to claim that there is no direct evidence that smoking causes cancer. Strictly speaking, they may be correct, because the studies have mainly been correlational. But given the amount of research that has substantiated a causal relationship between smoking and cancer, one would be foolish to ignore the research and trust the people who are making a profit from selling tobacco.

Finding that statistics anxiety and procrastination are related does not tell us much about the causal relationship between these two variables. It could be that increases in statistics anxiety cause increases in procrastination or maybe changes in procrastination cause changes in statistics anxiety. Alternatively, there might be other variables, such as neuroticism, that causes changes in both statistics anxiety and procrastination (see Figure 1.4). You can see, therefore, that establishing that a relationship exists between two variables does not necessarily tell us much about cause and effect.

Another example of this limitation in correlational designs is the relationship between anxiety and depression. It has been found in a great many studies that anxiety and depression are highly related (see Clark and Watson 1991). People who report high levels of anxiety also report high levels of depression. Could we say, then, that depression causes anxiety or anxiety causes depression? No, we could not. It is quite likely that some intervening variable links these two mood states. In fact, it has been found that anxiety

| Figure 1.4 | Possible causal relationships between neuroticism, statistics anxiety and procrastination |

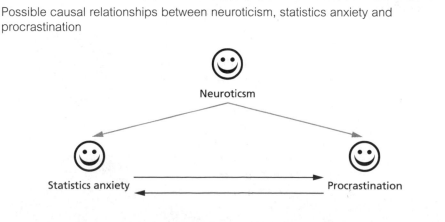

| **Figure 1.5** | Illustration of the common elements shared by anxiety and depression and the absence of a causal link between them |

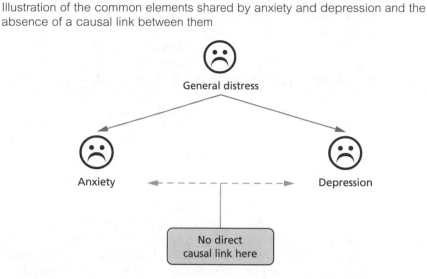

and depression have a common general distress element to them and it is this that explains the large relationship between them (see Figure 1.5).

It is possible to assess causal relationships using correlational designs but these situations are much more complex than simple correlational designs indicated in this section and involve measuring the variables at various time points.

1.3.4 The experimental design

In order for us to establish causal relationships between variables more easily we need to manipulate one of the variables systematically and see what effect it has on the other variables. Such a process is essentially that undertaken in *experimental designs*.

One of the most widely used designs in science is the experimental design, also called the *true experiment*. If you think back to the typical experiment you conducted or read about in chemistry or physics at school, this epitomises the experimental design. For example, we might want to see what happens to sodium when we expose it to air and compare this with when it is exposed to water. We would observe a slow reaction in the 'air' condition (the shiny surface of the sodium becomes dull) and a rapid reaction in the 'water' condition (the sodium fizzes about the surface of the water and may ignite). In an experiment we have one variable that we are measuring (the state of the sodium, called the dependent variable), and we wish to find out what effect another variable, called the independent variable (e.g. what sodium is exposed to), has on it. The variable manipulated by the experimenter is called the *independent variable* (IV), that is its value is not dependent upon (is independent of) the other variables being investigated. The other variable in such an experiment is called the *dependent variable* (DV). It is called the dependent variable because it is assumed to be dependent upon the value of the IV. Indeed, the purpose of the experiment is to establish or dismiss such dependence.

We can conduct such research in psychology: for example, we could find out whether dog-walking does influence the number of social encounters. If we conducted this study we could get a group of individuals and randomly allocate them to walking with a dog and walking alone. We might predict that walking with a dog would lead to more social encounters than walking alone. We have thus set up a hypothesis that we could test with statistics analyses.

Let us assume that we have conducted the above experiment and have found that the dog walkers have more social encounters than the walkers without dogs. It thus looks like we will have support for our prediction. However, there are a number of other factors that may have led to a difference in the number of social encounters between the two conditions (see Figure 1.2). How do we know that the difference we observe has been caused by our manipulation of the independent variable rather than one of the possible confounding variables? The answer is that we don't know. We can, though, limit the impact of the confounding variables upon our study by randomly allocating the participants to the conditions of our IV. By randomly allocating participants to conditions we can reduce the probability that the two groups differ on things like shyness, attractiveness and gender and thus eliminate these as possible causes of the difference in number of social encounters between our groups. If we randomly allocate participants to conditions we can be more confident in our ability to infer a causal relationship between the IV and the DV (walking with/without a dog and number of social encounters). It is this element of random allocation that makes experimental designs so useful for determining causal relationships among variables.

Thus, one of the major defining features of an experimental design is the *random allocation* of participants to conditions. To employ random allocation in the dog-walking example above, we could give each person who is participating a random number generated on a computer. We could then ask all those students whose number is below a certain number to walk with a dog and all those above the number to walk without a dog. In this way we would then have randomly allocated the participants to each of the two conditions.

Of course random allocation is most useful in controlling inter-personal factors such as shyness. There are other factors relating to experimental design that cannot be controlled by random allocation of participants to conditions. Take another look at Figure 1.2 and you will notice that confounding variables such as time of day and type of dog would not be controlled by random allocation of participants to conditions of the IV. These are issues that would need to addressed through other aspects of experimental design such as ensuring that a variety of types of dogs were used in the study and that both conditions were run at the same time of day and on the same days of the week.

1.3.5 Quasi-experimental designs

Often in psychology we want to look at variables that we cannot directly manipulate. If we want to compare males and females in some way, we cannot manipulate the group to which each participant belongs. We cannot randomly allocate participants to the male and female conditions; they are already either male or female. We therefore, strictly speaking, do not have an experimental design. To highlight the fact that such designs are not strictly experimental, they are called *quasi-experimental* designs.

As an example, suppose we conducted the dog-walking study above and we wanted to try to remove gender as a confounding variable. We could conduct a follow-up study where we try to find out whether females have more social encounters when walking (without dogs) than males. You can see that in this study the participants are not randomly allocated to conditions; they were already either female or male. We thus have a quasi-experimental design. If we found that the females had more social encounters than males, then we could argue that being female is more likely to encourage social interaction than being male.

One of the problems with quasi-experiments is that, because participants are not randomly allocated to the various conditions that make up the IV, we cannot be certain that our manipulation of the IV (or, should we say, pseudo-manipulation) is responsible for any differences between the various conditions. That is, it is harder to infer causation from quasi-experimental designs than from experimental designs. For instance, in the previous example, it could be that there is some other factor beyond gender that distinguishes the two groups (size, for example). It could be that females are seen as less threatening because they tend to be smaller than males. Thus, an important confounding variable has crept into our study. Because of the increased risk of confounding variables associated with quasi-experimental designs, experimental studies are to be preferred whenever they are possible.

If you are ever unsure whether you are dealing with an experimental or a quasi-experimental design, then look for random allocation of participants to conditions. If it is not a feature of the design, then you are most likely dealing with a quasi-experimental design.

Another important reason for preferring experimental to quasi-experimental designs is that many of the statistical techniques that we use assume that we have randomly allocated participants to conditions, and thus non-random allocation of participants may reduce the validity of the conclusions that are based upon these statistical techniques. In practice, this is not too much of a problem; but, you do need to be aware that the problem exists.

If you have used an experimental or a quasi-experimental design then some of the statistical techniques that are available to you are the t-test, Mann–Whitney U test, Wilcoxon test and analysis of variance (ANOVA). These are all covered later in this book.

1.3.6 Overview of research designs

We have now described three major research designs and how they influence the different types of statistical analyses we can use. Table 1.2 gives a brief summary of the main features of these designs along with the types of statistical tests that would be appropriate to use with such designs.

Table 1.2 Overview of the main features of the various research designs

Designs	Characteristics	Statistical test
Experimental	■ Manipulated IV ■ Random allocation of participants to groups ■ Analysis by comparison between groups	■ t-tests ■ ANOVA ■ Mann–Whitney U test
Quasi-experimental	■ Pseudo-manipulation of IV ■ Non-random allocation of participants ■ Analysis by comparison between groups	■ t-tests ■ ANOVA ■ Mann–Whitney U test ■ Wilcoxon
Correlational	■ Investigates the degree to which variables co-vary ■ Cannot infer causation from correlations ■ Analysed using correlation tests	■ Pearson's product moment correlation ■ Spearman's rho

Activity 1.2

Classify the following studies as either correlational, experimental or quasi-experimental:

(a) Relationship between caffeine intake and incidence of headaches
(b) Difference between males and females in verbal ability
(c) Effect on exam performance of participants being randomly assigned to high-noise and no-noise exam conditions
(d) Difference in self-esteem of tall and short people
(e) Relationship between stress and hours spent working
(f) Difference in anxiety scores between two randomly allocated groups of participants where one group is taught relaxation techniques and the other is not

1.4 Between-participants and within-participants designs

Another important feature of research designs is whether you get each participant to take part in more than one condition. Suppose we return to our example of dog-walking and social encounters. Here we have an experiment where the IV is whether the participants are walking a dog and the DV is the number of social encounters.

How would you allocate participants to the conditions in such an experiment?

■ You will recall that we suggested that the best thing to do would be to allocate participants randomly to the dog-walking and no-dog conditions.
■ There is an alternative, however, and that is to get each participant to walk both with a dog and again without a dog.

The former procedure is called a *between-participants design* (also sometimes known as an *independent* or *unrelated* design); the latter is called a *within-participants design* (sometimes called a *repeated measures* or *related* design). When deciding which of these designs to use you should bear in mind the advantages and disadvantages of each.

1.4.1 Within-participants designs

The main advantage of using within-participants designs is that you are able to control for many inter-individual confounding variables. When you use different groups of people in each condition you run the risk of there being some variable other than your IV that also distinguishes between your groups. You would, if this happened, have a confounding variable. When you use a within-participants design you have much greater control over such variables. Because you have the same people in all your conditions of the IV there will be much less extraneous variation between your conditions. By and large the same person will bring the same problems or qualities to all conditions of your IV.

A second very attractive point about using within-participants designs is that you need to find fewer participants in order to complete your research. For example, if you have two conditions and you would like a minimum of 12 people per condition, you would need 24 people if you used a between-participants design, but only 12 with a within-participants design. As you can probably imagine, if you are conducting a costly piece of research then this is an important consideration.

It is not, however, all rosy in the within-participants garden. If you think about the dog-walking study being run as a within-participants design you might be able to identify some possible problems. It could be the case that, if you use the same people in both conditions, familiarity with the walk and perhaps other people on the walking route will encourage them to talk to the participant. Thus, in the second condition the participants may have more social encounters because of familiarity rather than whether they had a dog. They may also start to get bored or tired when completing the walk in the second condition, which may also have an effect on the number of social encounters they have. These factors are thus confounding variables and could make the data difficult to interpret. Any differences in social encounters that you find between your two conditions may be due to these factors rather than the experimental manipulation of the IV. These are called *order effects*.

One way to eliminate order effects is to introduce *counterbalancing* into your design. In counterbalancing you get one half of your participants to complete the first condition followed by the second conditon. You then get the other half of your participants to do the two conditions in the opposite order, second condition followed by the first condition. To introduce counterbalancing in the dog-walking study, you could get half of the participants to walk with a dog first and then without the dog. You could then get the other half of the participants to walk first without the dog and then with the dog. Any practice, fatigue or boredom effects would thus be spread across both conditions of the IV and would therefore no longer constitute a confounding variable (see Figure 1.6). You also still have each participant undertaking the walk under both conditions and have therefore retained all the advantages of using a within-participants design.

| **Figure 1.6** | Illustration of the way order effects can be eliminated using counterbalancing |

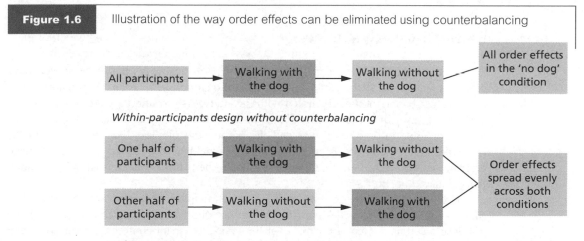

Within-participants design without counterbalancing

Within-participants design with counterbalancing

Another limitation of within-participants designs is that having participants take part in both conditions means that they are more likely to realise the purpose of the experiment. This is a problem because participants usually want to do what the experimenter wants them to and so may perform how they believe they should do rather than how they would normally have done. These are called *demand effects*. The reason why this is more likely in a within-participants design is that each participant is exposed to more of the experimental procedure than in the equivalent between-participants design. To a certain extent counterbalancing can also reduce but not necessarily eliminate such demand effects.

A further problem associated with within-participants designs is that you cannot use them in many quasi-experimental designs. For example, if you wanted to compare social encounters experienced by males and females while out walking you could not use a within-participants design. You cannot have one person being both male and female on two separate occasions, and so one person cannot take part in both conditions (unless of course they have a sex change between taking part in the two conditions).

Activity 1.3

How would you introduce counterbalancing into the following study?

A study is conducted that tests the effects of motivation on performance in a mirror drawing task. Participants are asked to trace the outline of a star using mirror drawing equipment. The time taken to complete the tracing of the star and the number of errors are recorded. Participants then have to complete the task again, but this time they are offered £5 if they complete the task in a faster time and with fewer errors.

1.4.2 Between-participants designs

One of the important features of between-participants designs is that because you have different groups of participants in each condition of the IV, each participant is less likely to get bored, tired or frustrated with the study. As a result, they are more likely to perform at an optimum level throughout. In a similar vein, your research is going to be less susceptible to practice effects and the participants are less likely to work out the rationale for the study. Between-participants designs therefore reduce order and demand effects, and you can, to a large extent, eliminate these factors as confounding variables from your study.

On the negative side, you will need more participants than you would for a completely within-participants design. Also, if you use different participants in each condition you lose a certain degree of control over the inter-participant confounding variables. For example, suppose we conducted the dog-walking study described in the previous section as a between-participants design. What if we did find that walking a dog leads to more social encounters? Before we can accept this at face value we have to ensure that there are no confounding variables. An important confounding variable in such a study might be the shyness of the walkers. It could be the case that, by chance, those in the no-dog condition were more shy and therefore it could be this variable that led to the lack of social encounters. If we had done this experiment as a within-participants design we would be able to control this confounding variable as each person walks with and without a dog. This means that the overall level of shyness is the same under both conditions and is thus not a confounding variable.

From the above discussion it can be seen that one of the problems of between-participants designs is that different people bring different characteristics to the experimental setting. When we are randomly allocating participants to conditions we might, by chance, allocate all participants with one characteristic to one group, and this might confound our results. The statistical techniques that we describe in this book give us an indication of the probability of such circumstances arising in our research.

Table 1.3 gives a summary of the advantages and disadvantages of within- and between-participants designs. It should be apparent that the advantages of within-participants designs tend to be disadvantages in between-participants designs and vice versa. When deciding upon a design for some research your decision about which to use needs to take these factors into account.

Table 1.3   Summary of the advantages and disadvantages of between- and within-participants designs

Design	Advantages	Disadvantages
Between-participants	■ Relative absence of practice and fatigue effects ■ Participants less likely to work out the purpose of the study	■ You need more participants ■ There is not as much control of confounding variables between conditions
Within-participants	■ Need fewer participants ■ Greater control of confounding variables between conditions	■ Increased likelihood of practice or fatigue effects ■ Participants more likely to guess the purpose of the study

Activity 1.4

How would you design a study to investigate a causal relationship between caffeine and mathematical ability?

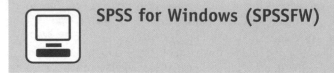

SPSS for Windows (SPSSFW)

This section provides a brief introduction to SPSS for Windows and explains how to enter and save some data into a file. It also explains the difference between entering data for between-participants and within-participants designs.

Basics

First you may need to know some basics about Windows-compatible software. Windows is a graphic user interface that allows the user to manipulate icons and textual information on the screen. Many programs, such as SPSS, present you with a number of different 'windows', which you are able to manipulate as and when you need to.

When you start up SPSS for Windows version 10, 11 or 12 (SPSSFW) you will be presented with a box asking you what you want to do with SPSSFW.

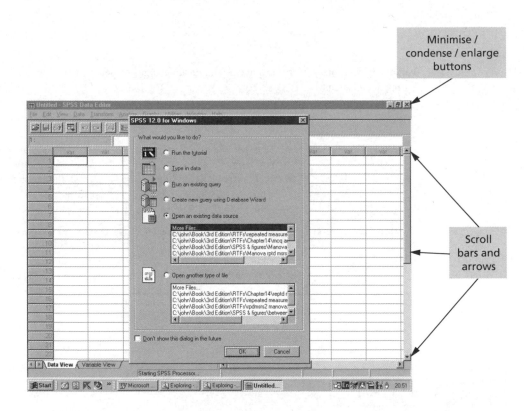

The first thing you need to decide is whether you want to open an existing datafile or input some new data. To open an existing file select the *Open an existing data source* option from the *What would you like to do?* dialogue box. You should then select the relevant file and press *OK* to continue. If you want to enter new data select the *Type in data* option and click on *OK*. Once you click on *OK* you will be presented with the following screen:

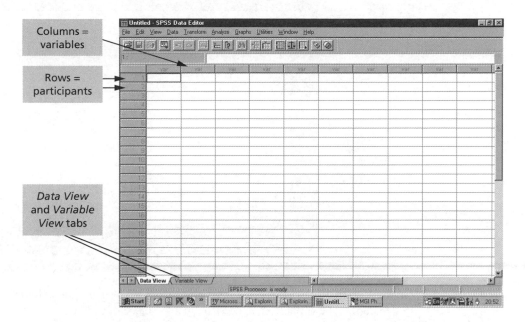

You may find that the active window is too small to display all the information available. You can increase the size of the active window by clicking on the *Minimise / Condense / Enlarge* buttons (_/⊟/□) in the top right-hand corner of the active window. Here the _ button will minimise the active window, ⊟ will condense an enlarged window, and □ will enlarge a condensed window. Minimising the active window decreases its size to an icon at the bottom of the screen, whereas condensing the window will leave the window open but reduce its size. If the window is already condensed you can see more information in it if you enlarge it by clicking the □ button. If the window is already in its enlarged state and you need to see more information you can scroll through the contents of the active window by clicking on the up and down scrolling arrows.

Data entry

Before you can carry out any analysis you need to enter your data. You will notice that there are *cells* arranged in columns and rows. Each row of data that you input will represent the data from one participant and each column represents the data from one variable. For example, suppose we have run a study looking at the relationship of statistics anxiety to procrastination. Let us assume that we have the following data to input:

Participants:	P1	P2	P3	P4	P5	P6
Statistics anxiety:	55	59	48	60	62	50
Procrastination:	125	132	94	110	140	96

The first thing to do is to set up the variables in SPSSFW. To set up variable names and other features of variables you need to select the *Variable View* tab at the bottom of the screen. The screen will change so that you can set up the variables in your data file.

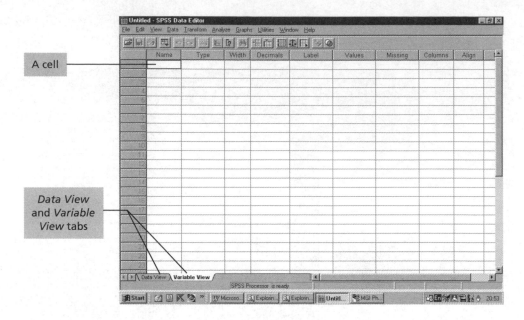

On the *Variable View* screen the rows represent variables and the columns some formatting feature of the variable. You need to input the name of each variable in the first column, headed *Name*. Click on the first row in this column and type in the variable name. We have two variables to set up, the statistics anxiety and procrastination variables. Type in the first variable name: call it *statsanxiety*. You have to stick with the following rules when naming variables:

- No longer than 16 characters long (e.g. *statsanxiety* is OK but *statisticsanxiety* is not)
- If you are using SPSSFW versions 10 and 11, variable names must be no longer than eight characters long, so you could call your variable *statsanx*.
- Must not contain punctuation marks or spaces (e.g. *statsanxiety* is OK but *stats anxiety* is not).
- Do not worry about capital letters as SPSSFW will automatically convert the names into lower case.

Once you have typed *statsanxiety* into the first cell, click on the next cell down and type in the variable name for the procrastination variable. Remember that it should be fewer than 16 characters (eight for SPSSFW 10 and 11) so you can call it *procrastination*. When you have completed this the screen should look similar to that below:

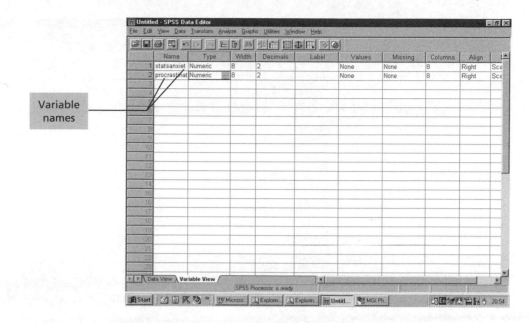

The variables have now been set up, so that you can now enter the data. To be able to do this you need to select the *Data View* tab at the bottom of the screen and this will present you with the following screen:

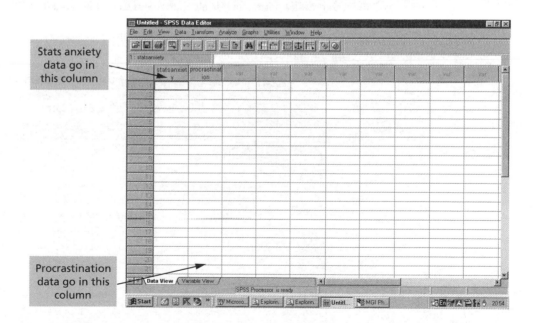

You should notice that the first two columns are labelled *statsanxiety* and *procrastination*. Remember that in the *Data View* screen columns refer to variables and rows refer to participants. Therefore all the data for *statsanxiety* will be input into the first column and that for *procrastination* into the second column. Go ahead and enter the data we presented earlier. Once you have done this the screen should resemble the one that follows:

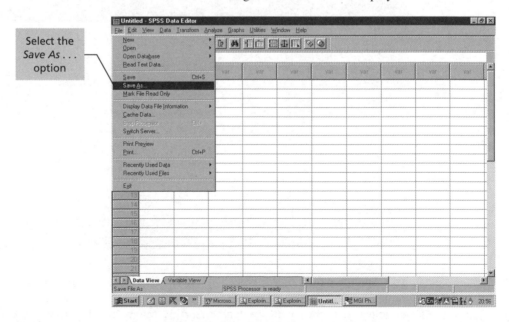

You can see here that the data have been input.

Saving your data

Once you have entered all your data it is a good idea to save it as a datafile. This will avoid having to type it all in again should you wish to do more analyses at some future time. To save your file you should move the mouse pointer over the *File* menu command and click the left button on the mouse. The following menu will then be displayed:

Move the mouse pointer and click on the *Save as . . .* option, and the following dialogue box will appear. It is called a dialogue box because this is where you tell SPSSFW what to do. You should simply type in the filename in the relevant box and click on the *OK* button. Your file will then be saved into this file.

Remember that your datafiles should be named in the following way:

■ the first part is a name that is meaningful for you, e.g. *statsanxiety*
■ the second part should always be *SAV* for a datafile (this is called the file extension)
■ the first and second parts are always separated by a full-stop.

Thus we have called our file *statsanxiety.sav*. Actually, you do not even have to type in the *.sav* part of the name as SPSSFW will automatically do this for you. Whenever you see filenames ending in *.sav* you can be reasonably confident that they are SPSSFW datafiles. If you forget what you have called a file then look for files with the *.sav* file extension.

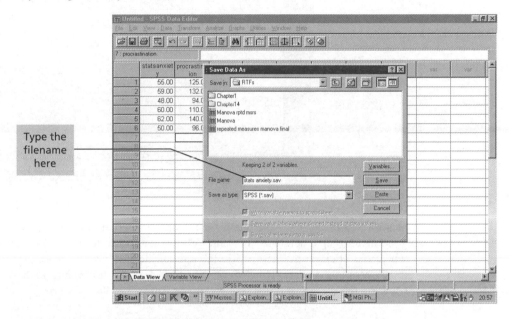

Type the filename here

Inputting data for between-participants and within-participants designs

We have just described how to input and save your data into SPSSFW. However, different designs need to have data input in different ways. We have just described the appropriate manner for correlational designs. If you wish to input data for a between-participants design you should proceed as follows. Let us assume that we have just conducted the dog-walking study as a between-participants design. Suppose we have recorded the following numbers of social encounters in each condition:

Walking with a dog: 9   7   10   12   6   8
Walking without a dog: 4   5   3   6   5   1

In this design walking with or without a dog is the IV and number of social encounters is the DV. When entering the data into SPSSFW we need to set up one variable for the IV and one for the DV. The first thing you need to do then is to name the variables on the *Variable View* screen. When setting up variables the IV variable is the one you need to pay most attention to as it is the one that many students find hard to deal with. When we have different groups of people in each condition of the IV we need to set up a *grouping variable* in SPSSFW. This simply lets SPSSFW know which of the two groups each participant was in. Set up the variables as in the following illustration:

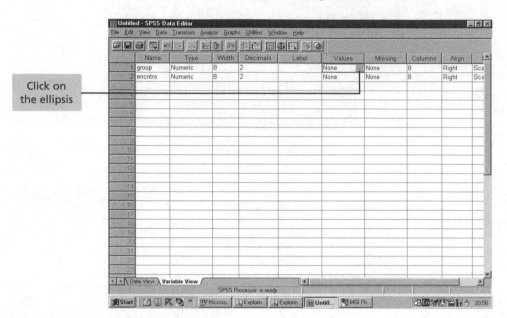

Click on the ellipsis

If we left the variable set up as it stands you might find the printouts difficult to interpret as they will not display any labels for the different conditions of the IV. It is therefore a good idea to input details of the names of the conditions of the IV. You should notice that when you click on the first cell in the column headed *Values* an ellipsis (grey box with three dots in it) appears. This indicates that you can add further information to this column. Click on the ellipsis and you will obtain the following dialogue box:

Type the group (1) number here

Type group name here

Click *Add* to confirm details

We have two conditions for the IV for which we need to assign group numbers. We will label the 'walking with a dog' group as group 1 and the 'walking without a dog' group as group 2 (this is an arbitrary decision). Type a *1* into the *Value* box and *Walking with a dog* in the *Value Label* box. Once you have done this click *Add* and you will see that the details appear in the bottom box. Now type a *2* in the *Value* box and *Walking without a dog* in the *Value Label* box and click *Add*. The dialogue box should look like this:

Click on *OK* and you will be returned to the *Data View* screen. Whenever you want to let SPSSFW know the names of your groups you can do so by adding the information to the *Values* column.

We have now set up the variables. To enter the actual data, click on the *Data View* tab. When we come to input our data into the *group* column, if the person was in the *with a dog* group then we input a *1* in the column, if the person was in the *without a dog* group we input a *2* in the column. You can therefore see that our first column of data contains only 1s and 2s.

In the second column we simply input each person's number of social encounters, as this is our DV. You should be able to tell from looking at the input screen that participant number 4 was in the walking with a dog group (1) and had 12 social encounters. Participant number 12 was in the walking without a dog group (2) and had a lonely walk with only one social encounter.

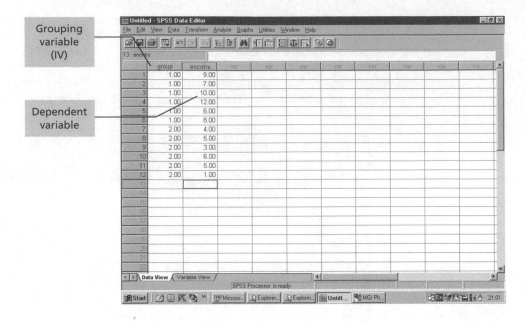

Within-participants designs

When we have within-participants designs we have to input the data in a different way. If we stick with the example above, in a within-participants design each person would complete the walking in both the dog and no-dog conditions. The data for such a study would look something like that shown below:

You might be wondering why we have to input the data differently for different designs. The reason is that each row on the data input screen represents the information from one participant. If you have a between-participants design you need to let SPSSFW know what each participant's score was and also which group they were in. When you have a within-participants design, each participant performs under two conditions and therefore has two scores. You need to let SPSSFW know what both of these scores are. Because each participant performs in both groups you do not need to let SPSSFW know their group with a grouping variable. You can therefore tell the difference between within- and between-participants designs by looking for a grouping variable. If there is one, then it is a between-participants design.

You should notice from the screenshot that we have set up two variables, one for the dog condition and one for the no-dog condition. Also, because we do not have a grouping variable we do not have to give group 'value' labels for any variables in the *Variable View* screen. Setting up the variables with such a design is therefore more straightforward than with between-participants designs.

Using SPSSFW help facilities

It is a good idea to practice using the SPSS for Windows help facilities. You could start off by running the tutorial which is made available to you. You can start the tutorial when you first open SPSSFW. You will notice that the first option on the first dialogue box that you see in SPSSFW is to run the tutorial.

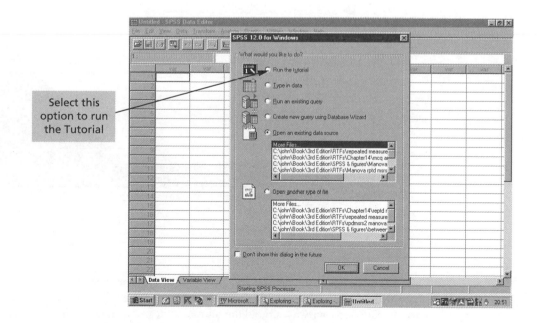

Select this option to run the Tutorial

You can also access the tutorials at any time during an SPSSFW session by clicking on the *Help* menu and selecting the *Tutorial* from there.

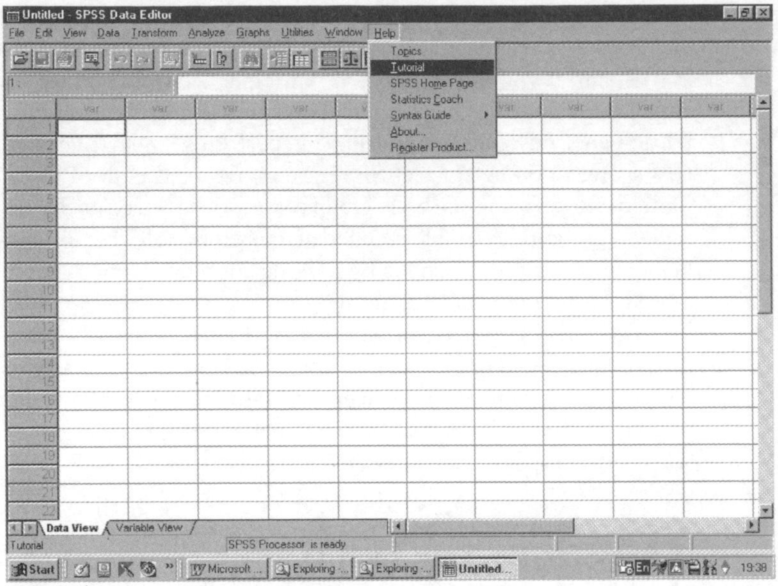

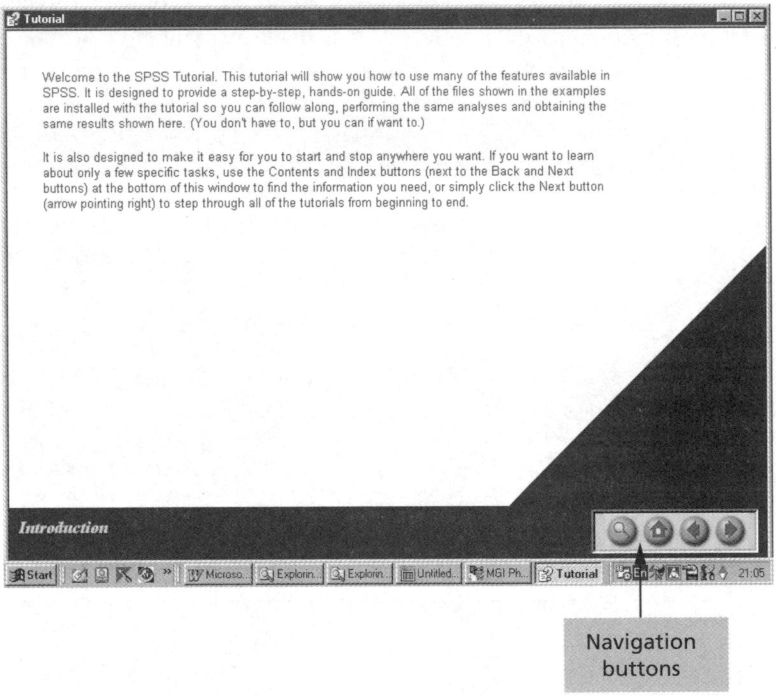

Navigation
buttons

Once you start up the tutorial you enter the Introduction to the help facilities in SPSSFW. You will notice four icons in the bottom right hand corner of the screen. These icons enable you to navigate your way around the tutorial topics. The magnifying glass takes you to an index of tutorial topics, the house takes you to the contents for the tutorial topics, while the left and right arrows take you to the previous and next screens respectively. When you click on the *Contents* icon (house) you will be presented with a contents list. You simply have to click on a topic of interest to get to a tutorial to help you.

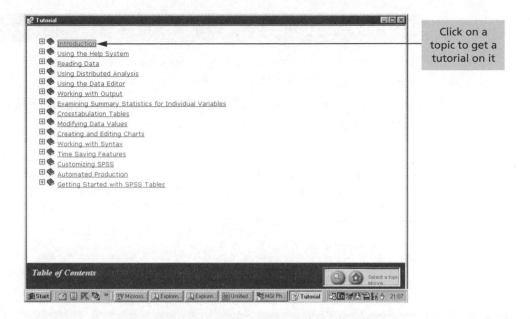

Remember, you can call up the tutorials whenever you need them.

Summary

In this first chapter we have introduced you to the basic concepts for an understanding of research and research design. You have learnt that:

■ Variables vary in terms of precision. That is, they can be:
  – continuous, taking any value within a given range (e.g. 10 or 10.2365)
  – discrete, able to take on only certain specified values within a given range (e.g. 9 or 10)
  – categorical, where the values that a variable can take are categories rather than purely numerical values (e.g. gender, male or female).

■ There are three main research designs:
  – Correlational designs examine relationships between variables and do not, strictly speaking, have IVs and DVs. You cannot infer causation from correlations.
  – Experimental designs involve the random allocation of participants to the conditions of the IV.
  – Quasi-experimental designs involve investigating intact groups such as males and females and therefore do not use random allocation of participants to conditions.

■ In experiments the independent variable (IV) is manipulated by the experimenter to see how it affects the dependent variable (DV).

■ Between-participants designs are those where we have different participants allocated to each condition of the IV.

■ Within-participants designs are those where each participant is measured under all conditions of the IV.

SPSSFW exercises

The answers to all exercises and multiple choice questions in the book can be found in the relevant sections at the end of the book.

Exercise 1

Dr Genius has conducted a study comparing memory for adjectives with that for nouns. She randomly allocates 20 participants to two conditions. She then presents to one of the groups of 10 participants a list of 20 adjectives and to the other group a list of 20 nouns. Following this, she asks each group to try to remember as many of the words they were presented with as possible. She collects the following data:

Adjectives: 10, 6, 7, 9, 11, 9, 8, 6, 9, 8
Nouns: 12, 13, 16, 15, 9, 7, 14, 12, 11, 13

1. What is the IV in this study?

2. What is the DV?

3. Is this a between- or within-participants design?

4. Is it an experimental, quasi-experimental or correlational design?

5. Enter the data into SPSSFW in the appropriate manner for the design of the experiment and save your data to a file.

Exercise 2

Using the data from Exercise 1:

■ If you input the data as a within-participants design, then input it now as a between-participants design.
■ If you input the data as a between-participants design, then input it now as a within-participants design.

Save the data to a file using a different filename.

MULTIPLE CHOICE QUESTIONS

1. Which of the following constitute continuous variables?
   (a) Number of times a score of 180 is achieved in a darts match
   (b) Gender
   (c) Temperature
   (d) All of the above

2. Experimental designs are characterised by:

   (a) Fewer than two conditions
   (b) No control condition
   (c) Random allocation of participants to conditions
   (d) None of the above

3. In a study with gender as the manipulated variable, the IV is:

   (a) Within participants
   (b) Correlational
   (c) Between participants
   (d) None of the above

4. Which of the following are true of correlational designs?

   (a) They have no IV or DV
   (b) They look at relationships between variables
   (c) You cannot infer causation from correlations
   (d) All of the above

5. Which of the following could be considered as categorical variables?

   (a) Gender
   (b) Brand of baked beans
   (c) Hair colour
   (d) All of the above

6. Between-participants designs can be:

   (a) Either quasi-experimental or experimental
   (b) Only experimental
   (c) Only quasi-experimental
   (d) Only correlational

7. Which of the following statements are true of experiments?

   (a) The IV is manipulated by the experimenter
   (b) The DV is assumed to be dependent upon the IV
   (c) They are difficult to conduct
   (d) (a) and (b) above

8. Quasi-experimental designs have:

   (a) An IV and a DV
   (b) Non-random allocation of participants to conditions
   (c) No IV or DV
   (d) (a) and (b) above

9. A continuous variable can be described as:

   (a) Able to take only certain discrete values within a range of scores
   (b) Able to take any value within a range of scores
   (c) Being made up of categories
   (d) None of the above

10. Which of the following are problems associated with within-participants designs?

    (a) There is an increased likelihood of practice or fatigue effects
    (b) Participants are more likely to guess the nature of the experiment
    (c) They cannot be used with quasi-experimental designs
    (d) All of the above

11. According to Streiner (2002) how efficient are studies that dichotimise continuous variables when compared with studies that do not?

    (a) 100%
    (b) 95%
    (c) 67%
    (d) 50%

12. A researcher has just conducted a correlational study investigating the relationship between amount of alcohol drunk by fans of the home team before a football match and the number of goals scored by the home team. They found that there was a relationship between the two variables. Which of the following statements are valid?

    (a) The amount of alcohol drunk was related to the home team's ability to score goals, but we cannot say it caused the team to score the goals
    (b) The home team's ability to score goals is not related to the amount of alcohol but to the amount of cheering by the drunken fans
    (c) The increase in the amount of alcohol drunk caused an increase in the number of goals scored
    (d) All of the above

13. In a within-participants design with two conditions, if you do not use counterbalancing of the conditions then your study is likely to suffer from:

    (a) Order effects
    (b) Effects of time of day
    (c) Lack of participants
    (d) All of the above

14. You have conducted a study that shows that the earlier people get up, the more work they get done. Which of the following are valid conclusions?

    (a) There is not necessarily a causal relationship between getting up early and amount of work done
    (b) People who get up early have a need to get more work done
    (c) Getting up early is the cause of getting more work done
    (d) Both (b) and (c) above

15. Which of the following designs is least likely to enable us to establish causal relationships between variables?

    (a) Experimental design
    (b) Quasi-experimental design
    (c) Correlational design
    (d) Within-participants design

16. Demand effects are possible confounding variables where:

    (a) Participants behave in the way they think the experimenter wants them to behave
    (b) Participants perform poorly because they are tired or bored
    (c) Participants perform well because they have practised the experimental task
    (d) None of the above

17. Suppose you wanted to conduct a study to see if depressed individuals bite their nails more than non-depressed individuals. Which of the following would be the best way to proceed?

    (a) Measure participants' depression with a questionnaire and ask them to give a rating of how much they bite their nails. Then classify participants as 'depressed' or 'non-depressed' on the basis of their questionnaire scores. We could then see if there was a difference in how much they bit their nails
    (b) As per (a) above but don't divide the participants into two groups; use actual depression scores in the analyses and see if there is a relationship between depression and biting nails
    (c) This sort of study is impossible to carry out and so we couldn't proceed with it
    (d) None of the above

18. Which of the following might be suitable IVs in a quasi-experimental study?

    (a) Gender
    (b) Whether or not someone had Generalised Anxiety Disorder
    (c) Students versus non-students
    (d) All of the above

19. In within-participant designs order effects occur when:

    (a) Participants get tired in later conditions
    (b) Participants perform equally well in all conditions
    (c) Participants have trouble obtaining their drinks at the bar
    (d) None of the above

20. Which of the following are problems associated with dichotomising continuous variables?

    (a) Loss of experimental power
    (b) Spurious effects may occur
    (c) There is a serious loss of information
    (d) All of the above

References

Aitken, M. (1982) 'A personality profile of the student procrastinator.' Unpublished Doctoral Dissertation, University of Pittsburg. (*Dissertation Abstracts International*, **43**: 722–732 A).

Clark, L.A. and Watson, D. (1991) 'Tripartite model of anxiety and depression: psychometric evidence and taxonomic implications', *Journal of Abnormal Psychology*, **100**: 316–36.

Cruise, R., Cash, R. and Bolton, D. (1985) 'Development and validation of an instrument to measure statistical anxiety.' Paper presented at the annual meeting of the Statistical Education Section and reprinted in Proceedings of the American Statistical Association.

Dorling, D., Eyre, H., Johnston, R. and Pattie, C. (2002) 'A good place to bury bad news? Hiding the detail in the geography on the Labour Party's website', *The Political Quarterly*, **73**: 476–92.

Egloff, B. and Hock, M. (2003) 'Assessing attention allocation toward threat-related stimuli: a comparison of the emotional Stroop task and the attentional probe task', *Personality and Individual Differences*, **35**: 475–83.

Maxwell, S.E. and Delaney, H.D. (1993) 'Bivariate median splits and spurious statistical significance', *Psychological Bulletin*, **113**: 181–90.

McNicholas, J. and Collis, G.M. (2000) 'Dogs as catalysts for social interactions: robustness of the effect', *British Journal of Psychology*, **91**: 61–70.

Spielberger, C.D., Gorsuch, R.L., Lushene, R., Vagg, P.R. and Jacobs, G.A. (1983) *Manual for the State–Trait Anxiety Inventory (Form Y)*. Palo Alto, CA: Consulting Psychologists Press.

Streiner, D.L. (2002) 'Breaking up is hard to do: the heartbreak of dichotomizing continuous data', *Canadian Journal of Psychiatry*, **47**: 262–6.

Walsh, J.J. and Ugumba-Agwunobi, G. (2002) 'Individual differences in statistics anxiety: the roles of perfectionism, procrastination and trait anxiety', *Personality and Individual Differences*, **33**: 239–51.

Note

[1] Correction to article made by the *Guardian* (published 10th October 2002):

In our report, 'Labour website spin like 'Orwell's 1984', page 7, October 8, we said: "Labour's webmasters are compared to Winston Smith, the character in George Orwell's novel 1984, who spent his time in the Ministry of Plenty rewriting history." In fact, Winston Smith worked for the Ministry of Truth. Among his tasks, however, was 're-adjusting' the figures of the Ministry of Plenty. 'It was not even forgery. It was merely the substitution of one piece of nonsense for another' (page 36 of the Penguin 1983 edition).

In our article we referred to the report under discussion as "unpublished". In fact, it appears in the October edition (Volume 73, issue 4) of Political Quarterly, published by Blackwells.

2 Descriptive statistics

Chapter overview

In Chapter 1 we outlined some important factors in research design. In this chapter we will be explaining the basic ways of handling and analysing data collected through quantitative research. These are *descriptive statistics*. An important step for anyone trying to understand statistical analyses is to gain a good grounding in the basics. Therefore, we will explain to you a number of basic statistical concepts which will help you to understand the more complex analyses presented later in the book. By the end of the chapter you should have a good understanding of the following:

- samples and populations
- measures of central tendency (e.g. the mean)
- graphical techniques for describing your data (e.g. the histogram)
- the normal distribution
- measures of variability in data (e.g. the standard deviation).

These are all important concepts, which will pop up in various guises throughout the book, and so it is important to try to understand them. Look at these as the initial building blocks for a conceptual understanding of statistics.

2.1 Samples and populations

In Chapter 1 we explained that statistics are essentially ways of describing, comparing and relating variables. When producing such statistics we have to be aware of an important distinction between *samples* and *populations*. When psychologists talk about populations they do not necessarily mean the population of a country or town; they are generally referring to distinct groups of people, e.g. all individuals with autism or all men who are left-footed. In statistical terms a population can even refer to inanimate objects, for example, the population of Ford cars.

A sample is simply a selection of individuals from the population (see Figure 2.1). Researchers use samples for a number of reasons, chiefly that samples are cheaper, quicker and more convenient to examine than the whole population. Imagine that we wanted to see if statistics anxiety was related to procrastination, as Walsh and Ugumba-Agwunobi

Figure 2.1   Illustration of several samples of five faces taken from a population of faces

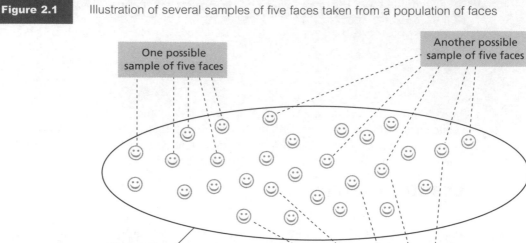

(2002) have done. We could simply measure everyone's levels of statistics anxiety and procrastination and observe how strongly they were related to each other. This would, however, be prohibitively expensive. A more convenient way is to select a number of individuals randomly from the population and find the relationship between their statistics anxiety and procrastination levels. We could then generalise the findings from this sample to the population. We use statistics, more specifically inferential statistics, to help us generalise from the sample to the whole population.

When conducting research we have to ensure that we know which population is relevant and choose our sample from that population. It is of no use conducting a study using a sample of males if the target population includes both sexes, and it is pointless conducting a study using a sample of tarantulas if the target population is zebras.

The ability to generalise findings from a sample to the population is vitally important in research. We therefore have to ensure that any samples used are truly representative of the target population. A simple example will illustrate some of the problems. Imagine that some researchers want to find out if walking a dog leads to more social encounters than walking without a dog. They decide to go to their nearest park and follow a number of dog owners and non-owners to count the number of social interactions they have. They find that non-owners tend to have more social encounters than dog owners do. They conclude that having a dog is bad for your social life.

Is this correct? We do not really know the answer to this from the research that these researchers have conducted. It might be correct, but they may not have used an appropriate sample upon which to base their conclusions, that is, they may have a *sampling problem*. The problem with this is that the dog owners they followed may for example have all been very shy, and it is this rather than having a dog that explains the difference in social encounters. There are many ways in which the researchers could have failed to obtain representative samples. There could be experimenter bias, where the experimenters unconsciously follow people who help support their hypothesis. There could be issues to do with the time of day in which people walk their dogs, for example people walking dogs early in the morning may be in a hurry in order to get to work and thus may be less sociable. Certain dogs may lead to fewer social interactions (e.g. walking with a pit bull terrier). As researchers we have to be aware of all these possibilities when designing our research in order to ensure such problems do not arise. We want to be able to generalise from our sample to the wider populations and therefore we want to avoid problems with the design that reduce our ability to do this. Many of the finer points of research design are attempts to ensure that we are able to generalise. The researchers in the above example could of course have gone to many different parks and followed many people on many occasions. In this way they would ensure that their samples are much more representative of the population.

The previous example illustrates a very important point, which is that our ability to generalise from samples to populations is dependent upon selecting samples that are truly representative of the target population.

We have now introduced you to the distinction between samples and populations. You will find when you read textbooks on statistics that statisticians have different ways of describing samples and populations. Strictly speaking, *statistics* describe samples. So if you calculate an average or mean for a sample it is a statistic. If you calculate the mean for a population, however, you should call it a *parameter*. While statistics describe samples, parameters describe populations. Thus a population mean is a parameter and a sample mean is a statistic. This is a technical distinction and one that need not worry you unduly, as long as you realise that there are differences between the statistical techniques that describe samples and those that describe populations. Typically we use sample statistics to estimate population parameters. More specifically, however, we tend to use *descriptive statistics* to describe our samples and *inferential statistics* to generalise from our samples to the wider populations.

Activity 2.1

If you wanted to find out which group, football fans or rugby fans, were least intelligent, which of the following samples would be most suitable?

- A group of people who are both football and rugby fans
- A random sample of people from the general population
- One group of football fans and one group of rugby fans
- One group of males and one group of females
- A group of psychology students
- A group of chimpanzees

2.2 Measures of central tendency

The first and perhaps most common form of descriptive statistics that you will come across are measures of *central tendency*. A measure of central tendency of a set of data gives us an indication of the typical score in that data set. There are three different measures of central tendency that are typically used to describe our data. We will begin with the most popular of these, the *mean*, which may be known to many of you as the *average*.

2.2.1 Mean

The mean is easily calculated by summing all the scores in the sample and then dividing by the number of scores in the sample. The mean of this sample (5, 6, 9, 2) of scores will be:

$$\frac{5 + 6 + 9 + 2}{4} = 5.5$$

As another example, if we obtained the following dataset 2, 20, 20, 12, 12, 19, 19, 25, 20, we would calculate the mean as follows:

- We would add the scores to get 149.
- We would then divide this by 9 (which is the number of scores we have in the sample) to get a mean of 16.56.

$$\frac{2 + 20 + 20 + 12 + 12 + 19 + 19 + 25 + 20}{9} = 16.56$$

This gives us an indication of the typical score in our sample. It is quite difficult to simply use the mean of a sample as an estimate of the population mean. The reason for this is that we are never certain how near to the population mean is our sample mean, although there are techniques we can use to help us in this regard (e.g. confidence intervals, see p. 103).

2.2.2 Median

A second measure of central tendency is the *median*, which is officially defined as the value that lies in the middle of the sample: that is, it has the same number of scores above as below it. The median is calculated by *ranking* all the scores and taking the one in the middle. For the data used above, to illustrate the calculation of the mean (2, 20, 20, 12, 12, 19, 19, 25, 20), we *rank* the data by putting them in ascending order, from lowest to highest score thus:

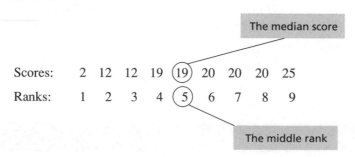

You can see that we have arranged the scores in ascending order (top row) and assigned each score a rank (bottom row). Thus, the lowest score gets a rank of 1, the next lowest a rank of 2, and so on.

Strictly speaking, however, when we have two or more scores the same (as in the above example) the ranks we assign to the equal scores should be the same. Therefore, ranks given to the data presented above should actually be as follows:

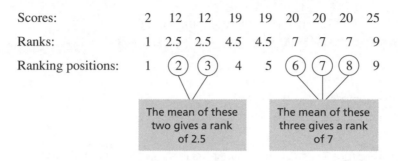

Scores: 2   12   12   19   19   20   20   20   25

Ranks: 1 2.5 2.5 4.5 4.5   7   7   7   9

Ranking positions: 1 ②   ③   4   5   ⑥   ⑦   ⑧   9

The mean of these two gives a rank of 2.5

The mean of these three gives a rank of 7

You can see here that all the scores that are equal have the same rank as each other. We work out the ranking in such cases by taking the mean of the ranking positions that these scores occupy, as illustrated above.

In order to find the median we need to locate the score that is in the middle of this ranked list. We have nine scores, therefore the middle score here is the fifth one. The median is thus 19, which is the fifth score in the list.

In the above example it was easy to work out the median as we had an odd number of scores. When you have an odd number of scores there is always one score that is the middle one. This is not the case, however, when we have an even number of scores. If we add the score of 26 to the above list we now have an even number of scores.

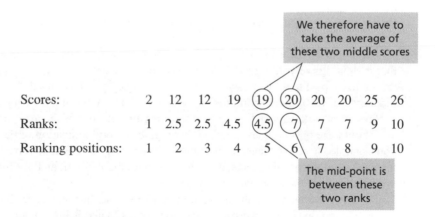

We therefore have to take the average of these two middle scores

Scores: 2   12   12   19 ⑲ ⑳ 20   20   25   26

Ranks: 1 2.5 2.5 4.5 ④⑤ ⑦   7   7   9   10

Ranking positions: 1   2   3   4   5   6   7   8   9   10

The mid-point is between these two ranks

In such a situation the median will be between the two middle scores, i.e. between the fifth and sixth scores. Our median is, in this case, the average of the two scores in the fifth and sixth positions: $(19 + 20) \div 2 = 19.5$.

2.2.3 Mode

A third measure of central tendency is the *mode*, which is simply the most frequently occurring score. In the set of scores given above to illustrate the mean and median the mode would be 20, which is the most frequently occurring score.

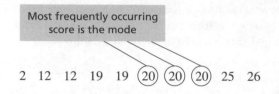

Most frequently occurring
score is the mode

2 12 12 19 19 (20) (20) (20) 25 26

Activity 2.2

For practice work out the mean, median and mode for the following sets of scores:

- 12, 23, 9, 6, 14, 14, 12, 25, 9, 12
- 1, 4, 5, 6, 19, 1, 5, 3, 16, 12, 5, 4
- 32, 56, 91, 16, 32, 5, 14, 62, 19, 12

2.2.4 Which measure of central tendency should you use?

We have described to you three different measures of central tendency: that is, three measures of the typical score in a sample. The question remains, however, which of these should you use when describing your data? The answer to this question is that it depends upon your data.

The important point to keep in mind when choosing a measure of central tendency is that it should give you a good indication of the typical score in your sample. If you have reason to suspect that the measure of central tendency you have used does not give a good indication of the typical score, then you have probably chosen the wrong one.

The mean is the most frequently used measure of central tendency and it is the one you should use once you are satisfied that it gives a good indication of the typical score in your sample. It is the measure of choice because it is calculated from the actual scores themselves, not from the ranks, as is the case with the median, and not from frequency of occurrence, as is the case with the mode.

There is a problem with the mean, however. Because the mean uses all the actual scores in its calculation, it is sensitive to extreme scores. Take a look at the following set of scores:

1 2 3 4 5 6 7 8 9 10

The mean from this set of data is 5.5 (as is the median). If we now change one of the scores and make it slightly more extreme we get the following:

1 2 3 4 5 6 7 8 9 20

The mean from this set of data is now 6.5, while the median has remained as 5.5. If we make the final score even more extreme we get the following:

1 2 3 4 5 6 7 8 9 100

We now get a mean of 14.5, which is obviously not a good indication of the typical score in this set of data. As we have the same number of scores in each of these sets of data and we have changed only the highest score, the median has remained as 5.5. The median is thus a better measure of central tendency in the latter two cases. This example illustrates the need for you to check your data for extreme scores (we will be introducing one way of doing this later in this chapter) before deciding upon which measure of central tendency to use. In the majority of cases you will probably find that it is acceptable to use the mean as your measure of central tendency.

If you find that you have extreme scores and you are unable to use the mean, then you should use the median. The median is not sensitive to extreme scores, as the above example illustrated. The reason for this is that it is simply the score that is in the middle of the other scores when they are put in ascending order. The procedure for locating the median score does not depend upon the actual scores themselves beyond putting them in ascending order. So the top score in our example could be 10, 20, 100 or 100 million and the median still would not change. It is this insensitivity to extreme scores that makes the median useful when we cannot use the mean.

As the mode is simply the most frequently occurring score it does not involve any calculation or ordering of the data. It thus can be used with any type of data. One of the problems with the median and mean is that there are certain types of data for which they cannot be used. When we have categories such as occupation as a variable it does not make sense to rank these in order of magnitude. We therefore cannot use the mean or the median. If you have this sort of data you have no choice but to use the mode. When using the mode, however, you need to make sure that it really is giving you a good indication of the typical score. Take a look at the following sets of data:

```
1   2   2   2   2   2   2   3   4   5   6   7   8
1   2   2   3   4   5   6   7   8   9   10  11  12
```

You should note that the first set of data contains many more 2s than any other score. The mode in this case would be a suitable measure of the central tendency as it is a reasonable indication of the typical score. In the second set of data, 2 would again be the mode because it is the most frequently occurring score. In this case, however, it is not such a good indicator of the typical score because its frequency of occurrence is only just greater than all the other scores. So in this case we should probably not choose the mode as our measure of central tendency. Sometimes you may find that none of the measures of central tendency is appropriate. In such situations you will just have to accept that there are no typical scores in your samples.

Activity 2.3

Which measure of central tendency would be most suitable for each of the following sets of data?

(a) 1 23 25 26 27 23 29 30
(b) 1 1 1 1 1 1 1 1 1 1 1 2 2 2 2 2 3 3 4 50
(c) 1 1 2 3 4 1 2 6 5 8 3 4 5 6 7
(d) 1 101 104 106 111 108 109 200

2.2.5 **The population mean**

The measures of central tendency we have just described are useful for giving an indication of the typical score in a sample. Suppose we wanted to get an indication of the typical score in a population. We could in theory calculate the population mean (a parameter) in a similar way to the calculation of a sample mean: obtain scores from everyone in the population, sum them and divide by the number in the population. In practice, however, this is generally not possible. Can you imagine trying to measure the levels of procrastination and statistics anxiety of everyone in the world? We therefore have to estimate the population parameters from the sample statistics.

One way of estimating the population mean is to calculate the means for a number of samples and then calculate the mean of these sample means. Statisticians have found that this gives a close approximation of the population mean.

Why does the mean of the sample means approximate the population mean? Imagine randomly selecting a sample of people and measuring their IQ. It has been found that generally the population mean for IQ is 100. It could be that, by chance, you have selected mainly geniuses and that the mean IQ of the sample is 150. This is clearly way above the population mean of 100. We might select another sample that happens to have a mean IQ of 75, again not near the population mean. It is evident from these examples that the sample mean need not be a close approximation of the population mean. However, if we calculate the mean of these two sample means we get a much closer approximation to the population mean:

$$\frac{75 + 150}{2} = 112.5$$

The mean of the sample means (112.5) is a better approximation of the population mean (100) than either of the individual sample means (75 and 150). When we take several samples of the same size from a population, some will have a mean higher than the population mean and some will have a lower mean. If we calculated the mean of all these sample means it would be very close to 100, which is the population mean. This tendency of the mean of sample means to equal the population mean is known in statistical circles as the *Central Limit Theorem*. Knowing that the mean of the sample means gives a good approximation of the population mean is important as it helps us generalise from our samples to our population.

2.3 Sampling error

Before reading this section you should complete Activity 2.4.

Activity 2.4

Above is a diagram containing pictures of many giant pandas. Each giant panda has a number that indicates its IQ score. To illustrate the problems associated with sampling error you should complete the following steps and then read the *sampling error* section. Imagine that this picture represents the population of giant pandas. The mean IQ score of this population is 100. We want you to randomly select ten samples from this population. Each sample should contain only two pandas. In order to do this we advise you to get a pencil and wave it over the picture with your eyes closed. With your free hand move the book around. When ready let the tip of the pencil hit the page of the book. See which panda the pencil has selected (if you hit a blank space between pandas then select the panda nearest to where your pencil falls). Make a note of the IQ of the panda that you have selected and do this twice for each sample. You should repeat this process ten times so that you have ten samples of two pandas drawn from the population of pandas. We realise that this doesn't actually represent random selection from the population but it will do for now to illustrate a point we wish to make.

We would now like you to repeat this whole process but this time selecting samples of ten pandas each time. Once you have done this calculate the mean for each of the samples that you have selected (all the two-panda samples and all the ten-panda samples).

You may now continue to read the section relating to sampling error.

One of the problems with sampling from populations is that systematic errors may affect our research and, as a result, make it difficult to interpret. For this reason, statistical error due to sampling is perhaps the biggest problem that we face when estimating population parameters from sample statistics. Whenever we select a sample from a population there will be some degree of uncertainty about how representative the sample actually is of the population. Thus, if we calculate a sample statistic we can never be certain of the comparability of it to the equivalent population parameter. The degree to which such sample statistics differ from the equivalent population parameter is the degree of *sampling error*. Why should there be such an error, and how can we minimise it?

Sampling error occurs simply because we are not using all the members of a target population. Once you start to use samples you will get some degree of sampling error. For example, supposing we wanted to measure the IQs of giant pandas. If we went out and tested all the pandas in the world then we would calculate the mean population IQ directly. We have tested the entire population and therefore the mean that we calculate will be the population mean.

Now suppose we tested only 90% of the population. We have effectively selected a sample. The mean we calculate from this sample will be a good estimate of the population mean, but it will not necessarily be exactly the same. Because we have not tested all the pandas we are likely to either overestimate or underestimate the population mean.

The fact that we have selected so many pandas means that, by chance, we are likely to select pandas from both extremes of the distribution. That is, we are likely to select both clever and not so clever pandas in the same sample. You should have seen from completing Activity 2.4 that when you selected samples containing ten pandas all the samples contained pandas whose IQs were above and below the mean. Thus with relatively large sample sizes, our samples are highly likely to contain clever and not so clever pandas. The sample mean is therefore likely to be a fairly good estimate of the population mean. Consequently, if we take lots of such samples, the degree of sampling error for each sample is likely to be quite small.

Let us now assume that we are researchers with very little money and as a result we can only afford to take sample sizes consisting of two pandas. What effect will this reduction in sample size have on the degree of sampling error? Again referring to Activity 2.4 you will probably have noticed that in some of the samples you selected both of the pandas were more clever than the population mean. This will mean that your sample mean is an overestimation of the population mean. You will also have found that in some of your samples both of your pandas were less clever than the population mean. Your sample mean in these cases will be an underestimate of the population mean. With such small sample sizes it is thus much more likely that the entire sample will be either more clever or less clever than the population mean. In such cases the sample mean will be a poor estimate of the population mean. We therefore have a much greater degree of sampling error with these small sample sizes.

As you increase your sample size you increase the probability that you will choose pandas that fall both above and below the population mean. You also decrease the likelihood that all the selected pandas are from the extremes of the distribution. You therefore decrease the degree of sampling error. You should have noticed from Activity 2.4 that the means calculated from the two-panda samples varied quite a lot, with some being a lot different from the population mean. Whereas for the ten-panda samples the sample means were probably pretty good estimates of the population mean. Thus, in general, the larger the samples the closer the sample mean will be to the population mean.

SPSSFW: obtaining measures of central tendency

To obtain measures of central tendency from SPSSFW you need to input your data as described in Chapter 1 and then click on the *Analyze* menu (see screenshot below).

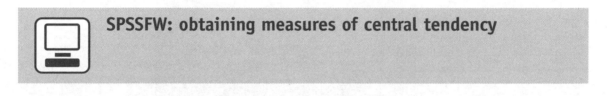

When you have displayed the *Analyze* menu click on the *Descriptive Statistics* option and then select the *Explore . . .* option of the final menu. You will then get the following dialogue box:

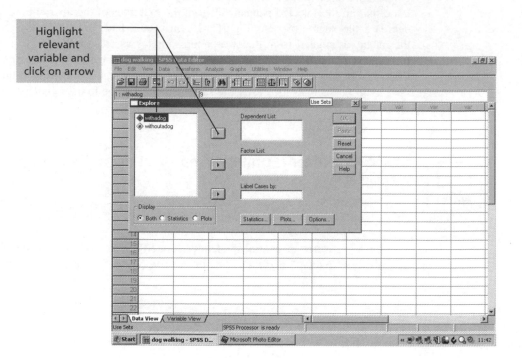

Highlight relevant variable and click on arrow

There are other options for displaying descriptive statistics but the *Explore* option is more flexible. The *Explore* option allows you to access a wider range of descriptive statistical techniques and so is a useful option to get familiar with. You will notice that there are a number of features in this dialogue box, including:

- variables list
- box for dependent variables (*Dependent List*)
- box for grouping variables (*Factor List*)
- *Display* options (at the bottom left)
- various option buttons (*Statistics*, *Plots*, *Options*).

To obtain measures of central tendency, move the non-grouping variables to the *Dependent List* box by highlighting the relevant variables and then clicking on the black arrow ▶ by the *Dependent List* box. You will see the variables move over to this box. See below:

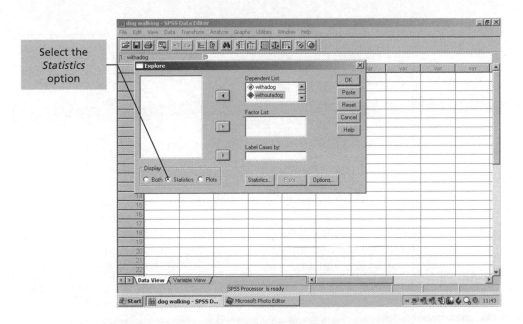

To obtain the relevant descriptive statistics you should select the *Statistics* option (middle one of the set of *Display* options) and then click on the *OK* button to obtain the measures of central tendency. When you do so you will get the following output from SPSSFW:

EXPLORE

Case Processing Summary

	Cases					
	Valid		Missing		Total	
	N	Percent	N	Percent	N	Percent
WITHDOG	6	50.0%	6	50.0%	12	100.0%
NODOG	6	50.0%	6	50.0%	12	100.0%

Descriptives

				Statistic	Std. Error
WITHDOG	Mean			8.6667	.8819
	95% Confidence Interval for Mean	Lower Bound		6.3996	
		Upper Bound		10.9337	
	5% Trimmed Mean			8.6296	
	Median			8.5000	
	Variance			4.667	
	Std. Deviation			2.1602	
	Minimum			6.00	
	Maximum			12.00	
	Range			6.00	
	Interquartile Range			3.7500	
	Skewness			.463	.845
	Kurtosis			−.300	1.741
NODOG	Mean			4.0000	.7303
	95% Confidence Interval for Mean	Lower Bound		2.1227	
		Upper Bound		5.8773	
	5% Trimmed Mean			4.0556	
	Median			4.5000	
	Variance			3.20	
	Std. Deviation			1.7889	
	Minimum			1.00	
	Maximum			6.00	
	Range			5.00	
	Interquartile Range			2.7500	
	Skewness			−.943	.845
	Kurtosis			.586	1.741

Mean and median

You will notice from the SPSSFW printout that you are presented with a lot of information. Do not worry too much if you do not understand most of it at this stage; we will explain it later in the book. For now, you should notice that for the two variables you can see the mean and median displayed. If you want the mode you should try using the *Frequencies*... option from the *Analyze*...*Descriptives* menus rather than the *Explore*... option. Once you get the *Frequencies* dialogue box open click on the *Statistics* button and select the mode from the next dialogue box – see the screenshot opposite:

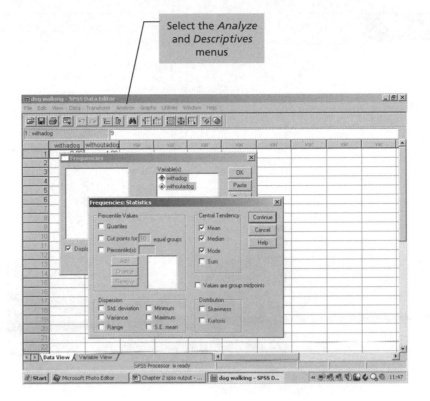

Select the *Analyze* and *Descriptives* menus

2.4 Graphically describing data

Once you have finished a piece of research it is important that you get to know your data. One of the best ways of doing this is through Exploratory Data Analyses (EDA). EDA essentially consists of exploring your data through graphical techniques. It is used to get a greater understanding of how participants in your study have behaved. The importance of such graphical techniques was highlighted by Tukey in 1977 in a classic text called *Exploratory Data Analysis*. Graphically illustrating your data should, therefore, be one of the first things you do with it once you have collected it. In the next section we will introduce you to the main techniques for exploring your data, starting with the *frequency histogram*. We will then go on to explain *stem and leaf plots* and *box plots*.

2.4.1 Frequency histogram

The frequency histogram is a useful way of graphically illustrating your data. Often researchers are interested in the frequency of occurrence of values in their sample data. For example, if you collected information about individuals' occupation you might be interested in finding out how many people were in each category of employment. To illustrate the histogram, consider a frequency histogram for the set of data collected in a study by Armitage and Reidy (unpublished). In this study investigating fear of blood

Figure 2.2   Frequency histogram showing frequency with which people rated colours as being their favourites (Armitage and Reidy, 2004)

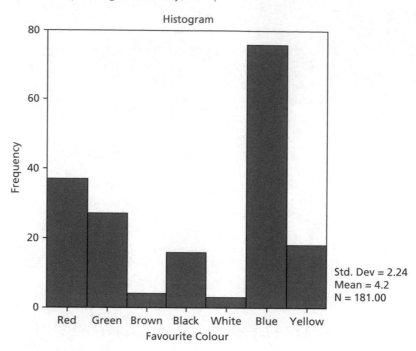

the researchers asked participants to indicate from a list of seven colours which was their favourite. The histogram representing this data is shown in Figure 2.2. You should be able to see from Figure 2.2 that people rated blue as being their favourite colour most often and white as their favourite least often.

The frequency histogram is a good way for us to inspect our data visually. Often we wish to know if there are any scores that might look a bit out of place. The histogram in Figure 2.3 represents hypothetical scores on a depression questionnaire. You can see from the histogram that the final score is much greater than the other scores. Given that the maximum score on this particular depression scale is only 63, we can see from the histogram that we must have made an error when inputting our data. Such problems are easier to spot when you have graphed your data. You should, however, be aware that the interpretation of your histogram is dependent upon the particular intervals that the bars represent. The histogram in Figure 2.3 has bars representing intervals of 1. Figure 2.4 shows how the depression score data would look with bars representing intervals of 5.

The frequency histogram is also useful for discovering other important characteristics of your data. For example, you can easily see what the mode is by looking for the tallest bar in your chart. In addition, your histogram gives you some useful information about how the scores are spread out, that is, how they are *distributed*. The way that data are distributed is important, as you will see when we come to discuss the *normal distribution* later in this chapter. The distribution of data is also an important consideration in the use of the *inferential statistics* discussed later in the book. We can see from the histogram of

Figure 2.3   Histogram of the depression questionnaire data

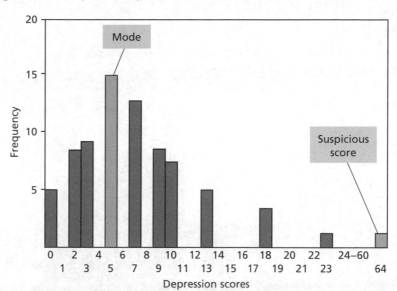

Figure 2.4   Histogram of the depression data grouped in intervals of 5

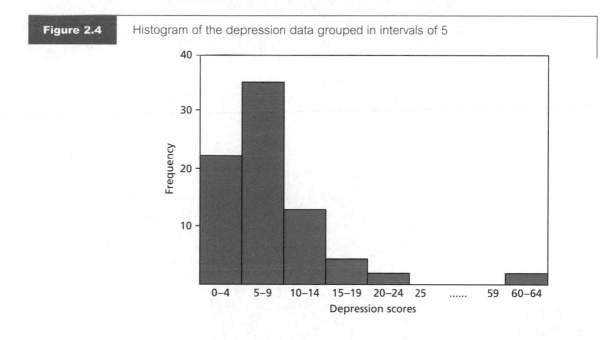

the depression questionnaire data that there is a concentration of scores in the 5 to 7 region and then the scores tail off above and below these points.

The best way of generating a histogram by hand is to rank the data first, as described earlier in the chapter for working out the median. You then simply count up the number of times each score occurs in the data; this is the frequency of occurrence of each score. This frequency is then plotted on a chart as above.

Activity 2.5

Given the following histogram, try to answer these questions:

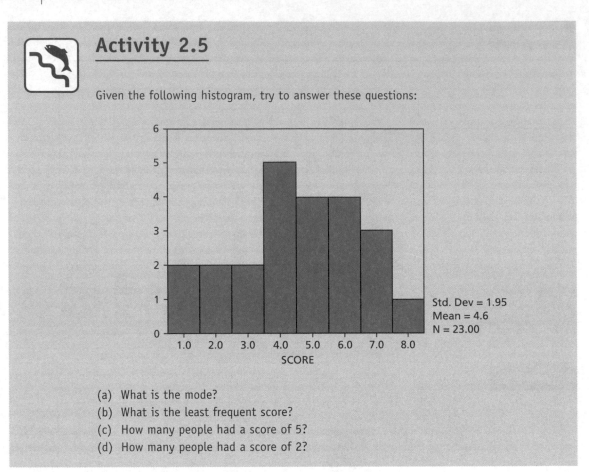

Std. Dev = 1.95
Mean = 4.6
N = 23.00

SCORE

(a) What is the mode?
(b) What is the least frequent score?
(c) How many people had a score of 5?
(d) How many people had a score of 2?

2.4.2 Stem and leaf plots

Stem and leaf plots are similar to frequency histograms in that they allow you to see how the scores are distributed. However, they also retain the values of the individual observations. Developed by Tukey (1977), they tend to be a lot easier to draw by hand than the histogram. The stem and leaf plot for the data we used to illustrate the calculation of the mean, median and mode (2, 12, 12, 19, 19, 20, 20, 20, 25) is presented in Figure 2.5.

| Figure 2.5 | Example of a stem and leaf plot |

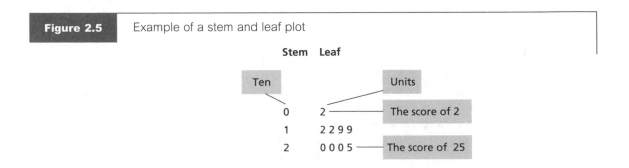

Stem   Leaf

Ten

Units

0   2 ——— The score of 2

1   2 2 9 9

2   0 0 0 5 ——— The score of 25

You can see the similarities between histograms and stem and leaf plots if you turn the stem and leaf plot on its side. When you do this you are able to get a good representation of the distribution of your data.

You can see that, in the example of Figure 2.5, the scores have been grouped in tens: the first line contains the scores from 0 to 9, the next line from 10 to 19 and the last line 20 to 29. Therefore, in this case the *stem* indicates the tens (this is called the *stem width*) and the *leaf* the units. You can see that a score of 2 is represented as 0 in the tens column (the stem) and 2 in the units column (the leaf), whilst 25 is represented as a stem of 2 and a leaf of 5.

The stem and leaf plot in Figure 2.6 comes from these scores: 1, 1, 2, 2, 2, 5, 5, 5, 12, 12, 12, 12, 14, 14, 14, 14, 15, 15, 15, 18, 18, 24, 24, 24, 24, 24, 24, 25, 25, 25, 25, 25, 25, 25, 28, 28, 28, 28, 28, 28, 28, 32, 32, 33, 33, 33, 33, 34, 34, 34, 34, 34, 34, 35, 35, 35, 35, 35, 42, 42, 42, 43, 43, 44. You can see from Figure 2.6 that the stem and leaf plot provides us with a concise way of presenting lots of data. Sometimes, however, the above system of blocking the tens is not very informative. Take a look at Figure 2.7, which shows the stem and leaf plot for the depression data that we presented in histogram form (Figure 2.3) earlier.

Figure 2.7 does not give us much information about the distribution of scores, apart from the fact that they are mostly lower than 20. An alternative system of blocking the scores is to do so in groups of five (e.g. 0–4, 5–9, 10–14, 15–19, etc.). The stem and leaf plot for the depression data grouped this way is presented in Figure 2.8. This gives a much better indication of the distribution of scores. You can see that we use a full stop (.) following the stem to signify the first half of each block of ten scores (e.g. 0–4) and an asterisk (*) to signify the second half of each block of ten scores (e.g. 5–9).

Figure 2.6   Stem and leaf plot for a larger set of data

Stem	Leaf
0	11222555
1	2222444455588
2	444444455555558888888
3	22333344444455555
4	222334

Figure 2.7   Stem and leaf plot for depression data grouped in blocks of ten

Stem	Leaf
0	000002222222233333333355555555555555555777777777777799999999
1	000000033333888
2	3
6	4

| Figure 2.8 | Stem and leaf plot for the depression data grouped in blocks of five |

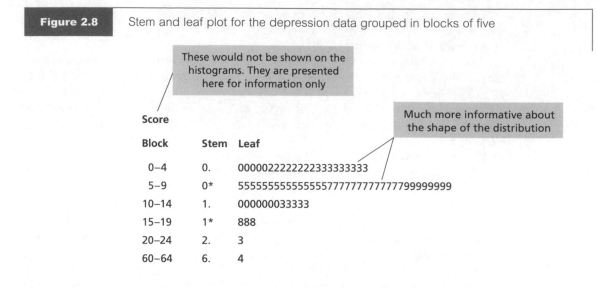

These would not be shown on the histograms. They are presented here for information only

Much more informative about the shape of the distribution

Score Block	Stem	Leaf
0–4	0.	00000222222222333333333
5–9	0*	5555555555555555777777777777799999999
10–14	1.	000000033333
15–19	1*	888
20–24	2.	3
60–64	6.	4

2.4.3 Box plots

Even though we can see that there is an extreme score in the depression example, it is often the case that the extreme scores are not so obvious. Tukey (1977), however, developed a graphical technique called the *box plot* or *box and whisker plot*, which gives us a clear indication of extreme scores and, like the stem and leaf plots and histogram, tells us how the scores are distributed.

Although you can get the computer to produce box and whisker plots, we will describe to you how to produce a box and whisker plot for the following data so that you know how to interpret them (the box plot for these data is presented in Figure 2.9):

2   20   20   12   12   19   19   25   20

■ First, find the median score as described above. This was position 5 (the actual median score was 19, but once the data had been ranked the score was in position 5).

2   12   12   19   (19)   20   20   20   25

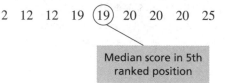

Median score in 5th ranked position

■ Then calculate the *hinges*. These are the scores that cut off the top and bottom 25% of the data (which are called the *upper* and *lower quartiles*): thus 50% of the scores fall within the hinges. The hinges form the outer boundaries of the *box* (see Figure 2.9). We work out the position of the hinges by adding 1 to the median position and then dividing by 2 (remember that our median is in position 5) thus:

$$\frac{5+1}{2} = 3$$

■ The upper and lower hinges are, therefore, the third score from the top and the third score from the bottom of the ranked list, which in the above example are 20 and 12 respectively.

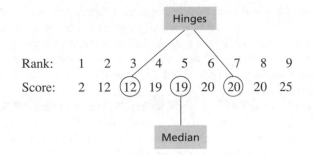

■ From these hinge scores we can work out the *h-spread*, which is the range of the scores between the two hinges. The score on the upper hinge is 20 and the score on the lower hinge is 12, therefore the h-spread is 8 (20 minus 8).

■ We define extreme scores as those that fall one-and-a-half times the h-spread outside the upper and lower hinges. The points one-and-half times the h-spread outside the upper and lower hinges are called *inner fences*. One-and-a-half times the h-spread in this case is 12, that is 1.5×8: therefore any score that falls below 0 (lower hinge, 12, minus 12) or above 32 (upper hinge, 20, plus 12) is classed as an extreme score.

■ The scores that fall between the hinges and the inner fences and that are closest to the inner fence are called *adjacent scores*. In our example, these scores are 2 and 25, as 2 is the closest score to 0 (the lower inner fence) and 25 is closest to 32 (the upper inner fence). These are illustrated by the cross-bars on each of the whiskers.

■ Any extreme scores (those that fall outside the upper and lower inner fences) are shown on the box plot.

You can see from Figure 2.9 that the h-spread is indicated by the box width (from 12 to 20) and that there are no extreme scores. The lines coming out from the edge of the box are called whiskers, and these represent the range of scores that fall outside the hinges

Figure 2.9 Example of a box plot

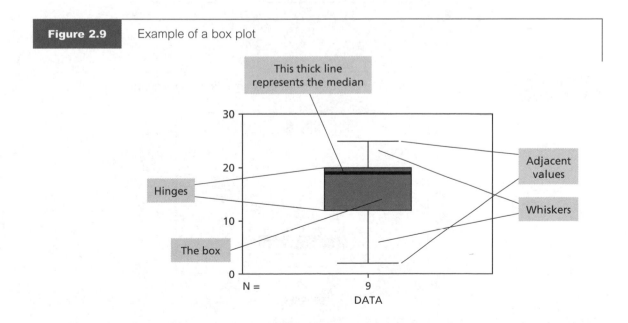

but are within the limits defined by the inner fences. Any scores that fall outside the inner fences are classed as extreme scores (also called outliers). You can also see from Figure 2.9 that we have no scores outside the inner fences, which are 0 and 32. The inner fences are not necessarily shown on the plot. The lowest and highest scores that fall within the inner fences (adjacent scores 2 and 25) are indicated on the plots by the cross-lines on each of the whiskers.

If we now add a score of 33 to the data set illustrated in Figure 2.9 the box plot would resemble that shown in Figure 2.10. You should notice that there is a score that is marked '10'. This is telling us that the tenth score in our data set (which has a value of 33) is an extreme score. That is, it falls outside the inner fence of 32. We might want to look at this score to see why it is so extreme; it could be that we have made an error in our data entry.

The box plot illustrated in Figure 2.11 represents the data from the hypothetical depression scores presented earlier in the chapter. You can see from this that the obvious

 Figure 2.10 Box plot illustrating an extreme score

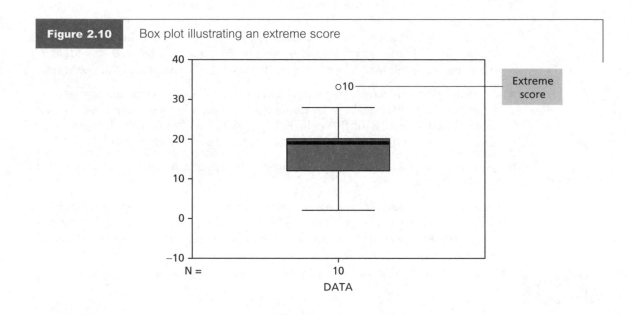

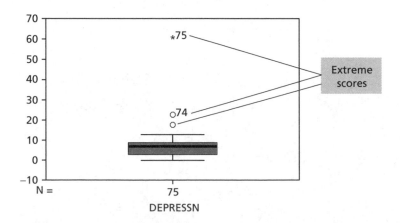 **Figure 2.11** Box plot for the questionnaire data illustrating several extreme scores

extreme score (the score of 64) is represented as such; however, there are less obvious scores that are extreme, the scores of 18 and 23. This clearly indicates that it is not always possible to spot which scores are extreme, and thus the box plot is an extremely useful technique for exploring your data. You will notice that the box plot has a whisker coming from the top of the box. This means that there are scores that fall outside the upper hinge but inside the inner fence (the scores of 13).

Why is it important to identify outlying scores? You need to bear in mind that many of the statistical techniques that we discuss in this book involve the calculation of means. You should recall that earlier (see page 40) we discussed how the mean is sensitive to extreme scores. We, thus, need to be aware of whether or not our data contain such extreme scores if we are to draw the appropriate conclusions from the statistical analyses that we conduct.

Strictly speaking we should not use most of the inferential statistical techniques in this book if we have extreme scores in our data. There are, however, ways of dealing with extreme scores. If you find that you have extreme scores then you should take the following steps:

■ Check that you have entered the data correctly.

■ Check that there is nothing unusual about the outlying (extreme) score. For example, do you recall from testing the person whether they looked as though they understood the instructions properly, did they complete your questionnaire properly? Is there any reason to think that they didn't complete the task(s) properly?
  – If you have a good reason then you can remove the participant (case) from the analysis. However, when you report your data analyses you should report the fact that you have removed data and the reason why you have removed the data.

■ If there is nothing unusual about the participant that you can identify apart from their extreme score then you should probably keep them in the analyses. It is legitimate, however, to adjust their score so that it is not so extreme and thus doesn't unduly influence the mean. Why is this so?
  – Remember, if you are using the mean then you must be interested in the typical score in a group. Clearly, an extreme score is not a typical score and so it is legitimate to adjust it to bring it more in line with the rest of the group.
  – To do this we adjust the extreme score so that it is one unit above the next highest score in the sample which is not an extreme score. In this way the participant is still recognised as having the highest score in the sample but their score is now having less of an impact upon the mean and thus less impact on our inferential statistical analyses.
  – As an example, refer to the depression scores we presented earlier (see Figure 2.11). Let us suppose that we had only one extreme score in this sample (the score of 64) and that this is a valid score (for the sake of illustration we will ignore the other two outliers in this sample). To adjust the extreme score we would find the highest score that is not extreme. In this case that is a score of 13. We would therefore adjust the extreme score so that it is one greater than 13. Our extreme score is therefore adjusted to 14.

■ Of course if you make such adjustments to the scores you need to report exactly what you have done when you come to write up the research so that your readers know that your analyses are based upon some adjusted scores.

We are not able to give a full discussion of this here but you can find a good account of it in Tabachnick and Fidell (2003).

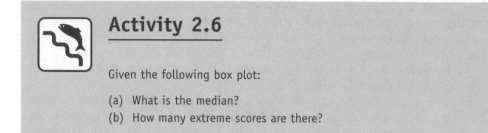

Activity 2.6

Given the following box plot:

(a) What is the median?
(b) How many extreme scores are there?

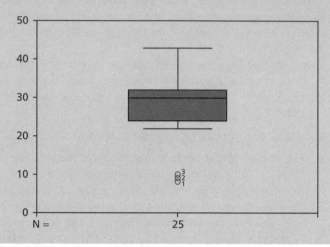

Example from the literature: emotional processing and panic disorder

It is rare for researchers to refer to box plots in their published articles, although we would presume that they do examine them before using many of the statistical techniques covered in this book. It is even more rare for researchers to actually present box plots in published articles. An exception to this is a recent paper published by Baker *et al.* (in press). In this article the authors report a study conducted to investigate differences between panic disorder patients and non-panic controls in their emotional processing. The authors concluded that panic patients appear to try to control their emotions more than non-panic controls. One of their measures of emotional control was the Courtauld Emotional Control Scale (CECS: Watson and Greer, 1983), which measures the degree to which respondents try to control their anger, anxiety and happiness. The questionnaire also gives a total score which represents respondents' degree of general emotional control. In their 'Results' section the authors present box plots for the total score on the CECS for the panic disorder group and the two control groups they used. However, the authors do not comment on what the box plots were suggesting about the distribution of the CECS scores in these groups. The box plots suggest that the distribution of CECS scores for the three groups were quite similar but panic disorder patients tended to have higher total CECS scores. Additionally, there were some outliers evident in one of their control groups.

SPSSFW: generating graphical descriptives

To obtain histograms, stem and leaf plots and box plots using SPSSFW you can use the *Explore* dialogue box. You should proceed as described earlier for obtaining measures of central tendency. If you wish to obtain measures of central tendency and the graphical descriptive you should select the *Both* option at the bottom left of the dialogue box (*Display* options). If, however, you only want to obtain graphical descriptives you should select the *Plots* option (see below):

Select *Plots* option and click on *Plots* button

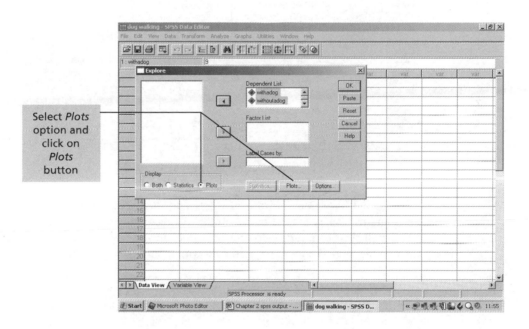

You should then click on the *Plots* button to specify which plots you want displayed. When you click on *Plots* you will be presented with the following dialogue box:

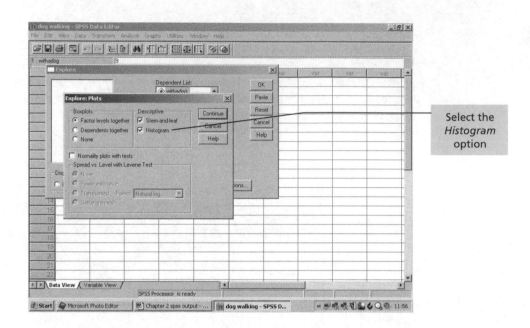

Select the *Histogram* option

The default selections are for *Boxplots* and *Stem-and-leaf plots*. To obtain frequency histograms also, select the option in this dialogue box and click on the *Continue* button. You will then be returned to the main dialogue box where you should click on *OK* to obtain the plots. You will be presented with the following output:

Figure 2.12 Output from SPSS giving histogram, stem and leaf diagram and box plot

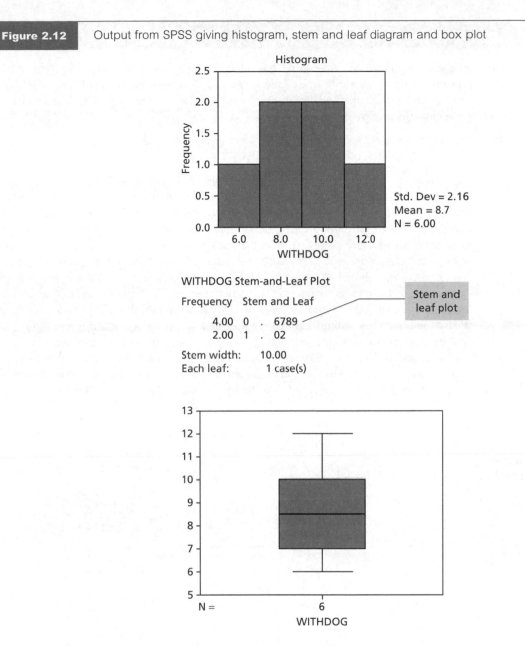

Histogram

WITHDOG

Std. Dev = 2.16
Mean = 8.7
N = 6.00

WITHDOG Stem-and-Leaf Plot

Frequency   Stem and Leaf

    4.00   0 . 6789
    2.00   1 . 02

Stem width: 10.00
Each leaf: 1 case(s)

Stem and leaf plot

WITHDOG

N = 6

You will be presented with a histogram, followed by the stem and leaf plot and finally the box plot. We have only presented the output for the with a dog condition here. SPSS will also give you the output for the without a dog conditon. You should note that SPSS may be set up to give you different bar intervals to those presented above and so you need to check what the bar intervals are on the ouput SPSS gives you.

2.5 Scattergrams

A useful technique for examining the relationship between two variables is to obtain a scattergram. An example of a scattergram can be seen in Figure 2.13 for the statistics anxiety and procrastination data presented in Chapter 1 (see page 19). These data are presented again below:

Statistics anxiety score: 50   59   48   60   62   55
Procrastination score: 96   132   94   110   140   125

A scattergram plots the scores of one variable on the *x*-axis and the other variable on the *y*-axis. Figure 2.13 gives scores for procrastination on the *x*-axis and statistics anxiety on the *y*-axis. It gives a good illustration of how the two variables may be related. We can see from the scattergram that generally, as statistics anxiety increases, so does procrastination. Thus there seems to be a relationship between the two variables. The scores seem to fall quite close to an imaginary line running from the bottom left corner to the top right corner. We call this a positive relationship.

Suppose that when you conducted your statistics anxiety study you found that, as statistics anxiety increased, procrastination decreased. What do you think the resulting scattergram would look like? You might find that it resembled the one presented in Figure 2.14.

You can now see from the scattergram in Figure 2.14 that, as procrastination increases, statistics anxiety decreases. The scores appear to cluster around an imaginary line running from the top left corner to the bottom right corner. We would call this a negative relationship. What would the scattergram look like if there were no discernible relationship between statistics anxiety and procrastination? The scattergram presented in Figure 2.15 gives an indication of what this might look like.

Figure 2.13   Scattergram for the statistics anxiety and procrastination data presented in Chapter 1

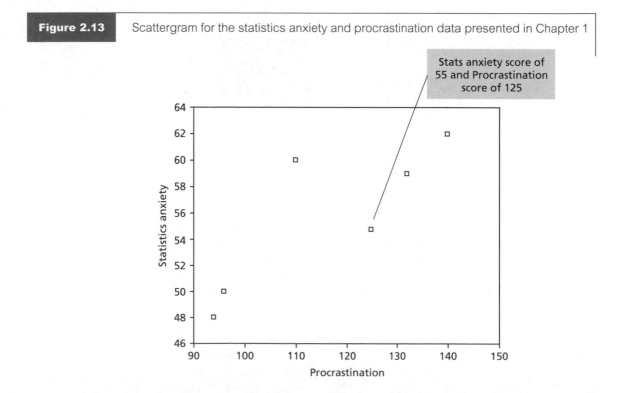

Stats anxiety score of 55 and Procrastination score of 125

Scattergram indicating that, as statistics anxiety decreases, procrastination increases

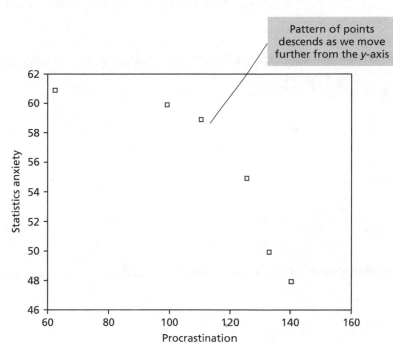

Scattergram indicating no relationship between statistics anxiety and procrastination

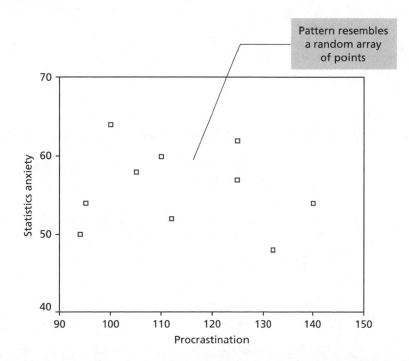

You can see that the arrangement of points in the scattergram illustrated in Figure 2.15 appears to be fairly random. Scattergrams are thus a very useful tool for examining relationships between variables, and will be discussed in more detail in Chapter 5.

Activity 2.7

Given the following scattergram, what would be the most sensible conclusion about the relationship between price of petrol and driver satisfaction?

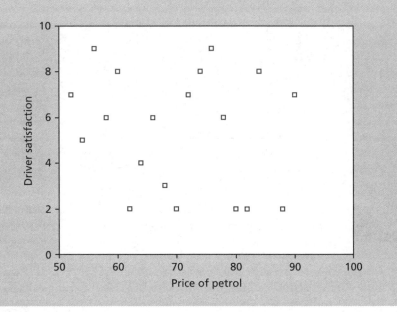

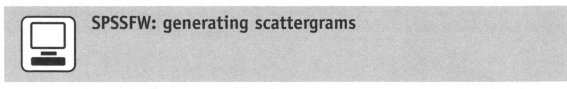

SPSSFW: generating scattergrams

To obtain a scattergram using SPSSFW you should click on the *Graphs* menu and then select the *Scatter . . .* option. You will be presented with the following option box:

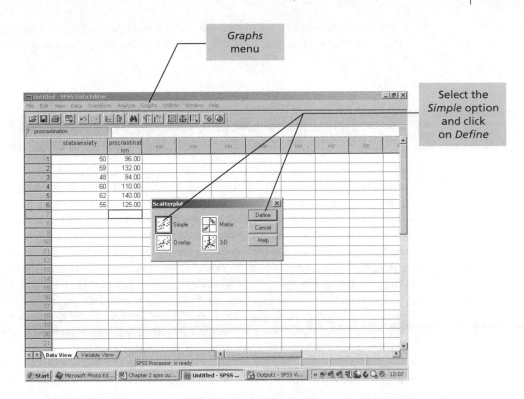

You should select the *Simple* option (which is the default selection) and click on the *Define* button. You will then be presented with a dialogue box where you can select various options for your scattergram (see below).

Move one variable to the *Y Axis* box and one other variable to the *X Axis* box using the ▶ buttons and then click on *OK* to obtain the scattergram. The graph should be similar to the one presented earlier (see Figure 2.13).

2.6 Sampling error and relationships between variables

You should recall that earlier in the chapter (see page 42) we explained the problems associated with sampling error. There we indicated that because of sampling error our sample mean need not necessarily be a good indicator or the population mean. You should note that sampling error is not restricted to circumstances where we wish to estimate the population mean. It is also an important concern when investigating relationships between variables. Suppose we conduct a study relating statistics anxiety to procrastination, and suppose that (unknown to us) there is actually no relationship between these two variables in the population. For the sake of illustration, let us assume that there are only 50 people in the population. The scattergram in Figure 2.16, therefore, represents the pattern of scores in the population. If you took two different samples from this population, one containing only three people and one containing 20 people, we might get scattergrams that look like Figure 2.17(a) and (b). In these scattergrams we can see that there does not appear to be a relationship between the two variables. As procrastination increases there is no consistent pattern of change in statistics anxiety. In this case our samples are good representations of the underlying population.

If we now select two more samples (one containing three people and one containing 20 people) we might obtain the scattergrams shown in Figure 2.18(a) and (b). In this case in the three-person sample we might conclude that there is a negative relationship between

| **Figure 2.16** | Scattergram of the population of procrastination and statistics anxiety scores |

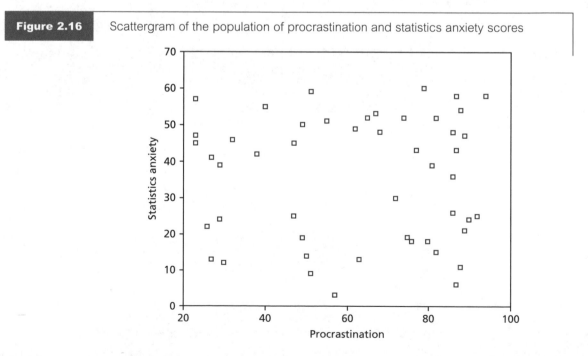

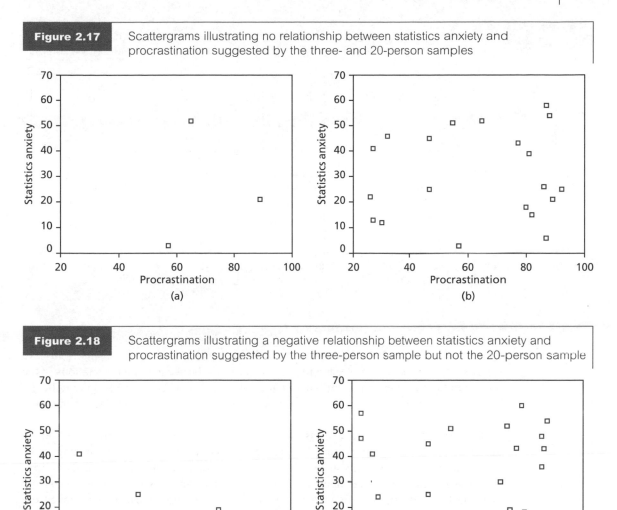

Figure 2.17 Scattergrams illustrating no relationship between statistics anxiety and procrastination suggested by the three- and 20-person samples

Figure 2.18 Scattergrams illustrating a negative relationship between statistics anxiety and procrastination suggested by the three-person sample but not the 20-person sample

the two variables. As statistics anxiety decreases, procrastination increases. In the 20-person sample, however, the suggestion is again that there is no real relationship between the two variables. You can see that here the smaller sample does not accurately reflect the pattern of the underlying population, whereas the larger sample does.

Finally, if we select two more samples we might get the pattern illustrated in Figure 2.19. Here you should be able to see that there does not appear to be a relationship between statistics anxiety and procrastination in the three-person sample but there does appear to be a relationship indicated by the 20-person sample. If you look at Figure 2.19 you should see that there appears to be a pattern for the 20-person sample that suggests as procrastination increases so does statistics anxiety. In this case the larger sample does not accurately represent the underlying population, whereas the smaller sample does.

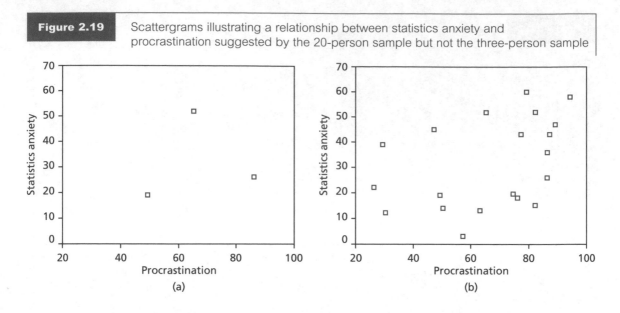

Figure 2.19 Scattergrams illustrating a relationship between statistics anxiety and procrastination suggested by the 20-person sample but not the three-person sample

You should note that you are much less likely to get the patterns indicated in Figure 2.19 than those in Figures 2.17 and 2.18. As we indicated earlier in the chapter, when you have larger sample sizes the samples are much more likely to be accurate representations of the underlying population. Although the scenario illustrated by Figure 2.19 is quite unlikely, however, it can occur and therefore we have to be careful when trying to generalise from samples to populations.

The main point of the above illustration is that the conclusions we draw from sample data are subject to sampling error. We can rarely be certain that what is happening in the sample reflects what happens in the population. Indeed, as the above scattergrams illustrate, our sample data can deceive us. They can show a pattern of scores that is completely different from the pattern in the underlying population. The larger the sample we take from the population, however, the more likely it is that it will reflect that population accurately.

2.7 The normal distribution

We have now presented you with four useful techniques for graphically illustrating your data. Why is it so important to do this? It is certainly not so that software giants can sell you fancy computer software. It is because the way that our data are distributed is important. Many of the statistical tests you will be presented with in this book make assumptions about how your data are distributed. That is, the tests are valid only if your data are distributed in a certain way. One of the most important distributions that you will come across is the *normal distribution*.

The curves illustrated in Figure 2.20 are all normal distributions. In everyday life many variables such as height, weight, shoe size, anxiety levels and exam marks all tend to be normally distributed, that is, they all tend to look like the curves in Figure 2.20. In our research we can use this information to make assumptions about the way that populations

| Figure 2.20 | Normal distributions |

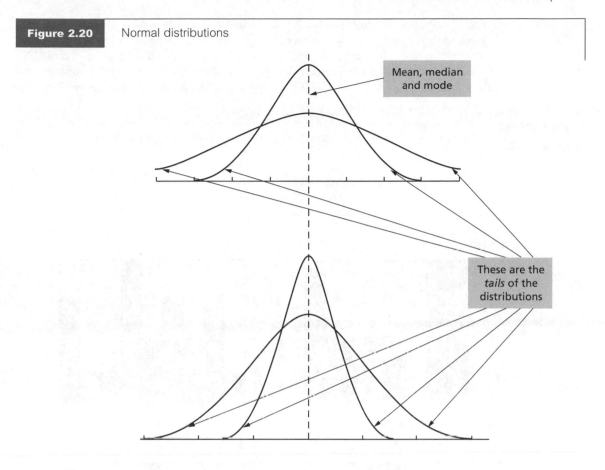

are distributed. It is for this reason that many of the most powerful statistical tools we use assume that the populations from which our samples are drawn are normally distributed.

For a distribution to be classed as normal it should have the following characteristics:

■ it should be symmetrical about the mean
■ the tails should meet the *x*-axis at infinity
■ it should be bell-shaped.

All the distributions in Figure 2.20 are normal; even though they are not exactly the same, they have the characteristics described above. You can see that they differ in terms of how spread out the scores are and how peaked they are in the middle. You will also notice, when you have a normal distribution, that the mean, median and mode are exactly the same. Another important characteristic of the normal distribution is that it is a function of its mean and standard deviation (we explain standard deviations later in this chapter). What this means is that, once we have the mean and standard deviation, we can plot the normal distribution by putting these values into a formula. We will not present the formula here; you just need to remember that the normal distribution can be plotted by reference to its mean and standard deviation.

As we pointed out earlier, when many naturally occurring variables are plotted they are found to be normally distributed. It is also generally found that the more scores from such variables you plot, the more like the normal distribution they become. A simple example may serve to illustrate this. If you randomly selected ten men and measured their heights in inches, the frequency histogram might look something like Figure 2.21(a). It is clear that this does not much resemble the normal distributions illustrated in Figure 2.20. If we select an additional ten men and plot all 20 heights, the resulting distribution might look like Figure 2.21(b), again not too much like a normal distribution. You can

| **Figure 2.21** | Histograms showing the progression to a normal distribution as more people are sampled |

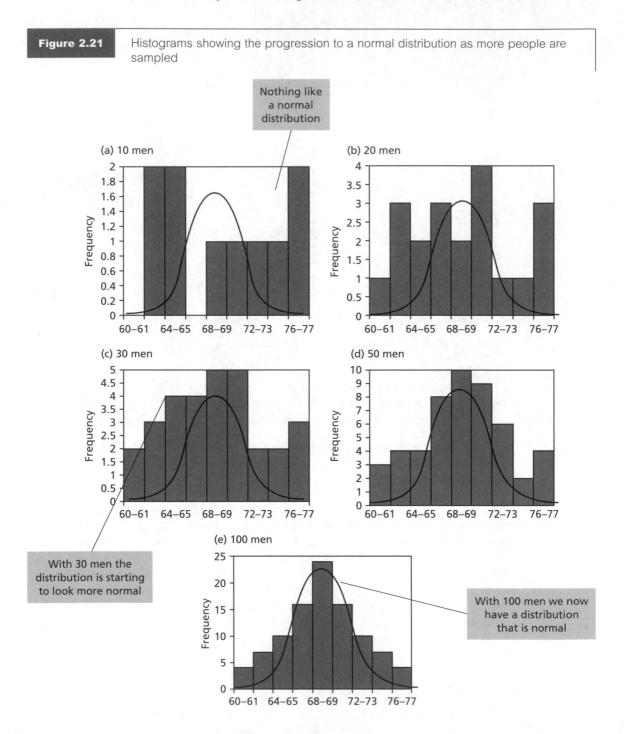

see, however, that as we select more and more men and plot the heights, the histogram becomes a closer approximation to the normal distribution (Figures 2.21(c) to (e)). By the time we have selected 100 men you can see that we have a perfectly normal distribution. Obviously we have made these data up to illustrate a point but in general this is what happens with many variables that you will come across.

We have given you an indication of what the normal distribution looks like; however, you need to be aware that there is not just one single normal distribution. As indicated in Figure 2.20, normal distributions represent a family of distributions. These distributions all have the characteristics of normal distributions (bell-shaped, symmetrical about the mean, etc.), but they differ from one another in terms of how spread out they are and how peaked or flat they are.

2.8 Variation or spread of distributions

We have introduced you to measures of central tendency, which give us an indication of the typical score in a sample. Another important aspect of a sample or population of scores is how spread out they are. Or, to put it another way, how much variation there is in your sample or population.

2.8.1 The range

One simple way of getting an indication of the spread of scores is to compare the minimum score with the maximum score in the sample or population. This is known as the *range*. The range is simply the difference between the minimum and maximum scores. For example, the range for the depression scores in Figure 2.3 is 64, that is 64 minus 0. In that example the lowest score is 0 and the highest score is 64 and so the range is 64.

Although the range tells us about the overall range of scores, it does not give us any indication of what is happening in between these scores. For example, take a look at the two distributions in Figure 2.22. These histograms were generated from two sets of data which have the same mean (16) and the same minimum and maximum scores (5 and 27). They both therefore have the same range, which is 22 (27 minus 5). They are, however, totally different distributions; the scores in distribution B are packed tightly around the mean whereas the scores in distribution A are generally more spread out. Ideally, we need to have an indication of the overall shape of the distribution and how much the scores vary from the mean. Therefore, although the range gives a crude indication of the spread of the scores, it does not really tell us much about the overall shape of the distribution of the sample of scores.

2.8.2 Standard deviation

A more informative measure of the variation in data is the *standard deviation* (SD). One of the problems with the range is that it does not tell us what is happening with the scores between the minimum and maximum scores. The SD, however, does give us an indication of what is happening between the two extremes. The reason why the SD is able to do this is that it tells us how much all the scores in a data set vary around the mean. The SD is a

Figure 2.22 Distributions with the same mean, minimum and maximum scores but which have very different distributions around the mean

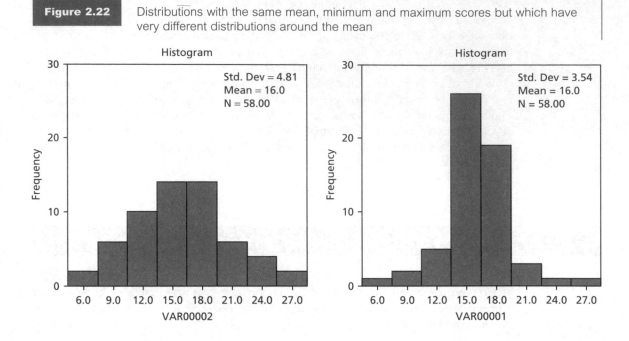

very important concept and so it is worth the effort spent now getting to understand it. It is important because it forms the basis of many of the statistical techniques we use to analyse our data.

The SD is a measure of how much the scores in your sample vary around the mean. Each score in a sample will deviate from the mean by some amount. If we subtract the mean from each score we get an indication of how far each score in the sample is from the mean. As with any group of scores we could then find the mean of the deviations from the mean. This mean, called the *mean deviation*, gives us an indication of how much the group as a whole differs from the sample mean. To calculate the mean deviation we have to sum the individual deviations and divide by the number of scores we have. There is a problem with such a procedure, however. The problem relates to the fact that the mean is a measure of central tendency (middle or typical score). As a result approximately half of the deviations from the mean will be negative deviations (the scores will be less than the mean) and half will be positive deviations (i.e. the scores will be greater than the mean). If we sum these deviations then we will get zero. This is illustrated below:

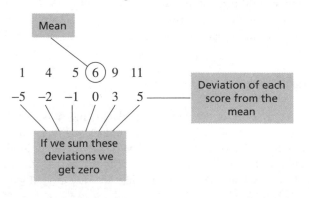

This is not a very informative indication of how the whole group is deviating from the mean, as for every sample we will get zero. A way out of this dilemma is to square each of the deviations from the mean; this eliminates all negative values (a negative number squared gives a positive value, e.g. $-5^2 = 25$). We can then calculate the mean of these squared deviations to give an indication of the spread of the whole group of scores. The resultant statistic is known as the *variance*. The problem with the variance is that it is based upon the squares of the deviations and thus it is not expressed in the same units as the actual scores themselves. It is expressed in the square of the unit of measurement. For example, if we had a set of scores expressed in seconds, the variance would be expressed in seconds^2. To achieve a measure of deviation from the mean in the original units of measurement we have to take the square root of the variance, which gives us the *standard deviation*.

A simple example will illustrate this. Suppose that we have the following group of scores collected from a study into the number of chocolate bars eaten by people each week: 1, 4, 5, 6, 9, 11. To work out the standard deviation we proceed as follows:

■ First, calculate the mean, which is 6.
■ The deviation of each score from the mean is: $-5, -2, -1, 0, 3, 5$ (if we add these up you see that we get zero).
■ We therefore need to square these deviations to get rid of the negative values, which gives us these scores: 25, 4, 1, 0, 9, 25.
■ Next, we calculate the mean of these scores, which is 10.67, i.e. $64 \div 6$, which gives us our variance.
■ Finally, we work out the standard deviation by taking the square root of the variance, which gives us 3.27.

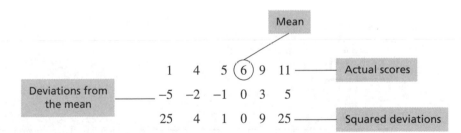

The standard deviation figure of 3.27 is useful as it gives us an indication of how closely the scores are clustered around the mean. Generally, you will find that nearly 70% of all scores fall within 1 standard deviation of the mean. In the above example the standard deviation is 3.27: this tells us that the majority of the scores in this sample are within 3.27 units above or below the mean. That is, nearly 70% of scores would fall between 2.73 (6 minus 3.27) and 9.27 (6 plus 3.27). The standard deviation is useful when you want to compare samples using the same scale. Suppose we took a second sample of scores and now had a standard deviation of 6.14. If we compare this with the SD of 3.27 from the initial example, it suggests that the initial sample of scores tends to be more closely clustered around the mean than the second sample.

Activity 2.8

If you have the variance of a set of scores, how would you calculate the standard deviation? Which of the following is (are) a reasonable definition of standard deviation?

(a) SD is the maximum score minus the minimum score
(b) SD is the total of the scores in a sample divided by the number of scores in the sample
(c) SD is a measure of the variation of the scores around the mean
(d) SD is the square-root of the variance

SPSSFW: obtaining measures of variation

To obtain measures of variation using SPSSFW you should follow the instructions presented earlier for generating measures of central tendency. If you use the *Explore* dialogue box as previously described, you will generate a printout similar to that presented below:

EXPLORE

Case Processing Summary

	Cases					
	Valid		Missing		Total	
	N	Percent	N	Percent	N	Percent
WITHDOG	6	50.0%	6	50.0%	12	100.0%
NODOG	6	50.0%	6	50.0%	12	100.0%

Descriptives

			Statistic	Std. Error
WITHDOG	Mean		8.6667	.8819
	95% Confidence	Lower Bound	6.3996	
	Interval for Mean	Upper Bound	10.9337	
	5% Trimmed Mean		8.6296	
	Median		8.5000	
	Variance		4.667	
	Std. Deviation		2.1602	
	Minimum		6.00	
	Maximum		12.00	
	Range		6.00	
	Interquartile Range		3.7500	
	Skewness		.463	.845
	Kurtosis		−.300	1.741
NODOG	Mean		4.0000	.7303
	95% Confidence	Lower Bound	2.1227	
	Interval for Mean	Upper Bound	5.8773	
	5% Trimmed Mean		4.0556	
	Median		4.5000	
	Variance		3.200	
	Std. Deviation		1.7889	
	Minimum		1.00	
	Maximum		6.00	
	Range		5.00	
	Interquartile Range		2.7500	
	Skewness		−.943	.845
	Kurtosis		.586	1.741

Variance, SD and range

You can see that the printout contains the range, variance and standard deviation.

2.9 Other characteristics of distributions

We have now covered ways to measure the spread of distributions. The other way in which distributions can differ from one another is in terms of how peaked or flat they are. The degree of peakedness or flatness is the *kurtosis* of the distribution. If a distribution is highly peaked it is said to be *leptokurtic*; if the distribution is flat it is said to *platykurtic*. A distribution that is between the more extremes of peakedness and flatness is said to be *mesokurtic* (see Figure 2.23).

You need not worry unduly about kurtosis at this stage of your statistical careers. We introduce it here for two reasons. First, for completeness, we want you to have a fairly comprehensive knowledge of the normal distributions and how they can differ from one another. Second, when you get SPSSFW to run descriptive statistics you will see a measure of kurtosis on the output. When you come across this you will now know what it refers to: positive values of kurtosis on the output suggest that the distribution is

| **Figure 2.23** | Normal distributions varying in terms of their peakness and flatness |

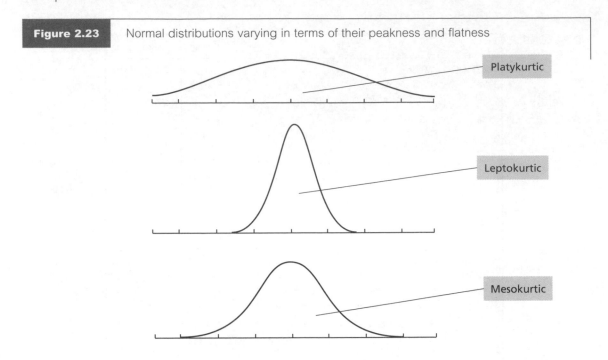

leptokurtic, whereas negative values suggest that it is platykurtic. A zero value tells you that you have a mesokurtic distribution.

2.10 Non-normal distributions

Although many variables, when plotted, roughly approximate the normal distribution, you will often find that variables deviate from this shape of distribution. Often such deviations from normal are the result of sampling error. It is important to check the shape of your distributions as most of the statistical techniques described in this book make the assumption that the data you are analysing are normally distributed. You can check the shape of the distributions by generating histograms. If you find that your data deviate markedly from the normal distribution you should consider using one of the statistical techniques that do not make the assumption of normally distributed data. These are called *distribution-free* or *non-parametric* tests and are covered in Chapter 15. The following descriptions illustrate some of the more common ways in which a distribution you may come across will deviate from the normal distribution.

2.10.1 Skewed distributions

The most often observed deviations from normality are the result of *skewness*. The distributions presented below are *skewed distributions* (Figure 2.24). You can see that in comparison with the normal distribution they are not symmetrical. The distribution that has an extended tail to the right is known as a *positively skewed* distribution (Figure 2.24(a)).

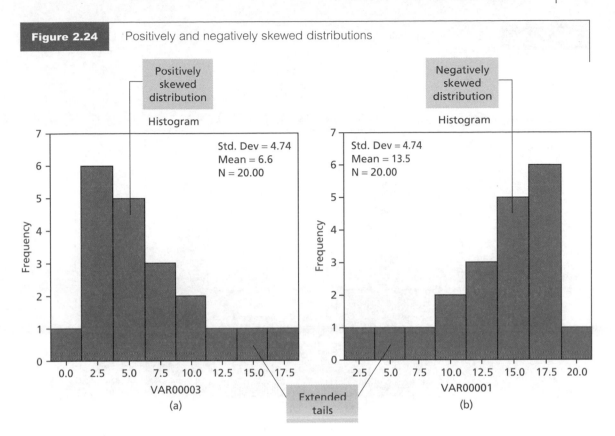

Figure 2.24 Positively and negatively skewed distributions

The distribution that has an extended tail to the left is known as a *negatively skewed* distribution (Figure 2.24(b)).

If you come across badly skewed distributions you should be cautious about using the mean as your measure of central tendency as the scores in the extended tail will be distorting your mean. In such cases you are advised to use the median or mode as these will be more representative of the typical score in your sample.

As with kurtosis, the output you get from SPSS for descriptive statistics also gives a measure of skewness. Here a positive value suggests a positively skewed distribution, whereas a negative value suggests a negatively skewed distribution. A value of zero tells you that your distribution is not skewed in either direction. If you look back at the output shown on page 75 you can see that we have a skewness value of 0.46 for the 'Withdog' condition indicating a small positive skew. We also have a value of −0.94 for the 'Nodog' condition indicating quite a large negative skew for these data. Values of skewness around about 1 (or −1) suggest deviations from normality which are too extreme for us to use many of the statistical techniques covered in this book.

2.10.2 Bimodal distributions

Occasionally you may come across a distribution like the one represented in Figure 2.25. This is known as a *bimodal distribution*. Essentially it has two modes, although in most cases the two humps of the distribution will not be equal in height. This is clearly a non-normal

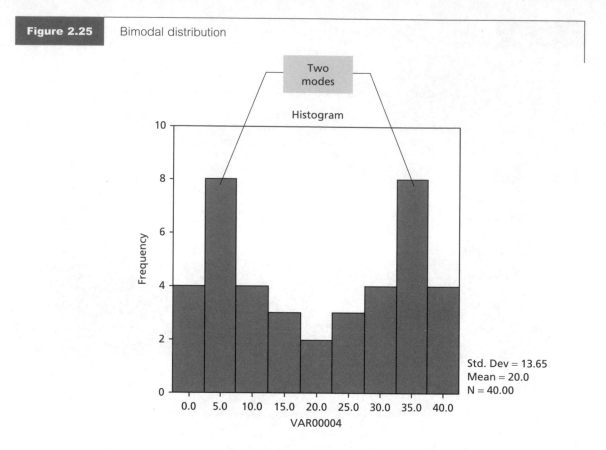

Figure 2.25 Bimodal distribution

distribution. If you come across such a distribution you should look closely at your sample as there may be some factor that is causing your scores to cluster around the two modal positions. It might be the case that you have to treat these as two separate populations. If all seems in order you should report that the distribution is bimodal and report the two modes.

A good example of bimodally distributed data is presented by Morris *et al.* (1981). In this study they looked at the relationship between memory for football scores and knowledge of football. Knowledge of football was measured using a football quiz. When the researchers examined the distribution of knowledge scores they found that it was bimodal. The explanation was that they had two distinct populations of people in the study, football enthusiasts and non-enthusiasts. The football enthusiasts scores clustered near the maximum possible score and the non-enthusiasts clustered near the minimum possible scores, thus forming a bimodal distribution.

We have now shown you what the normal distribution looks like and illustrated some of the ways in which actual distributions can deviate from normality. Because the normal distribution is so important in statistics, one of the main aims of graphically illustrating your data is to see whether they are normally distributed. Perhaps the best graphical techniques for establishing whether or not your data are normally distributed are histograms and stem and leaf plots. If you take another look at Figure 2.21(e) you will see an example of a histogram showing a normal distribution. On the other hand, Figure 2.3 is an example of a distribution that is slightly positively skewed. Compare it with Figure 2.24(a) and you will see that they are similar in shape.

One of the limitations of box plots is that it is often more difficult to tell when a distribution deviates from normality, but as a guide Figures 2.26(a) to (c) give examples of box plots illustrating normally and non-normally distributed data.

Figure 2.26(a) was generated from normally distributed data (1, 2, 2, 3, 3, 3, 4, 4, 4, 4, 5, 5, 5, 6, 6, 7) and shows that the median is in the centre of the box and we have whiskers of equal length coming from each side of the box. Also there are no outliers.

| **Figure 2.26** | Box plots illustrating (a) normally distributed, (b) negatively skewed and (c) bimodally distributed data |

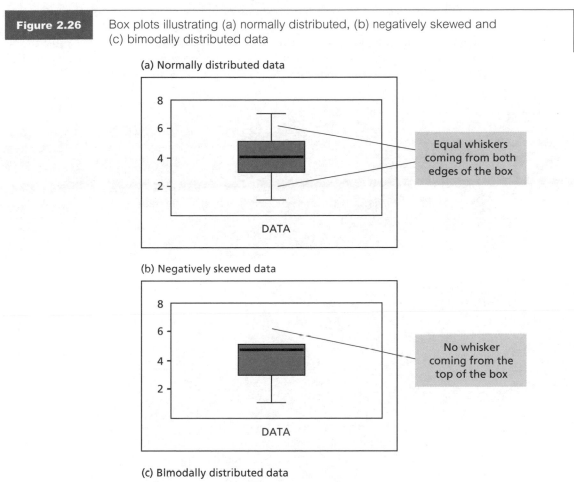

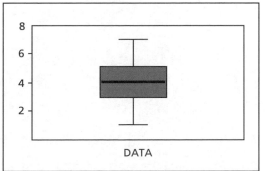

Figure 2.26(b) was generated from negatively skewed data (1, 2, 3, 3, 3, 4, 4, 4, 5, 5, 5, 5, 5, 5, 5, 5, 5) and shows that the median is shifted upwards in the box and is right near the top edge. Also there is no whisker coming out of the top of the box. This is an extreme example but whenever the median is shifted towards one edge of the box and you have a shortened or no whisker coming from that edge, you should suspect that you have skewed data.

Finally, Figure 2.26(c) was generated from bimodally distributed data (1, 2, 2, 3, 3, 3, 3, 3, 4, 4, 5, 5, 5, 5, 5, 6, 6, 7). Surprisingly, it looks exactly like Figure 2.26(a) and is a good illustration of the caution you should exercise when trying to interpret whether you have normally distributed data from box plots. This is why the histogram and, to a certain extent, stem and leaf plots are better for assessing whether you have normally distributed data. Thankfully, bimodally distributed data are not too common in research and so box plots can give a reasonable indication of the way your data are distributed.

Activity 2.9

Which of the following distributions are normal and which are not?

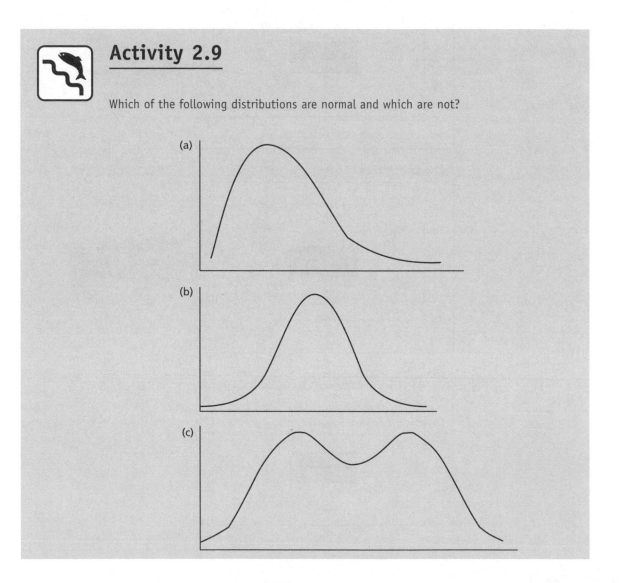

(a)

(b)

(c)

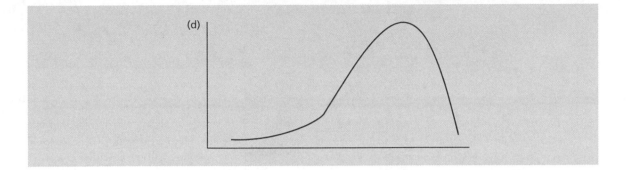

(d)

Example from the literature: experience of using computers and attitudes to computers

Even though we would expect that all researchers using the statistical techniques covered in this book would examine histograms it is quite rare to find researchers referring to histograms in published reports. A nice exception to this is a recent article published by Garland and Noyes (in press). In this study the researchers examined the aspects of computer use that best predicted attitudes towards computers. They concluded that current questionnaires measuring experience of computers are inadequate in terms of predicting attitudes to computers. Part of the questionnaire they administered to university students asked them for information about how much they use computers. The authors report analyses of this information by reference to histograms. They argue that given their relatively large sample size then it is more appropriate to use histograms to examine the distribution of response than other more sensitive measures of distribution. They suggested that the number of years participants report using computers is normally distributed, but some positive kurtosis is evident reflecting a peak for years of use between 9 and 11 years. They also suggest that the hours spent using computers was positively skewed and also showed positive kurtosis.

SPSSFW: displaying the normal curve on histograms

It is quite useful to get SPSSFW to display a normal distribution on your histograms to help you decide whether your data are normally distributed. Unfortunately, it is not possible to do this using the *Explore* dialogue box. In order to do this you should generate histograms using the *Graphs* menu instead of the *Analyze* menu. When you click on the *Graphs* menu you should notice that there are options for all the graphical descriptive techniques that we have shown you:

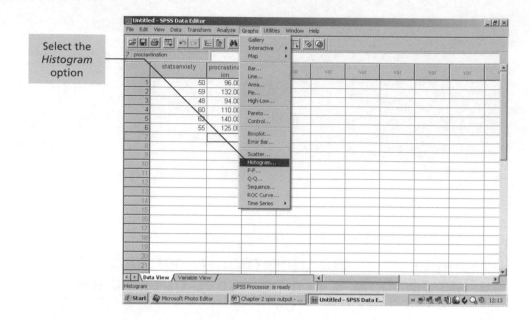

Select the *Histogram* . . . option and you will be presented with the following dialogue box:

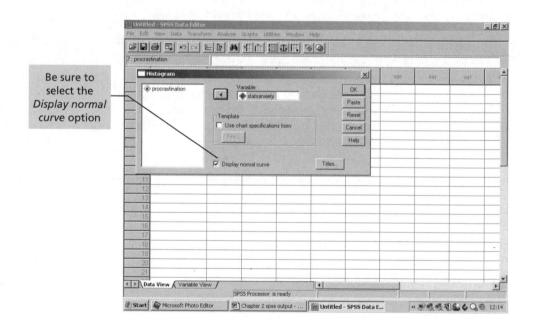

To generate a histogram with a normal curve on it you should move the relevant variable to the *Variable* box. You should then select the option that states *Display normal curve*. When you have made the correct selection, click on *OK* to generate the histogram. The resulting histogram will contain the normal curve, as indicated in Figure 2.27.

You can see from the histogram that the set of data that we have used corresponds quite closely to the normal curve.

Figure 2.27 SPSSFW histogram showing the normal distribution curve

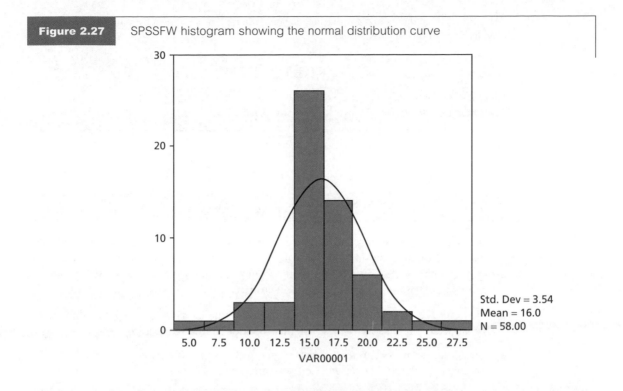

2.11 Writing up your descriptive statistics

Although it is good practice to examine the distribution of your data, you will find that most researchers do not routinely report the findings of such examinations. Typically, if your distributions deviate from normality then it is a good idea to report this fact. If the distributions are approximately normal in shape then it is up to you whether you report this. Whether or not you report the shape of your distribution, you should always examine this as the shape of your distribution has a bearing on the sorts of statistical techniques you can use to analyse your data.

If you wish to mention the way that your data are distributed then the following is perhaps how you should report your descriptive statistics. In a study conducted by Reidy and Keogh (1997) anxious and non-anxious individuals were compared on their interpretation of ambiguous information. There was also an examination of gender differences in such interpretations. We might present the descriptive statistics as follows:

There were 98 students in the study. The mean numbers of positive and negative interpretations were 10.06 and 7.95 respectively. The number of positive and negative interpretations given by males and females was compared. Table 2.1 shows the means and standard deviations for these two groups. The table shows that the males offered more negative interpretations than the females and about the same number of positive interpretations. Both genders gave more positive interpretations than they did negative interpretations. The standard deviations show that the two groups had similar levels of variability in terms of positive and negative interpretations. Examination of box and whisker plots revealed that the distributions were approximately normally distributed and that there were no extreme scores.

Table 2.1   Mean number of positive and negative interpretations shown by males and females (standard deviations in parenthesis)

	Females	Males
Positive interpretations	10.20 (2.32)	9.91 (3.01)
Negative interpretations	7.27 (2.99)	8.62 (3.55)

Summary

In this chapter we have introduced you to the ways of exploring and describing your data. We have highlighted the fact that it is important to become familiar with your data by using a number of descriptive statistical techniques, and we explained how to use and interpret such techniques. Thus, you have learnt:

- How to calculate means, medians and modes in order to get an indication of the typical score in a sample (these are measures of central tendency).

- Sampling errors occur when we take samples from populations, and the larger the sample we take, the lower will be the degree of sampling error.

- That there are a number of graphical techniques that help us to become more familiar with how our data are distributed; these include:
  - frequency histograms
  - stem and leaf plots
  - box plots
  - scattergrams.

- What the normal distribution looks like and why it is important in statistics.

- That there are a number of ways in which data that you gather can deviate from the normal distribution, including:
  - negatively skewed distributions
  - positively skewed distributions
  - bimodal distributions.

- That an important feature of any distribution is the degree to which the scores are spread out and that the most important measure of this is called the standard deviation.

- That the standard deviation is the degree to which the scores in a distribution deviate from the mean.

SPSSFW exercises

Exercise 1

You are given the job of finding out whether or not changing the lighting in an office from normal fluorescent lighting to red lighting will increase the alertness of data inputters and thereby decrease the number of errors they make. When you do this you find that 20 data inputters decrease their number of errors per day by the following amounts:

22, 22, 12, 10, 42, 19, 20, 19, 20, 21, 21, 20, 30, 28, 26, 18, 18, 20, 21, 19

1. What is the IV in this study?

2. What is the DV in this study?

3. Use SPSSFW to generate a box plot for the above set of scores:
    (a) Are the data normally distributed?
    (b) Are there any outliers shown on the box plot? If yes, which score(s) is (are) the outliers?
    (c) Using SPSSFW, what is the mean of the above set of scores? What is the standard deviation?

Exercise 2

A group of final-year students decides to see if the lecture material in Dr Boering's lectures can be made more memorable. They decide that the best way to do this would be to take hallucinogenic drugs during the lectures. At the end of term there was an exam and those students who took drugs during the lecture obtained the following marks (%):

23, 89, 62, 11, 76, 28, 45, 52, 71, 28

Those students in the class who did not take hallucinogenic drugs obtained the following marks:

45, 52, 68, 74, 55, 62, 58, 49, 42, 57

1. What is the IV in this study?

2. What is the DV? Is the DV continuous, discrete or categorical?

3. Use SPSSFW to plot histograms for the two sets of data and then answer the following:
    (a) Are the two sets of scores normally distributed?
    (b) Use SPSSFW to calculate the mean and standard deviations for both sets of scores.

MULTIPLE CHOICE QUESTIONS

1. Which one of the following represents the best estimate of the population mean?
    (a) The sample mean
    (b) The mean of several sample means
    (c) The mode of several sample means
    (d) The median of several sample means

2. If you obtained a sample of data that was relatively normally distributed and had no extreme scores, which measure of central tendency would you opt for?
    (a) Mode
    (b) Median
    (c) Mean
    (d) None of the above

3. Which of the following measures of central tendency are sensitive to extreme scores?
    (a) Mode
    (b) Median
    (c) Mean
    (d) None of the above

4. Given the following graph, how would you describe the distribution?

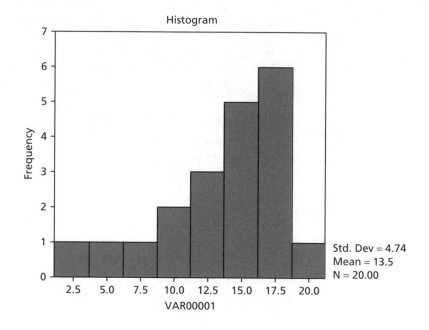

    (a) Normal
    (b) Positively skewed
    (c) Negatively skewed
    (d) Bimodal

5. The standard deviation is equal to:

   (a) The variance
   (b) The square-root of the variance
   (c) The variance squared
   (d) The variance divided by the number of scores

6. What is the relationship between sample size and sampling error?

   (a) The larger the sample size, the larger the sampling error
   (b) The larger the sample size, the smaller the sampling error
   (c) Sample size equals sampling error
   (d) None of the above

7. The mode is:

   (a) The frequency of the most common score divided by the total number of scores
   (b) The middle score after all the scores have been ranked
   (c) The most frequently occurring score
   (d) The sum of all the scores divided by the number of scores

8. In box plots an extreme score is defined as:

   (a) A score that falls beyond the inner fence
   (b) A score that falls between the hinges and the inner fence
   (c) A score that falls between the inner fence and the adjacent score
   (d) A score that falls between the two hinges

9. A normal distribution should have which of the following properties?

   (a) Bell-shaped
   (b) Be symmetrical
   (c) The tails of the distribution should meet the x-axis at infinity
   (d) All of the above

10. If you randomly select a sample of 20 pandas (sample A) and then select a sample of 300 pandas (sample B) and calculate the mean weight for each sample which is likely to give a better estimate of the population mean weight?

    (a) Sample A
    (b) Sample B
    (c) Both will give equally good estimates of the population mean
    (d) Neither will give a good estimate of the population mean

11. What sort of relationship is indicated by a scattergram where the points cluster around an imaginary line that goes from the bottom left-hand corner to the top right-hand corner?

    (a) Positive
    (b) Negative
    (c) Bimodal
    (d) Flat

12. What is the mean of the following set of scores: 5, 7, 10, 12, 18, 20, 24, 22, 24, 25?
    (a) 145
    (b) 17.2
    (c) 16.7
    (d) 167

13. If you have a negatively skewed distribution then:
    (a) The mean, median and mode are equal
    (b) The right-hand tail is extended
    (c) The left-hand tail is extended
    (d) None of the above

14. A perfectly normal distribution:
    (a) Is bell-shaped, symmetrical and has tails that cross the x-axis at infinity
    (b) Is only applicable for normal people
    (c) Has equal mean, median and modes
    (d) (a) and (c) above

15. When you have categorical variables and are simply counting the frequency of occurrence of each category then your measure of central tendency should be:
    (a) Mode
    (b) Median
    (c) Mean
    (d) None of the above

16. Given the following set of data (8, 7, 9, 12, 14, 10, 14, 11, 13, 14), what are the mean, median and mode?
    (a) 11.2, 11.5, 14
    (b) 112, 12, 14
    (c) 10, 5, 14
    (d) 10, 12, 14

17. If a distribution is described as platykurtic, then it is:
    (a) Very peaked
    (b) Very flat
    (c) Bimodal
    (d) Very thin

18. Having calculated the variance of a set of data with 12 participants to be 36, what would the standard deviation be?
    (a) 36
    (b) 1296
    (c) 6
    (d) 3

19. Which of the following statements are true?
    (a) Parameters describe samples and statistics describe populations
    (b) Statistics describe samples and populations
    (c) Parameters describe populations and statistics describe samples
    (d) Both (a) and (b) above

20. Given the following graph, how would you describe the distribution?

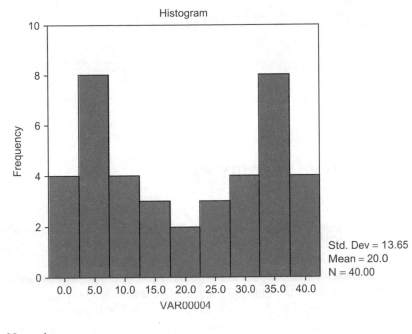

(a) Normal
(b) Positively skewed
(c) Negatively skewed
(d) Bimodal

References

Armitage, C. and Reidy, J. (unpublished) 'Development and validation of a new measure of blood fear'.

Baker, R., Holloway, J., Thomas, P.W., Thomas, S. and Owens, M. (in press) 'Emotional processing and panic', *Behaviour Research and Therapy*.

Garland, K.J. and Noyes, J.M. (in press) 'Computer experience: a poor predictor of computer attitudes', *Computers in Human Behaviour*.

Morris, P.E., Gruneberg, M.M., Sykes, R.N. and Merrick, A. (1981) 'Football knowledge and the acquisition of new results', *British Journal of Psychology*, **72**: 479–83.

Reidy, J. and Keogh, E. (1997) 'State and trait factors underlying the interpretation of threat/neutral homophones.' Paper presented at the British Psychological Society Cognitive Section Annual Conference.

Tabachnick, B. and Fidell, L.S. (2003), *Using Multivariate Statistics* (4th edn): Addison Wesley.

Tukey, J.W. (1977) *Exploratory Data Analysis*. Reading, MA: Addison-Wesley.

Walsh, J.J. and Ugumba-Agwunobi, G. (2002) 'Individual differences in statistics anxiety: the roles of perfectionism, procrastination and trait anxiety', *Personality and Individual Differences*, **33**: 239–51.

Watson, M. and Greer, S. (1983) 'Development of a questionnaire measure of emotional control', *Journal of Psychosomatic Research*, **27**: 299–305.

3 Probability, sampling and distributions

Chapter overview

In the previous two chapters we introduced you to the important aspects of experimental design and the initial processes of data analyses. In this chapter we will start you off on the road to drawing conclusions from your data. We will build upon your knowledge of samples and populations to explain how we are able to generalise our findings from samples to populations. We will show you how we use sample data to help us draw conclusions about our populations. That is, we will introduce you to *inferential statistics*. First we will give a brief introduction to the world of probabilities. We will then show how we can use probability distributions such as the standard normal distribution to draw inferences from sample data. Therefore in this chapter you will learn:

- probability and conditional probability
- applying probability to research
- standard normal distribution
- sampling distributions
- point and interval estimates
- standard error and confidence intervals
- error bar charts.

3.1 Probability

For an understanding of statistics you will need to understand the concept of probability. This should not be as difficult as it may seem, as probability is a common element of everyday life. Every time you toss a coin you are dealing with probabilities. Every time you roll a die or buy a lottery ticket, you are involved with probabilities. We hear about probabilities all the time in the news: for example, if you smoke cigarettes you greatly increase the probability that you will contract lung cancer. Similarly (and this one I like – JR), if you drink beer in moderation, you reduce the risk of coronary heart disease.

It is clear from the above examples that probabilities are an important aspect of everyday life. Let us now take a look at some of these examples in more detail. If you toss a coin, what is the probability of it landing with the heads side upwards? There is a 1 in 2 probability of getting heads when you toss a coin. This means that one in every two tosses of the coin is likely to turn out with heads being the exposed side of the coin. Usually, probabilities are expressed in the form of a decimal number ranging from 0 to 1, where 0 means that the event *definitely will not* happen and 1 means the event *definitely will* happen.

Activity 3.1

Which of these events has a probability of 0 (or very close to 0) and which has a probability of 1 (or very close to 1)?

■ Night following day
■ All politicians telling us the truth all the time
■ Your finding a cheque for a million pounds in the pages of this book
■ A wood fire being extinguished if you pour water on it
■ Authors having to extend the deadline for sending in manuscripts for books

To calculate the probability of an event occurring, such as tossing a coin, we simply divide the number of occurrences of the desired outcomes by the total number of possible outcomes. Thus, in the case of tossing the coin there is one desired outcome (heads) but two possible outcomes (heads or tails). The probability of getting heads is therefore 1/2 (or 0.5). You will also sometimes see probabilities expressed in terms of percentages. Such a format is often more familiar to people and helps them understand probabilities better. To calculate the percentage from the decimal you simply multiply it by 100. Therefore, the probability of obtaining heads when tossing a coin is 50% (0.5 × 100). The probability of 0 is 0% and a probability of 1 is 100%.

Activity 3.2

Express the following probabilities as percentages:

■ 0.25
■ 0.99
■ 1/3
■ 2/10

Express the following probabilities as decimals:

■ 1/8
■ 12/20
■ 30%
■ 14%

Let us now turn our attention to rolling the die. When we roll a die, what is the probability of our rolling a 6? Here we have *one* desired outcome (a 6) and *six* possible outcomes (1, 2, 3, 4, 5 or 6) and so we have a probability of 1 ÷ 6 or 0.1667 of rolling a 6. What is the probability of rolling a 1 or a 2? Here we have two desired outcomes (1 or 2) and six possible outcomes, therefore the probability is 2 ÷ 6 or 0.3333.

Try to work out the probability of rolling an even number (the answer is in the 'Answers' section of the book).

3.1.1 Conditional probabilities

For the purpose of research in psychology we need an understanding not only of probability but also of *conditional probability*. A conditional probability is the probability of some event taking place, which is dependent upon something else. For example, the probability of Arsenal winning the Cup Final this year might be 70% if they were playing against Enfield Town, but might be only 60% if they were playing Manchester United. These are conditional probabilities in that they are dependent upon which team Arsenal would be playing in the Cup Final. Another example of a conditional probability is the probability of someone buying this statistics book. Ordinarily, given that there are probably at least 99 other texts on the market, the probability of someone buying this book would be about 1 in 100 (or 1%). If a tutor recommends it, however, then the probability may change to about 1 in 5 (or 20%). This latter probability is a conditional probability; it is the probability of someone buying the book conditional upon a tutor recommending it. We mentioned two examples of conditional probabilities earlier in the chapter. The probability of contracting cancer if you smoke cigarettes is a conditional probability, as is the probability of coronary heart disease if you drink moderate amounts of beer. Try to ensure that you understand what conditional probabilities are as you will come across them more in Chapter 4 when we explain hypothesis testing.

Activity 3.3

Which of the following are conditional probabilities?

(a) The probability of being struck by lightning while playing golf
(b) The probability of winning the Lottery
(c) The probability of winning an Olympic gold medal if you do no training
(d) The probability of getting lung cancer if you smoke
(e) The probability of manned flight to Mars within the next ten years
(f) The probability of having coronary heart disease if you drink moderate levels of beer

3.1.2 Applying probabilities to data analyses: inferential statistics

Inferential statistics are techniques employed to draw conclusions from your data. When we conduct research we typically want to draw some conclusions about what we are observing, that is, we want to make inferences. The reason why we investigate the relationship between statistics anxiety and procrastination or that between cigarette smoking and short-term memory is to understand them better. Similarly, the reason why we would conduct a study on people who eat chocolate sponge with tomato ketchup at 6.30 in the morning is that we want to know why on earth they do it. To answer such questions we need to draw conclusions from our data.

Given the following description of events, what conclusion are you likely to draw?

> *On a busy afternoon in the centre of Wolverhampton a man was seen sprinting around a corner and running along the High Street. He was obviously in a hurry and did not care that he knocked people out of his way. About three seconds later a policewoman also came running around the corner and up the High Street.*

One likely conclusion from this description is that the policewoman is trying to catch up with and arrest the person running in front of her. In the majority of cases this would be a reasonable conclusion to draw from the description above. However, it could be that the policewoman is following a plain clothes officer and they are both rushing to the scene of a crime.

You can see how easy it is to jump to the wrong conclusion in real-life events. The same sorts of error can arise in psychological research, because we are trying to draw conclusions from statistical analyses. Remember, when we test a sample of individuals we are generally doing so to enable us to draw conclusions about the population from which the sample was drawn. If we wanted to find out whether statistics anxiety was related to procrastination we would randomly select a sample of individuals and get measures of these two variables. From these data we would then try to make some inferences about the relationship between the two variables in the population. This is what we use inferential statistical techniques for. It is, however, possible that we may draw the wrong conclusions from our statistical analyses. This is because the statistical techniques we use in order to draw conclusions about underlying populations are based upon probabilities. We therefore need to be constantly aware of the fallibility of such techniques.

Example from the literature: statistics anxiety and procrastination

Walsh and Ugumba-Agwunobi (2002) used inferential statistical techniques to assess the relationship between statistics anxiety and procrastination. They asked 93 people to complete a multidimensional measure of statistics anxiety and a procrastination questionnaire. Using Pearson's correlational coefficient as choice of inferential statistical technique, they found correlations between procrastination and three components of statistics anxiety, namely, fear of statistics teachers, fear of asking for help, and test and class anxiety. These statistical techniques enabled Walsh and Ugumba-Agwunobi to argue that they had support for their hypothesis that statistics anxiety is related to procrastination.

3.2 The standard normal distribution

We have explained what we mean by probability and also, in Chapter 2, described to you the family of distributions known as the normal distributions. We would now like to explain an even more important distribution known as the *standard normal distribution* (see Figure 3.1). As is indicated in Figure 3.1, the standard normal distribution (SND) is a normally shaped distribution with a mean of zero and a standard deviation of 1. Because of these and other characteristics the SND is a very useful distribution. Using this distribution we are able to compare scores from different samples, compare different scores from the same samples and much, much more.

In order to use the standard normal distribution for analysing our data we need to transform the scores in our samples to the standard normal scores. This is achieved by subtracting the mean from each score and then dividing by the standard deviation. The result is called a *z-score*. The z-score is expressed in standard deviation units, that is, the z-score tells us how many standard deviations above or below the mean our score is. If you have a negative z-score then your score is below the mean; if you have a positive z-score then your score is above the mean. Thus, a z-score of 1 tells us that it falls one standard deviation above the mean.

An example may help you to understand. The mean for IQ scores for many IQ tests is 100 and the standard deviation is 15. If you had an IQ score of 135 your z-score would be:

$$\frac{135 - 100}{15} = 2.33$$

This tells us that your score is 2.33 standard deviations above the mean: you have a z-score of 2.33.

Once we have converted our z-scores we can use the SND in a number of useful ways. The SND is known as a *probability distribution*. The beauty of probability distributions is that there is a probability associated with each particular score from the distribution. That is, we know the probability of randomly selecting any particular score from the distribution. We also know the probability of obtaining a score between any two values from the distribution,

| Figure 3.1 | The standard normal distribution |

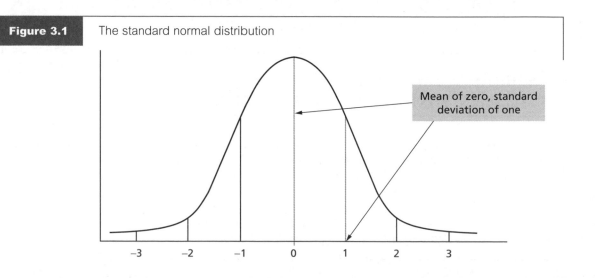

| **Figure 3.2** | Percentage of the curve falling between −1 and +1 standard deviations |

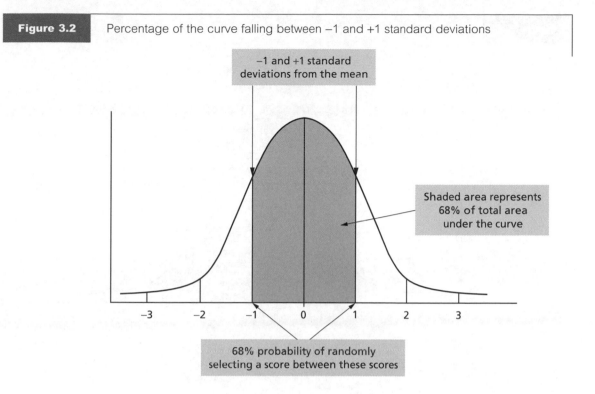

−1 and +1 standard deviations from the mean

Shaded area represents 68% of total area under the curve

−3 −2 −1 0 1 2 3

68% probability of randomly selecting a score between these scores

e.g. a score between −1 and +1. An important characteristic of probability distributions is that the area under the curve between any specified points represents the probability of obtaining scores within those specified points. For example, the probability of obtaining scores between −1 and +1 from the standard normal distribution is about 68% (see Figure 3.2). This means that 68% of the total area under the standard normal curve falls between the −1 and +1 standard deviations from the mean. We should emphasise that the probability being referred to here is the probability of randomly selecting scores from the distribution. Thus, there is a 68% probability of randomly selecting a score between −1 and +1.

Similarly, the probability of obtaining a score between −1.96 and +1.96 from the distribution is 95% (see Figure 3.3).

Because of these characteristics we can use the SND to work out the probability of obtaining scores within any section of the distribution. We could work out the probability of obtaining a z-score of 2 or above in the SND or we could find the probability of obtaining a z-score between 1 and 2. You will notice that extreme z-scores, say above 2 and below −2, have a much smaller chance of being obtained than scores in the middle of the distribution. That is, the areas of the curve above 2 and below −2 are small in comparison with the area between −1 and 1 (see Figure 3.4). We can relate this to more concrete variables such as men's height. If you think about scores falling above 2 and below −2 as the extremes of men's height, say above 6 ft 7 in (about 2.0 m) and below 4 ft 7 in (1.4 m), it is clear that we are much less likely to find men above and below these heights than, say, men between 5 ft 5 in (1.65 m) and 6 ft (1.83 m).

Fortunately, when working with the standard normal distribution, we do not have to work out the areas under the curve and convert them into probabilities; they have already been calculated for us and are conveniently listed in statistical tables for us to use. If you look at Appendix 1 you will see such a table.

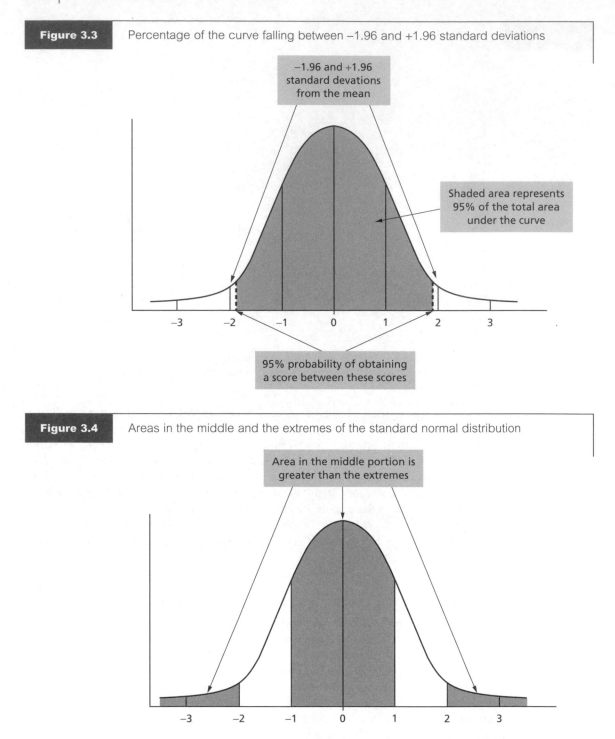

Figure 3.3 Percentage of the curve falling between −1.96 and +1.96 standard deviations

−1.96 and +1.96 standard devations from the mean

Shaded area represents 95% of the total area under the curve

95% probability of obtaining a score between these scores

Figure 3.4 Areas in the middle and the extremes of the standard normal distribution

Area in the middle portion is greater than the extremes

Another useful feature of the SND is that we can use it to calculate the proportion of the population who would score above or below your score. Remember, when we are talking about proportions here we want to think about the area under the standard normal curve. This is where we need to consult the standard normal distribution tables found in

| Figure 3.5 | Normal distribution showing the proportion of the population with an IQ of less than 135 (z-score of 2.33) |

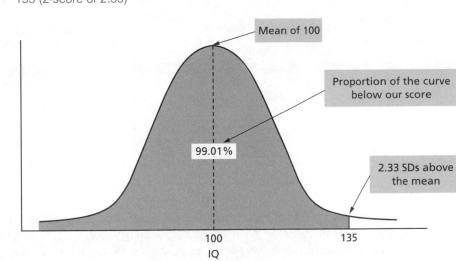

many statistical texts (see Appendix 1). If we look at Figure 3.5 we can see that the IQ score of 135 is 2.33 standard deviations above the mean. The shaded area represents the proportion of the population who would score less than you. The unshaded area represents those who would score more than you.

To find out what proportion of the population would score less than you, we can consult the standard normal distribution table. The normal distribution tables tend to come in different formats but the information in them is essentially the same. An extract from Appendix 1 can be seen in Table 3.1.

We can see from this that the values in the column headed 'Proportion below score' represent the proportion of area under the curve below any particular z-scores. The table shows us that the proportion falling below your z-score is 0.9901. This means that 99.01% of the area under the curve falls below your score. If you wanted to know what proportion of the curve was above your score, you could simply subtract the above proportion from 1. In this case you will find that 0.0099 of the curve is above your score, or less than 1%. This value is presented in the table in the 'Proportion above score' column.

Table 3.1 Extract from the statistical table giving details of the standard normal distribution

Details for the z-score of 2.33		Proportion of curve falling below your score
z-score	Proportion below score	Proportion above score
2.31	0.9896	0.0104
2.32	0.9898	0.0102
2.33	0.9901	0.0099
2.34	0.9904	0.0096
2.35	0.9906	0.0094

Figure 3.6 Illustration of proportions of the curve below positive z-scores and above negative z-scores

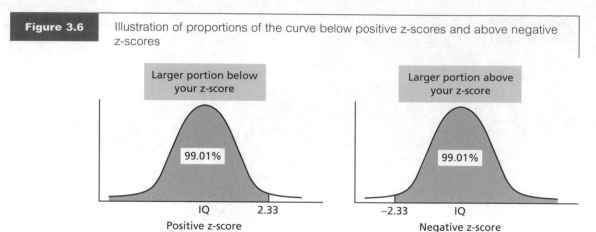

Larger portion below your z-score

99.01%

IQ   2.33

Positive z-score

Larger portion above your z-score

99.01%

−2.33   IQ

Negative z-score

You should note that the tables tend to contain only details of positive z-scores, that is, those that fall above the mean. If you have got a negative z-score you simply use the same tables but disregard the negative sign of the z-score to find the relevant areas above and below your score. However, because your score is below the mean, the proportion given in the 'Proportion below score' column now tells you the proportion of the curve that is above your score (see Figure 3.6).

Another example should help to make the calculation of such proportions clearer. Suppose that you had an off day when you took your IQ test and only scored 95. What percentage of the population falls below your score?

We can convert your score to a z-score, thus:

$$\frac{95 - 100}{15} = -0.33$$

You can see here that we now have a negative z-score. If we consult the SND tables we find that the proportion below your score is 0.3707 (37.07%). If you look at Figure 3.7 you

Figure 3.7 Proportion of the population scoring above and below an IQ score of 95

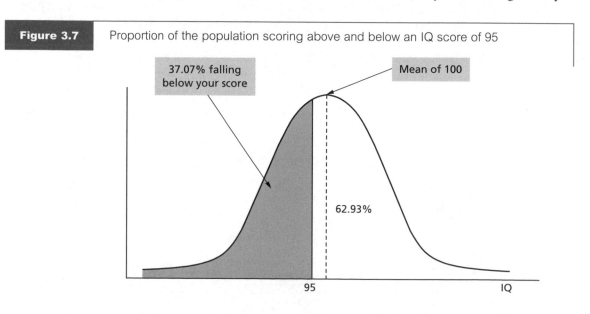

37.07% falling below your score

Mean of 100

62.93%

95

IQ

can see that, as your score is below the mean, the smaller portion will be that which is below your score. Therefore the tables tell us that 37.07% of the population score below and 62.93% score above your IQ. Remember when consulting Appendix 1 for negative z-scores that the proportion below your score will be found in the 'Proportion above score' column and *vice versa*.

Activity 3.4

If you have a negative z-score, does it fall above or below the mean? With a negative z-score do the majority of the population score higher or lower than you?

3.2.1 Comparing across populations

Another way that we can use the standard normal distribution is to compare across different situations. For example, suppose you were unsure about your future career but knew you would like to do pottery or weightlifting. You decide to take a course in each and see how you perform before deciding which career to choose. At the end of the courses you find that you were graded with 64% for pottery and 45% for weightlifting. On the face of it, you might feel justified in pursuing a career as a potter rather than a weightlifter. Have you made the correct decision? To get a better idea you need to compare yourself with the others in your groups. You might find that you are worse at pottery in comparison with the rest of the group than you are at weightlifting. To make such comparisons you need to convert your grades to z-scores. Let us suppose that the mean and standard deviation for pottery are 55% and 9% respectively and for weightlifting 40% and 4%. Your z-score for pottery would work out to be 1 and for weightlifting it would be 1.25.

$$\frac{64 - 55}{9} = 1 \qquad\qquad \frac{45 - 40}{4} = 1.25$$

z-score for pottery   z-score for weightlifting

This tells us that you were 1 standard deviation above the mean in pottery and 1.25 standard deviations above the mean for weightlifting. You are, therefore, comparatively better at weightlifting than pottery. Consequently, you would perhaps be better off choosing weightlifting as a career.

Activity 3.5

Suppose that your marks in Mathematics and English are 65% and 71% respectively. Which is your better subject in comparison with the others in your group if the group means and SDs are 60 and 5 (Mathematics) and 65 and 7 (English)?

3.3 Applying probability to research

We explained earlier in this chapter that the probability of some event happening can be expressed as a decimal or as a percentage. For example, when you roll a die you have a 0.1667 (16.67%) probability of rolling a 1. Similarly, if there was a probability of 0.05 (or 5%) of having an accident while driving your car, this would mean that in approximately one drive in every 20 you would probably have an accident. Such a probability may be dependent upon some other factor, such as using a mobile phone while driving. If this was the case we would state that there was a probability of 5% of your having an accident while driving your car when you are also using your mobile phone. This latter statement of probability is a conditional probability. The probability of 5% of having an accident when driving your car is conditional upon your driving while using the mobile phone.

You might be thinking, this is all very well but what has a knowledge of probability got to do with applying statistics to research? In research we usually generalise from samples to populations. As discussed in Chapter 2 (see page 42), whenever we use samples we are prone to sampling error. This means that we do not know whether the pattern of results we find in our samples accurately reflects what is happening in the populations or is simply the result of sampling error. It would be useful if we were able to work out the probability of the pattern of findings in our samples being the result of sampling error. If there is only a small chance that random sampling error by itself produced our pattern of results, we may wish to conclude that the samples accurately reflect the populations.

One of the simplest ways of applying probabilities to research and of estimating population parameters from sample statistics is to calculate confidence intervals. In the following sections we will explain the important concepts necessary for calculating confidence intervals and explain why they are useful for drawing conclusions from research. We will describe *sampling distributions* and highlight some important characteristics of these. Following this, we will explain how we can use sampling distributions of the mean to work out how good an estimate a sample mean is of a population mean, through the use of confidence intervals.

3.4 Sampling distributions

If you think back to Chapter 2, we explained that you could use the mean of the sample as an estimate of the mean of the population. We also explained that, if you took many samples and took the mean of the means of these samples, then this would be a better estimate of the population mean than the individual means (see page 42). The *Central Limit Theorem* states that, as the size of the samples we select increases, the nearer to the population mean will be the mean of these sample means. Thus, the larger the samples we obtain, the better estimate we can get of the population mean.

When you plot sample statistics from all of your samples as a frequency histogram you get something called the *sampling distribution*. Thus, if you plotted the sample means of many samples from one particular population you would have plotted the *sampling distribution of the mean*. An interesting property of sampling distributions is that, if they are plotted from enough samples, they are always approximately normal in shape. And

Figure 3.8 Histogram showing the distribution of the population of rolls of the die

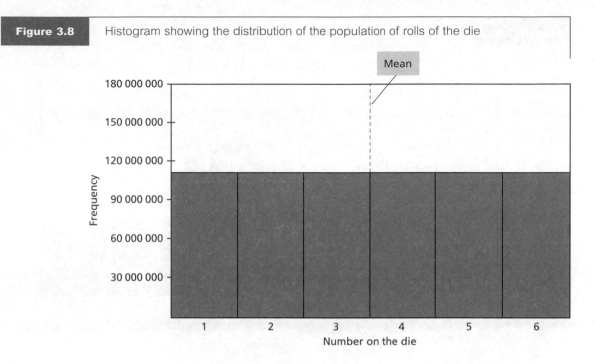

generally, the larger the samples we take, the nearer to normal the resulting sampling distribution will be.

Perhaps surprisingly, the sampling distribution of the mean will be normal in shape no matter how the overall population is distributed. The population could be skewed in some way or bimodally distributed or even be flat and we would still find that the sampling distributions would be normally distributed.

The following example will serve to illustrate this. Imagine that, when you were born, somebody started rolling a die and recording the numbers. This person rolled the die once every two seconds for the whole of your life, which we will assume is about 80 years (not a particularly interesting thing for someone to do but there we go). Now if we plotted the distribution of all the rolls of the die (the population of all the rolls of the die in your lifetime) it would probably look something like the distribution in Figure 3.8.

Because each number on the die has an equal probability of occurring (1 in 6), we would expect each number to have appeared with roughly equal frequency in your lifetime. Thus the population of rolls of the die in your lifetime has a flat distribution. Assuming that the numbers have occurred with equal frequency, then the mean of the population of rolls is 3.5. If we now randomly select five samples of ten rolls of the die from this population we might obtain the following:

Rolls of the die

1, 5, 1, 2, 6, 6, 4, 1, 4, 6   mean = 3.6

1, 2, 2, 2, 6, 5, 3, 3, 6, 4   mean = 3.4

4, 2, 1, 6, 6, 5, 3, 5, 5, 2   mean = 3.9

3, 5, 2, 4, 2, 2, 1, 4, 3, 4   mean = 3.0

4, 2, 1, 1, 2, 6, 6, 5, 3, 4   mean = 3.4

| Figure 3.9 | Histogram showing the distribution of the means from the five samples of ten rolls of the die drawn from the population of rolls of the die |

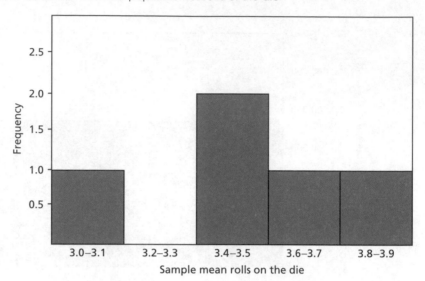

You can see that the means are relatively good approximations to the population mean of 3.5, although they do vary quite considerably. However, if we calculate the mean of the means we find that it is an even better approximation of the population mean:

$$\frac{(3.6 + 3.4 + 3.9 + 3 + 3.4)}{5} = 3.46$$

Now let us plot these sample means as a frequency distribution, that is, plot a sampling distribution – see Figure 3.9.

You can see from Figure 3.9 that the distribution is not flat like that of the population of rolls of the die. This is better illustrated, however, if we take more samples of ten rolls of the die. The graph in Figure 3.10 is the sampling distribution of 100 such sample means.

You can see that, even though the population has a flat distribution, the sampling distribution of the mean is approximately normal in shape. This would be the case for any sampling distribution that you cared to plot.

Activity 3.6

Suppose you took 100 different samples of four-year-olds and measured their reading ability. For each sample you calculate a mean and then plot the means of all the samples as a frequency histogram. What will be the shape of this frequency histogram?

| **Figure 3.10** | Histogram showing the distribution of the means from the 100 samples of ten rolls of the die drawn from the population of rolls of the die |

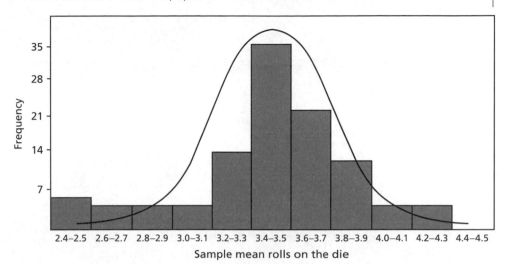

3.5 Confidence intervals and the standard error

Although we know that the sample mean is an approximation of the population mean, generally we are not sure how good an approximation it is. This is where *confidence intervals* help us.

Because the sample mean is a particular value or point along a variable, it is known as a *point estimate* of the population mean. It represents one point on a variable and because of this we do not know whether our sample mean is an underestimation or an overestimation of the population mean. Also we do not really know how close to the population mean our mean is. It would therefore be useful if we had some way of knowing approximately where on the variable the population mean lies. Fortunately, we do have some way of working this out by the calculation of confidence intervals. Confidence intervals of the mean are *interval estimates* of where the population mean may lie. That is, they provide us with a range of scores (an interval) within which we can be confident that the population mean lies.

For example, suppose we gave a sample of people the Beck Depression Inventory (BDI: Beck *et al.*, 1961). The questionnaire measures depression and scores can range from 0 to 63. Let us suppose that the mean of our sample on the BDI is 10.72. We do not know from this information how near our sample mean is to the population mean (see Figure 3.11 (a)). It would be very useful if we could give an indication of how near this figure was to the population mean. Let us think about this situation logically. As the minimum score on the questionnaire is 0 and the maximum is 63 we can be 100% confident that the population mean lies somewhere between these two scores (see Figure 3.11 (b)). This is a confidence interval. It is, though, not really that informative. We can use characteristics of sampling distributions to narrow this range down further, although we also reduce the degree of confidence that we can have concerning whether the interval we specify is likely to contain the population mean. We usually set up 95% confidence intervals and you will find that it is often the case that such intervals can be quite narrow (depending upon the size of your

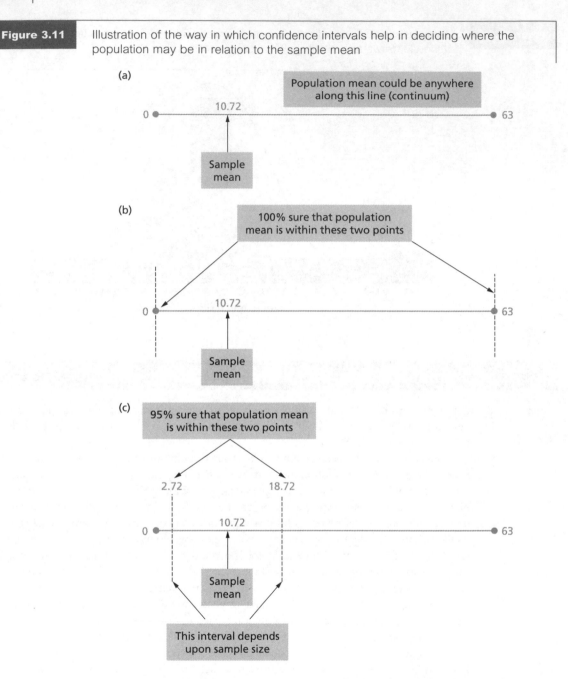

Figure 3.11 Illustration of the way in which confidence intervals help in deciding where the population may be in relation to the sample mean

samples). In our example, you can see that we are 95% confident that the population mean lies somewhere between 2.72 and 18.72 (see Figure 3.11 (c)). This is considerably more precise than stating that it lies between 0 and 63. This gives us a much better feel for where the population mean may lie in relation to our sample mean.

You should note, however, that because we are still only using estimates of population parameters it is not guaranteed that the population mean will fall within this range. We therefore have to give an expression of how confident we are that the range we calculate contains the population mean. Hence the term 'confidence intervals'.

Figure 3.12	Sampling distribution with unknown mean of sample means

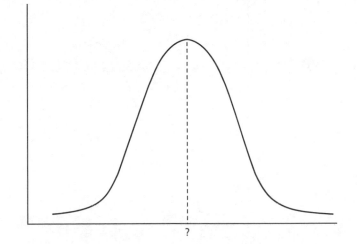

Previously we described how sampling distributions tend to be normally distributed. We also informed you that the mean of the sampling distribution of the mean is a very good approximation of the population mean. Such knowledge means that, regardless of the shape of the population distribution, we always know what the sampling distribution of the mean will look like. This is important as it gives us some very important insights about the population from sample statistics.

In Chapter 2 we informed you that the normal distribution is a function of its mean and standard deviation. This means that if we know the standard deviation and the mean then we can plot a normal curve from this information by putting it into a formula. Given that the sampling distribution of the mean is normally distributed it must also be a function of its mean and standard deviation. Consequently, once we know the mean and standard deviation of the sampling distribution of the mean, then we could easily plot it. We can then use this information to help us calculate confidence intervals.

Suppose we have the sampling distribution shown in Figure 3.12. The question mark in Figure 3.12 indicates that we do not know the value of the population mean (mean of the sample means). Now, let's say we took a sample and obtained the sample mean. Given that we do not know what the population mean is, we cannot be certain where in the distribution our sample mean will fall; it could be above, below or even exactly equal to the population mean (see Figure 3.13).

How do we go about tackling the difficult problem of identifying how close the population mean is to the sample mean? First of all we need to make use of the sampling distribution of the mean. We have previously explained two important characteristics of the sampling distribution of the mean:

■ it is always approximately normally distributed
■ its mean is a very good approximation to the population mean.

These two features mean that we can plot a normal distribution that we know contains a good approximation of the population mean. We can then use the characteristics of normal distributions to estimate how far our sample mean is from the population mean. Let us assume that Figure 3.14 is an example of such a sampling distribution.

Figure 3.13 Whereabouts of a sample mean in relation to the population mean is unknown

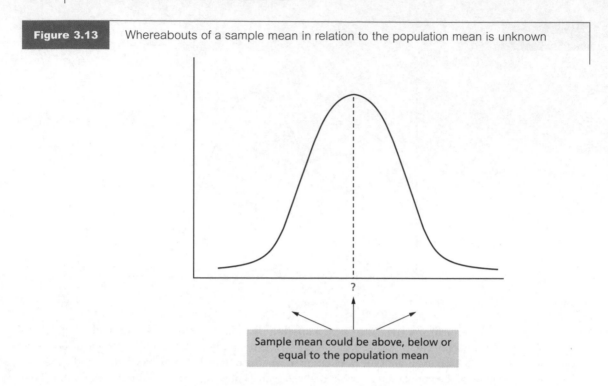

Figure 3.14 Sample mean is a certain number of standard deviations above or below the population mean

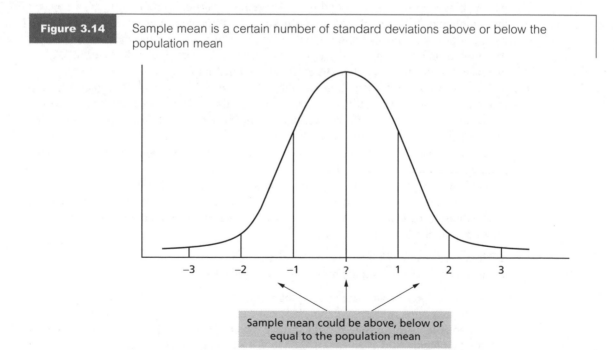

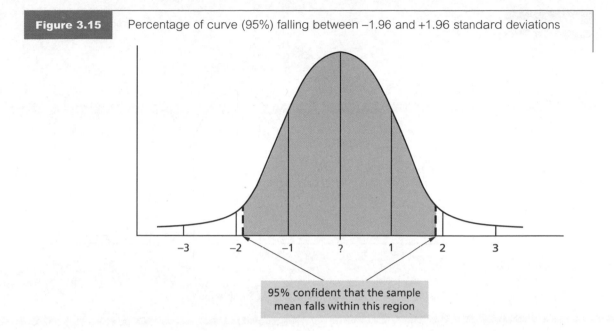

Figure 3.15 Percentage of curve (95%) falling between −1.96 and +1.96 standard deviations

95% confident that the sample mean falls within this region

We can see from Figure 3.14 that the sample mean is going to be a certain number of standard deviations above or below the population mean. Also, looking at the distribution we can be fairly confident that the sample mean will fall in the area between −3 and +3 standard deviations as this accounts for most of the scores in the distribution. In fact if we look at the z-scores from the normal distribution we can calculate the probability of a score falling in the area within −3 and +3 standard deviations. This probability works out to be 99.74%. This suggests that we can be 99.74% confident that the sample mean will be in the area enclosed by −3 and +3 standard deviations. Now suppose, as is usually the case, we want to be 95% confident that a certain area of the curve contains the sample mean. We work out this area again by referring to our z-scores. In section 3.2 we informed you that 95% of the area under the standard normal distribution falls within −1.96 and −1.96 standard deviations (see Figure 3.15). Thus, we can be 95% confident of the sample mean falling somewhere between −1.96 and +1.96 standard deviations from the population mean.

Now let us suppose for the sake of illustration that the sample mean is somewhere above the population mean. Now if we draw the distribution around the sample mean instead of the population mean we see the situation illustrated in Figure 3.16.

We can now apply the same logic as we have just done for predicting where the sample mean is in relation to the population mean. We can be fairly confident that the population mean falls somewhere within 1.96 standard deviations below the sample mean. Similarly, if the sample mean is below the population mean we can be fairly confident that the population mean is within 1.96 standard deviations above the sample mean (see Figure 3.17). Consequently, we can be fairly confident (95% confident) that the population mean is within the region 1.96 standard deviations above or below the sample mean. It is important to keep in mind that the standard deviation we are referring to here is the standard deviation of a sampling distribution, not the standard deviation of our sample. Armed with this information we can give an indication of how far the sample mean is from the population mean. All we need to know is the sample mean and the *standard deviation of the sampling distribution of the mean*.

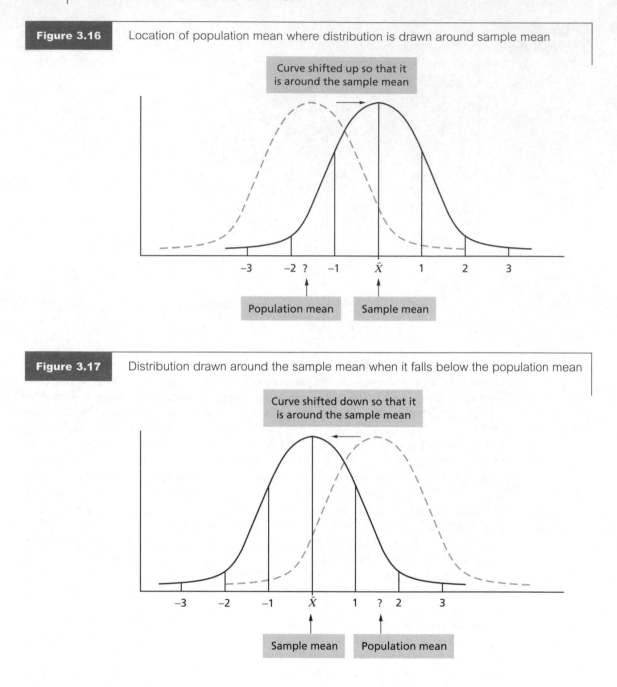

Figure 3.16 Location of population mean where distribution is drawn around sample mean

Figure 3.17 Distribution drawn around the sample mean when it falls below the population mean

3.5.1 Standard error

The standard deviation of the sampling distribution of the mean is an extremely import-ant concept and is usually called the *standard error*. The standard error, therefore, is a measure of the degree to which the sample means deviate from the mean of the sample means. Given that the mean of the sample means is also a close approximation of the population mean, the standard error of the mean must also tell us the degree to which the sample means deviate from the population mean. Consequently, once we are able to calculate the standard error we can use this information to find out how good an estimate our sample mean is of the population mean.

The problem we face here is a bit like the chicken and egg situation. If we knew the standard error then we could see how good an estimate our sample mean is of the population mean. However, in order to calculate the standard error of the mean we would have to select many samples from the population and then calculate the standard deviation of the means of these samples. This is not very helpful if we simply want to estimate the location of the population mean from the mean of one sample. Fortunately, statisticians have found that we can estimate the standard error quite easily from our sample statistics.

We explained earlier that sampling error is related to sample size (see section 2.2). The larger the sample size, the lower the sampling error. We explained that large samples tend to give means that are better estimates of population means. That is, they will not vary too much from the population mean. The means of small samples tend to vary a lot from the population mean. You should recall that the measure of the degree of variation around the mean is the standard deviation. The standard deviation of sample means is called the *standard error*. Consequently, for large sample sizes the standard error will tend to be less than that for small sample sizes. This means, therefore, that the standard error is also related to sample size. Consequently, for any given population, the larger the samples that we select, the lower the standard error. Conveniently, it has been shown that if, for any given sample, we divide the sample standard deviation by the square-root of the sample size, we get a good approximation of the standard error.

From any of our samples we can calculate a sample mean and standard deviation. Since we know that the standard error is approximately the standard deviation divided by the square-root of the sample size, we can also calculate the standard error. The standard error is the standard deviation of the sampling distribution of the mean. Consulting standard normal distribution tables we see that 95% of scores fall between 1.96 standard deviations above and below the mean. Applying this to the sampling distribution of the mean, we can therefore be 95% confident that the mean of the sampling distribution is within 1.96 standard deviations from the sample mean. Therefore the mean of the sampling distribution must lie within the region 1.96 × the standard error away from the sample mean. Given that the mean of the sampling distribution of the mean is a good approximation of the population mean we can be 95% confident also that the population mean lies within the region 1.96 × the standard error away from the sample mean.

An example may serve to clarify this for you. If we have the following sample data from a study (2, 5, 6, 7, 10, 12) we can calculate the mean and standard deviation, which are 7 and 3.58 respectively. The first step is to work out the standard error. Recall that the standard error is simply the standard deviation of the sample divided by the square-root of the sample size. The sample size here is 6 and thus the square-root of this is 2.45. If we divide the standard deviation (3.58) by this we get 1.46. Our standard error is therefore 1.46. To work out the 95% confidence interval we now have to multiply the standard error by 1.96, which gives us 2.86. Our confidence interval is therefore 7 ± 2.86 (or 4.14 to 9.86; see Figure 3.18(a)).

Our 95% confidence interval is quite a large range considering that the scores themselves only range from 2 to 12. The reason that our confidence interval is so large is that we have a small sample size. For the sake of illustration let us assume that we obtained the same mean and standard deviation with a sample size of 100. In this case the square-root of the sample size would now be 10. If we divide our standard deviation (3.58) by this, we get the standard error of 0.358. We can now multiply this standard error by 1.96 to set up

Figure 3.18   Confidence intervals with sample sizes of 6 and 100

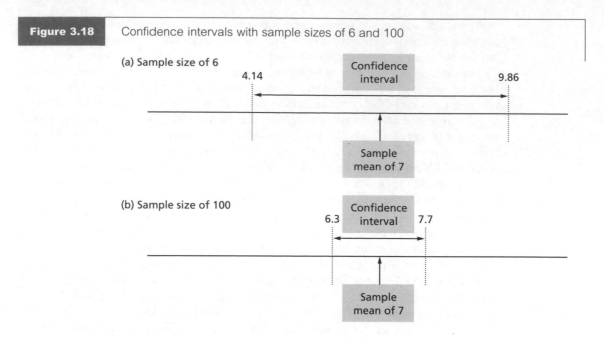

our 95% confidence interval. When we do this we find that our population mean should fall in the region that is 0.70 units above and below the mean (7). Thus we can now be 95% confident that the population mean falls between 6.30 and 7.70. This represents a much narrower range of scores and gives us a much clearer indication of where the population mean may be (see Figure 3.18(b)).

From this we can see the importance of sample size when trying to estimate population parameters from sample statistics. Generally, the larger the sample size, the better the estimate of the population we can get from it.

It may help to clarify what we have just explained by summarising it here:

■ A sample mean is a point estimate and we don't know how close it is to the population mean.

■ If we calculate confidence intervals around our sample mean we can get a good idea of how close it is to the population mean.

■ To calculate confidence intervals we need to make use of sampling distributions.

■ If we take lots of samples from a population and plot the means of the samples as a frequency histogram then we will have produced a sampling distribution of the mean.

■ Sampling distributions tend to be normal in shape.

■ The mean of the sampling distribution of the mean is a very good estimate of the population mean.

■ The standard deviation of the sampling distribution of the mean tells us how much our samples tend to vary around the population mean.

■ The standard deviation of the sampling distribution is called the *Standard Error* and is approximately equal to the standard deviation of a sample divided by the square-root of the sample size.

■ We know that 1.96 standard deviations above and below the mean encompasses 95% of the standard normal distribution.

■ Using this information we can generalise to our sampling distributions, which tend to be normal in shape.

■ Thus, we say that we are 95% confident that the population mean will be within 1.96 standard deviations (sampling distribution standard deviations) from our sample mean.

■ The sampling distribution standard deviation is the standard error and so we multiply this by 1.96 to get our confidence interval.

■ We say that we are 95% confident that the population mean will be within the region 1.96 × the standard error above and below our sample mean.

Activity 3.7

How confident can we be that the population mean is within 1.96 standard errors from the sample mean?

Suppose you have selected a sample of 20 spider phobics and obtained a measure of their fear of spiders. You find that the confidence interval for the mean is 1.5 to 5.6. What does this tell you? If you had selected 200 spider phobics, would the confidence interval have been larger or smaller than the one reported above?

SPSSFW: obtaining confidence intervals

It is fairly simple to obtain confidence intervals for the mean from SPSSFW. You follow the advice given earlier for descriptive techniques by selecting the *Explore* dialogue box:

Move variables to this box

Select *Statistics* option

Click on *Statistics* button

Move the relevant variables to the *Dependent List* box and click on the *Display*: *Statistics* option. To ensure that you generate confidence intervals you should click on the *Statistics* button. You will then be presented with the following dialogue box:

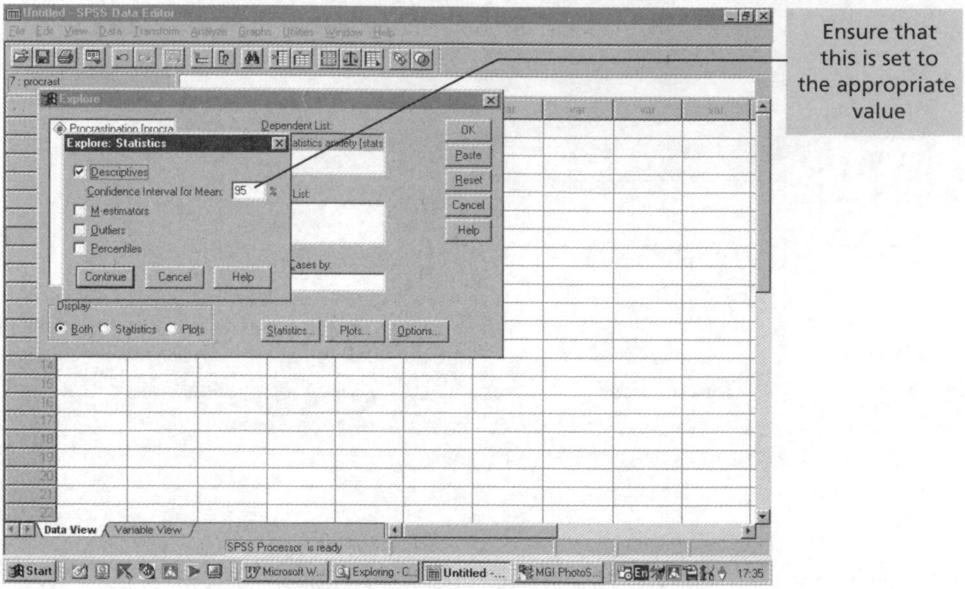

Ensure that this is set to the appropriate value

You should notice that SPSSFW is set up to generate 95% confidence intervals as the default. If you wish to generate confidence intervals other than 95% you should adjust the percentage to that which you desire. Ordinarily, however, you will not have to adjust this as you will usually be expected to generate 95% confidence intervals. Once you are happy that you have selected all the correct options, click on *Continue* followed by *OK* to generate the printout. An example printout can be seen below:

EXPLORE

Case Processing Summary

	Cases					
	Valid		Missing		Total	
	N	Percent	N	Percent	N	Percent
Statsanxiety	6	100.0%	0	.0%	6	100.0%

Descriptives

			Statistic	Std. Error
Statsanxiety	Mean		55.6667	2.3190
	95% Confidence	Lower Bound	49.7055	
	Interval for Mean	Upper Bound	61.6279	
	5% Trimmed Mean		55.7407	
	Median		57.0000	
	Variance		32.267	
	Std. Deviation		5.6804	
	Minimum		48.00	
	Maximum		62.00	
	Range		14.00	
	Interquartile Range		11.0000	
	Skewness		−.426	.845
	Kurtosis		−1.832	1.741

Confidence interval
(49.71 to 61.63)

3.6 Error bar charts

An extremely useful means of presenting confidence intervals in your research reports is to generate *error bar charts*. These simply display your means as a point on a chart and a vertical line through the mean point that represents the confidence interval. The larger the confidence interval, the longer the line is through the mean. Figure 3.19 shows the error bar charts for the confidence intervals that we have just calculated.

From Figure 3.19 it is easy to see the difference between the confidence intervals when the sample size is increased from 6 to 100.

| Figure 3.19 | Error bar chart showing the means and confidence intervals for sample sizes six and 100 |

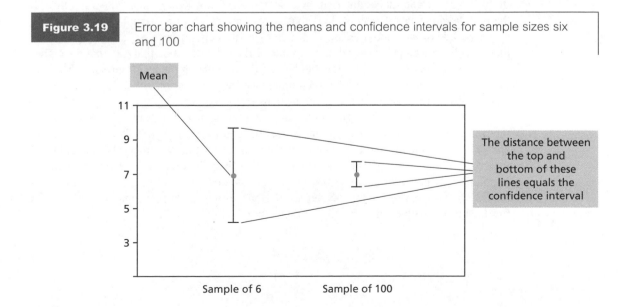

The distance between the top and bottom of these lines equals the confidence interval

Figure 3.20 Error bar chart showing overlapping confidence intervals for boys and girls in a mathematics exam

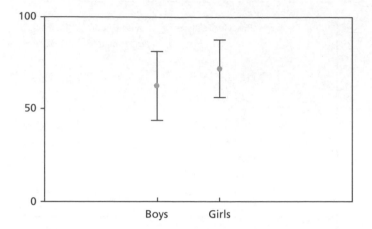

3.7 Overlapping confidence intervals

Suppose we wanted to see if two population means differed from each other. We could use confidence intervals to guide us. For example, imagine you wanted to see whether girls were better than boys in mathematics exams. You give a sample of students of each gender a mathematics exam. From these samples you calculate confidence intervals and obtain the error bar charts shown in Figure 3.20.

What would we be able to make of this? We can be 95% confident that the population means are within the intervals indicated in the chart. As there is substantial overlap between the two sets of confidence intervals we cannot be sure whether there is a difference in the population means. It seems likely that there is no real difference in the populations, or at the very least we cannot tell from our samples if such a difference exists. It might be that boys have a higher population mean than girls. Or it could be that girls have a higher population mean than boys. Or it could be that the population means of girls and boys are equal. We just do not know from the confidence intervals presented in Figure 3.20 and therefore we cannot draw any firm conclusions from these data.

Now suppose we obtained the confidence intervals shown in Figure 3.21. What should the conclusion be? In this case we can see that the confidence intervals do not overlap. We can be 95% confident that both population means fall within the intervals indicated and therefore do not overlap. This would suggest that there is a real difference between the population means. It would therefore appear that the population of girls do better at maths than the population of boys. You can see that examining confidence intervals gives us a fair idea of the pattern of means in the populations.

Figure 3.21

Error bar chart illustrating non-overlapping confidence intervals for boys and girls in the mathematics exam

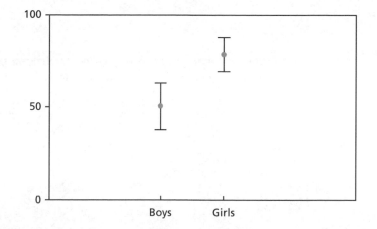

Activity 3.8

In which of the following error bar charts is there likely to be a real difference between the populations from which the two groups displayed were sampled?

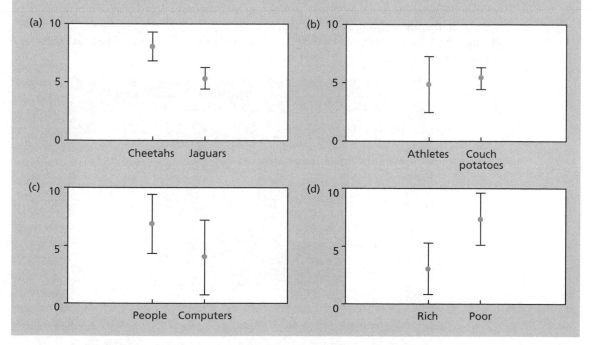

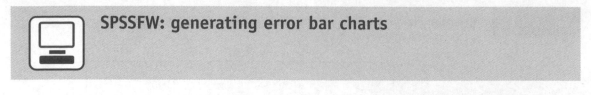

SPSSFW: generating error bar charts

To generate error bar charts in SPSSFW you should click on the *Graphs* menu and then select the *Error Bar . . .* option. You will be presented with the following dialogue box:

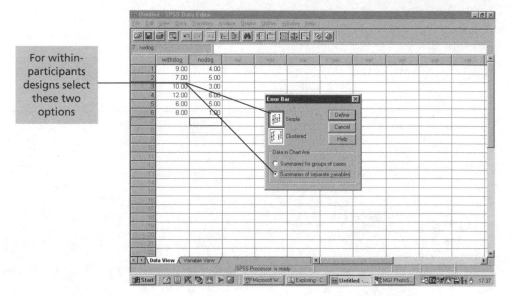

From the dialogue box the options you choose will depend upon the design of your study. If you have used a within-participants design and want to compare two (or more) variables, select the *Simple* and the *Summaries of separate variables* options. Click on *Define* and you will be presented with the following dialogue box:

Figure 3.22 Error bar chart for a dog-walking study as a within-participants design

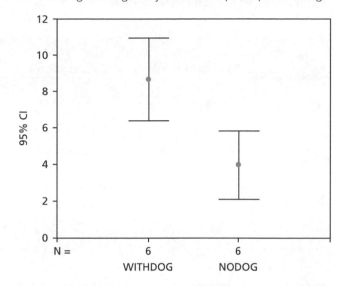

Move the relevant variables over to the *Error Bars* box as shown and click on *OK* to generate the error bar chart. The chart should resemble that shown in Figure 3.22.

You can see from the error bar chart that there are separate error bars for each condition of the within participants variable.

If you want to generate error bar charts and you have used a between-participants design, you should select the *Simple* and *Summaries for groups of cases* options in the initial options screen (see below):

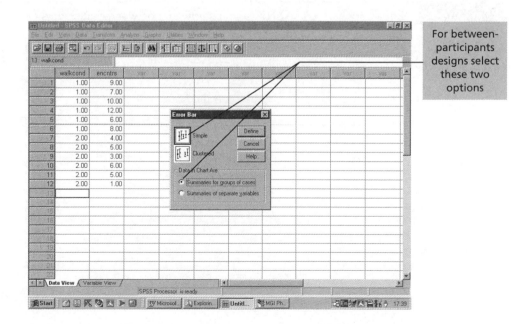

Click on *Define* and you will be presented with a slightly different dialogue box from that presented for within-participants designs:

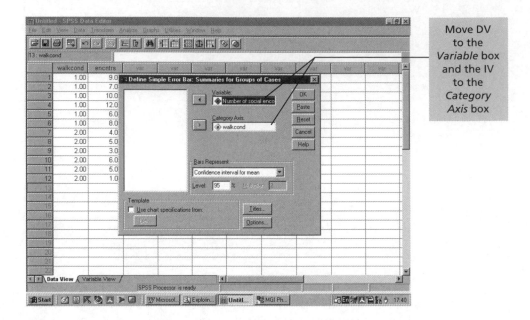

> Move DV to the *Variable* box and the IV to the *Category Axis* box

You will notice that there is a box for the dependent variable (*Variable*) and a separate box for the grouping variable (*Category Axis*). Move the dependent variable to the *Variable* box and the independent variable to the *Category Axis* box and click on *OK* to generate the error bar chart. It should resemble that shown in Figure 3.23.

Figure 3.23	Error bar chart for the dog-walking study as a between-participants design

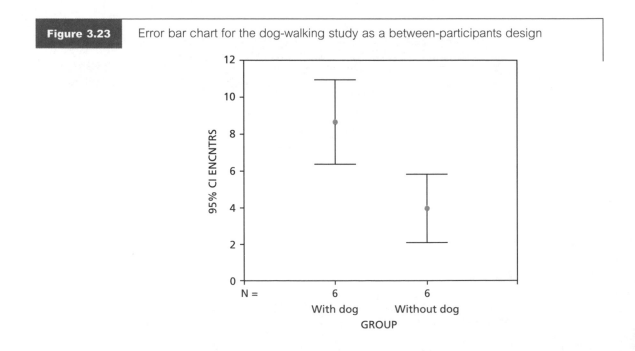

3.8 Confidence intervals around other statistics

We have illustrated confidence intervals around the mean to demonstrate the use of this technique. You should note that we are not restricted to means when working with confidence intervals. We can calculate confidence intervals for a number of different statistics, including the actual size of a difference between two means, correlation coefficients and t-statistics. We will explain these in more detail in Chapters 5 and 6. Basically, where a point estimate exists it is usually possible to calculate an interval estimate.

You should note that if you are investigating differences between groups then the confidence interval of the magnitude of the difference between the groups is very useful. If the confidence interval includes zero then it suggests that there is likely to be no difference between your groups in the population. This is explained further in Chapter 6.

Example from the literature: emotional processing and panic disorder

In Chapter 2 we described the study by Baker *et al.* (in press), which compared emotional control of panic disorder patients with that of two non-panic control groups (one from London and one from Aberdeen). They found that panic patients tended to try to control their emotions more than the two control groups. In this report the authors report the confidence intervals of the magnitude of the differences between the groups on the total score on the Courtaulds Emotional Control Scale (CECS). For example, they report that the mean difference between the panic group and the Aberdeen control group was 10.2 points with a 95% CI of 6.0 to 14.3. The mean difference between the panic group and the London control group was 13.4 with a 95% CI of 9.9 to 16.8. Finally, the mean difference between the two control groups was 3.2 with 95% CI of 0.06 to 5.9.

SPSSFW: using the Results Coach

Now that you are used to conducting some analyses using SPSSFW we would like to introduce you to a very useful feature of the program. Whenever you have the SPSSFW output on the screen you can use a utility called the *Results Coach* to help you interpret the output. One of the problems with SPSSFW is that it often gives us much more information than we need. One of the difficulties for students new to the program is trying to work out which parts of the printout is relevant to them. The *Results Coach* can be of great benefit in such situations.

To activate the *Results Coach* you need to have some output on the screen. We will demonstrate this feature with the descriptive statistics output for the statistics anxiety variable that we presented earlier in the chapter. With the 'Descriptives' table on the screen move the mouse cursor anywhere over the table and click on the right mouse button. You should be presented with a menu of options as illustrated in the following screenshot.

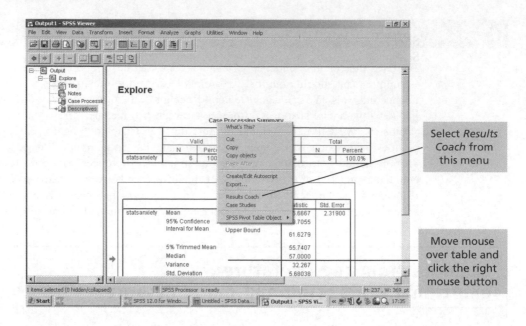

You should then click on the *Results Coach* option to activate the coach. You will be presented with an example of the output along with a description of what the table contains. You will notice that towards the bottom right-hand corner of the screen are the navigation buttons that we described in Chapter 1 when showing you the Tutorials. If you click on the right-hand arrow you will be taken through the table step by step and given a brief description of the contents. This can be extremely useful for helping you decide which bits of information you need to pay attention to.

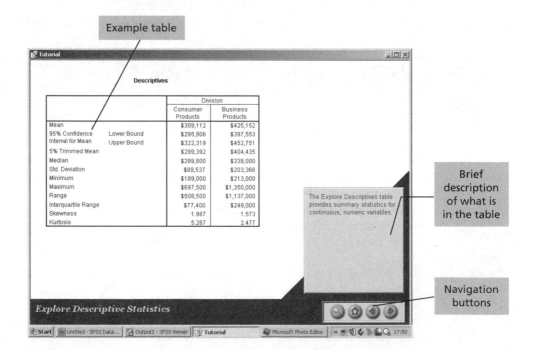

You should note that you can only use this feature for help with the tables that SPSSFW produces. It will not work with diagrams such as those for Error Bar Charts and Scattergrams.

To shut down the *Results Coach* click on the 'Close Window' button (the **×** button). This should take you back to the SPSSFW output screen.

Summary

In this chapter we have explained a number of important concepts that form the foundation for a thorough understanding of statistics. More specifically you have learnt that:

■ Probabilities can be represented in terms of odds (e.g. 1 in 5), decimals (0.2) or percentages (20%).

■ Conditional probabilities are probabilities associated with an event that is itself conditional upon another event happening.

■ We can use the standard normal distribution and z-scores to work out the proportion of a population that falls above or below a certain score or which falls between two scores.

■ If we take many samples from a population and plot the means of these samples as a frequency histogram then we have plotted a sampling distribution of the mean.

■ The more samples we take and the larger the sample sizes, the more likely the sampling distribution of the mean is to approximate the normal distribution, no matter how the population itself is distributed.

■ The standard deviation of the sampling distribution of the mean is the standard error, and this gives us an indication of how much the sample means deviate from the population mean.

■ The standard error is roughly equal to the standard deviation of a sample divided by the square-root of the size of the sample and can be used in conjunction with z-scores to calculate confidence intervals.

■ Confidence intervals give an interval within which we can be, say, 95% confident that the population mean falls.

■ We can conveniently illustrate confidence intervals using error bar charts.

SPSSFW exercises

Exercise 1

In the local dental surgery Nurse Nasher and Dr Payne decide that they want to try to reduce the anxiety levels of patients coming for treatment. They decide that the best way to do this would be to soundproof both of their waiting rooms so that the waiting patients cannot hear the screams of those being treated. They want to make sure that the soundproofing does reduce dental anxiety so they soundproof only one waiting room and compare the dental anxiety of patients put in that waiting room with those sent to the non-soundproofed room. Patients are randomly allocated to one of the waiting rooms when they arrive and are asked to fill in a dental anxiety questionnaire while they are waiting. The dental anxiety questionnaire gives a score based on many aspects of anxiety about going to the dentists: the higher the score, the higher the level of dental anxiety. Nurse Nasher and Dr Payne predict that there will be a difference in anxiety scores between the patients from the two waiting rooms. The following are the dental anxiety scores of the patients from each of the waiting rooms:

Soundproofed	Not soundproofed
12	16
11	26
8	20
4	21
3	19
13	20
10	22
10	18
9	20
11	17

1. Is this a between- or within-participants design?

2. Input the data from the table above into SPSSFW and obtain the following statistics for each group:
    - the mean
    - the standard deviation
    - the standard error
    - 95% confidence intervals.

3. (a) Use SPSSFW to generate error bar charts for each group.
    (b) Convert the first score in each condition into a z-score.

Exercise 2

Dr Doolittle has finally given up all pretence of being able to speak to animals and has decided to become an experimental animal psychologist. He is particularly interested in finding out whether or not cats are more intelligent than dogs. He develops an intelligence test specifically for the task, and tests samples of cats and dogs. He has been careful not to bias the test in any way and quite rightly claims to have developed a test that is not species bound, that is, it could be used with any species. Dr Doolittle predicts that there will be a difference between the intelligence scores of cats and dogs. The scores for cats and dogs are given in the table below.

Cats	Dogs
95	116
100	112
104	102
78	96
130	89
111	124
89	131
114	117
102	107
97	110

1. What sort of design is this study, quasi-experimental or experimental?

2. Is it a between-participants or a within-participants design?

3. Input the data above into SPSSFW and use the package to generate the following statistics for each group:
   ■ the mean
   ■ the standard deviation
   ■ the standard error
   ■ 95% confidence intervals.

4. (a) Use SPSSFW to generate error bar charts for each group.
   (b) Convert the first score in each condition into a z-score.

MULTIPLE CHOICE QUESTIONS

1. What is the probability 1 in 5 expressed as a percentage?
   (a) 14%
   (b) 25%
   (c) 20%
   (d) 32%

2. What is the relationship between sample size and sampling error?
   (a) The larger the sample size, the larger the sampling error
   (b) The larger the sample size, the smaller the sampling error
   (c) Sample size equals sampling error
   (d) None of the above

3. If we have a 95% confidence interval of 3 ± 2, what does it mean?
   (a) The population mean is definitely between 1 and 5
   (b) We are 95% sure that the population mean falls between 3 and 2
   (c) We are 95% sure that the population mean falls between 1 and 5
   (d) None of the above

4. What are the scores in the Standard Normal Distribution?

   (a) Extreme scores
   (b) z-scores
   (c) Standard deviation scores
   (d) Both (b) and (c) above

5. The standard error is:

   (a) The square-root of the mean
   (b) The square of the standard deviation
   (c) The standard deviation divided by the mean
   (d) The standard deviation divided by the square-root of the number of participants in the sample

6. If you have a probability of 33%, what is it expressed as a decimal?

   (a) 0.033
   (b) 0.33
   (c) 0.23
   (d) 0.133

7. The standard error tells us:

   (a) The degree to which our sample means differ from the mean of the sample means
   (b) The degree to which our sample means differ from the population mean
   (c) The degree to which the standard deviation differs from the population mean
   (d) Both (a) and (b) above

8. What would we multiply the standard error by to help us get our 95% confidence intervals?

   (a) 95
   (b) The square-root of the sample size
   (c) The standard deviation
   (d) 1.96

9. If you had a z-score of 2.33 this would tell you that:

   (a) Your score was 2.33 standard deviations above the mean
   (b) Your score was 2.33 standard deviations below the mean
   (c) There was a probability of 2.33 of obtaining a score greater than your score
   (d) There was a probability of 2.33 of obtaining a score less than your score

10. If an event has a probability of 95% of occurring, what does this mean?

   (a) The event is likely to occur 5 times out of every 100
   (b) The event is likely to occur 95 times out of every 100
   (c) The event is likely to occur 95 times out of every 95
   (d) None of the above

11. Which career should you choose if your weightlifting and pottery scores are as follows?

   Weightlifting: Your score is 52 (sample mean = 55, SD = 12)
   Potter: Your score is 50 (sample mean = 58, SD = 32)

   (a) Weightlifting
   (b) Pottery
   (c) Either as you are equally good compared with the populations
   (d) Neither because you are useless at both

12. Which of the following statements are true in reference to inferential statistics?

    (a) They merely describe our data
    (b) We are able to use them to draw conclusions about populations from sample data
    (c) They are used simply to make psychology look scientific
    (d) We are able to use them to draw conclusions about samples from populations

13. If you obtain a score of 13 on an anxiety questionnaire and you know that the population mean and standard deviation are 20 and 5 respectively, what is your z-score?

    (a) −2.33
    (b) −1.4
    (c) 1.33
    (d) 0

14. If you have a population of scores that has a flat (i.e. not normal) distribution, then the distribution of many sample means will be:

    (a) Flat
    (b) Bimodal
    (c) Negatively skewed
    (d) Normal

15. Which of the following gives the best estimate of the population mean?

    (a) Sample mean
    (b) The mean of several sample means
    (c) The standard deviation
    (d) The standard error

16. For a set of data we find that we have a standard deviation of 42 and a sample size of 16. What is the standard error?

    (a) 0.339
    (b) 2.95
    (c) 21.68
    (d) 10.5

17. If you draw 100 samples from a population and plot all their means as a frequency histogram, then you have a:

    (a) Mean distribution
    (b) Skewed distribution
    (c) Sampling distribution
    (d) None of the above

18. Given a standard error of 5.2 with a sample size of 9, what is the standard deviation?

    (a) 1.73
    (b) 15.6
    (c) 46.8
    (d) 0.556

19. Which of these could you not generate confidence intervals for?

    (a) A mean
    (b) A correlation coefficient
    (c) The mean difference between scores
    (d) None of the above

20. If we have a negatively skewed population, what shape will the sampling distribution of the mean of samples drawn from this population be?

    (a) Negatively skewed
    (b) Positively skewed
    (c) Normal
    (d) It is not possible to tell

References

Baker, R., Holloway, J., Thomas, P.W., Thomas, S. and Owens, M. (in press) 'Emotional processing and panic', *Behaviour Research and Therapy*.

Beck, A.T., Ward, C.H., Mendelson, M., Mock, J.E. and Erbaugh, J.K. (1961) 'An inventory for measuring depression', *Archives of General Psychiatry*, **4**: 561–71.

Walsh, J.J. and Ugumba-Agwunobi, G. (2002) 'Individual differences in statistics anxiety: the roles of perfectionism, procrastination and trait anxiety', *Personality and Individual Differences*, **33**: 239–51.

4 Hypothesis testing and statistical significance

Chapter overview

In Chapter 3 we started you off on the road to using inferential statistics. In this chapter we will move a little further down the road and explain how we can apply our knowledge of probabilities and sampling distributions to testing the hypotheses that we set up in our research. More specifically we will be explaining the following:

- the logic of hypothesis testing
- statistical significance and how it relates to probabilities
- how probability distributions form the basis of statistical tests
- the problems associated with basing conclusions on probabilities (i.e. Type I and Type II errors)
- one-tailed and two-tailed hypotheses
- how to choose the appropriate test to analyse your data.

4.1 Another way of applying probabilities to research: hypothesis testing

Suppose we were interested in examining the relationship between number of hours spent studying per week and exam grades. We would perhaps predict that the more time spent studying per week the higher the exam grades. Here we have set up a prediction that we would then test by conducting a study. In this study we could randomly select a number of students and record how many hours they spent per week studying and find out if it is related to their final exam grade. According to our prediction we would expect the population of scores to resemble that in the population illustrated in Figure 4.1. Here you can see there is a trend indicating that as the number of hours studied increases so do exam grades. Let us assume that this is the pattern in the underlying population. One of the problems we face when conducting research is that when we select samples from populations we might not get a sample that accurately reflects that population. If you think back to Chapter 2 we explained that due to sampling error the samples might not resemble the population. Figure 4.1 illustrates three samples taken from the population presented therein. You should notice that even though there is a positive relationship in the population of scores two of the samples do not reflect this. In fact, one of the samples actually suggests a negative relationship between hours studied and exam performance (as number of hours spent studying increases exam performance decreases). Another of the samples suggests that there is no relationship between the two variables. The remaining sample accurately reflects the underlying population by suggesting a positive relationship

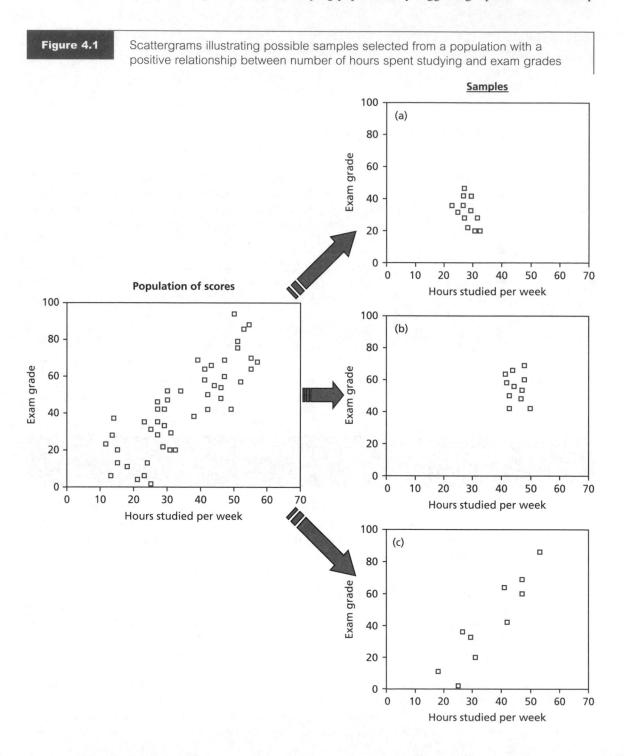

Figure 4.1 Scattergrams illustrating possible samples selected from a population with a positive relationship between number of hours spent studying and exam grades

between the two variables. The point to note here is that even though there is a relationship in the underlying population the sample we select might not reflect this.

Now take a look at Figure 4.2. In this example there is no relationship between amount of time spent studying and exam performance in the underlying population. Again, we have

Figure 4.2   Scattergrams illustrating possible samples selected from a population with no relationship between number of hours spent studying and exam grades

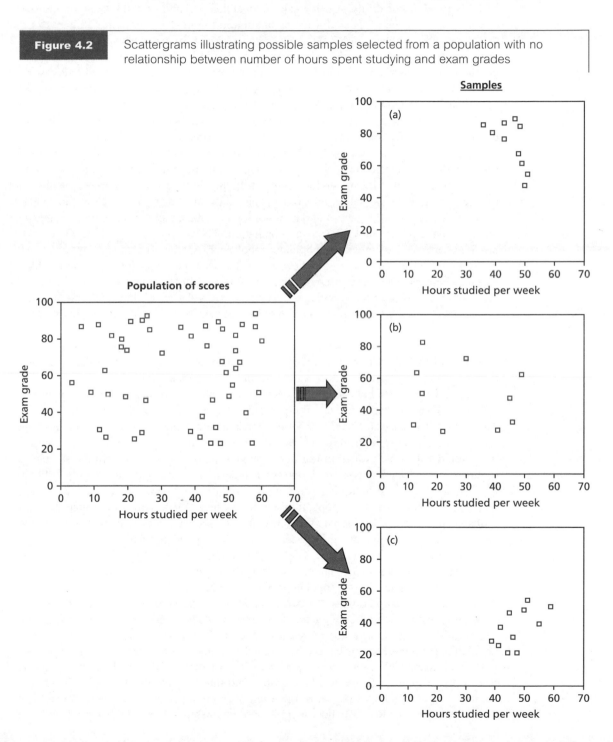

presented three samples that have been selected from the population. Yet again, only one of the samples accurately reflects the population. The fact is that, due to sampling error, the samples we select might not be a true reflection of the underlying population. From any particular population each of the patterns of sample scores we have presented will have a greater or lesser probability of being selected and this probability will depend on the size of the sample we select. Thus, for the population in Figure 4.1 we are more likely to get the pattern observed in sample (c) than in samples (a) and (b), particularly with reasonably large sample sizes. And for the population presented in Figure 4.2 we are more likely to get the pattern observed in sample (b) than in samples (a) and (c). You need to be aware though that sometimes simply due to sampling error we are likely to get patterns of scores in our samples that do not accurately reflect the underlying population.

One of the problems we face when conducting research is that we do not know the pattern of scores in the underlying population. In fact, our reason for conducting the research in the first place is to try to establish the pattern in the underlying population. We are trying to draw conclusions about the populations from our samples. Essentially, we are in a situation akin to that illustrated in Figure 4.3. In this figure everything above the dashed line relates to what we have observed in our study and everything below the line is unknown to us. From the pattern of data we observe in our sample we have to try to decide what the pattern may look like in the population. There may be an infinite number of possible patterns that reflect the population; however, we have given only two of these in the figure. From our sample we have to decide what we think the population is like. This is where we would use inferential statistical tests. Effectively what we do is observe the pattern of scores in the sample and decide which is the most plausible pattern in the population. Thus, given the pattern observed in the sample in Figure 4.3 we might argue that the pattern in population (b) is much more plausible than that shown in population (a). As is illustrated by Figures 4.1 and 4.2, however, the samples need not be an accurate reflection of the population. We therefore need some means of evaluating the likelihood that the sample we select is an accurate reflection of the population.

Our statistical tests help us in this decision but they do so in a way that is not very intuitive. What our statistical tests do is calculate a probability value, called the *p-value*. This probability tells us the likelihood of our obtaining our pattern of results due to sampling error if there is no relationship between our variables in the population. For example, they would tell us the probability of our obtaining the pattern of scores in the sample in Figure 4.3 if they came from population (a). If the pattern in our sample is highly unlikely to have arisen due to sampling error if the population resembles (a) then we might reasonably conclude that the population resembles that in (b). You should note that this probability value is a conditional probability. It is the probability of obtaining your sample data *if* there was no relationship between the variables in the population.

Hypothesis testing is often seen as a competition between two hypotheses. It is seen as a competition between our research hypothesis (that there is a relationship between study hours and exam grade in the population) and something called the *null hypothesis* (that there is no relationship between the two variables in the population). Thus, the process of hypothesis testing resembles Figure 4.3. We need to decide between populations (a) and (b). In this case population (a) represents the case if the null hypothesis were true and population (b) represents the case if the research hypothesis were true. The statistical tests we use tell us how likely it is that we would get our pattern of data if the null hypothesis were true. In Figure 4.3, we would probably find that the pattern of data in the sample would be highly unlikely to occur as the result of sampling error if they were drawn from a population resembling (a) where there is no relationship between hours spent studying

Figure 4.3 Scattergrams illustrating alternative underlying populations when a relationship is observed in a sample

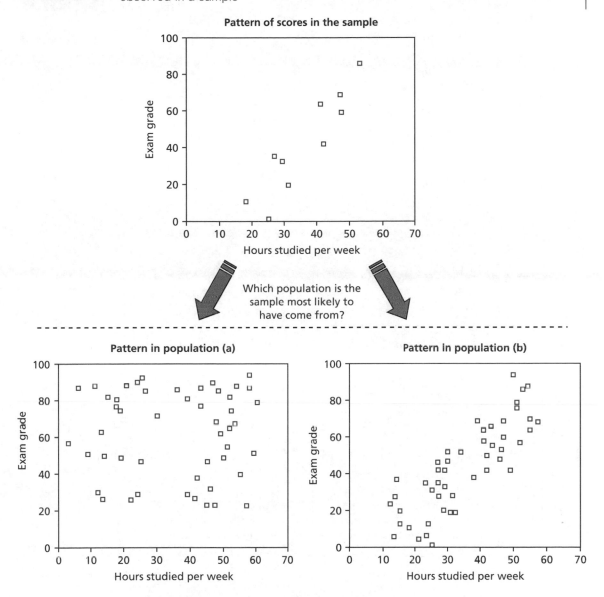

per week and exam grade. In fact, the probability turns out to be less than 1 in 1000. In this case it would make more sense to conclude that the data came from a population that resembles that illustrated in (b).

Now, let's have a look at the scenario represented by Figure 4.4. Remember that everything above the dashed line is what we observe from our study and everything below the line is unknown to us. Here you should be able to see that the sample appears to suggest that there is no discernible relationship between number of hours spent studying and exam grade. Intuitively, we would expect that this sample has come from a population resembling that shown in (a) rather than that shown in (b). However, again referring to Figure 4.1 you

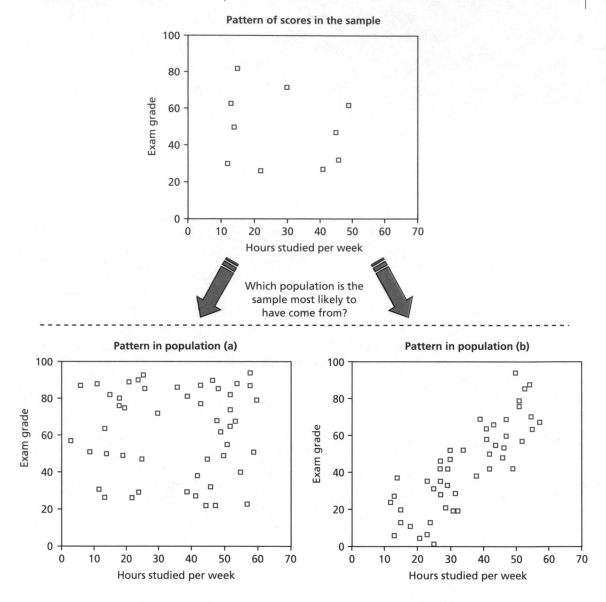

Figure 4.4 Scattergrams illustrating alternative underlying populations when no relationship is observed in a sample

should be able to see that even when there is relationship between two variables in the population we have the possibility that one will not be observed in our sample. This absence of a relationship in the sample would be the result of sampling error. So again in this case we could use inferential statistical tests to help us choose between the two hypotheses: the null hypothesis represented by population (a) or research hypothesis represented by population (b). The statistical test would inform us of the probability that we would obtain the pattern in our sample illustrated in Figure 4.4 if the population resembled the pattern shown in (a), that is, if the null hypothesis were true. In this case we would find that there is a high probability of obtaining the pattern observed in our sample if the null hypothesis were true. In fact, there is a 61% probability of obtaining this pattern from a population resembling that shown in (a). In this case we would probably decide that the population does in fact resemble population (a) rather than population (b). There are other issues that we would need to address, however, before we could come to this conclusion such as whether we had enough participants in our sample (see section 4.9 and Chapter 7).

4.2 Null hypothesis

We have just slipped a very important concept past you, which needs further explanation. The *null hypothesis* is very important to the process of hypothesis testing. We explained earlier that the probability we calculate in statistical testing is based upon the assumption that there is no relationship between the two variables in the population. This assumption is the *null hypothesis*. If the research hypothesis (often called the *experimental* or *alternate* hypothesis) states that there will be a relationship between two variables, then the null hypothesis states that there is absolutely no relationship between the two variables. Similarly, if you are interested in comparing groups of people, where the research hypothesis states that there will be a difference between two groups, the null hypothesis states that there is no difference between them.

You may find when reading psychological journals that the authors suggest that the null hypothesis could not be rejected. This simply indicates that the statistical probability they calculated meant that it was likely that the null hypothesis was the more sensible conclusion. If you read about researchers rejecting the null hypothesis, it means that the probability of obtaining their findings if the null hypothesis were true is so small that it makes more sense to believe in the research hypothesis. As we indicated earlier in this section this illustrates the competition between our null and research hypotheses. The importance of the null hypothesis is reflected by the fact that this whole approach to conducting research is called *null hypothesis testing (NHT)* or *null hypothesis significance testing (NHST)*.

4.3 Logic of null hypothesis testing

If you understand the preceding sections you should have no problems with grasping the general logic behind hypothesis testing, which is as follows:

- Formulate a hypothesis.
- Measure the variables involved and examine the relationship between them.
- Calculate the probability of obtaining such a relationship if there were no relationship in the population (if the null hypothesis were true).
- If this calculated probability is small enough, it suggests that the pattern of findings is unlikely to have arisen by chance and so probably reflects a genuine relationship in the population.

Put another way, if there is no real relationship in the population you are unlikely to find a relationship in your randomly selected sample. Therefore, if you do find a relationship in your sample, it is likely to reflect a relationship in your population. It is important that you understand this so take your time with this and ensure that you follow what we have just said.

Hypothesis testing is not restricted to the investigation of relationships between variables. If we are interested in studying differences between groups, we can also test hypotheses. The logic is broadly the same as that outlined for relationships above. For example, suppose we set up a study where we gave students two types of structured study, which differed only in the amount of time the students were required to study. In one group the students studied for 40 hours per week and the other group studied for 10 hours per week (this is the independent variable). We might hypothesise that the 40-hour group would achieve higher exam marks than the 10-hour group. This would be our research hypothesis. Our null hypothesis would be that there would be no difference between the two groups in their exam grades in the population. Once we have collected the data we could then see if there is a difference between the two study groups. If a difference did exist we would then need to work out the probability of obtaining such a difference by sampling error alone, that is, the probability of obtaining a difference of the size observed if the null hypothesis were true. If this probability is low, then it makes more sense to assume that the difference was due to the manipulation of the independent variable rather than to sampling error alone.

Activity 4.1

From the following research hypotheses, try to work out the null hypotheses.

- It is predicted that there will be a difference between males and females in spatial ability
- It is predicted that alcohol consumed will be related to number of driving errors
- It is predicted that reaction times will be different when participants are stressed than when they are relaxed
- It is predicted that the closer we get to a general election, the more lies will be told by politicians

DISCUSSION POINT: CRITICISMS AGAINST NULL HYPOTHESIS TESTING

Although null hypothesis testing is the dominant approach to research in psychology, today there is growing concern that it is inadequate in terms of providing useful insights into the variables that psychologists wish to investigate. For example, referring to hypothesis testing, Loftus (1991) says, 'I find it difficult to imagine a less insightful means of transiting from data to conclusions'. Loftus (1991, 1996) describes many problems associated with the use of hypothesis testing, but we will highlight two here. If you wish to read more there are two references at the end of this chapter.

One of the main problems highlighted by Loftus relates to the null hypothesis. When we are looking for a difference between two conditions we have to calculate the probability of obtaining our difference by chance if the null hypothesis is true. Remember, the null hypothesis states that there is *no* difference between the two conditions. The problem with the null hypothesis is that in few instances, in any science, will there be no difference between two conditions. It is quite unusual to find two things that are exactly equal, even in physics, and so to base our probability judgements on such a null hypothesis may be seriously misleading. This is just the gist of the point made by Loftus but it serves to illustrate one of the criticisms raised by Loftus.

The second problem that Loftus highlights is that, although we may report with some confidence that we have found a genuine difference between our two conditions and report the size of the difference, psychologists usually say very little about the underlying population means of the two conditions. Loftus argues that hypothesis testing lures us away from thinking about the population means. He suggests that we can avoid this trap by routinely reporting confidence intervals in our research reports.

Even though there are such criticisms levelled at the process of hypothesis testing it does not mean that we should abandon this approach completely; rather, we need to have a thorough understanding of what it means to engage in hypothesis testing. This is what we hope to give you in this book. Therefore, alongside the statistical tests that help us test our hypothesis (e.g. the t-test) you should, as Loftus suggests, routinely report descriptive statistics and confidence intervals. One useful way of presenting confidence intervals is by generating *error bar charts* and presenting these in your reports. We have shown you what these are like earlier in this book (see Chapter 3).

Activity 4.2

Which of the following descriptions represents a good summary of the logic behind hypothesis testing?

(a) We measure the relationship between the variables from our sample data and if it is large then there must be a genuine relationship in the population

(b) We measure the relationship between the variables from our sample and then find the probability that such a relationship will arise due to sampling error alone. If such a probability is large, then we can conclude that a genuine relationship exists in the population

(c) We measure the relationship between the variables from our sample and then find the probability that such a relationship will arise due to sampling error alone. If such a probability is small, then we can conclude that a genuine relationship exists in the population

(d) We measure a difference between our two conditions and then work out the probability of obtaining such a difference by sampling error alone if the null hypothesis were true. If the probability is small, then we can conclude that a genuine difference exists in the population

4.4 The significance level

Many of you, at this point, may be thinking that this is all well and good but how do we decide that the probability we calculate in null hypothesis testing is small enough for us to reject the null hypothesis? This is an excellent question and one that does not have a definitive answer. Most psychologists and indeed most reputable psychology journals use the convention that a probability of 5% is small enough to be a useful cut-off point. That is, given that the null hypothesis is true, if the probability of a given effect is less than 5% (0.05 or 1 in 20) then we have provided reasonable support for our research hypothesis. What this means is that, if you conduct a study 20 times, only once in those 20 studies would a relationship (or difference) as large as the one you observe come out by chance, if the null hypothesis were true. Given such a low probability, we can conclude with reasonable confidence that a real relationship (or difference) exists in the populations under investigation. The probability associated with each statistical test is often called the *p-value* or *alpha* (α). When this is printed on your SPSSFW output it will be printed as a decimal and, as with all probabilities expressed as a decimal, it ranges from 0 to 1.

In many journals you will typically see researchers reporting their findings as *significant* or *not significant*. On the assumption of the null hypothesis being true, if the probability of obtaining an effect due to sampling error was less than 5%, then the findings are said to be 'significant'. If this probability was greater than 5%, then the findings are said to be 'non-significant'. This way of thinking about your analysis has, however, come in for a good deal of criticism in recent years for the reasons discussed on pages 137–8.

The conventional view today is that we should report exact probability levels for our test statistics (the exact p-value or α) and shift away from thinking in terms of whether or not the findings are statistically significant. Therefore, when reporting the results of your analyses you should report the exact probability values that are associated with your findings. We have presented the significant/non-significant view here so that you will know what it means when you come across such statements in journal articles.

We recommend that you use the 5% level of α as a rough guide to what has traditionally been seen as an acceptable probability of your findings being due to sampling error. Therefore, if you find that your p-value is a lot less than the 5% level then you can be reasonably confident that this is generally acceptable as indicating support for your research hypothesis. However, you should report the actual p-value and evaluate your findings in terms of effect size (see Chapter 7) and your error bar charts.

Activity 4.3

Suppose you have conducted a study looking for a difference between males and females on preference for action films. When you run your study you find that there is a 0.005 probability of the difference you observe arising due to sampling error. How often is such a difference likely to arise by sampling error alone?

(a) 1 in 5000   (b) 1 in 2000   (c) 1 in 500   (d) 1 in 200   (e) 1 in 100

Suppose the probability was 0.01: which of the above is true in this situation?

4.5 Statistical significance

As suggested previously, when reading an article from a psychological journal or listening to eminent and not-so-eminent psychologists describe their research you will often hear/read the word 'significant'. Psychologists say things like:

Levels of negative affect preceding anger were rated as significantly *lower in driving than non-driving situations. (Parkinson, 2001)*

The panic disorder group did have significantly *more emotional processing difficulties than the control groups . . . (Baker* et al.*, in press)*

. . . and the association between trait anxiety and procrastination was also significant . . . (Walsh and Ugumba-Agwunobi, 2002)

What are we to make of statements such as these? In everyday life we interpret the word 'significant' to mean considerable, critical or important. Does this mean Parkinson found a considerable difference in anger between driving and non-driving situations? Or that Baker *et al.* found a critical difference between their panic and control groups, or perhaps Walsh and Ugumba-Agwunobi found an important relationship between procrastination and trait anxiety? In fact, they do not necessarily mean this. They are merely stating that what they found was *statistically significant*. Statistical significance is different from psychological significance. Just because a statistically significant difference is found between two samples of scores, it does not mean that it is necessarily a large or psychologically significant difference. For example, in the study cited above by Walsh and Ugumba-Agwunobi (2002) there was a statistically significant relationship between trait anxiety and procrastination. The overlap between these two variables was only 10%, however, which is not necessarily significant in psychological terms (we will explain this further in Chapter 5).

As we have already explained, the probability we calculate in inferential statistics is simply the probability that such an effect would arise if there was no difference between the underlying populations. This does not necessarily have any bearing on the psychological importance of the finding. The psychological importance of a finding will be related to the research question and the theoretical basis of that research. One of the main problems with the p-value is that it is related to sample size. If, therefore, a study has a large number of participants it could yield a statistically significant finding with a very small effect (relationship between two variables or difference between two groups). It is up to individual authors (and their audiences) to determine the psychological significance of any findings. Remember, *statistical significance does not equal psychological significance*.

DISCUSSION POINT: WHY REPORT THE EXACT P-VALUE (α)?

There is quite a debate going on in psychology concerning the use of the alpha criterion of significance. The generally accepted criterion of significance ($p < 0.05$) is coming under increasing criticism. There is nothing intrinsically wrong with the 5% cut-off, yet it has been argued that the pursuance of this as the Holy Grail in psychology is distorting the legitimate goals of psychological research. The problem with the 5% criterion is that we are often led to believe that just because some effect is statistically significant then it is psychologically significant, or even that it is a large or important effect. In fact, if we look at this criterion logically we can see the folly of this way of thinking. Suppose, for example, that you conducted a study looking at the relationship between statistics anxiety and procrastination. You find that, as statistics anxiety increases, so does procrastination. You find that the probability of obtaining such a relationship, if there really was no relationship in the population, is 4.9%. As this is less than the traditional 5% you conclude that this is a real relationship between statistics anxiety and procrastination. You then conduct a follow-up study (being the good researcher that you are) and again find a relationship between statistics anxiety and procrastination. This time, however, you find that the probability of such a relationship, given that the null hypothesis is true, is 5.1%. What are we to make of this? Do you now conclude that there is no real relationship between statistics anxiety and procrastination? You can see that there is only 0.2% difference in the probability values between these two studies. So it does not really make sense to argue that the sizes of the relationship in the two studies are different. Yet, in all probability, the first of these would get published in a psychological journal and the second would not.

One of the big problems with the p-value is that it is related to sample size. We could have two studies where one has a very small p-value (say 0.001) and one has quite a large p-value (say 0.15). Yet we would not be able to say that the first study shows a large effect (strong relationship or large difference between conditions) and the second study a small effect. In fact it could be the reverse situation because it might simply be the case that the first study has a very large sample size and the second a small one. Even very small effects will lead to significant statistical tests with very large sample sizes.

How can we get around this problem? The best approach to this is to try to get a measure of the magnitude of the experimental effect, that is, get information about the size of the relationship between statistics anxiety and procrastination. If you were looking for differences between groups you would get a measure of the size of the difference between your groups. This is called the *magnitude of effect* or *effect size*. A more detailed description of effect size can be found in Chapter 7. The preferred course of action when reporting your research findings is to report the exact probability level and the effect size. For example, you should report the probability level (i.e. $p = 0.027$) and the effect size (e.g. $r = 0.70$, $r^2 = 0.49$ or $d = 0.50$). In this way, whenever someone reads about your research he or she can get a fuller picture of what you have found. You should note that r is a correlation coefficient and indicates the strength of a relationship between variables (we explain this more in the next chapter); d is a measure of magnitude of effect used for differences between groups and is explained in Chapter 7. There is a very accessible discussion of effect sizes provided by Clark-Carter (2003).

4.6 The correct interpretation of the p-value

It is important to understand that the p-value is a conditional probability. That is, you are assessing the probability of an event's occurence, given that the null hypothesis is true. The p-value that you will observe on any computer printout represents this probability. It does not represent the probability that the relationship you observed simply occurred by chance. It represents the probability of the relationship occurring by chance if the null hypothesis were true. It is said to be a conditional probability. It is conditional upon the null hypothesis being true. A good discussion of the problems caused by misinterpreting what the p-value represents is given by Dracup (1995); however, we have summarised the main points in the discussion below. If you wish to read the original discussion the reference is given at the end of the chapter.

DISCUSSION POINT:
MISINTERPRETATION OF THE SIGNIFICANCE LEVEL (α)

Dracup (1995) has given a good discussion of the problems associated with the misinterpretation of the rationale behind hypothesis testing.

Many students new to statistics, and indeed those who perhaps should know better, equate the significance level (α) with the actual size of the experimental effect. The lower the significance level, the stronger, for example, the relationship between two variables. This is not what is meant by the significance of a finding. Alpha simply gives an indication of the likelihood of finding such a relationship if the null hypothesis were true. It is perhaps true that the stronger the relationship, the lower the probability that such a relationship would be found if the null hypothesis were true, but this is not necessarily so.

Dracup also highlights the fact that many statistical textbooks equate α with the probability that the null hypothesis is true. This is incorrect, as is clearly illustrated by Dracup. Alpha is the probability that we will get a relationship of an obtained magnitude if the null hypothesis were true. It is not the probability of the null hypothesis being true.

Related to this latter point, once someone has fallen into the trap of interpreting α as the probability of the null hypothesis being true, it is a relatively easy and convenient step to suggest that $1 - \alpha$ must be the probability that the research hypothesis is true. Thus, if we set α at the traditional 5% level and find a significant relationship, these people would assume that there is a 95% probability that the research hypothesis is true. This is incorrect. In fact, we do not know what the probability is that the research hypothesis is correct; our α probability is conditional upon the null hypothesis being true and has nothing to do with the truth or falsity of the research hypothesis.

It is important to remember that what we have just explained about relationships is also relevant when looking for differences between groups. Thus, the p-value is the probability of finding a difference between two groups if the null hypothesis (no difference in the population) were true.

Activity 4.4

Imagine that you have conducted two separate studies and found a relationship between head size and IQ in study 1 and head size and shoe size in study 2. The probability of observing the relationship in study 1 by chance is found to be 0.04, whereas in study 2 the probability is 0.001. Which of these findings is the most important psychologically?

4.7 Statistical tests

Imagine you are investigating the relationship between number of hours spent studying and exam performance. Now suppose you have conducted a study and have found a pattern of scores similar to that given in the sample presented in Figure 4.3. How do you go about calculating the probability that such a relationship is due to sampling error if the null hypothesis were true? This is where we need to use inferential statistical tests such as the Pearson Product Moment Correlation Coefficient (see Chapter 5). If you had conducted a study that examined the difference between two conditions of an independent variable, you would use a test such as the t-test to calculate your probability. In the rest of this section we hope to give a conceptual understanding of what statistical tests actually do.

When we look at the relationship between two variables (e.g. hours spent studying and exam grade) we are able to calculate a measure of the size or strength of the relationship (this is covered in more detail in the next chapter). Once we have a measure of the strength of a relationship we need to find out the probability of obtaining a relationship of such strength by sampling error alone. In order to calculate the probability we can make use of the probability distributions to which we introduced you in Chapter 3 (e.g. see page 94). Earlier we told you that the probability of obtaining any particular score from probability distributions is known. For example, the probability of obtaining a z-score of 1.80 or higher is only 3.8%. If we are able to convert the information we have about the strength of a relationship into a score from a probability distribution, we can then find the probability of obtaining such a score by chance. This would then give us an indication of the probability of obtaining the relationship we observe in our study by sampling error (by chance) if no such relationship really existed in the population. This is basically what significance testing involves. Converting the data from our samples into scores from probability distributions enables us to work out the probability of obtaining such data by chance factors alone. We can then use this probability to decide which of the null and experimental hypotheses is the most sensible conclusion. It should be emphasised here that these probabilities we calculate are based upon the assumption that our samples are randomly selected from the population.

Figure 4.5 shows the standard normal distribution and illustrates that the probability of obtaining scores in the extremes of the distribution is very small. You should remember that when looking at probability distributions the area under the graph represents probability. The larger the area above a positive score, the greater the probability of obtaining such a score or one larger. Similarly, the larger the area below a negative score, the greater the probability of obtaining that score or one smaller. Thus, once we have converted the degree of relationship between the variables into a score from a probability distribution, we can work out the probability of obtaining such a score by chance. If the score is in either of the two regions indicated in Figure 4.5, then we can conclude that the relationship is unlikely to have arisen by chance – that is, unlikely to have been the result of sampling error.

Of course if we were investigating differences between groups we could also use probability distributions to find out the probability of finding differences of the size we observe by chance factors alone if the null hypothesis were true. In such a case we would convert the difference between the two groups of the independent variable into a score from a probability distribution. We could then find out the probability of obtaining such

Figure 4.5   Diagram illustrating the extreme scores in a distribution

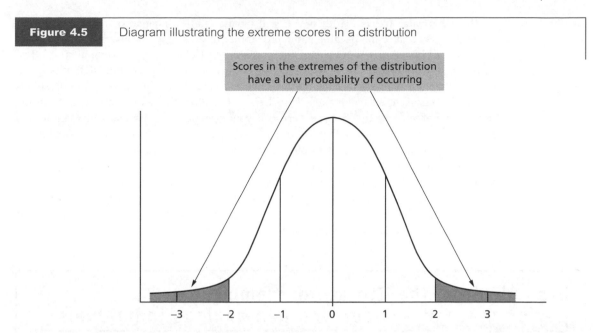

Scores in the extremes of the distribution
have a low probability of occurring

a score by sampling error if no difference existed in the population. If this probability is small, then it makes little sense to propose that there is no difference in the population and the difference between our samples is the result of sampling error alone. It makes more sense to suggest that the difference we observed represents a real difference in the population. That is, the difference has arisen owing to our manipulation of the independent variable.

It is important to note that when we convert our data into a score from a probability distribution the score we calculate is called the *test statistic*. For example, if we were interested in looking for a difference between two groups we could convert our data into a t-value (from the t-distribution). This t-value is called our test statistic. We then calculate the probability of obtaining such a value by chance factors alone and this represents our p-value.

4.8 Type I error

Suppose we conducted some research and found that, assuming the null hypothesis is true, the probability of finding the effect we observe is small – as would be the case represented in Figure 4.3. In this case we would feel confident that we could reject the null hypothesis. Now suppose there really is no such effect in our population and we have stumbled across a chance happening. We have obviously made a mistake if we conclude that we have support for our prediction. Statisticians would say that in rejecting the null hypothesis in this case we have made a Type I (one) error.

If your p-value (α) is 5% then you will have a 1 in 20 chance of making a Type I error. This is because the p-value is the probability of obtaining an observed effect, given that the null hypothesis is true. It is the probability of obtaining an effect as a result of sampling error alone if the null hypothesis were true. We argued that if this is small enough then it is unlikely that the null hypothesis is true. But as the above case illustrates we can be mistaken; we can make a Type I error. Therefore the p-value also represents the probability of your making a Type I error. If your p-value is 5% it means that you have a 5% probability of making a Type I error if you reject the null hypothesis. Although this probability is small it is still possible for it to occur. We can relate this to the National Lottery. There is only about a 1 in 14 million probability of your winning the lottery if you pick one line of numbers. Even though this represents a tiny chance of winning the possibility still exists, which is why people keep playing it. So beware, even if you find you have a p-value of only 0.001% there is still a very small probability of your making a Type I error if you decide to reject the null hypothesis.

Example from the literature: memory performance of anxious and non-anxious individuals

An example of a study in which the researchers may have made a Type I error is a study by Richards and French (1991). In this study the memory performance of anxious and non-anxious individuals for negative words was measured. They found that in a certain type of memory task the anxious individuals remembered more negative information than the non-anxious individuals. They therefore concluded that the difference was not due to sampling error and represented a genuine difference between the anxious and non-anxious individuals. Subsequent replications of this research by the same authors have, however, failed to support this initial finding. They have therefore concluded that the findings in the initial study were spurious and that there is no real difference between anxious and non-anxious individuals on this particular memory task.

These researchers made a Type I error because there is probably no real difference between anxious and non-anxious individuals in terms of their memory for generally negative information. This does not mean that this was a bad piece of research. On the contrary, it was an excellent piece of research; it just serves to illustrate that, as our judgements are based on probability, we are sometimes at the mercy of chance factors.

4.8.1 Replication

Suppose you run a study and find a relationship that has an associated probability of occurring if the null hypothesis were true of 0.01 (or 1%). In all likelihood you would be happy to reject the null hypothesis and claim that you had support for your research hypothesis. How confident could you be that there was a genuine relationship in the population? The answer to this question is difficult and in some respects depends upon the background to your research. If your study was the first in its field then you might be wise to treat your findings with a degree of caution. Remember, we are dealing with probabilities here, not certainties. Even if your findings had a small probability of occurring if the null hypothesis were true, that possibility is still there. When we take samples from populations each sample will be slightly different, and the differences between them are down to sampling error (we came across this previously in Chapter 2). It could be that you have been unfortunate enough that, owing to sampling error, the pattern you found is that 1 time in 100 when this arises. In other words, you would have been wrong to reject the null hypothesis. How should we proceed in such a situation? What you should do is try to replicate your findings by running another study. If you find the same sort of pattern and a similar probability of obtaining such a pattern if the null hypothesis were true, then you could be much more confident in your findings. Replication is one of the cornerstones of science. If you observe a phenomenon once, then it may be a chance occurrence; if you see it on two, three, four or more occasions, then you can be more certain that it is a genuine phenomenon.

4.9 Type II error

There is another sort of error that you can make when using the hypothesis testing approach to research and it is called a Type II (two) error. A Type II error is where you fail to reject the null hypothesis when it is, in fact, false.

Suppose you wanted to see if there was a relationship between amount of alcohol consumed and a person's coordination. You conduct a study and find that there is a large probability, say 0.8 (80%), that the relationship you observed in your sample arose by chance. You would, therefore, have to conclude that there is no relationship between alcohol and coordination. Would this be the correct conclusion? Clearly, this is an incorrect finding, as most evidence tells us that alcohol impairs our coordination. This is why we have drink-driving laws. In this case we would have made a Type II error: we have rejected the research hypothesis when it is in fact true.

The same sorts of errors can occur when investigating differences between groups. Suppose that you conducted a study to see if people can cover 100 m faster in a swimming pool or on a running track. Once you have analysed your data you find that there is a large probability that, if the null hypothesis were true, the difference you found was the result of sampling error. You therefore conclude that there is no difference in the times taken to complete 100 m on land or in water in the general population. You would clearly have made a Type II error.

In our research because we are never 100% certain that we can reject the null hypothesis or 100% certain that we can accept the null hypothesis we are likely to make errors some of the time. These are our Type I and Type II errors. You should recall from earlier that the probability of making a Type I error is denoted as α. The probability of making a Type II error is denoted as β (beta).

If you found yourself in the situations described above where you have made Type II errors you might ask yourself why, if there is a real relationship or difference in the population, you failed to detect it in your study. There are a number of reasons for this sort of outcome. The first is that, owing to chance factors, you may have selected people who have an unnatural tolerance of alcohol (or people who were truly as quick in the pool as on the track). More than likely, however, you will have had a poorly designed study or the sample sizes were too small. Factors such as these affect the sensitivity of your research to detect real differences in populations. The ability of a study to reject a null hypothesis when it is, in fact, false is said to be the *power* of the study and is calculated as $1 - \beta$. We say a lot more about power in Chapter 7.

Activity 4.5

Which of the following represent Type I and which represent Type II errors?

(a) You find in your study that a relationship exists between amount of tea drunk per day and amount of money won on the Lottery. You conclude that to win the Lottery you need to drinks lots of cups of tea

(b) You find in a study that there is no difference between the speed at which cheetahs and tortoises run. You conclude that tortoises are as fast as cheetahs

(c) You find in a study that there is a relationship between standard of living and annual income. However, because the probability associated with the relationship was 0.5 you conclude that there is no relationship between standard of living and annual income

4.10 Why set α at 0.05?

You may be wondering why we have a cut-off for α of 0.05? Who determined that 0.05 was an appropriate cut-off for allowing us to reject the null hypothesis rather than say 0.2 or 0.001? Although this is a fairly arbitrary cut-off there is a rationale behind it. Let us have a look at the situations where we set α at 0.2 and 0.001 respectively. If we set α at 0.2 we would be tolerating a Type I error in one case in every five. This is a very liberal criterion for significance. In one case in every five we would reject the null hypothesis when it is in fact true. On the positive side we would be much less likely to make a Type II error. That is, we would be much less likely to accept the null hypothesis when it is false. With such a liberal criterion for significance we are generally going to reject the null hypothesis more often and therefore are more likely to reject it when it is false (as well as more likely to reject it when it is true). This means a lower probability of a Type II error.

Ok, how about setting our α at 0.001? Here we are much less likely to make a Type I error. We are only likely to reject the null hypothesis when it is true one time in every thousand. This is a very conservative criterion for significance. On the face of it this would appear to be a very good thing. After all, we don't want to incorrectly reject the null hypothesis, and so why not set a conservative criterion for significance? The problem here is that although we reduce the probability of making a Type I error we also increase the probability of not rejecting the null hypothesis when it is false. We increase the probability of making a Type II error. The reason for this is that with such a conservative criterion for significance there are going to be fewer times where we reject the null hypothesis. Therefore, we are going to increase the likelihood of not rejecting the null hypothesis when it is false.

When setting our criterion for significance we therefore need to strike the right balance between making Type I and Type II errors. In most situations an α of 0.05 provides this balance. You should note that there are sometimes other considerations which should determine the level at which you set your criterion for significance. For example, if we were testing a new drug we should be much more conservative, as the consequence of making a Type I error could be very serious indeed. People may be given drugs that have nasty side-effects and yet not be effective in treating what they are supposed to treat. Another situation where you may want to set a different criterion for significance is where you conduct many statistical analyses on the same set of data. This is covered in more detail in Chapter 9 (see page 302).

4.11 One-tailed and two-tailed hypotheses

Earlier in this chapter we described a possible study investigating the relationship between number of hours spent studying per week and final examination grade (see section 4.1). We made the prediction (hypothesised) that, as hours of study increased, so would exam grades. Here we have made what we call a *directional hypothesis*. We have specified the exact direction of the relationship between the two variables: we suggested that, as study hours increased, so would exam grades. This is also called a *one-tailed hypothesis*. In this case we were sure of the nature of the relationship and we could thus make a prediction as to the direction of the relationship. However, it is often the case in psychology (and other disciplines) that we are not sure of the exact nature of the relationships we wish to examine. For example, suppose we wanted to investigate the relationship between anxiety and memory for negative information. Previous research in this area has yielded a number of contradictory findings. Mogg *et al.* (1987) found that anxious individuals remember fewer negative words than non-anxious individuals, whereas Reidy and Richards (1997) found that anxious individuals tend to remember more negative words. Here, then, we are not quite sure of the nature of the relationship between anxiety and memory for negative words. We therefore would want to predict only that there was a relationship between the two variables without specifying the exact nature of this relationship. In making such a prediction we are stating that we think there will be a relationship, but are not sure whether as anxiety increases memory for negative words will increase or decrease. Here we have made what we call a *bi-directional prediction*, better known as a *two-tailed hypothesis*.

You might be thinking to yourselves that these are bizarre terms to associate with these forms of hypotheses. Hopefully, all will become clear in the following explanation. To understand why we use the terms one- and two-tailed hypotheses you need to refer back to what we have taught you about distributions.

Previously we explained that a normal distribution (and other probability distributions) have *tails* at its extremes (see Figure 4.5). The probability of obtaining scores from these extremes (from the tails) is small compared with that of obtaining scores from the middle of the distribution (see Figure 4.6). For example, coming across a man who is 8 ft (244 cm) tall is highly unlikely, and this would thus be in the upper tail of the distribution of men's height.

You now need to think back to what we told you about statistical tests. We explained that we can use probability distributions to help us calculate the probability of a difference or a relationship occurring as a result of sampling error if one does not exist in the population. As an example, we showed you how we can use the standard normal distribution in such cases. We pointed out that, after we have transformed our sample details into a score from the distribution (remember this is called our test statistic), we could work out the probability of obtaining such a score as a result of sampling error. If this probability

Figure 4.6 Scores in the extremes have lower probability of occurrence than scores in the middle of the distribution

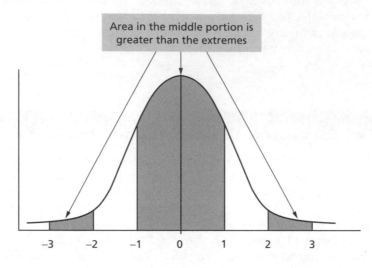

Area in the middle portion is greater than the extremes

is small, then we could argue with some confidence that we have a genuine relationship between our variables: that is, the relationship was not due to sampling error.

If you look at Figure 4.7 you will see that we have indicated the areas within the distribution where the probability of obtaining such a score is small. These scores are located in the extremes (the tails) of the distribution.

When we go through the process of calculating the relevant score from our sample information we are working with some measure of the strength of the relationship between the two. Suppose we have two studies, Study 1 and Study 2, both investigating the relationship between statistics anxiety and procrastination (see Table 4.1).

Figure 4.7 Illustration of scores in the tails of the distribution

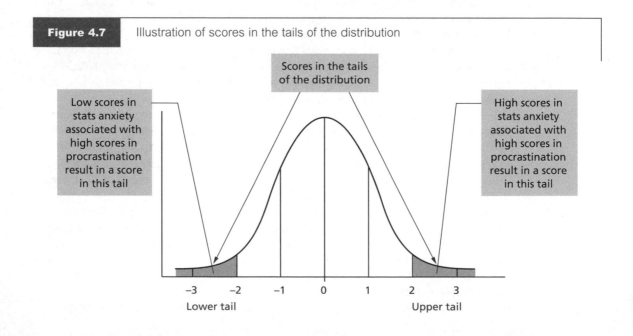

Scores in the tails of the distribution

Low scores in stats anxiety associated with high scores in procrastination result in a score in this tail

High scores in stats anxiety associated with high scores in procrastination result in a score in this tail

Lower tail   Upper tail

Table 4.1   Data for statistics anxiety and procrastination in Studies 1 and 2

Study 1		Study 2	
Statistics anxiety	Procrastination	Statistics anxiety	Procrastination
1	2	1	18
2	4	2	16
3	6	3	14
4	8	4	12
5	10	5	10
6	12	6	8
7	14	7	6
8	16	8	4
9	18	9	2

In both of these studies we might want to see if statistics anxiety and procrastination are related in some way. You should notice from the table that in each study there appears to be a relationship between statistics anxiety and procrastination. In Study 1, as the scores for statistics anxiety increase, so do those for procrastination. In this case when we calculate the score from the probability distribution we would probably obtain a value from the right-hand tail of the distribution (see Figure 4.7). If, on the other hand, as the values for statistics anxiety increased, the values for procrastination decreased (as in Study 2), then the resulting score we calculated would be in the left-hand tail of the distribution. This example illustrates the fact that the direction of the relationship between your variables determines the tail of the distribution in which the resulting score will be located.

When we do not predict the direction of the relationship between statistics anxiety and procrastination, then we are simply predicting that the score we calculate will fall in either one of the two tails. Hence, we have made a two-tailed prediction. If, on the other hand, we predict that, as the scores for statistics anxiety increase, so would the scores for procrastination, then we are predicting that the score we calculate will fall in the right-hand tail only. We have made a one-tailed prediction. That is, we are predicting the tail from which the score we calculate will be obtained.

If you make a two-tailed prediction, the calculated score can fall in either tail. Now suppose that we are sticking with convention and using the 5% significance level as our cut-off for rejecting the null hypothesis (we do not recommend that you use such a cut-off; we are merely using this to illustrate a point). We will be able to reject the null hypothesis only if there is 5% probability or less of obtaining our calculated score. Figure 4.8 shows that in either tail we take calculated scores that have a 2.5% probability of being obtained, that is, 5% divided between the two tails.

If we make a one-tailed prediction then we accept scores in only one of the tails and therefore our 5% probability region is all in the one tail: that is, it is not divided between the two tails. This effectively means that we can reject the null hypothesis for a greater number of scores in that tail than we can for a two-tailed test (see Figure 4.9).

Figures 4.8 and 4.9 illustrate the importance of being sure whether you have made a one- or two-tailed prediction. In the following chapters, when we come to describe how to carry out the various statistical tests using SPSSFW you will notice that there are options that allow us to calculate one- and two-tailed probabilities (p-values) for these statistics.

Figure 4.8 Areas (coloured) representing the regions where scores may fall for two-tailed hypotheses

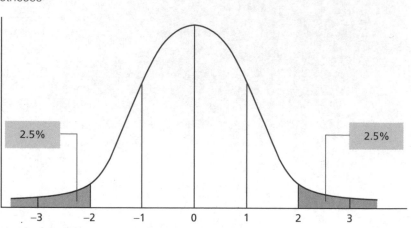

Figure 4.9 Area (coloured) representing the region where scores may fall for one-tailed hypotheses

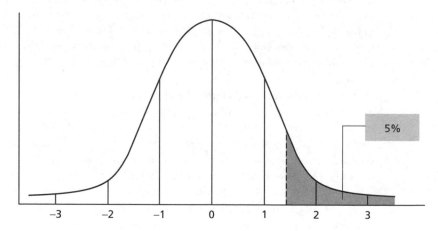

If, however, you have obtained a p-value for a two-tailed test and you want to know the corresponding probability for a one-tailed test, all you need to do is halve your p-value. For example, if you obtained a p-value of 0.03 for a two-tailed test, the equivalent value for a one-tailed test would be 0.015. Similarly, if you have obtained a p-value for a one-tailed test, to work out the equivalent probability for a two-tailed test you simply double the one-tailed probability. Note that you double the p-value, not the actual test statistic (e.g. correlation coefficient or t-value). The test statistic remains the same for both one- and two-tailed tests on the same set of data.

We should point out that, although we have illustrated the distinction between one-tailed and two-tailed predictions with reference to relationships between variables, you can also have both types of predictions when investigating differences between conditions.

Essentially, there are two ways that any two conditions (conditions A and B) can be different, that is:

■ condition A has higher scores than condition B, or
■ condition B has higher scores than condition A.

When making a two-tailed prediction about differences between two conditions we have only to specify that a difference exists between them. We do not have to specify which condition will have the higher scores. If we make a one-tailed prediction we would predict which of the above scenarios is most appropriate, that is, which condition will have the higher scores. We do not intend to go into any more detail here as this is covered in greater depth in Chapter 6.

Activity 4.6

Which of the following are one-tailed hypotheses and which are two-tailed?

(a) It is predicted that females will have higher empathy scores than males
(b) It is predicted that, as annual salary increases, so will the number of tomatoes eaten per week
(c) It is predicted that there will be a relationship between length of hair in males and number of criminal offences committed
(d) It is predicted that football fans will have lower IQ scores than opera fans
(e) It is predicted that there will be a relationship between the number of books read per week and range of vocabulary

4.12 Assumptions underlying the use of statistical tests

In the preceding sections and chapters of the book we have introduced the basic concepts underlying statistical testing. In the remainder of the book we will be explaining a wide range of statistical tests suitable for a number of different research designs. However, these tests require that a number of assumptions be met before they can be legitimately applied to sample data.

Most of the statistical techniques that we describe in this book make assumptions about the populations from which our data are drawn. Because population characteristics are called parameters (see Chapter 2) these tests are sometimes called *parametric tests*. Because the tests make these assumptions we have to ensure that our data also meet certain assumptions before we can use such statistical techniques. The assumptions are described in the following sections.

There are statistical techniques that do not make assumptions about the populations from which our data are drawn but these are not used as frequently as the parametric tests. Because they do not make assumptions about the populations they are often called *distribution-free tests*. We cover such tests in Chapter 15 of this book.

Assumptions underlying parametric tests

1. The populations from which the samples are drawn should be *normally distributed*. Parametric tests assume that we are dealing with normally distributed data. Essentially this assumption means that we should always check that the data from our samples are roughly normally distributed before deciding to use parametric tests. We have already told you how to do this using box plots, histograms or stem and leaf plots. If you find that you have a large violation of this assumption, then there are ways to transform your data legitimately so that you can still make use of parametric tests; as these are beyond the scope of this book, however, you should consult other more advanced texts. Howell (2002) gives a very good overview of such transformations. For your guidance, the distributions in Figure 4.10(a) and (b) are probably close enough to normal for you to use parametric tests. If your distributions are more like those in Figures 4.10(c) and (d), however, you should consider transforming your data.

2. The second assumption is that the variances of the populations should be approximately equal. This is sometimes referred to as the assumption of *homogeneity of variances*. If you remember when we explained how to calculate the standard deviation in Chapter 2, we told you that you calculate the variance as a step on the way to calculating the standard deviation. More specifically, we informed you that the standard deviation is the square-root of the variance. In practice, we cannot check to see if our populations have equal variances and so we have to be satisfied with ensuring that

---

Figure 4.10   Examples of distributions which could be considered approximately normal ((a) and (b)) and those that probably cannot ((c) and (d))

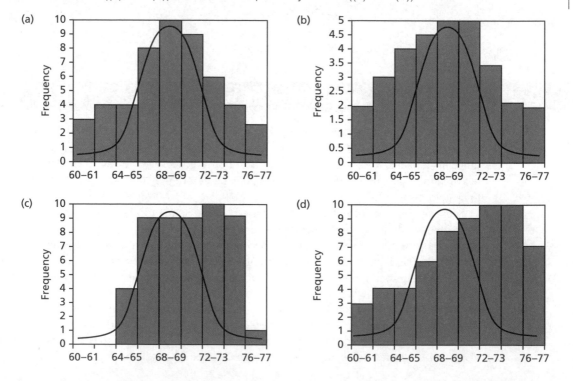

the variances of our samples are approximately equal. You might ask: *What do you mean by approximately equal?* The general rule of thumb for this is that, as long as the largest variance that you are testing is not more than *three times* the smallest, then we have roughly equal variances. We realise that this is like saying that a man and a giraffe are roughly the same height, but this does illustrate the reasonable amount of flexibility involved in some of these assumptions. Generally, a violation of this assumption is not considered to be too catastrophic as long as you have equal numbers of participants in each condition. If you have unequal sample sizes and a violation of the assumption of homogeneity of variance then you should definitely use a distribution-free test (see Chapter 15).

3. The final assumption is that we have no extreme scores. The reason for this assumption is easy to understand when you consider that many parametric tests involve the calculation of the mean as a measure of central tendency. If you think back to Chapter 2 you will recall that we explained that the mean is very sensitive to extreme scores and when these are present it is best to use some other measure of central tendency. If extreme scores distort the mean, then it follows that any parametric test that uses the mean will also be distorted. We thus need to ensure that we do not have extreme scores. If you find that you have extreme scores then you should see Chapter 2 for a discussion of what to do about them.

Given that there are these assumptions underlying the use of parametric tests, you might ask: why bother with them? Parametric tests are used very often in psychological research because they are more *powerful* tests. That is, if there is a difference in your populations, or a relationship between two variables, then the parametric tests are more likely to find it, provided that the assumptions for their use are met. Parametric tests are more powerful because they use more of the information from your data. Their formulae involve the calculation of means, standard deviations and some measure of error variance (these will be explained in the relevant chapters). Distribution-free or non-parametric tests, however, are based upon the rankings or frequency of occurrence of your data rather than the actual data themselves. Because of their greater power, parametric tests are preferred whenever the assumptions have not been grossly violated.

In this and previous chapters we have explained the important basic concepts for a good understanding of the most frequently used statistical tests. In addition to this we have presented you with a number of descriptive statistical techniques and some advice about when to use them. The preceding paragraphs have also presented advice on the criteria for choosing between various inferential statistical techniques. Before you move on to the nitty-gritty of the various inferential statistics it is perhaps a good idea to review all such advice and therefore we present it here in summary form. Figure 4.11 gives a rough pictorial guide to the way your design will affect your choice of statistics. It should be stressed that this flow-chart represents a general overview of the issues we have covered in the preceding chapters and should be used as such. Whenever you are uncertain as to which tests your data legitimately allow you to use, we recommend that you use the flow-chart in conjunction with the advice given previously.

Figure 4.11   Flow diagram as a guide to choosing the most suitable test for the design of a study

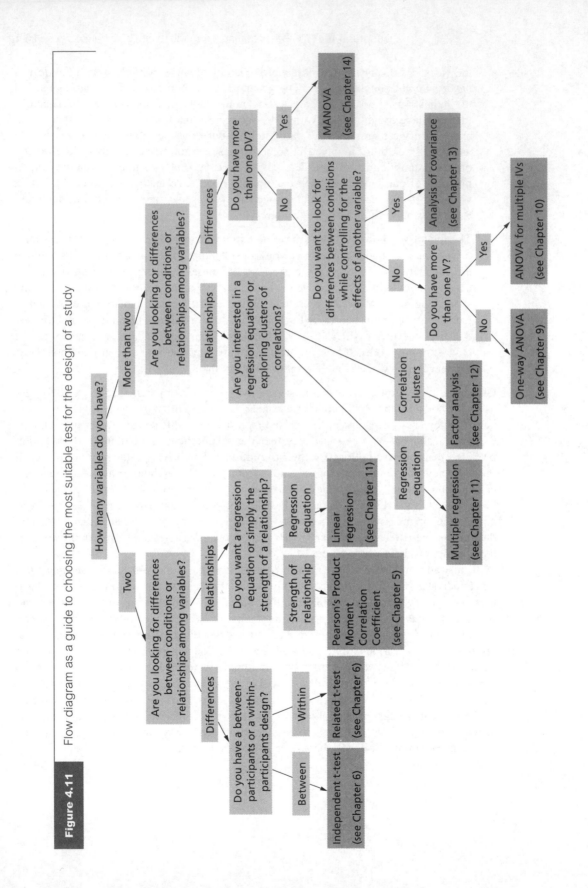

SPSSFW: Statistics Coach

Another useful feature of SPSSFW is the *Statistics Coach*. You can use the Statistics Coach in place of Figure 4.11 to find out which sort of analyses you should be doing on your data. You start the Statistics Coach through the *Help* menu:

Once the Statistics Coach starts you will be presented with a screen that asks you what you want to do. You are given a number of options to choose from such as *Summarize, describe or present data*, and *Compare groups for significant differences*.

Examples of SPSSFW output

Options to choose from

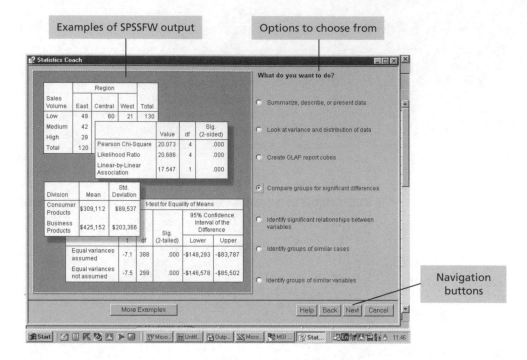

Navigation buttons

On the left-hand side of the screen you will be presented with examples of SPSS output. Towards the bottom right-hand part of the screen are a number of buttons to navigate your way through the Statistics Coach. Once you have made your selection click on the *Next* button and you will be presented with some more options related to what you want to do. As an example, we have selected the *Compare groups for significant differences* option.

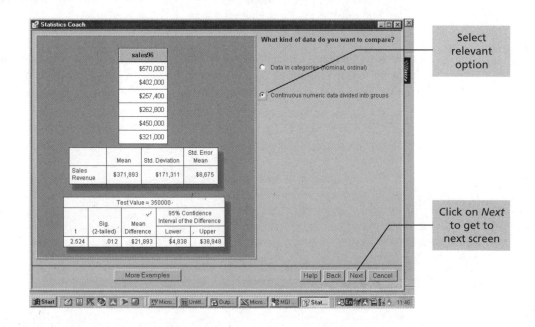

Select relevant option

Click on *Next* to get to next screen

You should then answer the relevant questions presented on the screens. After each set of options click on the *Next* button to move on to the next screen. As you make your selections you will notice that the examples of SPSSFW output on the left-hand part of the screen change to reflect the selections you have made.

Statistics Coach

How many groups or variables do you want to compare?

- ○ One group or variable compared to a known value
- ◉ Two groups or variables
- ○ Three or more groups

Division	Mean	Std. Deviation	Std. Error Mean
Consumer Products	$309,112	$89,537	$6,892
Business Products	$425,152	$203,366	$14,000

	t-test for Equality of Means		95% Confidence Interval of the Difference	
	Sig. (2-tailed)	Mean Difference	Lower	Upper
Equal variances assumed	.000	-$116,040	-$148,293	-$83,787
Equal variances not assumed	.000	-$116,040	-$146,578	-$85,502

More Examples   Help Back Next Cancel

Statistics Coach

How are your data organized?

- ◉ One continuous, numeric dependent variable divided into two unrelated groups
- ○ Two continuous, numeric variables that represent related data

division	sales96
Business Products	$402,000
Consumer Products	$257,400
Consumer Products	$262,800
Business Products	$450,000

Division	Mean	Std. Deviation	Std. Error Mean
Consumer Products	$309,112	$89,537	$6,892
Business Products	$425,152	$203,366	$14,000

	t-test for Equality of Means		95% Confidence Interval of the Difference	
	Sig. (2-tailed)	Mean Difference	Lower	Upper
Equal variances assumed	.000	-$116,040	-$148,293	-$83,787
Equal variances not assumed	.000	-$116,040	-$146,578	-$85,502

More Examples   Help Back Next Cancel

There will be a series of such screens for each type of analysis that you might want to carry out. Keep answering the questions and clicking on *Next* until you come to a screen that has a *Finish* button rather than a *Next* button.

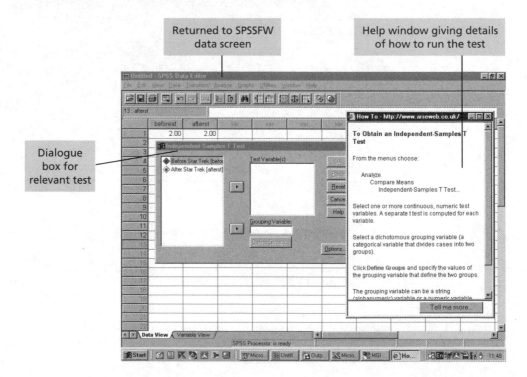

Once you have made your final selection click on the *Finish* button and SPSSFW will exit from the Statistics Coach and take you back to the SPSSFW Data screen. You will notice that the program has actually selected the relevant test from the menus. You will have a dialogue box displayed for the test you need. You will also be presented with an open Help window that contains information relevant to that particular test. So for example we have been presented with the dialogue box for the Independent t-test (see Chapter 6). You can then run the relevant analyses on your data.

Summary

In this chapter we have gone further into the realms of inferential statistics and have laid the final foundations for you to tackle the most frequently used inferential statistical techniques in psychology today. You have learned the following:

- The logic behind hypothesis testing and statistical significance.

- The null hypothesis represents the converse of the experimental hypothesis.

- How we can use probability distributions to work out the probability that the effects in our research are due to sampling error if the null hypothesis were true.

- Although hypothesis testing is the major research method in psychology there is growing concern over its inability to establish meaningful conclusions from our data.

- As a result of this we have suggested several ways of supplementing the results of your hypothesis testing with more meaningful statistics, for example effects sizes and confidence intervals.

- In hypothesis testing there are two general sorts of errors (Type I and Type II errors) that you could make when drawing conclusions from your analyses:
  - Type I errors are when you reject the null hypothesis when it is, in fact, true.
  - Type II errors are when you fail to reject the null hypothesis when it is false.

- What it means to make directional (one-tailed) and non-directional (two-tailed) predictions and how these are related to probability distributions.
  - Two-tailed predictions are those where we predict a difference between two conditions (or relationship between two variables) but do not specify the direction of the difference (or relationship).
  - One-tailed predictions are those where we specify the direction of a predicted difference (or relationship).

We hope that by this stage you have a good conceptual understanding of descriptive and inferential statistical approaches to analysing your data. In the remaining chapters, with the exception of Chapter 7, we will describe specific statistical tests in much more detail. However, you should always bear in mind when reading these chapters that these tests are based upon the concepts we have introduced to you in these opening chapters.

SPSSFW exercises

Exercise 1

Professor Yob is interested in crowd violence during football matches. She thinks that crowd violence is the result of uncomfortable seating in stadia. She therefore modifies two different stadia in England (where better for crowd violence?). In one stadium she puts in seating that is tightly packed and generally uncomfortable. In the other stadium she installs seating that is very comfortable, with lots of leg room and plenty of space between adjacent seats. She organises it so that one football club plays half of its games at one stadium and half of the games at the other stadium. She follows a group of 12 yobs who

Table 4.2   Number of arrests for each yob at the comfortable and uncomfortable stadia

Yob	Uncomfortable seating	Comfortable seating
1	8	3
2	5	2
3	4	4
4	6	6
5	4	2
6	8	1
7	9	6
8	10	3
9	7	4
10	8	1
11	6	4
12	7	3

support the club and records the number of times each one gets arrested or thrown out of each stadium. She predicts that there will be more arrests and ejections from the stadium with uncomfortable seating and obtains the data shown in Table 4.2.

1. Is this a between-participants or a within-participants design?

2. What sort of variable has Professor Yob measured, discrete or continuous?

3. (a) What is the IV?
   (b) What is the DV?

4. Is the prediction one-tailed or two-tailed?

5. What is the null hypothesis?

6. Input the data into SPSSFW and generate the following for each condition:
   ■ error bar charts
   ■ the mean
   ■ the standard deviation
   ■ the standard error
   ■ 95% confidence intervals.

7. Convert the first score from each condition into a z-score.

Exercise 2

Dr Pedantic has a passion for language and his particular dislike is the use of split infinitives (e.g. 'to *boldly go* where no man has gone before' contains a split infinitive, whereas 'to *go boldly* where no man has gone before' does not). He blames the popularity of *Star Trek* in the 1970s for the proliferation of split infinitives in journals reporting research. He therefore selects 12 researchers in psychology who have published research in journals before and after the *Star Trek* series was first televised. He goes through the last 20 publications of each researcher before *Star Trek* was televised and the first 20 publications

Table 4.3 Number of split infinitives used by researchers before and after the *Star Trek* series were originally shown

Researcher	Before *Star Trek*	After *Star Trek*
1	2	2
2	3	5
3	1	6
4	0	2
5	1	1
6	2	2
7	1	3
8	0	1
9	3	2
10	0	3
11	1	4
12	1	2

after *Star Trek* was televised and counts the number of split infinitives used. He predicts that the number of split infinitives would be greatest in the journals published after *Star Trek* was televised and obtained the data shown in Table 4.3.

1. Is this a between-participants or a within-participants design?

2. What sort of variable has Dr Pedantic measured: categorical, discrete or continuous?

3. (a) What is the IV?
   (b) What is the DV?

4. Is the prediction one-tailed or two-tailed?

5. What is the null hypothesis?

6. Input the data into SPSSFW and generate the following for each condition:
   ■ error bar charts
   ■ the mean
   ■ the standard deviation
   ■ the standard error
   ■ 95% confidence intervals.

7. Convert the first score from each condition into a z-score.

MULTIPLE CHOICE QUESTIONS

1. A Type II error occurs when:
   (a) The null hypothesis is not rejected when it should be
   (b) The null hypothesis is rejected when it should be
   (c) The null hypothesis is rejected when it should not have been
   (d) The null hypothesis is not rejected when it should not have been

2. What is the basis or logic of inferential statistical tests?

   (a) To work out the probability of obtaining an effect due to sampling error when the null hypothesis is true
   (b) To work out the probability of obtaining an effect due to sampling error when the null hypothesis is false
   (c) To work out the probability of making a Type II error
   (d) All of the above

3. If you obtain a one-tailed p-value of 0.02 then the equivalent two-tailed p-value is:

   (a) 0.01
   (b) 0.04
   (c) 0.02
   (d) 0.4

4. If you predict that two variables A and B will be related, what is the null hypothesis?

   (a) That there is no relationship between A and B
   (b) That A will be greater than B
   (c) That there is no difference between A and B
   (d) None of the above

5. The power of an experiment is:

   (a) α
   (b) The ability of the experiment to reject the null hypothesis if it is, in fact, false
   (c) The sensitivity of participants to your experimental manipulation
   (d) All of the above

6. When we predict that condition A will be greater than condition B, we have made:

   (a) A one-tailed prediction
   (b) A two-tailed prediction
   (c) A uni-directional prediction
   (d) Both (a) and (c) above

7. The probability that an effect has arisen due to sampling error given that the null hypothesis is true is denoted as:

   (a) Negligible
   (b) β
   (c) α
   (d) None of the above

8. If you obtain a two-tailed p-value of 0.02 the equivalent one-tailed p-value would be:

   (a) 0.01
   (b) 0.04
   (c) 0.02
   (d) 0.4

9. If we predict that there will be a difference between condition A and condition B, we have made:

   (a) A one-tailed prediction
   (b) A two-tailed prediction
   (c) A null prediction
   (d) Both (b) and (c) above

10. If you obtain a p value of 4%, what does this mean?

    (a) The probability that the null hypothesis is true is 4%
    (b) The probability that the null hypothesis is false is 4%
    (c) The probability of obtaining the effect you have due to sampling error if the null hypothesis were true is 4%
    (d) All of the above

11. If you predict that there will be a difference between condition A and condition B, what is the null hypothesis?

    (a) That condition A will be greater than condition B
    (b) That condition B will be greater than condition A
    (c) That condition A will be related to condition B
    (d) That there will be no difference between conditions A and B

12. If we reject the null hypothesis when it is, in fact, true then we have:

    (a) Made a Type I error
    (b) Made a Type II error
    (c) Made scientific progress
    (d) Both (b) and (c) above

13. Which of the following are the assumptions underlying the use of parametric tests?

    (a) The data should be normally distributed
    (b) The samples being tested should have approximately equal variances
    (c) You should have no extreme scores
    (d) All of the above

14. A Type II error means:

    (a) We have rejected the null hypothesis when it is, in fact, true
    (b) We have accepted the experimental hypothesis when it is false
    (c) We have accepted the null hypothesis when it is, in fact, false
    (d) None of the above

15. A researcher has conducted a study on reaction times with 20 participants in each of two conditions. She finds that the variance for the first condition is 2 seconds and for the second condition is 14 seconds. Which of the following statements are true?

    (a) She should not use parametric tests because she has failed to meet the assumption of homogeneity of variance
    (b) She has completely met all of the assumptions underlying the use of parametric tests
    (c) She has failed to meet the assumption of homogeneity of variance but could use parametric tests because she has equal sample sizes
    (d) None of the above

16. How do we denote power?

    (a) α
    (b) β
    (c) $1 - \alpha$
    (d) $1 - \beta$

17. Why do we usually set our criterion for significance at 0.05?

    (a) This is the traditional level used by most psychologists
    (b) This represents a good balance between making Type I and Type II errors
    (c) It is easier to get significant results with this α
    (d) Both (a) and (b) above

18. When we convert our data into a score from a probability distribution what do we call the value we obtain?

    (a) Significant
    (b) Not significant
    (c) The test statistic
    (d) The power of the study

19. Imagine we conduct two studies. In study A we have 1000 participants and obtain a p-value of 0.01, whereas in study B we have only 20 participants and a p-value of 0.05. In which of these two studies is there the largest effect?

    (a) Study A
    (b) Study B
    (c) The effect is the same in each study
    (d) We cannot answer this question from the information we have been given

20. If you find in a study that your p-value is 0.05, what is the probability of the alternative hypothesis being true?

    (a) 0.05
    (b) 1 minus 0.05
    (c) We cannot work out the probability of the alternative hypothesis being true
    (d) None of the above

References

Baker, R., Holloway, J., Thomas, P.W., Thomas, S. and Owens, M. (in press) 'Emotional processing and panic', *Behaviour Research and Therapy*.

Clark-Carter, D. (2003) 'Effect size: the missing piece of the jigsaw', *The Psychologist*, **16**: 636–8.

Dracup, C. (1995) 'Hypothesis testing – what it really is', *The Psychologist*, **8**: 359–62.

Howell, D.C. (2002) *Statistical Methods for Psychology*, (5th edn). Wadsworth.

Loftus, G.R. (1991) 'On the tyranny of hypothesis testing in the social sciences', *Contemporary Psychology*, **36**(2): 102–5.

Loftus, G.R. (1996) 'Psychology will be a much better science when we change the way we analyze data', *Current Directions in Psychological Science*, **5**: 161–71.

Mogg, K., Mathews, A. and Weinman, J. (1987) 'Memory bias in clinical anxiety', *Journal of Abnormal Psychology*, **96**: 94–8.

Parkinson, B. (2001) 'Anger on and off the road', *British Journal of Psychology*, **92**: 507–26.

Reidy, J. and Richards, A. (1997) 'A memory bias for threat in high-trait anxiety', *Personality and Individual Differences*, **23**: 653–63.

Richards, A. and French, C.C. (1991) 'Effects of encoding and anxiety on implicit and explicit memory performance', *Personality and Individual Differences*, **12**: 131–9.

Walsh, J.J. and Ugumba-Agwunobi, G. (2002) 'Individual differences in statistics anxiety: the roles of perfectionism, procrastination and trait anxiety', *Personality and Individual Differences*, **33**: 239–51.

5 Correlational analysis: Pearson's r

Chapter overview

In the first four chapters we have given you the basic building blocks that you will need to understand the statistical analyses presented in the remainder of the book. It is important that you understand all the concepts presented in those chapters, and you can get a good measure of your understanding by trying activities and multiple choice questions presented throughout the text and at the end of each chapter. If you find that there are certain things that you do not understand it is very much worth your while going back to the relevant chapter and making sure that you have grasped each concept fully. Once you feel confident that you have mastered these concepts you will be ready to tackle the more demanding statistical analyses presented from now on. Having a thorough understanding of these earlier concepts will smooth the way through the remainder of the book. In the first four chapters, you were introduced to the idea of looking at relationships between variables, for example the relationship between hours spent studying and performance in examinations. Psychologists often wish to know whether there is a significant relationship or association between two variables. This is the topic of the present chapter.

You will need to have an understanding of the following:

■ one- and two-tailed hypotheses (Chapter 4)
■ statistical significance (Chapter 4)
■ confidence intervals (Chapter 3).

In this chapter we will discuss ways in which we can analyse *relationships* or *associations* between variables. In the last chapter we talked about the relationship between time spent studying and exam performance. The way to find out whether such a relationship exists is to take a number of students and record how many hours per unit of time (e.g. per week) they spend studying, and then later take a measure of their performance in the examinations. We would then have two sets of data (or two variables). Correlational analysis gives us a measure of the relationship between them. In Chapter 4 (page 140) we suggested that we are able to calculate a measure of the strength of a relationship: correlational analysis gives such a measure.

In the present chapter we will discuss the following:

■ the analysis and reporting of studies using correlational analysis
■ *r* – a natural effect size
■ confidence limits around *r*.

5.1 Bivariate correlations

When we are considering the relationship between two variables, this is called *bivariate correlation*. If the two variables are associated, then they are said to be co-related (correlated). This means they co-vary; as the scores on one variable change, scores on the other variable change in a predictable way. In other words, the two variables are not independent.

5.1.1 Drawing conclusions from correlational analyses

A correlational relationship cannot be regarded as implying causation. Recall that in Chapter 1 we suggested that you cannot imply causation from correlations. That is, if a significant association exists between the two variables, this does not mean that *x* causes *y* or, alternatively, that *y* causes *x*. For instance, consider the following. It has been shown that there is a significant positive relationship between the salaries of Presbyterian ministers in Massachusetts and the price of rum in Havana. Now it is clearly inappropriate in this case to argue that one variable causes the other. Indeed, as Huff (1973), who supplied this example, observed, it is not necessary to infer causation because the more obvious explanation is that both figures are growing because of the influence of a third factor – the worldwide rise in the price level of practically everything!

Sometimes, then, two variables are statistically related, but there is no real association between them. Rather the significant results reflect the influence of a third variable.

It is also possible to produce a completely spurious significant correlation between two variables in the absence of any third variable influencing them. For instance, on one occasion we asked our students to perform a correlational analysis on several variables. When doing this on the computer, it is very easy to mistakenly include variables that are not relevant. One of our students included 'participant number' with the other variables, in error of course. She then showed us that 'participant number' had a high positive correlation with self-esteem, one of the other variables. It is as well, therefore, always to bear in mind the possibility that the relationship revealed by a correlational analysis may be spurious.

The exploration of relationships between variables may include the following steps:

1. Inspection of *scattergrams* (see below).
2. A statistical test called *Pearson's r*, which shows us the magnitude and degree of the relationship, and the likelihood of such a relationship occurring by sampling error, given the truth of the null hypothesis.
3. *Confidence limits* around the test statistic *r*, where appropriate.

5.1.2 Purpose of correlational analysis

The purpose, then, of performing a correlational analysis is to discover whether there is a relationship between variables, which is unlikely to occur by sampling error (assuming the null hypothesis to be true). The null hypothesis is that there is no real relationship between the two variables. This is not the only information, however, that a correlational analysis provides. It also enables us to determine the following:

- the direction of the relationship – whether it is positive, negative or zero
- the strength or magnitude of the relationship between the two variables – the test statistic, called the *correlation coefficient*, varies from 0 (no relationship between the variables) to 1 (perfect relationship between the variables).

These two points are discussed in greater detail below.

5.1.3 Direction of the relationship

Positive

High scores on one variable (which we call x) tend to be associated with high scores on the other variable (which we call y); conversely, low scores on variable x tend to be associated with low scores on variable y.

Negative

High scores on one variable are associated with low scores on the other variable.

Zero

Zero relationships are where there is no *linear* (straight-line) relationship between the two variables. (What precisely is meant by the term 'linear relationship' will be explained later. For now, just assume that no linear relationship means no relationship between the two variables.)

Now think about the *direction* of the relationships in the examples given above.

Number of hours spent studying and performance in examinations

You would expect that the number of hours spent studying would have a positive relationship with examination performance – the more hours a student spends studying, the better the performance.

Age of driver and motor accidents

Age of driver is associated with motor accidents – but this time the relationship is negative. Lawton *et al.* (1997) found that both age and sex were correlated with accident rate, young male drivers being more likely to have accidents.

5.1.4 Perfect positive relationships

We have already said that, in positive relationships, high scores on one variable are associated with high scores on the other, and vice versa. This can be seen by plotting the scores on a graph called a *scattergram*, or scatterplot. When performing a bivariate correlation, we have two sets of scores. When we plot the scores on a scattergram, we assign one variable to the horizontal axis – this is always called x. We assign the other variable to the vertical axis – this is always called y. It does not matter which variable we assign to x, and which variable to y.

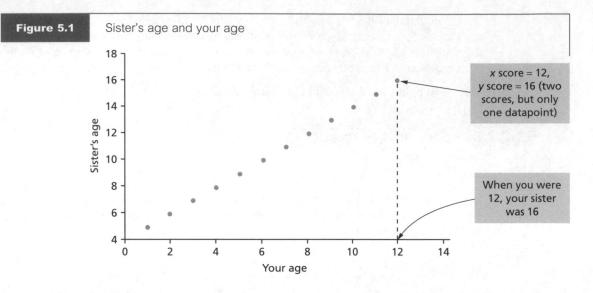

Figure 5.1 Sister's age and your age

To construct a scattergram, we take each person's score on *x* and *y*, and plot where the two meet. Each datapoint consists of two scores (*x* and *y*). You were introduced to the construction of scattergrams (using SPSSFW) in Chapter 2 section 5. Here we go into greater detail.

A perfect positive relationship is depicted in the scattergram in Figure 5.1. A perfect relationship is where all the points on the scattergram would fall on a straight line. For instance, think of your age plotted against your sister's age. (Of course, this is an unrealistic example. No one would really want to correlate their age with their sister's age – it is just an example.) In the example below, we have assumed that your sister is four years older than you. We have allotted your sister's age to the vertical axis (*y*) and your age to the horizontal axis (*x*), and for each pair of ages we have put one point on the scattergram. It should be immediately obvious that the relationship is positive: as you grow older, so does your sister. The relationship must be perfect as well: for every year that you age, your sister ages one year as well.

An important point to note is that the above example shows that you cannot draw any inferences about *cause* when performing a correlation. After all, your age increase does not cause your sister's age to increase, neither does her growing older cause you to age!

5.1.5 Imperfect positive relationships

Imagine that we have a number of students, whom we have measured on IQ and percentage marks in an exam. We want to see whether there is a relationship between IQ and exam marks. This does not mean that we are saying IQ *causes* students' exam marks; nor does it mean that the exam marks they achieved somehow had an effect on their IQ. Both high (or low) IQ and high (or low) exam marks could have been 'caused' by all sorts of factors – crammer courses, IQ practice tests, motivation, to mention just a few.

We decide to allot IQ to the vertical axis (*y*) and exam marks to the horizontal axis (*x*). Each student has two scores, an IQ score and an exam mark. However, each student contributes only one 'point' on the scattergram, as you can see in Figure 5.2.

Figure 5.2	Scattergram of IQ and exam marks

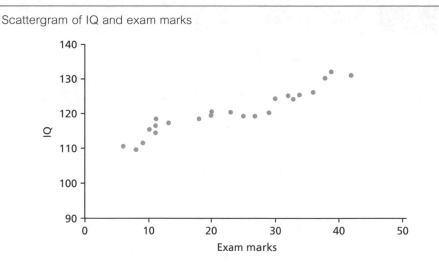

You can see from this scattergram that high IQs *tend* to be associated with high exam scores, and low IQ scores *tend* to be associated with low exam scores. Of course, in this instance the correlation is not perfect. But the trend is there, and that is what is important. That is, although the dots do not fall on a straight line, this is still a positive linear relationship because they form a discernible pattern going from the bottom left-hand corner to the top right-hand corner.

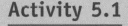

Activity 5.1

Try to think of some bivariate positive relationships. Are your examples likely to be *perfect* relationships? Discuss your examples with others. Do you agree with each other on whether your examples are good ones?

5.1.6   Perfect negative relationships

Again, because this relationship is perfect, the points on the scattergram would fall on a straight line. Each time *x* increases by a certain amount, *y decreases* by a certain, constant, amount.

Imagine a vending machine, selling chocolate. The cost is 50p per bar. At the beginning of the day, the machine is filled with ten chocolate bars. Assuming of course that it works as it should (that is, no chocolate bars get stuck, the money stays in, it gives you the right change etc. . . . well, perhaps this is a bit too unrealistic but never mind), each time someone puts in 50p, the chocolate bar is ejected, and one less remains. This can be seen in Figure 5.3.

As you can see, with a perfect negative linear relationship the dots still fall in a straight line, but this time they go from the top left-hand corner down to the bottom right-hand corner.

Figure 5.3 Graph of the relationship between chocolate bars in the machine and amount of money put in

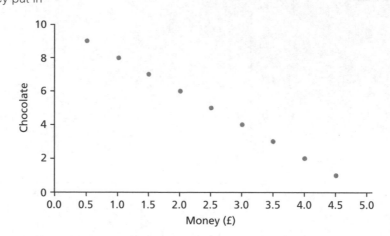

5.1.7 Imperfect negative relationships

With an imperfect negative linear relationship the dots do not fall on a straight line, but they still form a discernible pattern going from the top left-hand corner down to the bottom right-hand corner. For example, suppose we had collected data on attendances at cricket matches and the amount of rainfall. The resulting scattergram might look something like Figure 5.4.

Generally, the trend is for attendance at cricket matches to be lower when rainfall is higher.

5.1.8 Non-linear relationships

Note that, if a relationship is *not* statistically significant, it may not be appropriate to infer that there is *no* relationship between the two variables. This is because, as we have said before, a correlational analysis tests to see whether there is a *linear* relationship. Some

Figure 5.4 Scattergram of attendance at cricket matches and rainfall

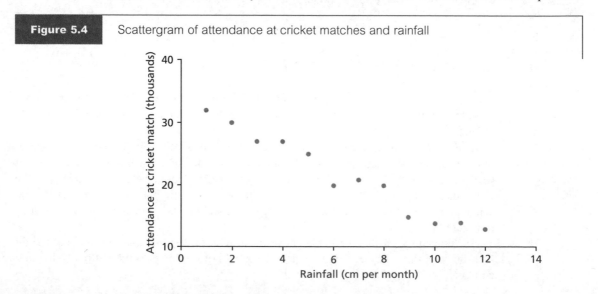

relationships are not linear. An example of such a relationship is that between arousal and performance. Although we would expect a certain level of arousal to improve sports performance, too much arousal could lead to a detriment in performance. Such a relation is described by the Yerkes–Dodson law (Yerkes and Dodson 1908). This law predicts an inverted curvilinear relationship between arousal and performance. At low levels of arousal, performance (e.g. athletic performance) will be lower than if arousal was a bit higher. There is an 'optimum' level of arousal, at which performance will be highest. Beyond that, arousal actually decreases performance. This can be represented as shown in Figure 5.5.

The same relationship can be represented by the scattergram in Figure 5.6, which shows a curvilinear relationship, i.e. *x* increases with *y* up to a certain extent, and then decreases with *y*. The point we are trying to make is that here there is undoubtedly a relationship between *x* and *y*, but the correlation coefficient would not be statistically significant because there is not a linear (straight line) relationship. For this reason, you should really always look at a scattergram before you carry out your analysis, to make sure that your variables are not related in this way, because if they are, there is not much point in using the techniques we are describing in this chapter.

Figure 5.5   The inverted-U hypothesis (Yerkes-Dodson Law, 1908)

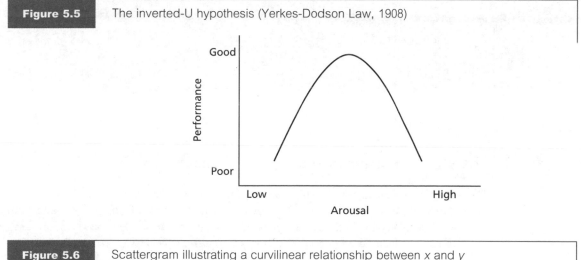

Figure 5.6   Scattergram illustrating a curvilinear relationship between *x* and *y*

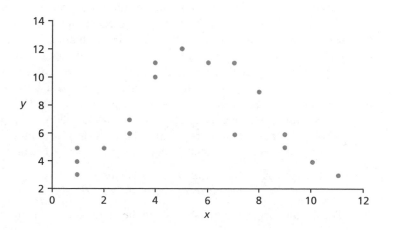

Activity 5.2

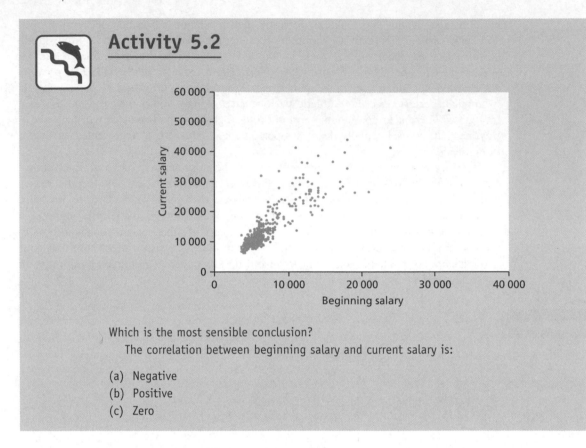

Which is the most sensible conclusion?

The correlation between beginning salary and current salary is:

(a) Negative
(b) Positive
(c) Zero

5.1.9 The strength or magnitude of the relationship

The strength of a linear relationship between the two variables is measured by a statistic called the *correlation coefficient*, also known as *r*, which varies from 0 to −1, and from 0 to +1. There are, in fact, several types of correlational tests. The most widely used are Pearson's *r* (named after Karl Pearson, who devised the test) and Spearman's Rho (Eta^2 and Cramer's V are two we mention in passing). The full name of Pearson's *r* is Pearson's product moment correlation; this is a parametric test and the one we will be discussing in this chapter. You will remember from Chapter 4, page 140, that, in order to use a parametric test, we must meet certain assumptions. The most important assumption is that data are drawn from a normally distributed population. If you have large numbers of participants, then this assumption is likely to be met. If you have reason to believe that this is *not* the case, then you should use the non-parametric equivalent of Pearson's *r*, which is called Spearman's Rho (see Chapter 15, page 523).

In Figure 5.1 above, the relationship is represented by +1: plus because the relationship is positive, and 1 because the relationship is perfect. In Figure 5.3 above, the relationship is −1: minus because the relationship is negative, and 1 because the relationship is perfect.

Remember: +1 = *perfect positive relationship*
−1 = *perfect negative relationship*

The diagram in Figure 5.7 shows you the various strengths of the correlation coefficents.

| Figure 5.7 | Illustration of the strength of positive and negative correlation coefficients |

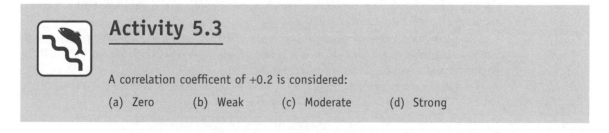

Perfect	+1		−1
Strong	+0.9 +0.8 +0.7		−0.9 −0.8 −0.7
Moderate	+0.6 +0.5 +0.4		−0.6 −0.5 −0.4
Weak	+0.3 +0.2 +0.1		−0.3 −0.2 −0.1
Zero		0	

The diagram in Figure 5.7 puts over the idea that −1 is *just as* strong as +1. Just because a relationship is negative does not mean that it is less important, or strong, than a positive one. As we have said before (but repetition helps), a positive relationship simply means that high scores on *x* tend to go with high scores on *y*, and low scores on *x* tend to go with low scores on *y*, whereas a negative relationship means that high scores on *x* tend to go with low scores on *y*.

You can see that we have assigned verbal labels to the numbers – these are only guides. A 0.9 correlation is a strong one. Obviously the nearer to 1 (+ or −) a correlation coefficient is, the stronger the relationship. The nearer to 0 (meaning no relationship), the weaker the correlation. Correlations of 0.4 to 0.5 are moderate. The correlation coefficient measures how closely the dots cluster together.

Activity 5.3

A correlation coefficent of +0.2 is considered:

(a) Zero   (b) Weak   (c) Moderate   (d) Strong

The scattergrams in Figures 5.8 and 5.9 give you some idea of what the correlation coefficients mean. Figure 5.8 shows that there is, then, a moderate positive association between age and general knowledge.

People vary as to how much they enjoy thinking and problem-solving. Psychologists have devised a scale to measure this construct, which is called need for cognition (Cacioppo

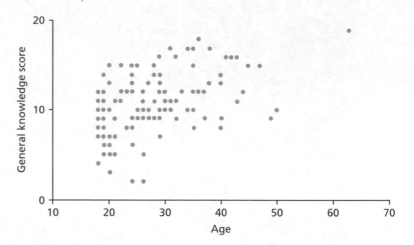

Figure 5.8 Correlation between age and general knowledge in a student sample ($n = 143$; $r = +0.44$)

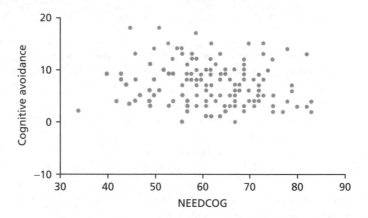

Figure 5.9 Scattergram showing the correlation between need for cognition and cognitive avoidance ($n = 143$; $r = -0.21$)

and Petty, 1982). People who enjoy problem-solving will have a higher need for cognition than people who dislike problem-solving. Some people avoid problem-solving tasks, showing cognitive avoidance.

The correlation between *need for cognition* (NEEDCOG) and *cognitive avoidance* in a student sample shows that there is a weak negative association between the need for cognition and cognitive avoidance (see Figure 5.9).

If a correlation is zero, the dots may appear to be random, and there is no discernible pattern. Thus there is no relationship between *x* and *y*.

Figure 5.10 shows that there is no association between *positive reappraisal* and the *need for cognition*.

Data correlating ($n = 11$; $r = +0.68$) days off school and being teased by others are represented in Figure 5.11. There is a moderately strong positive relationship between days off school and being teased by others.

There is a strong positive association between being teased and feeling different from others ($n = 11$; $r = +0.85$) (see Figure 5.12).

Figure 5.10

Zero relationship between positive reappraisal and need for cognition (NEEDCOG) on a student sample ($n = 143$; $r = -0.01$)

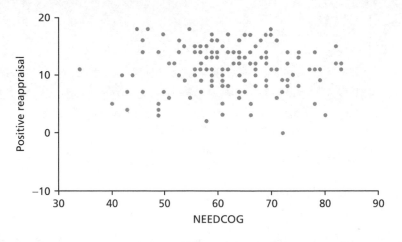

Figure 5.11

Correlation between being teased by others and number of days off school ($n = 11$; $r = +0.68$)

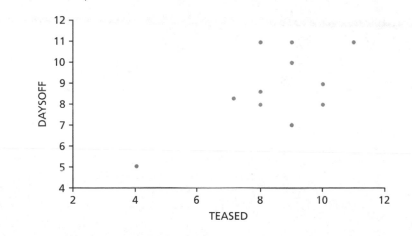

Figure 5.12

Correlation between being teased and feeling different from others ($n = 11$; $r = +0.85$)

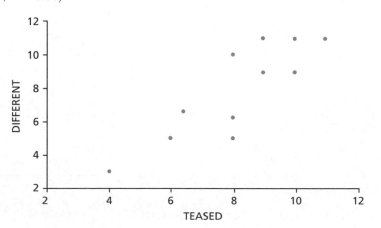

Activity 5.4

Have a look at the following scattergrams. Consider whether, just by looking at them, you can tell:

(a) The direction of the relationship (positive, negative or zero)
(b) The magnitude of the relationship (perfect, strong, weak or zero)

It is sometimes difficult to tell – which is when a test statistic like Pearson's *r* comes in handy!

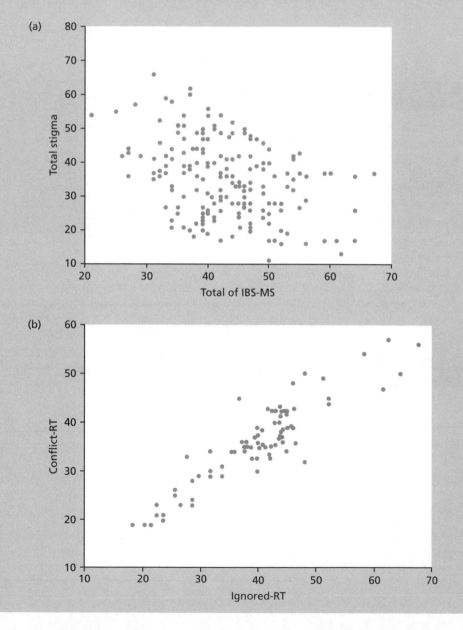

| **Figure 5.13** | Perfect linear relationship |

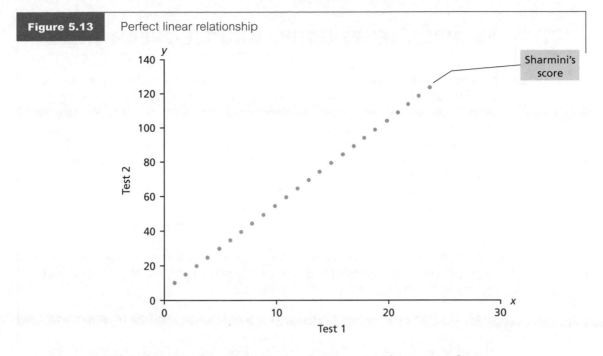

Think about this. Does going to church stop you getting pregnant?

> *There are about 118,000 teenage pregnancies a year, and half of all single parents are under 25. The UK has the highest divorce rate in Europe and the most teenage pregnancies, though other countries are coming up fast. The only reason detectable by statistics is connected to church-going. Britain's attendance figures began to drop before other countries, and everywhere as church attendance falls, divorce and single parenthood rise. (Polly Toynbee,* Radio Times, *20–26 March 1993)*

Let's look at a perfect relationship again (Figure 5.13).

Imagine that this represents the relationship between the scores on two tests, Test 1 and Test 2. The fact that this is a perfect correlation means that the relative position of the participants is exactly the same for each test. In other words, if Sharmini has the top score on Test 1 (in the above example it is 23) she will also have scored the top score on Test 2 (130). Conversely, the participant who has the lowest score on Test 1 will also have the lowest score on Test 2.

Now, as we said previously, perfect relationships are rare, but the same reasoning applies with imperfect relationships. That is, in order to calculate a correlation coefficient it is necessary to relate the relative position of each participant on one variable to their relative position on the second variable.

EXAMPLE: TEMPERATURE AND ICE-CREAM SALES

Let's imagine that we have carried out a correlational analysis on a number of ice-cream cones bought from a van outside your college, and temperature. We ask the vendor, called Sellalot, how many ice-cream cones have been sold each day. We take the measurements over 20 days. Now we need to know whether the number of ice-cream cones sold varies along with the temperature. We would expect that, according to previous literature, ice-cream sales would increase as temperature rises. This is a one-tailed hypothesis. The data are given in Table 5.1.

Now is it quite easy to see how to plot scattergrams by hand, although when you have many scores this could be tedious. Naturally, SPSSFW performs this task better than we can! Instructions for how to obtain scattergrams were given to you in Chapter 2, page 62.

From the scattergram in Figure 5.14 we can see that temperature and number of ice-cream cones sold are related. It is obviously not a perfect correlation, but just by looking at the data we can see that it is positive.

Table 5.1 Data for the number of ice-cream cones sold on days with different temperatures

Ice-cream cones sold	Temperature	Ice-cream cones sold	Temperature
1000	26	550	14
950	22	600	19
870	19	700	21
890	20	750	22
886	19	800	22
900	21	850	24
560	17	950	22
550	16	1050	26
400	12	1000	26
500	13	1000	26

| **Figure 5.14** | Scatterplot of the ice-cream cone data |

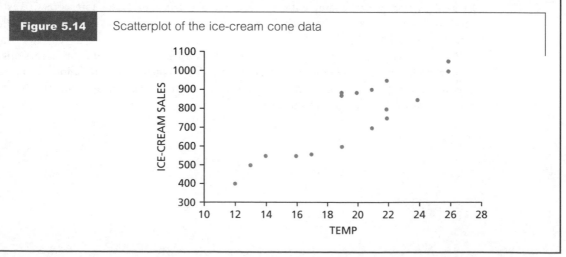

SPSSFW: bivariate correlations – Pearson's *r*

Now we want to know the value of the correlation coefficient and the associated probability, so again we turn to SPSSFW. Our data have already been entered into SPSSFW, so now we select *Analyze*, *Correlate*, *Bivariate*:

This brings you to the following dialogue box:

Move variables of interest from left hand box to here

Move both variables from the left-hand side to the right-hand side. Make sure the *Pearson* and *One-tailed* options are selected. Then click on *OK*. This will obtain your results.

Let's look at the output from SPSSFW. The important results for your write-ups are as follows:

- the correlation coefficient *r*; this shows us how strongly our variables relate to each other, and in what direction
- the associated probability level, letting us know the likelihood of our correlation coefficient arising by sampling error, assuming the null hypothesis to be true.

Results are given in the form of a matrix. A matrix is simply a set of numbers arranged in rows and columns. The correlation matrix is an example of a square symmetric matrix. You should find that each variable correlates perfectly with itself (otherwise something is amiss!). You will also note that results are given twice: each half of the matrix is a mirror image of itself. This means you have to look at one half (of the diagonal) only. SPSSFW also lets us know the number of pairs for each variable. You can see from the output below that the point where our variable ICECREAM meets our variable TEMP gives us the information we need. The first line gives us the correlation coefficient – it is usual for us to give this correct to two decimal places. The achieved significance level is given on the second line, and the third line confirms how many pairs we have in the analysis. Remember that, when SPSSFW gives a row of noughts, change the last nought to a 1 and use the < sign (i.e. $p < 0.001$, $n = 20$). Note that our correlation coefficient is *positive* – as temperature rises, so does the sale of ice-creams.

> The correlation coefficient (*r*) is given in the cell where 'ice cream' meets 'temperature', i.e. $r = +0.89$

Correlations

		Ice cream		temp
Ice cream	Pearson Correlation	**1.000**		**.8931**
	Sig. (2-tailed)	.		**.000**
	N	20		**20**
temp	Pearson Correlation	.8931		1.000
	Sig. (2-tailed)	.000		.
	N	20		20

> This is the achieved significance level. Remember that, when SPSSFW gives a row of noughts, change the last one to a '1' and use the < sign, i.e. $p < 0.001$

These results tell us that the sales of ice-cream cones are positively and strongly related to the temperature. The textual part of our analysis might therefore read as follows:

> The relationship between sales of ice-cream and outside temperature was found to be positively and strongly related ($r = +0.89$, $p < 0.001$). Thus as temperature rises, so does the sale of ice-cream.

This is all we can say at the moment, but as the chapter progresses you will see that we can add to this.

Activity 5.5

Look at the following output from SPSSFW:

Correlations

		Motivation	Hours	Age
Motivation	Pearson Correlation	1.000	.8801	−.0110
	Sig. (2-tailed)	.	.000	.811
	N	474	474	474
Hours	Pearson Correlation	.8801	1.000	−.1459
	Sig. (2-tailed)	.000	.	.001
	N	474	474	474
Age	Pearson Correlation	−0.110	−.1459	1.000
	Sig. (2-tailed)	.811	.001	.
	N	474	474	474

Which association is the strongest?

(a) Hours worked and motivation
(b) Age and motivation
(c) Age and hours worked

5.1.10 Variance explanation of the correlation coefficient

The correlation coefficient (r) is a ratio between the covariance (variance shared by the two variables) and a measure of the separate variances.

By now you should have a good idea of what a correlation coefficient means. For instance, if we tell you that two variables are associated at 0.9, you could probably draw the scattergram pretty well. Similarly, if we tell you to draw a scattergram representing a 0.1 association, you could probably do that fairly accurately as well. But there is another way of visualising what these coefficients mean, a way that will be very useful to you later on, when we go on to regression analysis. Let's take an example of number of hours of sunshine, and temperature (this example originated from Alt, 1990). These two variables are positively associated: the more hours of sunshine, the higher the temperature. When two variables are correlated, we say that they 'share' variance. For instance, the following circles represent sunshine hours and temperature.

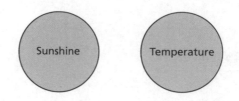

We have drawn these circles, representing sunshine and temperature, as if they are independent, but they are *not* independent. They share a lot of variance. How much variance do they share? The test statistic, a correlation coefficient, will give us the answer. We have already said that the correlation coefficient goes from 0 to +1, and 0 to −1. By *squaring* the correlation coefficient, you know how much variance, in percentage terms, the two variables share. Look at Table 5.2.

Table 5.2 Table demonstrating the relationship between correlations and squared correlations

Correlation (r)	Correlation squared (r^2)	Variance accounted for
0.0	0.0	0.00
0.1	0.1^2	0.01 (1%)
0.2	0.2^2	0.04 (4%)
0.3	0.3^2	0.09 (9%)
0.4	0.4^2	0.16 (16%)
0.5	0.5^2	0.25 (25%)
0.6	0.6^2	0.36 (36%)
0.7	0.7^2	0.49 (49%)
0.8	0.8^2	0.64 (64%)
0.9	0.9^2	0.81 (81%)
1.0	1.0^2	1.0 (100%)

Remember, negative correlations, when squared, give a positive answer. So −0.4 squared (-0.4×-0.4) = 0.16. So 16% of the variance has been accounted for by a −0.4 correlation, just the same as if the correlation is +0.4. If you have a correlation of 0.9, you have accounted for (explained) 81% of the variance. A Venn diagram will make this clearer. If two variables were *perfectly* correlated, they would not be independent at all. The two circles for x and y would lie on top of each other, just as if you had two coins on top of each other:

The two variables would correlate +1.00, and all the variability in the scores of one variable could be accounted for by the variability in the scores of the other variable. Take

sunshine hours and temperature, which we can assume to be correlated 0.9 (81%).[1] The two circles look like this:

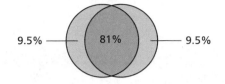

Remember, if 81% is shared variance, then 19% is not shared: it is what is known as unique variance – 9.5% is unique to sunshine, and 9.5% is unique to temperature. If the shared variance is significantly greater than the unique variances, then *r* will be high. If the unique variances are significantly greater than the shared variance, *r* will be low.

$$r = \frac{\text{a measure of shared variance}}{\text{a measure of the separate variances}}$$

The shaded part (81%) is the variance they share. In other words, 81% of the variation in number of hours of sunshine can be explained by the variation in temperature. Conversely, 81% of the variation in temperature can be accounted for by reference to the variation in number of hours of sunshine – 19% is 'unexplained', that is, the variation in scores must be due to other factors as well.

Activity 5.6

Look at the scattergram below:

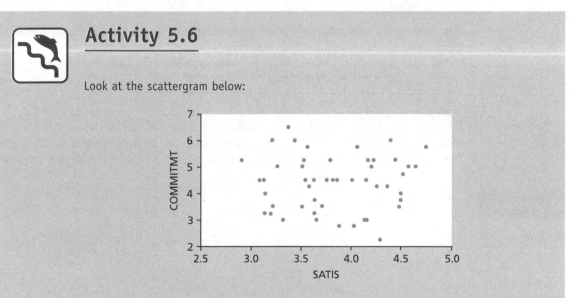

Which is the most sensible conclusion? The two variables show a:

(a) Moderate positive correlation
(b) Moderate negative correlation
(c) Strong negative correlation
(d) Zero correlation

---

[1] This example is from Alt (1990).

Figure 5.15   Diagram illustrating the amount of shared variance between two variables

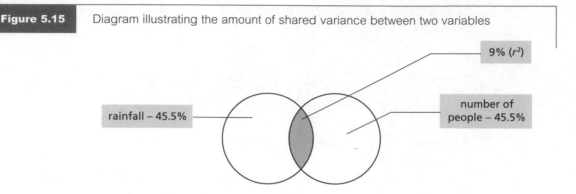

Take the case of number of inches of rainfall and attendance at cricket matches. Here we would expect a negative relationship: the more rain, the fewer people attending. Assume that the relationship is −0.3. This means that 9% (−0.3 × −0.3 = +0.09) of the variance has been explained (see Figure 5.15).

As another example (see Figure 5.16), assume that we measure and weigh a class of schoolchildren, and that height and weight correlate 0.7. How much of the variance has been accounted for? We multiply 0.7 by 0.7 = 0.49 (49%): this means that nearly half of the variation in the scores of height can be explained by the variation in weight. Conversely, nearly half of the variation in weight can be accounted for by reference to the variation in height.

This means, of course, that 51% is *unexplained*, that is, 51% is explainable by reference to other factors, perhaps age, genetics and environmental factors. A correlation coefficient can always be squared, to give you the 'variance explained' (r squared). Similarly, if you know r^2, you can use the square-root button on your calculator to give you the correlation coefficient, r (although this will not tell you the direction of the relationship). You should be able to see by this that a correlation of 0.4 is *not* twice as strong as a correlation of 0.2. A 0.4 correlation means that 16% of the variance has been explained, whereas 0.2 means that only 4% has been explained. So a correlation of 0.4 is, in fact, four times as strong as 0.2. A correlation coefficent is a good measure of effect size and can always be squared

Figure 5.16   A further illustration of shared variance

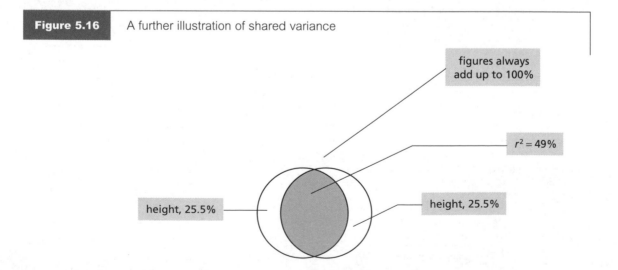

in order to see how much of the variation in scores on one variable can be explained by reference to the other variable.

Activity 5.7

When you are assessing the strength and significance of a correlation coefficient, it is important to look at:

(a) The significance level
(b) The value of the correlation coefficient
(c) Both (a) and (b)
(d) Neither (a) nor (b)

There is a (perhaps fictitious!) correlation between amount of ice-cream eaten and feelings of great happiness (+0.85). How much variation in the happiness scores can be explained by the amount of ice-cream eaten? How much variance is left unexplained?

5.1.11   Statistical significance and psychological importance

In the past, some people were more concerned about 'significance' than about the size of the correlation or the amount of variance explained. Sometimes people used to say that they had a highly significant correlation: they remembered the probability value (for instance, 0.005) but forgot the size of the correlation. The probability value means very little without reporting the *r* value. The correlation coefficient tells you how well the variables are related, and the probability value is the probability of that value occurring by sampling error.

So when you report your findings, report the correlation coefficient and think about whether *r* is meaningful in your particular study, as well as the probability value. Do not use the probability value on its own. *Remember, statistical significance does not necessarily equal psychological significance* (see Chapters 4 and 7 for further information).

EXAMPLE: ICE-CREAMS AND TEMPERATURE REVISITED

Now you know about variance explained, we can adjust the textual part of our results to include it. The textual part of our analysis might now read as follows:

> The sale of ice-cream cones was strongly associated with temperature; as temperature rises, so does the sale of ice-creams. The *r* of 0.89 showed that 79% of the variation in ice-cream sales was accounted for by the variation in the temperature. The associated probability level of 0.001 showed that such a result is highly unlikely to have arisen by sampling error, assuming the null hypothesis to be true.

Activity 5.8

Look at the following scattergram:

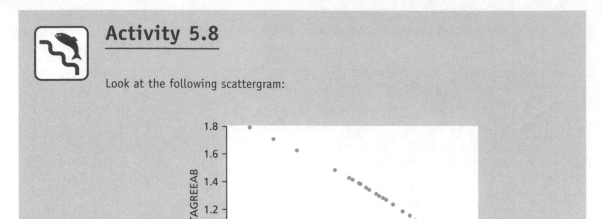

This shows that the variables show a:

(a) Strong negative association
(b) Moderate positive association
(c) Moderate negative association

EXAMPLE: COGNITIVE FUNCTION IN PEOPLE WITH CHRONIC ILLNESS

A study was carried out in which correlations between cognitive measures and illness variables were obtained. The measures were: IQ (both verbal and performance); a Stroop[2] score, duration of illness in years, and a depression measure. The hypotheses were two-tailed. Seventy participants provided data, and the results were as shown in Table 5.3.

The first row gives the *r* values, the second line gives the associated probability values, and the third gives the numbers of participants in each condition.

---

[2] The traditional Stroop test involves colour words (red, blue, yellow, green) being written in either a congruent colour (e.g. the word red is printed in red ink) or an incongruent colour (e.g. the word red is printed in blue ink). Participants typically take longer to name colours in the incongruent condition. Taking the difference in the reaction times between the two conditions gives the Stroop score reported in this study.

Table 5.3

Correlations

		verbal iq	performance iq	duration of illness in years	stroop	depression
verbal iq	Pearson Correlation	1	.615	−.175	−.227	−.327
	Sig. (2-tailed)	.	.000	.148	.059	.006
	N	70	70	70	70	70
performance iq	Pearson Correlation	.615	1	.043	−.231	−.094
	Sig. (2-tailed)	.000	.	.724	.055	.438
	N	70	70	70	70	70
duration of illness in years	Pearson Correlation	−.175	.043	1	.217	.398
	Sig. (2-tailed)	.148	.724	.	.072	.001
	N	70	70	70	70	70
stroop	Pearson Correlation	−.227	−.231	.217	1	.274
	Sig. (2-tailed)	.059	.055	.072	.	.022
	N	70	70	70	70	70
depression	Pearson Correlation	−.327	−.094	.398	.274	1
	Sig. (2-tailed)	.006	.438	.001	.022	.
	N	70	70	70	70	70

The textual part of your report might be written as follows:

As expected, verbal and performance IQ were strongly and positively related and a moderate correlation was found between duration of illness and depression. More interesting, however, was the finding that depression was related to verbal IQ ($r = -0.33$, $p = 0.006$) but not performance IQ ($r = -0.09$, $p = 0.44$). Depression was also related to the stroop measure – the more depressed the participant was, the more incongruent their scores ($r = 0.27$, $p = 0.022$)

You can also obtain a matrix of scattergrams through SPSSFW (see Figure 5.17). At a first glance, this looks confusing. However, it is interpreted in the same way as the correlational table above.

You really need to look at one half of the matrix only, as one half is a mirror image of the other. The scattergram for any two variables is shown at the square where they meet. So follow an imaginary vertical line upwards from 'duration of illness' and follow an imaginary horizontal line from 'verbal IQ' and this will result in the scattergram which plots 'duration of illness' against 'verbal IQ'.

▶

| Figure 5.17 | Scattergram matrices for cognitive and illness variables |

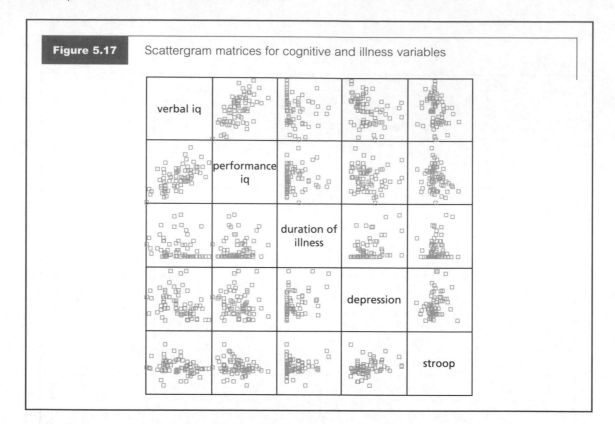

SPSSFW: obtaining a scattergram matrix

To obtain matrices, open up your data file, then select *Graphs*, *Scatter*:

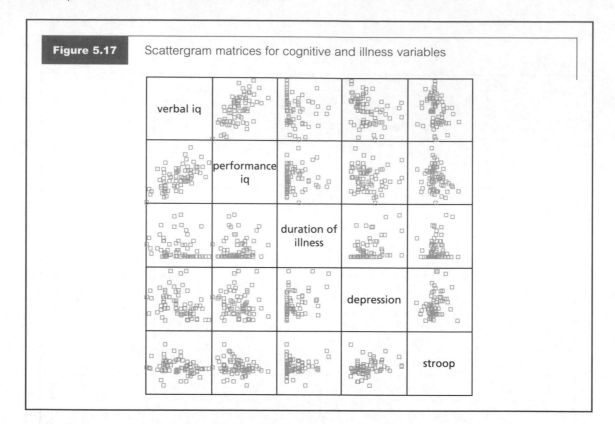

Next select *Matrix*, *Define*:

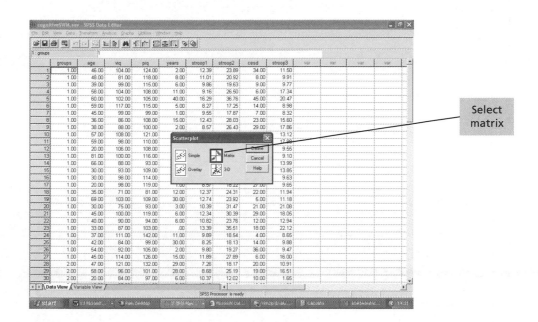

Move the variables that you wish to be included from the left-hand side of the dialogue box to the right by using the ▶ button. Click *OK*.

This will obtain the matrices.

EXAMPLE: IQ AND TEST SCORES

If you run a correlational analysis on several variables, you will obtain output such as that below, which is in the form of a correlational matrix:

Correlations

		iq	mathemat	score1	score2	score3
IQ	Pearson Correlation	**1.000**	**.5741**	**.0641**	**.0143**	**.1428**
	Sig.(1-tailed)	.	**.002**	**.383**	**.474**	**.253**
	N	24	**24**	**24**	**24**	**24**
mathemat	Pearson Correlation	.5741	1.000	**.0598**	**.0281**	**.2502**
	Sig.(1-tailed)	.002	.	**.391**	**.448**	**.119**
	N	24	24	**24**	**24**	**24**
score1	Pearson Correlation	.0641	.0598	1.000	**.9952**	**−.2153**
	Sig.(1-tailed)	.383	.391	.	**.000**	**.156**
	N	24	24	24	**24**	**24**
score2	Pearson Correlation	.0143	.0281	.9952	1.000	**.2188**
	Sig.(1-tailed)	.474	.448	.000	.	**.152**
	N	24	24	24	24	**24**
score3	Pearson Correlation	−.1428	−.2502	−.2153	−2188	1.000
	Sig.(1-tailed)	.253	.119	.156	.152	.
	N	24	24	24	24	24

Although we have correlated five variables with each other, we have only ten correlations to look at. This is because we ignore the correlations along the diagonals: these are $r = 1.00$, as each variable correlates perfectly with itself. Also, each half is a mirror image of the other, so we need only look at one half. We have emboldened the top half so that it is easier for you to see.

The output shows r and the exact probability of that particular correlation coefficient occurring by sampling error, assuming the null hypothesis to be true. It also gives the number of pairs of observations.

In this example, the mathematics score has a positive association with IQ ($r = 0.57$). This is a moderate correlation, but the association has an exact probability of $p = 0.002$: that is, there is only a small chance (0.2%) that this correlation has arisen by sampling error. The number of observations was 24.

If you look along the top row of the matrix, you will see that score1, score2 and score3 have rs that are all approximately zero. This means that there is no linear relationship between the variables, and this is confirmed by the probability values.

If you now look at the point at which score1 meets score2, you will see that there is a very strong, almost perfect relationship between them, showing that score1 and score2 must be measuring a very similar ability ($r = 0.9952$). The associated probability level ($p < 0.001$) shows that this result is unlikely to have arisen by sampling error, assuming the null hypothesis to be true. SPSSFW calculates the p-values to a number of decimal places (the user can change the settings so that the values are given to four decimal places as above ($r = 0.9952$) or to three decimal places (e.g. $r = 0.995$) or to any number. This is the same with p-values. (Remember that, when SPSSFW gives p as $p = 0.000$, you need to change the last zero to the number one, and use the $<$ sign as follows: $p < 0.001$.)

5.1.12 Confidence intervals around *r*

Rosnow and Rosenthal (1996) give the procedure for constructing 95% confidence limits (two-tailed $p = 0.05$) around *r*. The following is based on their text:

1. Consult a table to transform *r* to Fisher's Z_r (see Appendix 2, page 606).
2. Multiply $1/\sqrt{(n-3)}$ by 1.96.
3. Find the lower limit of the confidence interval by subtracting the result in 2. above from the figure in 1.
4. Find the upper limit of the confidence interval by adding the result of 2. above to the figure in 1.
5. Consult a similar table to transform the lower and upper Z_r values back to *r* values.

EXAMPLE

Let's try it for a correlation coefficient of +0.29 for an analysis with 133 people, that is: $r = 0.29$, $n = 133$.

1. We consult the table, which shows an *r* of 0.29 converts to Z_r of 0.299
2. Multiply $1/\sqrt{130}$ by 1.96.
    Thus multiply 1/11.40 by 1.96.
    Thus multiply 0.0877 by 1.96 = 0.1719.
3. Subtract 0.1719 from 0.299 = 0.1271 – this is the Z_r lower confidence limit.
4. Add 0.1719 to 0.299 = 0.4709 – this is the Z_r upper confidence limit.
5. Convert the figures in 3. and 4. to *r* (from Z_r). From tables,

    $Z_r = 0.1271 \rightarrow r = 0.126$
    $Z_r = 0.4709 \rightarrow r = 0.440$

Although the sample correlation coefficient is +0.29, we are 95% confident that the true population correlation coefficient is somewhere between 0.126 and 0.440.

So far we have been talking about the correlation between two variables, without taking any other variables into account. This sort of correlation is called a *zero-order correlation*.

5.2 First- and second-order correlations

Take our example of height and weight being highly correlated in children. A moment's thought will show you that age is correlated with both of these variables. We could run a correlational analysis on these three variables, to confirm this.

Correlations

		HEIGHT	WEIGHT	AGE
HEIGHT	Pearson Correlation	1.000	**.834**	**.970**
	Sig. (1-tailed)	.	.001	.000
	N	10	10	10
WEIGHT	Pearson Correlation	.834	1.000	**.802**
	Sig. (1-tailed)	.001	.	.003
	N	10	10	10
AGE	Pearson Correlation	.970	.802	1.000
	Sig. (1-tailed)	.000	.003	.
	N	10	10	10

** Correlation is significant at the 0.01 level (1-tailed).

We have emboldened the three correlation coefficients. You can see that all three variables are strongly related to each other.

If we want to discover the association between height and weight without the effect of age, we would have to find a sample of children who were all born on exactly the same day. If this was not possible, we could get rid of the age effect by 'partialling out' (removing the influence of) age, by statistical means. This is also known as 'holding age constant'. We correlate height and weight while getting rid of the effects of age; r would then be showing us the correlation between height and weight when the influence of age is removed.

Conceptually, this can be explained by looking at overlapping circles of variance. In the following diagram you can see that the relationship between height and weight (with age *not* partialled out) is $a + b$.

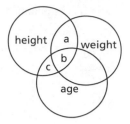

This relates to the *full correlation* between height and weight. However, part of the relationship between height and weight is due to age – the part represented by *b* alone. If the influence of age were removed (the area *b*), the correlation between height and weight would be reduced, as it would then be represented by *a* alone. This is a partial correlation – a correlation between two variables, with one (in this case) partialled out.[3]

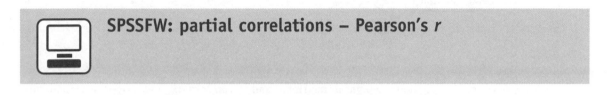

SPSSFW: partial correlations – Pearson's *r*

It is easy in SPSSFW to partial out a variable. The instructions are as follows.
After entering your data, choose *Analyze*, *Correlate*, *Partial*:

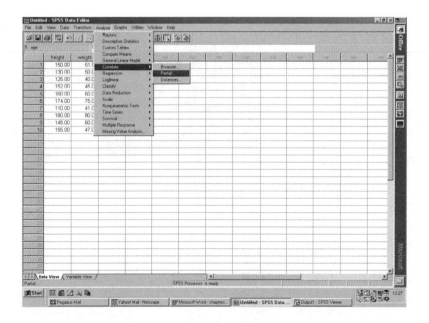

---

[3] This is a conceptual explanation, rather than a mathematical one. Thus mathematical accuracy is lost in the interests of conceptual understanding. The actual formula for calculating partial correlations is given by $r^2 = a/(a + \text{height})$ or $a/(a + \text{weight})$.

The following dialogue box is obtained:

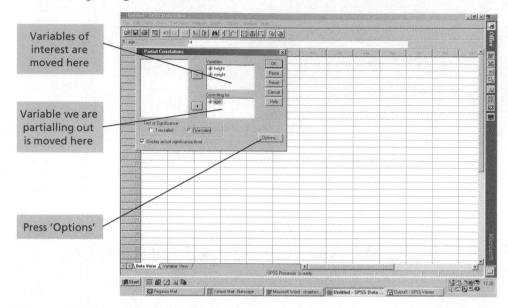

Variables of interest are moved here

Variable we are partialling out is moved here

Press 'Options'

We move height and weight to the right-hand *Variables* box, and move the variable that we wish to partial out (in this case, age) to the *Controlling for* box.

It would also be useful for us to know the value of the correlation coefficient for age and weight *without* controlling for age, so that we can compare the two. This is achieved by selecting *Options*, which gives you the dialogue box below. Check *Zero-order correlations* and press *Continue*.

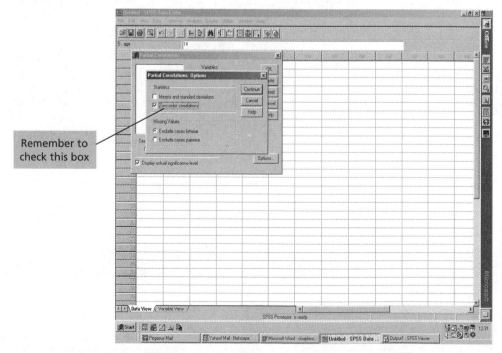

Remember to check this box

This brings you back to the *Partial Correlations* dialogue box, where you can click *OK*.

The zero-order correlations are printed first:

Partial Correlation Coefficients
Zero Order Partials

Relationship between variables *without* any
other variables being partialled out

		Height	Weight	Age
Height	Pearson Correlation	1.000	**.8339**	**.9695**
	Sig. (2-tailed)	.	**.002**	**.001**
	N	0	**8**	**8**
Weight	Pearson Correlation	.8339	1.000	**.8020**
	Sig. (2-tailed)	.002	.	**.006**
	N	8	0	**8**
Age	Pearson Correlation	.9695	.8020	1.000
	Sig. (2-tailed)	.001	.006	0
	N	8	8	0

The correlation
between height
and weight
(without age being
partialled out)
is strong: 0.84

This is exactly the same as given on page 186, except that the program has labelled the table *Zero Order Partials*.[4] This gives the relationship between the variables, without partialling out any other variable.

The output then gives the correlation between height and weight, with age partialled out:

Partial Correlation Coefficients
Controlling for . . Age

Shows that correlations in the table are
partial ones – age has partialled out

		Height	Weight
Height	Pearson Correlation	1.000	**.3853**
	Sig. (2-tailed)	.	**.306**
	N	0	**8**
Weight	Pearson Correlation	.3853	1.000
	Sig. (2-tailed)	.306	.

The correlation between height
and weight is now only 0.39
(because age has been
partialled out)

You can see that the correlation between height and weight has been reduced from 0.83 to 0.39 (correct to two decimal places). Thus we can see that, in this small sample, the association between height and weight was partially due to age. If the correlation of 0.83 had *not* been reduced when we partialled out age, this suggests that the association between height and weight is not affected by age.

In this case, we have partialled out one variable. This is called a first-order correlation. If we partialled out the effects of two variables, we would be performing a second-order correlation, and so on.

[4] Here figures are given to four decimal places.

How does the program (the formula) do this? Basically, it correlates age with height. Then it correlates age with weight. Then these figures are 'removed' from the height–weight correlation. This removes the influence of age from the correlation coefficient.

Activity 5.9

Look at the following results, taken from a study by Dancey *et al.* (2002):

Partial Correlation Coefficients
Zero Order Partials

		Total QOL	Total Stigma	Total Illness Intrusiveness
Total QOL	Pearson Correlation	1.000	–.4983	–.7161
	Sig. (1-tailed)	.	.000	.000
	N	117	117	117
Total Stigma	Pearson Correlation	–.4983	1.000	.4930
	Sig. (1-tailed)	.000	.	.000
	N	117	117	117
Total Illness Intrusiveness	Pearson Correlation	–.7161	.4930	1.000
	Sig. (1-tailed)	.000	.000	.
	N	117	117	117

Partial Correlation Coefficients
Controlling for . . Total Illness Intrusiveness

		Total QOL	Total Stigma
Total QOL	Pearson Correlation	1.000	–.2391
	Sig. (1-tailed)	.	.005
	N	117	117
Total Stigma	Pearson Correlation	–.2391	1.000
	Sig. (1-tailed)	.005	.
	N	117	117

(a) What is the zero-order correlation between QOL and Stigma?
(b) What is the value of the correlation between QOL and Stigma with Illness Intrusiveness partialled out?
(c) What can you conclude from this?

Example from the literature: memory and vocabulary

Many researchers use correlation coefficients in the reporting of their work, and journal articles often include correlational matrices for the reader to interpret. We have been advising you to report exact probability values, but sometimes the authors do not do this; they report either $p <$ or $p >$ a set level. Michas and Henry (1994) tested 24 boys and 24 girls (mean age 5.6 years) on various measures – the study investigated whether two measures of phonological memory, non-word repetition and non-word memory span were related to acquired vocabulary. Table 5.4 contains the correlations between all of the initial measures as well as the word-learning measures.

Note that the researchers have given us only half of the full correlation matrix. As we have said, we do not need to see the diagonals (all will be $r = 1.00$) and we need only one-half of the matrix. Also note that they have told us that any correlation with * after the figure is unlikely to have arisen by sampling error, assuming the null hypothesis to be true (using a 5% criterion value) and any correlation with ** after the figure is unlikely to have arisen by sampling error (using a 1% criterion). They have not given us the exact probability values, so we have no idea whether the correlation between age and non-word repetition, for instance (0.332*), had an associated probability of 0.049, or 0.02. Does it matter? You will have to read the critical discussion on page 137 and make up your own mind!

Note also that the researchers have given the *r* values correct to *three* decimal places. Not all studies do this; some report the figures correct to *two* decimal places.

Table 5.4   Pearson's Product Moment Correlation matrix

	Spatial memory	Non-word repetition	Memory span	Vocabulary	Word production	Word comprehension	Word definition
Age	0.049	0.332*	0.158	0.183	−0.023	−0.062	0.169
Spatial memory		0.185	0.114	0.211	0.200	−0.111	0.150
Non-word repetition			0.626**	0.484**	0.303*	0.278	0.391**
Memory span				0.476**	0.448**	0.291	0.347*
Vocabulary					0.279	0.378*	0.376*
Word production						0.496**	0.479**
Word comprehension							0.489**

* $p < 0.05$; ** $p < 0.01$.

Example from the literature: health beliefs and back pain

Harkapaa *et al.* (2000) studied health optimism and control beliefs to see whether they could predict successful treatment of people with back pain. As part of that study, they performed correlations between the variables. Their table is reproduced as Table 5.5.

Notice here that the researchers have given us the means to identify whether the correlation has reached a criterion significance level of < 0.05 or < 0.01. It is better, however, to use exact probabilities.

Table 5.5   Intercorrelations (Pearson's r) of baseline values of age, sex, functional capacity index (FCI) and the predictor variables (health optimism, three measures of locus of control, and depression)

	Health optimism	Others LOC	Internal LOC	Chance LOC	Depression
Age	−0.23	0.18	−0.23	0.18	0.10
Sex	0.02	0.06	−0.04	−0.01	0.08
FCI	0.29	−0.15	0.15	−0.11	−0.35
Health optimism	–	−0.34	0.51	−0.27	−0.20
Others LOC	−0.34	–	−0.13	0.43	0.38
Internal LOC	0.51	−0.13	–	−0.05	−0.09
Chance LOC	−0.27	0.43	−0.05	–	0.29
Depression	−0.20	0.38	−0.09	0.29	–

FCI = functional capacity index; LOC = locus of control.
$r > 0.208$, $p < 0.01$; $r > 0.159$, $p < 0.05$.

Example from the literature: stigma, illness intrusiveness and quality of life in irritable bowel syndrome

In this article (Dancey *et al.*, 2002), exact probabilities have been given where possible. However, as you have learned earlier, sometimes SPSSFW prints out a row of zeros ($p = 0.000$) and the convention is to change the last zero to a '1' and to use the $<$ sign ($p < 0.001$). This is what has been done here.

Table 5.6 is a (partial) table of results given in this article.

Look at the correlation between the intrusiveness of the illness into social role, and quality of life in women: $r = -0.51$. So, as the intrusiveness of the illness into the Social role aspect of life increases, quality of life decreases. This is a moderate correlation. However, if we partial out the variance due to symptom severity, the correlation reduces (to -0.37). This means that part of the relationship between the intrusiveness of the illness in respect of Social role was actually due to symptom severity.

Table 5.6 Full and partial correlations between illness intrusiveness and subscales of Quality of Life questionnaire reported by sex (partial correlations controlling for total symptom severity)

Variable*	Men		Women	
	Full	Partial	Full	Partial
Social role	−0.64 ($p < 0.001$)	−0.58 ($p < 0.001$)	−0.51 ($p < 0.001$)	−0.37 ($p = 0.002$)
Sleep	−0.36 ($p = 0.004$)	−0.25 ($p = 0.035$)	−0.30 ($p < 0.001$)	−0.15 ($p = 0.13$)
Physical role	−0.55 ($p < 0.001$)	−0.52 ($p < 0.001$)	−0.49 ($p < 0.001$)	−0.35 ($p < 0.001$)
Mental health	0.70 ($p < 0.001$)	−0.65 ($p < 0.001$)	−0.50 ($p < 0.001$)	−0.38 ($p < 0.001$)
Energy	−0.54 ($p < 0.001$)	−0.48 ($p < 0.001$)	−0.51 ($p < 0.001$)	−0.38 ($p < 0.001$)

* There are 13 items in the Illness Intrusiveness Ratings Scale; we have reproduced only five here.

Activity 5.10

Think about the *meaning* of the correlation coefficients opposite (health beliefs and back pain). What can you say about the size and significance of the various correlations?

5.3 Patterns of correlations

You should be able to see just by looking at a correlational matrix that patterns of correlations arise. For instance, look at the following correlational matrix:

Variables that 'hang'

Two variables that relate to each other but not with the others

Correlations

	relationship with spouse	family relationships	other social relationships	felt sad	satisfied with life	had crying spells
relationship with spouse	1.000	**.672**	**.547**	.321	**.500**	.119
family relationships		1.000	**.689**	.236	**.508**	.072
other social relationships			1.000	.165	**.584**	−.010
felt sad				1.000	.224	**.442**
less satisfied with life					1.000	−.117
had crying spells						1.000

If you look carefully, you can see that the variables that share most variance with each other are to do with quality of life – satisfaction with relationships and life. This is one pattern that you can see emerging from the data. These variables have correlated with each other; they form a natural 'group'. The other two variables, 'felt sad' and 'had crying spells', also correlate with each other (0.442) – but not with the other variables – so this shows a second pattern. So, from these six variables, we can distinguish two distinct patterns. Obviously in this example, with so few variables, the patterns are relatively easy to distinguish.

Psychologists who are designing or checking the properties of questionnaires make use of this 'patterning' to cluster variables together into groups. This is useful where a questionnaire has been designed to measure different aspects of, say, personality or quality of life. In the example above, the variables in the first group above are questions that made up a subscale of a quality of life (QOL) questionnaire. A questionnaire might have several questions relating to 'family life' (i.e. one subscale) and several others relating to 'financial situation' and perhaps another that could be called 'sex life'. The QOL questionnaire consists of these different subscales.

Using patterns of correlations to check that each set of questions 'hangs together' gives them confidence in their questionnaires. Psychologists do not, of course, simply look at correlational matrices. They use a technique called Factor Analysis, which effectively does the same thing, only better! This is discussed in greater detail in Chapter 12.

Summary

- If two variables are correlated, then they are not independent – as the scores on one variable change, scores on the other variable change in a predictable way.

- Correlations can be positive (high scores on x tend to be associated with high scores on y, and low scores on x tend to be associated with low scores on y); negative (high scores on x are associated with low scores on y); or zero (no linear relationship).

- Correlation coefficients range from −1 (perfect negative correlation) through zero to +1 (perfect positive correlation).

- Pearson's r is a parametric correlation coefficient; r is a natural effect size; r can be squared in order to give a measure of the variance explained, expressed in percentage terms.

- Confidence limits can be constructed around Pearson's r. If the sample r is found to be 0.5, and the confidence limits are 0.4 to 0.6 (95% limits), then we can be 95% confident that, in the population, r would be found to be within the range 0.4 to 0.6.

- Looking at patterns of correlations within a matrix can show us which variables 'hang together' – this is important in psychometrics.

SPSSFW exercise

Enter the following data into SPSSFW:

Case Summaries

		QOL	Illness intrusiveness	STIGMA
1		48.00	5.00	26.00
2		99.00	1.00	30.00
3		78.00	2.00	23.00
4		47.00	4.00	43.00
5		87.00	3.00	48.00
6		68.00	2.00	20.00
7		94.00	1.00	39.00
8		66.00	6.00	40.00
9		70.00	3.00	25.00
10		67.00	3.00	28.00
11		62.00	4.00	64.00
12		85.00	2.00	33.00
13		78.00	2.00	33.00
14		87.00	3.00	34.00
15		53.00	7.00	73.00
16		79.00	1.00	20.00
17		62.00	5.00	37.00
18		79.00	6.00	20.00
19		83.00	2.00	40.00
20		86.00	2.00	21.00
Total	N	20	20	20

Analyse the data:

1. obtaining a zero-order correlation between STIGMA and QOL

2. obtaining a correlation between STIGMA and QOL, partialling out the effects of illness intrusiveness. Use a one-tailed hypothesis.

3. Think about both the direction and magnitude of the correlation coefficients. What can you conclude from this analysis?

MULTIPLE CHOICE QUESTIONS

1. If 36% of the variation in scores on *y* has been accounted for by scores on *x*, how much variance is unexplained?
    (a) 64%
    (b) 36%
    (c) 6%
    (d) 0.6%

2. If two variables are totally independent, then the correlation between them is:
    (a) −0.1
    (b) −1.00
    (c) +1.00
    (d) zero

Questions 3 to 5 relate to the following table of results:

Correlations

		age	mood	qol	family relationships
age	Pearson Correlation	1.000	−.011	−.093	−.106
	Sig. (2-tailed)	.	.912	.332	.264
	N	113	112	111	112
mood	Pearson Correlation	−.011	1.000	.463	−.328
	Sig. (2-tailed)	.912	.	.000	.000
	N	112	118	115	117
QOL	Pearson Correlation	−.093	.463	1.000	−.598
	Sig. (2-tailed)	.332	.000	.	.000
	N	111	115	116	115
family relationships	Pearson Correlation	−.106	−.328	−.598	1.000
	Sig. (2-tailed)	.264	.000	.000	.
	N	112	117	115	118

3. Of those below, which two variables show the strongest relationship?
    (a) 'QOL' and 'family relationships'
    (b) 'QOL' and 'age'
    (c) 'mood' and 'QOL'
    (d) 'mood' and 'age'

4. Which correlation is the weakest?

   (a) 'QOL' and 'age'
   (b) 'mood' and 'age'
   (c) 'family relationships' and 'age'
   (d) 'family relationships' and 'mood'

5. What is the achieved significance level of 'family relationships' and 'mood'?

   (a) $p < 0.001$
   (b) $p = 0.011$
   (c) $p = 0.912$
   (d) $p < 0.01$

6. If you have a correlation coefficient of 0.5, how much variance is left unexplained?

   (a) 25%
   (b) 50%
   (c) 75%
   (d) None of the above

7. Someone who runs a correlational analysis says that an effect size of 64% has been found. What value of *r* did they obtain?

   (a) +0.8
   (b) −0.8
   (c) 0.8, we cannot tell whether the value is positive or negative
   (d) +0.64

8. If you have a correlation coefficient of 0.4, how much variance is left unexplained?

   (a) 16%
   (b) 40%
   (c) 84%
   (d) None of the above

9. Length of time working at the computer and poor eyesight are negatively correlated. What should we conclude?

   (a) People with poor eyesight are more likely to spend long hours working at the computer
   (b) Working for long hours is likely to cause a deterioration of eyesight
   (c) A particular type of personality may be more likely to both have poor eyesight and work long hours at the computer
   (d) Any of the above are possible – correlation does not imply causation

10. Look at the following scattergram:

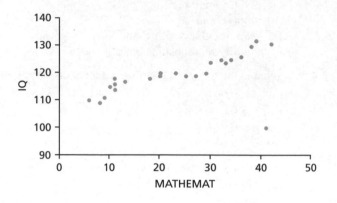

Which is the most sensible answer? The variables show a correlation of:

(a) +1.00
(b) −1.00
(c) +0.7
(d) −0.7

11. Look at the following scattergram:

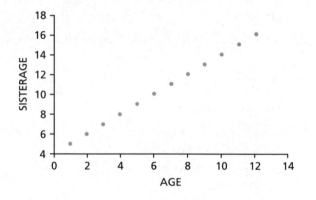

Which is the most sensible answer? The variables show a correlation of:

(a) −1.0
(b) −0.1
(c) +1.00
(d) +0.1

Questions 12 and 13 relate to the following table of results:

Correlations

	relationship with spouse	family relationships	other social relationships	felt sad	satisfied with life	had crying spells
relationship with spouse	1.000	.672	.547	.321	.500	.119
family relationships		1.000	.689	.236	.508	.072
other social relationships			1.000	.165	.584	−.010
felt sad				1.000	.224	.442
less satisfied with life					1.000	−.117
had crying spells						1.000

12. Of the following, which two variables show the strongest relationship?
    (a) 'family relationships' and 'relationship with spouse'
    (b) 'satisfied with life' and 'family relationships'
    (c) 'family relationships' and 'other social relationships'
    (d) 'felt sad' and 'had crying spells'

13. Which correlation is the weakest?
    (a) 'family relationships' and 'relationship with spouse'
    (b) 'family relationships' and 'other social relationships'
    (c) 'other social relationships' and 'had crying spells'
    (d) 'satisfied with life' and 'had crying spells'

14. A correlation of −0.5 has been found between height and weight in a group of schoolchildren. How much of the variance in height can be explained by weight, in percentage terms?
    (a) 5%
    (b) 50%
    (c) 25%
    (d) None of the above

15. A researcher wishes to look at the relationship between motivation and examination performance. However, she has reason to believe that IQ influences both of these variables and decides to obtain partial correlations. Which of the following options is most sensible? She should perform a correlation between:
    (a) Motivation and IQ controlling for examination performance
    (b) Motivation and examination performance controlling for IQ
    (c) IQ and examination performance controlling for motivation
    (d) None of the above options is sensible

Questions 16 and 17 relate to the following matrix. The cells have been labelled:

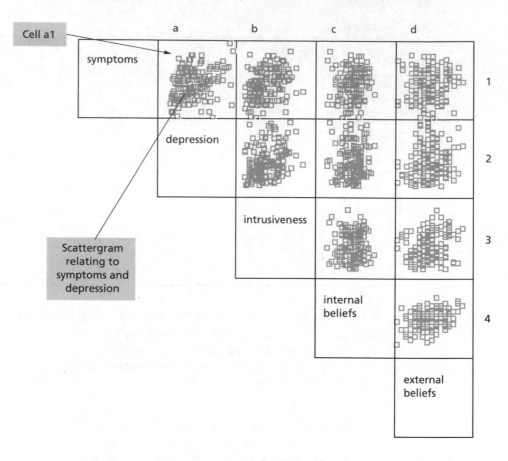

16. Which cell relates to the scattergram between 'internal beliefs' and 'external beliefs'?

    (a) d1
    (b) d2
    (c) d3
    (d) d4

17. The cell c3 relates to:

    (a) Intrusiveness and internal beliefs
    (b) Intrusiveness and external beliefs
    (c) Intrusiveness and symptoms
    (d) Depression and symptoms

18. A positive relationship means:

    (a) An important relationship exists
    (b) As scores on x rise, scores on y fall
    (c) As scores on x rise, so do those on y
    (d) High scores are frequent on x and y

19. If a correlation coefficient has an associated probability value of 0.02, then:

    (a) Our hypothesis is obviously true
    (b) Our results are important
    (c) There is only a 2% chance that our results are due to sampling error, assuming the null hypothesis to be true
    (d) There is only a 2% chance that our results are correct

20. SPSSFW prints the following: $p = .0000$. How should this be reported?

    (a) $p < 0.001$
    (b) $p < 0.0001$
    (c) $p > 0.001$
    (d) $p > 0.0001$

References

Alt, M. (1990) *Exploring Hyperspace*. McGraw-Hill.

Cacioppo, J.T. and Petty, R.E. (1982) 'The need for cognition', *Journal of Personality and Social Psychology*, **42**: 116–31.

Dancey, C.P., Hutton-Young, S.A., Moye, S. and Devins, G.M. (2002) 'Perceived stigma, illness intrusiveness and quality of life in men and women with irritable bowel syndrome', *Psychology, Health & Medicine*, **7**(4): 381–95.

Harkapaa, K., Jarvikoski, A. and Estlander, A. (2000) 'Health optimism and control beliefs as predictors for treatment outcome of a multimodal back treatment program', *Psychology & Health*, **12**(1): 123–34.

Huff, D. (1973) *How to Lie with Statistics*. London: Penguin.

Lawton, R., Parker, D., Stradling, G. and Manstead, A.S.R. (1997) 'Predicting road traffic accidents: the role of social deviance and violations', *British Journal of Psychology*, **88**: 249–62.

Michas, I.C. and Henry, L.A. (1994) 'The link between phonological memory and vocabulary acquisition', *British Journal of Developmental Psychology*, **12**(2): 147–63.

Rosnow, R.L. and Rosenthal, R. (1996) 'Computing contrasts, effect sizes and counternulls on other people's published data: general procedures for research consumers', *Psychological Methods*, **1**(4): 331–40.

Yerkes, R.M. & Dodson, J.D. (1908) 'The relation of strength of stimulus to rapidity of habit-formation', *Journal of Comparative Neurology and Psychology*, **18**: 459–82.

6 Analyses of differences between two conditions: the t-test

Chapter overview

In the previous chapters, you were introduced to the idea of looking at how scores on one variable related to scores on another variable, and for this analysis you learned about the parametric statistical test, Pearson's *r*. In this chapter, however, we will be looking at the *differences* between scores in two conditions. For instance, you could compare the memory ability of spider-phobics and non-phobics, to see how they differ. Such a design is called a *between-participants*, *independent* or *unrelated design*, since one group of participants gives scores in one condition, and a different group of people gives scores in a different condition. On the other hand, one group of participants may perform in both conditions, for instance one group of participants learn both high frequency words and low frequency words. They are then measured by the amount of recalled words. This is called a *within-participants*, *repeated measures* or *related design*, because the same people perform in both conditions. In this chapter we are going to discuss the analyses of two conditions by using the parametric test called the t-test. We are particularly interested in the differences between the two groups: specifically, the difference between the *mean* of the two groups. In this chapter we are going to show you how to analyse the data from such designs. Since the t-test is a parametric test, you must remember that your data need to meet the normal assumptions for parametric tests – that is, the data have been drawn from a population that is normally distributed. We tend to assume this is the case when your sample data are normally distributed. If you have reason to think this is not the case, then you need to use the non-parametric equivalents of the t-test, described in Chapter 15.

To enable you to understand the tests presented in this chapter you will need to have an understanding of the following concepts:

- the mean, standard deviation and standard error (Chapter 2)
- z-scores and the normal distribution (Chapter 3)
- assumptions underlying the use of parametric tests (Chapter 4)
- probability distributions like the t-distribution (Chapter 4)
- one- and two-tailed hypotheses (Chapter 4)
- statistical significance (Chapter 4)
- confidence intervals (Chapter 3).

6.1 Analysis of two conditions

The analysis of two conditions includes the following:

1. *Descriptive statistics*, such as means or medians, standard deviations; confidence intervals around the mean of both groups separately, where this is appropriate; graphical illustrations such as box and whisker plots and error bars.
2. *Effect size* – this is a measure of the degree to which differences in a dependent variable are attributed to the independent variable.
3. *Confidence limits* around the difference between the means.
4. *Inferential tests* – t-tests discover how likely it is that the difference between the conditions could be attributable to sampling error, assuming the null hypothesis to be true.

6.1.1 Analysis of differences between two independent groups

Twenty-four people were involved in an experiment to determine whether background noise (music, slamming of doors, people making coffee, etc.) affects short-term memory (recall of words). Half of the sample were randomly allocated to the NOISE condition, and half to the NO NOISE condition. The participants in the NOISE condition tried to memorise a list of 20 words in two minutes, while listening to pre-recorded noise through earphones. The other participants wore earphones but heard no noise as they attempted to memorise the words. Immediately after this, they were tested to see how many words they recalled. The numbers of words recalled by each person in each condition are as shown in Table 6.1.

Table 6.1 Raw data for NOISE/NO NOISE conditions

NOISE	NO NOISE
5.00	15.00
10.00	9.00
6.00	16.00
6.00	15.00
7.00	16.00
3.00	18.00
6.00	17.00
9.00	13.00
5.00	11.00
10.00	12.00
11.00	13.00
9.00	11.00
$\Sigma = 87$[a]	$\Sigma = 166$
$\bar{X} = 7.3$[b]	$\bar{X} = 13.8$
SD = 2.5	SD = 2.8

[a] Σ represents the total of the column
[b] $\bar{X}$ represents the mean (average)

Table 6.2 Mean, standard deviation and 95% confidence limits for NOISE/NO NOISE conditions

NOISE			NO NOISE		
$\bar{X}$	SD	95% CI	$\bar{X}$	SD	95% CI
7.3	2.5	5.7–8.8	13.8	2.8	12.1–15.6

6.1.2 Descriptive statistics for two-group design

The first thing to do is to obtain descriptive statistics through the *Explore* procedure in SPSSFW (see page 47). You can then gain insight into the data by looking at graphical illustrations, such as box and whisker plots and/or histograms. Summary statistics such as the means, standard deviations and confidence intervals are available through SPSSFW, which gives you the results in the form of tables. (These statistics are also given as part of the output when you analyse the data by using the t-test procedure.)

You can see in Table 6.2 that the means differ, in the expected direction. Participants in the NO NOISE condition recalled a mean of 13.8 words, while those in the NOISE condition recalled a mean of 7.3. People in the NO NOISE condition showed slightly more variability, as indicated by the *standard deviations*.

6.1.3 Confidence limits around the mean

The means you have obtained, for your sample, are *point estimates*. These sample means are the best estimates of the population means. If, however, we repeated the experiment many times, we would find that the mean varied from experiment to experiment. For example, the sample mean for the NO NOISE condition is 13.8. If we repeat the experiment we might find that the sample mean is 13.3. If you repeated the experiment many times, the best estimate of the population mean would then be the mean of all the sample means. It should be obvious, however, that our estimate could be slightly different from the real population mean difference: thus it would be better, instead of giving a point estimate, to give a *range*. This is more realistic than giving a point estimate.

The interval is bounded by a lower limit (12.1 in this case) and an upper limit (15.6 in the above example). These are called *confidence limits*, and the interval that the limits enclose is called the *confidence interval*. You came across these in Chapter 3. The confidence limits let you know how confident you are that the *population mean* is within a certain interval, that is, it is an interval estimate for the population (not just your sample).

Why are confidence limits important? When we carry out experiments or studies, we want to be able to generalise from our particular sample to the population. We also want to let our readers have a full and accurate picture of our results. Although our *sample* mean of the NOISE condition is 7.3, telling the reader that 'we are 95% confident that the *population mean* falls between 5.7 and 8.8' gives more information, and is more realistic, than simply reporting our sample mean. Confidence intervals are being reported more and more in journal articles, and so it is important for you to be able to understand them.

Figure 6.1 95% confidence limits for NOISE and NO NOISE conditions

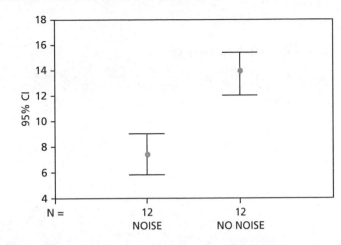

6.1.4 Confidence intervals between NOISE and NO NOISE conditions

For the noise condition, we estimate (with 95% confidence) that the population mean is within the range (interval) of 5.7 and 8.8. This can be represented graphically, as shown in Figure 6.1.

6.1.5 Measure of effect

We can also take one (sample) mean from the other, to see how much they differ:

$$7.3 - 13.8 = -6.5$$

This score on its own, however, tells us very little. If we converted this score to a *standardised score*, however, it would be much more useful. The raw score (the original score) is converted into a z-score. The z-score is a standardised score, giving a measure of effect which everyone can easily understand. This measure of effect is called *d*; *d* measures the extent to which the two means differ, in terms of standard deviations. This is how we calculate it:

$$d = \frac{x_1 - x_2}{\text{mean SD}}$$

This means that we take one mean away from the other (it does not matter which is which – ignore the sign) and divide it by the mean standard deviation.

Step 1: find mean sample SD

$$\frac{\text{SD of condition 1} + \text{SD of condition 2}}{2} = \frac{2.5 + 2.8}{2} = 2.65$$

Step 2: find *d*

$$\frac{x_1 - x_2}{\text{mean SD}} = \frac{7.3 - 13.8}{2.65} = \frac{6.5}{2.65} = 2.45$$

In this case, our means differ by 2.45 standard deviations. This is a very large effect size, an effect size not often found in psychological research.

6.1.6 The size of the effect

The effect size here, d, is expressed in standard deviations. Think of the normal curve of distribution:

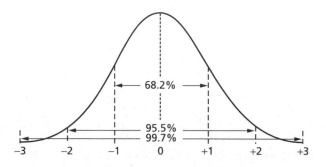

Z-scores are standardised so that the mean is zero and the standard deviation is 1. You can see that, if the means differed by 0.1, they would differ by only a tenth of a standard deviation. That is quite small, on our scale of 0 to 3. If the means differed by 3 standard deviations, that is a lot, using the scale of 0 to 3. There is no hard and fast rule about what constitutes small and large effects. Cohen (1988) gave the following guidelines:

Effect size	d	Percentage of overlap (%)
Small	0.2	85
Medium	0.5	67
Large	0.8	53

When there is little difference between our groups, the scores will overlap substantially. The scores for the groups can be plotted separately; for instance, scores for the NOISE condition can be plotted and will tend to be normally distributed. Scores for the NO NOISE condition can also be plotted, and will tend to be normally distributed. If there is little difference between them, the distributions will overlap:

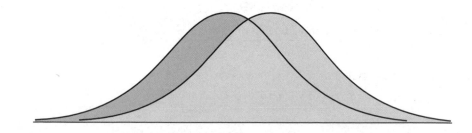

If there is a large difference between the two groups, then the distributions will be further apart:

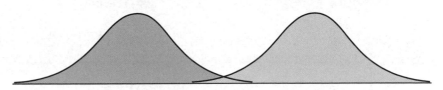

This is what is meant by the percentage of overlap. This measure of effect enables us to interpret our findings in a meaningful way. The exact extent of the overlap is given in the table below:

d	Percentage of overlap (%)
0.1	92
0.2	85
0.3	79
0.4	73
0.5	67
0.6	62
0.7	57
0.8	53
0.9	48
1.0	45
1.1	42
1.2	37
1.3	35
1.4	32
1.5	29

Effect sizes are discussed further in Chapter 7.

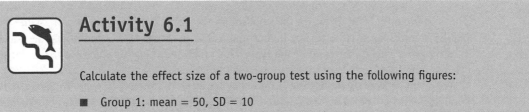

Activity 6.1

Calculate the effect size of a two-group test using the following figures:

■ Group 1: mean = 50, SD = 10
■ Group 2: mean = 70, SD = 5

6.1.7 Inferential statistics: the t-test

The t-test is used when we have two conditions. The t-test assesses whether there is a statistically significant difference between the means of the two conditions.

Table 6.3 Raw data for NOISE/NO NOISE conditions

NOISE	NO NOISE
5.00	15.00
10.00	9.00
6.00	16.00
6.00	15.00
7.00	16.00
3.00	18.00
6.00	17.00
9.00	13.00
5.00	11.00
10.00	12.00
11.00	13.00
9.00	11.00
$\Sigma = 87$	$\Sigma = 166$
$\bar{X} = 7.3$	$\bar{X} = 13.8$
SD = 2.5	SD = 2.8

The *independent t-test* is used when the participants perform in only *one* of two conditions, i.e. an independent, between-participants or unrelated design. The *related* or *paired t-test* is used when the participants perform in *both* conditions, i.e. a related, within-participants or repeated measures design.

The t-test was devised by William Gossett in 1908. Gossett worked for Guinness, whose scientists were not allowed to publish results of their scientific work, and so Gossett published results using his new test under the name of Student, which is why, of course, you will see it referred to in statistical books as Student's t.

Look again at our raw data for the NOISE/NO NOISE condition (Table 6.3). The first thing you should note is that participants vary *within* conditions. In the NOISE condition, the scores range from 3 through to 11. In the NO NOISE condition, the scores range from 9 to 18 (this within-participants variance can be thought of as variance *within* each column). You should recall from Chapter 2 that the standard deviation is a measure of variance – the larger the standard deviation, the greater the scores vary, within the condition. The participants differ *between* the conditions too. You can see that scores of the NO NOISE condition, in general, are higher than those in the NOISE condition – the means confirm our visual experience of the data. This is the *between-participants variance*, and can be thought of as the variance *between* the columns.

We want to know whether the differences between the means of our groups are large enough for us to be able to conclude that the differences are due to our independent variable – that is, our NOISE/NO NOISE manipulation. This is accomplished by performing mathematical calculations on our data. The formula for the t-test (not given here) results in a test statistic, which we call 't'. The t-test is basically a ratio between a measure of the between-groups variance and the within-groups variance. The larger the variance *between* the groups (columns), compared with the variance *within* the groups (rows), the larger the t-value.

Once we have calculated the t-value we (or rather the computer) can find the probability of obtaining such a t-value by chance (sampling error) if the null hypothesis were true.

Figure 6.2	Sampling distribution

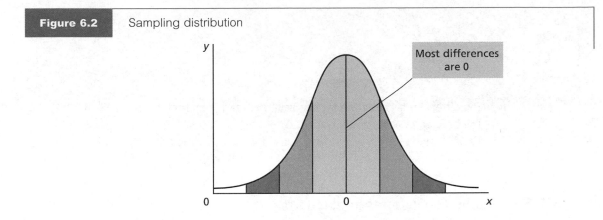

That is, if there were no differences between the NOISE condition and the NO NOISE condition, how likely is it that our value of *t* would be found?

If there were no real differences between the NOISE and the NO NOISE conditions, and we took repeated samples, most of the differences would fall around the zero mark (mean of NOISE condition and mean of NO NOISE condition would be almost the same). Sometimes, however, we would find a value larger than zero (maybe, for instance, participants in the NOISE condition would actually do *better* than participants in the NOISE condition). Sometimes we would find a very large difference. These differences are often chance differences, which arise just because we have used different samples each time – we say that these differences arise due to *sampling error*. The differences that we might find if we took repeated samples can be plotted as shown in Figure 6.2 (this is another example of a sampling distribution).

If there were no difference between the means of our particular experiment, it would be more likely that our *t* would fall in the middle region than in one of the 'tails' of the sampling distribution. This is because we know, through the Central Limit Theorem that most of our obtained values will fall in the middle range (see page 95). It would be rare (but possible) for our *t* to be found in the extreme edges of the tail as shown above. That is, if we perform 100 repeated NOISE/NO NOISE experiments, using different samples, in a small percentage of experiments we would find a *t* that falls in the extreme edges of the distribution. If, in practice, we obtain a *t* that is found in one of these tails, then we conclude that it is unlikely to have arisen purely by *sampling error*. We can put a figure on this 'unlikeliness' as well. Each obtained t-value comes with an exact associated probability level. If, for instance, our obtained *t* has an associated probability level of 0.03,[1] we can say that, assuming the null hypothesis to be true, a t-value such as the one we obtained in our experiment would be likely to have arisen in only 3 occasions out of 100. Therefore we conclude that there is a difference between conditions that cannot be explained by *sampling error*. As you have seen in Chapter 4, this is what is meant by 'statistical significance'. This does not necessarily mean that our finding is *psychologically* important, or that we have found a *large effect size*. We have to take into consideration our descriptive statistics and any measure of effect sizes, confidence intervals, etc., that we have also computed.

---

[1] Often psychologists call this Achieved Significance Level (ASL), and we use these terms interchangeably in this book.

Activity 6.2

What does the independent t-test examine?

(a) The difference between the median values for each condition
(b) The differences between the variances for each condition
(c) The differences between the mean scores for each condition

6.1.8 Output for independent t-test

In our experiment, the dependent variable is the number of words correctly recalled, and the independent variable is NOISE (either NOISE condition, or NO NOISE condition). All good computer packages, such as SPSSFW, will give the following information:

■ *Means of the two conditions* and the difference between them. What you want to know is whether the difference between the two means is large enough to be important (not only 'statistically significant', which tells you the likelihood of your test statistic being obtained, given that the null hypothesis is true).

■ *Confidence intervals*: SPSSFW, using the t-test procedure, gives you confidence limits for the *difference* between the means.[2] The difference between means, for your sample, is a *point estimate*. This sample mean difference is the best estimate of the population mean difference. If, however, we repeated the experiment many times, we would find that the mean difference varied from experiment to experiment. The best estimate of the population mean would then be the mean of all these mean differences. It is obviously better to give an interval estimate, as explained before. Confidence limits let you know how confident you are that the *population mean difference* is within a certain interval. That is, it is an *interval estimate* for the population (not just for your sample).

■ *t-value*: the higher the t-value, the more likely it is that the difference between groups is *not* the result of sampling error. A negative value is just as important as a positive value. The positive/negative direction depends on how you've coded the groups. For instance, we have called condition 1 NOISE and condition 2 NO NOISE. This was obviously an arbitrary decision; we could just as well have called condition 1 NO NOISE and condition 2 NOISE – this would result in exactly the same t-value, but it would have a different sign (plus or minus).

■ *p-value*: this is the probability of your obtained t-value having arisen by sampling variation, or error, given that the null hypothesis is true. This means that your obtained *t* is under an area of the curve that is uncommon – by chance, you would not expect your obtained t-value to fall in this area. The p-value shows you the likelihood of this arising by sampling error. For instance, $p = 0.001$ means that there is only one chance in a thousand of this result arising from sampling error, given that the null hypothesis is true.

---

[2] It is more important that you report the confidence interval for the difference between the means, than it is for you to report the confidence interval for both means separately.

■ *Degrees of freedom (DF)*: for most purposes and tests (but not all) degrees of freedom roughly equate to sample size. For a related t-test, DF are always one less than the number of participants. For an independent t-test, DF are $(n-1) + (n-1)$,[3] so for a sample size of 20 (10 participants in each group) DF = 18 (i.e. $9 + 9$). For a within-participants design with sample size of 20, DF = 19. DF should always be reported in your laboratory reports or projects, along with the t-value, p-value and confidence limits for the difference between means. Degrees of freedom are usually reported in brackets, as follows: $t(87) = 0.78$. This means that the t-value was 0.78, and the degrees of freedom 87.

■ *Standard deviations*: this gives you the standard deviation for your sample (see page 71).

■ *Standard error of the mean (SEM)*: this is used in the construction of confidence intervals (see page 108).

Degrees of freedom

This is a mathematical term that is often used in formulae for our statistical tests. There are mathematical definitions that are not useful for most psychologists, and there are working definitions, e.g. DF refers to the number of individual scores that can vary without changing the sample mean. Examples can help illustrate the concept. For instance, if we ask you to choose two numbers at random, with no constraints, then you have two degrees of freedom. If we ask you to choose two numbers that must add up to 10, however, then once you have chosen the first number, e.g. 7, the other is fixed: it is 3, and you have no choice in the matter! Thus the degrees of freedom are reduced to 1.

Let's take a non-mathematical example. Imagine you are hosting an important dinner party, and you need to seat ten people; a knowledge of where the first nine sit will determine where the tenth person sits – you would be free to decide where the first nine sits, and the tenth would be known, by a knowledge of the first nine (DF, then, is $10 - 1 = 9$). Imagine now that you are hosting a very old-fashioned formal dinner party, where you have five women and five men, and you need to sit each woman next to a man. In this case a knowledge of where the first four pairs sit (eight people) leads to the last pair (a man and a woman) being determined (DF, then, is $10 - 2 = 8$).

This is because, as can be seen in our dinner party example, we are free to vary all the numbers but one, in order to estimate the mean. The last number is determined by a knowledge of the others. The formulae we use in calculations often incorporate this restriction.

Of course psychologists are usually busy doing psychology, not going to dinner parties. So a more useful way of thinking about degrees of freedom is to say that DF are the number of observations made, minus the number of parameters which are estimated. When calculating statistical tests, we often have to 'estimate' figures Once we have to estimate a mean, we lose one degree of freedom. (This is why you often have to divide by $n - 1$ rather than n.) The more measures you have to estimate, the more you reduce your degrees of freedom. DF is a result of both the number of participants in the analysis, and the number of variables. It's not easy to find a statistical textbook that explains DF well, or shows you the relevance of DF. Dr Chong Ho Yu gives one of the best explanations of DF that we have seen, but much of the explanation is based on concepts which you will learn in Chapter 11, so we will be talking more about DF there. If you wish to hear and see Dr Chong Ho Yu's Degrees of Freedom tutorial on the web, the site address is given at the end of this chapter (Yu, 2003).

---

[3] *n* is the number of participants in each group.

Activity 6.3

It is easy to become confused sometimes when psychologists use several different names for the same thing! What are the alternative names for within-participants designs? What are the alternative names for between-participants designs?

6.1.9 Assumptions to be met in using t-tests

The t-test is a *parametric* test, which means that certain conditions about the distribution of the data need to be in force, i.e. data should be drawn from a normally distributed population of scores. We assume this is the case if our sample scores are normally distributed. You can tell whether your data are skewed by looking at histograms. In the past, in order to be able to use a t-test you would have been instructed to use interval data only. However, for many years now psychologists have used t-tests for the analysis of data from Likert-type scales (where variables have been rated on a scale of, say, 1 to 7).

The t-test is based on the normal curve of distribution. Thus, we assume that the scores of our groups, or conditions, are each normally distributed. The larger the sample size, the more likely you are to have a normal distribution. As long as your data are reasonably normally distributed, you do not need to worry, but if they are severely skewed, you need to use a non-parametric test (see Chapter 15).

At this stage, we recommend a simple eyeballing of the histograms for each variable (these can be obtained from the SPSSFW *Frequencies* program). You should do this for each group separately. Figures 6.3 to 6.6 are guidelines.

Remember that in using the t-test we compare a difference in *means*, and if our data are skewed, the mean may not be the best measure of central tendency.

In the past, psychologists were advised to perform a t-test only when the variances between the two groups were similar. This is because, in calculating part of the formula (for the t-test), the variances for the two groups are added together and averaged. If the variances are very unequal, the 'average' obtained will not be representative of either of the conditions. SPSSFW, however, uses a slightly different method of calculating a t-value when the variances are unequal, allowing you therefore to use the t-test under these conditions.

Figure 6.3 Slight positive skew

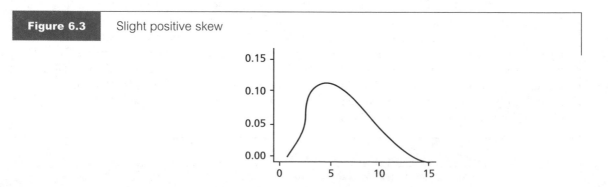

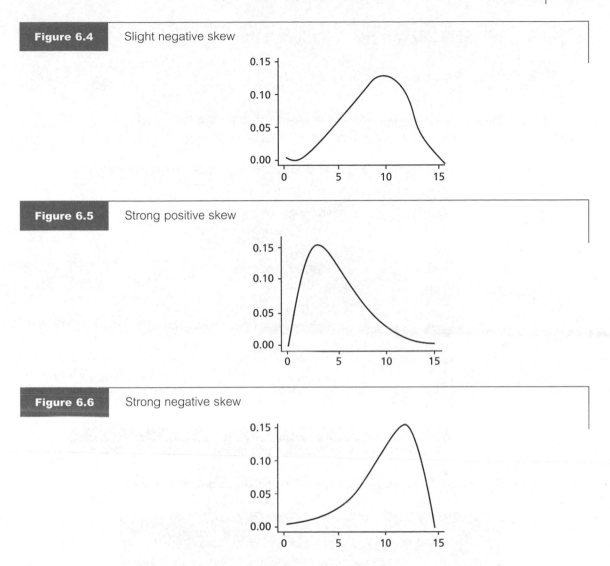

Figure 6.4 Slight negative skew

Figure 6.5 Strong positive skew

Figure 6.6 Strong negative skew

When we have different numbers of participants in the two groups, taking a simple average of the two variances might be misleading, because the formula would give the two groups equal weighting, when in fact one group might consist of more participants. In this case we would use a weighted average. The weighted average for the sample (called the pooled variance estimate) is used in order to obtain a more accurate estimate of the population variance.

If your data are extremely skewed and you have very small participant numbers, you will need to consider a non-parametric test (see Chapter 15). This is because non-parametric tests do not make assumptions about normality.

6.1.10 t-test for independent samples

Let's use our example of the NOISE/NO NOISE experiment to go through the SPSS instructions and output for a t-test for independent samples.

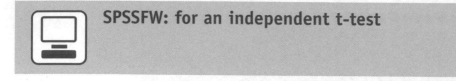

SPSSFW: for an independent t-test

Open your datafile. First you should set up a file suitable for independent designs. You have been shown how to do this in the SPSSFW section in Chapter 1, so please refer back to this.

This opens the *Independent-Samples T Test* dialogue box, as follows:

> Move the dependent variable(s) over from the left to the *Test Variable* list by highlighting them and using the > button

> Move the independent variable from the left to the *Grouping Variable* box, then click on the *Define Groups* button

This gives the *Define Groups* dialogue box:

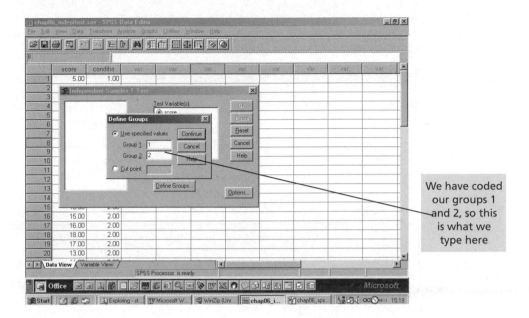

We have coded our groups 1 and 2, so this is what we type here

You then have to give the value you have assigned to the groups, i.e. if you have coded women as 0 and men as 1, then sex (0,1) is the correct format. In our example, however, our groups are coded as 1 and 2.

Click on *Continue*. This brings you back to the previous dialogue box; you can then click on *Options*. This gives you the following options box. It is here that you can change your confidence level, from 95% to 90%, for instance.

Click on *Continue*, and then *OK*.

Press *Continue*

The results will appear in the output window. Most outputs give you far more information than you need; at first glance, it might look just like a jumble of numbers. However, you'll soon learn to pick out what really matters for your particular experiment or study. Some of the output will simply tell you what you already know! For instance, in the first section of the output below we are given the following:

- the name of the two conditions
- the number of cases in each condition
- the mean of each condition
- the standard deviation and standard error of the mean, of the two conditions.

The above information can be scanned quite quickly; this information is already known to us. Once we know what to disregard, our output is fairly easy to read. These are the group statistics that appear first in the output:

Group Statistics

	noise and no noise	N	Mean	Std. Deviation	Std. Error Mean
SCORE	noise	12	7.2500	2.4909	.7191
	no noise	12	13.8333	2.7579	.7961

The next section of the output is what really interests us:

Independent Samples Test

		Levene's Test for Equality of Variances		t-test for Equality of Means						
		F	Sig.	t	df	Sig. (2-tailed)	Mean Difference	Std. Error Difference	95% Confidence Interval of the Difference	
SCORE	Equal variances assumed	.177	.678	−6.137	22	.000	−6.5833	1.0728	−8.8082	−4.3585
	Equal variances not assumed			−6.137	21.776	.000	−6.5833	1.0728	−8.8095	−4.3572

This shows that the variances are not significantly different ($p = 0.678$) so we use the equal variances assumed part of the output, as indicated by SPSSFW

Usually we give exact probabilities. When SPSSFW prints a row of zeros, however, change the last figure to a one, and use the $p <$ sign. Thus $p < 0.001$

This is the difference between the means

One of the things you will notice is that SPSSFW uses a test called Levene's Test for Inequality. This is used to test whether the conditions have equal variances. Equal variances across conditions is called 'homogeneity of variance'. Some statistical tests such as the t-test assume that variances are equal across groups or samples. The Levene test can be used to verify that assumption. The t-test gives two sets of results – one to use when we have met the assumption (i.e. variances are similar) and one to use when we have failed to meet this assumption (i.e. variances are different). Levene's test provides us with an F-value, which you have not come across yet, but it is a test statistic just like t – in fact when DF = 1, $t^2 = F$ or $t = \sqrt{F}$. So if $t = 3$, then you know that this is equal to an F-value of 9. You will come across the F-test statistic later, in Chapter 9.

Levene's Test is a test of homogeneity of variances that does not rely on the assumption of normality. In making our decision as to whether we have met the assumption of equal variances, we need to look at the p-value given alongside the F-value. Consistent with the traditional convention, we should conclude that our variances are different (unequal) if this p-value is less than 0.05. If the p-value is greater than 0.05 then we assume that our variances are roughly equal. SPSSFW uses a criterion value of $p < 0.05$ to decide whether the variances are equal. Obviously this decision is subject to the same constraints outlined for hypothesis testing in Chapter 4. For simplicity, however, we will adhere to the SPSSFW criterion, as explained above.

The textual part of the results might be reported as follows:

Participants in the NOISE condition recalled fewer words ($t(22) = 7.3$, SD = 2.5) than in the NO NOISE condition ($t(22) = 23.8$, SD = 2.8). The mean difference between conditions was 6.58, which is a large effect size ($d = 2.45$); the 95% confidence interval for the estimated population mean difference is between 4.36 and 8.81. An independent t-test revealed that, if the null hypothesis were true, such a result would be highly unlikely to have arisen ($t(22) = 6.14$; $p < 0.001$). It was therefore concluded that listening to noise affects short-term memory, at least in respect of recall of words.

EXAMPLE: NEED FOR COGNITION

Some people spend a lot of time actively engaged in problem-solving. Others do not. There are large individual differences in people's tendency to engage in and enjoy this 'cognitive activity'. This individual difference dimension is called need for cognition (NEEDCOG). In the following section of the output, men and women were compared on this dimension. There were far more men in the study. The means look similar, as do the standard deviation and the standard error of the mean.

Group Statistics

	Men and women	N	Mean	Std. Deviation	Std. Error Mean
NEEDCOG	Men	440	62.4886	9.942	.474
	Women	290	63.1586	8.484	.498

Here is the next section of the output:

Independent Samples Test

		Levene's Test for Equality of Variances		t-test for equality of means						
		F	Sig.	t	df	Sig. (2-tailed)	Mean Difference	Std. Error Difference	95% Confidence Interval of the Difference	
NEEDCOG	Equal variances assumed			−.94	728	.346	−.6700	.710	−2.064	.724
	Equal variances not assumed	14.577	.000	−.97	631.39	.330	−.6700	.688	−2.020	.680

The variances here are significantly different, i.e. not equal, so we use the 'equal variances not assumed' row

p = 0.33 – thus there is a 33% chance of these results being obtained by sampling error alone, assuming the null hypothesis to be true

You can see that the mean difference between conditions is 0.67. The variances between the two groups differ significantly, and so we use the 'equal variances not assumed' row. This shows a t-value of −0.97. The confidence interval shows that we are 95% confident that the population mean difference is between −2.02 and 0.68 – in other words, a very large range. The confidence interval includes zero – which means, if we repeat the study with a different sample, the women might score higher than the men (as in this case, where the mean difference is −0.67), the men might score higher than the women, or there might be absolutely no difference at all (zero). This is obviously not good enough for us, and we have to conclude that the groups do not differ on NEEDCOG. This is borne out by the small t-value (0.97) and the associated significance level of $p = 0.33$. This means that, assuming the null hypothesis to be true, we have a 33% chance of finding the t-value of 0.97.

CAUTION!

Remember that the minus sign when obtaining a t is equivalent to a plus sign. In other words, a t of, say, −5 is equivalent to a value of +5.

Example from the literature: psychosocial factors and coronary artery disease

Ketterer *et al.* (1996) were looking at psychosocial factors and coronary artery disease. Ketterer *et al.* presented a table showing a comparison of patients who completed their study with those who failed to do so. The t-tests compared these two groups on the variables listed in Table 6.4. Results are presented as means and standard deviations.

This is a useful table of results, because in one table it gives the means for both the groups (and the standard deviations). This enables us to see the direction of the difference. It gives exact probabilities, which gives us much more information than if we had read 'n.s.' (As you will see later, some authors do not report exact probability levels, but tell us only whether the results are 'significant' or 'non-significant' [n.s.]. With the advent of good statistical packages, however, we are able to report *exact* probability levels.) The variable that differentiated the groups at a statistically significant level was 'Education (in years)'. You can see from the means that participants who completed the study were significantly more educated (in terms of number of years) than participants who failed to complete the study. However, the two groups did not differ significantly on any of the other variables. Although we are not given the effect sizes, we can calculate them, as we have been given all the necessary information. Why not have a go?[4]

Table 6.4 Means, standard deviations and probability values for participants in Ketterer *et al.* (1996) study

	Compliant participants ($n = 175$)	Non-compliant participants ($n = 187$)	p
Age	58.0 (10.6)	58.9 (11.8)	0.435
Education (in years)	13.7 (2.8)	12.6 (3.3)	0.001
Pack-years of smoking	42.9 (43.6)	49.0 (44.4)	0.191
Hours of exercise (per week)	2.4 (4.5)	2.1 (4.3)	0.530
Caffeine	3.3 (3.9)	3.5 (3.7)	0.668
Body Mass Index	19.2 (2.6)	19.3 (3.3)	0.582
Alcohol (drinks per day)	0.5 (1.4)	0.7 (2.2)	0.373

6.1.11 Related t-test

The related t-test is also known as the paired t-test; these terms are interchangeable. As explained on page 206, the related t-test is used when the *same* participants perform under both conditions. The formula for this test is similar, not surprisingly, to the independent t-test. However, the related t-test is more sensitive than the independent t-test. This is because each participant performs in both conditions, and so each participant can be tested

---

[4] You can check your calculations with ours, on page 573.

against him- or herself. If we have 20 people in a related design (20 people taking part in both conditions), we would need 40 in an unrelated design (20 in each condition). So the formula for the related t-test takes into account the fact that we are using the same participants. If you compare an independent and related t-test using the same dataset, you will find that the related t-test gives a result with a higher associated probability value – this is because the comparison of participants with themselves gives rise to a reduced within-participants variance, leading to a larger value of t.

Imagine that we want to find out whether different types of visualisation help pain control. To make it simple, assume there are two types of visualisation:

- imagine performing an exciting t-test (statistics condition)
- imagine lying on a sunny beach, drinking cocktails (beach condition).

Participants sit down, and are taken through the visualisation as they plunge their hands into ice-cold water. Although we have not tried this, we are assured it is very painful. The dependent variable is the number of seconds that our participants are able to keep their hands in the iced water. Now, as we are running this as a within-participants design (because it is more sensitive), we cannot simply have the participants doing one condition, then the other (this might lead to order effects, or it might be that no one returns for the second condition!). Therefore half the participants do condition A, then condition B, and half do condition B, then A (see counter-balancing, Chapter 1). Now some people might think that our hypothesis is one-tailed, because they might think visualising lying on a sunny beach would help with pain control more than thinking about statistics. However, we advise you to determine whether your hypothesis is one- or two-tailed on the basis of previous research, not just a hunch you have! Since there is no research on this topic (as far as we know), we are going to have a two-tailed hypothesis. The data are shown in Table 6.5.

Table 6.5 Time (seconds) hands kept in water for each condition

Participant	Statistics condition	Beach condition
1	5	7
2	7	15
3	3	6
4	6	7
5	10	12
6	4	12
7	7	10
8	8	14
9	8	13
10	15	7

SPSSFW: two samples repeated-measures design – paired t-test

Open your datafile. Choose the *Paired-Samples T Test* from the *Compare Means* menu:

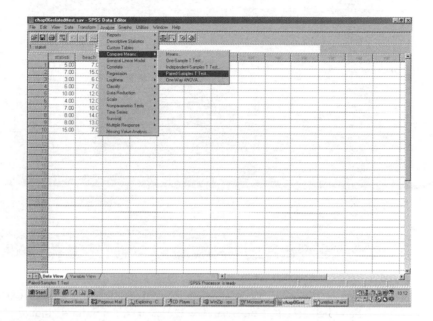

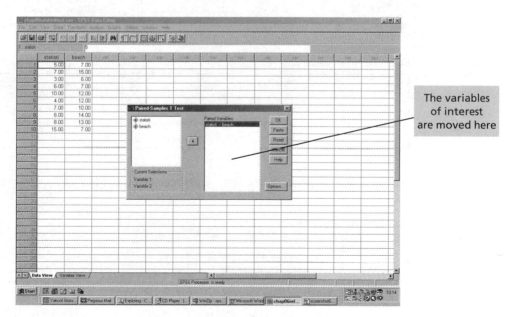

The variables of interest are moved here

To select a pair of variables:

1. Click on the first variable.
2. Click on the second variable.
3. Click on ▶ to move the pair over.

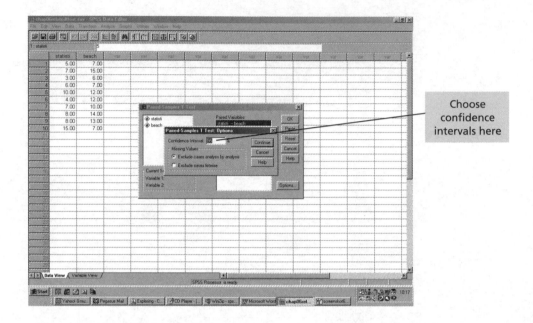

Choose confidence intervals here

Click on *Options*, if wanted (see above), then click on *Continue* within that dialogue box. Then click on *OK*. Your results will appear in the output window.

First of all, we obtain the group statistics. This gives the usual descriptive statistics: the mean, number of participants, standard deviation and standard error of the mean.

Paired Samples Statistics

		Mean	N	Std. Deviation	Std. Error Mean
Pair 1	STATISTI	7.3000	10	3.4010	1.0755
	BEACH	10.3000	10	3.3350	1.0546

The next section of the output provides us with a correlation between the two conditions:

Paired Samples Correlations

		N	Correlation	Sig.
Pair 1	STATISTI & BEACH	10	.070	.849

This shows that there is no relationship between scores in the BEACH condition and scores in the STATISTICS condition ($r = 0.07$, which is very weak indeed).

Then we come to the paired sample statistics:

Paired Samples Test

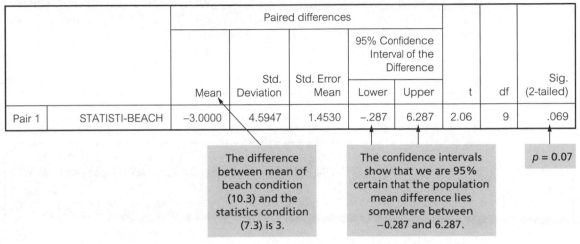

		Paired differences							
					95% Confidence Interval of the Difference				Sig.
		Mean	Std. Deviation	Std. Error Mean	Lower	Upper	t	df	(2-tailed)
Pair 1	STATISTI-BEACH	−3.0000	4.5947	1.4530	−.287	6.287	2.06	9	.069

The difference between mean of beach condition (10.3) and the statistics condition (7.3) is 3.

The confidence intervals show that we are 95% certain that the population mean difference lies somewhere between −0.287 and 6.287.

$p = 0.07$

Although we can see, oddly enough, that participants in the BEACH condition did keep their hands in the iced water longer (mean = 10.3 seconds as opposed to the mean of the statistics condition, 7.3 seconds), the analysis gave us a t-value of 2.06, with an associated probability level of 0.069. The confidence interval is wide – we can say, with 95% confidence, that the true population mean difference is somewhere within the interval −0.287 and 6.827. This means that we cannot really be sure, if we repeated the study, that the beach visualisation would have given the better result. Therefore we have to conclude that there is no evidence to suggest that this type of visualisation affects pain control.

Part of your textual analysis might read:

Although it can be seen that participants in the BEACH condition held their hands in ice-cold water for a mean of 10.3 seconds, as opposed to the mean of 7.3 in the STATISTICS condition, the 95% confidence limits show us that, if we repeated the experiment, the population mean difference between the conditions would lie somewhere between −0.287 and 6.287. Thus we cannot be sure that, in the population, the beach visualisation would give the better result ($t(9) = 2.06$; $p = 0.07$)

EXAMPLE: THE VERBAL AND PERFORMANCE IQ OF PEOPLE WITH CHRONIC ILLNESS

A study was carried out comparing the verbal IQ (VIQ) and the performance IQ (PIQ) of people with chronic illness. In a normal population you would expect the two IQ measures to be similar. The population mean IQ is 100.

SPSSFW provides us with a correlation between the two conditions:

Paired Samples Correlations

		N	Correlation	Sig.
Pair 1	verbal iq & performance iq	40	.680	.000

As would be expected, there is a strong and positive relationship between the two IQ measures.

Remember to scan the first part of the output, which confirms how many pairs you have, and the names of the variables:

Paired Samples Statistics

		Mean	N	Std. Deviation	Std. Error Mean
Pair 1	verbal iq	94.8750	40	12.03880	1.90350
	performance iq	109.1000	40	12.86777	2.03457

It can immediately be seen that the verbal IQ of the group is lower than their performance IQ.

Paired Samples Test

		Paired differences							
					95% Confidence Interval of the Difference				
		Mean	Std. Deviation	Std. Error Mean	Lower	Upper	t	df	Sig. (2-tailed)
Pair 1	verbal iq – performance iq	–14.2250	9.98842	1.57931	–17.4195	–11.0305	–9.007	39	.000

In this case, our sample mean paired difference (between verbal and performance IQ) is 14.23. Regarding the population mean difference, we are 95% confident that the value falls between 11.03 and 17.42.

$t(39) = -9.01$ has an associated p-value of $p < 0.001$, which means that, assuming the null hypothesis to be true, such a value would have occurred less than once in 1000 times. This is so unlikely that we conclude that the differences between the verbal and performance IQ of the group are unlikely to have arisen by sampling error.

Activity 6.4

Look at the following printout, which relates to the next *two* questions:

Group Statistics

	condition	N	Mean	Std. Deviation	Std. Error Mean
Memory	Con1	10	15.6000	5.621	.1778
	Con2	10	23.9000	11.130	3.520

Paired Samples Correlations

		N	Correlation	Sig.
Pair 1	Con1 and Con2	10	.786	.007

Paired Samples Test

		Paired differences							
					95% Confidence Interval of the Difference				Sig.
		Mean	Std. Deviation	Std. Error Mean	Lower	Upper	t	df	(2-tailed)
Pair 1	Con1 and Con2	−8.3000	7.558	2.390	−13.707	−2.893	−3.47	9	.007

1. The value of the test statistic is:
   (a) 0.007
   (b) −8.30
   (c) −3.47

2. The difference between the mean of condition 1 and 2 is:
   (a) −8.3
   (b) 7.558
   (c) 2.390

Example from the literature: perceived control and distress following sexual assault

Frazier (2003) collected data from women who had suffered a serious sexual assault, at four time-points after the assault. The data provided information relating to the way in which beliefs about controllability and distress change over the time following the assault. Descriptive statistics were as follows:

Variable	2 weeks (n = 88)		2 months (n = 98)		6 months (n = 89)		12 months (n = 92)	
	$\bar{X}$	SD	$\bar{X}$	SD	$\bar{X}$	SD	$\bar{X}$	SD
Control								
Behavioural self-blame	3.54	1.18	3.37	1.07	3.07	1.14	2.88	1.10
Rapist blame	3.85	0.95	3.65	1.15	3.73	1.16	3.47	1.21
Control over recovery	3.74	0.77	3.93	0.71	3.91	0.79	4.03	0.78
Future control	4.07	0.63	4.23	0.64	4.13	0.72	4.12	0.64
Future (un)likelihood of assault	2.40	0.76	2.63	0.84	2.72	0.75	2.81	0.75
Distress								
Anxiety	2.31	0.85	1.78	0.98	1.52	1.01	1.29	0.96
Depression	2.04	0.98	1.64	1.03	1.50	1.02	1.18	0.94
Hostility	1.58	0.90	1.44	0.96	1.31	1.04	1.03	0.88
Distress	2.00	0.74	1.63	0.85	1.45	0.92	1.17	0.82

The authors state that:

> *Rapist blame was more common than behaviour self-blame, with small effect sizes at 2 weeks, t(87) = −.78, p = .08, d = 0.19, and 2 months, t(94) = −.80, p = .07, d = 0.19, and medium effects at 6 months, t(84) = −4.61, p < .0001, d = 0.50, and 12 months, t(89) = −4.50, p < .0001, d = 0.48, postassault. According to Cohen's (1992) conventions for effect sizes (ds) for t tests, .20 is a small effect size, .50 is medium, and .80 is large.*

Note that the authors have performed four paired t-tests. That is, they have compared ratings on 'behavioural self-blame' with ratings on 'rapist blame' at four time-points. The first comparison was made two weeks after the assault. Although participants rated rapists more to blame than themselves, the difference between these two variables was small – the effect size is given as 0.19, which is, as the authors have told us, a weak effect. The difference between the two 'blame' variables at this time-point has an associated probability level of 0.08. A second t-test was performed on the same variables at two months – again the effect is weak. Six months later, however, when they perform the third t-test, the difference between the conditions becomes more marked. The two conditions here differ by half a standard deviation. At the fourth time-point, the difference is similar.

Multiple testing

If you perform several tests within one study or experiment, then some of your inferential statistical analyses will give rise to results with low associated probability levels (e.g. 0.001) by sampling error alone. To allow for this, we recommend that you interpret your results in the light of this knowledge. The easiest way to do this is to divide 0.05 (the traditional criterion variable for significance) by the number of tests you are performing (in any one study), and then interpret your ASL accordingly.

So if, in your experiment, you carry out three t-tests, then:

$$ASL = \frac{0.05}{3} = 0.0167$$

Any ASL > 0.0167 may be due to sampling error. Remember, however, that interpreting significance levels is just one piece of information contributing to the interpretation of your results. There are also effect sizes and confidence intervals.

Summary

- Confidence limits allow you to infer with a certain degree of confidence (usually 95%) that a population mean (or difference between means) falls within a certain range.

- d, an effect size, gives the magnitude of difference between two independent means, expressed in standard deviations.

- t-tests allow us to assess the likelihood of having obtained the observed differences between the two groups by sampling error: e.g. $p = 0.03$ means that, if we repeated our experiment 100 times using different samples, then assuming no real difference between conditions, we would expect to find our pattern of results three times, by sampling error alone.

- t-tests are suitable for data drawn from a normal population – they are parametric tests.

SPSSFW exercise

Twenty schoolchildren (ten boys and ten girls) have been measured on number of episodes of illness in one year, performance in a test at the beginning of the year, and performance in a similar test at the end of the year. Enter the following data into SPSSFW. Code the boys as group 1, and the girls as group 2.

Group	Episodes of illness	Test at beginning of year	Test at end of year
1	24	13	16
1	20	16	20
1	8	7	18
1	12	30	35
1	5	5	5
1	24	10	15
1	0	9	10
1	8	15	24
1	20	18	30
1	24	20	27
2	7	18	17
2	30	14	10
2	2	20	20
2	10	9	10
2	18	13	9
2	9	13	16
2	20	10	1
2	10	16	14
2	15	5	6
2	8	7	14

Assume that data are drawn from a normally distributed population.

1. Perform an independent t-test between boys and girls on 'episodes of illness', and on the end of year test.

2. Calculate the effect size, d, where appropriate.

3. Imagine that your friend does not understand the output you have obtained, nor does the friend know about effect sizes or confidence intervals. Write a few paragraphs explaining the meaning of the results to your friend.

4. Perform a repeated-measures t-test on performance on the test at the beginning of the year and the end of the year. Give a written explanation of the meaning of your results to your friend. The prediction is that the group will perform better at the end of the year.

MULTIPLE CHOICE QUESTIONS

1. The DF for an independent t-test analysis with 20 participants in each condition is:
   (a) 38
   (b) 20
   (c) 40
   (d) 68

2. For a paired t-test with 40 participants, the appropriate DF is:
   (a) 20
   (b) 39
   (c) 38
   (d) none of these

3. For an independent t-test with 15 participants in each condition, the appropriate DF is:
   (a) 28
   (b) 14
   (c) 30
   (d) 15

4. One hundred students were tested on their anxiety before and after an anxiety counselling session. Scores are drawn from a normally distributed population. Which statistical test is the most appropriate?
   (a) Independent groups t-test
   (b) Related measures t-test
   (c) Levene's Test
   (d) None of these

5. The most important assumption to meet when using a t-test is:
   (a) The variation in scores should be minimal
   (b) Scores should be drawn from a normally distributed population
   (c) Conditions should have equal means
   (d) All of the above

6. The higher the t-value, the more likely it is that the differences between groups are:
   (a) A result of sampling error
   (b) Not a result of sampling error
   (c) Similar to each other
   (d) None of the above

7. A t-value of −5 is:
   (a) Less important than a value of +5
   (b) More important than a value of +5
   (c) Equivalent to a value of +5
   (d) Less significant than a value of +5

Questions 8 to 10 relate to the following table of results:

Group Statistics

	SEX	N	Mean	Std. Deviation	Std. Error Mean
total of stigma	1.00	62	33.8710	12.1149	1.5386
	2.00	53	34.8302	13.0586	1.7937

Independent Samples Test

		Levene's Test for Equality of Variances		t-test for Equality of Means						95% Confidence Interval of the Difference	
		F	Sig.	t	df	Sig. (2-tailed)	Mean Difference	Std. Error Difference		Lower	Upper
total of stigma	Equal variances assumed	.755	.387	−.408	113	.684	−.9592	2.3493		−5.6136	3.6951
	Equal variances not assumed			−.406	107.199	.686	−.9592	2.3632		−5.6439	3.7255

8. The difference between the means of the groups is (correct to one decimal place):

(a) 0.41

(b) 0.69

(c) 0.96

(d) 0.76

9. The variances of the two groups are:

(a) Indeterminate

(b) Unequal

(c) Assumed equal

(d) Skewed

10. What can you conclude from the results?

(a) There are no statistically significant differences or important differences between the two groups

(b) There is a statistically significant difference but it is not important

(c) There is an important difference between the two groups but it is not statistically significant

(d) There are both statistically significant and important differences between the groups

11. The effect size for independent groups, d, can be calculated by:

(a) (mean 1 − mean 2) ÷ mean SD

(b) (mean 1 + mean 2) ÷ mean SD

(c) (mean 1 − mean 2) ÷ SEM

(d) (mean 1 + mean 2) ÷ SEM

12. If the 95% confidence limits around the mean difference (in a t-test) are $10.5 - 13.0$, we can conclude that, if we repeat the study 100 times, then:

(a) Our results will be statistically significant 5 times

(b) Our results will be statistically significant 95 times

(c) 95% of the time the population mean difference will be between 10.5 and 13.00; 5% of the time the population mean difference will be outside this range

(d) 5% of the time the population mean difference will be between 10.5 and 13.00; 95% of the time the population mean difference will be outside this range

13. In an analysis using an unrelated t-test, you find the following result:

Levene's Test for Equality of Variances: $F = 0.15$ $p = 0.58$

This shows that the variances of the two groups are:

(a) Dissimilar
(b) Similar
(c) Exactly the same
(d) Indeterminate

14. In the SPSSFW output, if $p = 0.000$, then you should report this as:

(a) $p = 0.000$
(b) $p = 0.0001$
(c) $p < 0.001$
(d) $p < 0.0001$

15. In an independent t-test, you would use the 'equal variances not assumed' part of the output when Levene's test is:

(a) Above a criterion significance level (e.g. $p > 0.05$)
(b) Below a criterion significance level (e.g. $p < 0.05$)
(c) When numbers of participants are unequal in the two conditions
(d) When you have skewed data

16. For a within-participants design using 20 people, the degrees of freedom are:

(a) 20
(b) 38
(c) 19
(d) 40

17. Levene's test is:

(a) A test of heterogeneity that relies on the assumption of normality
(b) A test of homogeneity that relies on the assumption of normality
(c) A test of heterogeneity that does not rely on the assumption of normality
(d) A test of homogeneity of variances that does not rely on the assumption of normality

Read the following excerpt from a results section of a journal article (Ratcliff et al., 2003) then answer question 18:

The changes in mean scores on all tests between Wave 4 and Wave 5 were statistically significant based on the paired t-test (all of the p values < .001, except MMSE, p = .012; Word List Learning, Delayed Recall, p = .009; Boston Naming, p = .019).

18. Why are 'all of the p values' reported as $p < 0.001$, when the other named variables have been reported with the exact probability values?

(a) The researchers could not work out the exact probability values
(b) The significance level in their statistical program calculated $p = 0.000$
(c) The unnamed variables are not as significant
(d) All of the above

Questions 19 and 20 relate to the following table:

Independent Samples Test

		Levene's Test for Equality of Variances		t-test for Equality of Means						
		F	Sig.	t	df	Sig. (2-tailed)	Mean Difference	Std. Error Difference	95% Confidence Interval of the Difference	
									Lower	Upper
Serious economic consequences	Equal variances assumed	.113	.738	.923	106	.358	.5258	.56951	−.60327	1.65494
	Equal variances not assumed			.882	16.607	.391	.5258	.59644	−.73481	1.78649

19. Which row would the researcher use to interpret the independent t-test results?

   (a) The equal variances row
   (b) The unequal variances row

20. Generalising to the population, what sign would the expected t-value take?

   (a) Positive
   (b) Negative
   (c) It could be either positive or negative

References

Cohen, J. (1988) *Statistical Power for Behavioral Sciences* (2nd edn). New York: Academic Press.

Cohen, J. (1992) 'A power primer', *Psychological Bulletin*, **112**: 155–9.

Frazier, P.A. (2003) 'Perceived control and distress following sexual assault: a longitudinal test of a new model', *Journal of Personality and Social Psychology*, **84**(6): 1257–69.

Ketterer, M.W., Kenyon, L., Foley, B.A., Brymer, J., Rhoads, K., Kraft, P. and Lovallo, W.R. (1996) 'Denial of depression as an independent correlate of coronary artery disease', *Journal of Health Psychology*, **1**(1): 93–105.

Ratcliff, G., Dodge, H., Birzescu, M. and Ganguli, M. (2003) 'Tracking cognitive functioning over time: ten-year longitudinal data from a community-based study', *Applied Neuropsychology*, **10**(2): 89–95.

Yu, C.H., Ho, W.J. and Stockford, S. (2001) 'Using multimedia to visualize the concepts of degree of freedom, perfect-fitting, and over-fitting'. Paper presented in August 2001 at the Joint Statistical Meetings, Atlanta, GA.

Yu, C.H. (2003) 'Illustrating degrees of freedom in multimedia', available at http://seamonkey.ed.asu.edu/~alex/pub/df/default.htm [accessed 10 March 2004].

7   Issues of significance

Chapter overview

In the last two chapters you learned to describe and analyse the *relationships* between variables and also to analyse the *differences* between two conditions. In those chapters, we encouraged you to use different methods of analysis in order to make sense of the data, and to give your readers (usually your lecturers who are marking your work) as full a picture as possible. Thus we encouraged you to describe your data, by using graphical illustrations, measures of central tendency and variability; we gave you a simple method by which you could calculate an effect size, and we introduced you to confidence intervals (CIs). We also encouraged you to report the achieved significance level (exact probability figure, ASL).

In this chapter, we are going to discuss the concepts above in greater depth. We are going to discuss the issues surrounding the reporting of probability levels, and we will introduce a new concept – the concept of *power*. Power is the ability to detect a significant effect, where one exists. It is the ability that the test has to reject the null hypothesis correctly. It is important to have an understanding of such issues before you run your own experiments and studies, which is why we are introducing them now.

In this chapter, you will learn about:

■ the relationship between power, effect size and probability levels
■ the factors influencing power
■ issues surrounding the use of criterion significance levels.

To enable you to understand the issues discussed in this chapter, you will need to have understood correlational analysis (Chapter 5) and the analyses of differences between two groups using the t-test (Chapter 6).

7.1 Criterion significance levels

As noted earlier in the book, it was common practice for many years simply to report probability values as being < 0.05 or > 0.05. This convention arose partly because, prior to the advent of powerful computer packages such as SPSSFW, the exact probability could not be determined easily. However, there are good reasons why the exact probability should always be reported.

For example, imagine that you run an experiment, analyse it and find an associated probability value of 0.049. Subsequently, you decide to replicate the experiment, but this time you find a probability level of 0.051. To report the first study as being 'significant' at the < 0.05 level and the second study as being 'non-significant' at the > 0.05 level is misleading, particularly given the fact that when you carry out a study there is always a certain amount of error (see Chapter 4, p. 138). That is, if you re-run the experiment you might well find an associated probability value of 0.06, or 0.04. Similarly, as Howell (2002) observes, is it reasonable to treat 0.051 and 0.75 as being equally non-significant by reporting them both as > 0.05? Moreover, should 0.049 and 0.00001 be thought of as being equally significant by reporting them both as $p < 0.05$?

Furthermore, an additional problem associated with the > 0.05/< 0.05 approach is that it tends to lead to a sort of 'mind-set' in which the 0.05 cut-off point is regarded as a rule that must never be broken. Consequently, people tend to assume that if a result is below this threshold it must be important, and if it is above this threshold it is of no interest. The problem is that this cut-off point was always intended simply as a guideline, not a cut-and-dried rule, because it was appreciated that statistical significance is not always equated with importance. This is because statistical significance is affected by sample size, as we will see later. Although exact p-values provide more information than reporting < 0.05 or > 0.05, the convention of using criterion probability values has its supporters, many of whom believe that the conventional method of reporting p-values provides a common standard for evaluating statistical claims. However, as Rosnow and Rosenthal (1989) said:

Surely God loves the 0.06 nearly as much as the 0.05.

The exact probability level lets your reader know the likelihood of your results having been obtained by sampling error, given that the null hypothesis is true. The probability level is one piece of information to be taken into account in interpreting your results. We are not arguing against reporting probability values! As Macdonald (1997) says:

Data should be seen as evidence to be used in psychological arguments and statistical significance is just one measure of its quality. It restrains researchers from making too much of findings which could otherwise be explained by chance.

The debate relating to the use of exact or criterion probability levels is just a small part of a larger controversy relating to the place of Null Hypothesis Significance Testing (NHST) in psychology. The controversy is not new – it has been going on for over 40 years, and eminent psychologists and statisticians can be found on both sides of the debate. There are many journal articles relating to this topic, and if you wish to read further, we suggest you look at Kranz (1999) or Nickerson (2000).

Activity 7.1

I. The problem

Oh, t is large and p is small
That's why we are walking tall.
What it means we need not mull
Just so we reject the null.
Or chi-square large and p near nil
Results like that, they fill the bill.
What if meaning requires a poll?
Never mind, we're on a roll!
The message we have learned too well?
Significance! That rings the bell!

II. The implications

The moral of our little tale?
That we mortals may be frail
When we feel a p near zero
Makes us out to be a hero.
But tell us then is it too late?
Can we perhaps avoid our fate?
Replace that wish to null-reject
Report the size of the effect.
That may not insure our glory
But at least it tells a story
That is just the kind of yield
Needed to advance our field.
(Robert Rosenthal, 1991)

Why do you think Rosenthal wrote this poem? What is he trying to tell us?

7.2 Effect size

You have learned, in Chapters 5 and 6, ways of calculating an effect size. An effect size is the magnitude of the difference between conditions, or the strength of a relationship. There are different ways of calculating effect sizes. In Chapter 5 you learned of a natural effect size (a correlation coefficient) and in Chapter 6 you learned how to calculate the size of the difference between means, in terms of standard deviations (d). In other words, by how many standard deviations did the means differ? Remember how easy it is to calculate d:

$$\frac{x_1 - x_2}{\text{mean SD}}$$

As mentioned above, *d* is the distance between the two means in terms of standard deviations. If there is a large overlap between the two groups, the effect size will be relatively small, and if there is a small overlap, the effect size will be relatively large.

Sometimes the effect size is easy to calculate (as in the case of two conditions); at other times it may be more difficult. Report the effect size, however, when you can. Sometimes psychologists know the size of the effect that they are looking for, based on a knowledge of previous work in the area. Statisticians have given us guidelines (remember – guidelines, not rules) as to what constitutes a 'small' effect or a 'large' effect, as we learned in the last chapter. These are guidelines developed by Cohen (1988)[1]:

Effect size	*d*	Percentage of overlap
Small	0.20	85
Medium	0.50	67
Large	0.80	53

There are other measures of effect, and these are covered later. However, *d* is widely reported and understood, so it is important that you understand how to calculate and interpret it.

7.3 Power

Sometimes you will hear people say things like 'the t-test is more powerful than a Mann–Whitney' or 'repeated-measures tests have more power'. But what does this really mean? Power is the ability to detect a significant effect, where one exists. And you have learned that by 'effect' we mean a difference between means, or a relationship between variables. Power is the ability of the test to find this effect. Power can also be described as the ability to reject the null hypothesis when false. Power is measured on a scale of 0 to +1, where 0 = no power at all. If your test had no power, you would be unable to detect a difference between means, or a relationship between variables; 0.1, 0.2 and 0.3 are low power values; 0.8 and 0.9 are high power values.

What do the figures 0.1, 0.2, etc. mean?

- 0.1 means you have only a 10% chance of finding an effect if one exists. This is hopeless. Imagine running a study (costing time and money!) knowing that you would be so unlikely to find an effect.
- 0.7 means that you have a 70% chance of finding an effect, where one exists. Therefore you have a good chance of finding an effect. This experiment or study would be worth spending money on.
- 0.9 means that you have a 90% chance of finding an effect. This rarely happens in psychological research.

---

[1] A table giving the percentage overlap for *d* values 0.1 to 1.5 was given in Chapter 6, page 211.

You can see, then, that if your power is 0.5, you have only a 50:50 chance of finding an effect, if one exists, which is really not good enough.

You can probably see that really we should find out about our power level *before* the experiment or study is run, as there is not much point doing all that work, finding nothing, and then realising that we had only a small chance of finding an effect.

7.4 Factors influencing power

- The size of the effect you expect to find
- The criterion significance level (i.e. the value of the significance level at which you are prepared to accept that results are probably not due to sampling error)
- The numbers of participants in the study
- The type of statistical test you use
- Whether the design is between-participants or within-participants
- Whether the hypothesis is one- or two-tailed.

7.4.1 Size of the effect

For calculating a power value, you need to have an idea of the effect size that you are looking for. How do you know this *before* carrying out the study or experiment? If there is past research in the area, you can look at the journal articles and try to find out the effect sizes found by the researchers. Sometimes authors will have given effect sizes; sometimes you will be able to calculate them. Past research is a good guide to the sort of effect you might find. If there is no past research in the area (unlikely) you can fall back on Cohen's values (Cohen, 1988). In psychology, small to medium effect sizes are more likely than large effect sizes.

A large effect size will be easier to detect than a small effect size. You will need more power to find small effect sizes.

7.4.2 Criterion significance level

This is the probability level that you are willing to accept as the likelihood that the results were due to sampling error. Let's say that Betty Beech decides to be reasonably strict, and will consider interpreting her results only if the associated probability level is 0.02. If her ASL does not reach this level, she is going to interpret any effect as 'probably being due to sampling error'. This means that her result will be interpreted only if it falls into the tail of the distribution shown in Figure 7.1.

Adam Ash, however, decides (for reasons best known to himself!) that he will interpret his results if the associated probability level is 0.16. If his ASL does not reach this level, he will interpret his result as being 'probably due to sampling error'. This means that his result will be interpreted if it falls into the tail of the distribution shown in Figure 7.2.[2]

---

[2] One-tailed hypothesis.

| Figure 7.1 | Normal distribution, showing area under the curve |

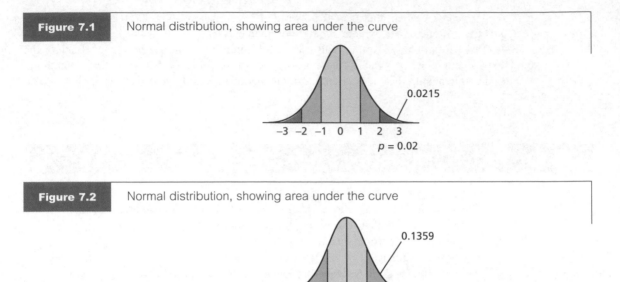

0.0215

−3 −2 −1 0 1 2 3

$p = 0.02$

| Figure 7.2 | Normal distribution, showing area under the curve |

0.1359

−3 −2 −1 0 1 2 3

$p = 0.16$

It should be evident that Adam Ash stands a much greater chance of finding an effect, since he has been more lax with his criterion.

When psychologists need to use a criterion significance level, they choose it carefully. Normally this varies from 0.01 to 0.05, but can be as high as 0.10, depending on the type of experiment or study they are running.

Activity 7.2

A power level of 0.7 means that a researcher has:

(a) 49% chance of finding an effect
(b) 7% chance of finding an effect
(c) 70% chance of finding an effect

7.4.3 Number of participants

The larger the sample size, the greater the power. You may have heard people say that, if you have a large sample size, you have a greater chance of a statistically significant result. This seems strange, since whether we declare a result 'statistically significant' seems to depend on sample size. This is, of course, a problem of relying too heavily on associated probability values, rather than on effect sizes and confidence intervals.

We can see this by using an example. Let's say that we are looking at the differences between the noise and no-noise groups in the examples in Chapter 6, using five participants.

Group Statistics

	noise and no noise	N	Mean	Std. Deviation	Std. Error Mean
SCORE	noise	2	9.5000	.707	.500
	no noise	3	13.6667	3.786	2.186

Independent Samples Test

		Levene's Test for Equality of Variances		t-test for Equality of Means							
		F	Sig.	t	df	Sig. (2-tailed)	Mean Difference	Std. Error Difference	95% Confidence Interval of the Difference	
SCORE	Equal variances assumed	5.660	.098	−1.46	3	.239	−4.1667	2.846	−13.225	4.892
	Equal variances not assumed			−1.86	2.20	.192	−4.1667	2.242	−13.012	4.678

There are so few participants in this study that, although it looks as if there is quite a difference between means (4.17 – and in the expected direction), this *could* have just been due to sampling error. It makes intuitive sense to think that, if we repeated this study with another five participants, they could have totally different scores, just by chance. Consequently, you have to find a much larger difference between the groups with this number of participants for your confidence intervals to be narrower and for the associated probability value to be lower. If you use a larger number of participants in each group, you would find that the test is declared 'statistically significant' with a smaller difference between the groups. In the present example, the confidence interval is wide. The mean population difference is expected (95% confidence) to be between −13.225 and +4.892. This means we are confident that, if we repeated the experiment, the mean of the noise group might be larger than the no-noise group (+), the no-noise group might be larger than the noise group (−), or they might be equal (0). This is similar to saying we are confident that it might be good, bad or neutral weather tomorrow. Not much use at all. *With so few participants, we have low power – if an effect exists, we are unlikely to find it, because any effect just might have been due to sampling error.*

Let's repeat the study, this time using 216 participants.

Group Statistics

	noise and no noise	N	Mean	Std. Deviation	Std. Error Mean
SCORE	Noise	110	9.1364	3.355	.320
	No noise	106	12.9623	3.570	.347

Independent Samples Test

		Levene's Test for Equality of Variances		t-test for Equality of Means						
		F	Sig.	t	df	Sig. (2-tailed)	Mean Difference	Std. Error Difference	95% Confidence Interval of the Difference	
SCORE	Equal variances assumed	1.024	.313	−8.12	214	.000	−3.8259	.471	−4.755	−2.897
	Equal variances not assumed			−8.11	211.92	.000	−3.8259	.472	−4.756	−2.896

This time, this difference between the means is actually smaller: −3.82. However, using so many participants means that we are much more certain that the result is not just due to chance, or sampling error. If we repeated the study with another 216 people, we have a lot more confidence that we would get similar results. This time the confidence intervals show us that we are confident that the difference lies between 4.8 and 2.9 (remember, if both signs are negative we can ignore the sign). That is, we can be 95% confident that the population figure for the no-noise condition will be significantly higher than for the noise condition. *With more participants, we have a greater likelihood of detecting a significant effect; we can be more certain that the effect is due to something other than sampling error.*

However, notice that our result has become 'more significant' if you home in on the significance level only. Has it really become more significant, even though the mean difference is smaller? The answer is no. We have more confidence in our ability to generalise to the wider population, using a greater number of participants, but in a way, finding a larger difference with a smaller number of participants is more impressive, because it is harder to find an effect with small participant numbers. Obviously, using five participants as in our first example is both unrealistic and not useful – because we cannot generalise, and using so few participants means that our results stand a high chance of being obtained by sampling error alone. Demonstrating that statistical significance depends on sample size is important, because it shows you that statistical significance does *not necessarily* mean practical or psychological importance. This is why you need other ways of assessing the importance of your study – such as effect sizes and confidence intervals.

Activity 7.3

A researcher runs an experiment with a large number of participants, and power is 0.9. They find *no effect* at all. Which is the most sensible conclusion?

(a) There is an effect but they did not have enough power to find it
(b) They had enough power to find an effect, so it seems likely that there really is no effect

7.4.4 Type of statistical test

Parametric tests are more powerful than non-parametric tests, provided that you meet the assumptions. Thus a t-test is more likely to find an effect than its non-parametric equivalent (see Chapter 15), provided that you have met the assumptions for a parametric test.

7.4.5 The design

Repeated-measures designs increase power because they reduce within-participants variability, as each participant acts as his or her own control. Consider a repeated-measures design rather than an independent design if you can.

7.4.6 One- or two-tailed test

If a one-tailed test is appropriate, then use it. Two-tailed hypotheses require larger sample sizes than one-tailed, to compensate for the loss of power.

7.5 Calculating power

The actual power level (e.g. 0.7) for a particular study or experiment can be calculated by the following:

1. Number of participants in the study.
2. Effect size you are looking for.
3. A criterion probability value (e.g. $p = 0.10$).

Say you decide to run a two-group, independent design, to be analysed with a between-participants t-test (two-tailed). You are thinking of running ten participants in each group and are looking for a medium effect size. Since you know (1), (2) and (3) above, you can calculate power. Often, we do not need to hand calculate because there are computer programs, or textbooks that provide tables (e.g. Stevens, 2002). For our example, we find that, with only ten participants in each group, we have a less than 20% chance of finding an effect, if one exists! Knowing this *before* we carry out our study, we can, if it is possible, increase the number of participants in the study. To have a good chance of finding an effect (e.g. power = 0.7), we will need to find 100 participants (50 in each group) for our study!

Now, if you run a study without calculating power, and then find a significant effect, it was obvious that you had enough power. After all, if you did not have enough power, you would not have found an effect! Therefore, after the experiment, a knowledge of power is more important when you do not find an effect. This is because then you cannot be sure whether (a) there was really no effect, or (b) there was an effect, but you did not have enough power to find it.

Power calculations for all sorts of statistical tests can be found in Howell (2002). The more complex the statistical analysis, the more complex the power calculations. However, hand calculations are becoming less common, with the advent of good statistical packages for power, especially those online programs.

7.5.1 Calculating the number of participants required

It follows from the above that, if you know (a) the power level you want, (b) the effect size and (c) the criterion significance level, then you will find (d) how many participants you need for the study or experiment you intend running. In fact, a knowledge of three of any one of these four parameters will enable you to calculate the fourth. However, students need most often to determine how many participants they need for a particular study. It might be thought that the best idea is to forget all these calculations and just run as many participants as you can, but normally this cannot be done. Often it would not be possible to finance such costly studies. Sometimes your participants are a minority population (e.g. children with brain damage or people with unusual health problems). In this case, it is often difficult to study large numbers of participants.

Anyway, why run hundreds of participants when it is not necessary? As long as you have enough participants, power-wise, you need not obtain more. Imagine a person who has heard about 'bigger sample = more power' and runs 2000 participants. In this case, a minute effect will be declared statistically significant at the $p = 0.0001$. This is a case of statistical significance, but no practical significance. In such cases, a tiny effect (either a small difference between means, or a weak relationship between variables) will have a low associated probability level. This is why you need to look at measures of effects, and confidence intervals, as well as probability levels.

The power calculations given in Howell (2002), for example, would enable you to calculate how many participants you would need for various types of statistical analyses. However, an easier way perhaps, if you decide to hand calculate, is to look at Kraemer and Thieman (1987), who show you how to calculate how many participants you will need for various types of analyses. Statistical power programs such as PASS, or GPOWER, however, present no problems. If you have access to the Internet, then you will be able to find information on various different power packages, some of which can be downloaded free of charge. Others can be performed online. Some statistical texts (such as Stevens, 2002) give useful power tables. SPSSFW gives you power values for some tests: for instance, the factorial ANOVA test (which you will learn about in Chapter 9) includes an estimate of power. However, in other cases you will probably need to use a program such as PASS or GPOWER, or an online power calculator. For those of you who like to hand calculate, see Howell (2002) or Kraemer and Thieman (1987).

7.5.2 The importance of power when no effect has been found

As we mentioned previously, power is particularly important when the effect size that we find is small or non-existent. This is because we cannot tell whether there really *is* an effect, and we have failed to find it, or whether there really is no effect. When you have small effect sizes, therefore, you need to be able to report the power level that you had. In reporting findings that have no statistical significance, some psychologists report how many participants would be needed to find an effect. In cases where the number of participants needed to find an effect is truly enormous (and in most cases it would be unreasonable to expect psychologists to run thousands of participants) this implies that the effect size is so small that *there really is no effect*.

Activity 7.4

Use a search engine on the Internet to find some power programs that you can either download or use online.

Example from the literature:
cognitive therapy and irritable bowel syndrome

Vollmer and Blanchard (1998) assigned patients with irritable bowel syndrome (IBS) to three treatment conditions: group cognitive therapy (GCT), individual cognitive therapy (ICT) and waiting list control (WL). In the GCT condition, there were only three to five patients. Treatment was for 10 weeks. They then compared groups on a variety of measures (e.g. symptom reduction). One of the comparisons they made was between the GCT and the ICT conditions. They calculated the effect size and found it was small. This is how they reported these findings and interpreted them:

A . . . comparison of the GCT and ICT conditions was not significant [F(1,21) = .11, p = .75].[3] The effect size for this comparison indicated that 4% of the variance is explained by the treatment conditions. An equation was generated to find the sample size needed to show a significant difference between the treated groups. With statistical power of .80 and a significance level of .05, 1158 subjects would be needed to obtain a significant difference between GCT and ICT. It thus seems apparent that the two active treatments were equivalent in efficacy for all practical purposes.

Vollmer and Blanchard had all the pieces of information needed to find how many participants they would need to have a good (80%) chance of finding an effect. They had:

- the criterion significance level (0.05)
- the power level they wanted (80%)
- the effect size (4%).

They were thus able to calculate (although they don't tell us how they did it!) the number of participants needed to find an effect. The fact that they would need over 1100 participants to have an 80% chance of finding an effect shows how small the effect is – so small, they conclude, as to be negligible.

7.6 Confidence intervals

Imagine that you ask people to estimate how many students are in the first year of a typical psychology BSc undergraduate degree course. Quite often you would get the reply '140 give or take 5 either way'. In other words, they will produce both a point estimate and

---

[3] *F* is a statistic that you will learn about in Chapter 9.

Table 7.1 A comparison of means for four obstetric groups on eight dependent variables (Maclean *et al.*, 2000, by permission of Taylor & Francis Ltd. www.tandf.co.uk/journals)

Dependent variables	Mode of delivery									f-ratio	f-prob.	Eta² (effect size)
	Spontaneous vaginal delivery (n = 10)		Induced vaginal delivery (n = 10)		Instrumental delivery (forceps & episiotomy) (n = 10)		Emergency caesarean section (n = 10)					
	Mean (SD)	95% confidence interval	Mean (SD)	95% confidence interval	Mean (SD)	95% confidence interval	Mean (SD)	95% confidence interval			
1 Self-perceived risk of serious injury	[a]1.30 (0.95)	0.62–1.98	[b]1.30 (0.48)	0.95–1.65	[abc]4.20 (0.79)	3.64–4.76	[c]1.50 (0.53)	1.12–1.88	*39.65	0.001	0.77
2 Satisfaction with pain relief during labour	2.30 (1.42)	1.29–3.31	2.70 (1.06)	1.94–3.46	4.00 (1.50)	3.25–4.75	1.50 (0.85)	0.89–2.11	*8.77	0.001	0.42
3 Self-reported level of distress during the birth	[a]2.20 (1.32)	1.26–3.14	[b]2.30 (0.95)	1.62–2.98	[abc]4.20 (0.79)	3.64–4.76	[c]2.60 (1.43)	1.58–3.62	*6.56	0.001	0.35
4 Social support: number of extended family living within 5 miles	3.60 (2.79)	1.59–5.60	3.80 (3.19)	1.51–6.08	0.00 (0.00)	0.00–0.00	2.50 (3.27)	0.15–4.84	4.25	0.01	0.06
5 Depressive affect (HAD)	3.20 (2.90)	1.13–5.27	6.90 (3.03)	4.73–9.07	4.20 (2.70)	2.27–6.13	3.70 (2.21)	2.12–5.28	3.66	0.02	0.23
6 Anxiety (HAD)	6.80 (5.14)	3.12–10.48	6.60 (4.01)	3.73–9.47	7.10 (3.35)	4.70–9.50	4.60 (2.91)	2.52–6.68	0.83	0.49	0.07
7 Avoidance response (IES)	4.60 (7.76)	−0.95–10.15	5.90 (3.98)	3.05–8.75	7.00 (6.02)	2.69–11.51	3.80 (2.94)	1.70–5.90	0.66	0.58	0.05
8 Intrusiveness response (IES)	8.00 (8.29)	2.07–13.93	7.10 (4.86)	3.62–10.58	11.30 (7.29)	6.09–16.51	7.90 (8.72)	1.66–14.14	0.63	0.60	0.05

Notes: means with a common superscript are significantly different on a Scheffé test; asterisked *f*-ratios are significant at $p < 0.0063$, the Bonferroni procedure (where $p = 0.05/N$-of-tests [i.e. 8 here] as after Dunn, 1961) having been employed.

an interval estimate. The 140 is their best guess (i.e. a point estimate), and the '5 either way' is an attempt to give a range within which they are fairly certain the correct number falls (i.e. an interval estimate).

The significance of the above is that parametric tests generally involve calculating point estimates of the population mean and population variance. The sample means that we obtain are point estimates of the population means. If we repeated the experiment, however, it is unlikely that we would obtain exactly the same sample means again, and this, of course, means that our estimates could be slightly different from the real population means. It would obviously be helpful, therefore, to obtain an interval estimate within which we could be fairly certain our population means fall. This is what confidence intervals around the mean, which are available under the *Explore* command in SPSSFW, provide. (Confidence intervals were introduced in Chapter 3, page 103)

In Chapter 5 you saw that confidence intervals could be constructed around Pearson's *r*. In Chapter 6 you saw that they could be constructed around means (for the independent t-test) and around the difference between means (for the paired t-test). In Chapter 11 you will see that we can construct confidence intervals around regression lines. For some statistical tests, where SPSSFW does not provide confidence intervals, it is not easy to calculate them. We suggest that, at this stage, you do not worry too much on the occasion when you find you cannot calculate them. Report them when you can, however – they will be very informative to your readers.

Obviously a narrow confidence interval is far more useful than a wide one. The more power your test has (as discussed above), the narrower your confidence intervals will be.

Example from the literature: women's emotional responses to childbirth practices

Maclean *et al.* (2000) compared four groups of women: those who had given birth by spontaneous vaginal delivery; induced vaginal delivery; instrumental vaginal delivery; or caesarean section. There were ten participants in each group. Women were compared on eight dependent variables, by a series of one-way ANOVAs. It is unusual to find a published article which has incorporated all the points of good practice we have mentioned. As you will see in Table 7.1 (opposite), the authors give means, confidence limits, exact probability values, and a measure of effect (Eta^2). You will note that they have used a criterion probability level against which to compare their achieved significance levels. They have given us full information on the way in which the criterion value ($p < 0.0063$) was arrived at. The table is reproduced in full – a template for good practice!

Summary

■ There are several issues to be taken into consideration when designing and running your own studies and experiments. These issues include power, effect size, probability value, number of participants, type of design and statistical test.

■ Power is the ability of the statistical test to find a significant effect, where one exists. Power is on a scale of 0 (no power) through to 1.0 (100% power). Thus 0.5 power would mean that you have a 50% chance of finding a significant effect, where one exists.

■ It is important to take such issues into consideration before running your study or experiment, so that you can maximise your chances of finding an effect. It is not cost effective to run a study that has little chance of finding a significant effect. This means that you should think carefully about your design: for instance, whether it is an independent or repeated-measures design, and the numbers of potential participants in the study.

■ It is important to report effect sizes and confidence intervals when you can.

MULTIPLE CHOICE QUESTIONS

1. The narrower the confidence intervals:
   (a) The more confidence you can place in your results
   (b) The less you can rely on your results
   (c) The greater the chance that your results were due to sampling error
   (d) None of the above

2. Statistical significance:
   (a) Is directly equivalent to psychological importance
   (b) Does not necessarily mean that results are psychologically important
   (c) Depends on sample size
   (d) Both (b) and (c) above

3. All other things being equal, repeated-measures designs:
   (a) Have exactly the same power as independent designs
   (b) Are often less powerful than independent designs
   (c) Are often more powerful than independent designs
   (d) None of the above

4. All other things being equal:
   (a) The more sample size increases, the more power decreases
   (b) The more sample size increases, the more power increases
   (c) Sample size has no relationship to power
   (d) The more sample size increases, the more indeterminate the power

5. Power is the ability to detect:
   (a) A statistically significant effect where one exists
   (b) A psychologically important effect where one exists
   (c) Both (a) and (b) above
   (d) Design flaws

6. Effect size is:
   (a) The magnitude of the difference between conditions
   (b) The strength of a relationship or association
   (c) Both of these
   (d) Neither of these

7. Sample means are:
   (a) Point estimates of sample means
   (b) Interval estimates of population means
   (c) Interval estimates of sample means
   (d) Point estimates of population means

8. All other things being equal, the more powerful the statistical test:
   (a) The wider the confidence intervals
   (b) The more likely the confidence interval will include zero
   (c) The narrower the confidence interval
   (d) The smaller the sample size

9. Power can be calculated by a knowledge of:
   (a) The statistical test, the type of design and the effect size
   (b) The statistical test, the criterion significance level and the effect size
   (c) The criterion significance level, the effect size and the type of design
   (d) The criterion significance level, the effect size and the sample size

10. A power level of 0.3 means:
    (a) You have a 30% chance of detecting an effect
    (b) You have a 49% chance of detecting an effect
    (c) You have a 70% chance of detecting an effect
    (d) You have a 0.7% chance of detecting an effect

11. Look at the following output for an independent t-test:

Independent Samples Test

		Levene's Test for Equality of Variances				t-test for Equality of Means				
									95% Confidence Interval of the Difference	
		F	Sig.	t	df	Sig. (2-tailed)	Mean Difference	Std. Error Difference	Lower	Upper
	Equal variances assumed			−6.807	38	.000	−27.7000	4.0692	−35.9377	−19.4623
	Equal variances not assumed	34.863	.000	−6.807	19.000	.000	−27.7000	4.0692	−36.2169	−19.1831

Which is the most appropriate answer?

We can be 95% confident that:

(a) The population mean difference is 27.7
(b) The population mean will fall between 19.18 and 36.21
(c) The population mean will fall between 19.46 and 35.93
(d) The results will be important

12. A researcher has found a correlation coefficient of $r = +0.30$, CI(95%) $= -0.2 - (+0.7)$. Which is the most sensible conclusion? We are 95% confident that the population regression line would be:

(a) Positive (+0.30)
(b) Zero
(c) Negative (−0.2)
(d) Between −0.2 and +0.7

13. Look at the following output from a paired t-test analysis:

Paired Samples Statistics

		Mean	N	Std. Deviation	Std. Error Mean
Pair 1	congruent-errors	7.500E-02	80	.2651	2.963E-02
	neutral-errors	.2250	80	.7111	7.951E-02

Paired Samples Correlations

		N	Correlation	Sig.
Pair 1	congruent-errors & neutral-errors	80	−.024	.836

Paired Samples Test

		Paired differences			95% Confidence Interval of the Difference		t	df	Sig. (2-tailed)
		Mean	Std. Deviation	Std. Error Mean	Lower	Upper			
Pair 1	congruent-errors − neutral-errors	−.1500	.7647	8.550E-02	−.3202	.02	−1.754	79	.083

Which is the most sensible answer?

(a) The sample mean difference is −0.15, and we are 95% confident that the population mean difference will fall between −0.32 and 0.02
(b) The sample mean difference is 0.76, and we are 95% confident that the population mean difference will fall between −0.32 and 0.02
(c) The sample mean difference is −0.15, and we are 95% confident that the population mean difference will fall between −0.15 and −0.17
(d) The results are important

14. It is more important to know the power of a study when:
    (a) The study has large participant numbers and is statistically significant
    (b) The study has large participant numbers and is not statistically significant
    (c) The study has small participant numbers and is statistically significant
    (d) The study has small participant numbers and is not statistically significant

15. Relative to large effect sizes, small effect sizes are:
    (a) Easier to detect
    (b) Harder to detect
    (c) As easy to detect
    (d) As difficult to detect

16. What are your chances of finding an effect (if one exists) when power = 0.6?
    (a) 50:50
    (b) 60:40
    (c) 40:60
    (d) 60:60

17. Confidence intervals around a mean value gives you:
    (a) A range within which the population mean is likely to fall
    (b) A range within which the sample mean is likely to fall
    (c) A point estimate of the population mean
    (d) A point estimate of the sample mean

18. As your statistical test grows more powerful, does your confidence interval become:
    (a) Wider
    (b) Narrower
    (c) It makes no difference

19. If $d = 0.89$, then the effect size is said to be:
    (a) Zero
    (b) Weak
    (c) Moderate
    (d) Strong

20. When is a knowledge of power more important?
    (a) When you find an effect
    (b) When you don't find an effect
    (c) It makes no difference

References

Cohen, J. (1988) *Statistical Power Analysis for the Behavioral Sciences* (2nd edn). New York: Academic Press.

Dunn, D.J. (1961) 'Multiple comparisons among means', *Journal of the American Statistical Association*, **56**: 52–64.

Howell, D.C. (2002) *Statistical Methods for Psychology* (5th edn). Boston: PWS-Kent.

Kraemer, H.C. and Thieman, S. (1987) *How Many Subjects?* London: Sage.

Krantz, D.H. (1999) 'The null hypothesis testing controversy in psychology', *Journal of the American Statistical Association*, **94**: 1372–81.

Macdonald, R. (1997) 'On statistical testing in psychology', *British Journal of Psychology*, **88**: 333–47.

Maclean, L.I., McDermott, M.R. and May, C.P. (2000) 'Method of delivery and subjective distress: women's emotional responses to childbirth practices', *Journal of Reproductive and Infant Psychology*, **18**(2): 153–62. Journal website http://www.tandf.co.uk/journals.

Nickerson, R.S. (2000) 'Null hypothesis significance testing: a review of an old and continuing controversy', *Psychological Methods*, **5**(2): 241–301.

Rosenthal, R. (1991) 'Cumulating psychology: an appreciation of Donald T. Campbell', *Psychological Science*, **2**(2): 213, 217–21.

Rosnow, R.L. and Rosenthal, R. (1989) 'Statistical procedures and the justification of knowledge in psychological science', *American Psychologist*, **44**(10): 1276–84.

Stevens, J. (2002) *Applied Multivariate Statistics for the Social Sciences* (4th edn). New Jersey: Lawrence Erlbaum Associates.

Vollmer, A. and Blanchard, E.B. (1998) 'Controlled comparison of individual versus group cognitive therapy for irritable bowel syndrome', *Behavior Therapy*, **29**: 19–33.

8 Measures of association

Chapter overview

In Chapter 5 you learned how to analyse the relationship between two variables, using Pearson's r. This test was useful in giving a measure of the association between two continuous variables. You have seen how to represent such relationships on scattergrams, or scatterplots. You learned what was meant by a correlation coefficient, and that r is a natural effect size. This chapter also discusses relationships, or associations, but this time we are going to discuss how to analyse relationships between *categorical* variables.

The measure of association that we are going to discuss in this chapter, χ^2 or chi square (pronounced kye-square), measures the association between two *categorical* variables. You have learned about categorical variables in Chapter 1. If, for instance, we classify people into groups based on which colour blouse or shirt they are wearing, this is a categorical category. In the same way, if we classify people by ethnic group, religion or the country in which they live, these are all categorical judgements; it does not make sense to order them numerically. In this chapter then, you will learn how to

- ■ analyse the association between categorical variables
- ■ report another measure of effect (Cramer's V)
- ■ report the results of such analyses.

The analyses of the relationships between categorical variables include the following:

- ■ *Frequency counts* shown in the form of a table; this will be explained later.
- ■ *Inferential tests* show us whether the relationship between the variables is likely to have been due to sampling error, assuming the null hypothesis is true.
- ■ *Effect size*: χ^2 can be converted to a statistic called Cramer's V – this is interpreted in the same way as any other correlation coefficient. Luckily, this is available through SPSSFW.

8.1 Frequency (categorical) data

The tests you have used so far have involved calculations on sets of scores obtained from participants. Sometimes, however, we have categorical data (i.e. data in the form of frequency counts). For example, let's imagine that we ask a sample of farmers (actually

Table 8.1   Numbers of farmers expressing preferences for pictures of pigs

Picture 1	Picture 2	Picture 3	Picture 4
150	220	60	114

544 of them) which of four pig pictures they prefer for a 'save our bacon' campaign. We would simply record how many chose picture 1, how many chose picture 2, and so on. The data would be frequency counts. Table 8.1 shows the sort of results we might obtain.

You can see, then, that most farmers preferred picture 2. These are frequency counts, so it does not make sense to give any other descriptive statistics.

The above example is known as a *one-variable* χ^2, because we have only one variable. The variable is 'pig pictures'; it has four levels (picture 1 to picture 4).

Note here that each participant can contribute only one count – if you prefer picture 2, you cannot be counted for another category. Categorical data here involve being in one category and one category only; no participant is allowed to be in more than one category. You can see that this makes sense. If we were talking about religion, or ethnic group, for instance, and a person is classified as Catholic, then he or she could not be classified as Salvation Army as well.

With frequency counts, the data are not scores, they are the number of participants that fall into a certain category. χ^2 is particularly appropriate for such data. It is a measure of a relationship, or an association, and was developed by Karl Pearson in 1900. It enables us to see whether the frequency counts we obtain when asking participants which category they are in are significantly different from the frequency counts we would expect by chance.[1] This will be clarified below.

The measures of association that we are going to discuss in this chapter are as follows:

- *One-variable* χ^2 (goodness-of-fit test) – used when we have one variable only, as in the example above.
- χ^2 *test for independence: 2 × 2* – used when we are looking for an association between two variables, with two levels (e.g. the association between drinking alcohol [drinks/does not drink] and smoking [smokes/does not smoke]). Hence the description 2 × 2.
- χ^2 *test for independence: r × 2* – used when we are looking for an association between two variables, where one has two levels (smokes/does not smoke) and the other has more than two levels (heavy drinker, moderate drinker, does not drink). This is called an *r × 2*, because there are several rows and two columns.

---

[1] χ^2 tests can be regarded as testing for an association or difference between categories – it depends on the way the problem is framed.

Activity 8.1

Measures of association test for a relationship between two or more variables. This means the design is:

(a) Repeated-measures
(b) Between-participants
(c) Correlational

8.2 One-variable χ^2 or goodness-of-fit test

This test enables us to discover whether a set of obtained frequencies differs from an expected set of frequencies. Usually the expected frequencies are the ones that we expect to find if the null hypothesis is true, but if we want to, we can compare our observed frequencies with any set of frequencies: we can then see how good the fit is. Details on how to do this follow on page 259. In this case we have one variable only. Working through the calculations for the one-variable test will enable you to understand the rationale underlying the χ^2 2×2 table, and the $r \times c$ tables.

EXAMPLE: PREFERENCE FOR CHOCOLATE BARS

A sample of 110 people were asked which of four chocolate bars they preferred. The numbers of people choosing the different bars were recorded in Table 8.2.

We want to find out whether some brands (or one brand) are preferred over others. If they are not, then we should expect roughly the same number of people in each category. There will not be *exactly* the same number of people in each category, but they should be near enough equal. Another way of saying this is: if the null hypothesis is true, and some brands are not preferred more than others, then all brands should be equally represented.

We have said that we expect roughly equal numbers in the categories, if the null hypothesis is true.

Table 8.2   Number of people preferring different types of chocolate bar

Chocolate A	Chocolate B	Chocolate C	Chocolate D
20 people	60 people	10 people	20 people

20 + 60 + 10 + 20 = 110 people altogether

There are 110 people, and four categories. If the null hypothesis is true then we should expect 110/4 to be in each category, so

110/4 = 27.5

This is because, if all brands of chocolate are equally popular, we would expect roughly equal numbers of people in each category – the numbers of people should be evenly distributed throughout the brands. (Of course, it is impossible to have 27.5 people; but for the purposes of calculating the test statistic, we don't worry about minor details such as this!)

The numbers that we find in the various categories are called the *observed frequencies*.

The numbers that we expect to find in the categories, if the null hypothesis is true (all brands are equally popular), are the *expected frequencies*.

What χ^2 does is to compare the observed frequencies with the expected frequencies. If all brands of chocolate are equally popular, the observed frequencies will not differ much from the expected frequencies. If, however, the observed frequencies differ a lot from the expected frequencies, then it is likely that all brands are not equally popular. It is often difficult to tell just by looking at the data. The chocolate-bar data are reproduced in Table 8.3, showing the way in which people usually set out data suitable for χ^2.

Table 8.3   Observed and expected frequencies for people preferring different types of chocolate bar

Frequencies	Chocolate A	Chocolate B	Chocolate C	Chocolate D
Observed	20	60	10	20
Expected	27.5	27.5	27.5	27.5

Activity 8.2

What's wrong with the following? One hundred people were asked: which is the best-looking cat from those below? The observed frequencies are below:

| 50 | 25 | 15 | 10 | 10 |

8.2.1 How do we find out whether the observed and expected frequencies are similar?

1. Take the expected frequencies away from the observed frequencies:

Observed	Expected	=	Difference
20	27.5	=	−7.5
60	27.5	=	32.5
10	27.5	=	−17.5
20	27.5	=	−7.5
110	110		

We ignore the sign (plus or minus) because we are interested in the absolute value of the differences. (In fact, squaring the numbers, as in step 2, gets rid of the negative signs anyway.)

2. Square all the numbers:

$7.5^2 = 56.25$
$32.5^2 = 1056.25$
$−17.5^2 = 306.25$
$−7.5^2 = 56.25$

3. Divide these figures by a measure of variance (this is similar to what happens in the t-test, or Pearson's r). In this case the measure of variance is the expected frequencies (27.5).

$$\frac{56.25}{27.5} = 2.05$$

$$\frac{1056.25}{27.5} = 38.41$$

$$\frac{306.25}{27.5} = 11.14$$

$$\frac{56.25}{27.5} = 2.05$$

4. The figures are then added to give:

Total = 53.65

So χ^2 is 53.65 (53.7)

The degrees of freedom (DF) is one less than the number of categories, so in this case DF = 3. We need to know this, for it is usual to report the DF, along with the value of χ^2 and the associated probability level.

The χ^2 value of 53.65 is rounded up to 53.7. This value is then compared with the value that would be expected, for a χ^2 with 3 DF, if the null hypothesis were true (i.e. all brands are preferred equally). We do not have to make this comparison, as the statistical package does it for us.

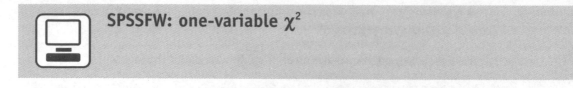

SPSSFW: one-variable χ^2

If you have your data in the form of frequency counts in a table such as the one we have used for the example above, then you can enter data as follows.

Data for the chocolate bars are entered into SPSSFW as follows:

Whenever we enter the data in this way, and perform χ^2, we have to weight the cases by the frequency count. This is done in order to 'tell' SPSSFW that our data are in the form of frequency counts (rather than raw data), and is accomplished as follows:

This opens the *Weight Cases* dialogue box, below:

Make sure the *Weight cases by* box has been checked; move the frequency variable over to the *Frequency Variable* box

Then move *freq* from the left box to the *Frequency Variable* box by clicking on the ▶ button. Click on *OK*. Now click on *Analyze*, *Non-parametric tests* and *Chi-Square* as follows:

This opens the *Chi-Square* dialogue box, as follows:

Click on *Options* if you wish, and then *OK*. The results will appear in the output window.

8.2.2 Output for one-variable χ^2

For a one-variable χ^2, it is important to report the value of the test statistic, the degrees of freedom, and associated probability level. However, the first section of the χ^2 output confirms our calculations in section 8.2.1:

CHOCOLAT

	Observed N	Expected N	Residual
1.00	20	27.5	−7.5
2.00	60	27.5	32.5
3.00	10	27.5	−17.5
4.00	20	27.5	−7.5
Total	110		

The second section of the output gives our test statistics:

Test Statistics

	CHOCOLAT
Chi-Square	53.636[a]
df	3
Asymp. Sig.[1]	.0000

> $p < 0.0001$ meaning that, assuming the null hypothesis is true, our χ^2 value is likely to have arisen only once in 10 000 times: in other words, extremely unlikely!

a. 0 cells (.0%) have expected frequencies less than 5. The minimum expected cell frequency is 27.5.

The textual part of the results might read:

The χ^2 value of 53.6, DF = 3 was found to have an associated probability value of 0.0001. This means that, if the null hypothesis were true, such a value would rarely occur (once in ten thousand). Thus we can accept that there is a significant difference between the observed and expected frequencies, and can conclude that all brands of chocolate are not equally popular. The table below shows that more people prefer chocolate B (60) than the other bars of chocolate.

Frequencies	Chocolate A	Chocolate B	Chocolate C	Chocolate D
Observed	20	60	10	20
Expected	27.5	27.5	27.5	27.5

Although our conclusion is that people do prefer some brands rather than others (not all brands are equally liked), we can say more than this: we can look at the table and say which brands are preferred – that is, we can talk about the direction of the difference, i.e. chocolate B is preferred more than the other chocolate bars.

Activity 8.3

The goodness-of-fit test is also known as the:

(a) $r \times c \; \chi^2$
(b) One-variable χ^2
(c) $2 \times 2 \; \chi^2$
(d) None of the above

---

[1] SPSS now gives 2 sorts of significance tests for crosstabs and non-parametric tests. Asymp. Sig. stands for Asymptotic Significance and is based on large samples. Exact Sig. is used when the data set is small, unbalanced or does not meet the assumption of normality.

8.2.3 Comparing observed frequencies with any set of expected frequencies

Sometimes we want to compare our observed frequencies with a particular set of expected frequencies. For instance, researchers have found that left-handed people are over-represented in people with Inflammatory Bowel Disease. That is, the prevalence of left-handers is higher than would be expected in that sample of people. Let's assume that we tested 150 people with IBD and found the following:

	Right-handed	Left-handed
Observed	120	30
Expected under the null hypothesis	75	75

If you simply divided 150 by 2 in order to find the expected frequencies under the null hypothesis, you would end up with 75. It should be immediately apparent that we do not expect there to be equal numbers of people who are right- and left-handed in the population, because we know that there are far fewer left-handed people in the population than right-handers. The real expected frequencies are the ones that we *know* from previous research that exist in the population. There is also a sex difference in handedness – the prevalence of left-handedness is greater in men than women. This means that men and women cannot be included together in one group. Approximately 10% of women are left-handed.

We decided to see whether there was a greater prevalence of left-handedness in women with Irritable Bowel Syndrome (IBS) rather than IBD. Three hunded and seventeen women were given a questionnaire that included questions on handedness; 268 of them were right-handed, and 49 were left-handed. As we expect 90% of women to be right-handed, then we would expect 285.3 of our sample to be right-handed (90% of 317 = 285.3). This means that we expect 31.7 of them to be left-handed (317 − 285.3 = 31.7).

	Right	Left
	n	*n*
Observed	268	49
Expected	285.3	31.7

We actually found that only 268 were right-handed – this represents 84.5% of the total 317. 49 were left-handed – representing 15.5% of the total, rather than the 10% that we would expect to find.

SPSSFW: one-variable χ^2: using frequencies different from those expected under the null hypothesis

Open up the datafile. Select *Data*, *Weight Cases*:

This opens up the *Weight Cases* dialogue box, as follows:

Move the 'Frequency' variable here

Check the *Weight cases by* option, and move the *frequency* variable from the left to the right, then click on *OK*. This brings you back to the original datafile.

Select *Analyze*, *Nonparametric Tests*, *Chi-Square*:

This opens the *Chi-Square Test* dialogue box, as follows:

The test variable, 'hand', is moved here

Make sure the correct variable (in this case *hand*) is moved from the left to the *Test Variable List*. Note that under *Expected Values* you can choose *All categories equal* (which is what we would use normally; it's the default) or *Values* (which means we choose the expected values ourselves). In this case, check *Values* and type in the expected frequency of the first category (right hand), which is 285.3. Then click on *Add*:

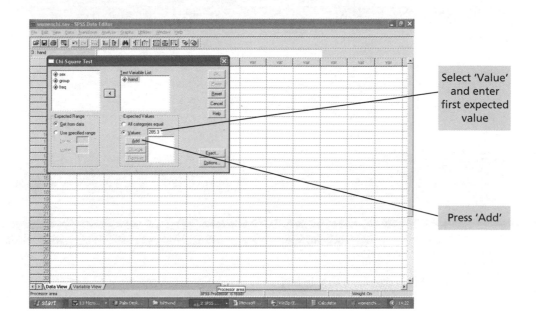

Type in the expected frequency of the second category (left hand), which is 31.7, and click on *Add*:

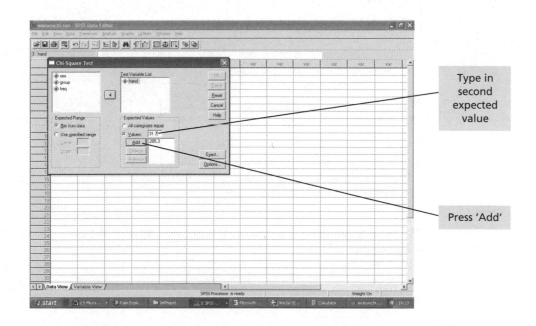

Finally, click on *OK*:

This obtains a simple output:

HAND

	Observed N	Expected N	Residual
right	268	285.3	−17.3
left	49	31.7	17.3
Total	317		

Test Statistics

	HAND
Chi-Square[a]	10.490
df	1
Asymp. Sig.	.001

a. 0 cells (.0%) have expected frequencies less than 5.
The minimum expected cell frequency is 31.7.

This shows that there is a significant difference between the observed and the expected frequencies.

8.3 χ^2 test for independence: 2 × 2

χ^2 enables us to discover whether there is a relationship or association between two categorical variables (e.g. the association between smoking [smokes/does not smoke] and drinking [drinks/does not drink]). This is categorical data, because we are not asking about how many cigarettes people smoke, or how much alcohol they drink. We are simply asking whether they smoke and drink. Such a design would look like Table 8.4.

This type of *contingency table* is called a 2 × 2 because there are two rows and two columns.

Table 8.4   2 × 2 contingency table

	Drink	Do not drink
Smoke		
Do not smoke		

EXAMPLE: ASSOCIATION BETWEEN SMOKING AND DRINKING

Is there a relationship between smoking cigarettes and drinking alcohol in students? If there is no significant association, then we conclude that the variables are independent of each other. (It is possible to ask each student how many cigarettes they smoke per week and how many units of alcohol they drink per week. In this case, you could use Pearson's *r*, as you would have continuous data.) If you simply asked the following questions:

A.   How many of you smoke and drink?
B.   How many smoke but do not drink?
C.   How many do not smoke but do drink?
D.   How many abstain from both?

you would not have interval, or ordinal, data. You would have frequencies; that is, the number of students in each group. Here we will be considering measuring an association when you have frequency, or categorical, data.

So we are using smoking and drinking as categorical data (i.e. we are not considering how many cigarettes they smoke, or how much alcohol they are consuming; we are simply asking which of the four categories they fall into).

You can represent this as a 2 × 2 table. Imagine that we have asked 110 students the above questions. Each student can fall into only one group. Thus we have four groups. We count the numbers of students falling into the groups, and write it in the form of a table (Table 8.5). Each 'box' is called a *cell*. We code the groups: (1) those who drink, (2) those who do not drink; (1) those who smoke, (2) those who do not smoke. We could, however, just as easily code it the other way round, and we do not have to use 1 and 2 as codes. Often psychologists use 0 and 1.

Table 8.5   2 × 2 contingency table with labelled codings

	Smoke (coded 1)	Do not smoke (coded 2)
Drink (coded 1)	50 (A)	15 (C)
Do not drink (coded 2)	20 (B)	25 (D)

We have chosen to call the cells by letters. Cell A is for people who both smoke and drink; cell D is for people who do neither. Thus:

Group 1: 50 (cell A)
Group 2: 20 (cell B)
Group 3: 15 (cell C)
Group 4: 25 (cell D)

The data can be written as shown in Table 8.6.

Table 8.6   Data table with codings

Smoke	Drink	Frequency
1	1	50
1	2	20
2	1	15
2	2	25

So, in smoke category 1 (do smoke) with drink category 1 (do drink) there are 50 students. This is represented by the 2 × 2 contingency table as cell A.

Note that no participant can be in more than one cell. *This is important.* Categories are mutually exclusive.

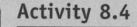

Activity 8.4

Decide whether the following situations are best suited to Pearson's *r* or χ^2. The relationships between:

(a) Height (cm) and weight (kg)
(b) Distance run (metres) and time taken (minutes and seconds)
(c) A person's body shape and occupational level (professional, clerical, manual)
(d) Length of finger and length of toe (cm)
(e) Handedness (right or left) and spatial ability (excellent, average, hopeless)

8.3.1 The rationale for 2 × 2 chi square

The test calculates the expected frequencies in the cells. In other words, there are 110 students. The test calculates how many we can expect to find in each cell, if there is really no relationship between smoking and drinking (i.e. the null hypothesis is true).

The expected frequencies for each cell are computed in a way similar to the one-variable case of χ^2, except that, since we have different numbers of people who smoke and drink, the expected frequencies in the cells will be different.

The resulting χ^2 value is compared with the value that would be expected to have arisen if the null hypothesis were true (i.e. there really is no association between the two variables). Your computer package calculates this for you – this is the meaning of the probability value – it is the probability of your particular value of χ^2 having arisen, assuming the null hypothesis is true.

We have to tell you now that the frequencies listed above are unrealistic. Now, we are more likely to get the following (Table 8.7).

The trouble with this is that χ^2 has an assumption: you must not have more than 25% of cells (in this case 25% of 4 = 1) with an *expected* frequency of less than 5. We cannot tell by looking at the table whether we have broken this assumption. SPSSFW will alert you to this problem, however, and proceed to calculate Fisher's Exact Probability Test for you; lucky, because the calculations can be tedious. Fisher's Test is appropriate only for 2 × 2 tables, however.

This test can be used instead of χ^2 when the assumption is broken, because the formula is not sensitive to small expected frequencies.

Table 8.7   2 × 2 contingency table

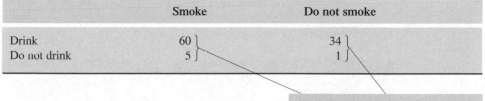

	Smoke	Do not smoke
Drink	60	34
Do not drink	5	1

These are the *observed* frequencies

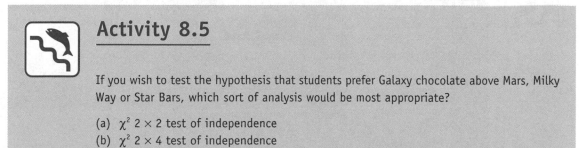

Activity 8.5

If you wish to test the hypothesis that students prefer Galaxy chocolate above Mars, Milky Way or Star Bars, which sort of analysis would be most appropriate?

(a) χ^2 2 × 2 test of independence
(b) χ^2 2 × 4 test of independence
(c) One-variable χ^2
(d) None of the above

SPSSFW: 2 × 2 χ^2

Weight your cases by following the same instructions as for the one-variable χ^2. Then choose *Analyze*, *Descriptive Statistics* and *Crosstabs*:

This brings up the following dialogue box:

'drink' is moved to the row

'smoke' is moved to the column

Move *drink* over to the rows box and *smoke* over to the columns box. Click on *Statistics*. This gives you the following dialogue box:

Check the statistics you require

You can then check the statistics you require, by checking *Chi-square* and *Cramer's V* (via the *Phi and Cramer's V* box).

Click on *Continue* (this brings you back to the previous dialogue box). If you want cell display, click on *Cells*. This gives you the following:

This will give you the observed and expected frequencies

Click on the options you require. You can choose to have a table of observed and expected frequencies on their own, or you can select to have row, column and total percentages. Click on *Continue*. Once back to the *Crosstabs* dialogue box, click on *OK*. Your results will appear in the output window. The observed and expected frequencies are given below:

DRINK * SMOKE Crosstabulation

			SMOKE		Total
			smoke	dont smoke	
DRINK	drink	Count	60	34	94
		Expected Count	61.1	32.9	94.0
	don't drink	Count	5	1	6
		Expected Count	3.9	2.1	6.0
Total		Count	65	35	100
		Expected Count	65.0	35.0	100.0

This shows we have broken one of the assumptions of chi square. That is, that there should not be more than 25% of cells with an expected frequency of less than 5. We have two cells where the expected frequencies are below 5. In this case we would probably want to increase the sample size. You might have to include considerably more participants in the study, to solve this problem.

8.3.2 Output for 2 × 2 χ^2

The output of χ^2 will give you information that is superfluous to your needs, so, as in previous tests, you learn to glance over it quite quickly. The first part of the output reproduces your 2 × 2 table: just glance at this to make sure it is correct.

χ^2 statistics

SPSSFW prints out several lines of statistics. However, the one you need is the first one listed. This is called *Pearson*, and you need to report the value of (Pearson's) χ^2, the degrees of freedom and the associated probability level.

Cramer's V

This is a measure of effect used for tests of association; it is a correlation coefficient, interpreted in the same way as Pearson's *r*.

This output uses the following data:

- 50 people both smoke and drink
- 15 people drink but do not smoke
- 20 people smoke but do not drink
- 25 people abstain from both.

The first section of the output confirms the categories and frequencies:

DO YOU DRINK * DO YOU SMOKE CROSSTABULATION

Count

			do you smoke		Total
			yes	no	
do you drink		yes	50	15	65
		no	20	25	45
Total			70	40	110

The next section of the output gives the test statistics:

$$\chi^2 = 12.12$$

Chi-Square Tests

	Value	df	Asymp. Sig. (2-sided)	Exact Sig. (2-sided)	Exact Sig. (1-sided)
Pearson Chi-Square	**12.121**[b]	**1**	**.000**		
Continuity Correction[a]	10.759	1	.001		
Likelihood Ratio	12.153	1	.000		
Fisher's Exact Test				.001	.001
Linear-by-Linear Association	12.011	1	.001		
N of Valid Cases	110				

a. Computed only for a 2 × 2 table
b. 0 cells (.0%) have expected count less than 5. The minimum expected count is 16.36.

The emboldened row is the one that interests us. You need to read the *Pearson Chi-square* row, which is the emboldened one above. So our χ^2 value is 12.12, DF = 1, $p < 0.001$. So the probability of obtaining a χ^2 of this magnitude is very remote – less than 1 in a 1000 chance . . . therefore we conclude that there is an association between smoking and drinking – in students anyway.

Our output also gives Cramer's V: this shows an effect size of 0.33. If you square 0.33 you will obtain a value of 0.1089. Thus nearly 11% of the variation in frequency counts of smoking can be explained by drinking.

Symmetric measures

		Value	Asymp. Std. Error[a]	Approx. T[b]	Approx. Sig.
Nominal by Nominal	Phi	.332			.000
	Cramer's V	**.332**			**.000**
Interval by Interval	Pearson's R	.332	.092	3.657	.000[c]
Ordinal by Ordinal	Spearman Correlation	.332	.092	3.657	.000[c]
N of Valid Cases		110			

a. Not assuming the null hypothesis.
b. Using the asymptotic standard error assuming the null hypothesis.
c. Based on normal approximation.

In your report, you would show the frequency counts in the form of a 2 × 2 cross-tabulation table, and also give the χ^2 value, DF and associated probability level.

The textual part of your report might read as follows:

A 2 × 2 χ^2 was carried out to discover whether there was a significant relationship between smoking and drinking. The χ^2 value of 12.12 had an associated probability value of < 0.001, DF = 1, showing that such an association is extremely unlikely to have arisen as a result of sampling error. Cramer's V was found to be 0.33 – thus nearly 11% of the variation in frequencies of smoking can be explained by drinking. It can therefore be concluded that there is a significant association between smoking and drinking.

Have you broken the assumptions for χ^2?

If you have, then Fisher's Exact Probability Test will be on your output, and the line saying *Cells with expected frequency < 5* will tell you the percentage of cells that you have with an expected frequency of less than 5.

In this case, instead of reporting the values in the paragraph above, you report the exact probability level given by Fisher's (e.g. Fisher's Exact Probability = 0.66). Fisher's does not have a *value* like a t-test or χ^2. The following output shows you what to expect if you have more than 25% of cells with an expected frequency of less than 5.

The first section of the output is simply the categories and frequency values:

DO YOU DRINK * DO YOU SMOKE CROSSTABULATION

Count

			do you smoke		Total
			yes	no	
do you drink	yes		60	34	94
	no		5	1	6
Total			65	35	100

We then have the test statistics:

Chi-Square Tests

	Value	df	Asymp. Sig. (2-sided)	Exact Sig. (2-sided)	Exact Sig. (1-sided)
Pearson Chi-Square[a]	.943[b]	1	.332		
Continuity Correction	.281	1	.596		
Likelihood Ratio	1.057	1	.304		
Fisher's Exact Test				**.662**	**.312**
Linear-by-Linear Association	.934	1	.334		
N of Valid Cases	100				

a. Computed only for a 2 × 2 table
b. 2 cells (50.0%) have expected count less than 5. The minimum expected count is 2.10.

Warning: assumption broken, therefore use Fisher's Exact Test (the emboldened row)

The emboldened row shows the probability of obtaining a value of 0.94 when the null hypothesis is assumed to be true – 66% for a two-tailed hypothesis, and 31% for a one-tailed hypothesis.

Symmetric Measures

		Value	Approx. Sig.
Nominal by Nominal	Phi	–.097	.332
	Cramer's V	**.097**	**.332**
N of Valid Cases		100	

This is the measure of effect

a. Not assuming the null hypothesis.
b. Using the asymptotic standard error assuming the null hypothesis.

The textual part of your report might read as follows:

Since 50% of the cells had an expected frequency of less than 5, the appropriate statistical test was Fisher's Exact Probability. This gave $p = 0.66$ for a two-tailed hypothesis. The value of Cramer's V was 0.10, showing that the relationship between smoking and drinking was almost zero. The conclusion, therefore, is that there is no evidence to suggest an association between drinking and smoking.

A 2×2 χ^2 square is easy to work out by hand once you are used to it, but we will not ask you to do it. The instructions on how to perform a 2×2 χ^2 analysis on SPSSFW were given on page 272.

CAUTION!

You cannot tell how many people are going to fall into each category when you start your study, so you need to obtain far more participants than you think you need, to make sure you have enough participants in each cell.

χ^2 is always positive (because a squared number is always positive).

Whereas degrees of freedom roughly equates to the number of participants in most statistical analyses, it does not in χ^2, as DF is calculated by number of rows minus 1 $(r-1)$ multiplied by number of columns minus 1 $(c-1)$. In this case, you can see that a 2×2 χ^2 will always have DF = 1 because $(r-1) \times (c-1) = (2-1) \times (2-1) = 1$.

Activity 8.6

Cramer's V is:

(a) A measure of difference
(b) A correlation coefficient
(c) An equivalent statistic to Fisher's Exact Probability Test
(d) A CV value

8.4 χ^2 test of independence: $r \times c$

What if you have more than two levels? It is perfectly possible to have more rows and columns. We still have two categorical variables, but this time we have more categories to choose from. χ^2 can handle this quite easily. Let's assume, staying with our smoke/drink example, that we have three levels of *smoke*: heavy smokers, light smokers and non-smokers. We could also have heavy drinkers, light drinkers and teetotallers (see Table 8.8).

This is a 3×3 contingency table, for obvious reasons. The calculations are worked out in exactly the same way as we have described for the 2×2 table. The degrees of freedom, however, will be different.

Table 8.8 3×3 contingency table

	Heavy smokers	Light smokers	Non-smokers
Heavy drinkers			
Light drinkers			
Teetotallers			

Remember: DF = $(c - 1) \times (r - 1)$
So: $2 \times 2 = 4$

It is also possible to have more than three levels (e.g. 6×4 or 7×3), but interpretation then becomes a problem. We do not just want to say 'there is a significant relationship between variable A and variable B'. We would also like to be able to say something about the *direction* of the relationship. For instance, in our smoke/drink example, we could see, from looking at the cells, that the significant relationship referred to the *positive* association between drinking and smoking. When we have larger contingency tables, it can be difficult to disentangle all the various relationships.

Also, for the test statistic to be reliable, remember:

■ No more than 25% of cells should have an *expected* frequency of less than 5.
■ No cell should contain less than 1 (if they do, you may be able to collapse cells, i.e. ex-smokers and smokers could be added together to form one group; however, sometimes it is not possible to collapse cells in this way, because the cells do not have enough in common).

You may be wondering why we have to meet these assumptions. It is because we assume that we are sampling from a normal population. If the expected cell sizes are so small, it is unlikely that we are sampling from a normal population. Our test statistic will be unreliable unless we meet the assumptions.

Check that participants do *not* appear in more than one cell. Remember that we are checking to see if the numbers of participants in each cell are independent – obviously they will not be if they are the same participants! So the same participants must *not* respond more than once. The total of the cell frequencies must equal the number of participants.

There is no reason why the χ^2 test cannot be used with quantitative variables – it is just that, with quantitative data, other tests, such as the parametric ones, will be more powerful.

Activity 8.7

True or false?

(a) χ^2 needs to have equal numbers of participants in each cell
(b) Each participant must contribute to every cell
(c) You must have < 50% of your cells with an expected frequency of 5 in order to perform χ^2
(d) The same participant can count in more than one category

8.4.1 χ^2: a one- or two-tailed test?

There are debates among statisticians as to whether we should use one- or two-tailed tests. You cannot go wrong if you use a two-tailed test, because you are less likely to declare a result *significant* when using such a test. Some people think you should always use a two-tailed hypothesis when using χ^2. The test *itself* is one-tailed: the χ^2 value will be the same whether the figures look like this:

15	40
36	22

or this:

36	15
22	40

like this:

22	36
40	15

or this:

40	22
15	36

The sampling distribution of χ^2 is always positive. That is, because χ^2 value is a *squared* figure, it is always positive. This is what we mean by saying that the test itself is one-tailed: it gives you values only in the positive range – it is impossible to obtain a negative χ^2 value.

However, your *hypothesis* can be two-tailed (there is an association, but you are not predicting the direction of the association) or, more likely, one-tailed (you predict the direction of the association, e.g. smoking and cancer are related in a positive way or, in a one-variable χ^2, brand A chocolate is preferred significantly more often than the other brands). However, one-tailed tests should be formulated on the basis of previous theory – not just because you felt that chocolate A was better than all the other bars. Some people feel that if we use a one-tailed test, and then the relationship is found to be opposite to the one we are predicting, then we have 'lost out', but of course that is the case with any one-tailed prediction (see Chapter 4, page 145 for more on this).

If we have good reason to specify a direction of the association, then it is quite valid to use a one-tailed hypothesis, but you must decide *before* you do your analysis (i.e. you have to think carefully about whether your hypothesis is one- or two-tailed *before* the study).

Example from the literature: social class and tranquillisers

Bish *et al.* (1996) wanted to see whether social class is associated with frequency of tranquilliser use. A group of people who managed to reduce their tranquilliser use, and a group who did not, were classified in terms of their social class. The results were as recorded in Table 8.9.

As you can see from Table 8.9, it appears that a larger percentage of the group who did not reduce their tranquilliser use are working class. χ^2 analysis, however, shows that the likelihood of obtaining the χ^2 value of 0.18, given the null hypothesis to be true (no association), is higher than is acceptable

Table 8.9   Results from Bish *et al.* (1996) study

	Tranquilliser reduction group	Tranquilliser non-reduction group
Middle class	9 (53%)	5 (38%)
Working class	8 (47%)	8 (62%)
$\chi^2 = 0.18$, n.s.		

and so we do not accept that there is a significant association between tranquilliser use and social class. Bish *et al.* do not give us the associated probability value for their χ^2 value of 0.18, but you can calculate this for yourself later.

Sometimes in the literature you will find researchers who have used Yates' correction for continuity. This is a slight adjustment to the formula, used when we have small expected frequencies, in a 2×2 table. In the late 1980s, psychologists were routinely advised to use Yates' correction, but now many people feel it is unreasonable and unnecessary to do this (see Howell, 2002, for debate on this issue). You will note that the SPSSFW output (see page 277) also reports a χ^2 value, corrected for continuity. We recommend that, as introductory students, you do not worry about such corrections. Note, however, that some of the journal articles you read will report the use of Yates' correction.

Example from the literature: family representations in relationship episodes of bulimic patients

Benninghoven *et al.* (2003) studied the ways in which patients suffering from bulimia nervosa differed from other patients in psychotherapy and from non-clinical control participants in terms of the way they perceived their ongoing and their past family relationships. It is often important to show that such groups do not differ on demographic variables – so that any differences on the variables of interest (in this case perception of relationships) cannot be attributed to differences in, say, age or professional status. As part of Benninghoven *et al.*'s study then, they looked at the association between the different groups in terms of professional status. They reported as shown in Table 8.10. It can be seen that this is a 3×4 χ^2. The degrees of freedom are $(n - 1) \times (n - 2)$ which is $(3 - 1) \times (4 - 1) = 6$. $\chi^2 = 3.5$ with an associated probability of 0.744. Thus there is no significant association between the three groups, and professional status.

Table 8.10   Groups by professional status: frequencies and χ^2 statistics

Professional status %	Bulimia	Clinical Controls	Non-clinical Controls	By χ^2 test		
				χ^2	DF	*p*
Worker	18	28	15	3.5	6	0.744
Trainee	12	11	10			
Student at university	71	56	75			
Housewife	0	6	0			

Summary

- For the analysis of relationships between categorical variables, χ^2 is the appropriate inferential statistic.

- A one-variable χ^2 (or goodness-of-fit test) has one variable with several levels. The test shows whether the frequencies in the cells are significantly different from what we would expect, assuming the null hypothesis to be true.

- A χ^2 test for independence shows whether there is a significant association between two variables (with two or more levels). The test statistic results from a calculation showing the degree by which the observed frequencies in the cells are different from the frequencies we would expect, assuming the null hypothesis to be true (i.e. no relationship).

- χ^2 has certain assumptions (see page 269). If these are broken, then for a 2 × 2 table, Fisher's Exact Probability Test can be performed. This is automatically done in SPSSFW.

- χ^2 can be converted to Cramer's V (a correlation coefficient) to give a measure of effect. This is performed automatically in SPSSFW.

SPSSFW exercises

Exercise 1

Use the data from Bish *et al.* (1996) on page 281 in order to perform a 2 × 2 χ^2 on SPSSFW. What do you note about their analysis?

Exercise 2

Perform a 2 × 2 analysis on your computer package.

	Smoke	Do not smoke
Drink		
Do not drink		

Is there a relationship between drinking and smoking in your class?

1. What is the χ^2 value?

2. What is the probability value?

3. What do the results tell you?

Exercise 3

Thirty-three people were given an animal preference questionnaire and classified as to whether they preferred mice, spiders, bats or snakes. The results were as follows:

Mice	Spiders	Bats	Snakes
10	8	11	4

1. What are the expected frequencies for the four cells?
2. What is the χ^2 value?
3. What is the probability value?
4. What can you conclude from the results?

Exercise 4

Perform a χ^2 on the following data:

	Smoke	Do not smoke
Drink	70	32
Do not drink	7	1

Report the results and explain what they mean.

DISCUSSION POINT: χ^2 OR T-TEST?

Look at the following newspaper cuttings and decide for each whether you would use χ^2 or t-test.

A: And there's a chance of rain on Thursdays

From Professor MJ
> *Sir, NP (Letters, 24th July) attempts to explain GN's findings (Letters, 22nd July) that Thursday is the wettest day of the week. No explanation is needed. The variation in the figures for the seven days is purely random, as any statistician can assure you.*
>
> *The total rainfall for all seven days is 938.9, giving an average of 134.13. This average is the expected figure for each day if rainfall is distributed equally over the seven days. A Chi-square test may be used to compare the seven observed figures with the expected one. The resultant Chi-square value of 1.28 for 6 degrees of freedom is far too small to demonstrate any significant difference from expectation. In fact, chance would produce this amount of difference at least 95 times out of 100.*

Yours faithfully,

B: The wettest day of the week put to test

From Mr AF

Sir, It may seem impertinent for a simple graduate to criticise his betters, but surely Professor MJ has used the wrong statistical test in his letter (27 July). The Chi-square test is used to test frequencies of occurrence. In this case we have interval data and should use a t-test, requiring a knowledge of the standard deviations of the sets of data. Notwithstanding this, the result will probably be similar.

In my view, Thursday is the wettest day as it is the first day of a Test Match. The selectors use this information to pick four seamers who then prove woefully inadequate for the remaining four dry days.

Yours faithfully,

MULTIPLE CHOICE QUESTIONS

1. Fisher's Exact Probability Test is used when:
    (a) The calculations for χ^2 are too difficult
    (b) You have more than 25% of cells with expected frequencies of less than 5 in a 2×2 design
    (c) You have more than 25% of cells with expected frequencies of less than 5 in a 3×2 contingency table
    (d) You have non-categorical data

2. Cramer's V is:
    (a) A victory sign made after performing Cramer's statistical test
    (b) A measure of effect based on standardised scores
    (c) A correlational measure of effect converted from χ^2
    (d) A measure of difference

Questions 3 to 5 relate to the following output:

DAY OF WEEK * SEX CROSSTABULATION

Count

			SEX		Total
		men	women		
day of week	tuesday am	21	210		231
	wednesday am	43	127		170
	evening	25	99		124
Total		89	436		525

Chi-Square Tests

	Value	df	Asymp. Sig. (2-sided)
Pearson Chi-Square	19.450[a]	2	.000
Likelihood Ratio	20.208	2	.000
Linear-by-Linear Association	10.429	1	.001
N of Valid Cases	525		

a. 0 cells (.0%) have expected count less than 5. The minimum expected count is 21.02.

3. How many women were in the Tuesday morning group?

   (a) 127
   (b) 43
   (c) 99
   (d) 210

4. Pearson's χ^2 has an associated probability of:

   (a) < 0.001
   (b) 0.00004
   (c) 0.00124
   (d) None of these

5. The number of people in this analysis is:

   (a) 231
   (b) 170
   (c) 124
   (d) 525

6. 290 people are asked which of five types of cola they prefer. Results are as follows:

Coca Cola	Pepsi	Diet Coke	Cheapo	Pepsi Lite
67	83	77	6	57

   What are the expected frequencies for the cells:

   (a) 57
   (b) 58
   (c) 290
   (d) None of the above

7. Look at the following output:

Chi-Square Tests

	Value	df	Asymp. Sig. (2-sided)
Pearson Chi-Square	14.3212	1	.00050
Likelihood Ratio	14.3722	1	.00004
Linear-by-Linear Association	14.3521	1	.00005

χ^2 has an associated probability of:

(a) 0.00005
(b) 0.00004
(c) 0.00200
(d) 0.00050

8. Look at the following table:

	Statistics	Child development	Psychobiology	Cognitive Psychology
observed	72	31	15	50
expected				

What is the value of the expected frequencies?

(a) 32
(b) 50
(c) 42
(d) 25

9. A one-variable χ^2 is also called:

(a) Goodness-of-fit test
(b) χ^2 test of independence
(c) χ^2 4×2
(d) 2×2 χ^2

10. The value of χ^2 will always be:

(a) Positive
(b) Negative
(c) High
(d) It depends

11. The Yates' correction is sometimes used by researchers when:

(a) Cell sizes are huge
(b) Cell sizes are small
(c) They analyse data from 2×2 contingency tables
(d) Both (b) and (c) above

Questions 12 to 14 relate to the following (partial) output, which is the result of a χ^2 analysis investigating the association between body shape and type of sports played:

Chi-Square Tests

	Value	df	Asymp. Sig. (2-sided)
Pearson Chi-Square	22.305[a]	9	.00796
Likelihood Ratio	21.516	9	.01055
Linear-by-Linear Association	12.162	1	.00049
N of Valid Cases	525		

a. 0 cells (.0%) have expected count less than 5. The minimum expected count is 21.02.

	Cramer's V	.09943	.00796

a. Not assuming the null hypothesis.
b. Using the asymptotic standard error assuming the null hypothesis.

12. The χ^2 value is:
    (a) 12.162
    (b) 21.516
    (c) 22.305
    (d) 525

13. The χ^2 value has an exact probability level of:
    (a) 0.0004
    (b) 0.05
    (c) 0.01055
    (d) 0.00796

14. The value of Cramer's V is:
    (a) 0.05
    (b) 0.008
    (c) 0.099
    (d) 0.010

15. Look at the following 2×2 contingency table, taken from 150 participants:

	Drink tea	Drink coffee
Feel terrific	70	50
Feel lousy	30	80

There is something wrong with the above, in that the numbers in the cells should:
    (a) Add up to 150
    (b) Add up to 100
    (c) Be equal
    (d) Be analysed by a 4×3 χ^2

16. 485 people are asked which of five types of bird pictures they prefer to be put on a 'stop all wars' campaign. Results are as follows:

| 162 | 84 | 57 | 94 | 88 |

What are the expected frequencies for the cells?

(a) 79
(b) 97
(c) 485
(d) 5

17. In order to find out the effect size after performing a χ^2 analysis, we:

(a) convert Cramers V to χ^2
(b) convert χ^2 to Cramers V
(c) Square the χ^2 value
(d) convert χ^2 to Fisher's Z

18. Look at the following table.

	Anxious	Not anxious
Dreadful job	210	150
Wonderful job	62	52

This is called a:

(a) 2×2 contingency table
(b) 3×2 contingency table
(c) 1×2 chi square table
(d) 2×2 chi square table

19. The general purpose for which a 2×2 χ^2 analysis is used is to discover whether:

(a) There is a significant association between two categorical variables
(b) There is an association between two continuous variables
(c) Two groups of participants differ on two variables
(d) None of the above

20. If you are performing a 4×4 χ^2 analysis and find you have broken the assumptions, then you need to:

(a) Look at the results for a Fisher's exact probability test
(b) Look to see whether it is possible to collapse categories
(c) Investigate the possibility of a t-test
(d) Give up

References

Benninghoven, D., Schneider, H., Sttrack, M., Reich, G. and Cierpka, M. (2003) 'Family representations in relationship episodes of patients with a diagnosis of bulimia nervosa', *Psychology & Psychotherapy*, **76**(3): 323–36.

Bish, A., Golombok, S., Hallstrom, C. and Fawcett, S. (1996) 'The role of coping strategies in protecting individuals against long-term tranquillizer use', *British Journal of Medical Psychology*, **69**(2): 101–15.

Howell, D.C. (2002) *Statistical Methods for Psychology* (5th edn). Boston: PWS-Kent.

9 Analysis of differences between three or more conditions: one-factor ANOVA

Chapter overview

In previous chapters you learned how to compare two conditions, and how to analyse relationships between two variables. As part of these analyses you learned how to report effect sizes, confidence intervals and achieved significance levels (ASLs). You now have all the tools you need to go on to a more complicated analysis – the analysis of three or more conditions. You are used to the idea of comparing two conditions (see Chapter 6), and the analysis of three or more conditions is just an extension of this. Instead of the t-tests, for two conditions, we now have ANOVA (for three or more conditions). ANOVA is the parametric equivalent of the t-test, for more than two groups. ANOVA is an acronym for Analysis of Variance. As in the t-test, you need to meet certain assumptions in order to be able to perform ANOVA. You will recognise these from your work on the t-test:

■ Scores must be drawn from a normally distributed population. We assume this is the case if our sample data show a normal distribution: the more participants we have in the study, the more likely it is that the distribution will be normal (see Chapter 2, page 70).
■ Homogeneity of variance. This means that the variances are similar for the different groups. SPSSFW will test for this. In the case of the independent ANOVA, the test is called Levene's Test. In the case of the repeated-measures ANOVA, it is F Max.
■ In a repeated-measures analysis, there is an additional assumption – that of sphericity. However, there is an adjustment used in repeated-measures ANOVA when this assumption has been violated. The adjustment is called the Greenhouse–Geisser Epsilon, and is given routinely in SPSSFW.

ANOVA is relatively robust in respect of these assumptions, so that small violations (e.g. you have normally distributed data, equal number of scores in the conditions but variances are not equal) mean that you can still go ahead. (Within-participants ANOVA is not robust to violations of sphericity, however, which is why the F must be routinely adjusted to take account of this.) If you have small numbers of participants, your data are skewed, and you have unequal numbers of scores in the different conditions, you must consider performing a non-parametric equivalent of ANOVA, which is covered in Chapter 15.

In this chapter you will:

■ gain a conceptual understanding of what is meant by the analysis of variance
■ learn how to analyse data by the use of parametric ANOVAs

■ learn about an overall measure of effect (partial eta^2)
■ learn how to present your results graphically.

The analysis of three or more conditions includes the following:

■ descriptive statistics, such as means, confidence intervals where appropriate, medians, standard deviations; graphical illustrations such as box and whisker plots
■ effect size – the magnitude of the difference between the conditions, called d, and an overall measure of effect, partial eta^2
■ inferential tests: a statistical test called Analysis of Variance (ANOVA) evaluates how likely it is that any differences between the conditions are due to sampling error.

9.1 Visualising the design

It is easy to visualise an analysis of the differences between three or more groups by representing it as follows:

Table 9.1 Independent participants (between groups)

Three levels (or conditions) of one factor (Factor A)

A1	A2	A3
P1	P11	P21
P2	P12	P22
.	.	.
.	.	.
.	.	.
.	.	.
.	.	.
.	.	.
P10	P20	P30

This is called a *one-way* design, because we have one factor – Factor A. This has three levels – A1, A2, A3. We can tell this is a between-groups design because each participant appears under only one level, e.g. Participant 1 (P1) appears only under the A1 condition.

Table 9.2 is also a one-way design,[1] because there is only *one* factor (called A). Factor A has three levels, or conditions (A1, A2, A3). You can tell that the design is repeated-measures, because each participant is shown to give a score under each level, e.g. P1 appears under A1, A2 and A3, as do Participants 2 to 10.

---

[1] Although sometimes a repeated-measures one-way design such as this is, confusingly, known as a two-way. This is because the repetition of participants over all conditions is itself called a factor.

Table 9.2   Repeated measures (within participants)

A1	A2	A3
P1	P1	P1
P2	P2	P2
.	.	.
.	.	.
.	.	.
.	.	.
.	.	.
.	.	.
.	.	.
P10	P10	P10

ANOVA looks to see whether there are differences in the means of the groups. It does this by determining the grand mean[2] and seeing how different each of the individual means is from the grand mean.

There are two types of ANOVA:

1. Independent ANOVA (used when the participants perform in only *one* condition of several, i.e. an independent or between-participants design).
2. Related ANOVA (used when the participants perform in *all* conditions, i.e. a related or within-participants design).

Related and independent ANOVAs test whether there is a significant difference between some or all of the means of the conditions by comparing them with the grand mean.

ANOVA is the t-test, generalised to more than two groups, and because of this, there is a direct relationship between them; in fact, if you use ANOVA on two conditions, the results will be equivalent to those obtained using a t-test.

9.2   Meaning of analysis of variance

Analysis of variance (ANOVA), as the name suggests, analyses the different sources from which variation in the scores arises. Look at the scores in Table 9.3.

You will note that scores do not vary at all in the first condition. The variance is greater in the second condition, and even greater in the third.

9.2.1   Between-groups variance

ANOVA looks for differences between the means of the groups. When the means are very different, we say that there is a greater degree of variation *between* the conditions. If there were no differences between the *means* of the groups, then there would be no variation.

---

[2] The grand mean is the mean of the means, e.g. $(M1 + M2 + M3)/3$.

Table 9.3   Scores for participants in three conditions

A1	A2	A3	
9	15	21	
9	15	25	
9	16	17	Variation within the third group (from 17 through to 26)
9	15	22	
9	16	26	
$\bar{X} = 9$	$\bar{X} = 15.4$	$\bar{X} = 22.2$	

Variation between the groups (9 to 22.2)

This sort of variation is called *between-groups variation*, e.g. you can see from Table 9.3 that the means vary from 9 to 22.2.

Between-groups variation arises from:

■ *Treatment effects*: When we perform an experiment, or study, we are looking to see that the differences between means are big enough to be important to us, *and* that the differences reflect our experimental manipulation. The differences that reflect the experimental manipulation are called the treatment effects.

■ *Individual differences*: Each participant is different, therefore participants will respond differently, even when faced with the same task. Although we might allot participants randomly to different conditions, sometimes we might find, say, that there are more motivated participants in one condition, or they are more practised at that particular task. So sometimes groups vary because of the unequal distribution of participants.

■ *Experimental error*: Most experiments are not perfect. Sometimes experimenters fail to give all participants the same instructions; sometimes the conditions under which the tasks are performed are different, for each condition. At other times equipment used in the experiment might fail, etc. Differences due to errors such as these contribute to the variability.

The between-groups variance can be thought of as variation *between the columns*. In the scores above, there *is* variation *between* the columns.

9.2.2   Within-groups variance

Another source of variance is the differences or variation *within* a group. This can be thought of as variation *within* the columns. You can see from the scores above that condition 1, A1, has *no variation* within it; all the participants have scored the same: 9. Condition 2, A2, has little variation. Condition 3, A3, has much more variation. We have given these scores in order to illustrate variation – we might not want to perform ANOVA on data like these, because one of the assumptions of ANOVA (see later) is that the variances in each group are similar. This is because the formula for ANOVA takes the variances of each group and calculates an average. It only makes sense to use such an average if the groups are similar.

Within-groups variation arises from:

■ *Individual differences*: In each condition, even though participants have been given the same task, they will still differ in scores. This is because participants differ among themselves – they have different abilities, knowledge, IQ, personality and so on. Each group, or condition, is bound to show variability – thus the scores in condition 1, A1, above are unrealistic.

■ *Experimental error*: This has been explained above.

9.2.3 Partitioning the variance

As you know, the purpose of ANOVA is to discover whether there are differences in the means of the groups, and it does this by first calculating a grand mean, and then looking to see how different each of the individual means is from the grand mean. It does this by what is known as *partitioning the variance*, as explained below. The variability in scores both across the groups and within the groups represents the total variance, and there are two sources that will determine this total variability – between-groups influences and within-groups influences. What ANOVA does is to partition this total variability into these two components. In order to do this ANOVA has to estimate how much variability is contributed by each of these components:

1. First, ANOVA calculates the *mean* for each of the three groups.
2. Then it calculates the *grand mean* (the three means are added together, then divided by 3).
3. For each group separately, the total deviation of each individual's score from the mean of the group is calculated. This is the *within-groups variation*.
4. Then the deviation of each group mean from the grand mean is calculated. This is the *between-groups variation*.

As you can see, these calculations involve the grand mean. For instance, the total variance of a group describes the distance between the grand mean and the furthest score (see Figure 9.1). The total variance can then be partitioned into that due to differences between the means of the groups (between-groups variance) and that due to random error, that is, they are not manipulated by the experimenter (within-participants variance).

This is done for each of the groups. Approximately speaking, the final calculations involve finding an average of the three groups' between-groups variance, the within-groups variance, and the total variance. The test statistic, F, is a ratio between the between-groups variance and the within-groups variance.

Between-groups variance ÷ within-groups variance = F ratio

As we said earlier, the F test has a direct relationship to the t-test. In fact when we have only two conditions,

$$t^2 = F$$

Figure 9.1	Three-group design showing partition of variance and distances from grand mean

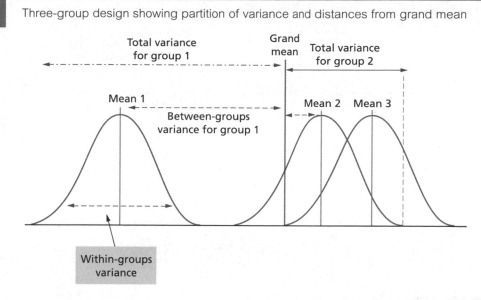

When we conduct our experiment, we hope that the within-groups variance is minimal – because this way, our F ratio will be larger. When the between-groups variance is very much larger than the within-groups variance, the F-value is large and the likelihood of such a result occurring by sampling error decreases.

In Figure 9.1 you can see that there is a lot of overlap between groups 2 and 3 suggesting that they do not differ from each other. Group 1, however, shows no overlap with groups 2 and 3. The grey vertical line is the grand mean (simply the three means added up and divided by 3). The distribution of scores on the left is for group 1. The total variance for group 1 starts at the edge of the distribution and finishes at the grand mean. This can be broken down into between-groups variance (from the mean of group 1 to the grand mean) and within-groups variance (from the edge of the distribution to the group mean).

You should be able to see that the total variance for both groups 2 and 3 is far smaller. The distance from the individual means of group 2 and group 3 to the grand mean (the between-groups variance) is much smaller than the distance from group 1's mean to the grand mean.

In Figure 9.2 you can see that there is a lot of overlap between the three groups, and that none of the individual group means will be far from the grand mean. The effect is small.

In Figure 9.3, you can see that there is a much smaller area of overlap, and that the individual group means will be much further from the grand mean. The effect will be larger.

The larger the (average) between-groups variance is in relation to the (average) within-groups variance, the larger the F ratio. This shows us that one (or more) of the individual group means is significantly different from the grand mean. It does not tell us which means are significantly different: this will require a further test.

| Figure 9.2 | Schematic representation of a small one-way effect |

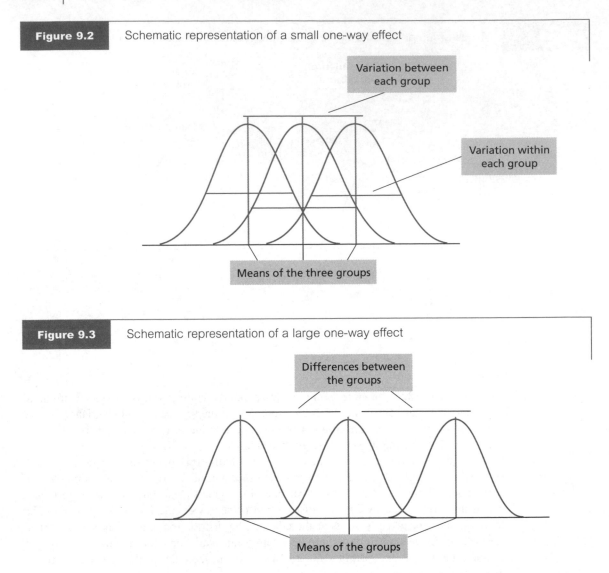

Variation between each group

Variation within each group

Means of the three groups

| Figure 9.3 | Schematic representation of a large one-way effect |

Differences between the groups

Means of the groups

Activity 9.1

Consider a design that has four independent conditions. Think of some reasons why scores in the different conditions might be different from each other. Then consider some of the reasons why participants might vary *within* each group.

EXAMPLE: ALCOHOL AND DRIVING ABILITY

Thirty-six people took part in an experiment to discover the effects of alcohol on driving ability. They were randomly assigned to three conditions: placebo (no alcohol), low alcohol and high alcohol. The non-alcoholic drink looked and tasted exactly the same as the other drinks(!). Participants were weighed and given the appropriate amount of drink. Thus the design is an independent one (between-participants). After half an hour of drinking, participants drove in a simulator for ten minutes, and the number of errors made was automatically registered by the computer. Data were as shown in Table 9.4.

Table 9.4   Data in three alcohol conditions

Placebo	Low alcohol	High alcohol
5	5	8
10	7	10
7	9	8
3	8	9
5	2	11
7	5	15
11	6	7
2	6	11
3	4	8
5	4	8
6	8	17
6	10	11
$\Sigma = 70^a$	$\Sigma = 74.00$	$\Sigma = 123.00$
$\bar{X} = 5.83^b$	$\bar{X} = 6.17$	$\bar{X} = 10.25$
SD = 2.69	SD = 2.33	SD = 3.05

[a] Σ = total
[b] $\bar{X}$ = mean

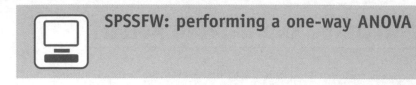

SPSSFW: performing a one-way ANOVA

Enter data in the usual way: save datafile. Select *Analyze*, *Compare Means*, and *One-Way ANOVA*.

This brings you to the following dialogue box:

The DV (score) is moved from the left hand box to the Dependent List on the right

The grouping variable is moved from the left hand box to the Factor on the right

If you want post-hoc tests, click on the *Post Hoc* box (post-hoc tests are explained on page 302):

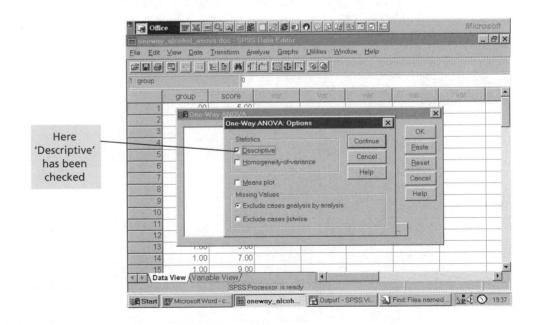

Check the tests you want

Check the test you require, then click on *Continue*. Click on *Options* if you require descriptive statistics for each condition.

Here 'Descriptive' has been checked

Then click on *Continue*, then *OK*. Your results will appear in the output window.

9.3 Descriptive statistics

The descriptive statistics option gives standard deviations, and confidence limits around the means. Look at Table 9.5.

Table 9.5 Descriptive statistics and confidence limits for three alcohol conditions

	Placebo	Low alcohol	High alcohol
$\bar{X}$	5.83	6.17	10.25
SD	2.69	2.33	3.05
CI	4.12–7.54	4.69–7.65	8.31–12.19

The means appear to be different; the variances are similar. Let's look at the means plotted on a graph, with the confidence intervals around the means – see Figure 9.4.

Although the means of the placebo group (5.83) and the low alcohol group (6.17) are slightly different, the confidence intervals overlap substantially. Thus any difference we see between the means could be due to sampling error. After all, the confidence limits for the placebo tell us that we are 95% confident that the population mean is between 4.12 and 7.54; the confidence limits for the low alcohol group tell us that we are 95% confident that the population mean for this group is 4.69–7.65. Thus, if we ran the experiment again on a different sample, we might find that the means were exactly the same!

The mean of the high alcohol group is much higher than the other two means, but, more importantly, the confidence interval of this group does not overlap at all with groups 1 and 2. Thus we can already see that any effect is between the high alcohol group and the other two groups.

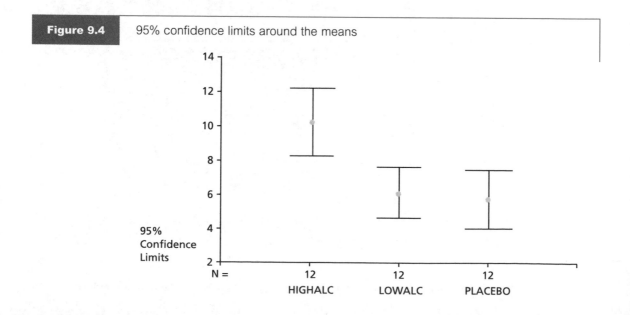

Figure 9.4 95% confidence limits around the means

The test statistics for a one-way independent ANOVA are as follows:

> The 'group' row is the between-groups statistics, and is the row of interest. Our analysis shows us $F(2,33) = 9.92$, $p < 0.001$. Remember in Chapter 5 we explained that a correlation coefficient could be squared in order to show the percentage of variation in scores on y accounted for by scores on x? Well, partial η^2 is a correlation coefficient that has already been squared. So in this case, we can simply read the number in the 'eta squared' column. The interpretation in the case of partial η^2 in this ANOVA is to say that 37.5% of the variation in driving ability is accounted for by which alcohol condition the participants were in

Tests of Between-Subjects Effects[3]
Dependent Variable: driving ability score

Source	Type III Sum of Squares	df	Mean Square	F	Sig.	Eta Squared
Corrected Model	145.167[a]	2	72.583	9.915	.000	.375
Intercept	1980.250	1	1980.250	270.500	.000	.891
GROUP	**145.167**	**2**	**72.583**	**9.915**	**.000**	**.375**
Error	**241.583**	**33**	7.321			
Total	2367.000	36				
Corrected Total	386.750	35				

a. R Squared = .375 (Adjusted R Squared = .337).

> The 'error' row contains the figures relating to the within-participants variation

Levene's Test of Equality of Error Variances[a]
Dependent Variable: driving ability score

F	df1	df2	Sig.
.215	2	33	.808

> Shows that the variances of the three groups are not significantly different from each other, therefore we have met the assumption of homogeneity of variance

Tests the null hypothesis that the error variance of the dependent variable is equal across groups.
a. Design: Intercept+GROUP

In journal articles, you will see that the F-value (9.9), the degrees of freedom (2,33) and the associated probability (here $p < 0.001$) are always reported in the text. It is useful to report the overall size of the differences between the groups, however. SPSSFW computes Partial^2 automatically under the ANOVA procedure. Here Partial^2 was given as 0.375. Thus 37.5% of the variation in the scores on driving ability is accounted for by the amount of alcohol consumed.

We now have a fair bit of information about the effect of alcohol on driving errors. Although it looks as if the differences between the groups are between the high alcohol condition and the other groups (rather than between placebo and low alcohol), ANOVA does not test for such comparisons. ANOVA lets us know whether there is a difference between some (or all) of the conditions, but that is as far as it goes. We can, however,

---

[3] This output table has been obtained with the General Linear Model > Univariate command rather than the One-Way ANOVA as used on the previous page.

obtain a further statistical test in order to confirm our belief that the differences that exist are between the high alcohol group and the others.

Multiple comparison procedures are used to assess which group means differ from means in the other groups.

9.4 Planned comparisons

Researchers can usually predict which means will differ from other means, and often such comparisons are planned in advance. These comparisons are usually carried out after the overall F ratio has shown that there are significant differences between two or more of the means. Although there are several tests for making such comparisons, we recommend you make your planned comparisons by using the t-test, since you are already familiar with this.

9.5 Controlling for multiple testing

Often researchers want to make several comparisons after running a one-way ANOVA. If you carry out multiple comparisons, then, as stated on page 231, you increase the likelihood of a Type I error. In order to take into consideration multiple testing you need to be more strict about the criterion used for declaring a result statistically significant. One way to control for multiple testing is to divide an acceptable probability value (e.g. 0.05) by the number of comparisons you wish to make. Thus, if you decide to make three pairwise comparisons, you divide 0.05 by 3. This gives you a value of 0.016. You then accept as statistically significant a probability level of less than 0.016. This avoids a Type I error.

9.6 Post-hoc tests

Sometimes researchers explore differences between the various sets of means without having specified these on the basis of theory. There are many post-hoc tests available to use, and these vary according to their power and ability to produce a Type I error – that is, they differ according to the extent to which they are liberal or conservative (these terms were explained in Chapter 4, page 144). When we perform post-hoc tests using SPSSFW, we do not have to correct for a Type I error (as explained in the paragraph above) because the tests available have been corrected to account for multiple testing. When you are making a large number of comparisons, you should choose a post-hoc test that is more conservative. Such a test is called the Tukey honestly significant difference (HSD) test. A test that tends to be more liberal is called the least significant difference test (LSD). Full discussion of these tests is not within the scope of this book; interested students are referred to Howell (2002) – or a search on the Internet!

If we (or rather our statistical package) perform a Tukey HSD on our alcohol data, we obtain the following:

Multiple Comparisons
Dependent Variable: SCORE
Tukey HSD

(I) condition	(J) condition	Mean Difference (I–J)	Std. Error	Sig.	95% Confidence Interval Lower Bound	Upper Bound
placebo	low alcohol	–.3333	1.1046	.951	–3.0438	2.3771
	high alcohol	**–4.4167***	**1.1046**	**.001**	**–7.1271**	**–1.7062**
low alcohol	placebo	.3333	1.1046	.951	–2.3771	3.0438
	high alcohol	**–4.0833***	**1.1046**	**.002**	**–6.7938**	**–1.3729**
high alcohol	placebo	4.4167*	1.1046	.001	1.7062	7.1271
	low alcohol	4.0833*	1.1046	.002	1.3729	6.7938

* The mean difference is significant at the .05 level.

This shows that there is a statistically significant difference between the placebo and high alcohol group, and between the low and high alcohol groups (emboldened). There is obviously no difference between the placebo and low alcohol group. You can now calculate the effect size, *d*, for the differences between the two conditions, in exactly the same way as you did for the t-test (see page 209). Just to remind you, the formula is as follows:

$$\frac{\text{Mean of condition 1} - \text{Mean of condition 3}}{\text{Mean SD}} = \frac{5.83 - 10.25}{\text{Mean SD}} = \frac{-4.42}{\text{Mean SD}}$$

So for conditions 1 and 3, the effect size is

$$\text{Mean SD} - \frac{2.69 + 3.05}{2} = 2.87$$

Ignore the sign

$$\text{Effect size} = \frac{-4.42}{2.87} = 1.54$$

Therefore the means of the placebo and high alcohol condition differ by 1.54 of a standard deviation; and this is statistically significant. If you calculate the effect size for the low and high alcohol conditions, you will find that they also differ by 1.54 SD. Calculation of the effect size for the placebo and low alcohol condition leads to a figure of 0.135. Thus these conditions differ by approximately one-seventh of a standard deviation. Such a difference could be due to sampling error. We now have plenty of information to write our report. The textual part of the analysis might be written as follows:

Descriptive statistics (Table x)[4] show that there were more errors made in the high alcohol condition than in the other two conditions. A one-way analysis of variance showed that any differences between conditions were unlikely to have arisen by sampling error,

---

[4] You should refer your readers to the table where you give your descriptive statistics.

assuming the null hypothesis to be true. $F(2,33) = 9.92$, $p < 0.001$ represented an effect size (partial η^2) of 0.375, showing that nearly 38% of the variation in driving errors can be accounted for by differing levels of alcohol. A post-hoc test (Newman–Keuls) confirmed that the differences between conditions 1 and 3, and 2 and 3 (both effect sizes $(d) = 1.54$) were unlikely to have arisen by sampling error. There was no significant difference between the placebo and low alcohol conditions (effect size $(d) = 0.14$).

Activity 9.2

In calculating an effect size between two conditions in a one-way ANOVA, you obtain an effect size (d) of 0.490. The conclusion is that the means differ by:

(a) About half a standard deviation
(b) About a quarter of a standard deviation
(c) 4.9 standard deviations
(d) None of the above

Example from the literature:
eating attitudes and irritable bowel syndrome

The following is a study on eating attitudes and the irritable bowel syndrome (IBS). Some people think there might be a link between eating disorders (such as bulimia or anorexia) and IBS. There is some research showing a coexistence of eating disorders and inflammatory bowel disease (similar symptoms to IBS but with a known cause for such symptoms). One questionnaire measuring the extent to which a person has an eating disorder is called the Eating Attitudes Test (EAT). Sullivan *et al.* (1997) gave the EAT to four groups of people: IBS sufferers, people with an eating disorder, people with inflammatory bowel disease and people without any disorder. Table 9.6 shows the results.

It can be seen immediately that, as expected, people with an eating disorder score higher than all other groups on the EAT. Indeed, if this were not the case, the EAT would not be a valid test.

Table 9.6   Table of results by Sullivan *et al.* (1997)

Group	Count	Mean score	95% CI for the mean
IBS	48	16.67	13.6–19.7
Eating disorder	32	56.7	48.7–64.8
Bowel disease	31	10.4	8.0–12.9
Controls	28	9.6	7.2–12.0

The confidence intervals show that the inflammatory bowel disease group and the control group overlap, showing that there are no important differences between these two groups on the EAT. The IBS group, however, not only has a higher sample mean than these two groups, but the confidence interval for the mean does not overlap with them, suggesting that any differences (discounting the eating disorders group) will be between the IBS group and the bowel disease/control groups. The confidence interval for the eating disorder group does not overlap with any of the other groups.

Sullivan *et al.* report as follows: 'When all four groups were compared using ANOVA ($F = 93.7217$) and multiple range testing using the Least Significant Difference test (LSD)[5] with a significance level of 0.05, both the eating disorder group and the IBS group achieved a significantly higher EAT score than the IBD group and the control group.'

Example from the literature: cognitive performance and use of Ecstasy

Dr Parrott and colleagues (Parrott *et al.*, 1998) carried out a study on cognitive performance in recreational users of Ecstasy. Previous work had shown memory deficits in users of Ecstasy. Parrott *et al.* assessed cognitive task performance (response speed, reaction time, choice reaction time, number vigilance and word recall) in three groups of young people: ten regular users, ten novice users and ten control participants who had never taken Ecstasy. The researchers analysed the data with a one-way ANOVA and Duncan test.[6]

Only two of the cognitive tasks generated a significant effect: immediate word recall and delayed word recall, as shown in Table 9.7.

Duncan comparisons showed that the differences between the controls and the novices, and the controls and the regular users, on both immediate and delayed word recall, were unlikely to be attributable to sampling error, assuming the null hypothesis to be true. However, the slight differences between novice and regular users could have been due to sampling error (we know this because Parrott *et al.* have not given us the significance levels for this comparison, therefore we assume it to be non-significant). It does seem that cognitive decrements may develop with the use of Ecstasy.

Table 9.7   Cognitive task performance in recreational MDMA (Ecstasy) users and non-users (group means and standard deviations)

	Non-user controls		Novice users		Regular users		ANOVA group effect	Control vs. novice	Control vs. regular	Novice vs. regular
Immediate word recall	8.2	1.6	5.3	1.1	6.5	1.3	$p < 0.001$	$p < 0.01$	$p < 0.05$	
Delayed word recall	6.9	1.6	4.6	1.0	5.1	1.4	$p < 0.01$	$p < 0.01$	$p < 0.01$	

---

[5] The LSD is one of the post-hoc tests available in SPSSFW.
[6] Another post-hoc comparison test.

9.7 Repeated-measures ANOVA

The repeated-measures ANOVA consists of one group of participants performing under all the conditions. You will remember that, for the independent design, we partitioned the variance into two parts:

- between-groups variance
- within-groups variance.

When we carry out a repeated-measures design, we can further partition the within-groups variance as follows:

1. The variability in scores due to individual differences.
2. The variability due to random error.

We can measure (1) above because, in the repeated-measures design, each participant is tested under all conditions. Thus we can compare each participant's overall score (scores on all conditions added up) with the other participants' overall scores.

You will probably remember that the F ratio for our independent groups design was a ratio:

$$F = \frac{\text{Between-groups variance}}{\text{Within-groups variance}}$$

The between-groups variance was made up of variation due to treatment effects, individual differences and experimental error. In a repeated-measures design, there is no between-groups variation due to individual differences, as the participants in each group are one and the same! The formula for calculating F in repeated-measures designs takes into account the fact that the participants are the same in each condition. Variation due to individual differences (which we can measure; see above) are removed from both the top and bottom of the equation; this tends to give rise to a more sensitive and powerful statistical test:

$$F = \frac{\text{Between-groups variance}}{\text{Within-groups variance (with individual differences removed)}}$$

Let's now imagine a situation where we re-run our alcohol experiment as a repeated-measures design. This means that each person will perform the task in all three conditions (placebo, low and high alcohol). It would not make sense for each person to perform all the conditions in one day, so the participants will have to be tested, say, every Monday for three weeks. In order to offset practice and order effects, the conditions will have to be counterbalanced. This is a more powerful design than the between-participants experiment, as each participant acts as their own control. We will assume that the scores, however, are the same (see Table 9.8).

The analysis starts in the same way as the between-participants design, with descriptive statistics and graphical illustrations.

Table 9.8 Data from participants in three alcohol groups

Participant	Placebo	Low alcohol	High alcohol
1	5	5	8
2	10	7	10
3	7	9	8
4	3	8	9
5	5	2	11
6	7	5	15
7	11	6	7
8	2	6	11
9	3	4	8
10	5	4	8
11	6	8	17
12	6	10	11
Σ	70	74	123

SPSSFW: instructions for repeated-measures ANOVA

From the menus, choose *Analyze*, *General Linear Model*, and *Repeated Measures*:

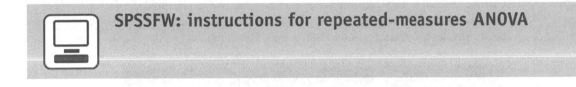

This brings you to the following dialogue box:

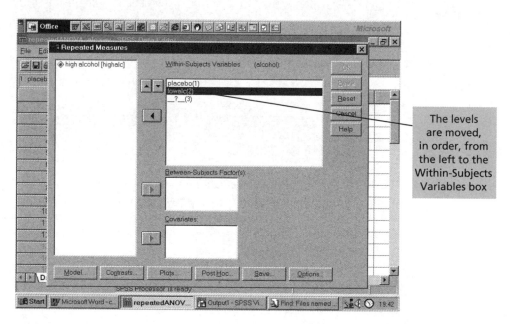

Change 'Factor 1' to a sensible name – in this case we have called the factor 'alcohol' – and insert the number of levels. Since we have PLACEBO, LOW and HIGH doses, we have three levels. Then press the *Add* button. Then click on *Define*.

Move the variables on the left, one at a time, into the *Within-Subjects Variables* box on the right. In the example, *placebo* is moved first, into the number one position, *low* is moved into the second position, and *high* the third. This represents our three levels. Then press *Options*.

(Ignore the *Between-Subjects Factor(s)* and the *Covariates* buttons, as we are not interested in these for our analysis.)

This gives you the following dialogue box:

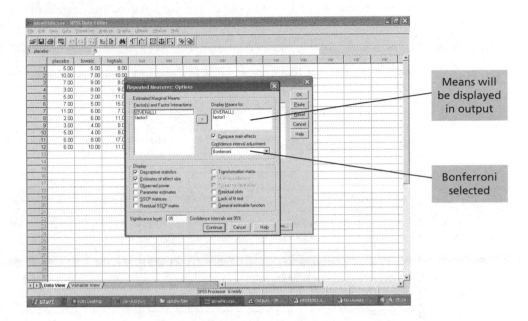

Means will be displayed in output

Bonferroni selected

Make sure that you check *Compare main effects*. You are then given a choice of three tests: *LSD*, *Bonferroni* or *Sidak*. We suggest you use *Bonferroni*, which corrects for the number of pairwise tests that you are carrying out (see Multiple testing on page 231).

You can then check the options you require. Here we have asked for descriptives, effect size, means and power. The confidence intervals are given routinely. Then press *Continue*. This brings you back to the *Repeated Measures ANOVA* dialogue box. Press *OK*. Your results will appear in the output window.

9.7.1 Sphericity

In ANOVA we start from the assumption that the conditions are independent. In repeated measures designs, however, we use the same participants in each condition, which means there is likely to be some correlation between the conditions. If you have three conditions, then there are three bivariate correlations: condition 1 vs condition 2, condition 2 vs condition 3, and condition 1 vs condition 3. We make the assumption that these correlations are similar. Thus we assume that all of the covariances are similar. The assumption of sphericity holds when the variance of the difference between the estimated means for any pair of groups is the same as for any other pair. Since this assumption is unlikely to be met, and violations of sphericity are deterimental to the accuracy of ANOVA, we recommend that you routinely interpret the 'Greenhouse–Geiser' row of the output. In other words, it's better to assume that we *have* broken the assumption. The Greenhouse–Geiser works (as you can see from the output overleaf) by adjusting the degrees of freedom. This correction formula makes our test more stringent, so that, even if we have broken the assumption of sphericity, we are less likely to make a Type I error.

9.7.2 Output for ANOVA

We have emboldened the row of interest. The degrees of freedom look odd in the SPSSFW output, because they are given to several decimal places. The degrees of freedom, instead of being given as 2, 22 (for the sphericity assumed rows) are given as 1.833 and 20.164. Don't use such precision when reporting your degrees of freedom when using the Greenhouse–Geiser rows – just round them to whole numbers – in this case, 2,20. Here you will see that $F = 10.83$, and $p = 0.001$. The effect size, rounded up, is 50%. Therefore 50% of the variation in scores measuring driving ability is accountable by the different amounts of alcohol consumed.

Tests of Within-Subjects Effects
Measure: MEASURE_1

Use the Greenhouse–Geisser row

Source		Type III Sum of Squares	df	Mean Square	F	Sig.	Eta Squared
ALCOHOL	Sphericity Assumed	145.167	2	72.583	10.826	.001	.496
	Greenhouse– Geisser	**145.167**	**1.833**	**79.194**	**10.826**	**.001**	**.496**
	Huynh-Feldt	145.167	2.000	72.583	10.826	.001	.496
	Lower-bound	145.167	1.000	145.167	10.826	.007	.496
Error (ALCOHOL)	Sphericity Assumed	147.500	22	6.705			
	Greenhouse– Geisser	147.500	20.164	7.135			
	Huynh-Feldt	147.500	22.000	6.705			
	Lower-bound	147.500	11.000	13.409			

Note that $F(2,20) = 10.83$, $p = 0.001$

9.7.3 Post-hoc tests/planned

This is the output obtained under the *Compare main effects* option, using Bonferroni:

Estimates
Measure: MEASURE_1

FACTOR1	Mean	Std. Error	95% Confidence Interval	
			Lower Bound	Upper Bound
1	5.833	.777	4.123	7.543
2	6.167	.672	4.687	7.646
3	10.250	.880	8.313	12.187

The above table shows the mean score for each of the conditions, plus the 95% confidence limits.

Pairwise Comparisons
Measure: MEASURE_1

(I) FACTOR1	(J) FACTOR1	Mean Difference (I–J)	Std. Error	Sig.[a]	95% Confidence Interval for Difference[a] Lower Bound	Upper Bound
1	2	−.333	.924	1.000	−2.939	2.272
	3	−4.417*	1.196	.011	−7.790	−1.043
2	1	.333	.924	1.000	−2.272	2.939
	3	−4.083*	1.033	.007	−6.997	−1.170
3	1	4.417*	1.196	.011	1.043	7.790
	2	4.083*	1.033	.007	1.170	6.997

Based on estimated marginal means
* The mean difference is significant at the .05 level.
a. Adjustment for multiple comparisons: Bonferroni.

The table above compares each condition with every other condition, giving the mean difference between every pair, the standard error, the probability value, and the 95% confidence limits around the mean difference.

The first row compares 1 (placebo) with 2 (low alcohol). The mean difference is 0.333. This is not statistically significant at any acceptable criterion value. This row also compares level 1 (placebo) with level 3 (high alcohol). The difference here is 4.417, and the associated probability level is 0.011. Have a go at interpreting the rest of the table yourself.

Activity 9.3

Think about what the confidence limits are telling us. How would you explain the meaning of the confidence interval of the mean difference to a friend who did not understand the output?

The write-up is similar to the independent groups ANOVA. This time, however, we can say:

A repeated-measures ANOVA was carried out on the data. Assumptions of normality, homogeneity of variance and sphericity were met. Results showed that differences between conditions were unlikely to have arisen by sampling error ($F(2,22) = 10.83$, $p = 0.001$); an overall effect size of 0.496 (partial η^2) showed that 50% of the variation in error scores can be accounted for by differing levels of alcohol. Pairwise comparisons showed that the difference between the placebo and low alcohol condition was minimal (1%) whereas the difference between the low alcohol and the high alcohol condition was large (partial $\eta^2 = 59$); $F(1,11) = 15.6$, $p = 0.002$). It can be concluded therefore that participants who consumed a high level of alcohol made more driving errors than when they performed in the placebo condition. The confidence interval showed that the population mean difference is likely (95%) to be found between 1.78 and 7.05.

Example from the literature: eyewitness confidence and accuracy

Kebbell *et al.* (1996) carried out two experiments on eyewitness confidence and accuracy. Some studies had found that witnesses (to accidents or other incidents) were more accurate in their recall when they were absolutely certain that they had remembered events correctly, than when they were less certain. Other researchers, however, found that there was very little correlation between accuracy and confidence. Kebbell *et al.* argued that researchers had not paid sufficient attention to the issue of item difficulty – for instance, it is much easier to remember, in an incident, that a person was a man or woman than to remember what colour hair they had.

Kebbell and colleagues devised two experiments that measured how confident participants were in remembering information in a short video film, and how accurate they were. First, however, they had to devise a pool of items that could be categorised as easy, medium and hard. This first part of their study is what concerns us here. As they state in their article, an easy question was 'What song was the woman singing?', a medium one was 'What was on the dish next to the TV set?', and a hard one was 'What was behind the Tabasco sauce bottle in the kitchen?' The researchers had to be sure that they had categorised the items correctly – it was no use categorising 'What song was the woman singing?' as 'easy' if none of the participants could answer it! Therefore, participants should answer easy questions more accurately than hard ones, if the items have been correctly categorised.

The dependent variable was the number of correct answers in each of the three categories; the independent variable is item difficulty with three levels (easy, medium and hard). This can be represented as shown in Table 9.9.

The most appropriate inferential statistical test is therefore a one-way repeated-measures ANOVA, which is what Kebbell *et al.* used; they then performed follow-up tests. They reported as follows:

A one-way repeated measures ANOVA showed a significant effect of question difficulty on the number of correct answers ($F(2,88) = 591.37$, $p < 0.0001$). Follow-up tests ($p < 0.05$) confirmed that these differences were in the appropriate direction; easy questions were more likely to be answered correctly than medium questions, which were in turn more likely to be answered correctly than hard questions. This again validated the categories of item difficulty.

Table 9.9   Illustration of design used by Kebbell *et al.* (1996)

Easy	Medium	Hard
P1	P1	P1
P2	P2	P2
P3	P3	P3
P.	P.	P.

Summary

■ ANOVAs allow us to test for differences between three or more conditions

■ ANOVAs are suitable for data drawn from a normal population – they are parametric tests.

■ ANOVA allows us to assess the likelihood of having obtained an observed difference between some or all of the conditions by sampling error.

■ Planned or post-hoc tests show us which conditions differ significantly from any of the other conditions.

■ Partial^2 is a correlation coefficient that can be used as a measure of effect in ANOVA. It lets us know, in percentage terms, how much variance in the scores of the dependent variable can be accounted for by the independent variable.

SPSSFW exercises

Exercise 1

Enter the data from Table 9.10 into SPSS, analyse it by the use of *ONEWAY* (which is in the Compare Means menu), and obtain the results. Perform a post-hoc test. Copy down the important parts of the printout. Interpret your results in terms of the experiment.

At the local university, students are randomly allocated to one of three groups for their laboratory work – a morning group, an afternoon group and an evening group. At the end of the session they were given 20 questions to determine how much they remembered from the session. Were there differences between the groups, and, if so, in which direction?

Table 9.10 Data from morning, afternoon and evening laboratory groups

Morning		Afternoon		Evening	
P1	15	P11	14	P21	13
P2	10	P12	13	P22	12
P3	14	P13	15	P23	11
P4	15	P14	14	P24	11
P5	17	P15	16	P25	14
P6	13	P16	15	P26	11
P7	13	P17	15	P27	10
P8	19	P18	18	P28	9
P9	16	P19	19	P29	8
P10	16	P20	13	P30	10

Exercise 2

There is some evidence to show that smoking cannabis leads to short-term memory loss and reduced ability in simple tasks. Seven students, smokers who normally did not take cannabis, were recruited to answer difficult arithmetic questions, under four different conditions. In the placebo condition they smoked a herbal mixture, which they were told was cannabis. In condition 2 they smoked a small amount of cannabis, increasing to a large amount in condition 4. Students were required to smoke cannabis alone. To avoid practice effects, there were four different arithmetic tests, all at the same level of difficulty. To avoid the effects of order and fatigue, the order in which participants took the tests was counterbalanced.

Results are as follows:

Participant number	Placebo	Low dose	Medium dose	High dose
1	19	16	8	7
2	14	8	8	11
3	18	17	6	3
4	15	16	17	5
5	11	14	16	7
6	12	10	9	8
7	11	9	5	11

Enter the data into SPSSFW, analyse with a repeated-measures ANOVA, and write up the results in the appropriate manner.

MULTIPLE CHOICE QUESTIONS

1. Parametric one-way independent ANOVA is a generalisation of:
   (a) The paired t-test
   (b) The independent t-test
   (c) χ^2
   (d) Pearson's r

Questions 2 to 4 are based on the following information:

Alice, a third-year student, noticed that she and her friends learned more statistics when they were in Madame MacAdamia's class than in Professor P. Nutt's. They could not determine whether this was due to the style of the teaching or the content of the lectures, which differed somewhat. For her third-year project, therefore, she persuaded three statistics lecturers to give the same statistics lecture, but to use their usual lecturing styles. First-year students were allotted randomly to the three different lecturers, for one hour. At the end of the lecture, they were tested on their enjoyment of the lecture (ENJOYMENT), and also on what they had learned in the lecture (KNOWLEDGE). Alice then conducted a one-way ANOVA on the results. This is the SPSSFW printout for ENJOYMENT:

ANOVA
ENJOYMENT

	Sum of Squares	df	Mean Square	F	Sig.
Between Groups	94.4308	2	47.2154	.4893	.6141
Within Groups	13798.1240	143	96.4904		
Total	13892.5548	145			

Descriptives
ENJOYMENT

	Mean
1.00	62.9063
2.00	61.2041
3.00	62.9091

2. Which is the most appropriate conclusion?

   (a) There are statistically significant differences between the three groups of students on ENJOYMENT
   (b) There are important differences between the three groups but these are not statistically significant
   (c) There are no statistical or important differences between the three groups
   (d) No conclusions can be drawn

3. The following is also given with the above printout:

Test of Homogeneity of Variances
ENJOYMENT

Levene Statistic	df1	df2	Sig.
1.3343	2	143	.267

What can you conclude from this?

   (a) The variances of the groups are significantly different from each other
   (b) The variances of the groups are similar
   (c) The variances are heterogeneous
   (d) None of the above

4. Here are the results for the KNOWLEDGE questionnaire, which the students completed after their one-hour lecture:

ANOVA
KNOWLEDGE

	Sum of Squares	df	Mean Square	F	Sig.
Between Groups	110.3100	2	55.1550	5.3557	.0057
Within Groups	1482.9689	144	10.2984		
Total	1593.2789	146			

Descriptives
KNOWLEDGE

		Mean
1.00	P.Nutt	10.5781
2.00	MacAdamia	10.0408
3.00	Cashew	12.3235

Which is the most sensible conclusion?

(a) There are significant differences between the groups on KNOWLEDGE; specifically, Colin Cashew's group retained more of the lecture than the other two groups
(b) There are significant differences between the groups on KNOWLEDGE; specifically, Madame MacAdamia's group retained more of the lecture than Professor P. Nutt's group
(c) There are significant differences between all of the groups on KNOWLEDGE; specifically, Professor P. Nutt's group retained more of the lecture than the other two groups
(d) There are no significant differences between the groups on KNOWLEGE

5. The F-ratio is a result of:

(a) Within-groups variance/between-groups variance
(b) Between-groups variance/within-groups variance
(c) Between-groups variance $\times$ within-groups variance
(d) Between-groups variance + within-groups variance

6. The relationship between the F-ratio and t-value is explained by:

(a) $t^3 = F$
(b) $F^2 = t$
(c) $t^2 = F$
(d) $f^3 = t$

7. Professor P. Nutt is examining the differences between the scores of three groups of participants. If the groups show homogeneity of variance, this means that the variances for the groups:

   (a) Are similar
   (b) Are dissimilar
   (c) Are exactly the same
   (d) Are enormously different

8. Differences between groups, which result from our experimental manipulation, are called:

   (a) Individual differences
   (b) Treatment effects
   (c) Experiment error
   (d) Within-participants effects

9. Herr Hazelnuss is thinking about whether he should use a related or unrelated design for one of his studies. As usual, there are advantages and disadvantages to both. He has four conditions. If, in a related design, he uses 10 participants, how many would he need for an unrelated design?

   (a) 40
   (b) 20
   (c) 10
   (d) 100

10. Individual differences within each group of participants are called:

    (a) Treatment effects
    (b) Between-participants error
    (c) Within-participants error
    (d) Individual biases

11. Dr Colin Cashew allots each of 96 participants randomly to one of four conditions. As Colin Cashew is very conscientious, he meticulously inspects his histograms and other descriptive statistics, and finds that his data are perfectly normally distributed. In order to analyse the differences between the four conditions, the most appropriate test to use is:

    (a) One-way between groups ANOVA
    (b) t-test
    (c) Pearson's r
    (d) Repeated-measures ANOVA

12. The assumption of sphericity means that:

    (a) The variances of all the sample groups should be similar
    (b) The variances of the population difference scores should be the same for any two conditions
    (c) The variances of all the population difference scores should be similar
    (d) The variances of all the sample groups should be dissimilar

13. If, in an analysis of variance, you obtain a Partial^2 of 0.52, then how much of the variance in scores on the dependent variable can be accounted for by the independent variable?

   (a) 9%
   (b) 52%
   (c) 25%
   (d) 27%

14. Calculating how much of the total variance is due to error and the experimental manipulation is called:

   (a) Calculating the variance
   (b) Partitioning the variance
   (c) Producing the variance
   (d) Summarising the variance

15. The following is output relating to a post-hoc test, after a one-way ANOVA:

Multiple Comparisons
Dependent Variable: Current Salary
Tukey HSD

(I) Employment Category	(J) Employment Category	Mean Difference (I–J)	Std. Error	Sig.	95% Confidence Interval Lower Bound	Upper Bound
Clerical	Custodial	–$3,100.35	$2,023.76	.276	–$7,843.44	$1,642.74
	Manager	–$36,139.26*	$1,228.35	.000	–$39,018.15	–$33,260.37
Custodial	Clerical	$3,100.35	$2,023.76	.276	–$1,642.74	$7,843.44
	Manager	–$33,038.91*	$2,244.41	.000	–$38,299.13	–$27,778.69
Manager	Clerical	$36,139.26*	$1,228.35	.000	$33,260.37	$39,018.15
	Custodial	$33,038.91*	$2,244.41	.000	$27,778.69	$38,299.13

* The mean difference is significant at the .05 level.

Which groups differ significantly from each other?

   (a) Clerical and custodial occupations only
   (b) Custodial and manager occupations only
   (c) Manager and clerical occupations only
   (d) Manager and clerical plus manager and custodial

16. Look at the following output, which relates to a repeated measures ANOVA with three conditions. Assume sphericity has been violated.

Tests of Within-Subjects Effects
Measure: MEASURE_1

Source		Type III Sum of Squares	df	Mean Square	F	Sig.	Partial Eta Squared
FACTOR1	Sphericity Assumed	542.857	2	271.429	7.821	.007	.566
	Greenhouse–Geisser	542.857	1.024	529.947	7.821	.030	.566
	Huynh-Feldt	542.857	1.039	522.395	7.821	.029	.566
	Lower-bound	542.857	1.000	542.857	7.821	.031	.566
Error (FACTOR1)	Sphericity Assumed	416.476	12	34.706			
	Greenhouse–Geisser	416.476	6.146	67.762			
	Huynh-Feldt	416.476	6.235	66.796			
	Lower-bound	416.476	6.000	69.413			

Which is the most appropriate statement?
The difference between the conditions represented by:

(a) $F(2,12) = 7.82, p = 0.007$
(b) $F(1,6) = 7.82, p = 0.030$
(c) $F(2,12) = 7.82, p = 0.030$
(d) $F = (1.6) = 7.82, p = 0.031$

17. Which is the most appropriate answer? The effect size is:

(a) 5.7%
(b) 57%
(c) 0.57%
(d) 5%

Questions 18 to 20 relate to the output below, which shows a repeated measures ANOVA with three levels. Assume sphericity has been violated.

Tests of Within-Subjects Effects
Measure: MEASURE_1

Source		Type III Sum of Squares	df	Mean Square	F	Sig.
COND	Sphericity Assumed	521.238	2	260.619	5.624	.019
	Greenhouse–Geisser	521.238	1.073	485.940	5.624	.051
	Huynh-Feldt	521.238	1.118	466.251	5.624	.049
	Lower-bound	521.238	1.000	521.238	5.624	.055
Error (COND)	Sphericity Assumed	556.095	12	46.341		
	Greenhouse–Geisser	556.095	6.436	86.406		
	Huynh-Feldt	556.095	6.708	82.905		
	Lower-bound	556.095	6.000	92.683		

Pairwise Comparisons
Measure: MEASURE_1

(I)COND	(J)COND	Mean Difference (I–J)	Std. Error	Sig.[a]	95% Confidence Interval for Difference[a] Lower Bound	Upper Bound
1	2	−11.857	3.738	.058	−24.146	.431
	3	−3.429	1.494	.184	−8.339	1.482
2	1	11.857	3.738	.058	−.431	24.146
	3	8.429	4.849	.339	−7.514	24.371
3	1	3.429	1.494	.184	−1.482	8.339
	2	−8.429	4.849	.399	−24.371	7.514

Based on estimated marginal means
a. Adjustment for multiple comparisons: Bonferroni.

18. Which is the most appropriate statement?

    (a) $F(2,12) = 5.62, p = 0.020$
    (b) $F(1,6) = 5.62, p = 0.050$
    (c) $F(2,12) = 5.62, p = 0.049$
    (d) $F(1,6) = 5.62, p = 0.055$

19. Which two conditions show the largest difference?

    (a) 1 and 2
    (b) 2 and 3
    (c) 1 and 4
    (d) They are identical

20. Assuming that the null hypothesis is true, the difference between conditions 1 and 2 has a:

    (a) 5% chance of arising by sampling error
    (b) 6% chance of arising by sampling error
    (c) 19% chance of arising by sampling error
    (d) 20% chance of arising by sampling error

References

Howell, D.C. (2002) *Statistical Methods for Psychology* (5th edn). Boston: PWS-Kent.

Kebbell, M.R., Wagstaff, G.F. and Covey, J.A. (1996) 'The influence of item difficulty on the relationship between eyewitness confidence and accuracy', *British Journal of Psychology*, **87**: 653–62.

Parrott, A.C., Lees, A., Garnham, N.J., Jones, M. and Wesnes, K. (1998) 'Cognitive performance in recreational users of MDMA or "ecstasy": evidence for memory deficits', *Journal of Psychopharmacology*, **12**(1): 79–83.

Sullivan, G., Blewett, A.E., Jenkins, P.L. and Allison, M.C. (1997) 'Eating attitudes and the Irritable Bowel Syndrome', *General Hospital Psychiatry*, **19**: 62–4.

10 Analysis of variance with more than one IV

Chapter overview

In Chapter 9 we introduced you to one of the most widely used statistical tests in psychology today, the analysis of variance (ANOVA). In this chapter we aim to:

- teach you about an extension of the one-way ANOVA to include two or more IVs
- describe three different ANOVA designs, each with two IVs:
  - the first ANOVA will have two between-participants IVs
  - the second will have two within-participant IVs
  - the third will have one between- and one within-participants IV
- explain, with all these designs, how the variance is allocated between the various conditions and how we might evaluate the degree of interaction between our two IVs
- illustrate how we can break down interaction effects to find out precisely how one IV is interacting with the second IV; such analyses are called *simple effects*.

10.1 Introduction

In Chapter 9 we explained how we can use analysis of variance (ANOVA) to test for differences between groups when we have more than two conditions of the IV. One of the most useful aspects of ANOVA, though, is that it allows us to analyse the effects of two or more IVs on a DV in one analysis. In addition to this, we can use ANOVA to find out if there is an interactive effect of our two variables on the DV, that is, whether one IV may behave differently in the two conditions of the second IV. You should note that ANOVA is not restricted to just two IVs. You could, if you so wished, have three or four or more IVs. The more IVs you have, however, the harder it becomes to interpret any interactive effects there are between them. Once we have shown you how to interpret interactions you will begin to appreciate how difficult it could get if we had a lot of IVs.

A simple example should illustrate what the factorial ANOVA offers us. Suppose we conducted a study to investigate the effects of alcohol and caffeine on driving ability. We might make several predictions in such an experiment:

1. High alcohol levels will impair driving ability.
2. High levels of caffeine might improve driving ability due to its arousing effect.
3. Given that old wisdom has it that coffee helps to sober us up, we might predict that increased caffeine intake will reduce the influence of alcohol on driving ability.

The first two of these predictions are called *main effects*. These refer to the overall effect of each of the IVs on the DV. That is, the overall effect of alcohol on driving performance regardless of which caffeine condition participants are in, or the overall effect of caffeine on driving regardless of the alcohol condition the participants are in. Prediction 3 above, which relates to the way that caffeine and alcohol interact to modify driving ability, is called the *interaction* between the two IVs. Thus, we have three predictions in this study and ANOVA allows us to test all three of these in one analysis.

10.2 Sources of variance

As the name of the test suggests, we use ANOVA to analyse all the possible sources of variance in our studies. When we measure participants on some DV we will get variation in their scores. Some of this variation will be attributable to the IVs, some of it attributable to the interaction between the IVs and some of it will be error variance. The purpose of ANOVA is to try to identify how much of the total variation in scores is accounted for by each of these factors (see Figure 10.1). Figure 10.1 shows that when we have two IVs variation in the DV can be attributed to the two IVs separately and the interaction between them. Any variation that is not accounted for by these factors is said to be error variance.

In Chapter 9 we explained that the one-way ANOVA assesses the degree to which the variance between conditions is greater than the variance within conditions. We explained that, if the between-conditions variance was considerably larger than that within conditions, then we could conclude that the between-groups difference was not due to sampling

Figure 10.1   Pie chart illustrating the sources of variation in the DV for a study with two IVs

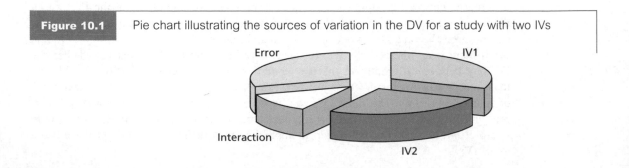

Figure 10.2 Pie chart illustrating the various sources of variation in the DV for a study with three IVs

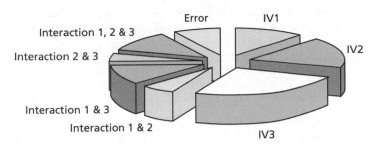

error. We suggested that in such a situation the difference between groups could probably be attributed to our manipulation of the IV. The logic of analysing more than one variable is similar to that of the one-way ANOVA. We essentially divide (or partition) the total variance into that which represents the two IVs separately and that which is attributable to the interaction between these IVs; we then compare these sources of variance with the within-conditions (or error) variance. These analyses allow us to assess the likelihood of a particular effect being the result of sampling error.

We suggested earlier that ANOVA allows us to analyse even more than two IVs in one analysis. In Figure 10.2 you can see how we would divide up the variation if we had three IVs. It is apparent from this diagram that there are many more sources of variation that we have to identify. In fact, with the addition of only one IV we double the number of sources of variation that we have to analyse. Thus, the complexity of the analyses is increased dramatically when we include more IVs (compare Figures 10.1 and 10.2 with the pie chart in section 9.2.3). In such designs it also becomes much more difficult to interpret the interactions between all the IVs. So, for those of you thinking of doing an experiment investigating the effects of age, gender, social class, anxiety and intelligence on ability to abseil and analysing the data using ANOVA, think again. Such an analysis is unwieldy and would prove extremely difficult to interpret. There are better ways of analysing such data, for example multiple regression (see Chapter 11), although there are drawbacks even to this.

We should point out that the partitioning of the variation illustrated in Figures 10.1 and 10.2 represents the case for completely between-participants designs only. When we have any within-participants IVs in the analyses things get a lot more complicated. We will cover such designs later in this chapter.

Activity 10.1

See if you can work out the various sources of variance when you have four IVs (variable A, variable B, variable C and variable D).

10.3 Designs suitable for factorial ANOVA

There are various designs that are suitable for factorial analysis of variance. The key feature of such designs is that they have only *one DV* and *two or more IVs*. In this chapter we will be explaining the rationale for three types of factorial ANOVA, those with:

- two between-participants IVs
- two within-participants IVs
- one between-participants IV and one within-participants IV.

All the ANOVAs we describe in this chapter will have IVs with two conditions. For example, in the alcohol and caffeine study described earlier we might have two alcohol conditions (no alcohol and high levels of alcohol) and two caffeine conditions (no caffeine and high levels of caffeine). If this study were a completely between-participants design, the allocation of participants to conditions would look something like that shown in Table 10.1.

We could conduct the same study as a totally within-participants design. In such a study, each participant would have to take part in all four conditions (see Table 10.2).

Finally, we might have one IV, say the alcohol one, as a between-participants variable and the other, caffeine, as a within-participants variable. The allocation of participants to conditions in such a study is illustrated in Table 10.3.

Table 10.1 Allocation of participants to conditions in a completely between-participants design

	No alcohol	Alcohol
No caffeine	P1	P4
	P2	P5
	P3	P6
	. . .	. . .
Caffeine	P7	P10
	P8	P11
	P9	P12
	. . .	. . .

Table 10.2 Allocation of participants to conditions in a completely within-participants design

	No alcohol	Alcohol
No caffeine	P1	P1
	P2	P2
	P3	P3
	. . .	. . .
Caffeine	P1	P1
	P2	P2
	P3	P3
	. . .	. . .

Table 10.3 Allocation of participants to conditions in one between-participants (alcohol/no alcohol) and one within-participants (caffeine/no caffeine) design

	No alcohol	Alcohol
No caffeine	P1	P4
	P2	P5
	P3	P6
	. . .	. . .
Caffeine	P1	P4
	P2	P5
	P3	P6
	. . .	. . .

10.4 ANOVA terminology

Often in the literature you will see ANOVA designs expressed as a *2 × 2 ANOVA* or a *3 × 4 ANOVA*, or perhaps a *3 × 2 × 2 ANOVA*.

Such terminology simply tells you how many IVs were used and how many conditions in each.

■ In the first example there were two IVs each with two conditions.
■ In the second example there were two IVs, one with three conditions, the other with four conditions.
■ In the final example there were three IVs, one with three conditions and two with two conditions.

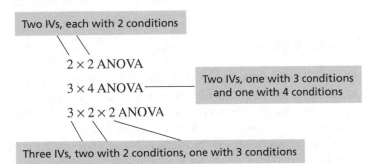

How would you describe the following analysis: a $4 \times 4 \times 2 \times 2 \times 2 \times 5 \times 6$ ANOVA? The official answer to the question is that it has seven IVs, one with six conditions, one with five conditions, two with four conditions and three with two conditions. However, we would describe such an analysis as crazy because it would be extremely difficult to interpret an interaction between all of these IVs. Remember, we explained that increasing the number of IVs dramatically increases the number of sources of variance in a design. It is perhaps for such reasons that we very rarely see published work that has analysed data using ANOVA with more than three IVs.

We should also note here that using many IVs in ANOVA means that we are testing many different effects against many different null hypotheses. We therefore have to bear in mind the increased probability of making Type I errors. An example should help to illustrate this. Suppose you conducted a study with four IVs (A, B, C and D). If you conducted ANOVA on these data you would be testing 15 different effects against their corresponding null hypothesis (main effects of A, B, C and D plus 11 interactions between these IVs). In doing this you would be drastically increasing the familywise error rate and thus increasing the probability of making a Type I error. We should therefore use common sense when deciding how to analyse the data from complex pieces of research.

Activity 10.2

Have a go at describing the following analyses:

(a) A 6 × 2 ANOVA
(b) A 3 × 3 × 3 ANOVA
(c) A 4 × 2 × 4 × 2 ANOVA
(d) A 2 × 2 × 2 × 2 × 2 ANOVA

10.5 Two between-participants independent variables

Let us return to the example experiment outlined previously concerning alcohol, caffeine and driving ability. Some invented data from such an experiment are presented in Table 10.4.

10.5.1 Initial analyses

As with the one-way ANOVA you need to run some exploratory data analyses to check that the assumptions for ANOVA are met. Some initial statistical analyses (mean, SD and 95% confidence intervals) are presented along with the data in Table 10.4. We can see from these analyses that there were fewest driving errors in the No alcohol–Caffeine condition (mean = 5.75) and most errors in the Alcohol–No caffeine condition (mean = 21.25). The means for the No alcohol–No caffeine and the Alcohol–Caffeine conditions are in between these two extremes (means of 7.92 and 9.00 respectively). We can also see that the standard deviations for all conditions are quite similar and thus we can be reasonably confident that the assumption of *homogeneity of variance* has not been violated with these data.

The next stage of our exploratory data analyses should involve obtaining some plots to establish whether our data are normally distributed. We can look at this using histograms, stem and leaf plots or box plots. Let us assume that we have generated such plots and are satisfied that we have no violations of assumptions underlying the use of parametric tests (remember, ANOVA is such a test). We can therefore proceed to analyse our data using ANOVA.

Table 10.4   Number of driving mistakes made by each participant in the four driving conditions (no alcohol & no caffeine, alcohol & no caffeine, no alcohol with caffeine, and alcohol with caffeine)

	No alcohol		Alcohol	
No caffeine	4	2	28	19
	9	11	22	16
	10	11	21	25
	8	10	27	17
	6	3	21	19
	11	10	20	20
	$\bar{X}$ = 7.92[a]; SD = 3.32		$\bar{X}$ = 21.25; SD = 3.72	
	95% CI: 5.81–10.02		95% CI: 18.89–23.61	
Caffeine	8	6	5	11
	4	3	6	8
	9	0	14	10
	0	8	8	11
	8	9	14	8
	6	8	5	8
	$\bar{X}$ = 5.75; SD = 3.28		$\bar{X}$ = 9.00; SD = 3.07	
	95% CI: 3.67–7.83		95% CI: 7.05–10.95	

[a] $\bar{X}$ = mean

Activity 10.3

Referring to Table 10.4, give your interpretation of the confidence intervals.

10.5.2 Sources of variance

How do we work out the sources of variance when this is a completely between-groups design? If you look at the predictions, you can see that we have already identified three possible sources of variance:

1.   The *main effect* due to alcohol.
2.   The *main effect* due to caffeine.
3.   The *interaction* between these two factors.

Are there any other sources of variance? If you think back to Chapter 9 you should recall that, for a one-factor between-participants design, there were two sources of variance, the between-groups variance and the within-groups (or error) variance. That is, we had one source of variance due to the between-groups factor and one due to differences between the participants within each condition. In the two-IV design we also have to take account of such variations between the participants within each condition. Consequently, as in the one-factor design, we have an extra source of variance relating to *within-groups* or *error variation*. We therefore have the following sources of variance:

- variance due to the effects of alcohol on driving ability (main effect of alcohol)
- variance due to the effects of caffeine on driving ability (main effect of caffeine)
- variance due to the interaction between these two factors
- variance due to difference between participants within each condition (error variance).

When you carry out a completely between-groups ANOVA you will get a printout that looks like the one below for the alcohol/caffeine data.

If you look at the printout for this analysis you will notice that we have the same information beside each entry as the ANOVA tables presented in Chapter 9. For each source of variance we have the sum of squares, the degrees of freedom (DF), the mean square, the F-value and the exact probability *p* (Sig.). You should recall that, to calculate the F-value, we simply divide the mean square for each source of variance relating to the IVs by the mean square error. Remember, in Chapter 9 we explained that the mean square is simply a measure of variance. Thus, in this analysis you can see that for the main effect of alcohol when we divide the mean square (825.02) by that for the error term (11.26) we get the F-value of 73.27. You can also see that the main effect of caffeine has an associated F-value of 55.38 (623.52 ÷ 11.26) and for the interaction there is an associated F-value of 27.09 (305.02 ÷ 11.26).

UNIVARIATE ANALYSIS OF VARIANCE

Between-Subjects Factors

		Value Label	N
alcohol	1.00	No alcohol	24
	2.00	Alcohol	24
caffeine	1.00	No caffeine	24
	2.00	Caffeine	24

Tests of Between-Subjects Effects
Dependent Variable: Driving errors

Source	Type III Sum of Squares	df	Mean Square	F	Sig.	Partial Eta Squared
Corrected Model	1753.562[a]	3	584.521	51.914	.000	.780
Intercept	5786.021	1	5786.021	513.880	.000	.921
alcohol	825.021	1	825.021	73.274	.000	.625
caffeine	623.521	1	623.521	55.377	.000	.557
alcohol * caffeine	305.021	1	305.021	27.090	.000	.381
Error	495.417	44	11.259			
Total	8035.000	48				
Corrected Total	2248.979	47				

a. R Squared = .780 (Adjusted R Squared = .765)
* The row that includes the asterisk is for the interaction

You can see from the printout that we have a probability of 0.000 associated with the main effects of both alcohol and caffeine and also the interaction (remember that $p = 0.000$ in SPSSFW means that $p < 0.001$). This tells us that, if the null hypotheses were true, we would be highly unlikely to get the observed main effects and interactions. What does all this mean? It is always a good idea when trying to understand what has happened in these more complex experimental designs to illustrate the means graphically. Following the recommendations of Loftus (1996) we have generated an error bar chart for the data in this example; this is presented in Figure 10.3. You should note that SPSSFW does not put in the solid lines linking the pairs of means. We have included these lines to help you understand the nature of the interaction between the two IVs.

The top line in Figure 10.3 represents driving ability without caffeine and the bottom line driving ability with caffeine. We can immediately see from this graph that the main effect due to caffeine appears to be telling us that driving ability is better when we have had a dose of caffeine (remember, these are made-up data, so don't try this at home!). There are more driving errors in the no-caffeine conditions (top line) than in the caffeine conditions (bottom line). The points on the right-hand ends of the two lines represent the alcohol conditions, and those on the left-hand ends the no-alcohol conditions. We can see here, although it is perhaps not as obvious (we have drawn line graphs to make this more obvious, see Figure 10.4), that there are more mistakes when alcohol has been consumed than when it has not. Perhaps the best way to visualise main effects when you have *equal* numbers of participants in each group is to mark a point halfway along each line for the main effect of caffeine (see Figure 10.4). The vertical difference between these two points represents the actual difference between the means of the caffeine and no caffeine conditions, ignoring the alcohol IV. This represents the main effect of the caffeine IV. For the alcohol IV you should mark a point halfway between the points on the right-hand end of the lines and another point between the points at the left-hand end of the lines. The vertical

---

Figure 10.3   Error bar chart for the alcohol/no alcohol and caffeine/no caffeine conditions

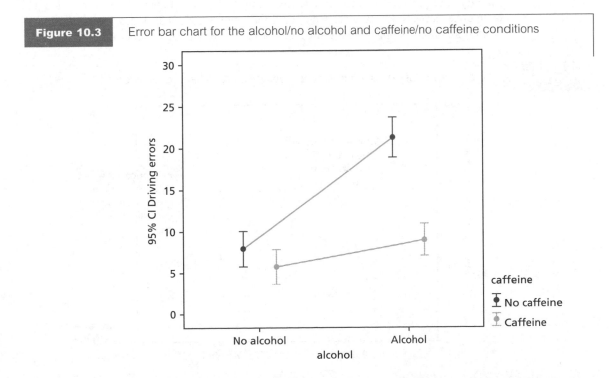

Figure 10.4   Line graph illustrating the main effects of alcohol and caffeine

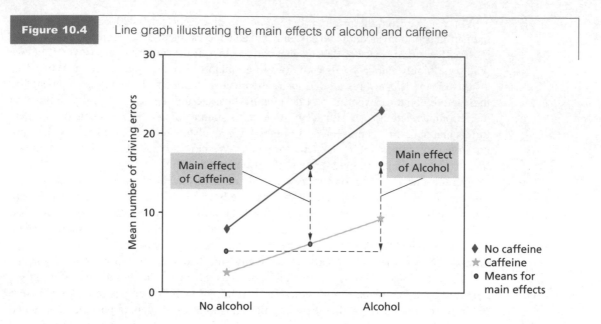

difference between these points represents the actual difference between the alcohol and no alcohol conditions, ignoring the caffeine IV. This represents the main effect of the alcohol IV. Remember, you can use this simple visual technique only when you have equal sample sizes. If you had different numbers of participants in each group you would have to calculate the means for the main effects and then draw them on the graph.

How do we interpret the interaction? If you have a significant interaction you can initially interpret the interaction visually using the graph. Figure 10.5 shows that the difference between the two caffeine conditions with no alcohol is much smaller than it is with alcohol. It appears, therefore, that caffeine has a greater moderating effect in the

Figure 10.5   Line graph illustrating the interaction between the caffeine and alcohol IVs

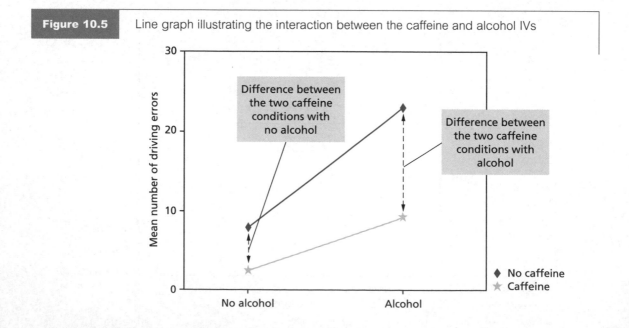

alcohol condition, as was predicted. The alternative interpretation is that, when there is no caffeine (look at the vertical difference between the two ends of the top line), alcohol has a greater detrimental effect on driving ability than when there is caffeine (difference between the two ends of the bottom line). These are both valid ways of interpreting the above data and are essentially saying exactly the same thing.

10.5.3　Interactions between variables

One of the golden rules of ANOVA is that once you find a significant interaction you should proceed to explore that interaction further. What does it mean to have an interaction between two variables? If you have two variables each with two conditions, an interaction is where one variable behaves differently in each condition of the other variable. For example, we suggested above that caffeine has an effect in both alcohol conditions. However, caffeine has a greater effect in the alcohol condition than in the no alcohol condition. An example from the research literature would be the finding that highly anxious individuals tend to direct their attention to negative stimuli in the environment, whereas non-anxious individuals direct attention away from negative stimuli (Mogg and Bradley, 1999). Here there is an interaction between the anxiety variable and the attention variable. A useful way of seeing whether you have an interaction between two variables is to generate line graphs. Take a look at the graphs illustrated in Figure 10.6.

Figure 10.6 shows that, when there is no interaction between two variables, the lines that represent the caffeine variable are parallel. When we observe such parallel lines we can be sure that we do not have an interaction between two variables. What do the parallel lines tell us? If you compare the alcohol and no alcohol conditions in all three examples given in Figure 10.6 you should see that there are more driving errors when drivers have no caffeine than when they have caffeine. That is, we have the same pattern of results in both the alcohol conditions, whereby having caffeine leads to fewer driving errors.

What does an interaction look like in graph form? Take a look at the graphs in Figure 10.7.

The graphs in Figure 10.7 illustrate the various patterns of lines that suggest you have an interaction. The key feature you should note about each of the graphs in Figure 10.7 is that the two lines are not parallel. Looking at each graph, we see that there is a different pattern of findings in each of the two alcohol conditions. In graph (a) we see that in the no alcohol condition there are more driving errors with caffeine than without it. In the alcohol condition, however, we find the opposite pattern: more errors without caffeine. In graph (b) we see no real difference between caffeine and no caffeine in the no alcohol

| **Figure 10.6** | Graphs illustrating no interactions between variables |

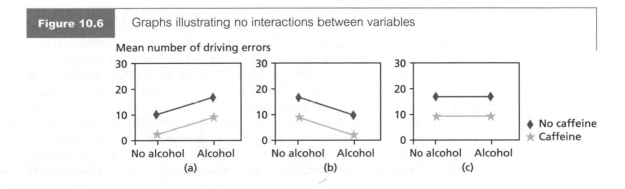

| Figure 10.7 | Graphs illustrating the pattern of lines for interaction |

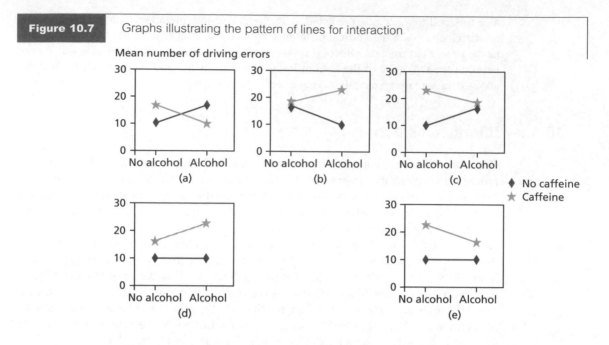

condition, whereas in the alcohol condition caffeine increases driving errors. Graph (c) shows the opposite to (b) in that there is no difference in the alcohol condition and caffeine increasing errors in the no alcohol condition. Moving on to graph (d) we see that in both the no alcohol and alcohol conditions, having caffeine has the effect of increasing numbers of driving errors. However, the graph shows that there is a greater impact on driving errors of caffeine in the alcohol condition. Graph (e) shows the opposite effect with a greater impact of caffeine in the no alcohol condition.

You should bear in mind that you cannot tell just by looking at line graphs whether or not you have a significant interaction between your IVs. The line graphs will give you an indication of this; however, you need to consult the ANOVA printout to find out if there is a significant interaction. You should, therefore, use the line graphs in association with the ANOVA printout to help you understand your pattern of findings.

10.5.4 Interpretation of main effects when there are significant interactions

You should be careful when interpreting main effects when you have significant interactions. They should be interpreted only if they are meaningful and/or they are interesting in the context of the research conducted. If they are not meaningful or interesting then it is perhaps best to concentrate on interpreting the interaction. There are difficulties for researchers when they interpret significant main effects in the presence of significant interactions. For example, the graph in Figure 10.7(b) suggests that there is no effect of caffeine in the no alcohol condition. In the alcohol condition, however, caffeine has the effect of impairing driving performance. Clearly there is not an effect of caffeine in all conditions. Therefore you should be wary of interpreting the main effect in such a way. For there to be a global main effect of caffeine it would have to influence driving performance in both of the alcohol conditions. The graph would probably resemble that shown in

Figure 10.7(d) rather than (b). If we simply relied upon the SPSSFW printout we might conclude that we have a global main effect of both IVs when, in fact, if Figure 10.7(b) is anything to go by, we do not. It is therefore very important to examine the graphical illustrations of your findings as well as the SPSSFW printout. To quote Howell (2002):

> *Among the points we should emphasise in our discussion of simple effects is that the experimenter must examine her data carefully. Plotting the data and considering what they mean is an important, if not the most important, part of an appropriate analysis of any set of data.*

Activity 10.4

Which of the following graphs suggest an interaction and which do not?

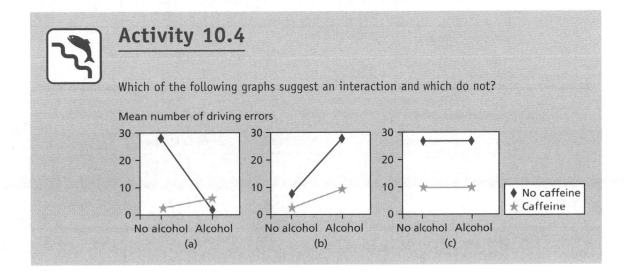

Mean number of driving errors

10.5.5 Simple effects

The various scenarios illustrated above highlight the importance of graphically illustrating your data to help you understand what has happened with your main effects and interactions. If you do get a significant interaction, you then need to find out what is really happening in each of your conditions. You can do this by analysing the simple effects (sometimes called *simple main effects*). A simple effect is the difference between any two conditions of one IV in *one* of the conditions of another IV. Thus, I might analyse the difference between the caffeine and no caffeine conditions in the no alcohol condition. This would be an analysis of a simple effect. Usually, we have already made a prediction about how these cell means will vary and we can use these predictions to guide which simple effect analyses we should carry out. Simple effect analyses are equivalent to t-tests but involve the calculation of F-values, and you can get SPSSFW to calculate them for you. However, in order for us to explain how to get SPSSFW to do this we would have to teach you the SPSSFW *Syntax Language*.[1] Such a task is beyond the scope of this book and so we recommend that you simply get SPSSFW to calculate t-tests for the simple effects you require. For the data presented in Table 10.4 (the initial between-participants analyses that we presented in this chapter) the simple effect t-tests are as follows:

---

[1] You could use the method recommended by Howell (2002). This involves running separate oneway ANOVAs on each simple effect and then recalculating the F-ratios using the mean square error from the original analysis in place of the one calculated for the simple effect. See Howell (2002) for details on how to do this.

T-TEST
ALCOHOL = NO ALCOHOL

Group Statistics[a]

	caffeine	N	Mean	Std. Deviation	Std. Error Mean
Driving errors	No caffeine	12	7.9167	3.31548	.95710
	Caffeine	12	5.7500	3.27872	.94648

a. alcohol = No alcohol

Independent Samples Test[a]

		Levene's Test for Equality of Variances		t-test for Equality of Means						95% Confidence Interval of the Difference	
		F	Sig.	t	df	Sig. (2-tailed)	Mean Difference	Std. Error Difference		Lower	Upper
Driving errors	Equal variances assumed	.027	.872	1.610	22	.122	2.16667	1.34606		−.62488	4.958
	Equal variances not assumed			1.610	21.997	.122	2.16667	1.34606		−.62490	4.958

a. alcgroup = No alcohol

The output above provides the test of the first simple effect. It tests the difference between the caffeine and no caffeine conditions in only the no alcohol condition. The means that it is comparing are indicated in Figure 10.8(a) by the arrow. The t-test tells us that the difference between the caffeine and no caffeine conditions in the no alcohol condition has an associated value of $t(22) = 1.61$, $p = 0.12$ and is not significant.

The second simple effect analysis is presented below:

ALCOHOL = ALCOHOL

Group Statistics[a]

	caffeine	N	Mean	Std. Deviation	Std. Error Mean
Driving errors	No caffeine	12	21.2500	3.72034	1.07397
	Caffeine	12	9.0000	3.07482	.88763

a. alcohol = Alcohol

Independent Samples Test[a]

| | | Levene's Test for Equality of Variances | | t-test for Equality of Means | | | | | | |
| | | F | Sig. | t | df | Sig. (2-tailed) | Mean Difference | Std. Error Difference | 95% Confidence Interval of the Difference | |
									Lower	Upper
Driving errors	Equal variances assumed	.173	.682	8.792	22	.000	12.25000	1.39330	9.360	15.140
	Equal variances not assumed			8.792	21.25	.000	12.25000	1.39330	9.355	15.145

a. alcgroup = Alcohol

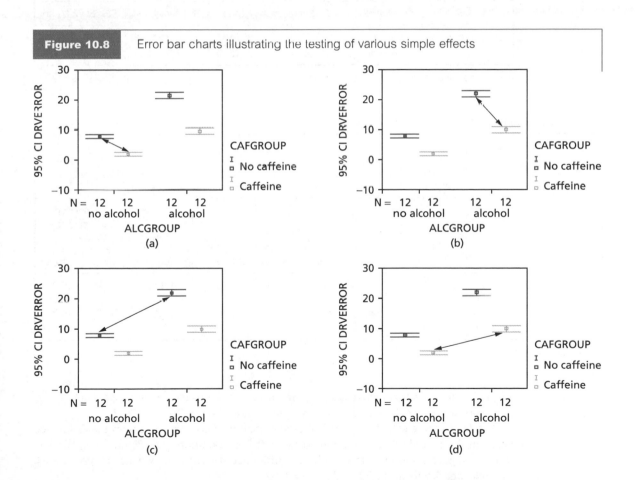

| Figure 10.8 | Error bar charts illustrating the testing of various simple effects |

(a)

(b)

(c)

(d)

This t-test shows us that in the alcohol condition there is a significant difference between the two caffeine conditions. The relevant details are $t(22) = 8.79$, $p < 0.001$. This analysis is illustrated in Figure 10.8(b). We have stated that p is less than 0.001 because SPSSFW has displayed the p-value as 0.000. This means that the actual p-value is less than 0.001, but SPSSFW cannot display such a value. We therefore cannot present the exact p-value as we have advised you to do when writing up your results. When you come across this in your analyses, report the p-value as we have done above.

The test of the difference between the two alcohol conditions in the no caffeine condition only is presented in the printout below. This t-test examines the two means indicated in Figure 10.8(c).

T-TEST
CAFFEINE = NO CAFFEINE

Group Statistics[a]

	alcohol	N	Mean	Std. Deviation	Std. Error Mean
Driving errors	No alcohol	12	7.9167	3.31548	.95710
	Alcohol	12	21.2500	3.72034	1.07397

a. caffeine = No caffeine

Independent Samples Test[a]

		Levene's Test for Equality of Variances		t-test for Equality of Means						
									95% Confidence Interval of the Difference	
		F	Sig.	t	df	Sig. (2-tailed)	Mean Difference	Std. Error Difference	Lower	Upper
Driving errors	Equal variances assumed	.005	.945	−9.269	22	.000	−13.33333	1.43856	−16.317	−10.350
	Equal variances not assumed			−9.269	21.714	.000	−13.33333	1.43856	−16.319	−10.348

a. cafgroup = No caffeine

The printout shows that there is a significant difference between the two alcohol conditions in the no caffeine condition. The relevant details are: $t(22) = 9.27$, $p < 0.001$.

The final simple effect analysis is presented below. This t-test examines the difference between the two alcohol conditions in the caffeine condition (see Figure 10.8(d)). The analysis suggests that there is a significant difference between the two alcohol conditions. The relevant details are: $t(22) = 2.51$, $p = 0.02$.

CAFFEINE = CAFFEINE

Group Statistics[a]

	alcgroup	N	Mean	Std. Deviation	Std. Error Mean
Driving errors	No alcohol	12	5.7500	3.27872	.94648
	Alcohol	12	9.0000	3.07482	.88763

a. cafgroup = Caffeine

Independent Samples Test[a]

		Levene's Test for Equality of Variances		t-test for Equality of Means							
										95% Confidence Interval of the Difference	
		F	Sig.	t	df	Sig. (2-tailed)	Mean Difference	Std. Error Difference	Lower	Upper
Driving errors	Equal variances assumed	.059	.810	−2.505	22	.020	−3.25000	1.29758	−5.941	−.5590
	Equal variances not assumed			−2.505	21.910	.020	−3.25000	1.29758	−5.942	−.5583

a. cafgroup = Caffeine

You should be able to see that there is an effect of alcohol in both the caffeine conditions which are unlikely to be due to sampling error, given that the null hypotheses are true. These analyses confirm to us that, in this case, there is a genuine main effect of the alcohol IV: that is, these are not spurious effects caused by the interaction between the two IVs. It is a genuine main effect as alcohol has a significant effect in *both* the caffeine conditions. For the caffeine IV, however, you should be able to see that there is only a significant effect of caffeine in the alcohol condition. This means that we should be cautious about the observed main effect of caffeine. Because there is not an effect of caffeine in the no alcohol condition we cannot state that caffeine, in general, affects driving performance. Caffeine seems to only have an effect when participants are also given alcohol. This finding clearly shows the importance of investigating any significant interactions when you get significant main effects.

In practice you should be careful when conducting simple effects analyses, as the more simple effects you calculate, the higher your familywise error rates will be. In Chapter 9 we explained to you that the familywise error rate relates to the overall error rate you have if you conduct many analyses. By conducting many analyses you have an increased probability of making a Type I error and so you should be selective in the simple effects analyses you conduct. Generally, when you have conducted an experiment that is of the factorial ANOVA design, you will have made some sort of prediction (as we have) about the interactive effects of your two IVs. You should use these predictions to guide you in your choice of simple effects analyses. Such analyses are often called *planned* or *a priori* comparisons. When your comparisons are post hoc or you are making many comparisons, you need to make some adjustment to your α (see the section on post-hoc testing in Chapter 9). As we have examined all possible simple effects in the printout presented here then we should really set our criterion for significance at 0.0125, that is $0.05 \div 4$. When we do this we find that the simple effect of the alcohol IV in the caffeine condition is non-significant ($p = 0.02$) and so we would want to treat this difference as possibly due to sampling error.

Activity 10.5

Which of the following describe simple effects?

(a) The difference between chewing gum and no chewing gum in the talking condition
(b) The overall difference between the tea and non-tea drinking groups
(c) The effects of noise in only the mathematics exam
(d) The effects of cognitive behaviour therapy on the fear responses of all groups of participants

10.5.6 Effect size

The calculation of effect size is similar to the case of the one-way analysis of variance described in Chapter 9. As stated previously, there are several measures of effect size in ANOVA designs; however, as SPSSFW presents you with *partial eta-squared* (η^2) this is the one we will explain here.

Partial η^2 is easily requested through SPSSFW for both between-participants designs and within-participants designs. You should note from the printout that the partial η^2 estimates do not add up to 1, as it is in fact a ratio of the effect sum of squares to the effect sum of squares plus the error sum of squares:

$$\text{Partial } \eta^2 = \frac{SS_{effect}}{SS_{effect} + SS_{error}}$$

For the main effect of alcohol, the partial η^2 (0.625) is calculated from:

$$\text{Partial } \eta^2 = \frac{825.021}{825.021 + 495.417}$$

All the partial η^2 details given in the ANOVA printout on page 328 are calculated in a similar way. These analyses tell us that 62.5% of the variation in driving errors is accounted for by our manipulation of the alcohol IV. Partial η^2 is useful for a global measure of magnitude of effect. If, however, you are interested in the magnitude of the difference between two conditions (the size of a simple effect) then you could use d as we have suggested in Chapter 9.

10.5.7 Writing up these analyses

When you have conducted such an analysis you might write it up as follows:

The means and 95% confidence intervals for number of driving errors in the alcohol/no alcohol and caffeine/no caffeine conditions are presented in Figure 10.9. This suggests that there is a considerable difference in driving performance between the caffeine and no caffeine conditions when participants have had alcohol but not necessarily when they have no alcohol. The figure also shows that there is little or no overlap of 95% CIs when comparing the alcohol and no alcohol conditions. This suggests that in both the caffeine conditions alcohol has a detrimental effect on driving performance. There is a hint of an interaction between the two IVs but it is not clear from the figure how large an interaction this is.

The number of driving errors was analysed using a factorial analysis of variance with two between-participant factors of alcohol (alcohol vs. no alcohol) and caffeine (caffeine vs. no caffeine). This analysis revealed that the main effects due to the alcohol ($F(1,44) = 73.27$, $p < 0.001$) and caffeine ($F(1,44) = 55.38$, $p < 0.001$) factors and the interaction between these ($F(1,44) = 27.09$, $p < 0.001$, partial $\eta^2 = 0.38$) were unlikely to have arisen due to sampling error. This suggests that there were more driving errors made when alcohol was consumed than with no alcohol (means of 15.13 and 6.83 respectively, partial $\eta^2 = 0.63$). In addition 63% of the overall variation in driving performance was attributable to the influence of the alcohol IV. The main effect of the caffeine suggests that there were fewer driving errors in the caffeine than in the no caffeine condition (means of 7.38 and 14.58 respectively, partial $\eta^2 = 0.56$). Thus, 56%

Figure 10.9 Error bar chart illustrating means and 95% CIs for the number of driving errors in the alcohol/no-alcohol and caffeine/no-caffeine conditions

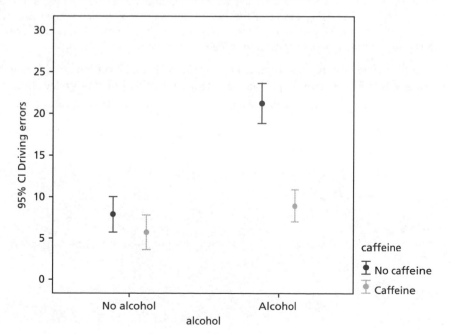

of the variance was due to the caffeine manipulation. Finally, the interaction between alcohol and caffeine was considerable and accounts for 38% of the overall variance. This interaction was further investigated using t-tests. Given that there were four tests of simple effects the criterion for significance was adjusted to 0.0125. These analyses showed that the effect of caffeine in the alcohol condition was such that it was unlikely to have arisen due to sampling error ($t(22) = 8.79$, $p < 0.001$, $d = 3.61$). There was no significant effect of caffeine in the no alcohol condition ($t(22) = 1.61$, $p = 0.1221$, $d = 0.66$). The effect of alcohol in the no caffeine condition was also unlikely to have arisen due to sampling error ($t(22) = 9.27$, $p < 0.001$, $d = 3.79$). However, there was no significant effect of the alcohol IV in the caffeine condition ($t(22) = 2.51$, $p = 0.02$, $d = 1.02$).

Example from the literature: gender differences in prejudice

Ekehammar *et al.* (2003) examined gender differences in implicit prejudice. In this study they presented males and females with a face recognition task involving either Swedish faces or those of immigrants to Sweden. They then assessed the degree to which these tasks influenced ratings of the character of a person described in a story. They were interested in the degree to which being presented with the faces influenced the negativity of the ratings given of the character described in the subsequent story:

> In the study the researchers used a 2 (faces: Swedish vs immigrant) × 2 (participant gender: women vs men) ANOVA to analyse responses to the character in the story. They found no significant main effect of the faces IV (F(1,39) = 0.94, p = 0.34) suggesting that overall there was no difference in rating of the character when participants were previously exposed to the Swedish or the immigrant faces. There was, however, a significant interaction between the faces and gender IVs (F(1,39) = 5.63, p = 0.02). They followed up this interaction by conducting post hoc Fisher's LSD test which showed that women showed greater negativity towards the described character than men when previously presented with immigrant pictures but not with Swedish pictures, thus suggesting greater implicit prejudice among women.

The statistical details are those reported by Ekehammar *et al.* You can see that they have reported the actual p-values rather than simply stating whether *p* was less than or greater than 0.05.

Activity 10.6

Which of the following measures of magnitude of effect are suitable for use with ANOVA?

(a) d
(b) r^2
(c) Partial η^2

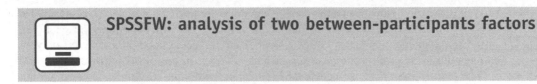

SPSSFW: analysis of two between-participants factors

Setting up the variables

As with all analyses the first thing you need to do is input your data. The way to do this is illustrated below:

Two grouping variables and one for the DV

Remember, when setting up a datafile for two between-groups IVs you will need to set up two grouping variables containing the numbers representing the group to which each participant belongs. Thus, if participant 15 is in the no alcohol/caffeine group, they will have a '1' in the *alcgroup* column and a '2' in the *cafgroup* column. Someone in the alcohol/no caffeine group would have a '2' in the *alcgroup* column and a '1' in the *cafgroup* column, and someone in the alcohol/caffeine group would have a '2' in both columns. The third variable that you need to set up is for the DV and simply contains each person's score, in this case, number of driving errors.

Obtaining descriptive statistics for each group of participants

The initial part of your analyses will be to obtain descriptive statistics for each group of participants. We have four groups of participants, but it is not a straightforward procedure to get the descriptive statistics for the four groups separately. In order to do this we need to split our datafile into two parts, one containing all the data for the no alcohol condition and one containing the data for the alcohol condition. Once we have done this we have to run our descriptive statistics on the driving error data for each condition of the caffeine IV. SPSSFW will give us the descriptive statistics for the caffeine conditions for each part of the split data file, that is, for both the alcohol and no alcohol conditions. In this way we can get all our descriptive statistics for each of our four groups of participants.

The first step therefore is to get SPSSFW to split the file into two parts. You can do this by clicking on the *Data*, *Split File* option:

Once you do this you will be presented with the following dialogue box:

Select this option and move the alcgroup variable over to this box

You will need to select the *Organize output by groups* option and then move the alcohol variable to the *Groups Based on* box. Once you have done this you should click on the *OK* button. Your file is now effectively split into two, those data for the no alcohol condition and those for the alcohol condition. Any analyses you now conduct will be carried out on both parts of the file separately. Therefore the next step is to get SPSSFW to produce descriptive statistics for us. You should set up the *Analyze*, *Descriptive Statistics*, *Explore* dialogue box as follows:

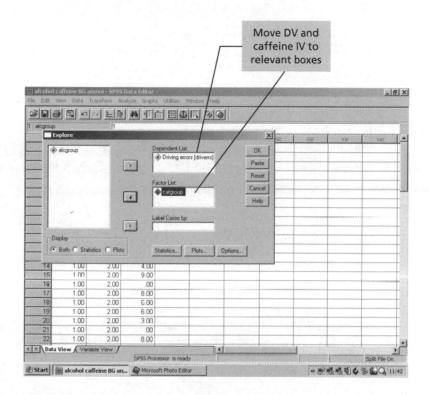

When SPSSFW carries out these analyses it will produce two lots of descriptive statistics, one lot for the no alcohol condition and one lot for the alcohol condition. In this way, you will have obtained the descriptive statistics (including box plots and histograms) for all four groups in the study.

When you have obtained the descriptive statistics for each of the four groups you will want to conduct the ANOVA on all the data. You will therefore need to tell SPSSFW to unsplit the datafile. If you did not do this you would find that SPSSFW tries to run the analysis on the two parts of the file separately, which would be incorrect. Therefore, you need to let SPSSFW know that it has to use all of the data together for the ANOVA. To do this you need to return to the *Data*, *Split File* dialogue box and reselect the *Analyze all cases, do not create groups* option as shown below:

Select *Analyze all cases* option

Running the ANOVA

To get SPSSFW to run the ANOVA you need to select the *General Linear Models* and *Univariate* options from the *Analyze* menu.

Move DV and IVs to relevant boxes

Click *Options* button

Once you have the *Univariate* dialogue box on the screen, move the DV and IVs across to the relevant boxes so that it resembles that shown in the screenshot. If you want to get information about effect sizes for each of your main effects and interaction you should then click on the *Options* button. Doing this will give you the following dialogue box:

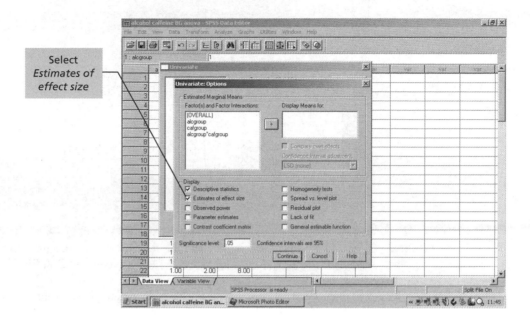

Select the *Estimates of effect size* option and click on *Continue* to return to the main ANOVA dialogue box. You should note that, if you select the *Descriptive statistics* option here, SPSSFW will display means and standard deviations as part of the ANOVA printout (and you do not need to split the file for this). Click on the *OK* button and SPSSFW will run the analysis for you. You should then be presented with a printout that is similar to that shown in the original analyses earlier (see page 328).

To investigate your simple effects you will need to carry out t-tests. However, it is not as straightforward as simply conducting t-tests on your DV between the two groups in each of your IVs. Remember, in simple effects analyses we are looking for the effects of one of our IVs in *one* condition of the other IV. Thus, the first two t-tests we might conduct are to look at the difference between the two alcohol conditions in the no caffeine condition and then again in the caffeine condition. We therefore need to let SPSSFW know that we want to split the file into two parts again. This time we would divide it on the basis of the caffeine variable and so we would set up the *Data*, *Split File* dialogue box as follows:

Once you have done this, click on *OK* and the file will be split again. You can then run your independent t-tests with alcohol as the IV and drive as the DV. SPSSFW will conduct t-tests for both the no caffeine and caffeine conditions.

You will then need to conduct more t-tests to examine the difference between the caffeine and no caffeine conditions in each of the alcohol conditions. You will therefore need to go back to the *Data, Split File* dialogue box and move the alcohol variable into the *Groups Based on* box instead of the caffeine variable. Once this has been done you will be able to conduct independent t-tests with caffeine as the IV and drive as the DV under both conditions of the alcohol variable.

Remember, when you have finished your analyses of simple effects you should tell SPSSFW to unsplit the file again so that any subsequent analyses you conduct will be based upon all of your data.

Generating the error bar charts

In order to generate the appropriate error bar charts you should select the *Error Bar . . .* option from the *Graphs* menu. You will be presented with the following dialogue box:

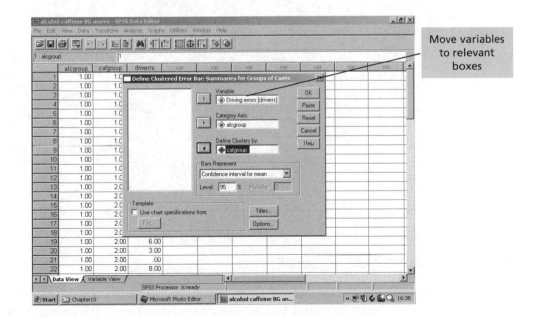

You will need to select the *Clustered* and *Summaries for groups of cases* options and then click on the *Define* button. You will be presented with a dialogue box resembling that shown below. You should move the driving errors variable to the *Variable* box, the *Alcgroup* variable to the *Category Axis* box and the *Cafgroup* variable to the *Define Clusters by* box. Then click on the *OK* button to generate the error bar chart. You should be presented with a chart similar to that presented in Figure10.3 (but without the solid lines connecting the error bars).

10.6 Two within-participants variables

We have shown you how ANOVA handles two between-participants variables and the interaction between these in one analysis; we will now move on to the case of two within-participants variables. We will remain with the same study and data as those used in the between-participants example so that we can highlight the important differences between the two types of analysis. The distribution of participants is now as shown in Table 10.5. Compare this with the previous completely between-participants design (Table 10.4).

You should be able to see that we have 12 participants taking part but each person has contributed a score in each of the cells in the table, that is, they have each taken part in all four conditions. Obviously this would be difficult to run in one session and so we would need to get the participants to come to four separate sessions.

We have the same data as for the completely between-participants design which means that the assumptions underlying the use of parametric tests are also met in the within-participants design. You should note, however, that this is only the case because we have only two conditions for each of our IVs. If we had more than two conditions in any of the within-participant IVs we would have to check also that the data do not violate the additional assumption of sphericity by consulting the Mauchley test of sphericity on the ANOVA printout. Remember, we explained that this was one of the assumptions underlying the use of within-participants ANOVA (see Chapter 9).

Table 10.5 Distribution of scores to conditions in the completely within-participants design

Participants	No alcohol		Alcohol	
	No caffeine	Caffeine	No caffeine	Caffeine
1	4	8	28	5
2	9	4	22	6
3	10	9	21	14
4	8	0	27	8
5	6	8	21	14
6	11	6	20	5
7	2	6	19	11
8	11	3	16	8
9	11	0	25	10
10	10	8	17	11
11	3	9	19	8
12	10	8	20	8

10.6.1 Sources of variance

When we conduct ANOVA we are trying to identify the possible sources of variance in our data. If you think back to when we explained about the sources of variance for a completely between-participants design, we suggested that the variance that was due to individual differences within each condition was classed as the error variance. When we have a within-participants design we have a constant source of variance due to using the same participants in each condition (this was explained in Chapter 9). Because we have this constant source of variance due to having the same participants in each condition we can subtract this from the error variance and as a result reduce the error term (this is often called *partialling out*). Why do we need to partial out the subject effects from the error term? When we have between-participants designs one of the assumptions of the statistical tests (one that we have not covered because it relates to the formulae, etc.) is that the data from each condition should be independent of the data from all other conditions. This is why such designs are also called 'independent' designs. This simply means that the conditions should be uncorrelated. Now this is a reasonable assumption for such designs. It is not such a reasonable assumption for within-participants designs. In such designs the conditions do tend to be correlated. For example, those participants who do well on the driving task in the no alcohol/no caffeine condition will also tend to do well compared with other participants in the other conditions. Similarly, those who tend to perform poorly in one condition will also tend to perform poorly in the other conditions. Now this is not necessarily the case for every study conducted but it is true for a great many. Therefore, the assumption of independence of conditions is lost for such designs.

How do we go about solving such a problem? The answer to this problem is to remove statistically the consistent effects of participants across all conditions. Once this is achieved the conditions will effectively be independent of each other and the analyses can continue. A useful feature of this statistical manipulation is that it tends to reduce the error term also. This means that in a great many cases the mean square for the effect is compared against a lower mean square for the error than would be the case for the equivalent between-participants analysis. The result of this procedure is that it often has the effect of making within-participants analyses more powerful than the equivalent between-participants analyses.

You will notice from the output for the within-participants analysis that there are many more entries than for the totally between-participants analysis. The reason for this is simply that we test each main effect and interaction against its own error term. That is, in within-participants designs, because we have the same participants in each condition, we are able to calculate the degree of error associated with each effect, whereas in the completely between-participants analysis we are able to calculate only the overall amount of error.

GENERAL LINEAR MODEL

Within-Subjects Factors
Measure: MEASURE_1

alcohol	caffeine	Dependent Variable
1	1	noalcnocaff
	2	noalccaff
2	1	alcnocaff
	2	alccaff

Multivariate Tests[b]

Effect		Value	F	Hypothesis df	Error df	Sig.	Partial Eta Squared
alcohol	Pillai's Trace	.882	82.331[a]	1.000	11.000	.000	.882
	Wilks' Lambda	.118	82.331[a]	1.000	11.000	.000	.882
	Hotelling's Trace	7.485	82.331[a]	1.000	11.000	.000	.882
	Roy's Largest Root	7.485	82.331[a]	1.000	11.000	.000	.882
caffeine	Pillai's Trace	.767	36.150[a]	1.000	11.000	.000	.767
	Wilks' Lambda	.233	36.150[a]	1.000	11.000	.000	.767
	Hotelling's Trace	3.286	36.150[a]	1.000	11.000	.000	.767
	Roy's Largest Root	3.286	36.150[a]	1.000	11.000	.000	.767
alcohol * caffeine	Pillai's Trace	.696	25.184[a]	1.000	11.000	.000	.696
	Wilks' Lambda	.304	25.184[a]	1.000	11.000	.000	.696
	Hotelling's Trace	2.289	25.184[a]	1.000	11.000	.000	.696
	Roy's Largest Root	2.289	25.184[a]	1.000	11.000	.000	.696

a. Exact statistic
b. Design: Intercept
   Within Subjects Design: alcohol+caffeine+alcohol*caffeine

Mauchly's Test of Sphericity[b]
Measure: MEASURE_1

Within Subjects Effect	Mauchly's W	Approx. Chi-Square	df	Sig.	Epsilon[a]		
					Greenhouse -Geisser	Huynh-Feldt	Lower-bound
alcohol	1.000	.000	0	.	1.000	1.000	1.000
caffeine	1.000	.000	0	.	1.000	1.000	1.000
alcohol * caffeine	1.000	.000	0	.	1.000	1.000	1.000

Tests the null hypothesis that the error covariance matrix of the orthonormalised transformed dependent variables is proportional to an identity matrix.

a. May be used to adjust the degrees of freedom for the averaged tests of significance. Corrected tests are displayed in the Tests of Within-Subjects Effects table.
b. Design: Intercept
   Within Subjects Design: alcohol+caffeine+alcohol*caffeine

Tests of Within-Subjects Effects
Measure: MEASURE_1

Source		Type III Sum of Squares	df	Mean Square	F	Sig.	Partial Eta Squared
alcohol	Sphericity Assumed	825.021	1	825.021	82.331	.000	.882
	Greenhouse-Geisser	825.021	1.000	825.021	82.331	.000	.882
	Huynh-Feldt	825.021	1.000	825.021	82.331	.000	.882
	Lower-bound	825.021	1.000	825.021	82.331	.000	.882
Error(alcohol)	Sphericity Assumed	110.229	11	10.021			
	Greenhouse-Geisser	110.229	11.000	10.021			
	Huynh-Feldt	110.229	11.000	10.021			
	Lower-bound	110.229	11.000	10.021			
caffeine	Sphericity Assumed	623.521	1	623.521	36.150	.000	.767
	Greenhouse-Geisser	623.521	1.000	623.521	36.150	.000	.767
	Huynh-Feldt	623.521	1.000	623.521	36.150	.000	.767
	Lower-bound	623.521	1.000	623.521	36.150	.000	.767
Error(caffeine)	Sphericity Assumed	189.729	11	17.248			
	Greenhouse-Geisser	189.729	11.000	17.248			
	Huynh-Feldt	189.729	11.000	17.248			
	Lower-bound	189.729	11.000	17.248			
alcohol * caffeine	Sphericity Assumed	305.021	1	305.021	25.184	.000	.696
	Greenhouse-Geisser	305.021	1.000	305.021	25.184	.000	.696
	Huynh-Feldt	305.021	1.000	305.021	25.184	.000	.696
	Lower-bound	305.021	1.000	305.021	25.184	.000	.696
Error(alcohol * caffeine)	Sphericity Assumed	133.229	11	12.112			
	Greenhouse-Geisser	133.229	11.000	12.112			
	Huynh-Feldt	133.229	11.000	12.112			
	Lower-bound	133.229	11.000	12.112			

Tests of Within-Subjects Contrasts
Measure: MEASURE_1

Source	alcohol	caffeine	Type III Sum of Squares	df	Mean Square	F	Sig.	Partial Eta Squared
alcohol	Linear		825.021	1	825.021	82.331	.000	.882
Error(alcohol)	Linear		110.229	11	10.021			
caffeine		Linear	623.521	1	623.521	36.150	.000	.767
Error(caffeine)		Linear	189.729	11	17.248			
alcohol * caffeine	Linear	Linear	305.021	1	305.021	25.184	.000	.696
Error(alcohol * caffeine)	Linear	Linear	133.229	11	12.112			

Tests of Between-Subjects Effects
Measure: MEASURE_1
Transformed Variable: Average

Source	Type III Sum of Squares	df	Mean Square	F	Sig.	Partial Eta Squared
Intercept	5786.021	1	5786.021	1022.772	.000	.989
Error	62.229	11	5.657			

Activity 10.7

How is the partial η^2 calculated for each effect in the above printout?

Essentially, in a within-participants design, ANOVA analyses each main effect as if it was a one-way ANOVA. It therefore calculates the overall amount of variability associated with each main effect (this will include all sources of variance, including error). ANOVA then subtracts from this overall variance the amount of the variability that can be attributed to the main effect and the amount of variability that can be attributed to the consistent effect of participants. The remaining variability is the variance that is unaccounted for and is, therefore, the error term. This is exactly the same procedure as was explained in Chapter 9 for the within-participants one-way ANOVA.

The rationale for the calculation of the interaction is similar to that explained for the between-participants ANOVA earlier. After we have calculated the main effects and their error terms there will probably be some that can be attributed to the interaction plus its error term. Once we have calculated the sum of squares for the interaction itself and for its error term, we can calculate the F-ratio. As a result of the calculations involved in the fully within-participants ANOVA you will notice on the printout that there is a separate error term for each of the main effects and the interaction.

In order to calculate the F-values in the within-participants design we have to divide the variance attributable to each effect (mean square$_{effect}$) by the error variance (mean square$_{error}$) that has been calculated for that effect. Thus, from the above printout, you can see that the F-value for the main effect of alcohol is

$$825.021 \div 10.021 = 82.331$$

You will also notice from the above printout that the overall number of degrees of freedom has been reduced from 44 in the between-participants design to 11 in this design. The reason for this is that we have only 12 participants in the latter example, whereas we have 48 people (12 in each condition) in the between-participants design.

10.6.2 Simple effects

The same advice about graphing your data in between-participants designs is applicable to within-participants designs. We have the same data as the example given for the between-participants design and so you should consult Figure 10.3 for the error bar chart for these data. The calculation of simple effects should be guided by the advice given earlier in this chapter and is essentially equivalent to the calculations of simple effects for the completely between-participants design. However, we have to use related t-tests instead of independent t-tests. The results of these analyses are presented below:

T-TEST

Paired Samples Statistics

		Mean	N	Std. Deviation	Std. Error Mean
Pair 1	No alcohol no caffeine	7.9167	12	3.31548	.95710
	No alcohol caffeine	5.7500	12	3.27872	.94648
Pair 2	Alcohol no caffeine	21.2500	12	3.72034	1.07397
	Alcohol caffeine	9.0000	12	3.07482	.88763
Pair 3	No alcohol no caffeine	7.9167	12	3.31548	.95710
	Alcohol no caffeine	21.2500	12	3.72034	1.07397
Pair 4	No alcohol caffeine	5.7500	12	3.27872	.94648
	Alcohol caffeine	9.0000	12	3.07482	.88763

Paired Samples Correlations

		N	Correlation	Sig.
Pair 1	No alcohol no caffeine & No alcohol caffeine	12	−.353	.260
Pair 2	Alcohol no caffeine & Alcohol caffeine	12	−.262	.410
Pair 3	No alcohol no caffeine & Alcohol no caffeine	12	−.153	.635
Pair 4	No alcohol caffeine & Alcohol caffeine	12	.225	.481

Paired Samples Test

		Paired Differences							
					95% Confidence Interval of the Difference				
		Mean	Std. Deviation	Std. Error Mean	Lower	Upper	t	df	Sig. (2-tailed)
Pair 1	No alcohol no caffeine − No alcohol caffeine	2.16667	5.42441	1.56589	−1.280	5.61317	1.384	11	.194
Pair 2	Alcohol no caffeine − Alcohol caffeine	12.250	5.41253	1.56246	8.8110	15.689	7.840	11	.000
Pair 3	No alcohol no caffeine − Alcohol no caffeine	−13.333	5.34846	1.54397	−16.73	−9.9351	−8.636	11	.000
Pair 4	No alcohol caffeine − Alcohol caffeine	−3.2500	3.95716	1.14233	−5.764	−.73574	−2.845	11	.016

It can be seen from the above printout that:

- the simple effect of the caffeine conditions without alcohol (see Figure 10.8(a)) has an associated t-value of $t(11) = 1.38, p = 0.194$
- the effect of the caffeine conditions with alcohol (Figure 10.8(b)) has a t-value of $t(11) = 7.84, p < 0.001$
- the effect of the alcohol conditions with no caffeine (Figure 10.8(c)) has a t-value of $t(11) = 8.64, p < 0.001$
- the effect of the alcohol conditions with caffeine (Figure 10.8(d)) has a t-value of $t(11) = 2.85, p = 0.016$

These analyses tell us that, with the exception of the two caffeine conditions in the no alcohol condition, the differences between each of the pairs of means are such that they are highly unlikely to have occurred due to sampling error, if the null hypotheses were true. However, if we use the more conservative criterion for significance of 0.0125 (0.05 ÷ 4) then we have to argue that the final simple effect is also not significant, although it is very close to reaching statistical significance.

It is important to recognise that for designs that include within-participants factors the analyses of simple effects can get complicated. The explanation for this is beyond the scope of this book, and so for now it is enough that you understand what simple effects are. You should also be wary of conducting too many analyses from one set of data so that you keep the familywise error rate to a minimum. If you wish to find out more about how the error terms for within-participants simple effects are determined you should consult one of the texts suggested at the end of this chapter.

10.6.3 Effect size

The most suitable measure of effect sizes for within-participants designs is again the partial eta-squared (partial η^2). You can see from the printout on page 351 that the partial η^2 for the main effect of alcohol is 0.88, for the main effect of caffeine it is 0.77 and for the interaction it is 0.70.

10.6.4 Writing up these analyses

The write-up for these analyses will be the same as for the completely between-participants example given earlier in this chapter. All you will need to do is alter the description of the ANOVA design, thus:

... The number of driving errors was analysed with a repeated measures ANOVA with two within-participants factors of alcohol (alcohol vs. no alcohol) and caffeine (caffeine vs. no caffeine) ...

The remainder of the write-up will be the same except that you will need to change the F, p and t values.

Example from the literature: women's ratings of attractiveness of body shapes

A study reported by Forestell *et al.* (2004) investigated womens' ratings of attractiveness of different female body shapes. They presented participants with a number of line drawings of people with different weights and waist-to-hip ratios (WHRs). There were three different categories for weight (light, moderate and heavy), and different WHRs ranging from 0.5 to 0.9. Previous research has shown that women tend to rate bodies with WHRs of 0.7 to be the most attractive.

The attractiveness ratings were analysed using a repeated measures (within-participants) ANOVA with body weight and WHR as the two IVs. The DV was the attractiveness rating given by the participants. The analyses revealed significant main effects of both body weight ($F_{(2,41)} = 11.70$, $p < 0.005$) and WHR ($F_{(4,39)} = 29.92$, $p < 0.001$). There was also a significant interaction between the two IVs ($F_{(8,35)} = 45.50$, $p < 0.001$). The researchers investigated this interaction by using Bonferonni pairwise tests which compared the various WHR for each body weight separately. They found that for all body weights the women tended to rate the WHRs of about 0.7 as the more attractive. However, for the moderate body weights a wider range of WHRs were rated as attractive when compared with the light and heavy body shapes.

SPSSFW: ANOVA with two within-participants factors

In the completely within-participants design we have four scores for each person and so we have to set up four variables in the data file (see below):

Set up four variables, one for each combination of conditions

	noalcnocaff	noalccaff	alcnocaff	alccaff
1	4.00	8.00	26.00	5.00
2	9.00	4.00	22.00	6.00
3	10.00	9.00	21.00	14.00
4	8.00	.00	27.00	8.00
5	6.00	8.00	21.00	14.00
6	11.00	6.00	20.00	5.00
7	2.00	6.00	19.00	11.00
8	11.00	3.00	16.00	8.00
9	11.00	.00	25.00	10.00
10	10.00	8.00	17.00	11.00
11	3.00	9.00	19.00	8.00
12	10.00	8.00	20.00	8.00

Once you have entered the data, click on the *Analyze* menu, followed by *General Linear Model*, followed by *Repeated Measures*:

Once you have selected *Repeated Measures* you will be presented with the following dialogue box. This should be familiar to you as it is the same procedure as for the one-way within-participants ANOVA:

Enter a name for each variable and the number of conditions and then click on *Add* to confirm details

When you name your within-participants variables, you need to remember which one you named first as this is important when you define each variable in the following dialogue box:

SPSSFW gives you a reminder of the order in which you named the variables

When you move the variables across to the relevant boxes, you need to do so in the correct order. This is why you need to remember the order in which you defined the variables in the previous dialogue box. In the *Within-Subjects Variables* box you can see that each entry has a two-digit code after it, for example (1, 2). This code informs us that this particular entry represents the first condition of variable 1 and the second condition of variable 2. Remember, we defined *alcohol* as the first variable and *caffeine* as the second variable. If you find that you cannot remember the order in which you named the variables, SPSSFW gives you a reminder near the top of the dialogue box. Consequently, each code represents the following conditions:

- (1, 1) = no alcohol/no caffeine
- (1, 2) = no alcohol/caffeine
- (2, 1) = alcohol/no caffeine
- (2, 2) = alcohol/caffeine

The variables therefore have to be moved into the appropriate slot in the *Within-Subjects Variables* box. When you are satisfied that you have moved the relevant variables across you should click on the *Options* button and check the *Effect Size* option as you did with the between-participants design above. Click on the *Continue* button and then the *OK* button to run the analysis. You should then be presented with output that is similar to that presented earlier.

The simple effects analyses are a bit more straightforward than for the completely between-participants design. In the completely within-participants design we do not have to tell SPSSFW to split the file, because every participant has contributed data to each condition. We therefore simply have to tell SPSSFW which two variables should go into each t-test (remember, we will be using related t-tests). So, if we wanted to examine the difference between the alcohol and no alcohol group in the no caffeine condition we would conduct a related t-test on the *noalnoca* and *alcnocaf* variables. If we wanted to examine the difference between the caffeine and no caffeine conditions in the alcohol condition we would conduct a related t-test on the *alcnocaf* and *alccaff* variables.

10.7 One between- and one within-participants variable

The final design we will be covering in this chapter is a mixture of between-participants and within-participants designs. Such an analysis is often called a *split-plot* ANOVA. We will be sticking with the alcohol/caffeine/driving example, but this time we will assume that the alcohol IV is a between-participants factor and the caffeine IV is assessed as a within-participants factor. The allocation of participants to conditions and their scores on the driving test are presented in Table 10.6.

Given that we are using the same data as the previous two analyses we can assume that we have met the assumptions underlying the use of parametric tests. Again, this is the case because we have only two conditions in our within-participants IV. If we had more than two conditions we would need to ensure that we had not violated the assumption of sphericity.

As with the two previous ANOVAs the first thing we need to think about is the possible sources of variance in the split-plot design. You can see from the printout for the current analysis that the between-participants IV has its own error term. The analysis of the between-participants IV is similar to conducting a one-way ANOVA on that factor, ignoring the within-participants IV.

Table 10.6 Distribution of scores to conditions in the split-plot design

	No alcohol			Alcohol	
Participant	No caffeine	Caffeine	Participant	No caffeine	Caffeine
1	4	8	13	28	5
2	9	4	14	22	6
3	10	9	15	21	14
4	8	0	16	27	8
5	6	8	17	21	14
6	11	6	18	20	5
7	2	6	19	19	11
8	11	3	20	16	8
9	11	0	21	25	10
10	10	8	22	17	11
11	3	9	23	19	8
12	10	8	24	20	8

GENERAL LINEAR MODEL

Within-Subjects Factors
Measure: MEASURE_1

cafgroup	Dependent Variable
1	nocaffeine
2	caffeine

Between-Subjects Factors

		Value Label	N
alcgroup	1.00	No alcohol	12
	2.00	Alcohol	12

Multivariate Tests[b]

Effect		Value	F	Hypothesis df	Error df	Sig.	Partial Eta Squared
cafgroup	Pillai's Trace	.659	42.474[a]	1.000	22.000	.000	.659
	Wilks' Lambda	.341	42.474[a]	1.000	22.000	.000	.659
	Hotelling's Trace	1.031	42.474[a]	1.000	22.000	.000	.659
	Roy's Largest Root	1.931	42.474[a]	1.000	22.000	.000	.659
cafgroup * alcgroup	Pillai's Trace	.486	20.778[a]	1.000	22.000	.000	.486
	Wilks' Lambda	.514	20.778[a]	1.000	22.000	.000	.486
	Hotelling's Trace	.944	20.778[a]	1.000	22.000	.000	.486
	Roy's Largest Root	.944	20.778[a]	1.000	22.000	.000	.486

a. Exact statistic
b. Design: Intercept+alcgroup
   Within Subjects Design: cafgroup

Mauchly's Test of Sphericity[b]
Measure: MEASURE_1

Within Subjects Effect	Mauchly's W	Approx. Chi-Square	df	Sig.	Epsilon[a]		
					Greenhouse-Geisser	Huynh-Feldt	Lower-bound
cafgroup	1.000	.000	0	.	1.000	1.000	1.000

Tests the null hypothesis that the error covariance matrix of the orthonormalised transformed dependent variables is proportional to an identity matrix.
a. May be used to adjust the degrees of freedom for the averaged tests of significance. Corrected tests are displayed in the Tests of Within-Subjects Effects table.
b. Design: Intercept+alcgroup
   Within Subjects Design: cafgroup

Tests of Within-Subjects Effects

Measure: MEASURE_1

Source		Type III Sum of Squares	df	Mean Square	F	Sig.	Partial Eta Squared
cafgroup	Sphericity Assumed	623.521	1	623.521	42.474	.000	.659
	Greenhouse-Geisser	623.521	1.000	623.521	42.474	.000	.659
	Huynh-Feldt	623.521	1.000	623.521	42.474	.000	.659
	Lower-bound	623.521	1.000	623.521	42.474	.000	.659
cafgroup * alcgroup	Sphericity Assumed	305.021	1	305.021	20.778	.000	.486
	Greenhouse-Geisser	305.021	1.000	305.021	20.778	.000	.486
	Huynh-Feldt	305.021	1.000	305.021	20.778	.000	.486
	Lower-bound	305.021	1.000	305.021	20.778	.000	.486
Error(cafgroup)	Sphericity Assumed	322.958	22	14.680			
	Greenhouse-Geisser	322.958	22.000	14.680			
	Huynh-Feldt	322.958	22.000	14.680			
	Lower-bound	322.958	22.000	14.680			

Tests of Within-Subjects Contrasts

Measure: MEASURE_1

Source	cafgroup	Type III Sum of Squares	df	Mean Square	F	Sig.	Partial Eta Squared
cafgroup	Linear	623.521	1	623.521	42.474	.000	.659
cafgroup * alcgroup	Linear	305.021	1	305.021	20.778	.000	.486
Error(cafgroup)	Linear	322.958	22	14.680			

Tests of Between-Subjects Effects

Measure: MEASURE_1

Transformed Variable: Average

Source	Type III Sum of Squares	df	Mean Square	F	Sig.	Partial Eta Squared
Intercept	5786.021	1	5786.021	738.106	.000	.971
alcgroup	825.021	1	825.021	105.245	.000	.827
Error	172.458	22	7.839			

The within-participants part of the ANOVA is divided into three parts: the main effect of caffeine, the interaction between the caffeine and alcohol factors, and the error term for this part of the analysis. Thus, in the split-plot design we have one error term for the between-participants part of the analysis and one error term for the within-participants part of the analysis. The interaction between alcohol (between-participants) and caffeine (within-participants) is part of the within-participants printout because it has a within-participants component. That is, one of the interaction terms (caffeine) is within-participants.

You can see from the above split-plot printout that the main effect of the alcohol factor has an F-value of 105.25 (825.02 ÷ 7.84) with an associated probability of $p < 0.001$. The main effect of the caffeine factor has an F-value of 42.47 (623.52 ÷ 14.68) with an associated probability of $p < 0.001$. And finally, the interaction has an F-value of 20.78 (305.02 ÷ 14.68) with a probability of $p < 0.001$.

10.7.1 Simple effects

Simple effects analyses are similar to those described above for the between- and within-participants designs. Again, you should be aware of the problems with familywise error rates and also the fact that, for any designs containing within-participants factors, the error terms are not straightforward. As in the previous examples you should stick to examining your simple effects using t-tests. The t-tests for these data are presented below. You should notice that in the split-plot design, because we have both between- and within-participants variables, you will need to use both the independent and related t-tests.

T-TEST
ALCGROUP = NO ALCOHOL

Paired Samples Statistics[a]

		Mean	N	Std. Deviation	Std. Error Mean
Pair 1	No caffeine	7.9167	12	3.31548	.95710
	Caffeine	5.7500	12	3.27872	.94648

a. alcgroup = No alcohol

Paired Samples Correlations[a]

	N	Correlation	Sig.
Pair 1 No caffeine & Caffeine	12	−.353	.260

a. alcgroup = No alcohol

Paired Samples Test[a]

		Paired Differences							
					95% Confidence Interval of the Difference				
		Mean	Std. Deviation	Std. Error Mean	Lower	Upper	t	df	Sig. (2-tailed)
Pair 1	No caffeine − Caffeine	2.167	5.42441	1.56589	−1.27984	5.61317	1.384	11	.194

a. alcgroup = No alcohol

ALCGROUP = ALCOHOL

Paired Samples Statistics[a]

		Mean	N	Std. Deviation	Std. Error Mean
Pair 1	No caffeine	21.2500	12	3.72034	1.07397
	Caffeine	9.0000	12	3.07482	.88763

a. alcgroup = Alcohol

Paired Samples Correlations[a]

	N	Correlation	Sig.
Pair 1 No caffeine & Caffeine	12	−.262	.410

a. alcgroup = Alcohol

Paired Samples Test[a]

	Paired Differences							
				95% Confidence Interval of the Difference				
	Mean	Std. Deviation	Std. Error Mean	Lower	Upper	t	df	Sig. (2-tailed)
Pair 1 No caffeine – Caffeine	12.250	5.41253	1.56246	8.8110	15.689	7.840	11	.000

a. alcgroup = Alcohol

T-TEST

Group Statistics

	alcgroup	N	Mean	Std. Deviation	Std. Error Mean
No caffeine	No alcohol	12	7.9167	3.31548	.95710
	Alcohol	12	21.2500	3.72034	1.07397
Caffeine	No alcohol	12	5.7500	3.27872	.94648
	Alcohol	12	9.0000	3.07482	.88763

Independent Samples Test

		Levene's Test for Equality of Variances		t-test for Equality of Means							
										95% Confidence Interval of the Difference	
		F	Sig.	t	df	Sig. (2-tailed)	Mean Difference	Std. Error Difference		Lower	Upper
No caffeine	Equal variances assumed	.005	.945	−9.269	22	.000	−13.33333	1.43856		−16.317	−10.350
	Equal variances not assumed			−9.269	21.714	.000	−13.33333	1.43856		−16.319	−10.348
Caffeine	Equal variances assumed	.059	.810	−2.505	22	.020	−3.25000	1.29758		−5.94101	−.55899
	Equal variances not assumed			−2.505	21.910	.020	−3.25000	1.29758		−5.94166	−.55834

These t-tests reveal that:

■ the effect of caffeine/no caffeine with no alcohol has a t-value of $t(11) = 1.38, p = 0.19$ (see Figure 10.8(a))

■ the effect of caffeine/no caffeine with alcohol has a t-value of $t(11) = 7.84, p < 0.001$ (see Figure 10.8(b))

■ the simple effect of alcohol/no alcohol without caffeine has an associated t-value of $t(22) = 9.27, p < 0.001$ (see Figure 10.8(c))

■ the effect of alcohol/no alcohol with caffeine has a t-value of $t(22) = 2.51, p = 0.02$ (see Figure 10.8(d)).

As we have the same data as in the previous two examples it is no surprise that all these t-tests give a similar pattern to that observed previously. There are significant effects of the caffeine IV in the alcohol condition and the alcohol IV in the caffeine condition. The other simple effects are not significant, assuming our criterion for significance has been adjusted to 0.0125 to take account of multiple testing.

10.7.2 Effect size

The most suitable measure of effect sizes for split-plot design is again the partial eta-squared (partial η^2). You can see from the printout on page 360 that the partial η^2 for the main effect of alcohol is 0.83, for the main effect of caffeine it is 0.66 and for the interaction it is 0.49.

Activity 10.8

Calculate *d* for the four simple effects comparisons above.

10.7.3 Writing up these analyses

The write-up for the split-plot analyses will be similar to that for the between-participants analyses presented earlier. All you will need to do is change the description of the ANOVA design and the way you describe the t-tests. The following is how you might describe the ANOVA design:

> . . . The number of driving errors was analysed with a split-plot ANOVA with alcohol group (alcohol vs. no alcohol) as the between-participants factor and caffeine group (caffeine vs. no caffeine) as the within-participants factor . . .

Example from the literature: gender differences in map-reading

A study reported by MacFadden *et al.* (2003) investigated gender differences in scanning of maps and in giving directions based upon the maps. In this study a map was presented on a computer screen and participants were asked to find a route from one place to another on the map (e.g. from a school to an airport). The participants were allowed two minutes to find a route and they were then asked to write directions on a sheet of paper so that another person would be able to find their way from the start point to the destination point. The researchers measured participants using an eye-tracker to see if there were any differences in the ways males and females scanned the map. They also examined the directions produced for gender related differences.

The scanning of the maps was analysed using a 2×2 ANOVA with gender as a between-participants IV and gaze points (either landmarks or compass legend) as a within-participants IV. The DV was the mean time spent focusing on the landmarks or the compass legend. They found a significant main effect of gaze point ($F(1,42) = 1504.220$, $p < 0.001$). They found that participants focused on the landmarks significantly more than the compass legend. There was no main effect of gender and no significant interaction. The authors did not report the Fs and ps for this main effect or interaction.

Analysis of the directions given by participants was designed to compare males and females for the number of landmarks and number of north, east, south, west directions. These data were converted to z-scores and analysed using a 2×2 ANOVA with gender as a between-participants IV and directions strategy (landmarks versus compass directions) as a within-participants IV. There was no significant main effect of gender [the authors don't give the F- and p-values for this]. There was, however, a significant interaction between gender and directions strategy ($F(1,42) = 4.458$, $p = 0.021$). This interaction was followed up with post hoc t-tests which suggested that males made more references to the compass points than did females ($t(43) = 2.699$, $p = 0.006$). The authors don't report the details of the other t-tests they conducted. They also don't report details of the main effect of directions strategy.

You should note from this that the authors have the tendency to under-report the non-significant statistical details. We advise that you report these in full when writing up your analyses.

SPSSFW: ANOVA with one between-participants and one within-participants factor

The datafile for a split-plot design is, not surprisingly, a combination of the between-participants and the within-participants design. We have to set up one grouping variable for the between-participants factor of alcohol/no alcohol and two variables representing the two conditions of the within-participants factor of caffeine/no caffeine. The datafile should therefore look like that below:

	alcgroup	nocaffeine	caffeine
1	1.00	4.00	8.00
2	1.00	9.00	4.00
3	1.00	10.00	9.00
4	1.00	8.00	.00
5	1.00	6.00	8.00
6	1.00	11.00	6.00
7	1.00	2.00	6.00
8	1.00	11.00	3.00
9	1.00	11.00	.00
10	1.00	10.00	8.00
11	1.00	3.00	9.00
12	1.00	10.00	8.00
13	2.00	28.00	5.00
14	2.00	22.00	6.00
15	2.00	21.00	14.00
16	2.00	27.00	8.00
17	2.00	21.00	14.00
18	2.00	20.00	5.00
19	2.00	19.00	11.00
20	2.00	16.00	8.00
21	2.00	25.00	10.00
22	2.00	17.00	11.00

Click on *Analyze*, *General Linear Model* and *Repeated Measures* to set up the analysis. This time you only need to set up one within-participants variable using the first dialogue box:

Click on the *Define* button and set up the variables as below:

When you have set up the variable click on *Options* to select effect size analyses and click on *OK* to run the analysis. The printout should look like the one shown to you above.

When you come to investigate your simple effects you need to bear in mind that one of the variables is a between-participants variable (in our case it is the *alc* variable). Therefore, if you wish to examine the difference between the caffeine and no caffeine conditions in each of the alcohol conditions you need to tell SPSSFW to split the file using the alcohol variable (*Data*, *Split File*). We have explained how to do this earlier in the chapter. You would then conduct related t-tests on the *nocaff* and *caff* variables. If you wanted to examine the difference between the alcohol and no-alcohol conditions in the caffeine condition you would not need to split the file but run an independent t-test with *alc* as the IV and *caff* as the DV. It is worth reiterating here that you should be careful when you use the split file option. You should make sure you unsplit the file after you have done your analyses so that any future analyses will be conducted on all your data. Thus, you should unsplit the file before you conduct the independent t-tests.

Summary

In this chapter we have explained:

- how factorial ANOVA is an extension of the one-way ANOVA we covered in Chapter 9

- how we can analyse data from a study that includes two or more IVs using factorial ANOVA

- the sources of variance for the following three designs:
  - two between-participants variables
  - two within-participants variables
  - one between-participants and one within-participants variable (split-plot design)

- how to examine the interaction between two IVs using the following:
  - error bar charts
  - line graphs
  - simple effects analyses

- how SPSSFW gives partial η^2 as the measure of effect size in factorial ANOVA, and that this is simply a ratio of the effect sum of squares to the effect sum of squares plus the error sum of squares

- that when we have a completely within-participants design, the main effects and interactions have their own error terms

- that a priori and post-hoc analyses of simple effects can be conducted using t-tests

- that when conducting more than one post-hoc (or a priori) comparison, you should adjust your α by dividing 0.05 by the number of comparisons being made.

SPSSFW exercises

Exercise 1

A researcher, Dr Bod, is interested in examining whether academic ability has fallen in the last 20 years. She therefore decides to compare the A-level performance of a sample of students who took the exams in 1997 and a sample who took them in 1977. Each student had taken an examination in both English and Mathematics. In order to ensure that the exams are marked to the same criteria she employs examiners to re-mark a sample of exams from each year group. The new marks awarded to each student for Mathematics and English are given in the table below:

Students from 1977		Students from 1997	
Mathematics	English	Mathematics	English
67	62	67	63
52	73	49	67
45	41	48	42
58	51	61	52
59	62	54	51
81	59	55	54
61	65	51	55
55	57	49	52
60	58	53	51
57	60	56	48
51	63	51	50
60	61	50	52

1. What sort of design is this study?

2. What are the IVs and DV?

3. Input the data into SPSSFW and conduct an ANOVA.

4. What are the F-values and associated probabilities for each main effect and any interactions?

5. Are there any effects that are probably not due to sampling error? If there are, which are they?

6. Which of the above effects has the largest magnitude of effect?

Exercise 2

A researcher, Dr Kid, is interested in whether boys and girls differ in the ability to perceive colours. She thinks that girls will be better than boys at perceiving differences in colours from a very early age. She therefore tests two different age groups (5-year-olds and

11-year-olds) on a standard colour perception test and compares the performance (marked out of 10) of boys and girls. The data are presented below:

5-year-olds		11-year-olds	
Boys	Girls	Boys	Girls
4	6	4	8
3	5	2	9
4	6	3	9
5	4	4	8
9	6	7	7
1	7	5	10
0	8	4	9
2	6	3	10
3	5	2	8
3	4	2	6
4	6	4	9
5	3	5	8

1. What sort of design is this?

2. What are the IVs and DV?

3. Input the data into SPSSFW and conduct an ANOVA.

4. What are the F-values and associated probabilities of the main effects and any interactions?

5. Are any of these effects probably not due to sampling error? Which ones?

6. What are the magnitudes of effects for the main effects and interactions?

7. Conduct simple effects analyses to find out if there was any improvement in colour perception with age for the boys and then do the same analysis for the girls.

MULTIPLE CHOICE QUESTIONS

1. How would you describe a $2 \times 2 \times 4$ ANOVA?
   (a) One IV with three conditions
   (b) One IV with four conditions and one IV with two conditions
   (c) One IV with four conditions and two IVs with two conditions
   (d) One IV with 16 conditions

2. ANOVA is useful for:
   (a) Teasing out the individual effects of factors on an IV
   (b) Analysing data from research with more than one IV and one DV
   (c) Analysing correlational data
   (d) All of the above

3. What are the various sources of variance in an ANOVA with two between-participants IVs?

   (a) Variance attributable to the populations
   (b) Variance attributable to the two IVs and the error
   (c) Variance attributable to the two IVs, the interaction between the two IVs and the error
   (d) Both (a) and (c) above

4. η^2 is:

   (a) A measure of the magnitude of the probability that the effects are due to sampling error
   (b) A measure of magnitude of effect used with ANOVA
   (c) A left-wing terrorist organisation
   (d) Both (a) and (b) above

5. When generating error bar charts for a study with two IVs, each with two conditions, which combination of options should you select in SPSFW?

   (a) *Simple* along with *Summaries of groups of cases*
   (b) *Simple* along with *Summaries of separate variables*
   (c) *Clustered* along with *Summaries of groups of cases*
   (d) *Clustered* along with *Summaries of separate variables*

Questions 6 to 9 relate to the following printout:

UNIVARIATE ANALYSIS OF VARIANCE

Between-Subjects Factors

		Value Label	N
CARBUS	1.00	Cars	20
	2.00	buses	20
AREA	1.00	Town	20
	2.00	Country	20

Tests of Between-Subjects Effects
Dependent Variable: Driving errors

Source	Type III Sum of Squares	df	Mean Square	F	Sig.	Eta Squared
Corrected Model	84.600[a]	3	28.200	23.178	.000	.659
Intercept	577.600	1	577.600	474.740	.000	.930
CARBUS	4.900	1	4.900	4.027	.052	.101
AREA	12.100	1	12.100	9.945	.003	.216
CARBUS * AREA	67.600	1	67.600	55.562	.000	.607
Error	43.800	36	1.217			
Total	706.000	40				
Corrected Total	128.400	39				

a. R Squared = .659 (Adjusted R Squared = .630)

6. What is the obvious conclusion from this printout?

    (a) That there is a main effect of AREA and an interaction, which are probably not due to sampling error
    (b) That there is only an interaction between the two IVs, which is probably not due to sampling error
    (c) That there are no main effects or interactions
    (d) Both (a) and (b) above

7. What is the p-value for the main effect of CARBUS?

    (a) 0.003
    (b) 9.945
    (c) 0.101
    (d) None of the above

8. How is the F-value for the interaction calculated?

    (a) $4.900 \div 12.100$
    (b) $12.100 \div 67.600$
    (c) $67.600 \div 1.217$
    (d) None of the above

9. How much variation in driving errors is accounted for by the interaction between CARBUS and AREA?

    (a) 93%
    (b) 5.2%
    (c) 60.7%
    (d) 65.9%

10. Look at the following error bar chart. What would be the sensible conclusion?

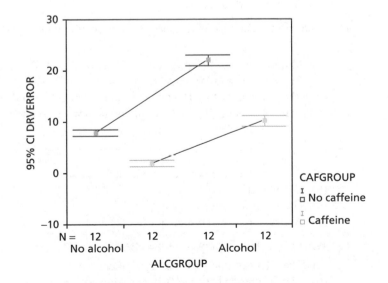

(a) That there are main effects of the two IVs and an interaction, which are probably not attributable to sampling error

(b) That there are no main effects or interactions

(c) That there is only one main effect

(d) That there are two main effects, which are probably not attributable to sampling error, but no interaction

11. How many effects are we comparing against their respective null hypotheses in a 2×2 ANOVA?

(a) 1

(b) 2

(c) 3

(d) 4

12. The Mauchley sphericity test is:

(a) A test of the assumption that the standard errors of the difference between means of the within-participants variables are equal

(b) A test that the data used in ANOVA are rounded in nature

(c) A well-known test developed at a well-known London psychiatric hospital

(d) None of the above

13. How would you describe a $2 \times 3 \times 5 \times 7 \times 7$ ANOVA?

(a) Sensible

(b) An ANOVA with two variables with three conditions, five variables with seven conditions and seven variables with one condition

(c) An ANOVA with one variable with two conditions, one variable with three conditions, one variable with five conditions, and two variables with seven conditions

(d) Both (a) and (c) above

14. What are the sources of variance in a completely within-participants design with two IVs?

(a) Main effect of IV^1 plus error, main effect of IV^2 plus the error, interaction between IV^1 and IV^2 plus error

(b) Main effects of IV^1, IV^2 and the interaction between these two plus the error

(c) Main effects of IV^1, IV^2 and the interaction between these two

(d) None of the above

15. Partial η^2 is:

(a) A measure of the power of your analyses

(b) Equal to η^2

(c) Usually much greater than η^2

(d) A measure of magnitude of effect

16. What is the definition of a simple effect?

(a) The effect of one variable on another

(b) The difference between two conditions of one IV at one level of another IV

(c) The easiest way to get a significant result

(d) All of the above

17. If you had an MS for your main effect of 12.4 and an MS for the error term of 3.1, what would your F-value be?

    (a) 6.2
    (b) 4.1
    (c) 3.1
    (d) 4

18. If you had a completely within-participants design, with each IV having two conditions, how would you examine the simple effects?

    (a) With independent t-tests, being careful to select the correct participants using the *Split File* command in SPSSFW
    (b) With independent t-tests, taking care to adjust the α to keep the familywise error rate low
    (c) With related t-tests, taking care to adjust the α to keep the familywise error rate low
    (d) None of the above

19. How many effects are we comparing against their respective null hypotheses in a $2 \times 2 \times 2$ ANOVA?

    (a) 3
    (b) 5
    (c) 7
    (d) 8

20. If you have a 2×2 between-participants design what should be the first step before generating descriptive statistics in SPSSFW?

    (a) Transform your data
    (b) Split the data file
    (c) Conduct t-tests
    (d) Conduct correlational analyses

References

Ekehammar, B., Akrami, N. and Araya, T. (2003) 'Gender differences in implicit prejudice', *Personality and Individual Differences*, **34**: 1509–23.

Forestell, C.A., Humphrey, T.M. and Stewart, S.H. (2004) 'Involvement of body weight and shape factors in ratings of attractiveness by women: a replication and extension of Tassinary and Hansen (1998)', *Personality and Individual Differences*, **36**: 295–305.

Howell, D.C. (2002) *Statistical Methods for Psychology* (5th edn). Wadsworth.

Loftus, C.R. (1996) 'Psychology will be a much better science when we change the way we analyze data', *Current Directions in Psychological Science*, **5**: 161–71.

MacFadden, A., Elias, L. and Saucier, D. (2003) 'Males and females scan maps similarly, but give directions differently', *Brain & Cognition*, **53**: 297–300.

Mogg, K. and Bradley, B.P. (1999) 'Some methodological issues in assessing attentional biases for threat faces in anxiety: a replication study using a modified version of the probe detection task', *Behaviour Research and Therapy*, **37**: 595–604.

11 Regression analysis

Chapter overview

Regression analysis is an extension of correlational analysis, which we covered in Chapter 5, so if you feel you have forgotten some of this material, it is probably best to go back and read that chapter. In the first part of this chapter we will be showing you how to assess the effect of one variable (x) on another variable (y). This is called *bivariate linear regression*. In the latter part of the chapter we will be showing you how to assess the effect of several variables (labelled x_1, x_2, and so on) on another variable (y). This is called *multiple regression*.

In this chapter you will:

- learn how to assess the relationship between a dependent variable and one or more explanatory variables
- learn how to predict a person's score on the criterion variable by a knowledge of their scores on one or more explanatory variables
- learn how to use confidence limits when analysing data by the use of multiple regression.

11.1 The purpose of linear regression

Psychologists are interested in using linear regression in order to discover the effect of one variable (which we denote by x) on another (which we denote by y). It is similar to simple correlational analysis, but while correlational analysis allows us to conclude how strongly two variables relate to each other (both magnitude and direction), linear regression will answer the question 'By how much will y change, if x changes?' In other words, if x changes by a certain amount, we will be able to estimate how much y will change.

Imagine we have data on the amount of diet cola bought and the price of diet cola. Now, if the price of diet cola becomes high enough, the sales of diet cola will decrease (people will swap to a cheaper alternative). A simple correlational analysis will show us that the price of diet cola and sales of diet cola are negatively correlated – we are able to say, then, that as the price increases, sales decrease. But we cannot tell by *how much* sales will decrease, for any given price rise. Psychologists use linear regression in order to be able to assess the effect that x has on y. Linear regression analysis results in a formula (a regression equation) that we can use to predict exactly how y will change, as a result of a change in x. For instance, we would be able to say something like: if the price of cola rises by 50%, sales will fall by 40%.

Since linear regression gives us a measure of the effect that x has on y, the technique allows us to predict y, from x. In our example above, if we know by how much diet cola sales decrease, as a result of every penny increase, then we are able to predict diet cola sales, from price. In an experimental situation, psychologists can use linear regression to *suggest* that a score on one variable influenced the score on the other variable. In this way they try to infer *causal* relationships.

Linear regression could be used to:

■ assess the effect of stress on symptoms of the common cold (e.g. runny nose, sore throat, cough)
■ predict children's mathematical ability from a measure of their reading ability.

When you carry out a linear regression, you proceed in exactly the same way as with a correlational design, that is, the two variables are examined to see if there is a linear relationship (a relationship that can be best described by a straight line) between them (see Chapter 5). This is explained further below.

For instance, consider the example of the relationship between marks in a mock statistics exam and marks in the final statistics exam. There is a positive relationship between these two variables: people who do well in the mock exam tend to do well in the final exam. The relationship is not perfect of course; some people will do really well in the mock, but perform badly in the final, and some who do badly in the mock will do well in the final. In order to carry out a regression analysis, we would collect data on the mock exam score and the final exam score for all the students in a particular year. If the relationship was positive and sufficiently strong to be predictive, then in the next year's set of students we could look at the scores from their mock exam and be able to have a good idea of how they would do in the final exam. Thus we could identify those students in danger of failing (before they have taken their final exam!) and perhaps offer additional support. This is an example of when psychologists would use the regression equation in order to predict.

Psychologists, however, do not usually use linear regression in order to predict in a new sample. The results of the regression analysis, however, will show the amount of change in y as a result of change in x. In the above example, performance in the mock exam does not actually cause the scores in the final exam. However, performance in the mock precedes performance in the final exam – both are related in a predictive, temporal sense. As mentioned previously, sometimes psychologists are able to suggest causal relationships by using this method. It is difficult to state that changes in one variable 'cause' changes in another, however, even when the two events occur at different timepoints, because another intervening variable may be influencing scores on both variables. This, of course, is a limitation of correlational designs.

11.1.1 The two variables, x and y

The variable that is being predicted is called a *criterion* or *dependent variable* (DV). This is also called y.[1] The variable that is predicting the DV is, not surprisingly, called the *predictor* (or *explanatory*) *variable* (IV); this is also called x.

---

[1] An actual value of y is simply represented by y, but a predicted value is labelled $\hat{y}$.

Sometimes the explanatory variables are called 'independent' variables. It can be a bit confusing, however, to call the variables 'independent' and 'dependent' because, of course, we are not manipulating the IV at all. For instance, we do not assign the students to groups. Studies using linear regression are correlational designs (i.e. you are looking to see whether the two variables are related, rather than looking for a difference between conditions, as we did in Chapter 6). In this chapter then, we call the variables that predict, or explain, scores on the dependent variable, the explanatory variables.

11.1.2 The regression line

If you have understood the chapter on correlation (Chapter 5), you should not have too much trouble with regression, because the two are very similar: for example, correlational analysis gives us a measure that represents how closely the datapoints are clustered around an (imaginary) line. It does not give us a measure of how much y changes as a result of x, and therefore it does not allow us to *predict* a person's score on y from x. As previously mentioned, linear regression does – because instead of an imaginary line, we draw (well, the computer does!) a *real* line.

Look at the data in Table 11.1.

We can plot these marks on a graph, just as we did with the data in the examples in Chapter 5. It is conventional to call the predictor variable x, as we use the x axis on the graph, and call the criterion variable y, as we use the y axis.

You can probably tell, just by looking at the scatterplot in Figure 11.1, that there is a positive correlation between x and y (actually +0.9), but all you can say at this point is that, as marks in the mock exam increase, marks in the final exam increase. The dots cluster quite tightly around an imaginary line, but how can we predict a person's final mark from his or her marks in the mock exam? The answer, of course, is linear regression. Linear regression is a method by which we fit a straight line to the data This line is drawn in the best place possible – that is, no other line would fit as well. This is why it is called the line of best fit – we talk about this more in the following paragraphs (see Figure 11.2).

Once we have a straight line representing the data, we can go further than just saying 'as x increases, y increases'. We can actually say that 'for every one unit change in x, y

Table 11.1 Percentage of marks in mock and final examination

% Marks in mock (predictor) x	% Marks in final (criterion) y
50	55
30	20
60	59
75	78
40	55
90	70
15	20
19	15
64	60
80	84

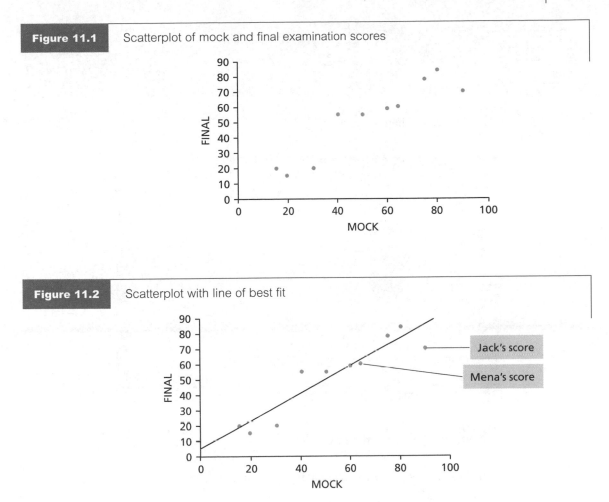

Figure 11.1 Scatterplot of mock and final examination scores

Figure 11.2 Scatterplot with line of best fit

Jack's score

Mena's score

changes by a certain amount'. In the above example, we are able to say: 'for every 20-mark increase in the mock exam, marks in the final increase by 18'.

Look at Figure 11.2. We can use the line to predict a person's score on y, from x. A person with a score of 60 on x is predicted to have a score of 59 on y. In fact, if you look at the person (Mena) with a score of 60 on x you will see that she has scored 59 on y – so the line was good at predicting for Mena. On the other hand, Jack, who has scored 90 on x, is predicted to score 86 on y, but he has scored only 70 on y. So the prediction, for Jack, is not so good. But the line will provide the *best* prediction possible, for the participants in general.

You may be wondering how we were able to work out the figures for the above; that is, how did we know that final marks increase by 18, for every 20-mark increase in the mock? Although we could work this out mathematically, it is simpler to get SPSSFW to do it! The slope of the line (called b) gives us a measure of how much y changes as x changes. The larger the value of b, the steeper the slope. Using a straight line, as above, allows us to predict a person's score on y, from x. You could not do that with a simple correlation. The trick is to draw the line in the right place! (Although, unlike us, SPSSFW doesn't have a problem with this. . . .)

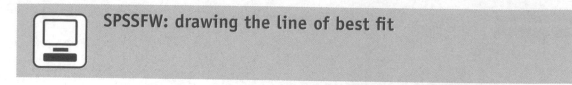

SPSSFW: drawing the line of best fit

Choose *Graphs*, then *Scatter*:

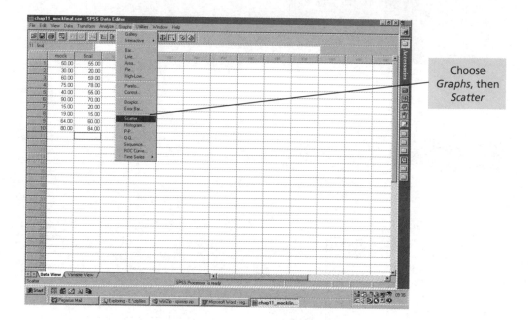

Choose
Graphs, then
Scatter

You need to choose the correct scattergram from four options: choose *Simple*:

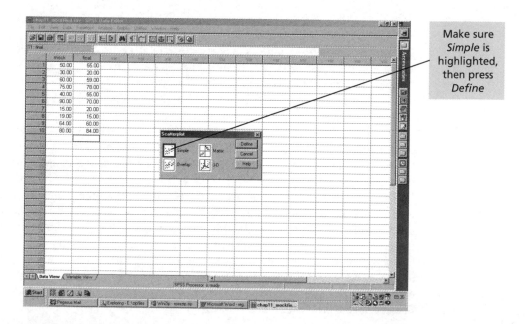

Make sure
Simple is
highlighted,
then press
Define

Both the predictor and criterion variables are moved from the variable list on the left to the appropriate boxes on the right-hand side:

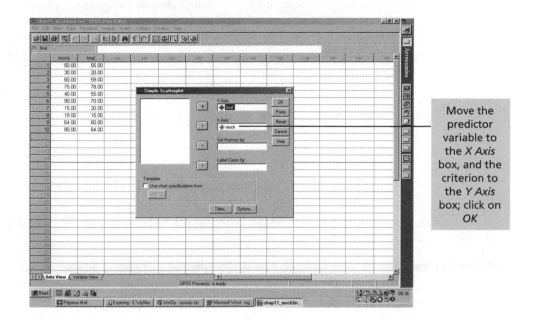

Move the predictor variable to the *X Axis* box, and the criterion to the *Y Axis* box; click on *OK*

After clicking on OK, your output will be shown as below. Make sure you double-click on the graph.

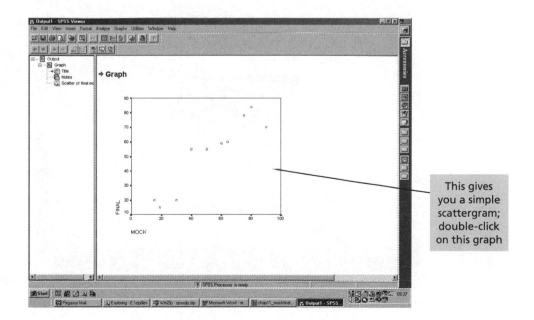

This gives you a simple scattergram; double-click on this graph

This will enable you to choose the chart options:

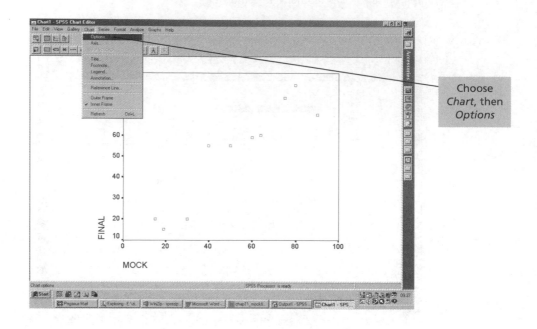

We now make sure we have chosen the *Fit Line Total* box:

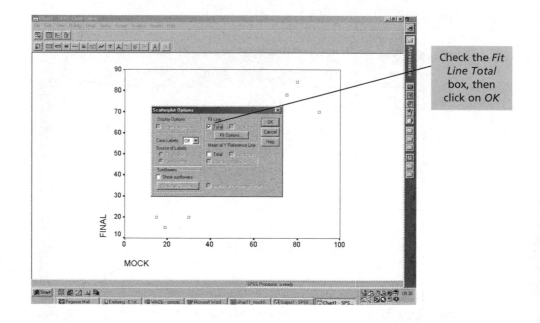

Choosing the *Fit Line Total* option gives the line of best fit:

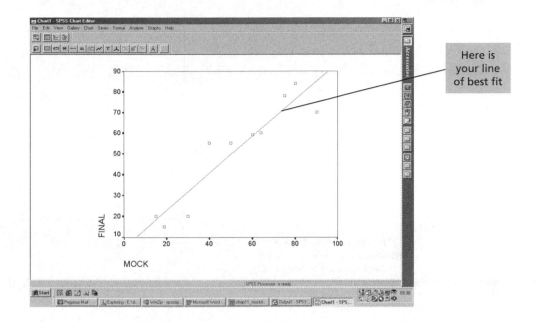

Here is your line of best fit

Activity 11.1

Have a go at explaining how regression analysis differs from simple correlation. What extra information does regression analysis give you?

11.1.3 Predicting from a straight line

In the next couple of sections we are going to look at how you can use a straight line to predict one variable from another. We will make it easy by starting with perfect relationships.

Perfect relationships – positive

Here we start with what you know already (Figure 11.3). You will immediately see that Figure 11.3 shows a perfect positive correlation. A straight line is drawn through the datapoints. Because the correlation is perfect, it is possible for the straight line to pass through every datapoint. The line of best fit here fits the data perfectly.

Figure 11.3   Plot of *x* with *y*

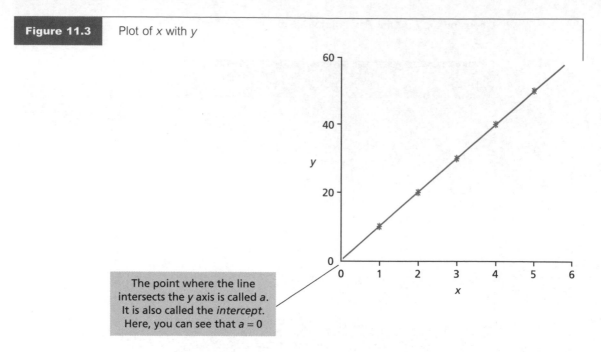

The point where the line intersects the *y* axis is called *a*. It is also called the *intercept*. Here, you can see that *a* = 0

Every time *x* increases by 1, *y* increases by 10. (Make sure you confirm this by looking at Figure 11.3.) The 0 is where the line intersects the *y* axis. This means that, when a person scores 0 on *x*, they score 0 on *y* too. For example:

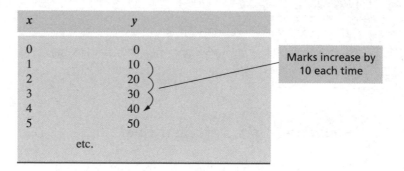

x	*y*
0	0
1	10
2	20
3	30
4	40
5	50
etc.	

Marks increase by 10 each time

You can see from the above table, too, that *y* increases by 10, with every unit change in *x* (i.e. 1). Note that this is a *constant* change.

The amount by which *y* changes, when *x* changes by 1, is known as *b*: *b* is the slope, or tilt, of the straight line.

11.1.4 The regression equation

When we perform a linear regression analysis, we obtain a regression equation, which shows the way in which *y* changes as a result of change in *x*. From this formula, we can calculate someone's score on *y* from their score on *x*. The general formula looks like this:

$$y = bx + a$$

or

$$y = a + bx$$

What this means is that, for any individual, y can be predicted by a value denoting the slope of the line multiplied by their particular score on x, added to a value denoted by a.

- y is the variable to be predicted
- x is the score on the variable x
- b is the value for the slope of the line
- a is the value of the constant, that is, the place where the straight line intercepts the y axis (also called the intercept).

The regression equation shows us the way in which y changes as a result of x changing. The steeper the slope (called b), the more y changes as a result of x. So the slope is an important part of your results, when reporting them in laboratory reports. In the regression equation below, the slope of the line is 10. This means that, every time x increases by one unit, y changes by 10. This is useful in itself, but as we have said previously, the regression allows you to predict. The equation below shows that y is able to be predicted by multiplying a person's score on x by b, which is 10, and then adding the constant, a (which is, in this case, zero).

In our example above, $a = 0$ (starting point on the graph, intercept, constant) and $b = 10$. So:

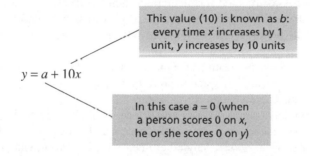

If we now tell you that a person has a score of 7 on x, then you will be able to predict his or her score on y.

$$y = 0 + (10 * 7) = 70$$

* means multiply

So a person who scores 7 on x is predicted to score 70 on y. If you look at the graph above, you will be able to confirm this.

Of course, it is easy to predict a person's score when all the points fall on a straight line. You always get it right! Some students become confused at this point, wondering why we are trying to predict a score when we know it already! However, if our regression equation was able to predict with a high degree of accuracy, this shows that we could use our equation in another sample, for whom we did *not* have information on y. This is rather like insurance companies, who have information to show that younger male drivers have more road accidents than other groups of people. When you try to buy car insurance for the first time, the company does not need to know how brilliantly you drive – your age and whether you are male or female will be noted in order to predict how likely it is that you will have an accident and cost the company money (there is no point in insisting you are an outlier!). Luckily (for us), lecturers over 40 will have cheaper premiums – even if they drive horrendously.

Activity 11.2

What is someone's predicted score on *y* when their score on *x* = 20? Assume *a* = 5 and *b* = 2.

Residuals

If we use our line of best fit to predict a person's score, unless we have a perfect relationship we will always make some errors. Look at the line of best fit for Burpacoke on page 389. Some datapoints are on the line, but others are further away. These represent errors of prediction.

If we use our line of best fit to predict sales for each price, then we will obtain a predicted sales figure. For this sample, we can compare it with the actual sales figures. If our line of best fit is really good for predicting, then the differences between the actual and predicted figures will be small; if the line of best fit is not good at predicting, then the differences will be large. The differences between the actual scores and predicted scores are called *residuals*. Residuals are particularly important in multiple regression, and so we will come across them again later in this chapter. SPSSFW gives you an output of residuals statistics; if you are interested to go further into the subject, there are many books with more advanced chapters on linear regression.

If there was no relationship between *x* and *y*, *y* could not be predicted by *x* at all and the line would be drawn as horizontal. In a case where *x* and *y* are not related at all, any line of best fit would be just as good as any other line, but it is conventional in this case for *b* to be drawn as a horizontal line, thus *b* = 0.

Figure 11.4 shows that *x* and *y* are not related at all (zero correlation −*r* = 0); *y* is not able to be predicted by *x* (*b* = zero).

Figure 11.4   Zero relationship

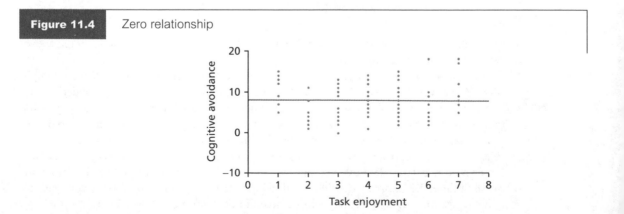

Figure 11.5 Plot of *x* with *y*

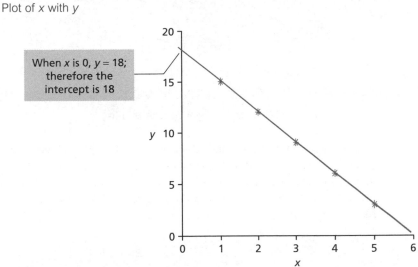

Perfect relationships – negative

It is not only in the case of positive relationships that we can predict. There are negative relationships too. For example, assume that *x* = number of hours watching television per night. Assume also that *y* is marks in a test at the end of the school week. Figure 11.5 is the graph (data are fictitious!). It can be seen that, as the number of television hours watched increases, marks in the test decrease. The relationship is perfect; that is, the straight line is able to be drawn in such a way that it goes through every datapoint.

If you look at Figure 11.5 you will see that *y* decreases by 3 every time *x* increases by 1. Look at the following data:

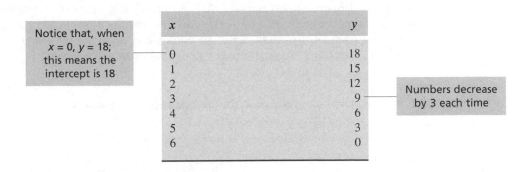

x	*y*
0	18
1	15
2	12
3	9
4	6
5	3
6	0

Here you can see that, every time *x* increases by 1, *y* decreases by 3. You can also see that the line of best fit has intercepted the *y* axis at 18.

- ■ $\hat{y}$ = marks in a test
- ■ *x* = number of television hours watched
- ■ *a* = 18
- ■ *b* = 3

So:

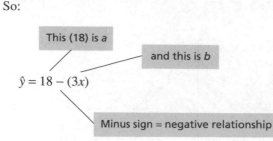

$$\hat{y} = 18 - (3x)$$

If we tell you that a person had watched 3.5 hours of television per night, what would you predict as the test score? You can find out from the graph, of course, by using a ruler upwards from 3.5 on the x axis to the straight line, and then using a ruler horizontally until it meets the y axis. However, you do not need to look at the graph; you can work it out from the formula:

$$\hat{y} = 18 - (3x)$$

So:

$$\hat{y} = 18 - (3 * 3.5)$$

The brackets show us that the sum inside the bracket should be calculated first. So:

$$18 - (3 * 3.5) = 18 - 10.5$$
$$= 7.5$$

Thus a person who watches 3.5 hours of television per night is predicted to score 7.5 in the test.

The minus sign means that it is a negative relationship: as one variable (x) increases, the other (y) decreases.

The intercept

In Figure 11.6, the line has started at 5. (This means that a person who has scored 0 on x would be predicted to score 5 on y. Of course, sometimes it would be impossible to score 0 on x – if x were IQ for instance. But we won't worry about this for now!) For every value of x, y increases by 5. So the formula you need in order to predict is:

$$\hat{y} = 5 + 5x$$

If a person has a score of 3 on x, the predicted score on y will be:

$$\hat{y} = 5 + (5 * 3)$$
$$= 5 + 15$$
$$= 20$$

So an x of 3 leads to a prediction of 20 on y. Check this by looking at the graph (Figure 11.6). Remember that a is also called the *constant*, and sometimes the *intercept*. The figure that is multiplied by x, as you have seen before, is called b; b is the *slope* of the line:

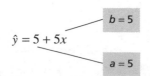

$$\hat{y} = 5 + 5x$$

Figure 11.6 Plot of *y* against *x*

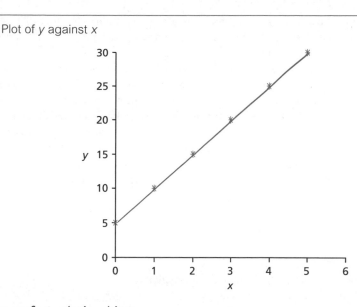

Non-perfect relationships

As we noted earlier, it is easy to predict from a perfect relationship because you always get it right. Consider, however, the following graph of a non-perfect relationship (Figure 11.7).

Here we cannot draw the straight line in such a way as to pass through every datapoint. It looks as if it would be impossible to predict *y* from *x*. It is possible, however. The line will not be perfect, as it will not pass through every datapoint, but if we could draw the line in the best place possible, it might have predictive power.

What you need to do is to draw the line in the best place possible, that is *the place where the maximum number of dots will be nearest the line – this will be the place that provides the 'best fit' to the scores.* The straight line must be drawn so that it will be as near as possible to the datapoints. This is difficult to do, by guesstimating. Most people try to draw the line through the 'middle' of the datapoints. But sometimes it is difficult to tell where the middle is.

Figure 11.7 Plot of *x* with *y*

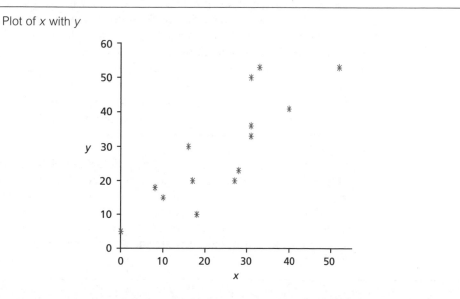

As an exercise, you are going to try guesstimating the line of best fit. Normally, you will not need to do this, because your computer package will calculate the line for you, and can even draw the line in!

Assume $a = 5$. This means that your line must intercept the y axis at 5 (see above). If you want to, draw the line in, using a light pencil line. Obviously there are many different lines you *could* draw. You have to try and draw the 'best' line. If you are working with other people, look to see if your line is in the same position as theirs; in other words, have they chosen the same straight line through the points as you have? Chances are, they haven't. So, at this point, we cannot tell what the formula (called the regression equation) will be, but we can write the formula anyway, using letters instead of numbers. One value we do know, though, is a. This is the starting point on the graph, the point at which the line intercepts the y axis. So at this point:

$$\hat{y} = 5 + bx$$

or

$$\hat{y} = bx + 5$$

It doesn't matter which; they are equivalent.

Note that we use the positive sign (+) in the general formula, and in the equation for this example, since we know the relationship is positive. However, if the relationship between x and y were negative (and thus the value of b would be negative) the '+' sign would change to a minus sign.

EXAMPLE: SALES OF DIET COLA

Let's go back to our example of diet cola. There are lots of alternative diet drinks, so if the price of ours, called Burpacoke, goes up too much, people will buy something else. The manufacturers of Burpacoke did some research and found the data shown in Table 11.2.

First, let's look at the scatterplot (Figure 11.8).

It can be clearly seen that there is a negative correlation between the price of Burpacoke and the sales figures. When the relationship between x and y is not perfect, we have to select from all the possible straight lines that could be drawn through the scores, as you have tried to do previously. We need the line that gives the best fit through the data. There are several methods by which the line of best fit can be calculated. One way, used by SPSSFW, is to minimise the vertical distances from the datapoints and the line. This is called the least-squares regression line. In the above example, the line of best fit has been drawn in by SPSSFW.

All the scores in Figure 11.8 are clustered around the line – the line, then, will be able to predict well. It 'fits' the data well. The formula used enables the line to be drawn in the best possible place (i.e. it will give us the best prediction possible). That is why it is called the line of best fit.

The data are not usually so accommodating, though. Look at Figure 11.9.

In this scatterplot, you can see that the dots do not cluster quite as closely to the line as in Figure 11.8. Here the line is in the best place possible – any other line would not be so good at predicting. But you can see that it will not be as good as Figure 11.8, because the distances from the dots to the line are greater.

Once the line of best fit has been drawn, we can predict from it, as explained on page 382.

Table 11.2   Price and sales of Burpacoke

Price per bottle	Thousands of sales
80	500
81	500
82	499
83	498
84	497
85	450
86	445
87	440
88	439
89	438
90	400
91	380
92	370
93	360
94	330

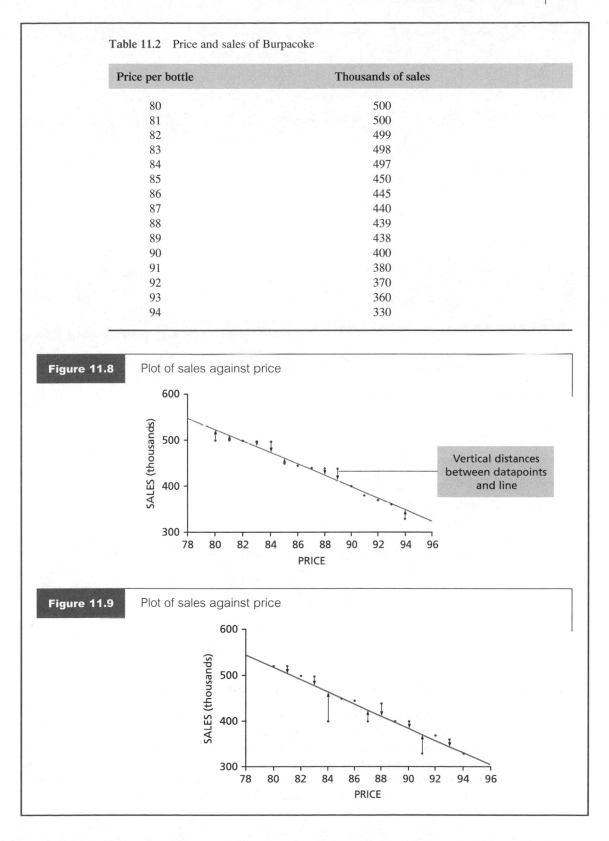

Figure 11.8   Plot of sales against price

Vertical distances between datapoints and line

Figure 11.9   Plot of sales against price

Activity 11.3

Which regression line gives the better prediction, (a) or (b)?

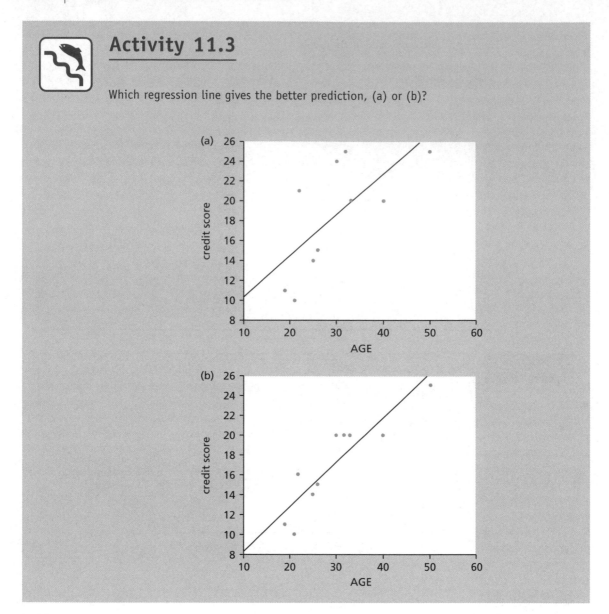

11.1.5 How do you know the values of *a* and *b*?

You could work out the values of *a* and *b* by a formula, given in most chapters of statistics books dealing with regression. However, most people use statistical packages such as SPSS to calculate linear regression. In writing this book we wanted to keep mathematical calculations to a minimum, so the formula is not included here! If you want to know how *a* and *b* are calculated, however, you will need to go to another textbook – we recommend several in the references sections at the end of every chapter.

When you perform regression analyses using a computer package, you obtain all the necessary information for writing your results section. SPSSFW gives you the correlation between x and y, and the figures for a (the intercept, or constant) and b (the slope of the line). Knowing the value of the slope, b, is essential, but you also want to know whether the height of the slope is significantly different from that which you would expect by sampling error. This is accomplished by an ANOVA summary table – which you are used to working with. The slope of the line, b, is also converted into a standardised score (beta). This answers the question, 'If x changes by one standard deviation, by how many standard deviations (or parts of standard deviations) will y change?' (standardised scores were discussed in Chapter 3, page 94).

SPSSFW: linear regression analysis

Select *Analyze*, *Regression*, *Linear*:

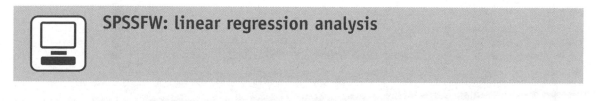

Choose *Regression*, then *Linear*

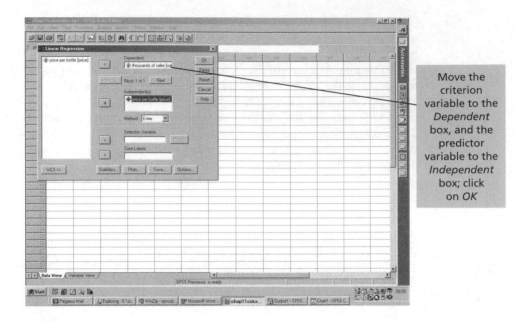

Move the criterion variable to the *Dependent* box, and the predictor variable to the *Independent* box; click on *OK*

Make sure the variable to be predicted (the criterion variable) is moved from the left-hand side to the *Dependent* box, and the predictor variable is moved to the *Independent* box. The *Method* box should read *Enter*. Then click on *OK*.

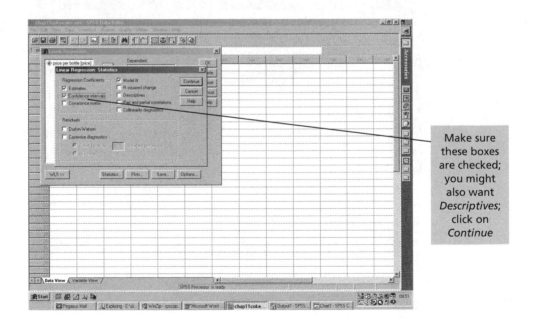

Make sure these boxes are checked; you might also want *Descriptives*; click on *Continue*

You need to check the *Confidence intervals* option; you may also want descriptives – if so, make sure that the appropriate box is checked.

This brings you back to the *Regression* dialogue box; click on *OK*.

11.1.6   Important parts of the output

Since the output for linear regression is quite long, we are going to break it down into more manageable chunks, and explain each part as we go along. The model summary is as follows:

Model Summary

Model	R	R Square	Adjusted R Square	Std. Error of the Estimate
1	.968[a]	.937	.932	14.8737

a. Predictors: (Constant), per bottle

The correlation between x and y

The correlation between x and y is a simple Pearson's r, and is represented on the output by R (also known as Multiple R). In our case, this is 0.968, which is a strong correlation.[2] We would report this as 0.97 (it is usual to round to two decimal places). This correlation is important, because it shows how well the datapoints cluster around the line of best fit. The prediction will obviously be better when the correlation is high. If the datapoints are further from the line, prediction will not be so good.

Variance explained

We have advised you to square a correlation coefficient, in order to obtain a measure of explained variance. However, in a linear regression analysis you do not have to tax yourself, as SPSSFW has done it for you! This is, as you can see, about 0.937. So 94% of the variation in sales of Burpacoke can be explained by the variation in price, for our sample.

Adjusted R Square

The R^2 is adjusted by SPSSFW to account for the number of participants and variables in the analysis. R^2 is too optimistic, as the line of best fit is based on a sample, not the population. We want our results to generalise to the population, so Adjusted R Square adjusts the figure to give a more realistic estimate. In our example, the variance explained is reported to be 93%.

Standard Error

Remember that our statistics are not free from error. We analyse our results with a particular sample and it may be that a sample on another day would give slightly different results. With repeated samples, we would find a range of values; the standard deviations of such distributions are called the *standard error* (see Chapter 3). The standard error gives us a measure of how accurate our estimation is likely to be. Standard errors are estimated. This figure is an estimate of the variance of y, for each value of x.

---

[2] Multiple R is never given as a negative value, for reasons that will not concern us here. The sign of the slope of the line will let you know whether the relationship is negative or positive, however; in our case it is negative.

Analysis of Variance

ANOVA[b]

Model		Sum of Squares	df	Mean Square	F	Sig.
1	Regression	42953.657	1	42953.657	194.162	.000[a]
	Residual	2875.943	13	221.226		
	Total	45829.600	14			

a. Predictors: (Constant), per bottle

The summary table, which you are used to, shows you whether your regression line (line of best fit) is significantly different from 0; that is, predicts better than would be expected by chance. Remember, if the slope $b = 0$, then the line of best fit is horizontal. In this case, the F-value is 194.16, with an associated probability of < 0.001. This means that such a result is highly unlikely to have arisen by sampling error, assuming the null hypothesis to be true.

Coefficients[a]

Model		Unstandardized Coefficients		Standardized Coefficients	t	Sig.	95% Confidence Interval for B	
		B	Std. Error	Beta			Lower Bound	Upper Bound
1	(Constant)	1513.957	77.427		19.553	.000	1346.686	1681.228
	per bottle	−12.386	.889	−.968	−13.934	.000	−14.306	−10.465

a. Dependent Variable: in thousands

This is *a*

This is *b*, the slope of the line

The slope, b

You can see that the value of *b* is −12.39. This means that, for every one pence rise in price, sales drop by 12.39 (thousands). While the standard error could be used as a measure of error of prediction, SPSSFW gives us the confidence limits, which are based on the standard error. The confidence limits show us that we are 95% confident that our population slope can be found within the interval −14.31 and −10.47. This is a fairly narrow interval, giving us confidence in our findings. The slope, *b*, has been converted into a standardised score, Beta, at the end of the line. The value is −0.97. This means that, for every one standard deviation increase in price, sales figures decrease by almost one standard deviation.

The intercept, a

The value of the intercept (1513.96) is also given, along with the standard error (77.43). In the output given by SPSSFW, the value of *a* is given in the row labelled 'Constant'. Confidence limits are also given. The values of *a* and *b* allow us to state the regression equation. We translate the algebraic formula

$$\hat{y} = bx + a$$

into the specific formula for this example, using the following:

- $\hat{y}$ = sales
- x = price
- a = 1513.96
- b = −12.39

sales = (−12.39 * x) + 1513.96.

The t-value above and achieved significance level show the statistical significance of the predictor variable.

11.1.7 Graphical illustration

We have said that the regression line, b, is −12.39. However, confidence limits allow us to state that we are 95% confident that the *population regression line* could be anywhere between −10.47 and −14.31. It is quite useful to see this graphically, and luckily it is easily accomplished in SPSSFW (Figure 11.10).

The slope for our sample is in the middle, this is b = −12.39. We are 95% confident that the population mean slope is somewhere between the lower line and the upper line.

11.1.8 Reporting your results

For your laboratory reports and projects, you will probably want to report the whole of the SPSSFW output. However, the textual part of the results section might say something like this:

Linear regression was carried out to determine the effect of price change on sales of Burpacoke. It was found that, for every one pence increase in price, sales decreased by 12 390, which represented almost one standard deviation. Confidence limits were narrow, showing that we are 95% confident that the population slope is between −14.31 and −10.47. $F(1,13)$ = 194.16 had an associated probability level of $p < 0.001$, showing that the results were unlikely to have arisen by sampling error, assuming the null hypothesis to be true.

11.1.9 Non-linearity

It is no good trying to do linear regression if the data are not linear. Remember what linear means: every time the value of x increases, y changes by a constant amount; a straight line can adequately describe the relationship between x and y. Look back at Chapter 5 if you have forgotten about this.

Figure 11.10 Regression line with lower and upper confidence limits

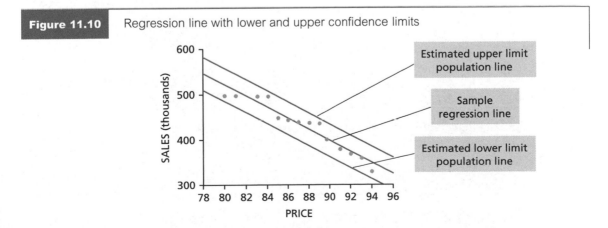

Study adds weight to old midwives' tale

The size of the box of chocolates given to midwives by parents of newborns rises in line with the baby's birthweight, according to research that confirms an age-old canon of obstetrics folklore. The correlation has been discovered by Andrew Nordin, a junior doctor in Taunton, Somerset. His six-month study involving midwives on the delivery suite and two postnatal wards at Musgrove Park Hospital is published in the American medical journal *Obstetrics and Gynecology*. Midwives were asked to record the weight of confectionery received from grateful parents and the birthweight of the baby.

Australian-born Dr Nordin, a registrar in obstetrics and gynaecology, dreamed up the chocolate study as part of routine medical auditing work. 'We take audit very seriously, but by tradition we try to have a bit of fun with the Christmas audit,' he said.

In his paper for the journal, Dr Nordin helpfully points out: 'Regression analysis found an association between birth weight and net chocolate weight, with a linear correlation equation of $\hat{y} = 3349 + 0.52058x$.'

Dr Nordin is preparing a presentation on his paper, at the autumn meeting of South West England's obstetricians and gynaecologists at the end of next month. He hopes his paper may inspire a more wide-ranging investigation of the links between parental gifts and babies' birthweights, perhaps involving the use of bottles of wine and tins of biscuits.

(From a national newspaper, 1993)

Activity 11.4

Look at this graph:

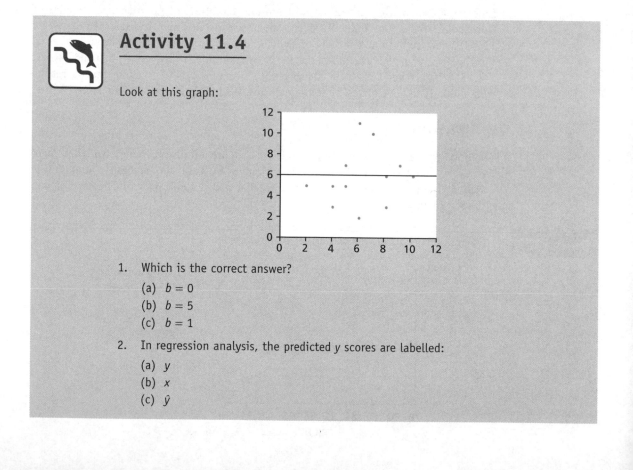

1. Which is the correct answer?

   (a) $b = 0$

   (b) $b = 5$

   (c) $b = 1$

2. In regression analysis, the predicted y scores are labelled:

   (a) y

   (b) x

   (c) $\hat{y}$

Degrees of freedom[3]

The concept of degrees of freedom is complicated, and there are different ways of explaining DF. Here we talk about DF in terms of sample size. Remember, this is a conceptual explanation of DF.[4] Dr Chong Ho Yu (2001) uses linear regression to explain degrees of freedom. Now that you have a good grounding in linear regression, his explanation will help you understand DF. Dr Yu shows that, in a linear regression scatterplot with only *one* datapoint, you have *no* degrees of freedom – you can't actually estimate the regression line.

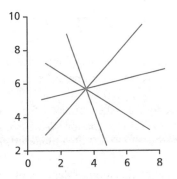

This diagram shows just one datapoint – if you try to draw a regression line, any line is as good as any other line. This isn't very useful! The degrees of freedom for regression are n − 1 (where n is the number of datapoints). So here, DF = 0 (1 − 1 = 0). As Dr Yu says '. . . the data has no "freedom" to vary, and you don't have any 'freedom' to conduct research with this data set'. In fact, if you try carrying out such an analysis in SPSSFW, you will obtain an error message.

Now imagine you have two datapoints for your linear regression.

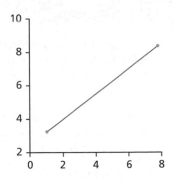

When there are only two points, a straight line will always be a perfect fit. In this case, there is one degree of freedom for estimation. DF = 1 (2 − 1 = 1). If you try this in SPSSFW, you will obtain output. However, the results mean nothing, because we already know the fit is perfect. With just two datapoints, it couldn't be any other way!

▶

---

[3] See also box on p. 215.
[4] Caution: DF are not always N − 1.

Now look at this scatterplot:

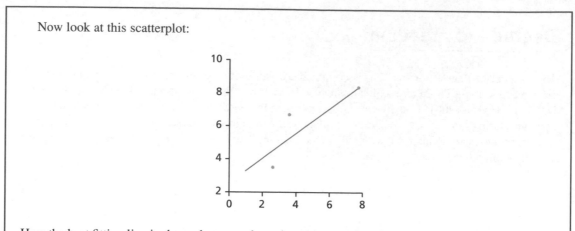

Here the best fitting line is shown between three datapoints, and so the degrees of freedom are 2. This time the line has more freedom to vary, since the line of best fit is not restricted to the path between two datapoints.

Dr Yu explains degrees of freedom as 'the number of pieces of useful information'. So that when we had DF = 0, there was no useful information. When we had DF = 1, there was not enough information to be useful to us. Even with DF = 2, there was still not enough useful information for us to perform a useful analysis.

Dr Yu has an on-line audio-visual explanation of degrees of freedom, with interactive activities. We have provided you with his website address so that you can learn more while having fun! (Yu, C.H., 2003)

11.2 Multiple regression

Multiple regression is an extension of linear regression. Psychologists are interested in using this technique in order to discover the ways in which several variables (called explanatory or predictor variables) are related to another (called the dependent or criterion variable). For instance:

- Psychologists want to discover the variables that predict 'burnout' in teachers.
- Researchers want to discover the ways in which gender, parenting style and fathers' education relate to health locus of control.

The criterion variable is still called y, but this time we have several explanatory variables, denoted x_1, x_2, x_3 and so on. Multiple regression is able to give us information on the ways in which the explanatory variables *combined* relate to the criterion variable, and it is also able to give us information on how each of the variables relates to the criterion variable, separately.

The equation is just an extension of the linear regression:

$$y = b_1x_1 + b_2x_2 + b_3x_3 \ldots + a$$

All this means is that y (the criterion variable) can be calculated by the slope of the first variable (multiplied by the score on the first variable), together with the slope of the second variable (multiplied by the score on the second variable), together with the slope of the third variable (multiplied by the score on the third variable) (and so on) plus the constant.

Remember that you *could* use the regression equation to predict *y* scores from a set of explanatory variables in a new population. However, psychologists do not usually set out to produce an equation that they can use to predict in a new sample (although this might be the case). They usually wish to discover the way in which variables they have selected relate to the criterion variable, and to see the relative contribution of each of these variables.

Multiple regression is a common technique – if you look through a selection of journal articles you will find many examples of multiple regression being used. There are several ways of performing a multiple regression, and we are going to use one of them – called the standard model. A discussion of other models is beyond the scope of this book (if you are interested in pursuing this further, see Tabachnick and Fidell, 2001).

11.2.1 Predicting the criterion variables from several explanatory variables

IQ alone might not predict examination success very well. Motivation, on its own, might not predict examination success either. However, *together* these two variables might predict examination success *much better*. In life, it is rare to find simple relationships where one variable predicts another, without the influence of anything else. It is more realistic to use multiple variables in statistical analyses.

Let's say you have collected information on examination success – percentage marks, for instance. You have also measured IQ and given a questionnaire on motivation levels. You could have more than two explanatory variables, of course, but for the purposes of explanation, it is easier to keep to *two* explanatory variables. How well does the combination of these two variables predict examination success? Multiple regression not only enables us to answer this question, it also allows us to discover the relative contribution of each separate variable.

So multiple regression shows us the cumulative effects of a set of explanatory variables (x_1, x_2, etc.) on a dependent variable (called *y*), and also the *separate* effects of these explanatory variables.

Let's say we wanted to do a simple linear regression, predicting exam success from IQ. We would obtain a scattergram, putting exam success on the *y* axis, as it is the criterion variable, and IQ on the *x* axis, as it is the explanatory variable. The scattergram, with line of best fit, might look like Figure 11.11.

The scattergram of motivation and examination, with line of best fit, might look like Figure 11.12.

Both might predict examination success, separately, but the prediction may be even better using both together.

In Figure 11.13, both IQ and motivation are shown (in 3D form) relating to examination success (on the *y* axis).

In this case, instead of a *line* of best fit, we have a *plane* of best fit. We can imagine this as a sheet of perspex, cutting through the cube. The best-fitting plane is one that has the dots closest to the perspex. It is not possible to imagine, or draw, in more than three dimensions, but SPSSFW has no problem in analysing data using many explanatory variables.

Multiple regression analysis is, not surprisingly, similar to the regression analysis using one explanatory variable. The following are the statistics that result from a multiple regression analysis.

Figure 11.11   Plot of examination success against IQ

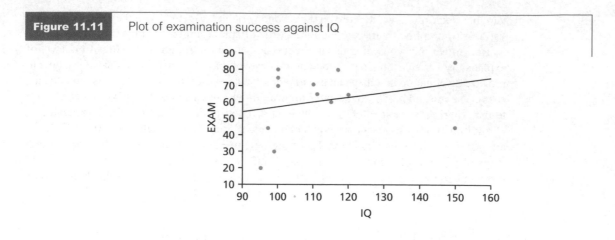

Figure 11.12   Plot of examination success against motivation

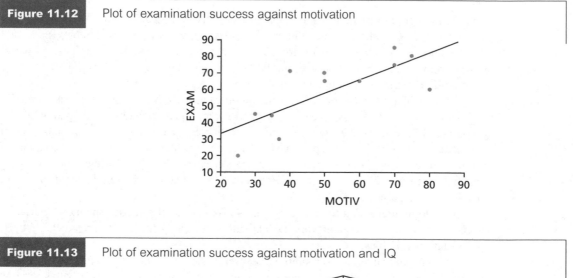

Figure 11.13   Plot of examination success against motivation and IQ

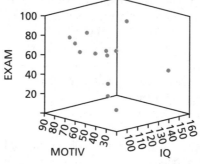

Important parts of the output

The first section confirms that both IQ and Motivation are entered, and that the criterion variable is EXAM. The method 'enter' means that both IQ and Motivation were entered together in order to predict exam success.

Variables Entered/Removed[b]

Model	Variables Entered	Variables Removed	Method
1	IQ, MOTIV[a]		Enter

a. All requested variables entered.
b. Dependent Variable: EXAM

Model summary

The R-value (0.762) is the correlation between EXAM and both of the explanatory variables. The R^2 (0.579) has been adjusted downwards to 0.52.

Model Summary

Model	R	R Square	Adjusted R Square	Std. Error of the Estimate
1	.762[a]	.579	.515	11.906

a. Predictors: (Constant), IQ, MOTIV

In Section 11.1.6, you had only one variable listed in the model summary. Remember that $r = b$ in that case. But here, however, we have two explanatory variables.

Remember that in linear regression this was simply Pearson's r, the correlation between x and y. In multiple regression, however, r becomes R, and it is the correlation between all the xs and y.[5] So in this case, it is the correlation between examination success, and IQ and motivation, y. In this study, R is 0.76.

R^2

If you square 0.76 you will obtain 0.58. R^2 represents the correlation between all the exploratory variables together with the criterion variable. This means all the variance (both shared and unique) of the exploratory variables in relation to the criterion variable. In our particular sample, 58% of the variance in exam success can be accounted for by IQ and motivation. However, SPSSFW adjusts this figure downwards to give an estimate of the population R^2, otherwise our r is too optimistic. This is because the sample regression line will always fit the sample better than it will the population (since it is the best fitting line for the sample). So we adjust downwards. The formula for this takes into account the number of participants and variables. Thus we can say we have accounted for 52% of the variance in y, by our explanatory variables.

11.2.2 The ANOVA summary table

This shows you that the explanatory variables together predict the criterion variable. The chance of the obtained results having been obtained by sampling error, assuming the null hypothesis to be true, is only 0.004.

---

[5] Multiple R actually represents the correlation between the actual y scores and the predicted y scores.

ANOVA[b]

Model		Sum of Squares	df	Mean Square	F	Sig.
1	Regression	2545.01291	2	1272.50646	8.97596	.004[a]
	Residual	1842.98709	13	141.76824		
	Total	4388.000	15			

a. Predictors: (Constant), IQ, MOTIV
b. Dependent Variable: EXAM

The ANOVA shows us that the regression plane for these variables significantly departs from 0 – in other words, we can predict y (exam success) from IQ and motivation together. Our prediction will not be perfect, of course, but it is better than chance alone ($F(2,13) = 8.97$, $p = 0.004$).

For the simple regression that we showed earlier in the chapter you had only one variable listed under the *Coefficients* column (see page 394). Remember that $r = b$ in that case. But here, however, we have two explanatory variables.

The coefficients

The following section gives the unstandardised (B) and standardised (Beta) weights for the variables IQ and motivation, along with t-values, probability values, and the 95% confidence limits around B.

Coefficients[a]

Model		Unstandardized Coefficients		Standardized Coefficients	t	Sig.	95% Confidence Interval for B	
		B	Std. Error	Beta			Lower Bound	Upper Bound
	(Constant)	−43.466292	27.919170		−1.557	.1435	−103.781988	16.849405
	MOTIV	.614508	.218457	.526770	2.813	.0147	.142561	1.086455
	IQ	.591585	.262691	.421726	2.252	.0422	.024075	1.159095

a. Dependent Variable: EXAM

Motivation

Motivation has a regression coefficient of 0.61. Thus, as motivation increases by one unit, exam success increases by 0.61. We can be 95% confident that the population coefficient is between 0.14 and 1.09. The t-value is 2.81 with an associated probability of 0.01, thus our regression coefficient is unlikely to have arisen by sampling error.

IQ

IQ has an unstandardised weight of 0.59, meaning that, as IQ increases by one unit, examination success rises by 0.59. The confidence limits show us that we are 95% confident that the true population regression coefficient is between 0.02 and 1.16. This is a fairly wide interval, but at least it does not include zero, or encompass a negative figure! Therefore, we can accept that the population regression slope is positive, although it could vary from 0.02 (almost horizontal) to 1.16. The t-value of 2.25 and associated probability of 0.04 tell us that the likelihood of such a result arising by sampling error, assuming that the null hypothesis is true, is only 4 in 100.

Comparison of explanatory variables

You can have a good idea of the importance of the explanatory variables by looking at the standardised weights (beta). It is no good comparing the unstandardised weights, because they are generally measured in different units (such as grams and inches, for example). Thus the weights are converted into the usual z-scores. This means, for IQ, that as IQ increases by one SD, examination success increases by 0.42 of a standard deviation.[6] As motivation increases by one SD, examination success increases by just over half a standard deviation (0.53). Thus motivation appears to contribute more to examination success than IQ. Remember to look at the *sign* of the regression coefficients. (If a coefficient is negative, it is interpreted in the same way as you would interpret a negative correlation coefficient.) We have no negative regression coefficients in our example.

Activity 11.5

In a multiple regression analysis Multiple R represents:

(a) The correlation between the first predictor variable and the criterion variable

(b) The correlation between all the predictor variables

(c) The correlation between the criterion variable and the entire set of predictor variables

11.2.3 The equation

You will remember that, in linear regression, the equation was:

$$y = bx + a$$

Our formula for multiple regression is similar. If you wanted to use the formula to predict examination success from IQ and motivation, you would need to use the unstandardised regression coefficients (b) and the constant (a). Thus

$\hat{y}$ (predicted examination success) = (0.591585 * IQ)
+ (0.614508 * MOTIVATION)
− 43.466292

> In hand calculations, two or three decimal places would be sufficient for our calculations

---

[6] This is conditional on the other explanatory variables remaining constant.

The formula enables us to hand calculate a predicted score, e.g. we can work out the examination mark that we predict the students to achieve, by using the scores they attained on their IQ and motivation tests. SPSSFW has calculated a value by which their individual motivation scores must be multiplied. In the SPSSFW output, the value is labelled B in the unstandardised coefficients column. You can see that, for motivation, $b = 0.614508$. For IQ, the score by which their individual IQ scores must be multiplied is 0.591585. So we calculate examination success by multiplying a person's motivation score by 0.614508, and then adding this to their IQ score, which has been multiplied by 0.591585. We then add or subtract a constant (which in this case is -43.466292). The resulting figure is their predicted examination score.

So, if you *did* want to predict a person's exam success, in a new sample, you would use the above equation. You would predict exam success with *both* variables, since they both contribute to examination success.

11.2.4 Textual part of the analysis

Remember that, as psychologists, most of us do not want to use the formula to predict in a new sample. We use multiple regression to see how certain variables (explanatory or predictor) relate to another variable (dependent or criterion).

Let's see how we might report the textual part of our analysis. This assumes that you have given your readers a table of results, much as they are printed above.

The association between the criterion and explanatory variables is moderately strong (Multiple $R = 0.76$). Together, IQ and motivation accounted for 51% of the variation in examination success (adjusted R^2). Both IQ and motivation positively related to examination success. The regression coefficient for IQ was 0.59 (95% CI $= 0.02 - 1.16$); and for motivation it was 0.61 (95% CI $= 0.14 - 1.09$). Since the confidence limits did not encompass a negative value, it can be concluded that the population regression coefficients for both IQ and motivation are positive (IQ $- t = 2.252$; $p = 0.04$/motivation $- t = 2.813$; $p = 0.01$). The standardised regression coefficients show that motivation is a stronger predictor than IQ. Both variables, however, are positively and significantly related to examination success.

Always remember that your results are specific to your sample. While we always have problems of how far we can generalise in any inferential statistical analysis, multiple regression is a mathematical maximisation technique – our plane of best fit is the best plane we can possibly have – for our sample. We do not know how well our results would generalise to the population. If you have enough participants and a few, good explanatory variables the chances of generalisation are better than if you have not met these conditions (see below).

11.2.5 Assumptions to be met when using multiple regression

1. *Make sure you have enough participants*: Psychologists have different opinions as to the numbers of participants required for using multiple regression. Often authors of statistical textbooks will recommend a participant/variable ratio. Assume you have four explanatory variables. The participant/variable ratio given in books tends to range from 15 participants per variable (which means you should have 60 participants in the

analysis) to 40 participants per variable (which means you should have 160 participants in the analysis). Quite a difference. Tabachnick and Fidell say that the simplest way of determining sample size is:

$N \geq 50 + 8M$.

where M is the number of explanatory variables. Thus if you have four explanatory variables, and simply wish to look at the combined effects of the explanatory variables (Multiple R) you should have at least:

$50 + (8 * 4) =$
$50 + (32) =$
>82 participants.

Often, however, researchers wish to look at the significance of each variable separately. In this case, Tabachnick and Fidell recommend the following calculation:

$N \geq 104 + m$
$= 104 + 4$
$= >108$

If you are looking at both the combined and separate results, choose the higher number. In this case, you need at least 110 participants. If you do not use enough participants, your results will be over-optimistic, and you would not know whether your results would be generalisable.

2. *The criterion variable should be drawn from a normally distributed population of scores*: the explanatory variables do not need to be normally distributed. It is the distribution of the criterion variable, *y* (conditional on the explanatory variables), which should be drawn from a normal distribution.

3. *Variables should be linearly related to the criterion variable*: Just as in linear regression, the explanatory variables should be linearly related to the criterion variable – otherwise there is not much point in doing multiple regression. Inspecting the scattergrams for your variables will let you know whether you have linear relationships (as compared with curvilinear relationships).

4. *Outliers may need to be eliminated*: You learned about outliers (extreme scores) in Chapter 2. Outliers can have a big influence on regression analysis. Univariate outliers (unusual and extreme score on one variable) are easy to spot, but multivariate outliers (extreme on two variables together) are more difficult. To give you an example of a multivariate outlier, a person aged 17 is not unusual, and earning a salary of £30,000 is not unusual (except for lecturers who write statistics books; they earn much less than this). However, to find a 17-year-old who earns such a salary *is* unusual. Sometimes it is quite hard to spot these sorts of outliers (SPSSFW can do this for you, although we do not cover it in this book).

   However, if you have a small data set, simply looking at the data might be enough. Then you might want to *consider* deleting *extreme* outliers from the analysis. However, it is obvious you cannot just delete outliers simply because they are outliers. It requires careful consideration, especially when you have <100 participants. Some students have asked us whether removing outliers is cheating, but we want the regression line (or plane) to reflect the 'average' subject, not somebody incredibly different from the rest.

5. *Multicollinearity*: The best situation occurs when the explanatory variables have high correlations with the criterion variable, but not with each other. You can inspect your correlational matrix before you perform multiple regression. You may find some variables correlate highly with each other (0.8 and above). Having such high inter-correlated variables is called multicollinearity. Your variables are obviously measuring much the same thing. Sometimes you can combine highly correlated variables, or you can omit one. This has the benefit of reducing the number of variables, of course, which helps with (1) above.

Example from the literature: pulmonary function and smoking

Emery *et al.* (1997) carried out a study to discover whether pulmonary function and smoking behaviour predict cognitive function in a British sample. One measure of cognitive function was simple reaction time (SRT). As part of their study, they first sought to discover whether age, gender, height and education could predict SRT. We report these results below.

Table 11.3 shows that, together, the predictors accounted for nearly 14% of the variance, that is, 14% of the variation in SRT scores can be accounted for by age, gender, height and education. Although the authors do not report Multiple R, all we have to do is to take the square-root of R^2. If you check using your calculator you will find this is 0.369. Thus the correlation between SRT and the other variables is 0.37 – a weak to moderate relationship. The authors then give the individual results: that is, the b weights (unstandardised slopes) for each of the variables separately. So, for instance, the slope of age predicting SRT is 0.2824. This means that, for every year a person ages, their simple reaction time is predicted to increase by 0.28 milliseconds (the association is positive). Height, however, has a virtually flat b weight, showing that the predictive power is almost zero.

Table 11.3 Results from Emery *et al.* (1997, by permission of Taylor & Francis Ltd. www.tandf.co.uk/journals)

Predictors	B	SRT (milliseconds) R^2
Age	0.2824	0.1362***
Gender (male/female)	0.0572	
Height	0.0100	
Education (less/more)	−0.1602	

*** $p < 0.001$

Example from the literature: job satisfaction among teleworkers

Konradt *et al.* (2003) investigated the effects of management behaviour and stress on job satisfaction among teleworkers. They performed a standard multiple regression, using the explanatory variables listed in Table 11.4.

All four variables *together* significantly predicted job satisfaction, as can be seen by the R^2 value and significance level given above. As expected, stressors showed a negative relationship with job satisfaction. For instance, an increase in every one task-related stressor was associated with a 0.21 decrease in job satisfaction. ($b = -0.21$ so that you know the relationship is negative.)

From the four predictors, Quality of management showed the strongest relationship with job satisfaction. You can see the weightings are positive for this variable. For every one unit increase in quality of management, job satisfaction increased by 0.96 of a unit. The beta weight (in the last column) gives us standardised scores. Therefore we can say that, for every one standard deviation increase in Quality of management, job satisfaction increases by just over half a standard deviation (0.52).

Table 11.4 Summary of simultaneous regression analysis for variables predicting job satisfaction of teleworkers ($n = 31$)

Explanatory variables	B	SEB	beta
Quality of management	0.96	0.30	0.52**
Task-related stressors	−0.21	0.34	−0.10
Task-related resources	0.01	0.28	0.05
Non-job-related stressors	−0.40	0.38	−0.17

$R^2 = 0.32$ ($p < 0.05$)
** $p < 0.01$

These are the unstandardised weights, see page 394.	These are the standard errors, see page 393.	These are the standardised weights.

Activity 11.6

Calculate the number of participants needed for the analysis reported above. Given the number of participants in the study, what conclusions can you draw from the results?

Summary

- Regression analysis allows us to predict scores on a dependent variable from a knowledge of the scores on one or more explanatory variables.

- Psychologists use regression to assess relationships between variables.

- The dependent variable is also called the criterion variable, and the exploratory variables are called the predictor variables.

- The line of best fit (the slope, b) can be used to determine how the criterion (y) changes as a result of changes in the predictor variable(s) (x).

- Confidence limits around b allow you to estimate the population slope with a certain degree of confidence.

SPSSFW exercises

Exercise 1

Enter the following data into SPSSFW and analyse it using the regression procedure: x is the score on examination anxiety and y is number of hours spent revising for examinations, in one week before the exam.

x	y	x	y
33	45	56	79
64	68	44	44
33	100	22	16
22	44	44	61
70	62	80	60
66	61	66	61
59	52	79	60
84	66		

Is anxiety about exams related to number of hours studied? How well does the regression equation predict?

Exercise 2

Professor Lemon wants to analyse the contribution made by social support (SOCSUP) and outgoing personality (OUTGO) to contentment at work (CONTENT), using his own colleagues as the participants.

Perform a multiple regression on the data below. Interpret the output for Professor Lemon, in the form of a written report, making sure that you let him know the contribution made by each of the predictor variables to the criterion variable.

SOCSUP	OUTGO	CONTENT
20.00	15.00	20.00
10.00	30.00	15.00
4.00	5.00	5.00
17.00	16.00	20.00
10.00	14.00	15.00
11.00	8.00	10.00
7.00	7.00	8.00
4.00	4.00	5.00
15.00	10.00	17.00
17.00	5.00	17.00
18.00	6.00	15.00
11.00	12.00	18.00
12.00	10.00	15.00
16.00	16.00	17.00
18.00	12.00	20.00
14.00	13.00	14.00
12.00	14.00	15.00
10.00	4.00	5.00
11.00	6.00	7.00
10.00	10.00	11.00

MULTIPLE CHOICE QUESTIONS

1. The line of best fit:
   (a) Minimises the distance between the scores and the regression line
   (b) Is the best of all possible lines
   (c) Maximises the correlation between x and y
   (d) All of these

2. In linear regression, where only *one* variable predicts y, and F is statistically significant at $p = 0.049$, then:
   (a) $t = 0.049$
   (b) $t = 0.0245$
   (c) $t = 0.098$
   (d) Cannot tell

3. In a linear regression analysis, the residuals are:
   (a) Actual scores minus the predicted scores
   (b) Actual scores plus the predicted scores
   (c) The correlation between the actual and predicted scores
   (d) None of the above

Questions 4–7 relate to the following output:

Model Summary

Model	R	R Square	Adjusted R Square	Std. Error of the Estimate
1	.319[a]	.102	.078	.639

a. Predictors: (Constant), MRL

ANOVA[b]

Model		Sum of Squares	df	Mean Square	F	Sig.
1	Regression	1.71690	1	1.71690	4.199	.048[a]
	Residual	15.12589	37	.40881		
	Total	16.84279	38			

a. Predictors: (Constant), MRL
b. Dependent Variable: PAIN

Coefficients[a]

			Unstandardized Coefficients		Standardized Coefficient	t	Sig.
Model		B	Std. Error		Beta		
1	(Constant)	1.757722	.15455			11.373	.000
	MRL	.01659	8.09626E-03		.31928	2.049	.0476

a. Dependent Variable: PAIN

4. Marks on MRL would be called:
   (a) The predictor variable
   (b) The criterion variable
   (c) The covariate
   (d) The constant

5. The exact probability value of the results having occurred by sampling error, assuming the null hypothesis to be true, is:
   (a) 0.0000
   (b) 0.05
   (c) 4.19978
   (d) 0.048

6. *b* is:
   (a) 2.049
   (b) 0.31928
   (c) 0.01659
   (d) None of these

7. *a* is:

    (a) 1.75772
    (b) 1.5455
    (c) 4.19978
    (d) 0.01659

8. How many degrees of freedom would you have where the linear regression scatterplot had only ONE datapoint? (very unrealistic we know . . .)

    (a) Zero
    (b) One
    (c) Two
    (d) Three

9. Psychologists use regression mainly to:

    (a) Assess relationships between variables
    (b) Use the regression formula for further research
    (c) Look at differences between groups
    (d) None of the above

Questions 10–15 relate to the partial output of the multiple regression analysis below:

Model Summary

Model	R	R Square	Adjusted R Square	Std. Error of the Estimate
1	.867[a]	.752	.711	3.2388

a. Predictors: (Constant), age, previous history rating

ANOVA[b]

Model		Sum of Squares	df	Mean Square	F	Sig.
1	Regression	381.457	2	190.729	18.182	.000[a]
	Residual	125.876	12	10.490		
	Total	507.333	14			

a. Predictors: (Constant), age, previous history rating
b. Dependent Variable: credit rating

Coefficients[a]

Model		Unstandardized Coefficients		Standardized Coefficient	t	Sig.	95% Confidence Interval for B	
		B	Std. Error	Beta			Lower Bound	Upper Bound
1	(Constant)	.790	3.471		.228	.824	−6.774	8.353
	previous history rating	.571	.241	.514	2.368	.036	.046	1.096
	age	.276	.145	.413	1.904	.081	−.040	.592

a. Dependent Variable: credit rating

10. The correlation between credit rating and the other variables is:
    (a) 0.867
    (b) 0.752
    (c) 0.711
    (d) 1.32

11. For every one standard deviation rise in previous history rating, credit rating:
    (a) Decreases by 0.5 of standard deviation
    (b) Increases by 0.5 of a standard deviation
    (c) Decreases by 0.3 of a standard deviation
    (d) Increases by 0.3 of a standard deviation

12. The predictor variables are called:
    (a) Credit rating and age
    (b) Credit rating and previous history rating
    (c) Previous history and age
    (d) The criterion variables

13. The achieved significance level associated with the F-value of 18.182 is:
    (a) 0.824
    (b) 0.36
    (c) < 0.001
    (d) None of these

14. The slope of the line (B) for previous history rating is:
    (a) 0.514
    (b) 0.790
    (c) 0.276
    (d) 0.571

15. a is:
    (a) 0.514
    (b) 0.790
    (c) 0.276
    (d) 0.571

16. Multicollinearity means:
    (a) There are high intercorrelations among the predictor variables
    (b) The predictor variables are positively correlated with the criterion variable
    (c) The variables show a skewed distribution
    (d) The variables show a peaked distribution

17. Kieran wants to perform a standard multiple regression using six explanatory variables. He is only interested in the overall R^2. According to Tabachnick and Fidell's formula, how many participants should he recruit?
    (a) 98
    (b) 56
    (c) 240
    (d) 120

18. Saeeda doesn't know about the necessity for large participant numbers in multiple regression. She's only got 20 participants in her study, and she has 10 explanatory variables. Which is the most appropriate statement? Compared with an analysis using 100 participants, Multiple R will be:

    (a) Conflated
    (b) Inflated
    (c) Deflated
    (d) No different

Questions 19 and 20 relate to the following, which is an extract from a results section in a journal:

All predictors significantly predicted blood pressure (adj. $r^2 = .42$; p = .002). Stress during the interview was the strongest predictor of increased blood pressure (beta = 0.49, p = .001) followed by age (beta = 0.18, p = .002).

19. Which is the most appropriate statement? The explanatory variables predicted

    (a) 6.5% of the variation in blood pressure
    (b) 42% of the variation in blood pressure
    (c) 6.5% of the variation in stress
    (d) 18% of the variation in age

20. Which is the most appropriate statement?

    (a) As stress increased by one standard deviation, blood pressure increased by nearly half a standard deviation
    (b) As stress increased by one standard deviation, age increased by 0.18 of a standard deviation,
    (c) As age increased by one year, blood pressure fell by 0.18 of a standard deviation
    (d) As age increased by one standard deviation, blood pressure increased by 18%

References

Emery, C.F., Huppert, F.A. and Schein, R.L. (1997) 'Do pulmonary function and smoking behavior predict cognitive function? Findings from a British sample', *Psychology and Health*, **12**(2): 265–75.

Konradt, U., Hertel, G. and Schmook, R. (2003) 'Quality of management by objectives, task-related stressors, and non-task-related stressors as predictors of stress and job satisfaction among tele-workers', *European Journal of Work and Organizational Psychology*, **12**(1): 61–79.

Tabachnick, B.G. and Fidell, L.S. (2001) *Using Multivariate Statistics* (4th edn). New York: HarperCollins.

Yu, C.H., Lo, W.J. and Stockford, S. (2001) 'Using multimedia to visualize the concepts of degree of freedom, perfect-fitting, and over-fitting'. Paper presented at the Joint Statistical Meetings, Atlanta, GA.

Yu, C.H. (2003) 'Illustrating degrees of freedom in multimedia', available at http://seamonkey.ed.asu.edu/~alex/pub/df/default.htm [accessed 10 March 2004]

12 Introduction to factor analysis

Chapter overview

You have made it this far and we hope that you now have a good conceptual understanding of the most widely used statistical techniques in psychology. In this and the next two chapters we would like to introduce you to another class of techniques, which are an extension of multiple regression and ANOVA. These tests come under the general heading of *multivariate statistics*. The particular statistical technique that we are going to introduce here is factor analysis. We gave a very brief idea of this technique in Chapter 5, page 197.

Here we will:

- give a conceptual understanding of factor analysis, by using one example from the psychological literature throughout
- show how to enter a data set into SPSS and analyse it by factor analysis
- show how to interpret the statistical output from such an analysis
- give examples from the literature to help you understand how factor analysis has been used in psychology.

12.1 What is the purpose of factor analysis?

The main methods of factor analysis were first used to study the structure of the mind, intelligence, and later personality, although now it has much wider applications. Factor analysis deals with *patterns* of correlations (see Chapter 5, page 197). So, for instance, in the 1950s psychologists noted that people who tended to do well on writing tests also tended to do well on tests of arithmetic, science and other tests. These variables were thus correlated with each other. Psychologists believed that there was a general *factor* that caused the *observed* patterns on correlations. The *factor* itself, which was called 'intelligence', could not be observed, but was revealed only through looking at the patterns of correlations for the observed variables.

The usual way of performing factor analysis is to take a sample of individuals, each of whom has given scores on a number of variables, e.g. they may have taken a battery of tests or answered some questionnaires. A matrix of correlation coefficients is calculated (in the same way as you learned in Chapter 5, page 197). Let's say that we have measured participants on six tests of ability. If we believe that each test we give to our participants calls for one specific ability, then what we are really saying is that none of the tests is related to any of the other tests.

Theoretically, all the correlations should be zero. In practice, however, this is very unlikely to happen. Some variables that are unrelated to each other would tend to show some correlation. In Table 12.1, the correlation coefficients hover around zero.

Now let's take the opposite view, and say that we believe that all tests call for the same ability. What we are really saying here is that each variable is related to all the others, and in Table 12.2 all the correlation coefficients would be, theoretically, 1. In practice they would be approximately 1.

Table 12.1 Hypothetical correlations between tests if we believe that each test calls for a specific ability

	Arithmetic test	Chemistry test	Art test	Written test	German language test	Music test
Arithmetic test	1	0.01	0.01	−0.01	0.001	−0.01
Chemistry test		1	−0.02	0.01	−0.000	0.02
Art test			1	0.00	0.01	0.11
Written test				1	0.00	−0.00
German language test					1	0.00
Music test						1

Table 12.2 Hypothetical correlations between tests when we believe that each test calls for the same ability

	Arithmetic test	Chemistry test	Art test	Written test	German language test	Music test
Arithmetic test	1	0.99	0.98	1.00	0.99	0.99
Chemistry test		1	0.99	0.99	0.98	1.00
Art test			1	0.99	1.00	0.99
Written test				1	0.99	0.98
German language test					1	1.00
Music test						1

Here the correlations hover near the 1 mark. These are two extremes. Normally some variables are related to others, and some are not. Factor analysis looks at the patterns of correlations. Groups of variables that relate highly to each other constitute a factor. A factor is conceived to be an underlying latent (hypothetical) variable along which individuals differ, just as they differ along a test scale. It is possible to perform factor analysis by working on either the correlation or the variance–covariance matrix.[1] At this stage we advise you to make sure that you choose the correlation matrix option when performing these techniques on your computer package, simply because it is safer. This is because

---

[1] A variance–covariance matrix is like a correlational matrix, except that the scores are not standardised. Standardised scores were covered in Chapter 3, page 94.

working on the correlation matrix is equivalent to standardising the data – if your variables are not measured in the same units or at least comparable, using the correlation matrix will standardise them so that they are comparable. Further discussion of this topic is beyond the scope of this book. The aim of factor analysis is to account for a large number of variables, in terms of a minimal number of primary factors.

Activity 12.1

It is not easy to explain the concept of factor analysis. If you were trying to explain what a factor analysis meant to a friend, what would you say?

12.2 The two main types of factor analysis

There are different kinds of factor analysis – here we are going to concentrate on the most familiar ones. One is called principal components analysis (PCA) and the other is usually referred to simply as factor analysis (although this usually means 'principal axis factoring'). Many people, including us, use these terms interchangeably. However, there *are* differences between them, and although you can treat them as if they are the same, we will spend just a few minutes discussing the differences.

12.2.1 Differences and similarities between PCA and factor analysis

Both PCA and factor analysis reduce data sets containing a larger number of variables into a smaller number of variables called components or factors respectively. The difference is mainly to do with the way variance is dealt with. In PCA, all the variance in the data is analysed, both shared and unique (see Chapter 5, page 181 for information on shared and unique variance). This assumes, of course, that there is no error. PCA actually transforms the original variables into a smaller set of uncorrelated components. With factor analysis, only the shared variance is analysed – unique variance is excluded, and some error variance is assumed.

It has been said that PCA is exploratory in nature – carried out simply in order to reduce a large data set to a smaller set. Often a researcher wants to perform a further analysis, for example multiple regression. To be reliable, multiple regression needs a good participant/ variable ratio (see Chapter 11). Thus PCA is sometimes performed in order to reduce a large set of variables into a more manageable set so that multiple regression can be performed. Factor analysis, on the other hand, has typically been used where researchers believe there is a smaller set of 'factors' that *cause* or in some way influence the observed variables. Factor analysis has thus been used in a confirmatory sense, in order to test hypotheses. In practice, however, researchers use both PCA and factor analysis as a means of exploring the data, and also to confirm hypotheses. Research has shown that, although factor analysis and PCA are not equivalent, the differences are relatively unimportant. This is especially so with large data sets and participant numbers. So when performing factor analysis, the advice is to try to use at least 100 participants in the analysis, and to have five times as many participants as variables. From now on we shall refer to both factor analysis–principal axis factoring and PCA as factor analysis.

12.3 Use of factor analysis in psychometrics

In psychometrics, factor analysis is particularly relevant to construct validity. When researchers design questionnaires, they usually have several questions relating to one construct or idea, i.e. certain questions correlate with each other because they are measuring the same construct. We *could* just look at the correlation matrix and try to see such patterns ourselves. However, this is very subjective and rather unreliable. Factor analysis can identify such patterns of correlations. The constructs, called factors (or sometimes components), can be used in describing the scales of a test. Factor analysis allows researchers to discover the *factorial validity* of the questions that make up each scale or construct. We shall be looking further at this on page 435.

The use of factor analysis is not limited to looking at cognitive abilities – it has also been used in other fields, as we will see from the examples that follow.

Example from the literature: shame and guilt

Alexander *et al.* (1999) investigated shame and guilt in a sample of depressed patients. They had 86 patients and used a ten-item scale by Gilbert *et al.* (1994). Five of these items were said to measure shame (reliability 0.74),[2] and five were said to measure guilt (reliability = 0.75). Alexander *et al.* decided to carry out a psychometric investigation of this scale. We are going to use this study in order to explain factor analysis. This is because it is fairly easy to understand, as the questionnaire has only ten items, and Alexander *et al.* wanted to check that there were two scales (shame and guilt) as suggested by Gilbert *et al.* These were the items on the questionnaire. You can see that items 1, 4, 5, 7 and 8 are said to measure SHAME (S) and 2, 3, 6, 9 and 10 are said to measure GUILT (G).

1	To do something embarrassing in public (S)
2	Secretly cheating on something you know will not be found out (G)
3	To hurt someone's feelings (G)
4	To be the centre of attention (S)
5	To appear inadequate to other people (S)
6	To behave in an uncaring way to others (G)
7	To have something unfavourable revealed about you (S)
8	To feel self-conscious in front of others (S)
9	To behave unkindly (G)
10	Not saying anything when a shop assistant gives you too much change (G)

---

[2] The reliability of scales within questionnaires is measured by a correlation coefficient. Any coefficient > 0.70 is strong, showing that these two scales can be considered reliable ones.

12.4 Visualising factors

You know how to visualise scatterplots, and know that a correlation coefficient of 0.7 means that 49% (that is 0.7 * 0.7 = 49) of the variation in scores on x can be accounted for by the variation in scores on y. You could draw overlapping circles to represent the correlation. In the example here, the original ten variables can be split up into two distinct patterns (see Figures 12.1 and 12.2).

Of course, when you perform a statistical analysis on your computer, you do not obtain such diagrams from your output. However, performing factor analysis allows you to see the patterns anyway, from the output. In this example, Alexander *et al.* found that the ten variables listed above could be accounted for by two distinct 'factors'. Shame was influencing the scores on five of the variables, and guilt was influencing the scores of the other five variables. Note that we have not measured guilt or shame directly – but we assume they are there, by the scores on the observed variables. Also note that it is worth performing factor analysis only if the variables *are* correlated with each other. If they are not, there would be no patterns of correlations to analyse.

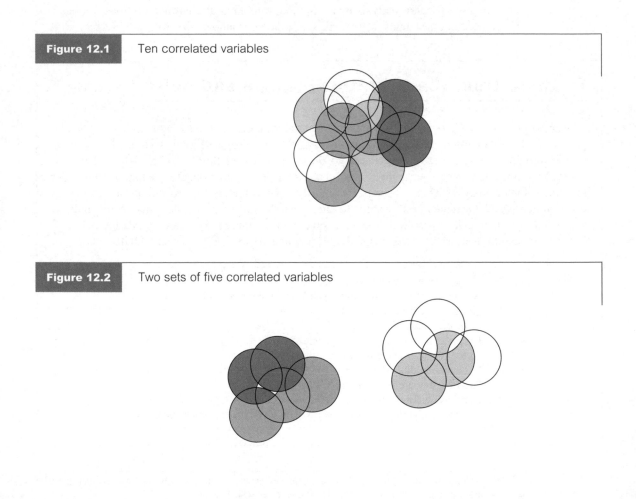

| Figure 12.1 | Ten correlated variables |

| Figure 12.2 | Two sets of five correlated variables |

12.5 Conceptualising factor analysis

One way to understand factor analysis is graphically. You already know that the relationship between variables can be represented by correlation coefficients, overlapping circles and scatterplots. However, there is another way of representing the relationship between variables, and that is by calculating the degree of angle between them.

Sticking with our example, let's assume that two of our variables, 'to feel self-conscious' and 'to do something embarrassing in public', are correlated, to the tune of 0.9. We can represent this relationship geometrically, by converting the 0.9 to the degree of angle between the two variables. To convert 0.9 to the degree of angle, you need to look at Table 12.3.

You can see that a correlation of 0.9 converts to a 26 degree angle. Use a horizontal line to represent one of the variables, e.g. 'to do something embarrassing in public'. You then use your protractor to measure 26 degrees, and to draw another line, which we can label 'to feel self-conscious' (see Figure 12.3).

This angle represents the degree of relationship between them. The lines we have drawn, with an arrow on them, are called *vectors*. A vector is simply a straight line that has a definite starting point, a definite direction and a definite length.

If our two variables were measuring absolutely the same thing, and they were perfectly correlated with each other, the angle between them would be zero, and both variables would lie along the same vector (see Figure 12.4).

Table 12.3 Conversion table from r to degree of angle (figures rounded to whole numbers)*

r	Degree of angle	r	Degree of angle	r	Degree of angle	r	Degree of angle	r	Degree of angle
0.00	90	0.30	72	0.50	60	0.70	46	0.90	26
0.11	84	0.31	72	0.51	59	0.71	45	0.91	25
0.12	83	0.32	71	0.52	59	0.72	44	0.92	23
0.13	83	0.33	71	0.53	58	0.73	43	0.93	22
0.14	82	0.34	70	0.54	57	0.74	42	0.94	20
0.15	82	0.35	70	0.55	57	0.75	41	0.95	18
0.16	81	0.36	69	0.56	56	0.76	41	0.96	16
0.17	80	0.37	68	0.57	55	0.77	40	0.97	14
0.18	80	0.38	68	0.58	54	0.78	39	0.98	11
0.19	79	0.39	67	0.59	54	0.79	38	0.99	8
0.20	78	0.40	66	0.60	53	0.80	37	1.00	00
0.21	78	0.41	66	0.61	52	0.81	36		
0.22	77	0.42	65	0.62	52	0.82	35		
0.23	77	0.43	65	0.63	51	0.83	34		
0.24	76	0.44	64	0.64	50	0.84	33		
0.25	76	0.45	63	0.65	49	0.85	32		
0.26	75	0.46	63	0.66	49	0.86	31		
0.27	74	0.47	62	0.67	48	0.87	30		
0.28	74	0.48	61	0.68	47	0.88	28		
0.29	73	0.49	61	0.69	46	0.89	27		

* Figures in this table computed by the authors

Figure 12.3 Diagram showing 26° angle between 'to feel self-conscious' and 'to do something embarrassing in public'

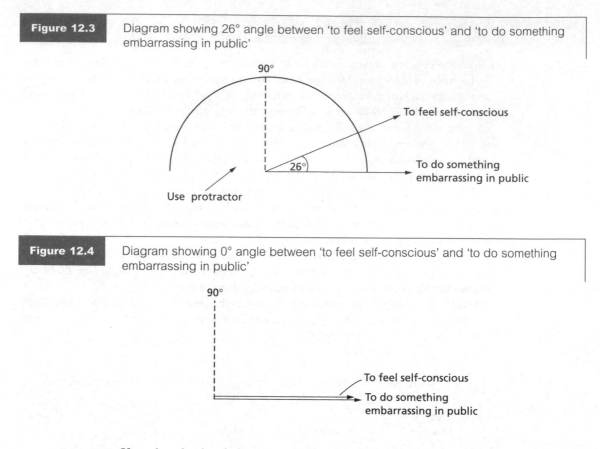

Figure 12.4 Diagram showing 0° angle between 'to feel self-conscious' and 'to do something embarrassing in public'

If, on the other hand, the two variables were totally unrelated, then they would lie at right angles to each other. The degree of relationship would be 90 degrees, which represents zero correlation (see Figure 12.5).

In order to perform factor analysis on these two variables (of course not likely, but an easy example to start off with) we need to find a new vector, which best represents the variables. We do this by drawing a new vector straight through the middle of x and y (see Figure 12.6).

Figure 12.5 Diagram showing 90° angle between 'to feel self-conscious' and 'to do something embarrassing in public'

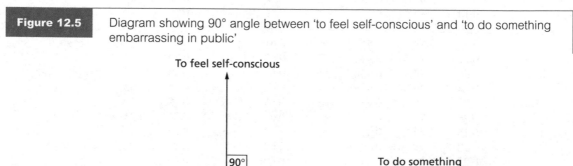

Diagram showing 26° angle between 'to feel self-conscious' and 'to do something embarrassing in public' with resultant factor

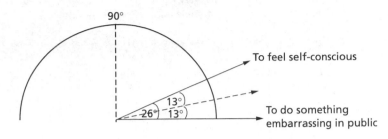

12.6 Naming the factors

The dotted line is the new factor, which we could call 'shame'. People 'name' factors by deciding what the related variables have in common. In this case, both of these variables have 'shame' in common. Since 'to feel self-conscious' and 'to do something embarrassing in public' could be represented by a 26-degree angle, you can see that the angle between 'to feel self-conscious' and the new vector must be 13, and the angle between 'to do something embarrassing in public' and the new vector must be 13 degrees. This can be seen in Figure 12.6.

12.7 Loadings of variables on factors

We can convert these angles back to correlation coefficients. Look at Table 12.4.

You will see that an angle of 13 degrees is equal to a correlation coefficient of 0.97. This is the correlation coefficient between 'to feel self-conscious' and the new resultant factor, and also between 'to do something embarrassing in public' and the new resultant factor. We say that both of these 'load highly' on SHAME. In fact, the new factor represents 94% of the relationship between them (0.97^2). The new factor groups together variables that are related (mathematically) to each other, but are different from other variables.

In our diagrams above, we have drawn only two variables, but factor analysis works in n-dimensional space. We cannot even adequately draw in 3D space, although we can try to explain by visualising such space. The example above used two variables in order to show how to obtain a new factor. There are, however, ten variables. Factor analysis looks at the patterns of correlations, and groups together the variables that explain most of the variation in scores.

Table 12.4 Conversion table from degrees of angle to correlation coefficients*

Degree of angle	r	Degree of angle	r	Degree of angle	r	Degree of angle	r
0	1.00	24	0.91	48	0.67	72	0.31
1	0.99	25	0.91	49	0.66	73	0.29
2	0.99	26	0.90	50	0.64	74	0.28
3	0.99	27	0.89	51	0.63	75	0.26
4	0.99	28	0.88	52	0.62	76	0.24
5	0.99	29	0.87	53	0.62	77	0.22
6	0.99	30	0.86	54	0.59	78	0.21
7	0.99	31	0.86	55	0.57	79	0.19
8	0.99	32	0.85	56	0.56	80	0.17
9	0.99	33	0.84	57	0.55	81	0.16
10	0.98	34	0.83	58	0.53	82	0.14
11	0.98	35	0.82	59	0.52	83	0.12
12	0.98	36	0.81	60	0.50	84	0.10
13	0.97	37	0.80	61	0.48	85	0.09
14	0.97	38	0.79	62	0.47	86	0.07
15	0.97	39	0.78	63	0.45	87	0.05
16	0.96	40	0.77	64	0.44	88	0.03
17	0.96	41	0.75	65	0.42	89	0.02
18	0.95	42	0.74	66	0.41	90	0.00
19	0.95	43	0.73	67	0.39		
20	0.94	44	0.72	68	0.37		
21	0.93	45	0.71	69	0.36		
22	0.93	46	0.69	70	0.34		
23	0.92	47	0.68	71	0.33		

* Figures in this table computed by the authors

Via matrix algebra,[3] vectors are then drawn in n-dimensional space, and a resultant vector (factor) is found, much the same as in our example in Figure 12.6. Once this factor (provisionally named Factor 1) has been found (extracted) then Factor 2 groups together a different set of variables, normally unrelated to the first. Each factor 'represents' a set of variables (the variables that are strongly related to the factor). We 'name' the factors by looking to see what such variables have in common.

Imagine that we have factor analysed 20 variables and that the program has obtained the correlation coefficients, converted them into degrees of angles, and found the resultant first factor for the first pattern of correlations. (This is calculated by using matrix algebra.) Although we cannot represent that here, the following diagram shows one way of visualising what is happening, although it is approximate. You can imagine the factor as an umbrella handle (upturned) with broken spokes. The spokes are the variables.

---

[3] You have heard of matrices: a data matrix, a correlation matrix, or a variance–covariance matrix, for instance. Matrix algebra is a special mathematical method by which these matrices are manipulated. In multivariate techniques such as factor analysis and MANOVA, matrix algebra is the method by which the matrices are analysed.

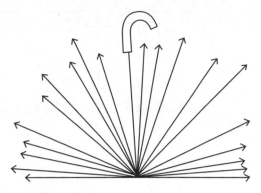

Some variables (the vectors furthest away from the handle) are hardly related to the new resultant factor at all, and these are not used for naming the factor. Other variables (the ones closest to the handle) are strongly related to the factor, and these are the ones we use for naming purposes. Variables that load highly on a factor are closer to the resultant factor. Although we do not see diagrams such as the ones above in our output, we do obtain a table of factor loadings (these are the correlation coefficients between the variables and the factors).

Activity 12.2

Look at the following diagram, which represents variables correlating with Factor 1. What name would you give to this factor?

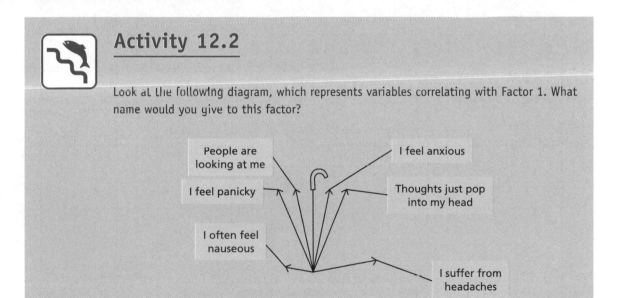

In our SHAME and GUILT example, we have ten variables.

12.8 The correlational matrix

The first thing the program does is obtain a matrix of correlation coefficients.

Correlations: r and p values for shame and guilt variables

	To do something embarrassing in public	Secretly cheating on something that you know will not be found out	To hurt someone's feelings	To be the centre of attention	To appear inadequate to other people	To behave in an uncaring way to others	To have something unfavourable revealed about you	To feel self-conscious in front of others	To behave unkindly	Not saying anything when a shop assistant gives you too much change
To do something embarrassing in public	**1.000** .	**.343** .001	**.215** .023	**.557** .000	**.476** .000	**.264** .007	**.416** .000	**.490** .000	**.239** .013	**.230** .017
Secretly cheating on something that you know will not be found out		**1.000**	**.450** .000	**.383** .000	**.306** .002	**.354** .000	**.176** .052	**.280** .005	**.503** .000	**.353** .000
To hurt someone's feelings			**1.000**	**.202** .031	**.376** .000	**.776** .000	**.137** .104	**.310** .002	**.748** .000	**.318** .001
To be the centre of attention				**1.000**	**.437** .000	**.168** .062	**.302** .002	**.469** .000	**.230** .017	**.122** .132
To appear inadequate to other people					**1.000**	**.371** .000	**.530** .000	**.745** .000	**.483** .000	**.177** .052
To behave in an uncaring way to others						**1.000**	**.256** .009	**.258** .008	**.739** .000	**.393** .000
To have something unfavourable revealed about you							**1.000**	**.567** .000	**.272** .006	**.209** .027
To feel self-conscious in front of others								**1.000**	**.342** .001	**.267** .006
To behave unkindly									**1.000**	**.436** .000
Not saying anything when a shop assistant gives you too much change										**1.000**

12.9 The unrotated and rotated matrices

The statistical program (e.g. SPSSFW) then performs matrix algebra on the figures, which results in a matrix showing the correlations of variables with factors. This first matrix is an unrotated matrix. We will be explaining the significance of this later. Matrix algebra is then used to rotate the matrix. The rotated matrix contains the factor loadings (correlations of variables with factors), which are used in interpreting the results, and the figures, which are used in reporting such results. The correlation coefficients in the rotated matrix (see Table 12.5) are also used in the construction of the diagrams below. The first diagram shows the relationship of the variables to the first resultant factor (see Figure 12.7).

You can see that all the variables closest to the handle are to do with items that relate to SHAME. Factor 1 is named 'shame'. The other variables that are not close to the handle are to do with something different.

Now the program looks at these other variables, the ones that were not related to Factor 1 (SHAME). It takes those variables and finds the resultant factor (see Figure 12.8).

You can see this time that all the variables close to the handle are to do with GUILT. Arising from the ten variables, then, there were two factors.

Looking at Table 12.5, then, we can see that the five items that loaded most highly on Factor 1 are grouped together, and that this factor can be named 'shame'. The other items load more highly on Factor 2, and these can be represented by 'guilt'. Alexander *et al.* mentioned in their article that the criterion that they used in deciding whether the factor loading was high was 0.5. You should note that this is a fairly arbitrary figure, and that other researchers might choose 0.4 or even 0.3. It is always good when an item loads highly on one factor only.

In Table 12.5 we have converted each factor loading into the degree of angle, so that you can check for yourselves (with your protractor) that we have drawn Figures 12.7 and 12.8 correctly.

Table 12.5 Rotated factor loadings

Item	Description	Factor 1		Factor 2	
		r	Degree of angle	*r*	Degree of angle
1	To do something embarrassing in public	**0.75**	**41**	0.15	82
2	Secretly cheating on something you know will not be found out	0.30	72	**0.57**	55
3	To hurt someone's feelings	0.11	84	**0.88**	28
4	To be the centre of attention	**0.71**	**45**	0.11	84
5	To appear inadequate to other people	**0.76**	**41**	0.32	**71**
6	To behave in an uncaring way to others	0.12	83	**0.87**	30
7	To have something unfavourable revealed about you	**0.71**	**45**	0.11	84
8	To feel self-conscious in front of others	**0.82**	**35**	0.21	78
9	To behave unkindly	0.20	78	**0.88**	28
10	Not saying anything when a shop assistant gives you too much change	0.15	82	**0.56**	56
	Variance %	43.9		17.5	

| Figure 12.7 | Degrees of angle represents relationship between F1 and the variable[4] |

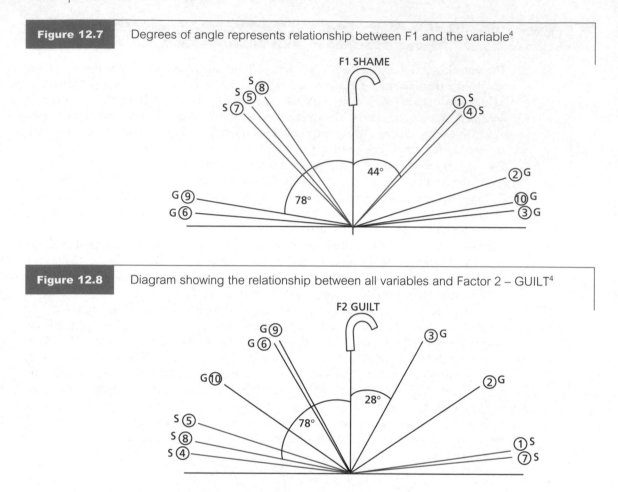

| Figure 12.8 | Diagram showing the relationship between all variables and Factor 2 – GUILT[4] |

We have emboldened all correlations above 0.5. All the emboldened figures in Factor 1 are to do with shame, and all the emboldened figures in Factor 2 are to do with guilt. Alexander *et al.* therefore confirmed that the Shame and Guilt Scale consisted of two scales, which could be called Guilt and Shame.

12.10 Plotting the variables in factor space

Another way of visualising the clusters of variables that form the factors is by drawing the factors as follows, and plotting the variables in the factor space (see Figure 12.9). Look at the first item, which loads 0.75 on F1 and 0.15 on F2. Go along to 0.75 on the horizontal axis (SHAME, F1) and then go up to 0.15 on F2, and write the item number where the two meet. The dotted lines show this for item 1.

---

[4] We have illustrated the degree of angle between the factor and two variables. Please use your protractor to measure the other angles.

| Figure 12.9 | Diagram showing variable 'to do something embarrassing in public' plotted in factor space |

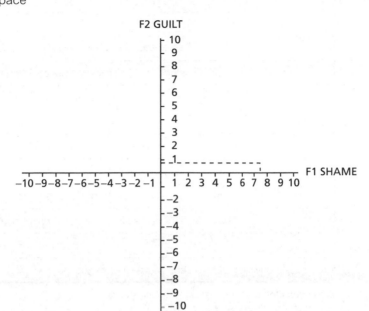

| Activity 12.3 |

Complete the rest yourselves, in pencil. Check your results against Figure 12.10.

| Figure 12.10 | Answer to exercise in Activity 12.3 |

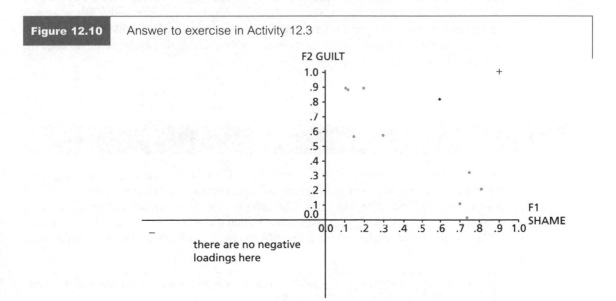

there are no negative loadings here

Component Matrix[a]

	Component	
	1	2
To do something embarrassing in public	.625	.433
Secretly cheating on something that you know will not be found out	.621	−.172
To hurt someone's feelings	.710	−.533
To be the centre of attention	.569	.441
To appear inadequate to other people	.758	.334
To behave in an uncaring way to others	.712	−.512
To have something unfavourable revealed about you	.574	.436
To feel self-conscious in front of others	.719	.450
To behave unkindly	.777	−.461
Not saying anything when a shop assistant gives you too much change	.507	−.277

Extraction Method: Principal Component Analysis.
a. 2 components extracted.

Of course, we can never draw more than Factor 1 plotted against Factor 2, so we are lucky in this example! You can see that there are clearly two clusters of variables, both by looking at the diagram (Figure 12.10) and by the rotated component matrix (Table 12.5). This is clear because we are working on the rotated matrix. This was what the matrix looked like before it was rotated.

It is hard to see the clusters of variables using this matrix – we cannot see which items relate to SHAME and which relate to GUILT, because all variables load significantly on the first factor. However, if we replot the variables in factor space using the unrotated component matrix, we can see that there are two clusters of variables, but that they are moderately correlated with both factors – you can see this both from the diagram (Figure 12.10) and from the output above.

12.11 Rotating the matrix

In order to aid interpretation, the axes are rotated.[5] There are several ways of rotating axes, but the most common is a method called varimax, the goal of which is to maximise high correlations and minimise low ones. The computer program rotates the matrix as long as you have selected the appropriate option. Rotation is a well-established technique that makes interpretation easier, because the differences in the loadings (of the variable with

---

[5] This is achieved by multiplying the unrotated component matrix by something called the component transformation matrix – also achieved by matrix algebra.

each factor) are emphasised.[6] When the data are strong and the patterns clear, then the choice of rotation doesn't matter so much, as the conclusions are similar.

Example from the literature: IBS

The use of factor analysis extends to Health Psychology. Invisible chronic illnesses, for instance, are ones in which the symptoms of the disorder persist, but are not apparent to other people. One such disorder is irritable bowel syndrome, which is a collection of symptoms, not all of which are to do with the bowel. People who have been diagnosed with IBS have been measured on a range of symptoms. The empirical data are, then, the scores that these people received on the tests conducted.

As part of a study investigating the features of eating disorders in IBS, Tang *et al.* (1998) collected information on nine gastrointestinal symptoms every day for two weeks. Sixty participants rated their symptoms on a five-point scale (0 – symptom not a problem and 4 – debilitating problem). Tang *et al.* then took the mean for each of the symptoms, which were: abdominal pain, abdominal tenderness, constipation, diarrhoea, flatulence, bloating, belching, nausea and vomiting.

12.12 Steps taken in performing a factor analysis

These are the steps taken to perform factor analysis:

1. *First a correlation matrix is produced*: The researchers themselves do not need to look at the correlational matrix, although the program uses the information from this matrix to perform further calculations.

2. *Then a set of factors is extracted*: In practice it is possible to extract as many factors as variables (if each variable was not highly correlated with any other) but this would defeat the object of factor analysis. We want to account for as much variance as possible, while keeping the number of factors extracted as small as possible. Although in our first example there were two clear factors, often things are not as simple as this, and the decision on how many factors to 'keep' is decided by the researchers on the basis of both statistical and theoretical criteria.

3. *Number of factors to retain*: When factor analysis is performed in SPSSFW, the program decides how many factors to keep on the basis of statistical criteria. Each factor that is extracted accounts for a certain amount of variance.

    (a) Eigenvalues show the proportion of variance accounted for by each factor. The sum of the eigenvalues is the number of variables in the analysis. Any factor that has an eigenvalue of 1.00 is kept.

---

[6] Varimax ensures that every factor is independent from the other factors. In real life most psychological variables are intercorrelated. Varimax is therefore artificial – even though it is a very common way of rotating.

It is a useful rule, but what happens if one of the factors has an eigenvalue of 0.99? Using this rule blindly would mean that the factor would not emerge, and yet it could be theoretically important. It is here that the researcher would consider whether to keep such a factor. If it is decided that the factor should be kept, then SPSSFW needs to be overruled.

(b) Scree plot. This is simply the number of factors plotted against variance accounted for. Here is a scree plot:

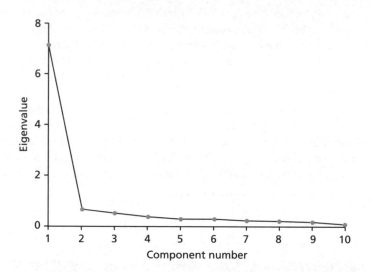

The idea is that factors drop off to some level and then plateau. The rule is that you look at the plot and see where the plateau levels out, and then choose the number of factors just before this point. Here we would choose two components. This is fine if your scree plot looks like the one above, but not if it looks like this:

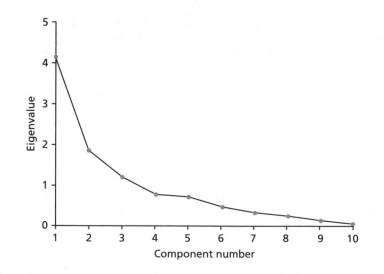

It is harder to say here how many components 'should' be kept.

(c) The third criterion is to look at how much variance the factors account for. It is good practice to try to account for approximately 75% of the variance. However, you need to try to explain the most variance with the least number of factors. Thus, all the criteria must be used together to decide how many factors to keep. A good researcher needs to take everything into consideration in coming to a decision on how many factors to retain.

Tang *et al.* say that they selected factors on the basis of eigenvalues of above 1 and that on this basis three factors emerged, which accounted for 64.5% of the variance.

4. *Unrotated factor loadings*: The program gives information on the strength of the relationships between the items and the factors. However, researchers are usually interested only in the rotated factor matrix – this tends to be easier to interpret (see page 428). Tang *et al.* tell us that they used varimax rotation (the default on SPSSFW).

5. *Naming the factors*: The researcher then looks at the *rotated* factor loadings, to see what the clusters of variables have in common. To do this, a decision must be taken on how strong a loading must be for it to be included in the naming process. As mentioned above, this tends to be fairly arbitrary and varies between 0.3 and 0.5. Tang *et al.* tell us that 'items with a rotated loading greater than 0.4 were incorporated within an index'. Factor 1 will normally account for the largest amount of variance, followed by Factor 2, and so on.

The table below shows the varimax rotated loadings of symptom severity ratings:

GI symptoms	Component I	Component II	Component III
Tenderness	**0.88**	−0.09	−0.02
Pain	**0.87**	0.28	−0.02
Bloating	**0.73**	0.13	0.03
Constipation	**0.61**	0.06	0.51
Flatulence	0.17	**0.86**	0.04
Belching	0.19	**0.85**	0.09
Diarrhoea	−0.04	0.37	0.12
Vomiting	−0.25	0.15	**0.81**
Nausea	0.38	0.18	**0.64**
Percent variance accounted for	30.1%	19.3%	15.1%

Tang *et al.* (1998)

We have emboldened the loadings above 0.4. Tang *et al.* do not mention that 'diarrhoea' has not loaded onto any of the components by the criterion of 0.4. Since this criterion is arbitrary, however, it seems that diarrhoea could be clustered with the other two variables that make Component II.

In Tang *et al.*'s study, then, they found that the nine variables listed above could be accounted for by three distinct components. Factor 1 consisted of tenderness, pain, bloating and constipation.

Tang *et al.* named the factors 'physical pain and discomfort', 'gaseousness' and 'vomiting'. Sometimes researchers have fun in thinking up names that are both suitable and amusing, but this was not the case with Tang *et al.*

Activity 12.4

Look at the following information:

Rotated Component Matrix

	Component		
	1	2	3
self-expression	.801		
active recreation	.766		
other social relationships	.737		
family relationships	.715		
work	.652		
sex life	.651		
community involvement	.638		
relationship with spouse	.623		
financial situation	.592		
health	.592		
passive recreation	.447		
religious expression	.431		
diet			
pleased		.673	
pleased accomplished something		.670	
proud		.626	
excited		.614	
on top of world		.480	
upset			.677
bored			.628
restless			.511
depressed			.460

Extraction Method: Principal Component Analysis.
Rotation Method: Varimax with Kaiser Normalization.
a. Rotation converged in 5 iterations.

Have a go at naming the factors – there are no 'right' answers!

Example from the literature: image questionnaire for adolescents

The third example is slightly more complicated in that the researchers performed three analyses in order to decide how many factors to keep. This is quite acceptable, because the decision on how many factors to keep is the researcher's, who needs to think through several alternatives in order to come to the best decision.

Patton and Noller (1994) wanted to discover the construct validity of an image questionnaire that they had developed for adolescents. They gave a 53-item questionnaire to over 216 adolescents. They performed three separate PCAs, one keeping four factors, one keeping five, and one keeping six. However, the sixth factor accounted for only an additional 2.16% of the variance (a very small amount of variance), and only two items loaded highly (criterion of > 0.4) on the sixth factor. (As a rule of thumb, factors are not usually kept when fewer than three variables load on them.) When Patton and Noller named the remaining five factors, they found they could confidently name them:

- Factor 1 – emotional self
- Factor 2 – social conscience
- Factor 3 – personal coping
- Factor 4 – family relationships
- Factor 5 – social relationships.

They did consider keeping just four factors in the final analysis, but that meant that a 'social' factor would not emerge, and they considered this important in the light of their previous knowledge. So they concluded that the factor analysis supported five dimensions of the self – which they had predicted.

Activity 12.5

Patton and Noller decided to keep five factors in the study described above. Think about the criteria they used in coming to this decision. Do you agree with their decision?

Example from the literature: why students decide to live on campus

Luzzo and McDonald (1996) carried out research to discover the reasons why students decide to live on campus. They first decided to check the psychometric properties of the questionnaire they intended using, which was called the On-Campus Questionnaire. They thus examined the factor structure of the questionnaire. Luzzo and McDonald specified the criteria they would use in deciding how many factors to retain.

Luzzo and McDonald followed the usual steps in producing the analysis, and they used 0.4 as the criterion figure for deciding which items should be used in the naming and interpretation of factors. Here is a table of their rotated factor loadings:

Item	Factor 1	Factor 2	Factor 3	Factor 4	Factor 5
To be more independent	**0.87**	0.08	0.17	0.16	0.18
For freedom	**0.91**	−0.03	0.21	0.12	0.06
To get away from parents	**0.82**	0.11	0.10	−0.13	−0.08
For safety	0.19	**0.68**	0.05	0.24	0.16
Because of the cost	−0.04	**0.66**	0.04	0.03	−0.07
My parents wanted me to	0.01	**0.64**	0.10	−0.36	0.05
To be with friends	0.26	0.26	**0.67**	−0.06	−0.06
To meet new people	0.04	0.20	**0.85**	0.13	0.05
To meet significant others	0.11	−0.10	**0.81**	−0.12	−0.30
To have the whole college experience	0.12	0.07	**0.73**	0.19	0.36
To party	0.38	−0.21	0.56	−0.21	0.30
For convenience	0.07	0.08	0.02	**0.87**	−0.11
My scholarship required it	0.03	−0.08	−0.04	−0.25	**0.85**
Opportunity for involvement in academic activities	0.13	0.39	0.35	0.20	**0.60**

We have emboldened the loadings that are above 0.4. It is possible to get the computer program to omit loadings that fall below the criterion level chosen and also to order the correlations so that those that load most highly appear first. Choosing these options makes it easier to pick out which items load most highly on the factors.

Activity 12.6

Have a go at naming the factors. Look to see what the cluster of items loading most highly on Factor 1 have in common, and think of a name that reflects this commonality. Then do the same with the other factors. There are no 'right' answers to this task of course, but you can see the names that Luzzo and McDonald gave to the factors on page 590.

12.13 Use of factors or components in further analyses

Most of the research articles that we have discussed present results based on the factors that were extracted. It is very common to use the factor scores in further analysis – often the factor scores are correlated with other variables. For instance, Alexander *et al.* (1999) confirmed that there were two factors in the Shame and Guilt Questionnaire that they used. The scores achieved by participants on these factors (actually a composite score made up of the variables that made up the scales) were correlated with a measure of depression (Becks Depression Inventory – BDI) and a questionnaire measuring submissive behaviour. Here are the (partial) results:

	Shame	Guilt
BDI	0.07	0.28**
Submissive behaviour	0.53***	0.35***

$** \ p < 0.01 \quad *** \ p < 0.001$

Activity 12.7

What can you conclude from the results above?

Tang *et al.* (1998) also performed correlations between the newly extracted factors and variables relating to eating disorders:

	Physical pain and discomfort	Gaseousness	Vomiting
Body dissatisfaction	0.09	−0.04	0.23
Perfection	0.34*	−0.03	0.14
Ineffectiveness	0.34*	0.14	0.35*
Bulimia	0.04	0.13	0.35*
Weight discrepancy	−0.02	0.22	0.31*

$* \ p < 0.05$

Activity 12.8

Look at the above table. If you had to interpret the results to a friend, what would you say?

12.14 The meaning of negative loadings

Negative loadings mean that the variable in question is negatively correlated with the factor. Sometimes it could be difficult to interpret negative loadings. For instance, if you found that an arithmetic test was negatively correlated with a factor called MENTAL ABILITY you would suspect you had done something wrong! Usually a negative loading simply means that the variable in question was worded in the negative. For example, look at the following items, which made up a factor that we called 'EXTREME HAPPINESS'.

Item	Description	Loading
1	I feel content	+0.75
2	I feel like singing in the rain	+0.68
3	Work is wonderful	+0.62
4	I feel like I love everyone	+0.61
5	I feel absolutely awful	−0.61

All the above load highly on the factor, except that the first four items load positively, and the last one loads negatively. This makes sense, because 'I feel absolutely awful' is a negative statement. The first four items are clustered with what is actually the opposite of 'I feel absolutely awful'. If the loading of item 5 had been positive, we would suspect we had made a mistake.

Activity 12.9

The following table represents correlations between three test scores:

	1	2	3
1	–	0.866	0.6428
2		–	0.1736
3			–

(a) Convert these to degrees of angle using the table on page 419.
(b) Using a ruler and a protractor, draw one diagram to represent the relationship between the three tests.

SPSSFW: factor analysis – principal components analysis

Load up your data. Choose *Analyze*, *Data Reduction*, then *Factor*.

This gives you the following dialogue box:

Choose only those variables that you want to factor analyse to be moved into the *Variables* box

The variables that you wish to factor analyse should be moved from the left into the *Variables* list on the right. Make sure you choose only the variables that should be factor analysed – it is very easy to make a mistake and move irrelevant variables over, e.g. group number.

In order to obtain descriptives, you click on the *Descriptives* option to obtain the following dialogue box:

Initial solution should be checked. You can also choose to select descriptives and a correlational matrix

Click on *Continue* to return to the previous dialogue box, then click on *Extraction*. The *Extraction* option gives you the following dialogue box:

PCA is the default. Check the Scree plot if you wish

You can change the *Method* from PCA to one of the other ways of factor analysing your data – but PCA is the default. You could also choose to have the program analyse the covariance matrix rather than the correlation matrix. You may want to deselect the unrotated solution – at this stage this may not be of interest to you.

The first thing we want to do is to look at the initial solution – that is, the default. We can defer choosing how many factors to keep until we have seen that. Thus we do not, at this stage, select how many factors we wish to retain. Press *Continue*.

Choosing *Rotation* will give you the following dialogue box:

Here you can select which method of rotation you require – *Varimax* is probably the one you would need. Make sure the *Rotated solution* option is selected. Press *Continue*.

Selecting *Scores* will give you the following:

This is where we can ask for the factor scores (the composite score made up from the variables correlated with the factor) to be saved; we can then use these scores in a further analysis, e.g. regression or a correlation.

Choosing *Options* gives the following:

Here we can ask the program to sort the correlations by size, and to blank out any values below a criterion level; here we have chosen to blank out any correlations below 0.4. This often makes a table of rotated factor loadings easier to read. Then click on *OK*.

Total Variance Explained

Component	Initial Eigenvalues			Rotation Sums of Squared Loadings		
	Total	% of Variance	Cumulative %	Total	% of Variance	Cumulative %
1	**7.141**	**59.511**	**59.511**	**7.111**	**59.260**	**59.260**
2	**1.044**	**8.698**	**68.209**	**1.074**	**8.950**	**68.209**
3	.957	7.974	76.183			
4	.665	5.543	81.726			
5	.540	4.502	86.229			
6	.362	3.015	89.244			
7	.299	2.491	91.735			
8	.278	2.320	94.055			
9	.246	2.053	96.108			
10	.211	1.755	97.863			
11	.165	1.377	99.240			
12	9.122E-02	.760	100.000			

Extraction Method: Principal Component Analysis.

Here the default SPSS program has chosen two factors, on the basis of eigenvalues above 1; 68.2% of the variation in scores can be explained by these two factors. However, a third component has an initial eigenvalue of 0.96 – perhaps the researcher would want to look at that component to see if it was useful or meaningful.

Rotated Component Matrix[a]

	Component	
	1	2
Mathematics makes me feel uncomfortable and nervous	.900	
Mathematics makes me feel uneasy and confused	.891	
My mind goes blank and I am unable to think clearly when working mathematics	.864	
I usually don't worry about my ability to solve maths problems	−.861	
I get really uptight during maths tests	.850	
I get a sinking feeling when I think of trying hard maths problems	.849	
I have usually been at ease in maths courses	−.837	
I almost never get uptight while taking maths tests	−.819	
I have usually been at ease during maths tests	−.815	
It wouldn't bother me at all to take more maths courses	−.715	
achieved GCSE		.856
achieved GNVQ or higher		−.535

Extraction Method: Principal Component Analysis.
Rotation Method: Varimax with Kaiser Normalization.
a. Rotation converged in three iterations.

Here we can see that there are clearly two factors: most variables load highly on Factor 1, which we could call MATHS, and only two variables load on the second factor, both of which are concerned with qualifications. Thus we could be original and call this factor QUALIFICATIONS.

However, what happens if we want to ask the program to keep three factors, rather than two? We go back to the appropriate dialogue box and re-run the analysis:

Here we have gone back via *Analyze*, *Data Reduction* and *Factor*, and we have chosen the *Extraction* option. We have changed the number of factors to three. Then we press *Continue*.

We have also chosen to ask the program to display the factor scores by choosing *Scores* and selecting the appropriate option:

Then press *Continue*. This time the output includes our third factor:

Total Variance Explained

Component	Initial Eigenvalues			Rotation Sums of Squared Loadings		
	Total	% of Variance	Cumulative %	Total	% of Variance	Cumulative %
1	7.141	59.511	59.511	7.088	59.064	59.064
2	1.044	8.698	68.209	1.030	8.582	67.646
3	.957	7.974	76.183	1.024	8.537	76.183
4	.665	5.543	81.726			
5	.540	4.502	86.229			
6	.362	3.015	89.244			
7	.299	2.491	91.735			
8	.278	2.320	94.055			
9	.246	2.053	96.108			
10	.211	1.755	97.863			
11	.165	1.377	99.240			
12	9.122E-02	.760	100.000			

Extraction Method: Principal Component Analysis.

As you can see, the third factor accounts for almost as much variance as the second. Let's see what the table of factor loadings looks like, and whether the components make sense when we try to label them.

Rotated Component Matrix[a]

	Component		
	1	2	2
Mathematics makes me feel uncomfortable and nervous	.896		
Mathematics makes me feel uneasy and confused	.895		
My mind goes blank and I am unable to think clearly when working mathematics	.867		
I get really uptight during maths tests	.863		
I usually don't worry about my ability to solve maths problems	−.859		
I get a sinking feeling when I think of trying hard maths problems	.854		
I have usually been at ease in maths courses	−.824		
I almost never get uptight while taking maths tests	−.820		
I have usually been at ease during maths tests	−.809		
It wouldn't bother me at all to take more maths courses	−.712		
achieved GNVQ or higher		.993	
achieved GCSE			.989

Extraction Method: Principal Component Analysis.
Rotation Method: Varimax with Kaiser Normalization.
a. Rotation converged in four iterations.

Well, not really. There is not much point in accounting for more variance when only one variable loads on a factor. So we will go no further; we will accept that two factors adequately represent the data.

Total Variance Explained

Component	Rotation Sums of Squared Loadings		
	Total	% of Variance	Cumulative %
1	7.111	59.260	59.260
2	1.074	8.950	68.209

Extraction Method: Principal Component Analysis.

Together these two factors account for 68.2% of the variance.

You can see, then, that the researchers need to be able to use their skill and judgement in interpreting the results from a factor analysis.

Summary

In this chapter we have given you a brief introduction to factor analysis/principal components analysis. We have:

- given you a conceptual understanding of factor analysis

- explained the similarities and differences of the most common form of factor analysis (principal axis factoring) and principal components analysis

- explained how to carry out a factor analysis on SPSSFW

- shown you how to interpret the output from such an analysis

- taken you through one example from the psychological literature in detail (Alexander *et al.*)

- used several other examples in order to illustrate this important statistical technique.

MULTIPLE CHOICE QUESTIONS

1. In order to name factors that have been extracted, researchers look at:
   - (a) The rotated factor loadings
   - (b) The unrotated factor loadings
   - (c) The table of eigenvalues
   - (d) None of the above

2. The differences between factor analysis and principal components analysis are relatively unimportant when the data set is:
   - (a) Large and the participant numbers are high
   - (b) Large and the participant numbers are low
   - (c) Small and the participant numbers are high
   - (d) Small and the participant numbers are low

3. A factor is thought of as an underlying latent variable:
   - (a) That is influenced by observed variables
   - (b) That is unexplained by unobserved variables
   - (c) Along which individuals differ
   - (d) Along which individuals are homogeneous

4. Look at the following diagram.

Variable 1

Variable 2

Theses variables are:

(a) Perfectly related to each other
(b) Totally unrelated to each other
(c) Share a moderate correlation with each other
(d) None of the above applies

5. A vector is:

(a) A curved line with an indefinite length
(b) A straight line with an indefinite length
(c) A straight line with a definite length
(d) A curved line with a definite length

6. Factor analysis deals with:

(a) Patterns of correlations
(b) Patterns of mean values
(c) Frequency counts
(d) None of the above

7. Factor analysis requires that variables:

(a) Are not related to each other
(b) Are related to each other
(c) Have only a weak relationship with each other
(d) Are measured in the same units

8. Using the correlational matrix to perform factor analysis rather than the variance–covariance matrix ensures that the data:

(a) Will be statistically significant
(b) Are standardised
(c) Are unstandardised
(d) None of these

9. The decision on how many factors to keep is decided on:

(a) Statistical criteria
(b) Theoretical criteria
(c) Both (a) and (b)
(d) Neither (a) nor (b)

10. The original unrotated matrix is usually rotated so that:

(a) The factors are more significant
(b) The mathematical calculations are easier
(c) Interpretation is easier
(d) All of these

11. A scree plot is a number of:

(a) Variables plotted against variance accounted for
(b) Variables plotted against factor loadings
(c) Factors plotted against correlation coefficients
(d) None of the above

12. It is possible to extract:

(a) As many factors as variables
(b) More factors than variables
(c) More variables than factors
(d) None of the above

Questions 13 to 15 relate to the following output:

Total Variance Explained

Component		Initial Eigenvalues			Rotation Sums of Squared Loadings		
	Total	% of Variance	Cumulative %		Total	% of Variance	Cumulative %
1	5.804	26.383	26.383		5.235	23.795	23.795
2	2.030	9.227	35.611		2.438	11.081	34.877
3	1.511	6.869	42.480		1.673	7.603	42.480
4	1.305	5.930	48.410				
5	1.176	5.344	53.754				
6	1.139	5.177	58.931				
7	.972	4.420	63.351				
8	.863	3.925	67.276				
9	.779	3.541	70.817				
10	.752	3.419	74.236				
11	.717	3.259	77.495				
12	.671	3.051	80.546				
13	.615	2.795	83.341				
14	.561	2.552	85.893				
15	.524	2.382	88.275				
16	.488	2.218	90.493				
17	.462	2.099	92.593				
18	.412	1.872	94.465				
19	.364	1.656	96.120				
20	.315	1.431	97.551				
21	.299	1.357	98.908				
22	.240	1.092	100.000				

Extraction Method: Principal Component Analysis.

13. How many components have an eigenvalue above 1?

    (a) 3
    (b) 4
    (c) 5
    (d) 6

14. If a three-factor solution is retained, approximately how much variance has been accounted for?

    (a) 43%
    (b) 35%
    (c) 24%
    (d) 10%

15. How many variables were in this analysis?

    (a) 3
    (b) 10
    (c) 22
    (d) Impossible to tell

16. What is the minimum number of participants recommended for a factor analysis?

    (a) 50
    (b) 70
    (c) 100
    (d) 500

Questions 17 to 20 relate to the table and text below, taken from Romero et al. *(2003).*

Researchers were investigating the components of self-control construct in the general theory of crime, evaluated by various questionnaires. They found that the analysis 'extracted 4 factors with eigenvalues greater than 1, which together explained 57.31% of the variance. The factors resulting from the rotation are listed in the table below (F1–F4)'.

	F1	F2	F3	F4
I like to take chances	0.78			
The things I like to do best are dangerous	0.75			
I enjoy roller coaster rides	0.63			
Even when I'm not in a hurry, I like to drive at high speeds	0.62			0.40
I enjoy activities where there is a lot of physical contact	0.54			
The best way to solve an argument is to sit down and talk things out, even if it takes an hour		−0.80		
If someone insulted me, I would be likely to hit or slap them		0.61		
I like to read books		−0.57		
I'd rather spend my money on something I wanted now than to put it in the bank			0.79	
If I see something in a store that I want, I just buy it			0.77	
I don't deal well with anything that frustrates me				0.81
I really get angry when I ride behind a slow driver				0.72

17. Which factor represents 'risk seeking'?

    (a) Factor 1
    (b) Factor 2
    (c) Factor 3
    (d) Factor 4

18. Which factor represents 'non-verbal orientation'?

    (a) Factor 1
    (b) Factor 2
    (c) Factor 3
    (d) Factor 4

19. On Factor 2, only one of the items is positive. This is because:

    (a) The authors have made a mistake
    (b) The positive item is coded in the opposite way to the other two items
    (c) The three items are coded in the same direction
    (d) There is no significance in the direction of the loadings

20. Only the most 'significant' loadings are shown in this table. This is because it is customary to blank out loadings below:

    (a) 0.4
    (b) 0.5
    (c) 0.6
    (d) 0.7

References

Alexander, B., Brewin, C.R., Vearnals, S., Wolff, G. and Leff, J. (1999) 'An investigation of shame and guilt in a depressed sample', *British Journal of Medical Psychology*, **72**: 323–38.

Gilbert, P., Pehl, J.B. and Allan, S. (1994) 'The Phenomenology of shame and guilt: an empirical investigation', *British Journal of Medical Psychology*, **67**(1): 23–36.

Luzzo, D.A. and McDonald, A. (1996) 'Exploring students' reasons for living on campus', *Journal of College Student Development*, **37**(4): 389–95.

Patton, W. and Noller, P. (1994) 'The Offer self-image questionnaire for adolescents: psychometric properties and factor structure', *Journal of Youth and Adolescence*, **23**(1): 19–41.

Romero, E., Gomez-Fraguela, J.A., Luengo, M.A. *et al.* (2003) 'The self-control construct in the general theory of crime: an investigation in terms of personality psychology', *Psychology and Crime Law*, **9**(1): 61–86.

Tang, T.N., Toner, B.B., Stuckless, N., Dion, K.L., Kaplan, A.S. and Ali, A. (1998) 'Features of eating disorders in patients with irritable bowel syndrome', *Journal of Psychosomatic Research*, **45**(2): 171–8.

13 Analysis of three or more groups partialling out effects of a covariate

Chapter overview

This chapter will introduce you to a technique that is based on both analysis of variance (ANOVA) and linear regression. This technique is called *analysis of covariance* (ANCOVA) and it builds on the material you have learned in previous chapters. A simple ANCOVA shows you whether your groups differ on a dependent variable, while partialling out the effects of another variable, called the *covariate*. A covariate is a variable that has a linear relationship with the dependent variable. You have already learned about removing (partialling out) the effects of a variable, in Chapter 5 (page 190), on correlational analysis. In ANCOVA, the variable that is partialled out is called the *covariate*. In this chapter, we are going to discuss the analysis of a one-way, between-participants design, and the use of one covariate.

As the material in this chapter is based on the one-way ANOVA, everything we talked about in relation to the analysis of a one-way, between-participants design (in Chapter 9) applies here. In other words, the analysis of a one-way design includes the following:

1. Descriptive statistics, such as means, standard deviations, graphical illustrations such as box and whisker plots, and error bars.
2. Effect size – either the magnitude of the difference between the conditions (d), and/or an overall measure of effect such as Eta^2 (η^2).
3. An inferential test: in this case ANCOVA, which shows us (assuming the null hypothesis to be true) how likely it is, after partialling out the effects of the covariate, that differences between the conditions are due to sampling error.

In this chapter you will:

■ gain a conceptual understanding of ANCOVA
■ learn the conditions under which it is appropriate to use ANCOVA
■ understand the assumptions that you must meet in order to perform ANCOVA
■ learn how to present results using graphical techniques.

There are two main reasons for using ANCOVA:

1. To reduce error variance.
2. To adjust the means on the covariate, so that the mean covariate score is the same for all groups.

EXAMPLE

Imagine that new students are assigned at random to three different introductory statistics groups, using three different teaching methods. They have an hour's session.

1. Group 1 has an hour of traditional 'chalk 'n' talk'.
2. Group 2 has an hour of the same, only the lecture is interactive in that students can interrupt and ask questions, and the lecturer will encourage this. This is traditional plus interactive.
3. Group 3 is highly interactive in that the students work in groups with guidance from the lecturer.

In order to discover which method has worked best, we give the students a 20-question test to see which group has retained the most material from the one-hour session. Let's say we expect Group 3 to retain the most material (i.e. the highly interactive method is expected to be the most effective teaching method).

We *could* perform a simple one-way ANOVA, using teaching method as the independent variable (three levels). This would show us whether there were differences between the groups, in retention of the statistics material. However, assume that the ability to retain material in the lecture is related to IQ, irrespective of teaching method. If IQ and ability to retain such material are associated, we would expect the association to be positive; that is, IQ and scores on the statistics test should be positively correlated.

Imagine that we have collected data on IQ and marks in a statistics test; the scattergram might look something like Figure 13.1.

Although the correlation is positive, it is a moderate one: +0.49 in fact.

What happens in ANCOVA is that IQ (called the covariate, because it varies with the dependent variable) is taken into account in the mathematical calculations. What the formula does is to *remove* the variance due to the association between statistics performance and IQ. As we have said above, this will reduce our error variance.

A good way to visualise what is happening is with a graph (Figure 13.2). This shows you our three different teaching method groups (called traditional, mixed and interactive). The instructions on how to obtain a chart of regression lines such as the ones in Figure 13.2 follow.

Figure 13.1 Scattergram of IQ and marks in statistics test

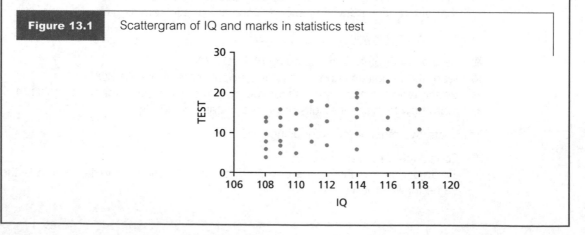

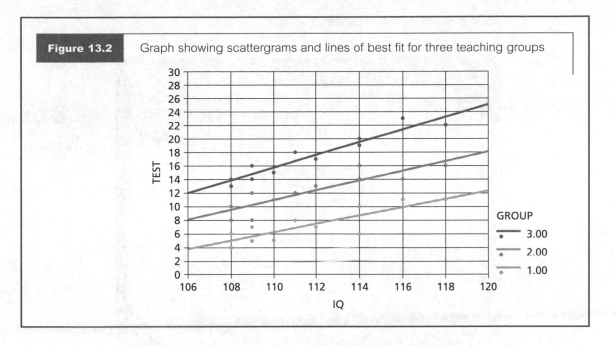

Figure 13.2 Graph showing scattergrams and lines of best fit for three teaching groups

SPSSFW: obtaining a chart of regression lines

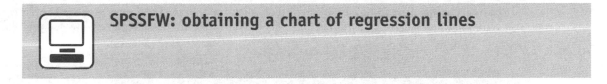

Select *Graphs*, then *Scatter* as follows:

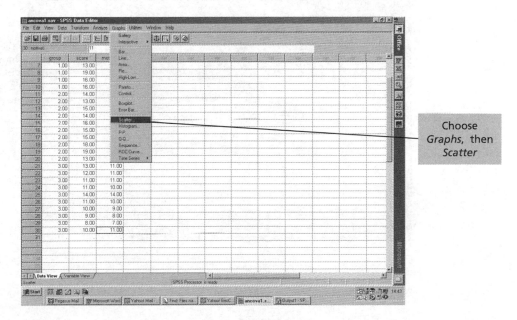

Choose *Graphs*, then *Scatter*

This gives you the following dialogue box:

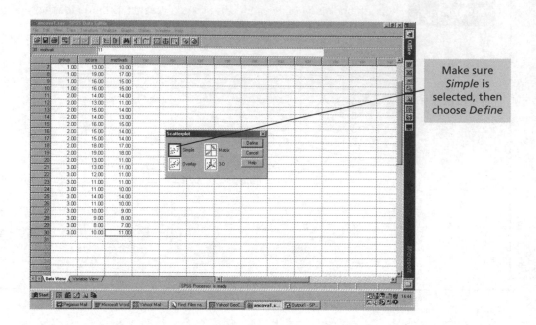

Make sure *Simple* is selected, then choose *Define*

Ensure that the *Simple* box is selected, then click on *Define*. This gives you the simple scatterplot dialogue box as follows:

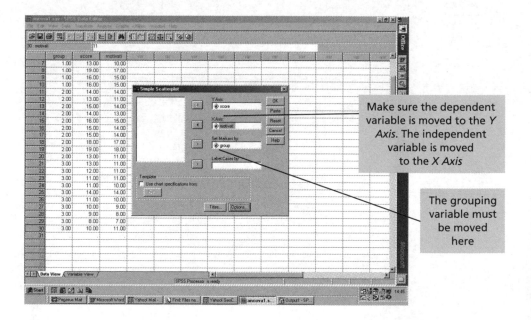

Make sure the dependent variable is moved to the *Y Axis*. The independent variable is moved to the *X Axis*

The grouping variable must be moved here

The variables are moved from the left-hand side to the right. *Score* is moved to the *Y Axis* box, *Motiv* to the *X Axis* box, and we move the *Group* to the *Set Markers by* box. This is important because it enables you to obtain separate regression lines for each group.

Click on *OK*. This leads to the following:

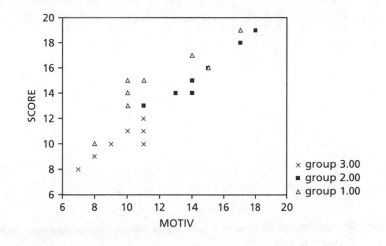

Once you have done this, you double-click on the graph and obtain the following:

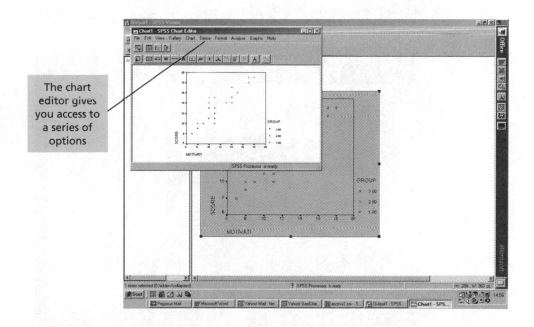

The chart editor gives you access to a series of options

You can maximise the window if you want to. Then choose *Chart* and *Options* as follows:

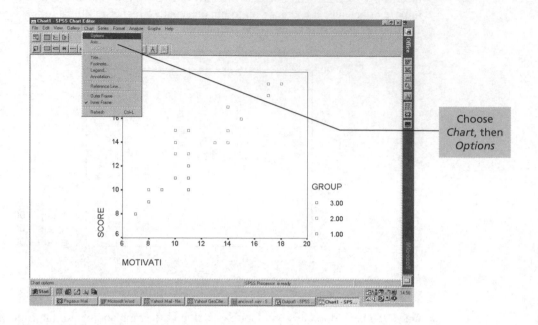

Choose *Chart*, then *Options*

This leads to the following:

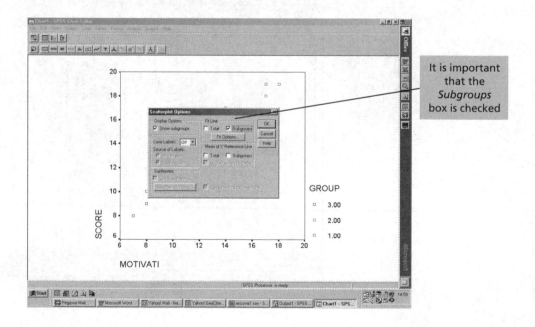

It is important that the *Subgroups* box is checked

Make sure that the *Subgroups* options have been checked.

Click on *Fit Options* to proceed to the following:

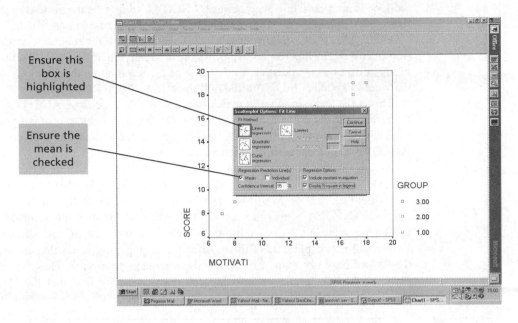

Click on *Continue*, then *OK*. This will give you the regression line for the three groups, separately.

You are used to seeing a line of best fit, for one group of participants. In Figure 13.2, however, we have drawn a separate line of best fit for each group (1, 2 and 3). In this fictional example you can see that interactive students have higher scores on their statistics tests than the mixed group, who have higher scores than the traditional students. For all three groups, however, scores on the statistics test are positively related to IQ (the covariate) – you can see this because the regression lines are positive for all three groups. In other words, students who have low IQs tend to score low marks in their statistics test, and students who have high IQs tend to score highly in the statistics test. However, Group 3 has obviously done better on the statistics test than Group 2, who have performed better, on average, than Group 1.

Notice, however, that the mean of the groups on IQ (*x*, the covariate) is the same. This is what we would expect, as we allocated our students randomly to the three teaching methods. Obviously, we have no reason to think that our three groups will differ in their IQ scores. It would be a bit unusual, however, to find the means being *exactly* the same, because even when there are no basic differences between groups, you expect there to be slight variations in the figures. For our example, however, we have used this unlikely event – all three groups have a mean IQ of 111![1] If you draw a horizontal line from each group's mean IQ to the *y* axis, you will see that the interactive group has a mean of 16 on the statistics test, the mixed group a mean of 12 and the traditional group a mean of 7. These are the means that ANOVA would work on. ANCOVA does not

▶

---

[1] All figures in this example rounded to the nearest whole number.

work on these means, however, because ANCOVA adjusts the means to take into account the relationship between IQ and statistics ability. This is explained below.

Figure 13.2 shows clearly that, for all three groups, IQ is related to statistics retention (measured by this test anyway). All we are really interested in is whether the three groups differ on the statistics test because of the teaching method they were under, so we would like to get rid of (partial out) the effects due to IQ.

This is the ideal situation in which to use ANCOVA, because ANCOVA gets rid of the effects due to the covariate (in this case IQ), that is, it reduces error variance, which, as we have said previously, leads to a larger F-value. Therefore the first purpose of ANCOVA is to reduce error variance.

Assume that we have a situation where the means on the covariate differ significantly. ANCOVA is still useful in that it adjusts the means on *y* (the statistics marks) to what they would be, had the groups had *exactly* the same means on IQ. So this is the second purpose: ANCOVA adjusts the means on the covariate for all of the groups, which leads to an adjustment in the means of the *y* variable – in this case, statistics marks.

We will now explain this further, using the example of groups that are pre-existing, that is, we have *not* randomly allocated participants to groups. These are also called *non-equivalent* or *intact* groups. In such cases, we may find that the groups differ significantly on the covariate.

Activity 13.1

A covariate is a variable that has a:

(a) Curvilinear relationship with the dependent variable
(b) Linear relationship with the dependent variable
(c) Curvilinear relationship with the independent variable
(d) Linear relationship with the independent variable

13.1 Pre-existing groups

Imagine a case where there are three groups of women (nightclub hostesses, part-time secretaries and full-time high-powered scientists). These are naturally occurring groups (i.e. we cannot allot participants to these groups, they are in them already). We wish to test the hypothesis that the more complex the occupation, the higher the testosterone level. Testosterone is known as a 'male' hormone, but although men do have a much higher level of testosterone, women produce testosterone too. There has, in fact, been research that shows a weak association between occupational level and testosterone. Can you think of other variables that might be related to the dependent variable (testosterone level)? Remember, these variables are called the *covariates*. You can probably think of several – the timing of the menstrual cycle for one: hormones fluctuate according to the day of the

| **Figure 13.3** | Scattergram showing the relationship between age and testosterone levels |

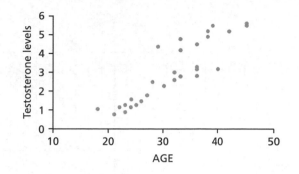

cycle. If we were measuring testosterone in the groups, we would like them to be measured on the same day of the cycle. Age is another. But in order to keep it simple, we will stick to one covariate – age. Assume that age is positively related to testosterone levels.

The scattergram in Figure 13.3 (fictional data) shows this relationship for all three groups combined.

Now think of your three groups. Is it likely that the mean age of the three groups would be the same? Why not?

It is not likely, of course. It is more likely that the high-powered scientists would be significantly older than the nightclub hostesses. So now if we use ANCOVA, we are using it in a slightly different way. Not only does ANCOVA reduce the error variance by removing the variance due to the relationship between age (covariate) and the DV (testosterone) (the first purpose), it also *adjusts* the means on the covariate for all of the groups, leading to the adjustment of the *y* means (testosterone).

In other words, what ANCOVA does is to answer the question: 'What would the means of the groups be (on *y*) if the means of the three groups (on *x*) were all the same?' The formula *adjusts* the *y* means to what they would be if the three groups *had the same mean on age* (*x*). The analysis goes on to answer: 'How likely is it that differences among the groups on the *adjusted statistics* means have occurred by sampling error?'

First, look at Figure 13.4, which shows regression lines for each group separately.

Look to see how each group differs on mean age. The scientists, for instance, have a mean age of 38. If you use your ruler to go across to the *y* axis, you will see that this shows you that the mean testosterone level of this group is 5. Have a look at the mean ages and mean testosterone levels of the other two groups. It is probably obvious to you that part of the differences in the mean testosterone is due to the groups' having a different mean age.

Before we go any further, remember how you obtain a *grand mean*? This is the mean of the means! The means of the ages for the three groups are as follows:

■ Group 1 scientists = 38
■ Group 2 secretaries = 34
■ Group 3 hostesses = 23

Therefore the grand mean is 38 + 34 + 23 divided by 3, which equals 31.6. We will round this up to 32 for the purposes of the example. Now we can see how far each mean is from the grand mean (Figure 13.5).

Look at the mean of the scientists – the dot labelled *a*. A vertical line upwards shows the grand mean, *p*. If you look along (or use your ruler) to the *y* axis, you can see that

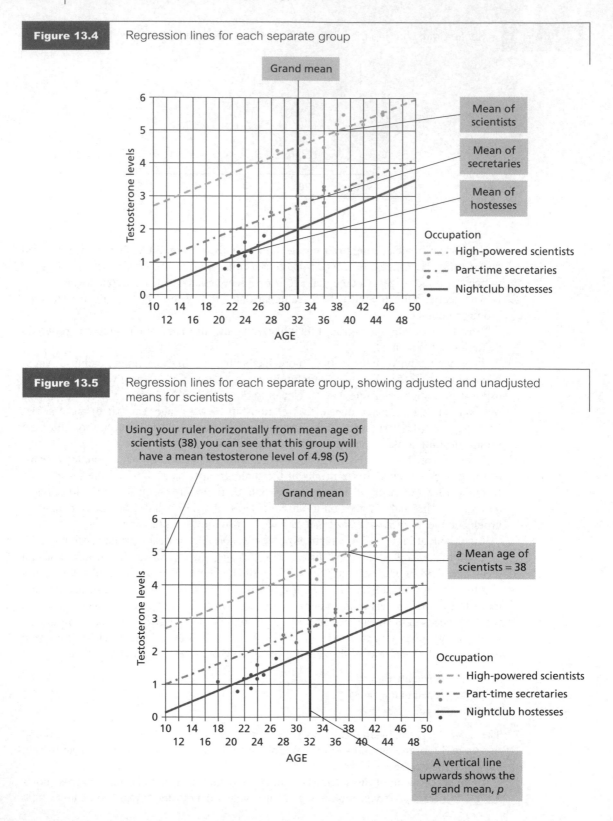

Figure 13.4 Regression lines for each separate group

Figure 13.5 Regression lines for each separate group, showing adjusted and unadjusted means for scientists

Figure 13.6   Regression line for scientists, showing adjusted and unadjusted means

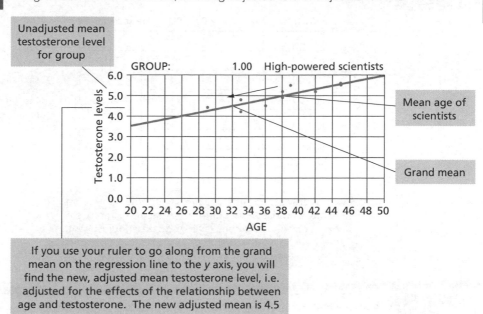

Unadjusted mean
testosterone level
for group

GROUP: 1.00   High-powered scientists

Mean age of
scientists

Grand mean

If you use your ruler to go along from the grand
mean on the regression line to the y axis, you will
find the new, adjusted mean testosterone level, i.e.
adjusted for the effects of the relationship between
age and testosterone. The new adjusted mean is 4.5

scientists have a mean testosterone level of 5. These are the unadjusted means, that is, we have not yet adjusted the means in the light of the relationship between age and testosterone. What ANCOVA does is use the *grand mean* for each of the groups, instead of the 'real' mean. So, for the scientists, ANCOVA does not use the mean age of 38, in order to find the mean testosterone level.

Look at Figure 13.6 and imagine pulling this dot along the regression line until it meets the grand mean.

Imagine doing the same thing with the mean of the secretaries (Figure 13.7) and the nightclub hostesses (Figure 13.8).

If you look at the new position of your dots, they are all 'set' at the grand mean (i.e. treated as if the groups have the same mean age). Use your ruler to go along from the new dots (the dots set at the same mean age) to confirm the new y means (i.e. the adjusted testosterone means). Figure 13.9 shows what it looks like.

It should be clear that ANCOVA has given you an estimate of what the mean testosterone levels would be, if age were held constant (i.e. the mean ages of the groups were the same). The unadjusted and adjusted means are shown in Table 13.1.

Using ANCOVA for the first purpose – reducing error variance – is uncontroversial. This is because when you randomly allocate participants to conditions (groups) ANCOVA meets the assumptions for ANCOVA, described below. First, in using ANCOVA you must make sure you meet the same assumptions as those for ANOVA (look back to Chapter 9 if you have forgotten these!).

In addition, for most purposes:

■ the covariate must be linearly related to the dependent variable
■ the covariate should be measured without error (i.e. reliably)
■ the regression lines for the different groups must be parallel to each other.

Figure 13.7 Regression line for part-time secretaries, showing adjusted and unadjusted means

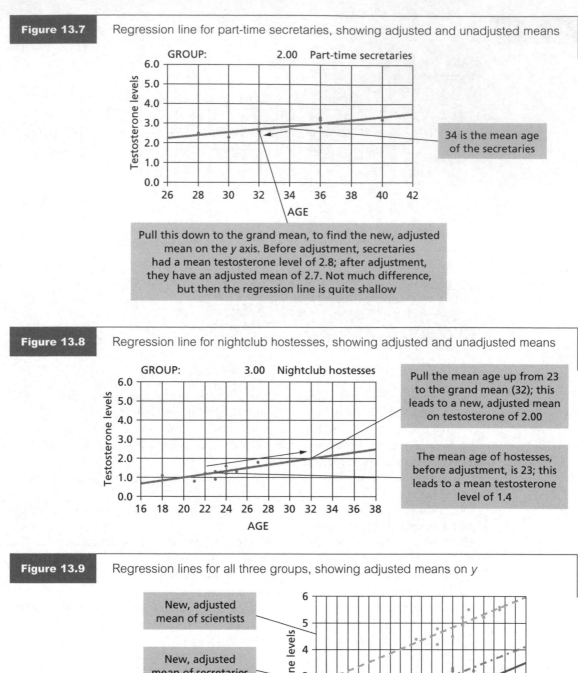

GROUP: 2.00 Part-time secretaries

34 is the mean age of the secretaries

Pull this down to the grand mean, to find the new, adjusted mean on the *y* axis. Before adjustment, secretaries had a mean testosterone level of 2.8; after adjustment, they have an adjusted mean of 2.7. Not much difference, but then the regression line is quite shallow

Figure 13.8 Regression line for nightclub hostesses, showing adjusted and unadjusted means

GROUP: 3.00 Nightclub hostesses

Pull the mean age up from 23 to the grand mean (32); this leads to a new, adjusted mean on testosterone of 2.00

The mean age of hostesses, before adjustment, is 23; this leads to a mean testosterone level of 1.4

Figure 13.9 Regression lines for all three groups, showing adjusted means on *y*

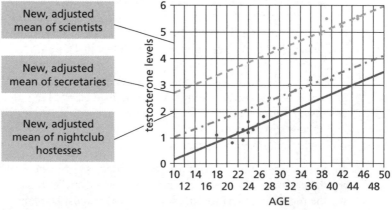

New, adjusted mean of scientists

New, adjusted mean of secretaries

New, adjusted mean of nightclub hostesses

Table 13.1   Unadjusted and adjusted means

Group	Mean age	Mean testosterone	Adjusted mean testosterone
1	38	5.0	4.5
2	34	2.8	2.7
3	23	1.4	2.0

ANOVA would look at the difference between means

ANCOVA looks at the differences in adjusted means

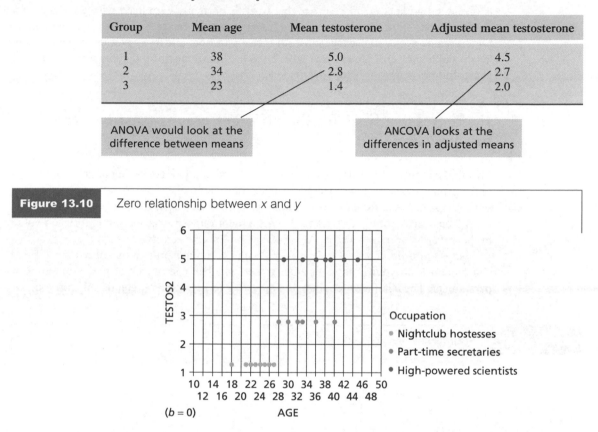

Figure 13.10   Zero relationship between *x* and *y*

13.1.1 The covariate must be linearly related to the dependent variable

Stop to think about this. There is not much point in performing ANCOVA if this is not the case. The graph in Figure 13.10 shows what would happen if there was *no* linear relationship between these two variables.

You can adjust your means so that the dots are set on the line marked grand mean   but the mean *y* values (testosterone) would be the same!

13.1.2 The covariate should be measured without error (i.e. reliably)

This means that, if you were to measure your participants' scores on the covariate on different occasions, there should be a high correlation between the scores they obtain on those different occasions. So IQ, for example, is a reliable covariate; it is made without significant measurement error: there is a high correlation between your IQ score this week and your IQ score on the next week. If you score 110 this week, you probably will *not* score exactly the same next week; remember, this is not what is implied by a high correlation. It does mean that people who have low scores this week will have low scores next week, and people who have high scores this week will have high scores next week. Age is measured without error: your age this week is perfectly correlated with your age next week. In your work at college, at some time, you may design your own questionnaires. Let's say you decide to use the data from such a questionnaire as a covariate. Do you know how reliable they are? Unless you have tested the questionnaire and know it to be reliable, you could be measuring your covariate *with error*.

13.1.3 The regression lines for the different groups must be parallel to each other

This makes sense. If the slopes are not parallel, using a procedure that adjusts the means of the groups to an 'average' (the grand mean) does not make sense. Is it possible to have a sensible grand mean, from three very different slopes, such as those shown in Figure 13.11?

The answer is no: the differences between the groups are *not* the same, for each value of the covariate. So in this case, ANCOVA would not be sensible.

Luckily you do not have to draw (or get the computer program to draw) the regression lines for all your groups, in order to see whether you have met the assumption of parallelism. The computer program you are using (e.g. SPSSFW) can do this for you.

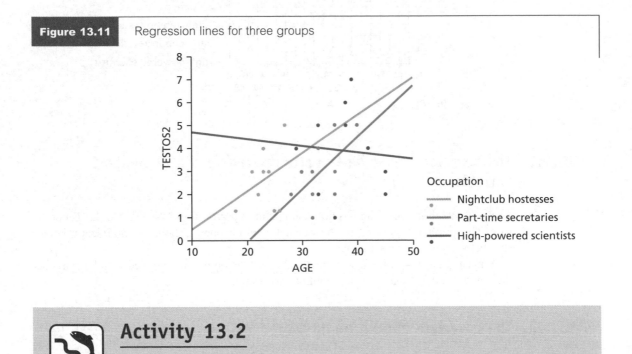

Figure 13.11 Regression lines for three groups

Activity 13.2

ANCOVA:

(a) Reduces between-groups variance
(b) Reduces the F-ratio
(c) Reduces error variance

13.2 Pretest–posttest designs

One of the most common designs in which ANCOVA is used is the pretest–posttest design. This consists of a test given *before* an experimental condition is carried out, followed by the *same* test *after* the experimental condition. In this case, the pretest scores are used as the covariate. Students often ask us why we use ANCOVA on these designs. They suggest taking the posttest scores from the pretest scores, and using the difference scores as the dependent variable in a one-way ANOVA (or t-test, for two groups). Although this is simple, this may not be the best way to analyse such data. Dugard and Todman (1995) demonstrated that change score analyses are usually unsatisfactory for such designs. When carrying out a pretest–posttest study, researchers often wish to partial out (remove, hold constant) the effect of the pretest, in order to focus on possible change following the intervention. Using difference scores does not achieve this, since the pretest score will normally be correlated with the change (difference) score (thus the variation in pretest scores is not removed).

The following is a data set for two groups on a pretest and, following an intervention, a posttest. Subtracting the posttest scores from the pretest scores gives each participant a difference score. A simple independent-groups t-test will be performed using the difference scores as the dependent variable:

Pre	Post	Group	Difference
150.00	51.00	1.00	98.10
130.00	50.00	1.00	80.00
125.00	40.00	1.00	85.00
152.00	45.00	1.00	107.00
160.00	60.00	1.00	100.00
174.00	75.00	2.00	99.00
110.00	41.00	2.00	69.00
180.00	80.00	2.00	100.00
145.00	60.00	2.00	85.00
140.00	55.00	2.00	85.00

First, however, note that, as expected, pretest scores correlate with posttest scores. Since the pre- and posttest scores are highly correlated, it is usual to find the pretest score highly correlated with the difference score:

Correlations

		PRE	POST	DIFF
PRE	Pearson Correlation	1.000	**.878**	**.837**
	Sig. (2-tailed)	.	.001	.003
	N	10	10	10
POST	Pearson Correlation	.878	1.000	.467
	Sig. (2-tailed)	.001	.	.173
	N	10	10	10
DIFF	Pearson Correlation	.837	.467	1.000
	Sig. (2-tailed)	.003	.173	.
	N	10	10	10

A high correlation exists between the pretest scores and the difference scores

There *is* a difference between the pre- and posttest scores, if the participants are considered as one group. However, the idea here is to see whether the two groups differ.

An independent groups t-test analysis gives the following output:

Independent Samples Test

		Levene's Test for Equality of Variances		t-test for Equality of Means						
									95% Confidence Interval of the Difference	
		F	Sig.	t	df	Sig. (2-tailed)	Mean Difference	Std. Error Difference	Lower	Upper
DIFF	Equal variances assumed	.007	.935	**.850**	8	**.420**	6.4200	7.5565	**−11.0053**	**23.8453**
	Equal variances not assumed			.850	7.874	.421	6.4200	7.5565	−11.0539	23.8939

Here you can see that $t(8) = 0.850$, $p = 0.420$. There are no significant differences between the two groups on the difference scores (the confidence intervals confirm this). The researcher would conclude, then, that the intervention affected the two groups similarly.

However, performing an ANCOVA using the posttest scores as the dependent variable and the pretest scores as a covariate gives the following:

Tests of Between-Subjects Effects
Dependent Variable: POST

Source	Type III Sum of Squares	df	Mean Square	F	Sig.
Corrected Model	1480.516[a]	2	740.258	34.184	.000
Intercept	65.387	1	65.387	3.019	.126
PRE	1058.016	1	1058.016	48.858	.000
GROUP	232.054	1	232.054	**10.716**	**.014**
Error	151.584	7	21.655		
Total	32657.000	10			
Corrected Total	1632.100	9			

a. R Squared = .907 (Adjusted R Squared = .881)

We can conclude here that the two groups differ on the posttest measure, after adjustment for the pretest scores. In general, ANCOVA tends to provide a more powerful test of the hypothesis than difference scores.

13.2.1 What can you do if your study does not conform to the conditions necessary for ANCOVA?

First, think of controlling *experimentally* as well as, or instead of, controlling statistically (which is what we are doing when performing an ANCOVA). In our example, we could (although it might be difficult!) manage to find some younger high-powered scientists, and/or older nightclub hostesses or secretaries. In this way, we could match the groups on age (Table 13.2).

Of course, here it would not be possible to match 19-year-old secretaries or nightclub hostesses with high-powered scientists of the same age. However, if you have thought about your design carefully *before* carrying out your studies, you should not find yourself in this sort of awkward situation.

Table 13.2 Matching participants on age

Nightclub hostesses	Secretaries	Scientists
25	25	25
30	30	31
50	50	50
41	41	42
39	39	39

Let's imagine you have matched your participants on age. This will mean that your groups have the same mean age on the covariate. You can still use ANCOVA profitably – in this case it will be for the first purpose we mentioned – in order to reduce error variance – error due to the correlation between the dependent variable and the covariate.

Activity 13.3

ANCOVA adjusts the means of the group on the covariate to:

(a) The grand mean
(b) The harmonic mean
(c) The arithmetic mean

At this point we will show you how to obtain output for an ANCOVA on SPSSFW.

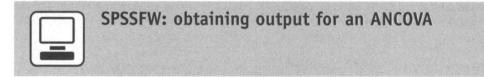

SPSSFW: obtaining output for an ANCOVA

Open your data file. Choose *Analyze*, *General Linear Model*, *Univariate*:

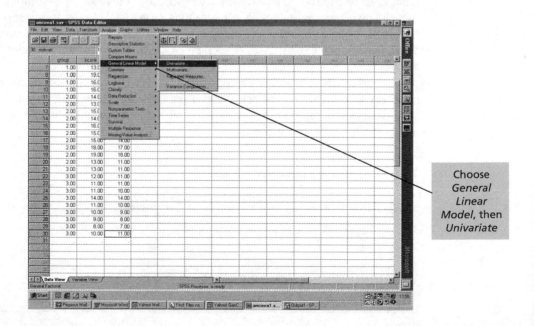

Choose *General Linear Model*, then *Univariate*

This gives you the following dialogue box:

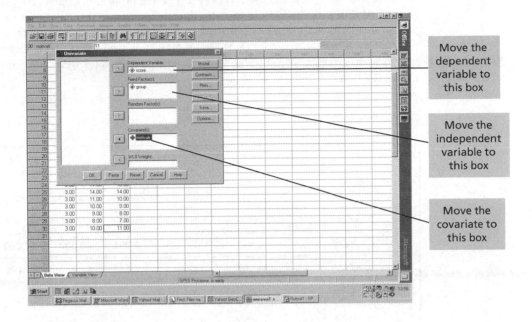

This brings you back to the *General Factorial ANOVA* dialogue box. Click on *Options*, and the following dialogue box appears;

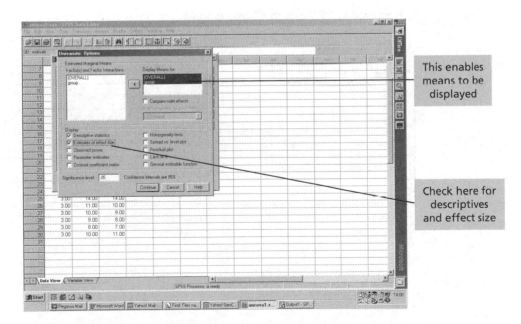

Moving the grouping variable to the *Display Means* will give you both the unadjusted and adjusted (estimated marginal) means. You can also check the boxes for descriptive statistics and estimates of effect size. Power can be checked if wanted. Notice that the confidence intervals will be given automatically.

Click on *Continue*; then press *OK*. This obtains your output.

Also, you do not have to use ANCOVA on three groups, of course. As you know, you can use ANOVA, or ANCOVA, on more than three groups, but sometimes students do not realise that they can use these techniques on two groups. Normally there is no point in performing ANOVA on two groups; you may just as well use a t-test. However, what if you had two groups and you wanted to control for a covariate? Here, of course, you could use ANCOVA.

Tests of Between-Subjects Effects
Dependent Variable: testosterone

Source	Type III Sum of Squares	df	Mean Square	F	Sig.	Eta Squared
Corrected Model	69.273[b]	3	23.091	313.806	.000[a]	.973
Intercept	6.521E-02	1	6.521E-02	.886	.355	.033
AGE	**2.981**	**1**	**2.981**	**40.509**	**.000**	**.609**
GROUP	**14.265**	**2**	**7.133**	**96.933**	**.000**	**.882**
Error	1.913	26	7.358E-02			
Total	353.320	30				
Corrected Total	71.187	29				

a. Computed using alpha = .05
b. R Squared = .973 (Adjusted R Squared = .970)

Estimates
Dependent Variable: testosterone

profession	Mean	Std. Error	95% Confidence Interval	
			Lower Bound	Upper Bound
scientists	4.466	.119	4.222	4.711
secretaries	2.663	.090	2.477	2.848
hostesses	2.071	.140	1.784	2.358

a. Evaluated at covariates appeared in the model: AGE = 31.6000.

Pairwise Comparisons
Dependent Variable: testosterone

(I) profession	(J) profession	Mean Difference (I–J)	Std. Error	Sig.[a]	95% Confidence Interval for Difference	
					Lower Bound	Upper Bound
scientists	secretaries	1.804*	.133	.000	1.530	2.077
	hostesses	2.395*	.227	.000	1.928	2.863
secretaries	scientists	−1.804*	.133	.000	−2.077	−1.530
	hostesses	.592*	.184	.003	.214	.969
hostesses	scientists	−2.395*	.227	.000	−2.863	−1.928
	secretaries	−.592*	.184	.003	−.969	−.214

Based on estimated marginal means
* The mean difference is significant at the .05 level.
a. Adjustment for multiple comparisons: Least Significant Difference (equivalent to no adjustments).

The relationship between age and testosterone is unlikely to be explained by sampling error, assuming the null hypothesis to be true ($F(1,26) = 40.5$, $p < 0.001$). The groups differ on testosterone, once the effects of age are partialled out ($F(2,26) = 96.9$, $p < 0.001$).

The above output clearly shows that age is related to testosterone, therefore an ANCOVA is appropriate.

EXAMPLE

Think back to the example used in Chapter 9, page 297. This was an experiment designed to discover whether alcohol (placebo, low alcohol, high alcohol) affected driving, measured by errors made on a driving simulator. For the independent-groups design, we found that the high alcohol group differed from the placebo and low alcohol groups. The F-ratio was found to be 9.91, with an associated probability of 0.004.

Now we may make the perfectly reasonable assumption that driving experience relates to errors made in driving, even on a driving simulator. The more experienced the driver, the fewer the errors. Thus driving experience is negatively associated with driving errors. Assume that we have found out how many months the participants (all drivers) had been driving. The data are as recorded in Table 13.3.

A Pearson's r calculated between driving errors and experience results in $r = -0.62$. Although the means of the three groups do differ on driving experience, this could have been due to sampling error (a one-way ANOVA would show you this).

If we plot the regression lines, separately for each group, we obtain Figure 13.12.

Table 13.3 Driving experience and driving errors

Placebo		Low alcohol		High alcohol	
Errors	Experience	Errors	Experience	Errors	Experience
5	12	5	21	8	29
10	5	7	16	10	8
7	9	9	7	8	26
3	24	8	15	9	20
5	15	2	30	11	18
7	6	5	21	15	6
11	3	6	12	7	12
2	30	6	13	11	7
3	20	4	26	8	15
5	10	4	24	8	9
6	7	8	9	17	3
6	8	10	6	11	7
$\Sigma_1 = 70$	$\Sigma_2 = 149$	$\Sigma_3 = 74$	$\Sigma_4 = 200$	$\Sigma_5 = 123$	$\Sigma_6 = 160$
$\hat{y}_1 = 5.83$	$\hat{y}_2 = 12.417$	$\hat{y}_3 = 6.17$	$\hat{y}_4 = 16.583$	$\hat{y}_5 = 10.25$	$\hat{y}_6 = 13.333$
$SD_1 = 2.69$	$SD_2 = 8.306$	$SD_3 = 2.35$	$SD_4 = 7.704$	$SD_5 = 3.05$	$SD_6 = 8.338$

Figure 13.12 Regression lines for each group

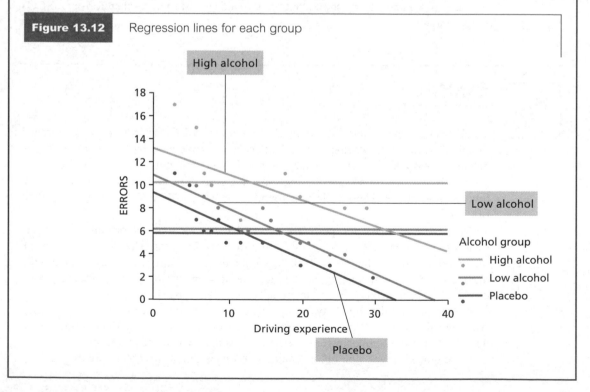

This time we have also obtained horizontal lines: at the point where the horizontal line meets the regression line (for each separate group) is the mean of x and y. You can see that driving experience is negatively related to driving errors, for all groups. We meet the assumptions for ANCOVA quite easily.

The covariate is measured reliably, the lines are (more or less) parallel. Performing the ANCOVA, we obtain the output – much of this is not needed for our simple analysis. Make sure you focus on the following parts of the output:

Tests of Between-Subjects Effects
Dependent Variable: testosterone

Source	Type III Sum of Squares	df	Mean Square	F	Sig.[a]	Eta Squared
Corrected Model	294.697[b]	3	98.232	34.148	.000	.762
Intercept	1035.760	1	1035.760	360.058	.000	.918
Experience	**149.531**	**1**	**149.531**	**51.981**	**.000**	**.918**
GROUP	**136.334**	**2**	**68.167**	**23.697**	**.000**	**.597**
Error	92.053	32	2.877			
Total	2367.000	36				
Corrected Total	386.750	35				

a. Computed using alpha = .05
b. R Squared = .762 (Adjusted R Squared = .740)

The source labelled 'Experience' shows that driving experience is related (negatively) to errors made, and that this relationship is unlikely to have arisen by sampling error, assuming the null hypothesis to be true.

The GROUP line shows that our three groups differ on the adjusted means. This difference is unlikely to have arisen by sampling error, assuming the null hypothesis to be true.

The SPSS output gives a table giving the actual, observed (unadjusted) means:

Descriptive Statistics
Dependent Variable: errors made

Alcohol	Mean	Std. Deviation	N
Placebo	5.8333	2.6912	12
Low	6.1667	2.3290	12
High	10.2500	3.0488	12
Total	7.4167	3.3242	36

A separate table is given for the estimated marginal means (these are the adjusted means):

Estimates
2. alcohol
Dependent Variable: errors made

alcohol	Mean	Std. Error	95% Confidence Interval	
			Lower Bound	Upper Bound
Placebo	5.383[a]	.494	4.377	6.388
Low	6.828[a]	.498	5.813	7.843
High	10.039[a]	.490	9.040	11.038

a. Evaluated at covariates appeared in the model: driving experience = 14.1389.

The confidence limits around the adjusted means are also given. Thus the adjusted sample mean for the placebo group is 5.838. We are 95% confident that the true population adjusted mean is between 4.38 and 6.39 (correct to two decimal places).

ANOVA would have shown the difference between the observed means, but by performing ANCOVA we have looked at the differences between the adjusted means.

Because we have partialled out the effects of driving experience, we have a more sensitive design. The F-ratio is now 51.91. Our overall η^2 was originally 0.375; it is now 0.584. Thus 58% of the variation in driving errors can be explained by differing levels of alcohol, once driving experience is controlled for (held constant, partialled out).

The textual part of our analysis might read as follows (the first and last parts of the following are simply a repetition of pages 303–4):

Descriptive statistics (Table X)[2] show that there were more errors made in the high alcohol condition than in the other two conditions. The observed and adjusted means are shown in Table X.[2] Although the mean errors made in the low-alcohol group were higher than those made in the placebo condition, the difference was slight and, in fact, confidence limits around the means show that the intervals in which the population means for these two conditions are likely to be found overlap substantially. It was found that driving experience was negatively associated with driving errors ($r = -0.64$); a one-way analysis of covariance, using driving experience as the covariate, showed that there was a significant difference between condition(s) ($F(2,32) = 23.7$, $p = 0.001$); this represented an effect size of 0.584, showing that, once driving experience was held constant, 58% of the variation in driving errors can be accounted for by differing levels of alcohol. A post-hoc test (Newman Keuls) confirmed that significant differences existed between conditions 1 and 3, and 2 and 3 (both effect sizes (d) = 1.54). There was no significant difference between the placebo and low alcohol conditions (effect size (d) = 0.14).

---

[2] You should refer your readers to the table where you give your descriptive statistics.

Activity 13.4

ANCOVA assumes that:

(a) The covariate must be linearly related to the dependent variable
(b) The regression lines must not be parallel
(c) The covariate need not be reliable

Example from the literature: IBD and IBS

Attree *et al.* (2003) studied the cognitive function of people with Inflammatory Bowel Disease and people with Irritable Bowel Syndrome. A healthy comparison group was included in the study. Participants completed three types of cognitive function assessment and a depression scale. The researchers wished to see whether the illness groups would differ when compared with each other and a healthy comparison group, on several measures, including IQ. Attree *et al.* performed split plot two-way analyses of covariance. However, here we report the results for verbal IQ only, which were not given in their 2003 article. Attree *et al.* had hypothesised that verbal deficits would occur in the illness groups.

The following table shows the adjusted means for the three groups (group 1 = IBS; group 2 – IBD; group 3 = healthy comparison group).

Estimates
Dependent Variable: verbal iq

iv conditions	Mean	Std. Error	95% Confidence Interval	
			Lower Bound	Upper Bound
1.00	95.785[a]	2.076	91.635	99.934
2.00	94.237[a]	3.156	87.929	100.545
3.00	107.038[d]	2.456	102.129	111.946

a. Evaluated at covariates appeared in the model: depression = 15.3286, participant's gender = 1.8571, age of participant = 43.0000, duration of illness in years = 7.2643, years of education = 12.2286.

Results are as recorded below:

Tests of Between-Subjects Effects
Dependent Variable: verbal iq

Source	Type III Sum of Squares	df	Mean Square	F	Sig.	Partial Eta Squared
Corrected Model	5422.225[a]	7	774.604	7.081	.000	.444
Intercept	2331.156	1	2331.156	21.311	.000	.256
CESD	542.165	1	542.165	4.956	.030	.074
GENDER	.159	1	.159	.001	.970	.000
AGE	960.120	1	960.120	8.777	.004	.124
YEARS	211.936	1	211.936	1.937	.169	.030
SCHOOL	1954.830	1	1954.830	17.870	.000	.224
GROUPS	**1309.983**	**2**	**654.991**	**5.988**	**.004**	**.162**
Error	6782.118	62	109.389			
Total	709008.000	70				
Corrected Total	12204.343	69				

a. R Squared = .444 (Adjusted R Squared = .382)

Preliminary analysis by Attree *et al.* showed that groups differed on levels of depression and (for illness groups) length of illness, and so these variables were used as covariates. Age, sex, and years of education were also included as covariates. This was in order to reduce variance attributable to these variables, although their effect might have been minimal.

If you look at the GROUPS row in the table above, you will see that $F(2,62) = 5.988$, $p = 0.004$. The groups thus differed on verbal IQ, with the other variables (listed in the first column) partialled out. Partial η^2 shows us that 16.2% of the variation in scores on verbal IQ was due to the independent variable (that is, the illness groups).

The researchers then wished to look further into the data.

Contrasts can be obtained via SPSSFW. This produces the following set of results:

Pairwise Comparisons
Dependent Variable: verbal iq

(I) iv conditions	(J) iv conditions	Mean Difference (I–J)	Std. Error	Sig.ᵃ	95% Confidence Interval for Difference[a]	
					Lower Bound	Upper Bound
1.00	2.00	1.548	3.635	1.000	–7.397	10.492
	3.00	–11.253*	3.388	.005	–19.590	–2.916
2.00	1.00	–1.548	3.635	1.000	–10.492	7.397
	3.00	–12.801*	4.554	.020	–24.007	–1.594
3.00	1.00	11.253*	3.388	.005	2.916	19.590
	2.00	12.801*	4.554	.020	1.594	24.007

Based on estimated marginal means
* The mean difference is significant at the .05 level.
a. Adjustment for multiple comparisons: Bonferroni.

The results to report from the Test of Between-Subject Effects table are emboldened. In the Pairwise Comparisons table, it can be seen that there is no important difference between IBS and IBD participants. The difference is between the illness groups and the healthy comparison group.

The results could be reported in the following way:

Preliminary analysis showed that groups differed significantly on depression, and length of illness. To reduce the variance attributable to these variables and other social demographic measures (age, sex, and years of education) these were entered as covariates in further analyses. First, the IQ measures were considered. Data were entered into a one-way analysis of covariance (ANCOVA) with verbal IQ as the dependent variable and groups as the independent factor. The illness groups were found to score considerably lower than the healthy comparison group ($F(2,62) = 5.59$, $p = 0.004$, $\eta^2 = .162$). Pairwise comparisons confirmed that the difference between the illness groups was negligible (mean IBS 95.8; mean IBD 94.2 $p = 1.00$) but that the difference between the illness groups and the healthy comparison group (mean 107) was considerable (IBS vs. HC:p = 0.005; IBD vs. HC:p = 0.020).

Summary

In this chapter you have learned that:

- a one-way independent-groups ANCOVA is used to discover whether there are differences between conditions while partialling out the effects of another variable, called the covariate

- the covariate is a variable that has a linear relationship with the dependent variable

- the ANCOVA reduces error variance, and so gives a more powerful test

- in order for us to have confidence in the results produced by ANCOVA, the assumptions of ANCOVA must be met.

SPSSFW exercise

Open the data file that you used for Chapter 9, page 313. These were the data you used for a one-way ANOVA, on three groups of students, allotted to morning, afternoon or evening laboratory groups. As part of a student project, you have decided to analyse differences between the groups, once motivation has been controlled. The data are as follows. Remember, you probably already have these data in a file – you just need to add in the motivation scores.

Group	Score	Motivation	Group	Score	Motivation
1.00	15.00	10.00	2.00	15.00	14.00
1.00	10.00	8.00	2.00	15.00	14.00
1.00	14.00	10.00	2.00	18.00	17.00
1.00	15.00	11.00	2.00	19.00	18.00
1.00	17.00	14.00	2.00	13.00	11.00
1.00	13.00	10.00	3.00	13.00	11.00
1.00	13.00	10.00	3.00	12.00	11.00
1.00	19.00	17.00	3.00	11.00	11.00
1.00	16.00	15.00	3.00	11.00	10.00
1.00	16.00	15.00	3.00	14.00	14.00
2.00	14.00	14.00	3.00	11.00	10.00
2.00	13.00	11.00	3.00	10.00	9.00
2.00	15.00	14.00	3.00	9.00	8.00
2.00	14.00	13.00	3.00	8.00	7.00
2.00	16.00	15.00	3.00	10.00	11.00

1. Obtain a scattergram with three separate regression lines for the groups. Do you meet the assumptions for ANCOVA?

2. Perform ANCOVA on the data. How is this different from the one-way that you performed in Chapter 9? Write down your interpretation of the results.

MULTIPLE CHOICE QUESTIONS

1. ANCOVA shows us how likely it is that differences between conditions are due to sampling error, once means have been adjusted for the relationship between:
   (a) The dependent variable and the covariate
   (b) The independent variable and the covariate
   (c) The dependent variable and the independent variable
   (d) All of the above

2. ANCOVA adjusts the means on the covariate, so that the mean covariate score is:
   (a) The same for all groups
   (b) Different for all groups
   (c) The same for all participants
   (d) It depends

3. The use of ANCOVA is sometimes controversial when:
   (a) Randomly allocating participants to conditions
   (b) Assumptions have not been met
   (c) Using intact groups
   (d) (b) and (c)

Questions 4 to 6 relate to the following output:

Tests of Between-Subjects Effects
Dependent Variable: Beginning Salary

Source	Type III Sum of Squares	df	Mean Square	F	Sig.	Eta Squared
Corrected Model	18267473987.605	3	6089157995.868	259.385	.000	.623
Intercept	29047525437.055	1	29047525437.055	1237.361	.000	.725
PREVEXP	341929455.308	1	341929455.308	14.565	.000	.030
JOBCAT	18207781455.753	2	9103890727.876	387.806	.000	.623
Error	11033430977.848	470	23475385.059			
Total	166546277625.000	474				
Corrected Total	29300904965.454	473				

4. The dependent variable is:
   (a) Beginning Salary
   (b) Prevexp
   (c) Jobcat
   (d) None of the above

5. The covariate is:
   (a) Beginning Salary
   (b) Prevexp
   (c) Jobcat
   (d) None of the above

6. The difference between the groups is:

   (a) Unlikely to have occurred by sampling error, assuming the null hypothesis to be true ($F(2,470) = 387.806$; $p < 0.001$)

   (b) Unlikely to have occurred by sampling error, assuming the null hypothesis to be true ($F(2,470) = 14.565$; $p < 0.001$)

   (c) Likely to have occurred by sampling error, assuming the null hypothesis to be true ($F(2,470) = 387.806$; $p < 0.001$)

   (d) Likely to have occurred by sampling error, assuming the null hypothesis to be true ($F(2,470) = 14.565$; $p < 0.001$)

7. Four groups have the following means on the covariate: 35, 42, 28, 65. What is the grand mean?

   (a) 43.5

   (b) 42.5

   (c) 56.7

   (d) None of the above

8. You can perform ANCOVA on:

   (a) Two groups

   (b) Three groups

   (c) Four groups

   (d) All of the above

9. When carrying out a pretest–posttest study, researchers often wish to:

   (a) Partial out the effect of the dependent variable

   (b) Partial out the effect of the pretest

   (c) Reduce the correlation between the pretest and posttest scores

   (d) None of the above

Questions 10 and 11 relate to the following:

Dr Ozzy Oak is analysing scores on a memory test for four groups of people who have taken different amounts of alcohol. He has an idea that memory is related to IQ, so he decides to control for that and chooses ANCOVA for his inferential test.

10. Which is the covariate?

   (a) Scores on the memory test

   (b) The amounts of alcohol

   (c) IQ

   (d) None of the above

11. His analysis would show:

   (a) Differences between groups on the memory test, partialling out the effects of IQ

   (b) Differences on IQ, partialling out the effects of IQ

   (c) Differences on IQ, partialling out the effects of alcohol

   (d) Differences between groups on the memory test, partialling out the effects of alcohol

Questions 12 to 14 relate to the following output:

Tests of Between-Subjects Effects
Dependent Variable: reaction time

Source	Type III Sum of Squares	df	Mean Square	F	Sig.	Eta Squared
Corrected Model	76.252	3	25.417	3.647	.064	.578
Intercept	4.792	1	4.792	.688	.431	.079
AGE	4.252	1	4.252	.610	.457	.071
GROUP	41.974	2	20.987	3.012	.106	.430
Error	55.748	8	6.969			
Total	1860.000	12				
Corrected Total	132.000	11				

12. The independent variable is:
    (a) Reaction time
    (b) Group
    (c) Age
    (d) None of the above

13. The covariate is:
    (a) Reaction time
    (b) Group
    (c) Age
    (d) None of the above

14. The dependent variable is:
    (a) Reaction time
    (b) Group
    (c) Age
    (d) None of the above

15. Using difference scores in a pretest–posttest design does not partial out the effect of the pretest for the following reason:
    (a) The pretest scores are not normally correlated with the posttest scores
    (b) The pretest scores are normally correlated with the difference scores
    (c) The posttest scores are normally correlated with the difference scores
    (d) None of the above

Questions 16 to 20 relate to the following output:

2. iv conditions
Dependent Variable: vocabulary, verbal knowledge, fund of information

iv conditions	Mean	Std. Error	95% Confidence Interval	
			Lower Bound	Upper Bound
1.00	46.725[a]	1.908	42.915	50.536
2.00	46.246[a]	2.521	41.210	51.281
3.00	54.425[a]	2.017	50.398	58.453

a. Evaluated at covariates appeared in the model: age of participant = 43.0000, depression = 15.3286.

Tests of Between-Subjects Effects
Dependent Variable: vocabulary, verbal knowledge, fund of information

Source	Type III Sum of Squares	df	Mean Square	F	Sig.	Partial Eta Squared
Corrected Model	1603.644[a]	4	400.911	4.277	.004	.208
Intercept	14104.574	1	14104.574	150.459	.000	.698
AGE	102.805	1	102.805	1.097	.299	.017
CESD	114.653	1	114.653	1.223	.273	.018
GROUPS	804.984	2	402.492	4.294	.018	.117
Error	6093.341	65	93.744			
Total	179809.000	70				
Corrected Total	7696.986	69				

a. R Squared = .208 (Adjusted R Squared = .160)

16. The highest level of verbal ability is shown by:

   (a) Group 1
   (b) Group 2
   (c) Group 3
   (d) They are all identical

17. Which is the most appropriate statement? The differences between the groups are:

   (a) Likely to have arisen by sampling error alone $F(1,65) = 150.46, p < 0.001$
   (b) Likely to have arisen by sampling error alone $F(1,65) = 1.22, p = 0.273$
   (c) Unlikely to have arisen by sampling error alone $F(2,65) = 4.29, p = 0.018$
   (d) Unlikely to have arisen by sampling error alone $F(4,65) = 4.28, p = 0.0004$

18. The effect size for the differences between the groups is approximately:

   (a) 2%
   (b) 12%
   (c) 21%
   (d) 70%

19. The strongest difference between the groups is between:
    (a) 1 + 2 versus 3
    (b) 2 + 3 versus 1
    (c) 1 + 3 versus 2
    (d) They are all identical

20. The group with the widest confidence interval around the mean level of verbal ability is:
    (a) Group 1
    (b) Group 2
    (c) Group 3
    (d) They are all identical

References

Attree, E.A., Dancey, C.P., Keeling, D. and Wilson, C. (2003) 'Cognitive function in people with chronic illness: inflammatory bowel disease and irritable bowel syndrome', *Applied Neuropsychology*, 10(2): 96–104.

Dugard, P. and Todman, J. (1995) 'Analysis of pre-test–post-test group designs in educational research', *Educational Psychology*, 15(2): 181–98.

14 Introduction to multivariate analysis of variance (MANOVA)

Chapter overview

So far all of the analyses we have covered in this book, with the exception of factor analysis, have been univariate analyses. In this chapter we will describe another multivariate technique that is an extension of ANOVA: this is *multivariate analysis of variance*. It is not our intention in this chapter to give you a thorough grounding in multivariate analysis of variance (MANOVA); rather we wish to give you a feel for what such methods offer us.

We will explain:

■ what MANOVA is
■ the assumptions underlying the use of MANOVA, including:
  – multivariate normality
  – homogeneity of variance–covariance matrices
■ MANOVA with:
  – one between-participants IV and two DVs
  – one within-participants IV and two DVs
  – each of these will be IVs with two conditions
■ post-hoc testing of the contribution of each individual DV to the multivariate difference between conditions of the IV.

14.1 Multivariate statistics

We introduced the concept of multivariate statistics when explaining factor analysis. As discussed in Chapter 12, multivariate statistics are extensions of the simpler univariate (and bivariate) techniques to the situations where we have more than one DV as well as one or more IV. In this chapter we will give a brief introduction to multivariate analysis of variance (MANOVA). The reasons for this are twofold. First, this technique is a logical extension of the ANOVA models we have already described in Chapters 9 and 10 (in fact, ANOVA is really a special case of MANOVA). Second, SPSSFW uses MANOVA as the basis of its within-participants ANOVA; therefore it will be useful for you to have some idea of the logic and rationale behind such analyses. It will also help you understand the various details on the printout of both MANOVA and within-participants ANOVA.

14.2 Why use multivariate analyses of variance?

Why should we use multivariate analysis of variance when we have perfectly adequate univariate ANOVA to use? Quite often we may have research questions where univariate ANOVA is not adequate. For example, suppose you wanted to compare the well-being of churchgoers and atheists. Here we have an IV of belief (churchgoers vs. atheists) and a DV of well-being. But what do we mean by *well-being* and, perhaps more importantly, how do we measure it? There are many possible answers to this question, for example well-being might be measured using a number of possible indices, including:

■ optimism about the future
■ happiness
■ enthusiasm for life
■ satisfaction with personal relationships.

Which of these indices of well-being is the most suitable? There is no right or wrong answer to such a question: to a certain extent it depends on the particular circumstances of the people you may ask. However, if you did use these indices as a guide to well-being you would probably find that each index would give you a different pattern of findings. For example, someone with a terminal illness might not be optimistic about the future but might have high levels of satisfaction with personal relationships and high enthusiasm for life, whereas another person might feel optimistic about the future but might have low satisfaction with personal relationships.

Because well-being has many facets, the sensible thing to do is to look at all such indices and then see whether churchgoers will be different overall from atheists. If we were to collect all this information we could then conduct several t-tests to see which group had higher levels of well-being. If we opted for this approach we would conduct a separate t-test with each of our measures of well-being as a DV and see if there were any differences between the two groups (IV) on these separately. We could then look at the overall pattern of these t-tests to give us an indication of which group, if any, came out best in terms of well-being.

Can you identify any problems with such an approach? The main problem was described to you back in Chapter 9 when we discussed post-hoc testing. If we take all these measures and conduct separate t-tests we increase the familywise error rate and as a result we increase the likelihood of making a Type I error. Remember, the more t-tests you do on a set of data, the more likely it is you will make a Type I error. What we really need is to be able to analyse all these indices (DVs) in one analysis. Fortunately, this is where multivariate statistics are useful. Multivariate statistics will allow us to analyse all our indices (DVs) in one analysis.

14.3 Multivariate analysis of variance

In Chapters 9 and 10 we introduced ANOVA to you. In all the examples we gave in those chapters we had one or more IVs with only one DV. MANOVA allows us to have more than one IV along with more than one DV. You can see that in this book we have progressed from tests that allow one IV and one DV, through those that have one DV and one or more IV to MANOVA, where we can have more than one IV *and* more than one DV:

- one DV and one IV with two conditions (t-tests)
- one DV and one IV with more than two conditions (one-way ANOVA)
- one DV and one or more IVs, each with two or more conditions (ANOVA)
- one DV with two or more IVs (multiple regression)
- two or more DVs with one or more IVs (MANOVA).

Activity 14.1

For which of the following studies would MANOVA be the appropriate analyses?

(a) A researcher, interested in the effects of overcrowding on trains, conducts a study comparing the stress experienced by commuters with that experienced by leisure travellers. Stress is measured using a heart-rate monitor at the end of each journey

(b) A researcher wants to find out if 'a bit of naughtiness' is good for your health. He compares one group who are allowed to have treats (e.g. eating chocolate or drinking beer) during one year and one group who are to abstain from such treats. Health is measured by number of illnesses in that year and a full fitness check at the end of the year

(c) A researcher wants to find out if males or females are more anxious about statistics. Groups of male and female students are given a questionnaire that measures several components of statistics anxiety (e.g. fear of statistics teachers, fear of asking questions in class)

(d) Researchers are trying to find out whether listening to music is good for revision. They think that listening to classical music will be better than rock music. They compare two groups of students, one listening to classical music and one listening to rock while revising for exams. They want to see whether there is a difference between the two groups in terms of overall exam performance

14.4 Logic of MANOVA

The logic of MANOVA is quite simple when thought of in the context of ANOVA. In ANOVA we partition the variability in the DV into that attributable to the IVs and their interaction plus that attributable to error. Obviously in MANOVA, because we have multiple DVs, things are not quite as straightforward. When we have multiple DVs MANOVA simply forms a *linear combination* of the DVs and then uses this linear combination in the analysis in place of the individual DVs. That is, it combines the DVs into a new variable and then uses this new variable as the single DV in the analyses.

Consequently the analysis tells us whether there is any effect of the IVs on the linear combination of the DVs. This is obviously an oversimplification but is in essence all that MANOVA does.

Using our example of the well-being of churchgoers and atheists, we would put all of the indices of well-being into the analysis as DVs and have an IV of belief (churchgoers or atheists). MANOVA would then combine the DVs and assess the amount of variability in this combined score that is attributable to the IV.

We have stated that MANOVA assesses the degree to which the IVs account for the variance of a linear combination of the DVs. A linear combination is a simple additive combination of the DVs. For example:

Well-being = Happiness + Enthusiasm + Optimism + Relationships

or perhaps:

Well-being = (3 × Happiness) + Enthusiasm + (Optimism × 2) + Relationships

Hence, we are simply combining the variables in the way illustrated above. A common instance of a linear combination of variables is when psychologists combine subtest scores on a questionnaire to form a total test score. For example, the Profile of Mood States questionnaire measures a number of mainly negative mood states as subtests (e.g. depression and anxiety) and then sums these to get an overall measure of mood disturbance. The total score on the questionnaire is simply a linear combination of the subtest scores. Thus:

Mood Disturbance = Depression score + Anxiety score + . . .

You are also already familiar with linear combinations in multiple regression. The linear regression equations we introduced in Chapter 11 are excellent examples of linear combinations:

$$y = b_1 x_1 + b_2 x_2 + b_3 x_3 \ldots + a$$

In this equation we are predicting y from a linear combination of the IVs (x_1, x_2 and x_3).

You may, at this point, be wondering how MANOVA decides, from all the possible combinations of the DVs, which is the most appropriate combination for the analysis. This is a good question, given that for any set of DVs there will be an infinite number of ways of combining them. Essentially, MANOVA uses the combination of the DVs that maximises the differences between the various conditions of the IVs. In order to find such a combination MANOVA uses a number of heuristics (rules of thumb). When you see your output for MANOVA you will notice that there are four different statistics that are computed in order to calculate the F-value. These are:

1. Wilks' lambda (λ).
2. Pillai's trace.
3. Hotelling's trace.
4. Roy's largest root.

These tests use different rules of thumb for combining the DVs in order to maximise the differences between the conditions of the IVs, and then calculate an F-value. We will discuss these further when we go through the MANOVA printout.

Activity 14.2

Which of the following are linear combinations?

(a) $a + b + c + d + e$
(b) $A \times B \times C \times D \times E$
(c) $(a + b + c + d + e)/2$
(d) Extraversion + 2 * Neuroticism − 3 * Psychoticism

14.5 Assumptions of MANOVA

As with any parametric statistics there are a number of assumptions associated with MANOVA that have to be met in order for the analysis to be meaningful in any way.

14.5.1 Multivariate normality

If you think back to the assumptions underlying the use of ANOVA, you should recall that one of these is that we have normally distributed data. Not surprisingly, we have a similar assumption underlying the use of MANOVA. However, the assumption for MANOVA is a little more complex. In this case we have to ensure that we have *multivariate normality*; that is, each of the individual DVs and all linear combinations of these DVs should be normally distributed.

In practice, assessment of multivariate normality is difficult because we would have to look at the distributions of each DV and *all* possible linear combinations of these to check that they are normal. It is, therefore, recommended that we at least check each DV to ensure they are normally distributed. It is worth noting that MANOVA is still a valid test even with modest violations of the assumption of multivariate normality, particularly when we have equal sample sizes and a reasonable number of participants in each group. By 'reasonable' we mean that for a completely between-participants design you have at least 12 participants per group and for a completely within-participants design at least 22 participants overall. It therefore makes sense, when planning to use MANOVA, to ensure that you have at least satisfied these conditions; you will then not need to worry too much if you have modest violations of this assumption.

14.5.2 Homogeneity of variance–covariance matrices

The second assumption underlying the use of MANOVA is that we should have equal *variance–covariance matrices*. Put simply, this assumption is equivalent to the assumption of homogeneity of variance for the univariate statistics we have covered earlier in the book. We will not attempt to explain this much further as it means going into matrix algebra, and you would never forgive us if we did that. It is enough for you to know that this assumption is equivalent to the homogeneity of variance assumption applicable with other parametric tests. If you are interested in reading more about this, however, there are good explanations in the texts listed at the end of this chapter. If you think of this assumption as being similar to the assumption of homogeneity of variance, that should suffice for now.

In general, when you have equal sample sizes this assumption is not too much of a problem. However, if you do find that you have unequal sample sizes then you will need to consult a more advanced text for guidance.

There is a test of the assumption of homogeneity of variance–covariance matrices that can be run in SPSSFW called Box's M test. If this test is significant ($p < 0.05$) then you have a violation of this assumption and you need to consider the various options to ensure that your MANOVA is reliable. In practice, however, Box's M test is a conservative test and so it is of most use when you have unequal and small sample sizes.

EXAMPLE

Let us assume that we have conducted the well-being study described earlier in this chapter but we have decided to use only two indices of well-being, Happiness and Optimism. We have then obtained the appropriate data (see Table 14.1) from 12 people who are regular churchgoers and 12 who are atheists.

Before we conduct the MANOVA we need to look at descriptive statistics in order to ensure that the assumptions for MANOVA are not violated.

We should initially establish that the data for each DV for each sample are normally distributed. For this we can get SPSSFW to produce box plots, histograms or stem and leaf plots. The box plots for the data in Table 14.1 are presented in Figure 14.1.

Table 14.1   Data for the well-being experiment

Churchgoers		Atheists	
Happiness	Optimism	Happiness	Optimism
4.00	3.00	5.00	3.00
5.00	4.00	4.00	4.00
5.00	8.00	8.00	5.00
6.00	7.00	9.00	4.00
6.00	6.00	7.00	2.00
6.00	5.00	6.00	3.00
7.00	6.00	7.00	4.00
7.00	6.00	5.00	3.00
7.00	5.00	6.00	2.00
8.00	5.00	4.00	4.00
8.00	7.00	5.00	5.00
9.00	4.00	6.00	3.00
$\bar{X} = 6.50$	$\bar{X} = 5.5$	$\bar{X} = 6.00$	$\bar{X} = 3.50$
SD = 1.45	SD = 1.45	SD = 1.54	SD = 1.00
95% CI = 5.58–7.42	95% CI = 4.58–6.42	95% CI = 5.02–6.98	95% CI = 2.86–4.14

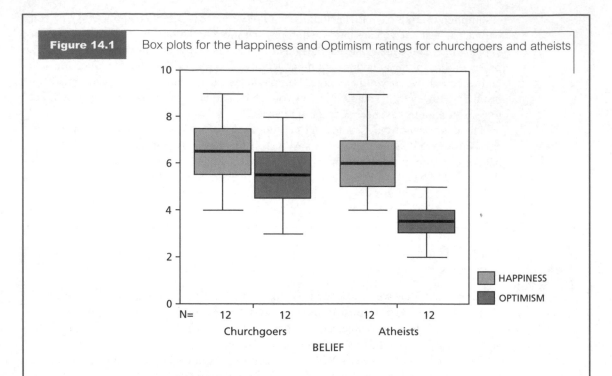

Figure 14.1 Box plots for the Happiness and Optimism ratings for churchgoers and atheists

You can see from these box plots that for both DVs in both conditions the distributions are approximately normal. These findings, along with the fact that we have equal numbers of participants in each condition, mean that we can continue with our MANOVA with some confidence that we do not have serious violations of the assumption of multivariate normality.

The second assumption, that of homogeneity of variance–covariance matrices, is assessed by looking at the MANOVA printout, and therefore we will go through this shortly.

Before we conduct the MANOVA it is instructive to look at the plots of the means and 95% confidence intervals around the means for the two DVs separately (see Figure 14.2).

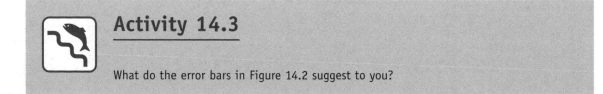

Activity 14.3

What do the error bars in Figure 14.2 suggest to you?

Figure 14.2 suggests that there is a real difference between the two groups in terms of their Optimism, but not necessarily in terms of Happiness ratings. You should be able to see that there is no overlap of the 95% CI for Optimism, but there is a large overlap for Happiness.

Figure 14.2 Means and 95% CI around the means for the Happiness and Optimism ratings for churchgoers and atheists

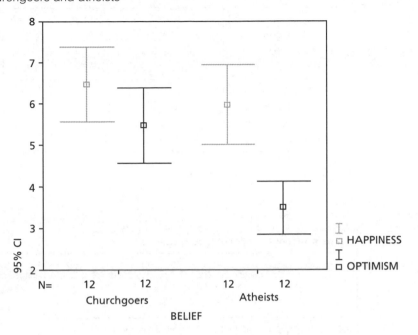

When we conduct the MANOVA on these data we get the following printout from SPSSFW:

GENERAL LINEAR MODEL

Between-Subjects Factors

		Value Label	N
BELIEF	1.00	Churchgoers	12
	2.00	Atheists	12

Box's Test of Equality of Covariance Matrices[a]

Box's M		1.508
F		.453
df1		3
df2		87120.000
Sig.		.715

Tests the null hypothesis that the observed covariance matrices of the dependent variables are equal across groups.
a. Design: Intercept+Belief

Multivariate Tests[b]

Effect		Value	F	Hypothesis df	Error df	Sig.
Intercept	Pillai's Trace	.969	327.224[a]	2.000	21.000	.000
	Wilks' Lambda	.031	327.224[a]	2.000	21.000	.000
	Hotelling's Trace	31.164	327.224[a]	2.000	21.000	.000
	Roy's Largest Root	31.164	327.224[a]	2.000	21.000	.000
Belief	Pillai's Trace	.418	7.547[a]	2.000	21.000	.003
	Wilks' Lambda	.582	7.547[a]	2.000	21.000	.003
	Hotelling's Trace	.719	7.547[a]	2.000	21.000	.003
	Roy's Largest Root	.719	7.547[a]	2.000	21.000	.003

a. Exact statistic
b. Design: Intercept+Belief

Levene's Test of Equality of Error Variances[a]

	F	df1	df2	Sig.
Happiness	.000	1	22	1.000
Optimism	1.571	1	22	.223

Tests the null hypothesis that the error variance of the
dependent variable is equal across groups.
a. Design: Intercept+Belief

Univariate tests

Tests of Between-Subjects Effects

Source	Dependent Variable	Type III Sum of Squares	df	Mean Square	F	Sig.
Corrected Model	Happiness	1.500[a]	1	1.500	.673	.421
	Optimism	24.000[b]	1	24.000	15.529	.001
Intercept	Happiness	937.500	1	937.500	420.918	.000
	Optimism	486.000	1	486.000	314.471	.000
Belief	Happiness	1.500	1	1.500	.673	.421
	Optimism	24.000	1	24.000	15.529	.001
Error	Happiness	49.000	22	2.227		
	Optimism	34.000	22	1.545		
Total	Happiness	988.000	24			
	Optimism	544.000	24			
Corrected Total	Happiness	50.500	23			
	Optimism	58.000	23			

a. R Squared = .030 (Adjusted R Squared = −.014)
b. R Squared = .414 (Adjusted R Squared = .387)

The first part of the printout gives us a test of the assumptions that we outlined earlier. We are given a test of the assumptions of homogeneity of the variance–covariance matrices (Box's M). If this has an associated p-value of less than 0.05 then we have violations of the assumption of homogeneity of the variance–covariance matrices. Given that this test, in the above printout, has a p-value that is greater than 0.05, we can assume that we have not violated this assumption. If you get a violation of this assumption and you have unequal sample sizes then you should use alternative analyses and perhaps consult one of the recommended texts detailed at the end of the chapter.

The rest of the printout relates to the actual analyses. You can see that SPSSFW gives us both multivariate and univariate analyses for the IVs and DVs. The multivariate statistics inform us of the effects of the IV on a linear combination of the DVs, whereas the univariate statistics give us the ANOVA results of the IV with each DV separately.

14.6 Which F-value?

As we explained earlier, SPSSFW gives us several different multivariate tests; that is, it uses several different ways of combining the DVs and calculating the F-value. These tests are:

- Wilks' lambda
- Pillai's trace
- Hotelling's trace
- Roy's largest root.

Ordinarily you will find that these different tests give you F-values that are the same as or at least very similar to each other, and so it does not really matter which of these you report. However, if you conduct an analysis and get different F-values from these tests you need to decide which one to use. As is often the case in statistics, there is no real consensus as to which is the most appropriate statistic to report. This is complicated by the fact that the most appropriate test is dependent upon the type of data you are analysing. However, consistent with the advice of Tabachnick and Fidell (1997), we suggest that you report the Wilks' lambda as this is the most commonly reported of the four tests.

The Wilks' lambda F-value reported in the above printout shows that the combined DVs successfully distinguish between the two belief groups. That is, given that the null hypothesis is true, the probability of finding a multivariate difference between the two belief groups as large as that observed with these data is so small that it is unlikely to be the result of sampling error. When we say multivariate difference, we simply mean a difference in terms of the linear combination of the DVs. Consequently, if we are to assume that these DVs measure well-being, we would conclude that there was a difference between the well-being of churchgoers and atheists.

Activity 14.4

Which of the following represents a method of calculating multivariate F-values in SPSSFW?

(a) Hotelling's trace
(b) Phil's mark
(c) Seth's weakest link
(d) Wilks' lambda (λ)
(e) Hayley's gamma
(f) Pillai's trace
(g) Crossroad's track
(h) Roy's largest root

14.7 Post-hoc analyses of individual DVs

It is apparent from the above SPSSFW printout that we have a considerable multivariate difference between our two belief groups. What does this actually mean? The problem we face in answering this question is similar to that which we face with ANOVA when we find a main effect of an IV with three or more conditions. The ANOVA simply tells us that there is a difference due to our IV. We subsequently have to carry out post-hoc (or a priori) analyses to find out where the difference(s) is (are). In the multivariate analyses, where we have more than one DV, once we find a multivariate difference, we need to find out which DVs are contributing to this difference. We need to do this because it is likely, especially if we have many DVs, that not every DV will contribute to the overall difference that we have observed.

In order to establish which DVs are contributing to this effect we have to conduct post-hoc univariate analysis of the individual DVs. As with post-hoc analyses of ANOVA designs, there is a variety of ways in which we can proceed with post-hoc analysis, and different authors prefer different techniques. If we get a multivariate difference for a two-group IV design, as we have, one approach recommended by Stevens (1997) is simply to conduct univariate t-tests and adjust the α to take account of the number of analyses we are conducting. Such an adjustment of α is necessary to control the familywise error rate. You came across this problem in Chapters 9 and 10. This is the approach that we will take; however, for a fuller discussion on this topic you are advised to consult one of the texts suggested at the end of the chapter.

The approach recommended by Stevens (1997) is to set a level for your overall α (we will set ours at 5%) and then divide this by the number of comparisons that you are going to make. We have two DVs, therefore we will need two t-tests, and thus our α for each t-test should be

$$0.05 \div 2 = 0.025$$

We then conduct our t-test analyses on both our Optimism and Happiness DVs separately with belief area as the IV in each case, setting our alpha for each at 0.025. If we find the probabilities associated with our t-tests are at or around the 0.025 level then we can feel relatively confident that our findings are unlikely to have arisen due to sampling error.

If we had five DVs we would need to conduct five t-tests (one for each DV). We would therefore divide the 5% α by 5:

$$0.05 \div 5 = 0.01$$

In this case we would need to set our α for each t-test at 1% (remember that 5% is equal to a probability of 0.05 and 1% is equivalent to 0.01).

Sample analysis

When we conduct the post-hoc analyses of our DVs we get the following results:

T-TEST

Group Statistics

	BELIEF	N	Mean	Std. Deviation	Std. Error Mean
Happiness	Churchgoers	12	6.5000	1.44600	.41742
	Atheists	12	6.0000	1.53741	.44381
Optimism	Churchgoers	12	5.5000	1.44600	.41742
	Atheists	12	3.5000	1.00000	.28868

Independent Samples Test

		Levene's Test for Equality of Variances		t-test for Equality of Means							
										95% Confidence Interval of the Difference	
		F	Sig.	t	df	Sig. (2-tailed)	Mean Difference	Std. Error Difference	Lower	Upper
Happiness	Equal variances assumed	.000	1.000	.821	22	.421	.50000	.60927	−.76355	1.76355
	Equal variances not assumed			.821	21.918	.421	.50000	.60927	−.76383	1.76383
Optimism	Equal variances assumed	1.571	.223	3.941	22	.001	2.00000	.50752	.94747	3.05253
	Equal variances not assumed			3.941	19.563	.001	2.00000	.50752	.93982	3.06018

You can see from these t-tests that only the Optimism DV has an associated probability of being due to sampling error that is less than the 2.5% level of α. We should, therefore, conclude that the two groups (churchgoers and atheists) differ only in terms of their level of optimism. If we are to assume that this is a valid measure of well-being, then it appears that there is a difference between these two groups in terms of their well-being. This point illustrates that even though we have conducted some quite sophisticated analyses on our data we still have to relate our findings to the real world; we have to make the judgement of whether or not optimism on its own is a sufficient indicator of well-being. If the answer to such a question is 'no', then our analyses suggest that overall there is no difference in well-being between the two communities beyond that which is attributable to differences in optimism.

You should note that the univariate F-values reported in the original analyses are equivalent to the t-tests (the F-values are simply the t-values squared). You could, therefore, use these to establish which DVs are contributing to the multivariate effects, but you should still set your α at 0.025.

14.8 Correlated DVs

The above post-hoc procedure is recommended when we have DVs that are not correlated with each other. Problems arise, however, when the DVs are correlated. The reason why such problems arise is not hard to explain. When we get a multivariate difference in our DVs we then have to evaluate the contribution of each DV to this overall effect (as we have just done). If we have uncorrelated DVs then there is no overlap between their contribution to the linear combination of the DVs. In such a situation, the univariate tests give a pure indication of the contribution of each DV to the overall difference. A simple analogy should help you understand what we mean here. Suppose that you find some oil and water in a container and you want to know how much of each liquid you have. If you poured this into a measuring beaker you would probably find that the oil and water did not mix. The oil would separate out on top of the water. Therefore you could tell simply by looking how much each liquid contributed to the total in the beaker (see Figure 14.3(a)). This is similar to the case when you have uncorrelated DVs: because they do not mix (they are uncorrelated) we can tell the relative contribution of each to the combined DVs by looking at the individual t-tests.

| Figure 14.3 | Illustration of the way (a) oil and water and (b) alcohol and water mix |

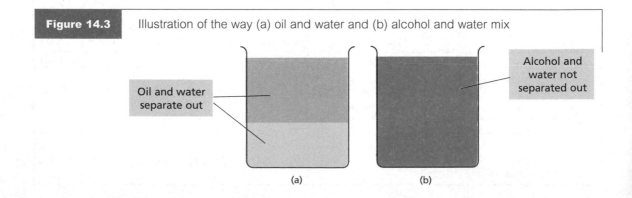

Oil and water separate out

Alcohol and water not separated out

(a)   (b)

When we have correlated DVs, however, it is a bit like having a mixture of alcohol and water rather than oil and water. If you had unknown quantities of alcohol and water in a beaker you could not tell by looking how much of each liquid you had because they mix (Figure 14.3(b)). In order to calculate how much of each liquid you had, you would have to use some complex procedure for separating the liquids (e.g. distillation). The same applies when you have correlated DVs. We cannot tell by looking at the t-tests what is the relative contribution of each because the contributions of the DVs are mixed up, rather like the alcohol and water. Therefore, to calculate the relative contribution of each DV you need to use rather complicated procedures for separating out the contribution of each DV (e.g. stepdown analysis). Such analyses are beyond the scope of this introduction to MANOVA but the two recommended texts give good discussions of this issue. We have highlighted the problem here so that you are aware that it exists.

The DVs in our example are not correlated and therefore we can use t-tests to calculate the relative contribution of each DV to the combined DVs.

CORRELATIONS

Correlations

		Happiness	Optimism
Happiness	Pearson Correlation	1	.166
	Sig. (2-tailed)	.	.437
	N	24	24
Optimism	Pearson Correlation	.166	1
	Sig. (2-tailed)	.437	.
	N	24	24

14.9 How to write up these analyses

The textual part of your analysis might look like this:

Box plots showed that the data for each DV in each condition of the IV were approximately normally distributed and therefore, given that there were equal sample sizes, we can be reasonably confident that we have no major violations of the assumption of multivariate normality. Box's M test indicated that there was also no violation of the assumption of homogeneity of the variance–covariance matrices. Error bar charts showed that there was quite a large difference, with no overlap of the 95% CIs, between the two groups in terms of their optimism but the difference in terms of happiness was relatively small and this was associated with a large overlap of the 95% CIs.

The well-being data were analysed with a one-factor belief (religious vs. atheist) MANOVA with Optimism and Happiness scores as DVs. The analysis revealed that there was a multivariate difference between the two groups that was unlikely to have resulted from sampling error alone ($F(2,21) = 7.55$, $p = 0.003$; Wilks' $\lambda = 0.582$). As the two dependent variables were not significantly correlated ($r = 0.17$, $n = 24$, $p = 0.44$) independent t-tests were conducted on the DVs separately. These analyses showed that there was a difference between the two groups in terms of optimism that was not attributable to sampling error ($t(22) = 3.94$, $p = 0.001$) but no such difference in terms of happiness ratings ($t(22) = 0.82$, $p = 0.42$).

Note: You could, if you wish, simply report the univariate F details instead of the t-tests when reporting the analysis of the individual DVs. Reporting the univariate Fs is the best approach when you have more than three conditions in your IVs.

Example from the literature:
mental toughness of rugby players

In a study by Golby and Sheard (2004) mental toughness and hardiness of rugby league players was measured using questionnaires. Mental toughness was measured using the Psychological Performance Inventory (PPI: Loehr, 1986). This scale measures seven components of mental toughness including self-confidence, negative energy control (handling negative emotions), attention control (keeping focused), visualisation and imagery control (using positive imagery), motivation, positive energy (enjoyment), and attitude control (maintaining a positive attitude). The measure of hardiness was the Maddi and Khoshaba (2001) Personal Views Survey III-R, which measures three components of hardiness. These components are commitment, control and challenge. The study involved the administration of the questionnaires to players who represented three different levels in rugby league. These included international players, Super League players and Division One players. These are the top three levels of rugby league in Great Britain. The researchers were trying to establish if there were differences in mental toughness and hardiness between players representing the three different levels of rugby league. To examine such differences they conducted MANOVA with follow-up univariate ANOVAs. It was found that there was a significant multivariate difference between the three levels of rugby league. The authors reported the Wilks' λ as 0.40 and F-value of 5.98, $p < 0.001$. The authors also reported a partial η^2 of .37 suggesting that 37% of the variation in the linear combination of the DVs is accounted for by level of rugby league being played. This is quite a high effect size for such psychological research. The researchers then reported the univariate ANOVAs which showed that there were significant group differences in terms of all three of the hardiness factors (commitment, control and challenge) and two of the factors relating to mental toughness (negative energy control and attention control). The authors noted that there were moderate correlations among some of the DVs and so they also conducted stepdown analyses (see Stephens, 1997). As we suggested earlier, such analyses are beyond the scope of this book but you can consult more advanced texts to find out more if you wish.

SPSSFW: conducting MANOVA with one between-participants IV and two DVs

To conduct a MANOVA on our data on optimism and happiness from earlier in the chapter you need to set up three variables in the data window. The first will be the grouping variable (IV) and the two remaining variables will contain the information about Optimism and Happiness rating for each person (DVs).

Once you have input the data you should click on the *Analyze* and *General Linear Model* options. When you are conducting an analysis for a completely between-participants MANOVA you then need to click on the *Multivariate* option:

The following dialogue box should then appear:

You should move the variables across to the relevant boxes. The two DVs should be moved to the *Dependent Variables* box and the IV should be moved to the *Fixed Factor(s)* box.

In order to get SPSSFW to display tests of homogeneity of variance, etc., you need to click on the *Options* button. You will be presented with the following dialogue box:

If you want SPSSFW to give you a test of homogeneity of the variance–covariance matrices (Box's M test) you should check the *Homogeneity tests* option. It is useful to get measures of the effect size, therefore you should also select this option. Once you have made your selections, click on *Continue* and you will get back to the previous screen. You then need to click on the *OK* button to proceed with the analysis. The output will be similar to that presented earlier.

14.10 Within-participants designs

One point we should clarify is that multivariate analyses of variance are not simply within-participants ANOVAs. Although the multiple DVs are, strictly speaking, within-participants measures, the analyses of these are different from the analyses of within-participants IVs. The key distinction here is between DVs and IVs. Remember that MANOVA deals with multiple DVs whereas within-participants ANOVA deals with within-participants IVs.

For example, suppose we wanted to find out whether a new therapy for spider phobia was effective. We could measure participants' fear of spiders, give them the new therapy and then measure their fear of spiders after the therapy. If the therapy were effective we would expect the participants' fear of spiders after therapy to be lower than before therapy. An important consideration in such a study is how we measure fear of spiders. There are a number of questionnaires that may be useful such as the Fear of Spiders Questionnaire (FSQ: Szymanski and O'Donohue, 1995). The FSQ is an 18-item questionnaire designed to assess spider phobia. Szymanski and O'Donohue found that the questionnaire was able to successfully discriminate between spider phobics and nonphobics and was more sensitive than other questionnaires to decrements in fear following treatment. This then would seem an ideal candidate for measuring fear of spiders. The total score on the questionnaire gives an indication of a person's level of fear of spiders. The higher the score on the questionnaire the higher the fear.

In our study we could, therefore, give participants the FSQ before and after treatment. We could then compare the two scores using a t-test to see if there was any decrease in FSQ score after treatment. Although this study would be fine it would be good to include a different measure of spider fear. One such measure is the Behavioural Approach Test (BAT), which involves participants being asked to move nearer a live spider in stages until eventually the spider is placed in the palm of their hand (see Öst *et al.*, 1998). Participants can stop this process at any stage and we thus get a behavioural measure of their fear of spiders. Öst *et al.* had 13 stages in their procedure and participants were given a score depending upon how near they got to the spider. A score of 0 was given if the participant refused to enter the room where the spider was (maximum fear) and a score of 12 was given if the participants were able to have the spider in the palm of their hand for at least 20 seconds (minimum fear). In our study we could include both of the FSQ and the BAT as measures of fear of spiders in order to assess as many aspects of fear as possible. We have a self-report measure (FSQ) where a high score equals high fear and a behavioural measure (BAT) where a high score equals low fear.

Clearly this is a within-participants design as we are testing the same participants before and after their treatment for spider phobia. The data for 22 participants from such a study along with the means, SDs and 95% confidence intervals are presented in Table 14.2.

Table 14.2 Possible data for the study investigating the effects of treatment on fear of spiders

Pre-treatment		Post-treatment	
FSQ	BAT	FSQ	BAT
92	8	51	11
126	2	120	5
126	7	111	8
121	10	84	8
84	4	67	6
67	4	45	6
19	10	21	11
65	5	96	7
73	1	55	7
107	5	91	6
101	0	72	3
83	6	63	6
110	7	109	8
21	11	31	11
68	8	69	9
42	4	67	3
106	9	110	9
89	6	75	10
88	5	91	6
33	10	41	10
55	6	56	5
33	7	42	10
$\bar{X} = 77.68$, SD $= 33.19$	$\bar{X} = 71.23$, SD $= 27.67$	$\bar{X} = 6.14$, SD $= 2.96$	$\bar{X} = 7.50$, SD $= 2.44$
95% CI $= 62.97$–92.40	95% CI $= 58.96$–83.49	95% CI $= 4.82$–7.45	95% CI $= 6.42$–8.58

Our initial step in analysing the data should be to ensure that our data do not violate the basic assumptions underlying the use of MANOVA. The SPSSFW box plots are presented in Figures 14.4(a) and (b).

Figures 14.4(a) and (b) show that we have no obvious outliers and that our data are reasonably normally distributed. We can therefore assume that we have not violated the assumption of multivariate normality.

We can also get SPSSFW to produce the error bar graphs for the 95% confidence intervals around the mean (Figures 14.5(a) and (b)).

It can be seen from Figures 14.5(a) and (b) that there is a substantial overlap of the 95% CIs for the FSQs pre- and post-treatment. We would probably find that there is no significant difference between these two measures. The overlap in 95% CIs for the BAT scores is a good deal less but we could still not tell from these whether or not there is likely to be a significant difference between these two measures. We thus appear to have a possible difference in the behavioural measure of fear of spiders but not the self-report measure.

Figure 14.4 Box plots for (a) scores on the FSQ and (b) scores from the BAT in the pre- and post-treatment conditions

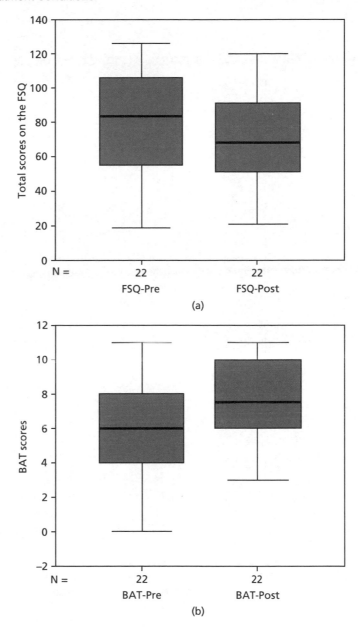

Figure 14.5 Error bar graphs for (a) the FSQ scores and (b) the BAT scores pre- and post-treatment

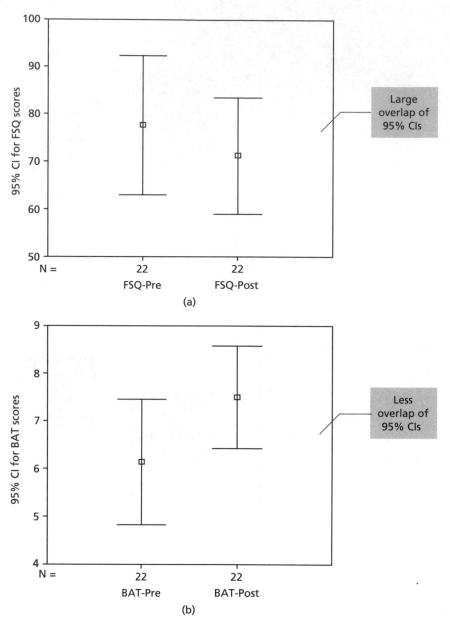

14.10.1 MANOVA printout

The MANOVA printout for the fear of spiders data is presented below:

GENERAL LINEAR MODEL

Within-Subjects Factors

Measure	treatmnt	Dependent Variable
fsq	1	fsqpre
	2	fsqpost
bat	1	batpre
	2	batpost

Multivariate Tests[b]

Effect			Value	F	Hypothesis df	Error df	Sig.
Between Subjects	Intercept	Pillai's Trace	.956	216.797[a]	2.000	20.000	.000
		Wilks' Lambda	.044	216.797[a]	2.000	20.000	.000
		Hotelling's Trace	21.680	216.797[a]	2.000	20.000	.000
		Roy's Largest Root	21.680	216.797[a]	2.000	20.000	.000
Within Subjects	treatmnt	Pillai's Trace	.379	6.110[a]	2.000	20.000	.008
		Wilks' Lambda	.621	6.110[a]	2.000	20.000	.008
		Hotelling's Trace	.611	6.110[a]	2.000	20.000	.008
		Roy's Largest Root	.611	6.110[a]	2.000	20.000	.008

a. Exact statistic
b. Design: Intercept
   Within Subjects Design: treatmnt

Mauchly's Test of Sphericity[b]

Within Subjects Effect	Measure	Mauchly's W	Approx. Chi-Square	df	Sig.	Epsilon[a]		
						Greenhouse-Geisser	Huynh-Feldt	Lower-bound
treatmnt	fsq	1.000	.000	0	.	1.000	1.000	1.000
	bat	1.000	.000	0	.	1.000	1.000	1.000

Tests the null hypothesis that the error covariance matrix of the orthonormalised transformed dependent variables is proportional to an identity matrix.
a. May be used to adjust the degrees of freedom for the averaged tests of significance. Corrected tests are displayed in the Tests of Within-Subjects Effects table.
b. Design: Intercept
   Within Subjects Design: treatmnt

TESTS OF WITHIN-SUBJECTS EFFECTS

Multivariate[b,c]

Within Sbjects Effect		Value	F	Hypothesis df	Error df	Sig.
treatmnt	Pillai's Trace	.379	6.110[a]	2.000	20.000	.008
	Wilks' Lambda	.621	6.110[a]	2.000	20.000	.008
	Hotelling's Trace	.611	6.110[a]	2.000	20.000	.008
	Roy's Largest Root	.611	6.110[a]	2.000	20.000	.008

a. Exact statistic
b. Design: Intercept
   Within Subjects Design: treatmnt
c. Tests are based on averaged variables.

Univariate Tests

Source	Measure		Type III Sum of Squares	df	Mean Square	F	Sig.
treatmnt	fsq	Sphericity Assumed	458.273	1	458.273	2.731	.113
		Greenhouse-Geisser	458.273	1.000	458.273	2.731	.113
		Huynh-Feldt	458.273	1.000	458.273	2.731	.113
		Lower-bound	458.273	1.000	458.273	2.731	.113
	bat	Sphericity Assumed	20.455	1	20.455	12.084	.002
		Greenhouse-Geisser	20.455	1.000	20.455	12.084	.002
		Huynh-Feldt	20.455	1.000	20.455	12.084	.002
		Lower-bound	20.455	1.000	20.455	12.084	.002
Error(treatmnt)	fsq	Sphericity Assumed	3523.727	21	167.797		
		Greenhouse-Geisser	3523.727	21.000	167.797		
		Huynh-Feldt	3523.727	21.000	167.797		
		Lower-bound	3523.727	21.000	167.797		
	bat	Sphericity Assumed	35.545	21	1.693		
		Greenhouse-Geisser	35.545	21.000	1.693		
		Huynh-Feldt	35.545	21.000	1.693		
		Lower-bound	35.545	21.000	1.693		

Tests of Within-Subjects Contrasts

Source	Measure	treatmnt	Type III Sum of Squares	df	Mean Square	F	Sig.
treatmnt	fsq	Linear	458.273	1	458.273	2.731	.113
Error(treatmnt)	bat	Linear	20.455	1	20.455	12.084	.002
	fsq	Linear	3523.727	21	167.797		
	bat	Linear	35.545	21	1.693		

Tests of Between-Subjects Effects
Transformed Variable: Average

Source	Measure	Type III Sum of Squares	df	Mean Square	F	Sig.
Intercept	fsq	243913.091	1	243913.091	143.555	.000
	bat	2045.455	1	2045.455	156.457	.000
Error	fsq	35680.909	21	1699.091		
	bat	274.545	21	13.074		

We can see from this analysis that we have an effect of the within-participants IV on the linear combination of the DVs, which is unlikely to have arisen by sampling error. We can see this by looking at the 'Multivariate' table in the 'Tests of Within-Subjects Effects' section of the printout. Thus, we have a multivariate difference between the pre- and post-treatment conditions. You should be able to see that we have a Wilks' λ of 0.621, which equates to an F-value of 6.11 and a p-value of 0.008. As with the between-participants analysis presented previously, we now need to examine the relative contribution of each of the DVs to this multivariate difference.

14.10.2 Evaluation of each DV

In order to evaluate each DV we first need to see whether they are correlated; we can check this by conducting Pearson's Product Moment Correlations. The correlations are shown below:

	Pre-treatment		**Post-treatment**
	fsq		fsq
bat	-0.32	bat	-0.35
	(22)		(22)
	$p = 0.16$		$p = 0.11$

It is evident from the above correlation coefficients that there is no correlation between the two DVs beyond that attributable to sampling error. We can therefore investigate the relative contribution of each DV to the linear combination of the DVs by conducting related t-tests (remember, if you get correlated DVs you should consult a more advanced text). When we conduct the t-tests we get the following results:

T-TEST

Paired Samples Statistics

		Mean	N	Std. Deviation	Std. Error Mean
Pair 1	fsq-pre	77.6818	22	33.18833	7.07578
	fsq-post	71.2273	22	27.66626	5.89847
Pair 2	bat-pre	6.1364	22	2.96480	.63210
	bat-post	7.5000	22	2.44462	.52120

Paired Samples Correlations

		N	Correlation	Sig.
Pair 1	fsq-pre & fsq-post	22	.834	.000
Pair 2	bat-pre & bat-post	22	.785	.000

Paired Samples Test

		Paired Differences							
					95% Confidence Interval of the Difference				Sig.
		Mean	Std. Deviation	Std. Error Mean	Lower	Upper	t	df	(2-tailed)
Pair 1	fsq-pre – fsq-post	6.45455	18.31920	3.90567	–1.66773	14.57682	1.653	21	.113
Pair 2	bat-pre – bat-post	–1.36364	1.83991	.39227	–2.17941	–.54786	–3.476	21	.002

From the above printout it is clear that only the behavioural measure of fear (BAT) significantly contributes to the difference in the combined DVs, and that there is no difference in the self-report measure of fear (FSQ) pre- and post-treatment beyond that attributable to sampling error.

You might write up these analyses as follows:

Box plots showed that the data for each DV in each condition of the IV were approximately normally distributed and therefore we can be reasonably confident that we have no major violations of the assumption of multivariate normality. Error bar charts showed that there was substantial overlap of the 95% CIs for the FSQ pre- and post-treatment suggesting no real effect of treatment on this measure of fear. The overlap in CIs for the BAT measure was not nearly as large and so there may have been more effect of treatment on the behavioural measure of fear.

A repeated-measures MANOVA with one within-participants factor of treatment (pre- vs. post) was conducted with FSQ and BAT scores as the dependent variables. This revealed that there was a multivariate difference between the pre- and post-treatment conditions that was not attributable to sampling error ($F(2,20) = 6.11$, $p = 0.008$, Wilks' $\lambda = 0.621$). As the two dependent variables were uncorrelated, separate univariate related t-tests were conducted on each of the dependent variables. These analyses suggested that there was a contribution, not attributable to sampling error, of the behavioural measure of fear (BAT) to the multivariate difference between the pre- and post-treatment conditions ($t = 3.48$, DF $= 21$, $p = 0.002$). However, there was no contribution of the scores on the FSQ to the multivariate difference between the pre- and post-treatment conditions ($t = 1.65$, DF $= 21$, $p = 0.113$). The confidence interval for the difference between the pre- and post-treatment conditions for the BAT showed that the population mean difference is likely (95%) to fall between −2.18 and −0.55.

Note: As with the between-participants design, you could report the univariate F details here instead of the t-tests.

Activity 14.5

Which of the following would be appropriate for following up a multivariate difference between the two conditions of the IV?

(a) First, need to see if the DVs are correlated. If they are, then use some complex analyses such as stepdown analysis to calculate the contribution of each DV to the mulitvariate difference between the conditions of the IV

(b) See if the DVs are correlated. If they are not, use individual t-tests with a suitable adjustment of α

(c) See if the DVs are correlated. If they are not, use the univariate analyses from the MANOVA printout

(d) No need to worry about correlations. Simply conduct t-tests on the DVs separately

SPSSFW: one within-participants IV and two DVs

In order to analyse the fear of spiders study data we need to set up four variables:

1. Pre-treatment FSQ score.
2. Post-treatment FSQ score.
3. Pre-treatment BAT score.
4. Post-treatment BAT score.

Once you have set up the variables and entered your data you should click on *Analyze* followed by *General Linear Model*, and then select the *Repeated Measures* option:

You should be presented with the following dialogue box. This box is exactly the same as the boxes we showed you in Chapters 9 and 10 when we explained how to use repeated-measures ANOVA. As before, you need to define your repeated-measures variables. You can see below that we have simply called the repeated-measures variable in our study *treatmnt* and that it has two conditions.

In Chapters 9 and 10 we told you that after defining the within-participants variables you should click on the *Define* button. When we are using multivariate analyses, however, we need to specify how the DVs are to be recognised. We do this by clicking on the *Measures* >> button, which will expand the current dialogue box:[1]

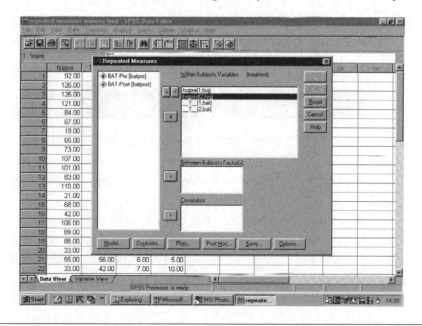

We have two DVs, each measured in both conditions of the IV. In the *Measure Names* box we need to indicate what the two DVs are to be called. Remember that the names you input here should be different from any of the variable names that you have already set up. You can see from the diagram that we have called the first DV *fsq* and the second DV *bat*. When you have the correct details in this dialogue box you should click on the *Define* button.

---

[1] You should note that SPSS version 12 does not present the screen as above; it presents the screen as per the next screenshot. Therefore you do not have to click on the *Measures>>* button to enlarge the dialogue box.

You will notice that in the *Within-Subjects Variables* box you have two slots available for the *fsq* DV and two slots available for the *bat* DV. You should move the relevant variables across from the variable list to fill these slots. We have two variables set up for each DV and so you need to move the FSQ variables (*fsqpre* and *fsqpost*) across to fill the *fsq* slots and the two BAT variables (*batpre* and *batpost*) across to fill the *bat* slots. You should then select the *Options* button to request effect-size calculations (see below).

Once you have set up the options to your satisfaction you should click on *Continue* and *OK* to run the analysis. The resulting printout should resemble the one we presented earlier.

Summary

In this chapter we have given you a brief introduction to multivariate statistical techniques. We have explained:

■ that multivariate analyses are used where we have one or more IVs with more than one DV

■ how MANOVA is an extension of ANOVA.

■ that MANOVA forms a linear combination of your DVs and then looks for a difference between the conditions of your IV in terms of this linear combination of DVs

■ the assumptions that underlie the use of MANOVA:
  – that multivariate normality means we have normally distributed DVs *and* all linear combinations of the DVs
  – that homogeneity of the variance–covariance matrices is equivalent to the homogeneity of variance assumption underlying ANOVA

■ that SPSSFW has several ways of working out the multivariate F, which are:
  – Wilks' lambda
  – Pillai's trace
  – Hotelling's trace
  – Roy's largest root

■ that the most commonly used value is Wilks' lambda

■ that when you get a significant multivariate F-value you need to find out which DVs are contributing to this by conducting univariate analyses on each of the DVs

■ that you need to adjust your α when you conduct more than one univariate test after your MANOVA

■ that you have to be careful when you have correlated DVs as this makes the task of examining the individual DVs with univariate statistics more complicated.

SPSSFW exercises

Exercise 1

An oil company has invented two new forms of fuel that are compatible with petrol engined cars. One of the fuels is made out of carrot juice (of course, this will also help the driver to see better at night); the other is made from mushy peas (not as useful for night driving but very green). Before the company markets the fuel, it wishes to find out which fuel is the best. The company decides to conduct some road trials with 12 cars running on the carrot juice fuel and 12 cars running on the mushy pea fuel. Each car is driven non-stop for 12 hours at a constant 70 kilometres per hour. The company decides that it should compare the fuel using several different indices, two of which are ratings out of 10 for damage to the engine of the cars (as assessed by a mechanic) and number of kilometres travelled per litre of fuel. The following are the data from this study:

Carrot juice fuel		Mushy pea fuel	
Engine condition rating	km per litre	Engine condition rating	km per litre
4	10	3	14
5	10	6	14
8	9	4	14
5	9	5	12
6	7	5	12
2	11	9	11
4	12	6	11
7	11	2	9
3	10	7	15
6	6	7	15
7	12	8	16
5	13	6	17

Enter these data into SPSSFW. Conduct a MANOVA on the data and answer the following questions:

1. Is the assumption of homogeneity of variance–covariance violated?

2. What is the F-value as calculated by Wilks' lambda?

3. Is there a multivariate difference, beyond that attributable to sampling error, between the two types of fuel?

4. According to the univariate F-tests, which DV(s) is (are) contributing to the multivariate difference between the two fuel types?

5. Conduct correlational analyses to ensure that the univariate ANOVAs are the most appropriate way of examining the contribution of each DV to the combined effect of the DVs.

6. What is the effect size of each DV separately?

Exercise 2

A beer company has formulated a new alcoholic drink that it thinks is going to revolutionise the drinking habits of young men. The drink is brewed like a stout but is stored and fermented like a lager and thus the company has called it Lout. They decide to do some testing of the drink before launching it (not literally) across Europe. They ask a group of 12 young men to compare the new drink with the most popular lager and give ratings on a number of characteristics of the drinks. On the first day of testing, half of the group are given six pints of Lout to drink and then give their ratings. The rest of the group are given the lager to drink. On the second day of testing the six men who were given Lout to drink are now given lager and the group who were given lager are now given Lout to drink and rate. Two of the rated characteristics (taste and pleasurable effects) are presented in the following table. The ratings are all out of a maximum of 15.

Lager		Lout	
Taste	Pleasurable effects	Taste	Pleasurable effects
5	8	8	9
11	7	11	8
9	2	14	7
11	3	14	7
10	4	15	2
12	7	10	3
9	6	10	4
6	6	15	5
8	5	11	5
10	5	13	6
9	5	13	6
8	4	13	6

Enter the data into SPSSFW. Conduct a MANOVA on the data and answer the following questions:

1. Is there a multivariate difference, beyond that attributable to sampling error, between the two drinks?

2. How would you examine the relative contribution of the two DVs to the difference of the combined DVs? Conduct these analyses.

3. Which DV(s) is (are) contributing to the difference in the combined DVs?

MULTIPLE CHOICE QUESTIONS

Questions 1 to 3 refer to the following study and printout:

Researchers were interested in the difference between males and females in their verbal ability. They thus measured writing skills and comprehension ability in a group of male and female students. The DVs were found not to be correlated. The following printout represents the output from a MANOVA conducted with their data:

GENERAL LINEAR MODEL

Between-Subjects Factors

		Value Label	N
GENDER	1.00	female	10
	2.00	male	10

Box's Test of Equality of Covariance Matrices[a]

Box's M	8.486
F	2.488
df1	3
df2	58320
Sig.	.058

Tests the null hypothesis that the observed covariance matrices of the dependent variables are equal across groups.
a. Design: Intercept+GENDER

Multivariate Tests[b]

Effect		Value	F	Hypothesis df	Error df	Sig.
Intercept	Pillai's Trace	.963	222.465[a]	2.000	17.000	.000
	Wilks' Lambda	.037	222.465[a]	2.000	17.000	.000
	Hotelling's Trace	26.172	222.465[a]	2.000	17.000	.000
	Roy's Largest Root	26.172	222.465[a]	2.000	17.000	.000
GENDER	Pillai's Trace	.426	6.308[a]	2.000	17.000	.009
	Wilks' Lambda	.574	6.308[a]	2.000	17.000	.009
	Hotelling's Trace	.742	6.308[a]	2.000	17.000	.009
	Roy's Largest Root	.742	6.308[a]	2.000	17.000	.009

a. Exact statistic
b. Design: Intercept+GENDER

Levene's Test of Equality of Error Variances[a]

	F	df1	df2	Sig.
Comprehension	.012	1	18	.915
Writing skills	.611	1	18	.444

Tests the null hypothesis that the error variance of the
dependent variable is equal across groups.
a. Design: Intercept+GENDER

Tests of Between-Subjects Effects

Source	Dependent Variable	Type III Sum of Squares	df	Mean Square	F	Sig.
Corrected Model	Comprehension	2.450[a]	1	2.450	1.100	.308
	Writing skills	20.000[b]	1	20.000	13.235	.002
Intercept	Comprehension	572.450	1	572.450	256.960	.000
	Writing skills	460.800	1	460.800	304.941	.000
GENDER	Comprehension	2.450	1	2.450	1.100	.308
	Writing skills	20.000	1	20.000	13.235	.002
Error	Comprehension	40.100	18	2.228		
	Writing skills	27.200	18	1.511		
Total	Comprehension	615.000	20			
	Writing skills	508.000	20			
Corrected Total	Comprehension	42.550	19			
	Writing skills	47.200	19			

a. R Squared = .058 (Adjusted R Squared = .005)
b. R Squared = .424 (Adjusted R Squared = .392)

1. What is the value of Box's M?

    (a) 8.49
    (b) 58320
    (c) 0.058
    (d) 3

2. What is the value of Wilks' lambda?

    (a) 9
    (b) 0.574
    (c) 0.742
    (d) None of the above

3. What is the most appropriate conclusion to be drawn from the above printout?

    (a) There is a multivariate difference, not attributable to sampling error, between males and females
    (b) Writing skills but not comprehension contributes to the difference in the combined DVs
    (c) The assumption of homogeneity of variance–covariance matrices is not violated
    (d) All of the above

4. Which of the following is true of MANOVA?

    (a) It analyses multiple IVs only
    (b) It analyses multiple DVs with one or more IVs
    (c) It can be used only with categorical data
    (d) All of the above

5. Which of the following are multivariate methods of calculating F?

    (a) Wilks' lambda
    (b) Pillai's trace
    (c) Hotelling's trace
    (d) All of the above

6. Box's M test:

    (a) Is a test of the homogeneity of variance assumption underlying ANOVA
    (b) Should be ignored at all times
    (c) Is a test of the homogeneity of variance–covariance matrices
    (d) Is applicable only for split-plot designs

7. If you have correlated DVs in a MANOVA with a two-group IV you should:

    (a) Cry
    (b) Conduct t-test analyses of the single DVs
    (c) Conduct χ^2 analyses of the DVs followed by t-tests
    (d) None of the above

8. For uncorrelated DVs how do we examine the relative contributions of the individual DVs to the combined DVs when our IV has only two conditions?

    (a) Conduct separate t-tests and adjust α to keep down the familywise error rate
    (b) Look at the multivariate effect size of the combined DVs
    (c) Check that Box's M is significant
    (d) Both (a) and (b) above

9. If we had three DVs and found a multivariate difference, what level of α would we set for each t-test to keep the overall α at 5%?

    (a) 5%
    (b) 1%
    (c) 1.67%
    (d) 3.33%

10. Which of the following are true of MANOVA?

    (a) It forms a linear combination of the IVs
    (b) It forms a linear combination of the DVs
    (c) It is an extension of χ^2
    (d) It correlates the IVs with all of the DVs

11. The assumption of multivariate normality means that:

    (a) Only the DVs should be normally distributed
    (b) All DVs and all IVs should be normally distributed
    (c) All DVs and all possible linear combinations of the DVs should be normally distributed
    (d) All of the above

12. Which of the following are linear combinations?

    (a) $A + B + C + D$
    (b) $b_1x_1 + b_2x_2 + b_3x_3 \ldots + a$
    (c) The Lottery numbers
    (d) Both (a) and (b) above

13. Which of the following are assumptions underlying the use of multivariate statistics?

    (a) Homogeneity of variance–covariance matrices
    (b) That we have equal sample sizes
    (c) That we have nominal-level data
    (d) None of the above

14. Which part of the MANOVA printout gives us information about differences between the conditions of the IVs in terms of the linear combination of the DVs?

    (a) The Box's M tests
    (b) The univariate F-statistics
    (c) The multivariate F-statistics
    (d) All of the above

15. If you have correlated DVs, which of the following are applicable?

    (a) You should use t-tests to examine the contribution of the individual DVs to the linear combination of the DVs
    (b) You should not use t-tests to examine the contribution of the individual DVs to the linear combination of the DVs
    (c) You should not water down your alcohol
    (d) Both (a) and (b) above

Questions 16 to 20 refer to the following printout:

GENERAL LINEAR MODEL

Within-Subjects Factors

Measure	condtion	Dependent Variable
anxiety	1	anxiety1
	2	anxiety2
depress	1	depression1
	2	depression2

Descriptive Statistics

	Mean	Std. Deviation	N
Anxiety1	39.5455	16.75518	22
Anxiety2	56.3636	15.79797	22
Depression2	5.8182	4.17060	22
Depression1	8.0000	3.03942	22

Multivariate Tests[b]

Effect			Value	F	Hypothesis df	Error df	Sig.
Between Subjects	Intercept	Pillai's Trace	.964	264.762[a]	2.000	20.000	.000
		Wilks' Lambda	.036	264.762[a]	2.000	20.000	.000
		Hotelling's Trace	26.476	264.762[a]	2.000	20.000	.000
		Roy's Largest Root	26.476	264.762[a]	2.000	20.000	.000
Within Subjects	condtion	Pillai's Trace	.497	9.889[a]	2.000	20.000	.001
		Wilks' Lambda	.503	9.889[a]	2.000	20.000	.001
		Hotelling's Trace	.989	9.889[a]	2.000	20.000	.001
		Roy's Largest Root	.989	9.889[a]	2.000	20.000	.001

a. Exact statistic
b. Design: Intercept
   Within Subjects Design: condtion

Mauchly's Test of Sphericity [b]

Within Subjects Effect	Measure	Mauchly's W	Approx. Chi-Square	df	Sig.	Epsilon [a]		
						Greenhouse -Geisser	Huynh-Feldt	Lower-bound
condition	anxiety	1.000	.000	0	.	1.000	1.000	1.000
	depress	1.000	.000	0	.	1.000	1.000	1.000

Tests the null hypothesis that the error covariance matrix of the orthonormalised transformed dependent variables is proportional to an identity matrix.

a. May be used to adjust the degrees of freedom for the averaged tests of significance. Corrected tests are displayed in the Tests of Within-Subjects Effects table.

b. Design: Intercept
   Within Subjects Design: condtion

TESTS OF WITHIN-SUBJECTS EFFECTS

Multivariate [b,c]

Within Subjects Effect		Value	F	Hypothesis df	Error df	Sig.
condtion	Pillai's Trace	.497	9.889[a]	2.000	20.000	.001
	Wilks' Lambda	.503	9.889[a]	2.000	20.000	.001
	Hotelling's Trace	.989	9.889[a]	2.000	20.000	.001
	Roy's Largest Root	.989	9.889[a]	2.000	20.000	.001

a. Exact statistic

b. Design: Intercept
   Within Subjects Design: condtion

c. Tests are based on averaged variables.

Univariate Tests

Source	Measure		Type III Sum of Squares	df	Mean Square	F	Sig.
condtion	anxiety	Sphericity Assumed	3111.364	1	3111.364	9.410	.006
		Greenhouse-Geisser	3111.364	1.000	3111.364	9.410	.006
		Huynh-Feldt	3111.364	1.000	3111.364	9.410	.006
		Lower-bound	3111.364	1.000	3111.364	9.410	.006
	depress	Sphericity Assumed	52.364	1	52.364	6.407	.019
		Greenhouse-Geisser	52.364	1.000	52.364	6.407	.019
		Huynh-Feldt	52.364	1.000	52.364	6.407	.019
		Lower-bound	52.364	1.000	52.364	6.407	.019
Error(condtion)	anxiety	Sphericity Assumed	6943.636	21	330.649		
		Greenhouse-Geisser	6943.636	21.000	330.649		
		Huynh-Feldt	6943.636	21.000	330.649		
		Lower-bound	6943.636	21.000	330.649		
	depress	Sphericity Assumed	171.636	21	8.173		
		Greenhouse-Geisser	171.636	21.000	8.173		
		Huynh-Feldt	171.636	21.000	8.173		
		Lower-bound	171.636	21.000	8.173		

Tests of Within-Subjects Contrasts

Source	Measure	condtion	Type III Sum of Squares	df	Mean Square	F	Sig.
condtion	anxiety	Linear	3111.364	1	3111.364	9.410	.006
	depress	Linear	52.364	1	52.364	6.407	.019
(condtion)	anxiety	Linear	6943.636	21	330.649		
	depress	Linear	171.636	21	8.173		

Tests of Between-Subjects Effects
Transformed Variable: Average

Source	Measure	Type III Sum of Squares	df	Mean Square	F	Sig.
Intercept	anxiety	101184.091	1	101184.091	506.776	.000
	depress	2100.364	1	2100.364	113.786	.000
Error	anxiety	4192.909	21	199.662		
	depress	387.636	21	18.459		

16. What are the DVs in this study?

    (a) Condition and intercept
    (b) Anxiety and depression
    (c) Greenhouse and Geisser
    (d) None of the above

17. How many conditions are there in the IV?

    (a) 1
    (b) 2
    (c) 3
    (d) 4

18. Is there a multivariate difference between the conditions of the IV?

    (a) Yes
    (b) No
    (c) Can't tell from the above printout
    (d) Yes but none of the DVs individually contribute significantly to the multivariate difference

19. Which of the following would you report in a write-up?

    (a) Pillai's trace = 0.497
    (b) Wilks' lambda = 0.503
    (c) Hotelling's trace = 0.989
    (d) Roy's largest root = 0.989

20. Are there any univariate differences present?

    (a) Yes, for anxiety only
    (b) Yes, for depression only
    (c) Yes, for anxiety and depression
    (d) There are no univariate differences present

References

Golby, J. and Sheard, M. (2003) 'Mental toughness and hardiness at different levels of rugby league', *Perceptual and Motor Skills*, **96**: 455–62.

Loehr, J.E. (1986) *Mental Toughness Training for Sports: Achieving Athletic Excellence*. Lexington, MA: Stephen Greene Press.

Maddi, S.R. and Khoshaba, D.M. (2001) *Personal Views Survey* (3rd edn, revised). Newport Beach, CA: The Hardiness Institute.

Öst, L., Stridh, B. and Wolf, M. (1998) 'A clinical study of spider phobia: prediction of outcome after self-help and therapist-directed treatments', *Behaviour Research and Therapy*, **36**: 17–35.

Stevens, J. (1997) *Applied Multivariate Statistics for the Social Sciences* (3rd edn). Lawrence Erlbaum Associates.

Szymanski, J. and O'Donohue, W. (1995) 'Fear of spiders questionnaire', *Journal of Behavior Therapy and Experimental Psychiatry*, **26**: 31–4.

Tabachnick, B.G. and Fidell, L.S. (1997) *Using Multivariate Statistics* (3rd edn). HarperCollins.

15 Non-parametric statistics

Chapter overview

In previous chapters you were introduced to parametric tests. Parametric tests, as you know, have certain assumptions. Data need to be drawn from a normally distributed population (see Chapter 4). When you meet the assumptions of parametric tests, they are more powerful than non-parametric tests, and psychologists prefer them. In many research situations we cannot use parametric tests because our data do not meet the assumptions underlying their use. For example, we might have skewed data with very small or unequal sample sizes – we would then be unsure as to whether our data were drawn from a normally distributed population. Non-parametric tests make no assumptions about the data and you can safely use the tests described in this chapter to analyse data when you think you might not be able to meet the assumptions for parametric tests.

In this chapter, you will learn about alternatives to:

- Pearson's *r* (Spearman's rho)
- t-test (Mann–Whitney for independent samples and Wilcoxon Signed Rank Test (Wilcoxon) for related samples)
- ANOVA (Kruskal–Wallis for independent samples and Friedman for related samples).

To enable you to understand the tests presented in this chapter you will need to have an understanding of the following concepts:

- one- and two-tailed hypotheses (Chapter 3)
- statistical significance (Chapter 3)
- confidence intervals (Chapter 3)
- Pearson's *r* (Chapter 5)
- t-test (Chapter 6)
- ANOVA (Chapter 9).

15.1 Alternative to Pearson's *r*: Spearman's rho

Pearson's *r* and Spearman's rho are very similar, not surprisingly. They are both correlation coefficients, interpreted in the same way. Pearson's *r* is used when your data meet the assumptions for a parametric test. Spearman's rho is used when your data do not conform to these assumptions – perhaps one or more variables are ratings given by participants (e.g. the attractiveness of a person), or they have to put pictures in rank order of preference. In these cases, data might not be normally distributed. When you have small participant numbers and are uncertain as to whether you meet the assumptions for Pearson's *r*, use Spearman's rho. Spearman's rho transforms the original scores into ranks before performing further calculations.

Look at the following data. Nine people were asked to rate the attractiveness of a target person, and then rate themselves (myattrac) on a 10-point scale from 1 (awful) to 10 (wonderful). Small participant numbers, the nature of the data and the fact that many participants rated themselves as near-wonderful should make you suspicious about such data conforming to the assumptions for a parametric test:

attrac	myattrac	attrac	myattrac
7.00	9.00	6.00	8.00
5.00	4.00	1.00	3.00
5.00	5.00	2.00	5.00
8.00	9.00	8.00	9.00
9.00	9.00		

SPSSFW: correlational analysis – Spearman's rho

Open your datafile. Choose *Analyze*, *Correlate*, *Bivariate*:

This brings you to the bivariate correlations dialogue box, just as you learned in Chapter 5:

However, this time you must make sure that you check the *Spearman* option.

Move the variables of interest from the left-hand side to the variable list on the right. To obtain descriptive statistics, choose *Options*. However, these may not be relevant. Clicking on *OK* obtains the following output:

Correlations

			my attractiveness	attractiveness of person
Spearman's rho	**my attractiveness**	**Correlation Coefficient**	**1.000**	**.921****
		Sig. (1-tailed)	.	**.000**
		N	9	9
	attractiveness of person	Correlation Coefficient	.921**	1.000
		Sig. (1-tailed)	.000	.
		N	9	9

** Correlation is significant at the .01 level (1-tailed).

As in the matrix from Pearson's *r*, we only need to focus on one half of the matrix. You can see here that there are nine sets of scores, and that the correlation between the ratings given to a target person and oneself is 0.92. Such a strong correlation has only a very tiny chance of arising by sampling error ($p < 0.001$) assuming the null hypothesis to be true. The way we rate others according to their attractiveness is related to how attractive we believe ourselves to be.

Example from the literature: pain and uterine contractions during breast feeding

Holdcroft *et al*. (2003) carried out a study that included discovering whether abdominal pain and uterine contractions differed according to parity (that is, the number of previous live births experienced) in women who were breast-feeding their babies. A visual analogue scale (VAS) and the McGill Pain Questionnaire (MPQ) were used to measure pain intensity. This questionnaire has four dimensions (sensory, affective, evaluative and miscellaneous). Each of these has varying numbers of subclasses. A total pain intensity index (TPI) can then be calculated. The researchers then used Spearman's rho to analyse relationships between variables.

Although the researchers tell us in their paper that they set their significance levels at $p < 0.05$, they ensure that the readers are given full information by reporting both the correlation coefficient and exact p-values.

The researchers report some of their results as text:

. . . a significant positive correlation was found for the relationship between the subjects' TPI and VAS scores during breast feeding, and the mean duration of uterine contractions (TPI: rho = 0.49, p = 0.006; VAS: rho = 0.40, p = 0.03), but not the number of uterine contractions. Neither the TPI nor the VAS scores reported for menstruation was significantly correlated with either the number or duration of uterine contractions during breast feeding.

Some of their results are given as a table (see Table 15.1). We report only part of their results table – the part that relates to the 'sensory' dimension. This has ten subclasses. Ratings on these subclasses were correlated with pain during breast feeding and pain during menstruation. Here we report the results for 'pain during breast feeding' only.

The researchers give a short summary in their article, drawing the reader's attention to the results that they consider are important.

Table 15.1   Spearman's rank correlation coefficients and p-values for parity for breast feeding for the sensory subclasses

Subclass	rho	*p*
Temporal	0.33	0.02
Spatial	0.28	0.05
Punctate pressure	0.21	0.14
Incisive pressure	0.04	0.80
Constrictive pressure	0.34	0.02
Traction pressure	0.12	0.42
Thermal	0.19	0.18
Brightness	−0.10	0.50
Dullness	0.39	0.005
Miscellaneous	0.09	0.54

Interpreting the results in Table 15.1 is a matter of looking at the strength, direction, and associated probability values together. It can be seen that 'Miscellaneous' is not related to parity. Even without knowledge of the associated probability value (0.54) the correlation coefficient is near zero. The scatter-plot would show no particular pattern. Although 'Brightness' has a negative correlation coefficient, this is very weak and the associated probability of 0.50 means this probably occurred by sampling error.

Activity 15.1

(a) Which is the strongest correlation from those in Table 15.1?

(b) Give the probability value for the weakest correlation coefficient.

SPSSFW exercise

Exercise 1

A German language teacher takes a group of five students. She hypothesises that the higher the confidence, the better the performance. She rank orders them in order of how confident they are when speaking (1 – extremely confident, 3 – not at all confident) and wants to correlate this with performance in the oral examination. A different teacher has given ratings of how well the students spoke in the oral exam (1 – hopeless, 5 – excellent).

Person	Confidence	Oral exam performance
Ahmed	2	5
Bella	3	3
Carol	1	5
Darren	4	4
Elke	5	1

Enter the data into SPSSFW, perform the appropriate analysis and then answer the following questions. Use a one-tailed hypothesis.

1. What is the value of the correlation coefficient?

2. What is the achieved significance level?

3. What can you conclude from this analysis?

15.2 Alternatives to the t-test: Mann–Whitney and Wilcoxon

The Mann–Whitney and Wilcoxon tests *assess whether there is a statistically significant difference between the mean ranks of the two conditions*. The *Mann–Whitney test* is used when you have different participants in each condition. The *Wilcoxon test* is used when you have the same, or matched participants in both conditions.

The Wilcoxon is equivalent to the Mann–Whitney, although the formulae for the two tests are slightly different, because in the Wilcoxon we can make use of the fact that the *same* participants are performing in both conditions. These tests are far more simple than the t-tests in that they do not involve calculations of means, standard deviations and standard errors. Both tests involve scores from the two conditions being ranked, and then the test statistic is calculated from these rankings.

15.2.1 Mann–Whitney (independent design)

Consider the following study. Twelve participants took part in an experiment to rate the attractiveness of a woman and a man who were shown on a video either in a good mood or a bad mood. Since the participants performed under one condition only, the design is a between-participants, or independent, design. The data given in Table 15.2 are ratings given by participants (out of 20) for a woman in either a good mood or a bad mood. The woman, an actor, was the same individual in both conditions. There were meant to be six participants in each group, but unfortunately an error occurred, and one participant who was meant to be in the GOOD MOOD condition was accidentally placed in the BAD MOOD condition. Our experimental hypothesis is that there will be a significant difference between the ratings given by participants in the GOOD MOOD and BAD MOOD conditions. Note, for the purposes of this example, that the hypothesis is two-tailed, that is, we have not predicted the direction of the difference.

Table 15.2   Ratings given by participants watching someone in a good mood or bad mood

GOOD MOOD	BAD MOOD
7.00	4.00
15.00	6.00
14.00	11.00
3.00	7.00
17.00	9.00
	4.00
	7.00

15.2.2 Descriptive statistics

From the *Explore* procedure in SPSSFW, the statistics shown in Table 15.3 have been obtained.

It can be seen from Table 15.3 that ratings in the GOOD MOOD condition are higher than those in the BAD MOOD condition; scores in the GOOD MOOD have greater variability, as shown by the standard deviation. Inspection of histograms (not shown here) shows us that data are not normally distributed, and we have a small sample as well. Therefore the most appropriate measure of central tendency is the median rather than the mean. Additionally, we should not use the t-test, using instead its non-parametric equivalent, which in this case is the Mann–Whitney.

In the case of Mann–Whitney, all the participants' scores are ranked from lowest to highest, and then the test calculates the number of times one condition is ranked higher than the other.

Table 15.3 Descriptive statistics obtained from the *Explore* procedure for participants in GOOD MOOD and BAD MOOD conditions

GOOD MOOD				BAD MOOD		
Mean	SD	Median		Mean	SD	Median
11.2	5.9	14.0		6.9	2.5	7.0

The table below shows the ratings given for the two conditions, and the ranks given to the scores. Although there are two conditions, both sets of scores are considered together in the ranking process. You have learned how to rank scores in Chapter 2. Here the lowest score is 3 (in the GOOD MOOD condition) and therefore this is given the first rank. The second lowest score is 4 (which occurs twice in the BAD MOOD condition). Therefore we have to share ranks 2 and 3 between the two scores $(2 + 3 \div 2 = 2.5)$. Once we have ranked all the data, we add the ranks, separately for each condition.

GOOD MOOD		BAD MOOD	
Score	Rank 1	Score	Rank 2
7.00	6	4.00	2.5
15.00	11	6.00	4
14.00	10	11.00	9
3.00	1	7.00	6
17.00	12	9.00	8
		4.00	2.5
		7.00	6
$n_1 = 5$ $\Sigma = 40$		$n_2 = 7$ $\Sigma = 38$	
Mean rank = 8		Mean rank = 5.4	

Lowest score, so we rank this 1

If there is no difference between the two groups, then high ranks and low ranks will occur roughly equally in the two groups, and then the sum of the ranks will be similar. As you can see above, most of the high ranks are in one group, i.e. the GOOD MOOD group, and most of the low ranks in the BAD MOOD group. Therefore the sum of the ranks is higher in the GOOD MOOD group. However, since there are different numbers of participants in the two conditions, we need to find the mean rank. Just looking at the data is often quite useful, but it is quite difficult to see whether the high and low ranks are equally distributed throughout both conditions just by looking at the raw data. It can be seen that the mean rank of the GOOD MOOD group (8) is higher than the mean rank of the BAD MOOD group (5). This tells us that the groups are different, and the statistic (U) that is calculated (based on the number of participants in each group, and the sum of the ranks) will be associated with a low probability value. This will tell us the likelihood of such a result occurring by sampling error. So how likely is it that our difference in ranks has arisen by sampling error?

SPSSFW: two-sample test for independent groups – Mann–Whitney

Choose *Analyze*, *Nonparametric Tests* and *2 Independent Samples*:

This opens up the *Two-Independent-Samples* dialogue box:

Move the independent variable to the *Grouping Variable* box – then click on *Define groups*, as you did with the t-test. Make sure you define them!

Define the groups in the same way as you did for the t-test and press *Continue*. Make sure the *Mann–Whitney U* option is checked:

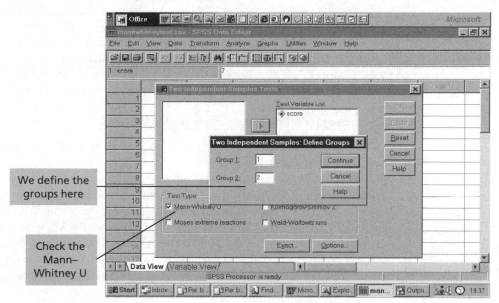

We define the groups here

Check the Mann–Whitney U

Press *Continue*, then *OK*. This gives you your output.

Look at the following output from SPSSFW. The first section of the output shows the mean ranks of both groups, and the sum of ranks. You can check the number of participants in each condition:

Ranks

	mood	N	Mean Rank	Sum of Ranks
SCORE	good mood	5	8.00	40.00
	bad mood	7	5.43	38.00
	Total	12		

The next section shows the value of the test statistic, in this case the Mann–Whitney U, which is 10.00.

Test Statistics[b]

	SCORE
Mann–Whitney U	10.000
Wilcoxon W	38.000
Z	−1.229
Asymp. Sig. (2-tailed)	.219
Exact Sig. [2*(1-tailed Sig.)]	.268[a]

This is the probability level associated with our two-tailed hypothesis

a. Not corrected for ties.
b. Grouping Variable: mood

15.2.3 Important parts of the output

The output shows you the value of Mann–Whitney U, which is 10 (and also the equivalent value of W). We are only interested in U, however, although the conversion to a z-score is useful to us, because a z-score gives us a measure of effect size (see page 95). The associated probability level is 0.22. This means that, assuming the null hypothesis to be true, there is a 22% chance of finding a U-value of 10. We are not willing to take such a risk, and so we conclude that we do not have enough evidence to conclude that participants' ratings of attractiveness are influenced by whether the actor is in a good or bad mood.

The textual part of the results might read as follows:

Histograms for the two conditions were inspected separately. As data were skewed, and participant numbers were small, the most appropriate statistical test was Mann–Whitney. Descriptive statistics showed that participants who rated the attractiveness of an actor in a GOOD MOOD gave higher ratings (median = 14) than participants who rated her in a BAD MOOD (median = 7). However, the Mann–Whitney U was found to be 10 ($z = -1.23$) with an associated probability of 0.22, which shows that it is possible that the higher ratings in the GOOD MOOD condition were due to sampling error. There is not enough evidence, then, to conclude that participants are influenced by the mood of actors when making judgements on their attractiveness.

Example from the literature: pregnant women and HIV

The results shown in Table 15.4 are taken from a paper written by Sherr *et al.* (1996) on HIV. They compared pregnant women who said they would have an HIV test if offered, and pregnant women who said they would not, on different variables ($n = 76$). A subset of the results that they presented are reported below.

You can see that Sherr *et al.* reported the 'non-significant' comparisons as well as the ones declared statistically significant. Notice that they have reported exact probability levels of the variables that they consider statistically significant. Giving the z-value as well as the U-value (the Mann–Whitney test statistic) also enables you to visualise the strength of the difference. For instance, 'Worry about having HIV test' shows that the difference between the expected mean difference (between the two

Table 15.4 Results section from Sherr *et al.* (1996, by permission of Taylor & Francis Ltd. www.tandf.co.uk/journals)

Variable	Test of independence Mann–Whitney U test	Significance
Age	$U = 199.5, z = -0.269$	n.s.
Number of previous pregnancies	$U = 130.0, z = 1.975$	0.05
Duration of current pregnancy	$U = 195.0, z = -0.369$	n.s
Amount known about HIV/AIDS	$U = 152.5, z = 1.428$	n.s.
Worry about having HIV test	$U = 91.0, z = 2.363$	0.02
Resentment at having HIV test	$U = 79.5, z = 2.055$	0.05

conditions) and the actual mean difference is almost 2.5 standard deviations.[1] From the table presented, however, you cannot tell the *direction* of the difference. In other words, which group scores the highest on 'Worry about having HIV test'? We cannot tell from the table presented; we would need to look at a table of means or read the paper in its entirety. Also, some U-values are associated with positive z-values, and some with negative values. This reflects the direction of the difference. However, we would need to read the original article to interpret the results in more detail. (The reference is given at the end of this chapter, in case you want to do so.) Since the authors have given us exact probabilities of some of the results, they could have also let us know the exact probabilities for the others. So that in addition to seeing 'n.s.' against 'Age', why not report the exact probability as well? It is good practice to report exact probabilities, so that the reader can confirm the results for themselves, rather than relying totally on the interpretation given by the authors of the paper.

Activity 15.2

Look at the following output for a Mann–Whitney analysis carried out on an experimental vs. control group. The dependent variable was a rating called SCORE. The researcher hypothesises that the experimental group will score significantly higher.

Mann–Whitney
Ranks

	GROUP	N	Mean Rank	Sum of Ranks
SCORE	experimental	5	9.30	46.50
	control	7	4.50	31.50
	Total	12		

Test Statistics[b]

	SCORE
Mann-Whitney U	3.500
Wilcoxon W	31.500
Z	−2.298
Asymp. Sig. (2-tailed)	.022
Exact Sig. [2*(1-tailed Sig.)]	.018[a]

SPSS now gives two sorts of significance tests for crosstabs and non-parametric tests. Asymp. Sig. stands for Asymptotic Significance and is based on large samples. Exact Sig. is used when the data is small, unbalanced or does not meet the assumption of normality

a. Not corrected for ties.
b. Grouping Variable: GROUP

What can you conclude from this analysis?

---

[1] In this case we are referring to differences in ranks rather than raw scores.

SPSSFW exercise

Exercise 2

A psychology lecturer is carrying out a small pilot study to discover whether students prefer learning her advanced statistics module by means of traditional lectures or a problem-based learning (PBL) approach. There are only 12 people in the group. Six are allocated to the 'traditional' group and six to the PBL group. She thus delivers the module twice on different days (she is very keen!). As she wants to know what the students feel about their learning, as well as taking performance measures she asks them to rate their enjoyment of the course (1–7, where 1 is not at all enjoyable and 7 is extremely enjoyable), along with various other measures. She does not make a prediction as to which approach will be the most enjoyable for students. Here are the data:

PBL	Traditional
5	4
7	6
4	4
5	4
7	1
6	2

Enter the data into SPSSFW and perform a Mann–Whitney test. Give a written explanation of the meaning of the results.

15.2.4 Alternative to the paired t-test: the Wilcoxon

The Wilcoxon test also transforms scores to ranks before calculating the test statistic (see page 537).

Consider the following study: general nurses were given a questionnaire that measured how sympathetic they were to ME sufferers; for each nurse, a total score (out of 10) was calculated. They then took part in an hour's discussion group, which included ME sufferers. Later, a similar questionnaire was given to them. This is obviously a within-participants design, as the same participants are being measured in both the 'before' and 'after' conditions. We will make a directional hypothesis here. A directional hypothesis should be made when there is evidence to support such a direction, e.g. from past research. Our hypothesis is that there will be a significant difference between the scores before and after the discussion, such that scores after the discussion will be higher. Note that this is a one-tailed hypothesis, because we have specified the direction of the difference. The nurses' scores on the questionnaires are shown in Table 15.5.

With small samples, sometimes data are skewed, and the mean may not be appropriate – in which case, report the median. You will need to look at histograms to discover whether this is the case.

Table 15.5 Nurses' sympathy scores before and after discussion

Before discussion	After discussion
5.00	7.00
6.00	6.00
2.00	3.00
4.00	8.00
6.00	7.00
7.00	6.00
3.00	7.00
5.00	8.00
5.00	5.00
5.00	8.00

Although the histogram for the BEFORE condition does not look too skewed (see Figure 15.1), the AFTER condition shows negative skew (see Figure 15.2). However, the means and medians are very similar. Summary statistics are shown in Table 15.6.

Figure 15.1 Histogram showing frequency distribution for scores in the BEFORE condition

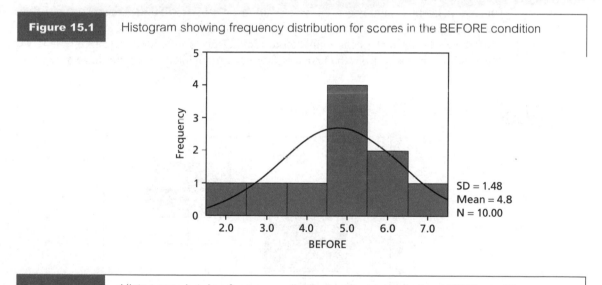

SD = 1.48
Mean = 4.8
N = 10.00

Figure 15.2 Histogram showing frequency distribution for scores in the AFTER condition

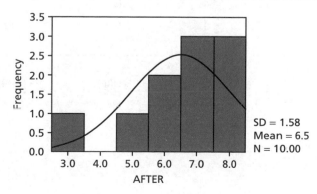

SD = 1.58
Mean = 6.5
N = 10.00

Table 15.6   Summary statistics

BEFORE condition			AFTER condition		
$\bar{X}$	SD	Median	$\bar{X}$	SD	Median
4.8	1.48	5	6.5	1.58	7

Box and whisker plots, again, can give you a good feel for your data (see Figure 15.3). In this case, the box and whisker plot confirms what we have seen from the histograms: the median of the AFTER condition is higher than the BEFORE condition and the BEFORE condition has a larger spread.

Inspection of the descriptive statistics told us that the data in the AFTER condition were negatively skewed. Given that this is the case and we have only ordinal data and a relatively small sample, we would be wise to use a non-parametric test. The most appropriate for this study would thus be the Wilcoxon test. There are essentially two stages in calculating the Wilcoxon test: (a) differences between each set of scores are obtained, and (b) the differences are ranked from lowest to highest. We could not do this in the case of the independent design, because it would not make sense to find differences using different participants. Here we have the same participants in both conditions, and so finding the differences between the conditions before ranking gives us a more sensitive test. If we take the second score from the first score for each participant, some will have a negative

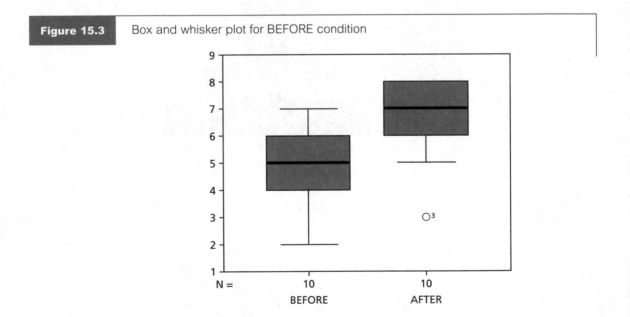

Figure 15.3   Box and whisker plot for BEFORE condition

difference (their rating was higher in the AFTER condition) and some will have a positive difference (their rating was lower in the AFTER condition). Some will be zero, and so we ignore these because they do not give us any information. If there were no significant differences between the two conditions, there would be a similar number of pluses and minuses, as the differences between one participant and another (some positive, some negative) would tend to cancel each other out.

You can see from the table below that there are far more negative signs than positive. The test also takes into account the strength of the differences – by ranking the differences.

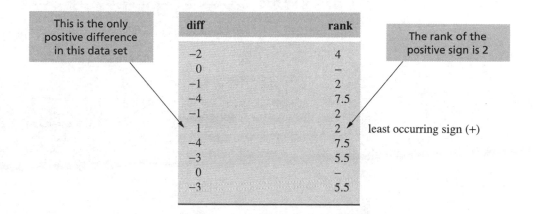

	This is the only positive difference in this data set	diff	rank	The rank of the positive sign is 2	
		−2	4		
		0	–		
		−1	2		
		−4	7.5		
		−1	2		
		1	2		least occurring sign (+)
		−4	7.5		
		−3	5.5		
		0	–		
		−3	5.5		

Once we have found the difference between scores, we rank the scores in the same way as before, ignoring the signs. (Of course, we keep talking about 'we' doing this, and 'we' doing that, but in reality it will be the statistical package that is doing it – we are only going into this detail in order to help you conceptualise what is happening when the test is performed.) We ignore ties where the difference between the two scores is zero – these are not ranked at all. The lowest score is 1, and there are three of them. So the mean of ranks 1, 2 and 3 is 2 $((1 + 2 + 3) \div 3 = 2)$.

The sum of the ranks of the least occurring sign (in the above case, the pluses) gives us our test statistic, which we call t. In this case, a positive rank has occurred once only. There are seven negative ranks. Therefore the 'least occurring sign' is positive. We then add up the *ranks* of the positive differences. (If there had been three participants who had scored lower in the AFTER condition, there would have been three positive scores; then we would have added up the ranks of the three pluses.) There is only one plus sign, and this has the rank of 2. Therefore, $t = 2$. What we want now is for our computer package to confirm our hand calculations and to give us the likelihood of $t = 2$ having occurred by sampling error.

SPSSFW: two-sample test for repeated measures – Wilcoxon

Choose *Analyze*, *Nonparametric Tests* and *2 Related Samples*:

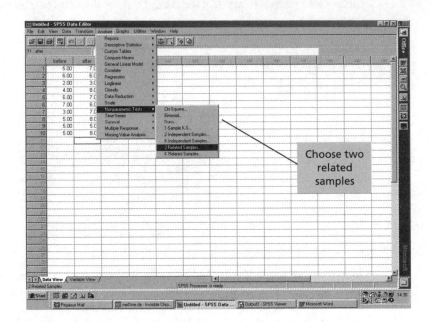

This gives the *Two-Related-Samples Test* dialogue box:

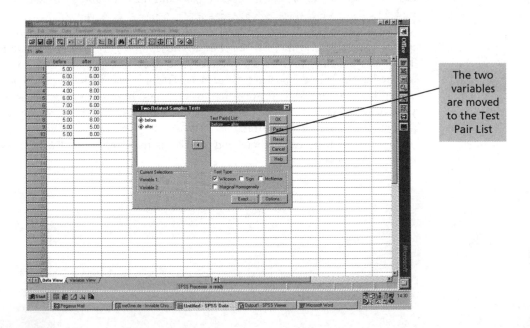

Move the two variables of interest from the left-hand side to the *Test Pair(s) List* on the right-hand side. Make sure the *Wilcoxon* option is checked.

If you want descriptive statistics, you will need to press the *Options* button. Then press *OK*.

This will give you the following SPSSFW output:

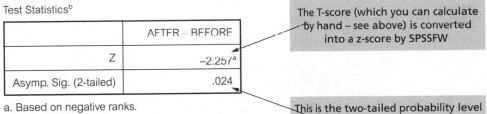

Mean rank of the positive cases

Ranks

		N	Mean Rank	Sum of Ranks
BEFORE – AFTER	Negative Ranks	7[a]	4.86	34.00
	Positive Ranks	1[b]	2.00	2.00
	Ties	2[c]		
	Total	10		

a. BEFORE < AFTER
b. BEFORE > AFTER
c. AFTER = BEFORE

There were two ties (we ranked these as zero)

The next part of our output gives the test statistics:

Test Statistics[b]

	AFTER – BEFORE
Z	−2.257[a]
Asymp. Sig. (2-tailed)	.024

a. Based on negative ranks.
b. Wilcoxon Signed Ranks Test

The T-score (which you can calculate by hand – see above) is converted into a z-score by SPSSFW

This is the two-tailed probability level

The ASL is 0.024. This is a two-tailed probability level, however, and since we made a definite directional prediction, we use a one-tailed probability. To obtain this, we divide the two-tailed probability level by 2, as shown in (2) below:

1. The mean rank of the positive and negative ranks can be obtained. In our example, the mean positive rank = 2. This represents the smallest rank total (t) and the mean negative rank = 4.86. Verify this for yourself from the information above.
2. The t-score is converted into a standardised score (z-score) by SPSSFW. This enables you to visualise how large the t-score is, relative to the mean of the distribution. In our case (see output above) the t-score is over two standard deviations away from the mean of the sampling distribution (which is always 0). The ASL is given, in this case 0.0251. However, since our hypothesis was directional, we halved this figure, to obtain 0.013. Assuming the null hypothesis to be true, therefore, a t of 2 would occur only once in 13/1000 (once in 77) repeat studies, as a result of sampling error.

The textual part of your results might say:

Since the sample size was small, the appropriate measure of central tendency was the median, and the appropriate statistical test was the Wilcoxon test. From Table x^2 it can be seen that the median of the AFTER condition (7.00) is higher than that of the BEFORE condition (5). The Wilcoxon test ($t = 2$) was converted into a z-score of -2.24 with an associated one-tailed probability of 0.01. It can therefore be concluded that the attitude towards ME by nurses is more sympathetic after the nurses have participated in a discussion group, and that such a difference is highly unlikely to have arisen by sampling error.

Activity 15.3

Look at the following output, where participants performed in both of the two conditions. The researcher hypothesised that the groups would differ, but did not make a specific prediction of direction of the difference:

Wilcoxon
Ranks

			N	Mean Rank	Sum of Ranks
COND2 – COND1	Negative Ranks		1[a]	2.00	2.00
	Positive Ranks		6[b]	4.33	26.00
	Ties		0[c]		
	Total		7		

a. COND2 < COND1
b. COND2 > COND1
c. COND1 = COND2

Test Statistics[b]

	COND2 – COND1
Z	–2.028[a]
Exact Sig. (2-tailed)	.043

a. Based on negative ranks.
b. Wilcoxon Signed Ranks Test

What can you conclude from the analysis?

---

[2] You should refer your readers to the table where you give your descriptive statistics.

Example from the literature: medical procedures and HIV

Treloan *et al.* (1996) designed a study on the result of education on medical procedures aimed to minimise exposure to HIV infection. Participants were doctors, nurses and other medical staff. The researchers took measures of how much participants complied with guidelines on minimising exposure to HIV (such as wearing gloves, disposing of needles properly, etc.). This was the PRETEST condition. They then gave the participants an education programme designed to make them aware of the different things they could do to minimise infection (this is called an INTERVENTION). They then measured them later, again on the same measures (this is called the POSTTEST condition). Partial results were as shown in Table 15.7.

The researchers have given the score on the pretest, and the score on the posttest; they then calculated that the change, in the expected direction, was 14%. There were 80 participants in the study. The Wilcoxon test was performed on the data, and the statistic has been converted to a z-score. A z-score of 3.44, as you know, is a large score (nearly 3.5 standard deviations above zero). An associated *p* of 0.0006 shows that such a result is unlikely to have occurred by sampling error, if the null hypothesis is true. Thus they conclude as follows: 'The median difference between pre-education and post-education global compliance scores was 14%, which was significantly different from 0%.'

Table 15.7   Results from Treloan *et al.* (1996)

Median compliant score (%)			Wilcoxon sign rank		
PRETEST	**POSTTEST**	**Change (%)**	*n*	*z*	*p*
67.0	83.0	14	80	3.44	0.0006

SPSSFW exercise

Exercise 3

Six students who had a phobia about mice rated their fear (1 – no fear; 5 – extreme fear) both before and after a behavioural programme designed to overcome that fear. The hypothesis was one-tailed: fear would be reduced after the programme.

Participant	Before	After
1	5	3
2	4	4
3	4	2
4	3	1
5	5	3
6	5	4

Enter the data into SPSSFW and perform a Wilcoxon test. Give a written explanation of the meaning of the results to your friend.

15.3 Alternatives to ANOVA

15.3.1 Kruskal–Wallis one-way analysis of variance (for independent groups)

Kruskal–Wallis is the non-parametric equivalent of ANOVA, and is a generalisation of the Mann–Whitney test. In other words, it is like a Mann–Whitney, but is used when you have more than two groups. The Kruskal–Wallis is used when your data do not meet the assumptions required for the parametric ANOVA. You do not have to worry about the shape of the distribution of scores for Kruskal–Wallis; they do not need to be normally distributed. All the conditions should have a similar shape, however. The formula for Kruskal–Wallis is based on the *ranks* of the scores, rather than the scores themselves. The test looks for a significant difference between the mean ranks of some or all of the conditions (similar to ANOVA above). Again, this test will not tell you which conditions are different from each other – just that there *is* a difference, somewhere.

Just as in the Mann–Whitney, the scores are ranked across the groups. Then the mean rank for each group is calculated. If there are no significant differences between the groups, the mean ranks will tend to be similar. So far we have discussed cases where we have randomly allotted participants to groups. This is the best situation for us, as psychologists, because then we are more certain that our experimental manipulation caused the observed effect, if one is found. Sometimes, however, we want to find differences between already existing groups (e.g. police officers, firefighters and paramedics). These are sometimes called intact groups. If we wanted to find differences between people in different occupations, we would have to find intact groups, as it would not be possible to allocate randomly.

If you hand-calculated Kruskal–Wallis, you would arrive at a test statistic called *H*. Statistical packages often convert test statistics into another statistic – for instance, into z, or χ^2, and this is just what SPSSFW does. In the following example, the intact groups were: security officers (coded 3), college trainees (coded 4) and cooks (coded 5). Kruskal–Wallis was used here because such small participant numbers, and unequal groups of participants, meant that the scores on the dependent variable (work experience) were unlikely to be normally distributed. The question to be answered was: did they differ on a measure of work experience?

Group	Experience
3.00	13.00
3.00	15.00
3.00	11.00
3.00	12.00
4.00	4.00
4.00	4.00
4.00	6.00
4.00	2.00
4.00	5.00
4.00	3.00
4.00	4.00
5.00	9.00
5.00	10.00
5.00	10.00
5.00	5.00

SPSSFW: independent samples test for more than two conditions – Kruskal–Wallis

Select *Analyze, Nonparametric Statistics, K Independent Samples*:

This brings you to the following dialogue box:

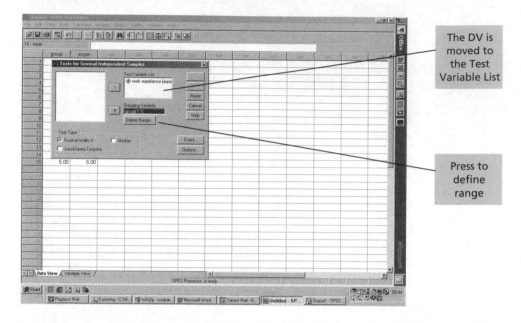

The DV is moved to the Test Variable List

Press to define range

Move the dependent variable from the left-hand side to the *Test Variable List* on the right-hand side. Move the independent variable (the grouping variable) from the left-hand side to the *Grouping Variable* box on the right-hand side. Then press the *Define Range* button. This enables you to define the range of the groups. Here, our groups are coded 3, 4 and 5, so the range is 3–5.

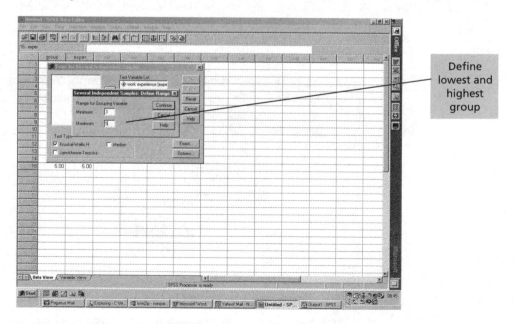

Define lowest and highest group

Enter the range into the dialogue box and press *Continue*. Ensure that the *Kruskal–Wallis H* box is checked. If you require descriptives, then press the *Options* button and select those you require. Otherwise, press *OK*. This gives the following output:

Ranks

	job category	N	Mean Rank
work experience	security officers	4	13.50
	college trainees	7	4.21
	cooks	4	9.13
	Total	15	

The first part of the output shows the mean rank of work experience for each job category. Here, security officers have the most experience.

Test Statistics[a,b]

	work experience
Chi-Square	11.442
df	2
Asymp. Sig.	.003

a. Kruskal Wallis Test
b. Grouping Variable: job category

The test statistics show that χ^2 is 11.44. The achieved significance level is $p = 0.003$.

15.3.2 Pairwise comparisons

Just as in the parametric ANOVA, you cannot tell where the significant differences lie. In the example above, it looks clear that security officers differ from college trainees. Do they differ from cooks, though? What about college trainees and cooks? Unlike ANOVA, there are no post-hoc tests following naturally from Kruskal–Wallis or Friedman's. You can, however, decide to make two comparisons by performing pairwise comparisons by Mann–Whitney tests. Remember that you will need to assess the value of your achieved significance level in the light of your knowledge of multiple testing (see page 231).

Now we come to our write-up. There is no easy way to construct confidence intervals, or effect sizes, because our measure of central tendency is the median rather than the mean. Still, you must do the best you can by reporting the descriptive statistics and giving graphical illustrations where appropriate. The textual part of the analysis might read as follows:

> Since sample size was small, and data were not normally distributed, a Kruskal–Wallis one-way ANOVA was performed on the three occupational groups. As expected, college trainees had the least work experience (median = 4 years) and security officers had the most (median = 12.5 years). Cooks had a median of 9.5 years. Results gave a χ^2 of 11.44 with an associated probability value of 0.003. Thus it was concluded that there are significant differences in the work experience of security officers, college trainees and cooks.

Activity 15.4

Look at the following output, which has been run on three groups of participants. The researcher expects that there will be a difference between the three groups, and that participants in condition 3 will score significantly lower than participants in the other two groups.

Kruskal–Wallis
Ranks

	GROUP	N	Mean Rank
RATING	condition 1	6	10.25
	condition 2	5	9.10
	condition 3	5	5.80
	Total	16	

Test Statistics[a,b]

	RATING
Chi-Square	2.586
df	2
Exact Sig.	.274

a. Kruskal–Wallis Test
b. Grouping Variable: GROUP

What can you conclude from this analysis?

Example from the literature: thinking in mood-disturbed people

Byrne and MacLeod (1997) conducted a study to examine aspects of future thinking in mood-disturbed participants. Participants who were either anxious, anxious and depressed (mixed) or neither were presented with a range of future positive and negative events and asked to provide explanations as to why those events would or would not happen to them.

There were 25 participants in each group. As a manipulation check (to check that the depressed participants showed higher depression scores than the other groups and that the anxious participants showed higher anxiety scores than the other groups, and so on) the authors tested whether the three groups were significantly different. The authors say:

> *Group differences in anxiety and depression scores were considered using Kruskal–Wallis . . . since parametric assumptions were not met. There were significant group differences on both measures ($p < .001$). Anxious mixed groups differed significantly from controls on the anxiety measure. . . . All three groups differed significantly on the depression measure (mean scores were 0, 1 and 4.2 for control, anxious and mixed groups respectively).*

SPSSFW exercise

Exercise 4

As part of their joint year project on the usefulness of therapy for sufferers of migraine, Nyashia and George have randomly allotted 18 migraine sufferers to three groups. Group 1 has six one-hour sessions of group counselling with a trainee counsellor; group 2 has six one-hour self-help sessions (not led by a facilitator; the agenda is determined by the group members themselves); and group 3 consists of migraine sufferers who would like to take part in the group therapy or self-help, but who have to wait. Nyashia and George expect that the counselling and self-help groups will rate themselves as suffering less than the waiting list control group when they rate themselves at the second time point. At the beginning of the study, sufferers rate their symptoms, over the past month, from 0 (not suffering) to 5 (terrible suffering). Fourteen weeks later, they rate their symptoms (in the past month) again. The data follow. Enter the data in SPSSFW and save this as a datafile.

Since the group sizes are small the scores are self-ratings and the data are not normally distributed; non-parametric tests are recommended. Perform *two* Kruskal–Wallis, one on the symptoms at the beginning of the study, and one on the symptoms 14 weeks later.

Write up the results in the form of a short paragraph, explaining the meaning of the results in terms of the study.

Group	Symptom 1	Symptom 2
1.00	3.00	1.00
1.00	4.00	3.00
1.00	5.00	4.00
1.00	2.00	2.00
1.00	3.00	1.00
2.00	4.00	2.00
2.00	5.00	5.00
2.00	4.00	3.00
2.00	2.00	2.00
2.00	3.00	5.00
2.00	2.00	2.00
3.00	4.00	5.00
3.00	5.00	3.00
3.00	4.00	4.00
3.00	2.00	4.00
3.00	3.00	6.00
3.00	2.00	2.00
3.00	3.00	3.00

15.3.4 Friedman's analysis of variance test: repeated-measures design

Friedman's ANOVA is the non-parametric equivalent of the repeated-measures ANOVA, and is a generalisation of the Wilcoxon test. In other words, it is the Wilcoxon test applied to more than two groups. As in the Kruskal–Wallis, the formula for this test involves the ranks of the scores rather than the scores themselves.

The test, confusingly, is called a two-way ANOVA. This is because some people consider the participants as a factor, in a repeated-measures design, as we have mentioned previously (see Chapter 9, page 292). It is, however, what we know as a one-way. In the following output, participants rated how alert they felt at various times of the day (on a scale of 1–5).

Morning	Lunchtime	Afternoon
1.00	2.00	3.00
2.00	4.00	5.00
1.00	2.00	2.00
2.00	1.00	3.00
1.00	3.00	3.00
2.00	5.00	5.00
1.00	2.00	3.00
2.00	2.00	2.00
1.00	3.00	3.00
2.00	1.00	3.00

SPSSFW: repeated-measures test for more than two conditions – Friedman's test

Select *Analyze, Nonparametric Tests, K Related Samples*:

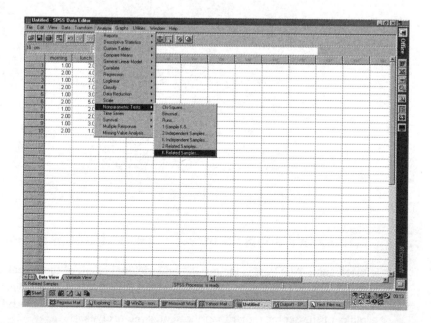

This brings you to the following dialogue box:

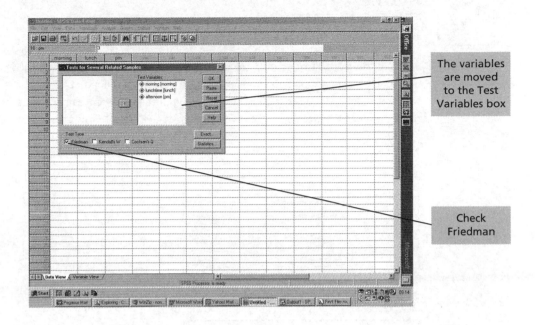

Move the test variables from the left-hand side to the right-hand side. Ensure that the *Friedman* box is checked. Choosing the *Statistics* option will enable you to obtain descriptives. Press *OK*. This obtains the following output:

Ranks

	Mean Rank
morning	1.30
lunchtime	2.00
afternoon	2.70

Test Statistics[a]

N	10
Chi-Square	12.250
df	2
Asymp. Sig.	.002

a. Friedman Test

The χ^2 value is 12.25, with an associated probability of 0.002. The differences found between participants at different times of the day are unlikely to be due to sampling error.

Activity 15.5

Look at the following output from a three-group analysis. Participants were people with a chronic illness, who declined to take part in a behavioural intervention designed to help them. Measures of depression were taken at three timepoints for all participants. The researcher predicted that there would be significant differences between scores at the three different timepoints, but he did not predict the direction of the difference.

Friedman
Ranks

	Mean Rank
TIME1	1.31
TIME2	1.88
TIME3	2.81

Test Statistics[a]

N	8
Chi-Square	12.250
df	2
Exact Sig.	.002

a. Friedman Test

What can you conclude from this analysis?

Example from the literature:
brain injury and stability of outcome

A high percentage of the estimated 5 000 000 traumatic brain injuries in the United States every year occur in young people, who will face many years of neurobehavioural and economic consequences. Ashley *et al.* (1997) looked at 332 people up to 14 years after discharge from post-acute rehabilitation after traumatic brain injury. They wanted to find which variables best predicted stability of outcome. Many of their variables were suitable for analysis by parametric statistics but one was not – the Occupational Status Scale (OSS). Ashley *et al.* wanted to determine whether occupational status changed over three timepoints – admission for traumatic brain injury, discharge after rehabilitation and at follow-up. They therefore used a Friedman's ANOVA – and found that occupational status showed a significant decrease in status at follow-up.

SPSSFW exercise

Exercise 5

Ten participants in a cognitive experiment learn low, medium and high frequency words. Later they repeat as many words as they can remember in three minutes. The under-graduate student carrying out this project hypothesises that there will be a greater number of words recalled in the high frequency condition. The scores under the three conditions are as follows:

Low	Medium	High
10.00	15.00	25.00
5.00	8.00	17.00
7.00	9.00	18.00
8.00	16.00	25.00
10.00	9.00	8.00
15.00	18.00	20.00
21.00	29.00	31.00
18.00	25.00	31.00
20.00	36.00	40.00
8.00	16.00	30.00

Perform a Friedman's ANOVA for participants at the three timepoints. Was the hypothesis supported? Give your results, making sure you explain them in terms of the experiment.

Summary

- The tests used in this chapter are non-parametric tests, to be used when it is not possible to use parametric tests.

- Non-parametric tests transform the data as a first stage in calculating the test statistic.

- Non-parametric tests do not require normally distributed data nor large samples.

- The non-parametric equivalent of Pearson's r is Spearman's rho.

- The non-parametric equivalents of the t-test are Mann–Whitney for independent samples, and the Wilcoxon for related samples.

- The non-parametric equivalents of ANOVA are the Kruskal–Wallis for independent samples, and Friedman's ANOVA for related samples.

MULTIPLE CHOICE QUESTIONS

1. The Wilcoxon matched pairs signed-ranks test (the Wilcoxon) is appropriate for:
   (a) Within-participants designs
   (b) Between-participants designs
   (c) Matched-participants designs
   (d) Both (a) and (c) above

2. To assess the difference in scores from two conditions of a between-participants design, with ranked data, you would use:
   (a) The independent t-test
   (b) The Wilcoxon
   (c) Related t-test
   (d) Mann–Whitney

3. Look at the following partial printout of a Mann–Whitney U analysis from SPSSFW:

Ranks

	group	N	Mean Rank	Sum of Ranks
SCORE	Group 1	8	8.50	68
	Group 1	8	8.50	68
	Total	16		

Test Statistics[a]

	SCORE
Mann–Whitney U	32.0
Wilcoxon W	68.0

The above information suggests that:
   (a) There will be a statistically significant difference between conditions
   (b) There will not be a statistically significant difference between conditions
   (c) The results are indeterminate
   (d) None of the above

4. The Wilcoxon matched-pairs signed ranks test can be used when:
   (a) There are two conditions
   (b) The same participants take part in both conditions
   (c) There is at least ordinal level data
   (d) All of the above

5. The Mann–Whitney U involves:
    (a) The difference in the means for each condition
    (b) The sum of the ranks for each condition
    (c) Finding the difference in scores across conditions, then ranking these differences
    (d) The difference in ranks across conditions

6. A Mann–Whitney test gives the following result:

    $U = 9, p = 0.1726$ (2-tailed probability)

    The researcher, however, made a prediction of the direction of the difference, and therefore needs to know the one-tailed probability. This is:
    (a) 0.0863
    (b) 0.863
    (c) 0.1726
    (d) Indeterminate

7. If, in a repeated-measures design with two conditions, you have a small number of participants, with skewed, ordinal data, the most appropriate inferential test is:
    (a) Unrelated t-test
    (b) Related t-test
    (c) Mann–Whitney U test
    (d) Wilcoxon

8. If a Wilcoxon test shows that $t = 3$ with an associated probability of 0.02, this means:
    (a) Assuming the null hypothesis to be true, a t-value of 3 would occur 2% of the time through sampling variation
    (b) We are 98% certain that our results are statistically significant
    (c) Given our data, we expect to find a t-value of 3 occurring 2% of the time through chance
    (d) If the null hypothesis is not true, then a t-value of 3 would occur 2% of the time through sampling variation

9. A t-value of 3 has been converted into a z-score of −3.2. This means:
    (a) The calculations are incorrect
    (b) There is not likely to be a statistically significant difference between conditions
    (c) There is likely to be a statistically significant difference between conditions
    (d) The results are indeterminate

Questions 10 to 12 relate to the following output:

Kruskal–Wallis
Ranks

	GROUP	N	Mean Rank
SCORE	1.00	5	4.00
	2.00	5	7.30
	3.00	5	12.70
	Total	15	

Test Statistics[a,b]

	SCORE
Chi-Square	9.785
df	2
Asymp. Sig.	.008

a. Kruskal–Wallis Test
b. Grouping Variable: GROUP

10. Which is the most sensible conclusion?

   (a) There are no significant differences between the three groups, $p > 0.05$
   (b) There are significant differences between the groups, $p = 0.008$
   (c) There are no significant differences between the groups, $p = 0.008$
   (d) Impossible to tell

11. Which group had the highest scores?

   (a) Group 1
   (b) Group 2
   (c) Group 3
   (d) Cannot tell

12. How many participants were in the study?

   (a) 5
   (b) 10
   (c) 15
   (d) 20

Questions 13 to 15 relate to the following output:

Friedmans
Ranks

	Mean Rank
BEFORE	1.50
AFTER	2.29
FOLLOWUP	2.21

Test Statistics[a]

N	7
Chi-Square	2.960
df	2
Asymp. Sig.	.228

a. Friedman Test

13. Which is the most sensible conclusion?

   (a) There are differences between the groups, but these stand a 23% chance of being due to sampling error
   (b) There are differences between the groups, and these are unlikely to be due to sampling error
   (c) There are no differences between the three groups at all
   (d) None of the above

14. How many participants were in the study?

   (a) 7
   (b) 14
   (c) 21
   (d) Cannot tell

15. The participants were measured:

   (a) At two timepoints
   (b) At three timepoints
   (c) At four timepoints
   (d) Cannot tell

Questions 16 to 17 relate to the following table, taken from Holdcroft et al. *(2003):*

Spearman rank correlation coefficients for affective measures and pain

	Pain	P value
Tension	0.04	0.78
Autonomic	−0.09	0.55
Fear	−0.13	0.36
Punishment	−0.24	0.09

16. Which is the most appropriate statement? In general terms, the affective measures and pain show a:

   (a) Weak relationship
   (b) Moderate relationship
   (c) Strong relationship
   (d) Perfect relationship

17. The strongest relationship is between pain and:

   (a) Tension
   (b) Autonomic
   (c) Fear
   (d) Punishment

18. Look at the following text, taken from Daley, Sonuga-Barke and Thompson (2003). They were making comparisons between mothers of children with and without behavioural problems.

> Mann–Whitney U tests were used ... significant differences indicated that mothers of children with behavioural problems displayed less positive initial statements ($z = -4.24$) and relationships ($z = -4.25$), less warmth ($z = -5.08$) and fewer positive comments ($z = -2.82$), all p's < .01

Of the four comparisons, which was the strongest?

(a) Initial statements
(b) Relationships
(c) Warmth
(d) Positive comments

19. Look at the output below.

Correlations

			Rating1	Rating2
Spearman's rho	Rating1	Correlation Coefficient	1.000	.600
		Sig. (2-tailed)	.	.000
		N	70	70
	Rating2	Correlation Coefficient	.600	1.000
		Sig. (2-tailed)	.000	.
		N	70	70

Which is the most appropriate statement? The relationship between the two ratings is

(a) Strong (rho = 0.7, $p < 0.000$)
(b) Strong (rho = 0.6, $p < 0.001$)
(c) Moderate ($r = 0.7$, $p < 0.001$)
(d) Moderate ($r = 0.6$, $p < 0.000$)

20. Look at the following table. Professor Green predicted that strength would relate positively to motivation. Unfortunately the Professor meant to obtain one-tailed p-values. Professor Green wants you to interpret the results below, *for a one-tailed hypothesis*.

Correlations

			Strength	Motivation
Spearman's rho	Strength	Correlation Coefficient	1.000	.347
		Sig. (2-tailed)	.	.094
		N	16	16
	Motivation	Correlation Coefficient	.347	1.000
		Sig. (2-tailed)	.094	.
		N	16	16

The relationship between Strength and Motivation is:

(a) Strong (rho = 0.35, p = 0.094)
(b) Strong (rho = 0.35, p = 0.047)
(c) Moderate (rho = 0.35, p = 0.094)
(d) Moderate (rho = 0.35, p = 0.047)

References

Ashley, M.J., Persel, C.S., Clark, M.C. and Krych, D.K. (1997) 'Long-term follow-up of post-acute traumatic brain injury rehabilitation: a statistical analysis to test for stability and predictability of outcome', *Brain Injury*, **11**(9): 677–90.

Byrne, A. and MacLeod, A.K. (1997) 'Attributions and accessibility of explanations for future events in anxiety and depression', *British Journal of Clinical Psychology*, **36**: 505–20.

Daley, D., Sonuga-Barke, E.J.S. and Thompson, M. (2003) 'Assessing expressed emotion in mothers of preschool AD/HD children: psychometric properties of a modified speech sample', *British Journal of Clinical Psychology*, **42**: 53–67.

Holdcroft, A., Snidvongs, S., Cason, A., Dore, C.J. and Berkley, K. (2003) 'Pain and uterine contractions during breast feeding in the immediate post-partum period increase with parity', *Pain*, **104**: 589–96.

Sherr, L., Jefferies, S., Victor, C. and Chase, J. (1996) 'Antenatal HIV testing – which way forward?' *Psychology, Health & Medicine*, **1**(1): 99–112.

Treloan, C.J., Higginbotham, N., Malcolm, J., Sutherland, D. and Berenger, S. (1996) 'An "academic detailing" intervention to decrease exposure to HIV infection among health-care workers', *Journal of Health Psychology*, **1**(4): 455–68.

Answers to activities, SPSSFW exercises and multiple choice questions

Chapter 1

Activity 1.1

Which of the following are continuous, which are discrete and which are categorical?

- Wind speed – continuous
- Degrees offered by a university – categorical
- Level of extraversion – continuous
- Makes of car – categorical
- Football teams – categorical
- Number of chess pieces 'captured' in a chessgame – discrete
- Weight of giant pandas – continuous
- Number of paintings hanging in art galleries – discrete

Activity 1.2

Classify the following studies as either correlational, experimental or quasi-experimental:

(a) Relationship between caffeine intake and incidence of headaches – correlational
(b) Difference between males and females in verbal ability – quasi-experimental
(c) Effect on exam performance of participants being randomly assigned to high noise and no-noise exam conditions – experimental
(d) Difference in self-esteem of tall and short people – quasi-experimental
(e) Relationship between stress and hours spent working – correlational
(f) Difference in anxiety scores between two randomly allocated groups of participants where one group is taught relaxation techniques and the other is not – experimental

Activity 1.3

In the mirror drawing study you would introduce counterbalancing by dividing the participants into two groups. One group would receive the motivation instructions (reward of £5 for doing well) the first time they completed the mirror drawing task, and then have no motivation the second time. The second group of participants would complete the mirror drawing task first without motivation and then they would be offered the motivation the second time they completed the task.

Activity 1.4

To examine the causal relationship between caffeine and mathematical ability you should have several groups that differ in terms of the amount of caffeine taken by participants. You could, for example, have four groups: one group has no caffeine, one group low levels of caffeine, one group moderate levels of caffeine and the final group high levels of caffeine. You would then give each group the same mathematics test to complete. You could then compare the performance of each in the maths test to try to establish a causal relationship between the variables. You could also conduct the study as a within-participants design with each person taking part under all four conditions. Obviously in such a case you would need to use different but equivalent maths tests each time they completed it.

SPSSFW exercises

Exercise 1

1. The IV in Dr Genius's study is whether the participants were presented with adjectives or nouns.
2. The DV in this study is the number of words correctly remembered by each participant.
3. This is a between-participants design because the adjectives were presented to one group and the nouns to another group.
4. This is an experimental design because Dr Genius has randomly allocated the 20 participants to the two conditions.
5. The data for this particular study should be set up as shown below. There should be two variables. The first one should be a grouping variable and contain just a series of 1s and 2s. In our case, 1 might represent the adjective condition and 2 the noun condition. The second variable would contain the number of words remembered by each participant.

Exercise 2

The data from the adjective/noun study should be input as follows if it were a within-participants design:

When we input the data for a within-participants design we need to set up two variables, one for each of the conditions. The first variable we have set up is for the adjectives condition and the second one for the nouns condition.

Multiple choice questions

1. c, 2. c, 3. c, 4. d, 5. d, 6. a, 7. d, 8. d, 9. b, 10. d, 11. c, 12. a, 13. a, 14. a, 15. c, 16. a, 17. b, 18. d, 19. a, 20. d

Chapter 2

Activity 2.1

The most suitable sample for the rugby vs. football fans study would be one group of football fans and one group of rugby fans (although perhaps some would argue that the group of chimpanzees is just as appropriate).

Activity 2.2

The means, medians and modes are as follows:

- Mean = 13.6, median = 12, mode = 12
- Mean = 6.75, median = 5, mode = 5
- Mean = 33.9, median = 25.5, mode = 32

Activity 2.3

The most appropriate measures of central tendency are as follows:

(a)   1 23 25 26 27 23 29 30 – median
(b)   1 1 1 1 1 1 1 1 1 1 1 2 2 2 2 2 3 3 4 50 – mode
(c)   1 1 2 3 4 1 2 6 5 8 3 4 5 6 7 – mean
(d)   1 101 104 106 111 108 109 200 – median

Activity 2.4

No answers needed for this activity.

Activity 2.5

The following are the answers to the questions about the histogram:

(a)   The mode is 4
(b)   The least frequent score is 8
(c)   Four people had a score of 5
(d)   Two people had a score of 2

Activity 2.6

The following are the answers to the questions about the box plot:

(a)   The median is 30
(b)   There are three extreme scores below the box plot itself

Activity 2.7

The scattergram suggests that there is no real relationship between petrol prices and driver satisfaction. The dots in the scattergram appear to be randomly scattered between the axes.

Activity 2.8

If you have the variance of a set of scores you can calculate the standard deviation by taking the square-root of the variance.

The most reasonable definitions of the standard deviation are (c): the standard deviation is a measure of the variation of the scores around the mean and (d): SD is the square-root of the variance.

Activity 2.9

The only one of the examples given that is a normal distribution is (b).

SPSSFW exercises

Exercise 1

1. The IV in the lighting study is the presence or absence of red lighting.
2. The DV is the number of errors made by each data inputter.
3. The box plot for the difference in errors between the two conditions is presented below:

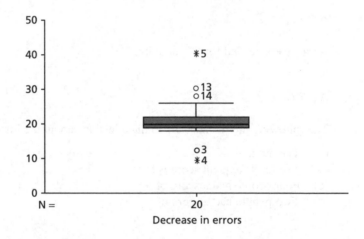

(a) The shortened whisker extending from the lower edge of the box plus the fact that the median is nearer this edge than the middle suggests that the distribution is positively skewed.
(b) The box plot shows several outliers both above and below the inner fences. The outliers are from scores 3, 4, 5, 13 and 14.
(c) The mean and standard deviation of the above set of scores can be obtained using the *Explore* option from the *Summarize* menu: the mean is 21.40 and the standard deviation 6.61.

Exercise 2

1. The IV in the drug study is whether or not the students took drugs during Dr Boering's lectures.
2. The DV is the marks obtained in the end-of-term exam and this is a continuous variable measured with a discrete scale. It is continuous because the underlying knowledge of students of the subject tested in the exam is assumed to be continuous. It is simply measured on a discrete scale (%).

3. The histograms for the data from each condition are as follows:

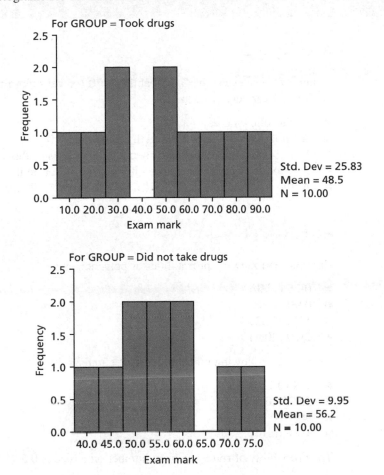

(a) One could perhaps argue the case for both sets of scores being approximately normally distributed. The most frequently occurring scores are in the middle of the distributions and they tail off above and below the modes.

(b) Fortunately, the means and standard deviations for both sets of scores are presented with the histograms. Ordinarily we would have used the *Explore* command to generate both the histograms and the descriptive statistics. The mean and standard deviation for the drugs condition are 48.5 and 25.83 respectively. The mean and standard deviation for the no-drugs conditions are 56.2 and 9.95 respectively. You should be able to see from these that taking drugs has not really made a difference to the overall mean scores but has led to a much greater variability of scores. The standard deviation of the drugs condition is over 2.5 times that for the no-drugs condition.

Multiple choice questions

1. b, 2. c, 3. c, 4. c, 5. b, 6. b, 7. c, 8. a, 9. d, 10. b, 11. a, 12. c, 13. c, 14. d, 15. a, 16 a, 17. b, 18. c, 19. c, 20. d

Chapter 3

Activity 3.1

Which of these events has a probability of 0 (or very close to 0) and which has a probability of 1 (or very close to 1)?

- Night following day – 1
- All politicians telling us the truth all the time – 0
- You finding a million pound cheque in the pages of this book – 0
- A wood fire being extinguished if you pour water on it – 1
- Authors having to extend the deadline for sending in manuscripts for books – 1

Activity 3.2

Express the following probabilities as percentages:

- 0.25 (25%)
- 0.99 (99%)
- 1/3 (33.33%)
- 2/10 (20%)

Express the following probabilities as decimals:

- 1/8 (0.125)
- 12/20 (0.60)
- 30% (0.30)
- 14% (0.14)

The probability of rolling an even number on a dice is 0.5.

Activity 3.3

Which of the following are conditional probabilities?

(a) The probability of being struck by lightning while playing golf – conditional probability
(b) The probability of winning the Lottery – not conditional
(c) The probability of winning an Olympic gold medal if you do no training – conditional probability
(d) The probability of getting lung cancer if you smoke – conditional probability
(e) The probability of manned flight to Mars within the next ten years – not conditional
(f) The probability of having coronary heart disease if you drink moderate levels of beer – conditional probability

Activity 3.4

If you have a negative z-score it will be below the mean. With negative z-scores the majority of the population will score above you.

Activity 3.5

Your z-score for Mathematics would be 1 ((65 − 60)/5). For English it would be 0.86 ((71 − 65)/7). Therefore, your better subject in comparison with the others in your group is Mathematics.

Activity 3.6

The frequency distribution of the means of your samples would be normal in shape.

Activity 3.7

How confident can we be that the population mean is within 1.96 standard errors from the sample mean? We can be 95% confident.

Suppose you have selected a sample of 20 spider phobics and obtained a measure of their fear of spiders. You find that the confidence interval for the mean is 1.5 to 5.6. What does this tell you? This tells us that we could be 95% confident that the population of spider phobics would have a mean fear of spiders between 1.5 and 5.6.

If you had selected 200 spider phobics, would the confidence interval have been larger or smaller than the one reported above? The confidence interval would be smaller than the one reported above.

Activity 3.8

Of the error bar charts presented, only in (a) and (d) are there likely to be real differences between the two groups.

SPSSFW exercises

Exercise 1

1. The dental surgery study is a between-participants design.
2. The descriptive statistics for each group are as follows:

	Soundproofed	Not soundproofed
Mean	9.10	19.90
Standard deviation	3.28	2.81
Standard error	1.04	0.89
95% CIs	6.75–11.45	17.89–21.91

3. The error bar chart for this study is presented below:

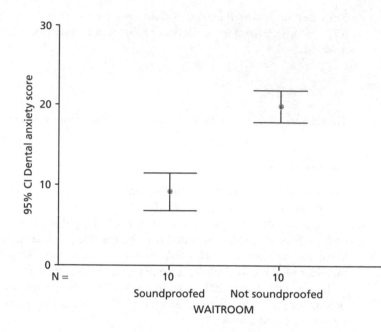

(a) The error bar chart shows that the anxiety scores for the soundproofed waiting room are considerably lower than for the non-soundproofed waiting room. There is also no overlap of the 95% CIs of the two conditions.

(b) Z-score for the first score in the Soundproofed condition = 0.88. Z-score for the first score in Not soundproofed condition = −1.39.

Exercise 2

1. The study conducted by Dr Doolittle is a quasi-experimental design because he has not randomly allocated the participants to the conditions. The conditions consist of natural categories (cats and dogs), therefore he cannot use random allocation.

2. The design is also between-participants because each animal cannot be in both the dog and cat conditions. They are either a cat or a dog, not both.

3. The descriptive statistics for the two species are presented in the following table:

	Dogs	Cats
Mean	110.40	102.00
Standard deviation	12.62	14.28
Standard error	3.99	4.52
95% CIs	101.37–119.43	91.78–112.22

4. The error bar chart is presented below.

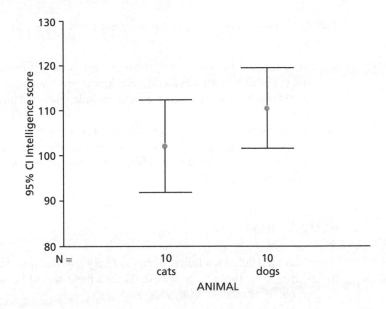

(a) The error bar chart shows that dogs have a higher mean IQ score than do cats; however, there is also a considerable overlap of the 95% CIs of the two species. This might suggest that there is no real difference between the two species because the population means may, in fact, be equal. Remember, with these CIs we are saying that we are 95% confident that the population means fall within the CIs. Therefore, the population means could be the same.

(b) Z-score for the first score for cats = −0.49. Z-score for the first score for dogs = 0.44.

Multiple choice questions

1. c, 2. b, 3. c, 4. d, 5. d, 6. b, 7. d, 8. d, 9. a, 10. b, 11. c, 12. b, 13. b, 14. d, 15. b, 16. d, 17. c, 18. b, 19. d, 20. c

Chapter 4

Activity 4.1

The following are the relevant null hypotheses:

- There will be no difference between males and females in spatial ability
- There will be no relationship between alcohol and number of driving errors
- There will be no difference in reaction times when relaxed and when stressed
- There will be no relationship between the time to the general election and the number of lies told by politicians

Activity 4.2

The descriptions in both (c) and (d) represent the best summaries of the logic of hypothesis testing.

(c)   We measure the relationship between the variables from our sample and then find the probability that such a relationship will arise due to sampling error alone. If such a probability is small, then we can conclude that a genuine relationship exists in the population.

(d)   We measure a difference between our two conditions and then work out the probability of obtaining such a difference by sampling error alone if the null hypothesis were true. If the probability is small, then we can conclude that a genuine difference exists in the populations.

Activity 4.3

If you have a 0.005 probability, then it is likely that one time in 200 will turn out this way by chance. If the probability was 0.01, then there would be a 1 in 100 probability of it turning out by chance.

Activity 4.4

We cannot really tell from the information given which of the two findings are the more important psychologically. Remember statistical significance does not equal psychological significance. Even though Study 2 has a much lower p-value it might have had a very large sample size. We need much more information before we can determine which study is most important psychologically, such as sample size and effect size.

Activity 4.5

Which of the following represent Type I and which represent Type II errors?

(a)   You find in your study that a relationship exists between amount of tea drunk per day and amount of money won on the Lottery. You conclude that to win the Lottery you need to drinks lots of cups of tea – Type I error

(b)   You find in a study that there is no difference between the speed at which cheetahs and tortoises run. You conclude that tortoises are as fast as cheetahs – Type II error

(c)   You find in a study that there is a relationship between standard of living and annual income. However, because the probability associated with the relationship was 0.5 you conclude that there is no relationship between standard of living and annual income – Type II error

Activity 4.6

Which of the following are one-tailed hypotheses and which are two-tailed?

(a) It is predicted that females will have higher empathy scores than males – one-tailed

(b) It is predicted that as annual salary increases so will number of tomatoes eaten per week – one-tailed

(c) It is predicted that there will be a relationship between length of hair in males and number of criminal offences committed – two-tailed

(d) It is predicted that football fans will have lower IQ scores than opera fans – one-tailed

(e) It is predicted that there will be a relationship between the number of books read per week and range of vocabulary – two-tailed

SPSSFW exercises

Exercise 1

1. Professor Yob has conducted a within-participants design as she collects data from each yob at both stadia.

2. Professor Yob has measured the number of arrests, which is a discrete variable (someone cannot be half-arrested).

3. (a) The IV in this study is the change of seating conditions (comfortable vs. uncomfortable).
    (b) The DV is the number of arrests and ejections from the stadia.

4. The prediction is one-tailed because, not only has Professor Yob predicted that there will be a difference between the two stadia, she has also predicted the direction of the difference, i.e. that the comfortable stadium will have fewer arrests/ejections.

5. The null hypothesis would state that there will be no difference between the two stadia in terms of the number of arrests/ejections.

6. The error bar chart will be as follows:

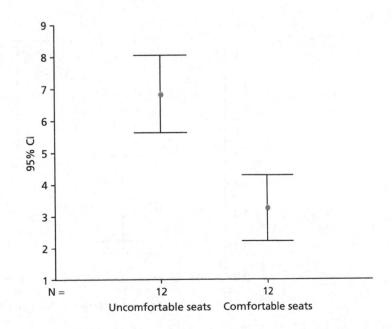

The descriptive statistics for the two stadia are presented in the following table:

	Uncomfortable seating	Comfortable seating
Mean	6.83	3.25
Standard deviation	1.90	1.66
Standard error	0.55	0.48
95% CIs	5.63–8.04	2.20–4.30

7. Converting the first scores in each condition into z-scores gives us a score of 0.62 for the uncomfortable seating condition and a score of -0.15 for the comfortable seating condition.

Exercise 2

1. Dr Pedantic has designed a within-participants study as he is comparing number of split infinitives used by each author before and after *Star Trek*.
2. Dr Pedantic has measured number of whole split infinitives written and is thus examining a discrete variable.
3. (a) The IV in this study is before and after the first showing of *Star Trek*.
    (b) The DV is the number of split infinitives written by the authors.
4. The prediction is one-tailed because Dr Pedantic has predicted the direction of the difference, i.e. that the number of split infinitives will be greatest after showing *Star Trek*.
5. The null hypothesis is that there will be no difference in the number of split infinitives written before and after *Star Trek*.
6. The error bar chart will look like this:

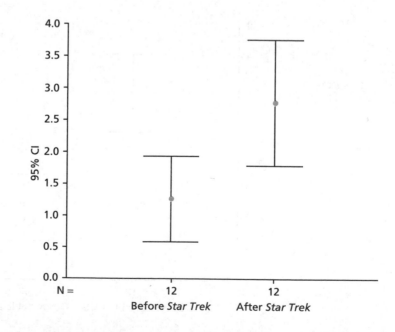

The relevant descriptive statistics are as follows:

	Before *Star Trek*	After *Star Trek*
Mean	1.25	2.75
Standard deviation	1.06	1.54
Standard error	0.30	0.45
95% CIs	0.58–1.92	1.77–3.73

7. Converting the first scores in each condition into z-scores gives us a score of 0.71 for the before-*Star Trek* condition and a score of -0.49 for the after-*Star Trek* condition.

Multiple choice questions

1. a, 2. a, 3. b, 4. a, 5. b, 6. d, 7. c, 8. a, 9. b, 10. c, 11. d, 12. a, 13. d, 14. c, 15. c, 16. d, 17. d, 18. c, 19. d, 20. c

Chapter 5

Activity 5.1

It is hard to find perfect relationships, but you should be able to think of many non-perfect ones.

Activity 5.2

(b)

Activity 5.3

(b)

Activity 5.4

(i) Negative and weak
(ii) Positive and strong

Activity 5.5

(a)

Activity 5.6

(d)

Activity 5.7

(c)

Activity 5.8

(a)

Activity 5.9

1. −0.4983. This would usually be rounded to −0.50.
2. −0.2391. This would usually be rounded to −0.24.
3. The relationship between stigma and QOL is lower after partialling out illness intrusiveness. This shows that the relationship between stigma and QOL is affected (or mediated) by illness intrusiveness.

Activity 5.10

Although some of these correlations are statistically significant at acceptable levels of significance, some (e.g. health, optimism and age) are weak and may not have practical significance.

SPSSFW exercise

1. The correlation between STIGMA and QUALITY OF LIFE is a weak-to-moderate negative association ($r = -0.32$), which may be due to sampling error (0.088).
2. Once ILLNESS INTRUSIVENESS is partialled out, the correlation between the STIGMA and QUALITY OF LIFE reduces considerably ($r = -0.01$, $p = 0.476$), showing that the observed relationship between STIGMA and QUALITY OF LIFE was almost totally due to their relationship with ILLNESS INTRUSIVENESS.

Multiple choice questions

1. a, 2. d, 3. a, 4. b, 5. a, 6. c, 7. c, 8. c, 9. d, 10. c, 11. c, 12. c, 13. c, 14. c, 15. b, 16. d, 17. a, 18. c, 19. c, 20. b

Chapter 6

Activity 6.1

$(70 - 50)/7.5 = 20/7.5 = 2.66$

Activity 6.2

(c)

Activity 6.3

Within participants – repeated measures; related design.
Between participants – independent groups; unrelated design.

Effect sizes (page 223)

1. Age = 0.080
2. Education = 0.361
3. Pack years = 0.139
4. Hours exercised = 0.068
5. Caffeine = 0.053
6. BMI = 0.034
7. Alcohol = 0.111

Calculated as follows:

Age $\qquad \dfrac{58 - 58.9}{\left(\dfrac{10.6 + 11.8}{2}\right)} = \dfrac{-0.9}{11.2} = -0.080$

Pack years $\qquad \dfrac{42.9 - 49}{\left(\dfrac{43.6 + 44.4}{2}\right)} = \dfrac{-6.1}{44} = -0.139$

Hours exercised $\dfrac{2.4 - 2.1}{\left(\dfrac{4.5 + 4.3}{2}\right)} = \dfrac{0.3}{4.4} = 0.068$

Caffeine $\qquad \dfrac{3.3 - 3.5}{\left(\dfrac{3.9 + 3.7}{2}\right)} = \dfrac{-0.2}{3.8} = -0.053$

BMI $\dfrac{19.2 - 19.3}{\left(\dfrac{2.6 + 3.3}{2}\right)} = \dfrac{-0.1}{2.95} = -0.034$

Alcohol $\dfrac{0.5 - 0.7}{\left(\dfrac{1.4 + 2.2}{2}\right)} = \dfrac{-0.2}{1.8} = -0.111$

Educ $\dfrac{13.7 - 12.6}{\left(\dfrac{2.8 + 3.3}{2}\right)} = \dfrac{1.1}{3.05} = 0.361$

Activity 6.4

1. (c)
2. (a) – although the sign does not matter: it could easily have been positive if we had coded/labelled the groups in the reverse order.

SPSSFW exercise

1. An independent groups t-test is suitable for the end-of-year test and episodes of illness.

Group Statistics: episodes of illness

illness	N	Mean	Std. Deviation	Std. Error Mean
boys	10	14.5000	8.960	2.833
girls	10	12.9000	8.048	2.545

Independent Samples Test

		Levene's Test for Equality of Variances		t-test for Equality of Means						
		F	Sig.	t	df	Sig. (2-tailed)	Mean Difference	Std. Error Difference	95% Confidence Interval of the Difference	
ILLNESS	Equal variances assumed	.823	.376	.42	18	.679	1.6000	3.808	−6.401	9.601
	Equal variances not assumed			.42	17.80	.679	1.6000	3.808	−6.408	9.608

Group Statistics: end-of-year test

TEST	N	Mean	Std. Deviation	Std. Error Mean
boys	10	20.000	9.189	2.906
girls	10	11.7000	5.638	1.783

Independent Samples Test

		Levene's Test for Equality of Variances		t-test for Equality of Means						
		F	Sig.	t	df	Sig. (2-tailed)	Mean Difference	Std. Error Difference	95% Confidence Interval of the Difference	
TEST	Equal variances assumed	2.018	.173	2.43	18	.026	8.3000	3.409	1.137	15.463
	Equal variances not assumed			2.43	14.93	.028	8.3000	3.409	1.030	15.570

2. The effect sizes are as follows. Means and standard deviations have been obtained from the above printouts.

   Episodes of illness:

   $$\frac{14.5 - 12.9}{(8.96 + 8.048)/2} = 1.6/8.504 = 0.19$$

   End-of-year test:

   $$\frac{20 - 11.7}{(9.189 + 5.638)} = 8.3/7.414 = 1.12$$

3. This is the sort of thing you would tell your friend:

   We wanted to see whether there were any significant differences between boys and girls on episodes of illness and the end-of-year test. For the episodes of illness, the difference between the two means was very small, only 1.6, which represented 0.19 of a standard deviation. The 95% CI showed that, in the population, the mean difference was likely to lie anywhere between −6.40 and 9.6, which means that if the study were to be replicated, we might find boys to have more episodes of illness, girls to have more episodes of illness, or they would both have the same number of episodes. The t-value of 0.42 gives an associated probability level of 0.679, showing that this result was highly likely to have arisen by sampling error, given that the null hypothesis is true.

On the end-of-year test, however, the boys have performed significantly better than the girls (a mean of 20 and 11.7 respectively). The difference (8.3) represents an effect size of 1.12 standard deviations – a large effect size. The 95% confidence interval shows that the mean population difference is likely to fall somewhere between 1.14 and 15.46. Assuming the null hypothesis to be true, our t-value of 2.43 is unlikely to have arisen by sampling error ($p = 0.026$). We therefore conclude that boys are likely to do better in this test than girls. We might also conclude test bias!

Paired Samples Statistics – Test at beginning and end of year

		Mean	N	Std. Deviation	Std. Error Mean
Pair 1	test at beginning of year	13.400000	20	6.0991803	1.3638182
	test at end of year	15.850000	20	8.5549309	1.9129407

Paired Samples Test

	Paired Differences							
				95% Confidence Interval of the Difference				
	Mean	Std. Deviation	Std. Error Mean	Lower	Upper	t	df	Sig. (1-tailed)
test at beginning of year – test at end of year	–2.450000	5.2763125	1.1798193	–4.919390	.019390	–2.077	19	.026

The group as a whole performed better in the end of year test (mean 15.85) than they did at the beginning of the year (mean 13.4). This difference stood a 2.6% chance of having arisen by sampling error, assuming the null hypothesis to be true.

Multiple choice questions

1. a, 2. b, 3. a, 4. b, 5. b, 6. b, 7. c, 8. c, 9. c, 10. a, 11. a, 12. c, 13. b, 14. c, 15. b, 16. c, 17. d, 18. b, 19. a, 20. c

Chapter 7

Activity 7.1

Rosenthal believes that it is more important to report an effect size than the test statistic and a probability value.

Activity 7.2

(c)

Activity 7.3

(b)

Activity 7.4

This requires you to use the Internet to find some power programs.

Multiple choice questions

1. a, 2. d, 3. c, 4. b, 5. a, 6. c, 7. d, 8. c, 9. d, 10. a, 11. b, 12. d, 13. a, 14. d, 15. b, 16. b, 17. a, 18. b, 19. d, 20. b

Chapter 8

Activity 8.1

(c)

Activity 8.2

The numbers do not add up to 100.

Activity 8.3

(b)

Activity 8.4

(a) Height (cm) and weight (kg) – Pearson's r
(b) Distance run (metres) and time taken (minutes and seconds) – Pearson's r
(c) A person's body shape and occupational level (professional, clerical, manual) – χ^2
(d) Length of finger and length of toe (cm) – Pearson's r
(e) Handedness (right or left) and spatial ability (excellent, average, hopeless) – χ^2

Activity 8.5

(c)

Activity 8.6

(b)

Activity 8.7

None of these is true.

SPSSFW exercises

Exercise 1

Bish *et al.* have used Yates' correction. The probability value = 0.68.

Exercise 2

This is based on your own data.

Exercise 3

1. 8.25
2. $\chi^2 = 3.48$
3. $p = 0.32$
4. Although the results look as if people have a significant preference for certain animals, our results show that a χ^2 result of 3.48 is quite likely to arise from sampling error alone, assuming there are no preferences for particular animals.

Exercise 4

The χ^2 value is 1.26, $DF = 1$, $p = 0.26$. The relationship between smoking and drinking can be explained by sampling error alone. There is no evidence from this study to suggest a relationship between drinking and smoking.

Multiple choice questions

1. b, 2. c, 3. d, 4. a, 5. d, 6. b, 7. d, 8. c, 9. a, 10. a, 11. d, 12. c, 13. d, 14. c, 15. a, 16. b, 17. b, 18. a, 19. a, 20. b

Chapter 9

Activity 9.1

Reasons why scores vary between groups: (a) manipulation of the independent variable: people differ because of the different conditions which they are in; (b) individual differences; (c) experimental error.

Reasons for participants varying within a condition: (a) individual differences and (b) experimental error.

Activity 9.2

(a)

Activity 9.3

The difference between the two sample means for our particular study is a point estimate. If we repeated the study with a different sample, we would find the mean difference was a bit higher, or lower. The confidence limits tell us that we can be confident (expressed as a percentage, e.g. 95%) that the population mean difference will fall somewhere between the lower limit and the upper limit.

SPSSFW exercises

Exercise 1

ONE-WAY ANOVA

ANOVA
SCORE

	Sum of Squares	df	Mean Square	F	Sig.
Between Groups	112.867	2	56.433	12.687	.000
Within Groups	120.100	27	4.448		
Total	232.967	29			

MULTIPLE COMPARISONS

Dependent Variable: SCORE
Tukey HSD

(I) lab groups	(J) lab groups	Mean Difference (I–J)	Std. Error	Sig.	95% Confidence Interval	
					Lower Bound	Upper Bound
morning	afternoon	−4.000	.943	.906	−2.7386	1.9386
	evening	3.9000*	.943	.001	1.5614	6.2386
afternoon	morning	.4000	.943	.906	−1.9386	2.7386
	evening	4.3000*	.943	.000	1.9614	6.6386
evening	morning	−3.9000*	.943	.001	−6.2386	−1.5614
	afternoon	−4.3000*	.943	.000	−6.6386	−1.9614

* The mean difference is significant at the .05 level.

The overall ANOVA shows that there are differences between some or all of the groups that are unlikely to be attributable to sampling error ($F(2,27) = 12.7$, $p < 0.001$); Tukey post-hoc comparisons show that there are no significant or important differences between morning and afternoon groups. However, the evening group differs from the other two groups.

Exercise 2

REPEATED-MEASURES ANOVA

Tests of Within-Subjects Effects
Measure: MEASURE_1

Source		Type III Sum of Squares	df	Mean Square	F	Sig.	Eta Squared
DRUG	Sphericity Assumed	197.821	3	65.940	4.278	.019	
	Greenhouse-Geisser	197.821	2.111	93.693	4.278	.036	
	Huynh-Feldt	197.821	3.000	65.940	4.278	.019	
	Lower-bound	197.821	1.000	197.821	4.278	.084	
Error(DRUG)	Sphericity Assumed	277.429	18	15.413			
	Greenhouse-Geisser	277.429	12.668	21.900			
	Huynh-Feldt	277.429	18.000	15.413			
	Lower-bound	277.429	6.000	46.238			

2. DRUG
Measure: MEASURE_1

DRUG	Mean	Std. Error	95% Confidence Interval	
			Lower Bound	Upper Bound
1	14.286	1.229	11.279	17.293
2	12.857	1.421	9.379	16.335
3	9.857	1.792	5.473	14.242
4	7.429	1.110	4.713	10.144

An inspection of the means showed that means for all conditions were in the expected direction. There was a trend downwards; participants scored highest in the *placebo* condition and lowest in the *high dose* condition. These differences in scores were unlikely to have arisen by sampling error, assuming the null hypothesis to be true ($F(2,13) = 4.28$, $p = 0.036$). It is concluded that the more cannabis smoked, the less well students will perform in arithmetic tests.

Multiple choice questions

1. b, 2. c, 3. b, 4. a, 5. b, 6. c, 7. a, 8. b, 9. a, 10. c, 11. a, 12. b, 13. b, 14. b, 15. d, 16. b, 17. b, 18. b, 19. a, 20. b

Chapter 10

Activity 10.1

With four variables you would have the following sources of variance:

- Main effects: A, B, C, and D
- Interactions: AB, AC, AD, BC, BD, CD, ABC, ABD, ACD, BCD, ABCD
- Error

Activity 10.2

Have a go at describing the following analyses:

(a)   A 6×2 ANOVA – one IV with six conditions and one with two conditions
(b)   A $3 \times 3 \times 3$ ANOVA – three IVs each with three conditions
(c)   A $4 \times 2 \times 4 \times 2$ ANOVA – two IVs with four conditions and two with two conditions
(d)   A $2 \times 2 \times 2 \times 2 \times 2$ ANOVA – five IVs with two conditions

Activity 10.3

Referring to Table 10.4, there is no overlap between the no alcohol and alcohol conditions with no caffeine, suggesting a real difference in the populations. There is little overlap of the CIs for these conditions with caffeine, again suggesting a possible difference in the populations. Comparing the no caffeine and caffeine conditions with no alcohol there is considerable overlap in CIs, suggesting perhaps no real difference in the population. For the no caffeine and caffeine conditions with alcohol, however, there is no overlap of CIs, again suggesting a real difference in the populations.

Activity 10.4

Of the graphs shown, those in (a) and (b) suggest that an interaction is present.

Activity 10.5

Which of the following describe simple effects?

(a) The difference between chewing gum and no chewing gum in the talking condition – simple effect
(b) The overall difference between the tea and non-tea drinking groups – main effect
(c) The effects of noise in only the mathematics exam – simple effect
(d) The effects of cognitive behaviour therapy on the fear responses of all groups of participants – main effect

Activity 10.6

The measures of magnitude of effect that are appropriate for use with ANOVA are both partial η^2 and d.

Activity 10.7

Partial η^2 is calculated as follows:

■ For the main effect of alcohol: 825.021/(825.021 + 110.229)
■ For the main effect of caffeine: 623.521/(623.521 + 189.729)
■ For the interaction: 305.021/(305.021 + 133.229)

Activity 10.8

The d for the simple effects are as follows:
    The differences between caffeine and no caffeine:

■ With alcohol = 3.68
■ Without alcohol = 0.66

The differences between alcohol and no alcohol:

- With caffeine = 1.02
- Without caffeine = 3.79

SPSSFW exercises

Exercise 1

1. The study conducted by Dr Bod is a split-plot design with the year of taking exam a between-participants variable and the subject taken the within-participants variable.
2. One IV is the year of taking the exam (1977 or 1997); the other IV is the subject taken (Maths or English). The DV is the mark given by the examiner for each exam.
3. The ANOVA output is presented below:

GENERAL LINEAR MODEL

Within-Subjects Factors
Measure: MEASURE_1

	SUBJECT	Dependent Variable
	1	MATHS
	2	ENGLISH

Between-Subjects Factors

		Value Label	N
YEAR	1.00	1977	12
	2.00	1997	12

Multivariate Tests[b]

Effect		Value	F	Hypothesis df	Error df	Sig.	Eta Squared
SUBJECT	Pillai's Trace	.000	.001[a]	1.000	22.000	.982	.000
	Wilks' Lambda	1.000	.001[a]	1.000	22.000	.982	.000
	Hotelling's Trace	.000	.001[a]	1.000	22.000	.982	.000
	Roy's Largest Root	.000	.001[a]	1.000	22.000	.982	.000
SUBJECT * YEAR	Pillai's Trace	.004	.088[a]	1.000	22.000	.769	.004
	Wilks' Lambda	.996	.088[a]	1.000	22.000	.769	.004
	Hotelling's Trace	.004	.088[a]	1.000	22.000	.769	.004
	Roy's Largest Root	.004	.088[a]	1.000	22.000	.769	.004

a. Exact statistic
b. Design: Intercept+YEAR
   Within Subjects Design: SUBJECT

Mauchly's Test of Sphericity[b]
Measure: MEASURE_1

Within Subjects Effect	Mauchly's W	Approx. Chi-Square	df	Sig.	Epsilon[a]		
					Greenhouse-Geisser	Huynh-Feldt	Lower-bound
SUBJECT	1.000	.000	0	.	1.000	1.000	1.000

Tests the null hypothesis that the error covariance matrix of the orthonormalised transformed dependent variables is proportional to an identity matrix.

a. May be used to adjust the degrees of freedom for the averaged tests of significance. Corrected tests are displayed in the Tests of Within-Subjects Effects table.

b. Design: Intercept+YEAR
   Within Subjects Design: SUBJECT

Tests of Within-Subjects Effects
Measure: MEASURE_1

Source		Type III Sum of Squares	df	Mean Square	F	Sig.	Eta Squared
SUBJECT	Sphericity Assumed	2.083E-02	1	2.083E-02	.001	.982	.000
	Greenhouse-Geisser	2.083E-02	1.000	2.083E-02	.001	.982	.000
	Huynh-Feldt	2.083E-02	1.000	2.083E-02	.001	.982	.000
	Lower-bound	2.083E-02	1.000	2.083E-02	.001	.982	.000
SUBJECT * YEAR	Sphericity Assumed	3.521	1	3.521	.088	.769	.004
	Greenhouse-Geisser	3.521	1.000	3.521	.088	.769	.004
	Huynh-Feldt	3.521	1.000	3.521	.088	.769	.004
	Lower-bound	3.521	1.000	3.521	.088	.769	.004
Error(SUBJECT)	Sphericity Assumed	879.958	22	39.998			
	Greenhouse-Geisser	879.958	22.000	39.998			
	Huynh-Feldt	879.958	22.000	39.998			
	Lower-bound	879.958	22.000	39.998			

Tests of Within-Subjects Contrasts
Measure: MEASURE_1

Source	SUBJECT	Type III Sum of Squares	df	Mean Square	F	Sig.	Eta Squared
SUBJECT	Linear	2.083E-02	1	2.083E-02	.001	.982	.000
SUBJECT * YEAR	Linear	3.521	1	3.521	.088	.769	.004
Error(SUBJECT)	Linear	879.958	22	39.998			

Tests of Between-Subjects Effects
Measure: MEASURE_1
Transformed Variable: Average

Source	Type III Sum of Squares	df	Mean Square	F	Sig.	Eta Squared
Intercept	151762.521	1	151762.521	2262.107	.000	.990
YEAR	391.021	1	391.021	5.828	.025	.209
Error	1475.985	22	67.089			

4. The F-values and associated p-values are:

Effect	F-value	p-value
Main effect of year	5.83	0.025
Main effect of subject	0.00	0.982
Interaction	0.09	0.769

5. These analyses show that only the main effect of year is probably not attributable to sampling error, if the null hypothesis were true. The main effect of subjects and the interaction have associated probabilities, which suggests that these effects probably are attributable to sampling error.
6. We can see from the ANOVA printout that partial η^2 for the year main effect (0.209) is much larger than the partial η^2 for the main effect of subjects (0.000) and that for the interaction (0.004).

Exercise 2

1. The study carried out by Dr Kid is a completely between-participants design.
2. One IV of age of child (5- and 11-year-old) and one IV of gender (boys and girls). The DV in this study is the score of each participant on the colour perception test.
3. The printout for the ANOVA is presented below:

UNIVARIATE ANALYSIS OF VARIANCE

Between-Subjects Factors

		Value Label	N
AGE	1.00	5 year olds	24
	2.00	11 year olds	24
GENDER	1.00	boys	24
	2.00	girls	24

Tests of Between-Subjects Effects
Dependent Variable: Colour Perception

Source	Type III Sum of Squares	df	Mean Square	F	Sig.	Eta Squared
Corrected Model	181.229[a]	3	60.410	22.702	.000	.608
Intercept	1354.687	1	1354.687	509.093	.000	.920
AGE	28.521	1	28.521	10.718	.002	.196
GENDER	130.021	1	130.021	48.862	.000	.526
AGE * GENDER	22.688	1	22.688	8.526	.006	.162
Error	117.083	44	2.661			
Total	1653.000	48				
Corrected Total	298.313	47				

a. R Squared = .608 (Adjusted R Squared = .581)

4. The F-values and associated p-values are:

Effect	F-value	p-value
Main effect of age	10.72	0.002
Main effect of gender	48.86	0.000
Interaction	8.53	0.006

5. The p-values shown above suggest that the main effects of age and gender and the interaction between these two IVs were unlikely to have arisen from sampling error if the null hypotheses were true.

6. The partial η^2 for the main effects of age and gender and the interaction are 0.196, 0.526 and 0.162 respectively. Thus, the magnitude of the effect due to gender is largest.

7. The interaction can be examined using individual t-tests. The results of such analysis are presented below:

T-TEST
GENDER = BOYS

Group Statistics[a]

	AGE	N	Mean	Std. Deviation	Std. Error Mean
Colour Perception	5 year olds	12	3.5833	2.2747	.6566
	11 year olds	12	3.7500	1.4848	.4286

a. GENDER = boys

Independent Samples Test[a]

		Levene's Test for Equality of Variances		t-test for Equality of Means						
									95% Confidence Interval of the Difference	
		F	Sig.	t	df	Sig. (2-tailed)	Mean Difference	Std. Error Difference	Lower	Upper
Colour Perception	Equal variances assumed	.772	.389	−.213	22	.834	−.1667	.7842	−1.7929	1.4596
	Equal variances not assumed			−.213	18.933	.834	−.1667	.7842	−1.8083	1.4750

a. GENDER = boys

GENDER = GIRLS

Group Statistics[a]

	AGE	N	Mean	Std. Deviation	Std. Error Mean
Colour Perception	5 year olds	12	5.5000	1.3817	.3989
	11 year olds	12	8.4167	1.1645	.3362

a. GENDER = girls

Independent Samples Test[a]

		Levene's Test for Equality of Variances		t-test for Equality of Means						
									95% Confidence Interval of the Difference	
		F	Sig.	t	df	Sig. (2-tailed)	Mean Difference	Std. Error Difference	Lower	Upper
Colour Perception	Equal variances assumed	.312	.582	−5.591	22	.000	−2.9167	.5216	−3.9985	−1.8349
	Equal variances not assumed			−5.591	21.386	.000	−2.9167	.5216	−4.0003	−1.8331

a. GENDER = girls

These t-tests show that for the boys there is no difference in colour perception scores between the 5- and 11-year-olds, beyond that attributable to sampling error ($t(22) = -0.21$, $p = 0.824$). The difference in colour perception scores between 5- and 11-year-old girls is, however, probably not due to sampling error ($t(22) = -5.59$, $p < 0.001$).

Multiple choice questions

1. c, 2. b, 3. c, 4. b, 5. c, 6. a,[1] 7. d, 8. c, 9. c, 10. a,[2] 11. c, 12. a, 13. c, 14. a, 15. d, 16. b, 17. d, 18. c, 19. c, 20. b

Chapter 11

Activity 11.1

Correlational analysis gives us a measure of how closely the datapoints cluster around an imaginary line (r). With linear regression a real line is drawn through the datapoints, in the place where total error is minimised. The line fits the data in the best place possible. The line can therefore be used to assess exactly how much y will change, as a result of change in x.

Activity 11.2

$5 + (2 * 20) = 5 + 40 = 45$

Activity 11.3

The line in the second diagram will predict best, since the datapoints in diagram (b) are nearer to the line of best fit than the datapoints in diagram (a).

Activity 11.4

1. (a)
2. (c)

Activity 11.5

(c)

---

[1] Although there is only a significant main effect of AREA, the p-value for the CARBUS IV (0.052) is close to the traditional criterion for significance and so you probably would want to discuss this main effect.

[2] It is difficult to tell from the graph if there is definitely an interaction and so you would probably want to look at the analysis for a decision on this. If, however, you look at the vertical difference between the two points on the left-hand end of the lines and compare this with the difference between the right-hand end of the lines it does suggest an interaction.

Activity 11.6

Where the researchers are looking at separate variables as well as the joint contribution of variables, you must use Tabachnick and Fidell's second formula (N > 104 + M). As there are four explanatory variables this means the researchers should have used > 104 + 4. So they should have had at least 108 participants.

SPSSFW exercises

Exercise 1

The researcher wanted to find out whether anxiety about examinations was related to the number of hours studied – perhaps people with examination anxiety study less (because studying increases anxiety) or maybe, being anxious, they would study more. The correlation coefficient between the two variables was moderate (0.35). The adjusted R^2 value (0.055) showed that only a small amount in the variation in hours studied could be accounted for by anxiety. The F-value of 1.822 had an associated probability level of 0.20. The slope of the regression line was .393. The confidence limits around the line were −0.236 to +1.021. Thus, in the population, we cannot be sure whether the regression line would be negative or positive. There is no evidence, then, to suggest that anxiety and hours studied are related.

Exercise 2

Professor Lemon wants to see whether Social Support and Personality predict Contentment. Social Support and Personality combined show a very strong relationship with Contentment (0.90). Adjusted R^2 shows that 78% of the variation in Contentment scores can be explained by Social Support and Personality. The F-value of 35.29 shows this result is unlikely to have arisen by sampling error, given that the null hypothesis is true ($p < 0.001$). Both Personality and Social Support contribute to the prediction of Contentment. For every one standard deviation (SD) rise in Social Support, Contentment rises by 0.73 SD and, for every one SD rise in Personality, Contentment rises by 0.38 SD. Thus both Personality and Social Support contribute strongly to Contentment.

Multiple choice questions

1. d, 2. d, 3. a, 4. a, 5. d, 6. c, 7. a, 8. a, 9. a, 10. a, 11. b, 12. c, 13. c, 14. d, 15. b, 16. a, 17. a, 18. b, 19. b, 20. a

Chapter 12

Activity 12.1

There are several ways of explaining a factor. A factor is a hypothetical entity, an underlying construct, of a composite measure that includes a number of correlated variables.

Activity 12.2

Possible names are 'fearful', 'agitated' or 'afraid'. You might have others.

Activity 12.3

See Figure 12.10 on page 427.

Activity 12.4

Three possible names are (1) Quality of Life, (2) Happy, (3) Feeling Down. You probably have other names just as suitable.

Activity 12.5

You must come to your own conclusions!

Activity 12.6

F1 = independence and freedom; F2 = external sources of motivation; F3 = social development; F4 = convenience; F5 = academic motivation.

Activity 12.7

Both shame and guilt are moderately related to submissive behaviour. Guilt shows a weak–moderate association with depression; shame does not.

Activity 12.8

Perfection and ineffectiveness show a moderate association with Factor 1, which was named Physical pain and discomfort. The factor named Gaseousness shows no important relationship with any of the eating disorder variables, whereas the factor that represents Vomiting does – vomiting shows moderate positive relations with ineffectiveness, bulimia and weight discrepancy.

Activity 12.9

(a)

	1	2	3
1	–	30	50
2		–	80
3			–

(b)

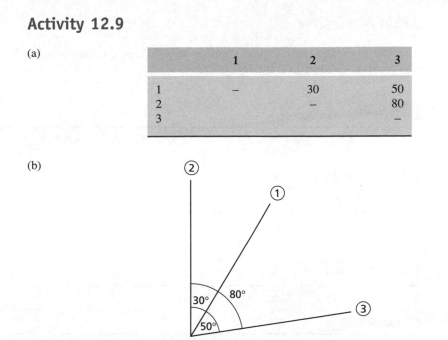

Multiple choice questions

1. a, 2. a, 3. c, 4. b, 5. c, 6. a, 7. b, 8. b, 9. c, 10. c, 11. d, 12. a, 13. d, 14. a, 15. c, 16. c, 17. a, 18. b, 19. b, 20. a

Chapter 13

Activity 13.1

(b)

Activity 13.2

(c)

Activity 13.3

(a)

Activity 13.4

(a)

SPSSFW exercise

1. The scattergram shows that the lines for all three groups are parallel; we therefore meet the assumptions for ANCOVA.

Tests of Between-Subjects Effects
Dependent Variable: SCORE

Source	Type III Sum of Squares	df	Mean Square	F	Sig.[a]	Eta Squared
Corrected Model	214.627[b]	3	71.542	101.425	.000	.921
Intercept	16.204	1	16.204	22.973	.000	.469
MOTIV	101.760	1	101.760	144.264	.000	.847
GROUP	28.335	2	14.167	20.085	.000	.607
Error	18.340	26	.705			
Total	5809.000	30				
Corrected Total	232.967	29				

a. Computed using alpha = .05
b. R Squared = .921 (Adjusted R Squared = .912)

Motivation is clearly related to scores, and so ANCOVA is appropriate. The analysis shows that the differences between conditions ($\eta^2 = 0.61$) are large, and unlikely to have arisen by sampling error ($F = 20.085, p < 0.001$).

Multiple choice questions

1. a, 2. a, 3. d, 4. a, 5. b, 6. a, 7. b, 8. d, 9. b, 10. c, 11. a, 12. b, 13. c, 14. a, 15. b, 16. c, 17. c, 18. b, 19. a, 20. b

Chapter 14

Activity 14.1

Of the studies described, those from (b) and (c) are suitable for analysis using MANOVA.

Activity 14.2

(a) $a + b + c + d + e$: linear combination
(b) $A \times B \times C \times D \times E$: not a linear combination
(c) $(a + b + c + d + e)/2$: linear combination
(d) Extraversion + 2 * Neuroticism − 3 * Psychoticism: linear combination

Activity 14.3

An interpretation of Figure 14.2 is given in the text after the figure.

Activity 14.4

(a) Hotelling's trace – yes
(b) Phil's mark – no
(c) Seth's weakest link – no
(d) Wilks' lambda – yes
(e) Hayley's gamma – no
(f) Pillai's trace – yes
(g) Crossroad's track – no
(h) Roy's largest root – yes

Activity 14.5

(a) Appropriate
(b) Appropriate
(c) Appropriate
(d) Inappropriate

SPSSFW exercises

Exercise 1

1. The assumption of homogeneity of variance–covariance matrices is tested using Box's M test. The details of this are presented below.

Box's Test of Equality of Covariance Matrices[a]

Box's M	2.246
F	.675
df1	3
df2	87120
Sig.	.567

Tests the null hypothesis that the observed covariance matrices of the dependent variables are equal across groups.
a. Design: Intercept+FUEL

If the p-value associated with Box's M is less than 0.05 then we have a violation of the assumption of variance–covariance matrices. In this case the p-value is much greater than 0.05 and so we do not have a violation of this assumption.

The multivariate statistics for this study are as follows:

GENERAL LINEAR MODEL

Between-Subjects Factors

		Value Label	N
FUEL	1.00	Carrot juice fuel	12
	2.00	Mushy pea fuel	12

Box's Test of Equality of Covariance Matrices[a]

Box's M	2.246
F	.675
df1	3
df2	87120
Sig.	.567

Tests the null hypothesis that the observed covariance
matrices of the dependent variables are equal across groups.
a. Design: Intercept+FUEL

Multivariate Tests[b]

Effect		Value	F	Hypothesis df	Error df	Sig.	Eta Squared
Intercept	Pillai's Trace	.973	384.381[a]	2.000	21.000	.000	.973
	Wilks' Lambda	.027	384.381[a]	2.000	21.000	.000	.973
	Hotelling's Trace	36.608	384.381[a]	2.000	21.000	.000	.973
	Roy's Largest Root	36.608	384.381[a]	2.000	21.000	.000	.973
FUEL	Pillai's Trace	.386	6.598[a]	2.000	21.000	.006	.386
	Wilks' Lambda	.614	6.598[a]	2.000	21.000	.006	.386
	Hotelling's Trace	.628	6.598[a]	2.000	21.000	.006	.386
	Roy's Largest Root	.628	6.598[a]	2.000	21.000	.006	.386

a. Exact statistic
b. Design: Intercept+FUEL

Levene's Test of Equality of Error Variances[a]

	F	df1	df2	Sig.
Engine condition	.184	1	22	.672
Number of km per litre	.760	1	22	.393

Tests the null hypothesis that the error variance of the dependent variable is equal across groups.
a. Design: Intercept+FUEL

2. The F-value as calculated using Wilks' lambda is 6.598.
3. As the associated p-value is only 0.006 we can be reasonably confident that the observed multivariate difference between the two fuels is unlikely to have arisen due to sampling error, given that the null hypothesis is true.

4. The univariate ANOVA tests are presented below:

Tests of Between-Subjects Effects

Source	Dependent Variable	Type III Sum of Squares	df	Mean Square	F	Sig.	Eta Squared
Corrected Model	Engine condition	1.500[a]	1	1.500	.421	.523	.019
	Number of km per litre	66.667[b]	1	66.667	13.750	.001	.385
Intercept	Engine condition	704.167	1	704.167	197.766	.000	.900
	Number of km per litre	3266.667	1	3266.667	673.750	.000	.968
FUEL	Engine condition	1.500	1	1.500	.421	.523	.019
	Number of km per litre	66.667	1	66.667	13.750	.001	.385
Error	Engine condition	78.333	22	3.561			
	Number of km per litre	106.667	22	4.848			
Total	Engine condition	784.000	24				
	Number of km per litre	3440.000	24				
Corrected Total	Engine condition	79.833	23				
	Number of km per litre	173.333	23				

a. R Squared = .019 (Adjusted R Squared = –.026)
b. R Squared = .385 (Adjusted R Squared = .357)

The univariate F-tests suggest that only the number of kilometres per litre contributes to the multivariate difference. If we set our overall α at 0.05 we need to divide this by two because we have two univariate tests. We therefore need to check the p-values associated with each of our univariate tests to see if they are in the region of 0.025 or less. If they are in this region then we can be reasonably confident that they are contributing to the multivariate difference. In this case only kilometres per litre has a p-value in this region and therefore this is the only DV that is contributing to the multivariate difference.

5. The correlational analyses are presented below and suggest that there is no correlation between the two variables beyond that attributable to sampling error.

CORRELATIONS

Correlations

		Engine condition	Number of km per litre
Engine condition	Pearson Correlation	1.000	.164
	Sig. (2-tailed)	.	.443
	N	24	24
Number of km per litre	Pearson Correlation	.164	1.000
	Sig. (2-tailed)	.443	.
	N	24	24

6. The effect size for each DV is shown with the univariate analyses. The η^2 for fuel consumption is 0.39 and that for engine condition is 0.02. These suggest that, when fuel consumption is the DV in the univariate analyses, 39% of the variation in fuel consumption is attributable to differences in fuel type. When engine condition is the DV, then only 2% of the variation in engine condition is attributable to differences in fuel type.

Exercise 2

The multivariate analyses for the drinks study are presented below:

GENERAL LINEAR MODEL

Within-Subjects Factors

Measure	DRINK	Dependent Variable
TASTE	1	LAGTASTE
	2	LOUTASTE
EFFECTS	1	LAGPLEAS
	2	LOUTPLSE

Multivariate Tests[b]

Effect			Value	F	Hypothesis df	Error df	Sig.	Eta Squared
Between Subjects	Intercept	Pillai's Trace	.995	984.826[a]	2.000	10.000	.000	.995
		Wilks' Lambda	.005	984.826[a]	2.000	10.000	.000	.995
		Hotelling's Trace	196.965	984.826[a]	2.000	10.000	.000	.995
		Roy's Largest Root	196.965	984.826[a]	2.000	10.000	.000	.995
Within Subjects	DRINK	Pillai's Trace	.600	7.516[a]	2.000	10.000	.010	.600
		Wilks' Lambda	.400	7.516[a]	2.000	10.000	.010	.600
		Hotelling's Trace	1.503	7.516[a]	2.000	10.000	.010	.600
		Roy's Largest Root	1.503	7.516[a]	2.000	10.000	.010	.600

a. Exact statistic
b. Design: Intercept
 Within Subjects Design: DRINK

1. These analyses show that there is a multivariate difference between the two drinks beyond that attributable to sampling error. The F-value of 7.516 has an associated probability of $p = 0.010$.
2. The decision about how to evaluate the relative contribution of the individual DVs to the multivariate difference is dependent upon whether or not the DVs are correlated. The correlation coefficients for the two DVs are shown below:

CORRELATIONS

		Lager: taste	Lager: pleasurable effects
Lager: taste	Pearson Correlation	1.000	−.229
	Sig. (2-tailed)	.	.475
	N	12	12
Lager: pleasurable effects	Pearson Correlation	−.229	1.000
	Sig. (2-tailed)	.475	.
	N	12	12

CORRELATIONS

		Lout: taste	Lout: pleasurable effects
Lout: taste	Pearson Correlation	1.000	−.264
	Sig. (2-tailed)	.	.407
	N	12	12
Lout: pleasurable effects	Pearson Correlation	−.264	1.000
	Sig. (2-tailed)	.407	.
	N	12	12

These correlational analyses show that there are no correlations beyond that attributable to sampling error between the taste and pleasure effects of lager and the taste and pleasure effects of Lout. We could therefore use the univariate tests on the MANOVA printout to examine the relative contribution of each DV to the multivariate difference. This printout is presented below:

Univariate Tests

Source	Measure		Type III Sum of Squares	df	Mean Square	F	Sig.	Eta Squared
DRINK	TASTE	Sphericity Assumed	63.375	1	63.375	16.165	.002	.595
		Greenhouse-Geisser	63.375	1.000	63.375	16.165	.002	.595
		Huynh-Feldt	63.375	1.000	63.375	16.165	.002	.595
		Lower-bound	63.375	1.000	63.375	16.165	.002	.595
	EFFECTS	Sphericity Assumed	1.500	1	1.500	.465	.509	.041
		Greenhouse-Geisser	1.500	1.000	1.500	.465	.509	.041
		Huynh-Feldt	1.500	1.000	1.500	.465	.509	.041
		Lower-bound	1.500	1.000	1.500	.465	.509	.041
Error(DRINK)	TASTE	Sphericity Assumed	43.125	11	3.920			
		Greenhouse-Geisser	43.125	11.000	3.920			
		Huynh-Feldt	43.125	11.000	3.920			
		Lower-bound	43.125	11.000	3.920			
	EFFECTS	Sphericity Assumed	35.500	11	3.227			
		Greenhouse-Geisser	35.500	11.000	3.227			
		Huynh-Feldt	35.500	11.000	3.227			
		Lower-bound	35.500	11.000	3.227			

3. These univariate tests suggest that only the taste DV is contributing to the multivariate difference between the two drinks. The difference in the ratings for pleasurable effects between the two drinks is probably attributable to sampling error ($p = 0.509$). The difference in taste ratings is probably not due to sampling error ($p = 0.002$), suggesting that the young men preferred the taste of Lout to lager.

Multiple choice questions

1. a, 2. b, 3. d, 4. b, 5. d, 6. c, 7. d, 8. a, 9. c, 10. b, 11. c, 12. d, 13. a, 14. c, 15. b, 16. b, 17. b, 18. a, 19. b, 20. c

Chapter 15

Activity 15.1

(a) The strongest correlation is between Dullness and parity (+0.39).
(b) The probability value for the weakest correlation (incisive pressure and parity (0.04)) is $p = 0.80$.

Activity 15.2

The experimental group did score significantly higher than the control group (mean rank 9.30 and 4.50 respectively). The Mann–Whitney value was 3.5 with an associated probability value (one-tailed) of 0.018. The likelihood of this result occurring as a result of sampling error, assuming the null hypothesis to be true, is < 2%.

Activity 15.3

There was a difference in scores between the two conditions – the two-tailed p-value was 0.043. The likelihood of these results occurring by sampling error, assuming the null hypothesis to be true, is less than 5%.

Activity 15.4

It looks as though the researcher's predictions have been confirmed – the mean rank in condition 3 (5.8) is lower than the mean rank of condition 1 (10.25) and condition 2 (9.10). The likelihood of these results being due to sampling error is, however, higher than we are willing to accept ($p = 0.274$).

Activity 15.5

Depression seems to have increased over the three timepoints (mean ranks 1.31, 1.88 and 2.81). The Chi Square value is 12.25. The likelihood of this value occurring by sampling error, given the truth of the null hypothesis, is 0.002. We conclude that the people who declined to take part in the behavioural intervention programme became significantly more depressed over the three timepoints.

SPSSFW exercises

Exercise 1: Spearman's rho

			ORAL	CONFID
Spearman's rho	ORAL	Correlation Coefficient	1.000	−.872
		Sig. (1-tailed)	.	.027
		N	5	5
	CONFID	Correlation Coefficient	−.872	1.000
		Sig. (1-tailed)	.027	.
		N	5	5

The correlation between confidence and performance in the oral examination is −0.872 ($p = 0.027$). Although this is a negative correlation, note that confidence has been coded in the opposite way from performance in the oral examination. Thus the positive relationship between these two variables is confirmed – the more confident the student, the better their performance. The relationship is strong, and is unlikely to have arisen by sampling error.

Exercise 2: Mann–Whitney

Ranks

	GROUP	N	Mean Rank	Sum of Ranks
SCORE	pbl	6	8.67	52.00
	traditional	6	4.33	26.00
	Total	12		

Test Statistics[b]

	SCORE
Mann–Whitney U	5.000
Wilcoxon W	26.000
Z	−2.131
Asymp. Sig. (2-tailed)	.033
Exact Sig. [2*(1-tailed Sig.)]	.041[a]

a. Not corrected for ties.
b. Grouping Variable: GROUP

As the lecturer did not make a prediction as to which approach would be the most enjoyable for the students, she uses a 2-tailed significance level.

The PBL group has scored higher on enjoyment than the traditional group. ($U = 5$, $z = -2.13$, $p = .041$). Her small pilot study shows it might be worth trying out the PBL approach with students taking an advanced statistics module.

Exercise 3: Wilcoxon

WILCOXON SIGNED RANKS TEST

Ranks

		N	Mean Rank	Sum of Ranks
after the programme – before the programme	Negative Ranks[a]	5	3.00	15.00
	Positive Ranks[b]	0	.00	.00
	Ties[c]	1		
	Total	6		

a. after the programme < before the programme
b. after the programme > before the programme
c. before the programme = after the programme

Test Statistics[b]

	after the programme – before the programme
Z	–2.121[a]
Exact Sig. (1-tailed)	.031

a. Based on positive ranks
b. Wilcoxon Signed Ranks Test

Levels of fear were reduced after the programme ($z = 2.12$, $p = 0.031$). It can be seen that the mean rank before the programme (3.00) was reduced to zero after the programme. A z-score of 2.12 has less than a 2% likelihood of arising by sampling error, assuming the null hypothesis to be true (one-tailed hypothesis). We can conclude, then, that the programme was effective in reducing fear.

Exercise 4: Kruskal–Wallis

KRUSKAL–WALLIS

Ranks

	GROUP	N	Mean Rank
SYMPTOM1	1.00	5	9.80
	2.00	6	9.50
	3.00	7	9.29
	Total	18	
SYMPTOM2	1.00	5	6.10
	2.00	6	9.42
	3.00	7	12.00
	Total	18	

Test Statistics[a,b]

	SYMPTOM1	SYMPTOM2
Chi-Square	.029	3.714
df	2	2
Exact Sig.	.994	.157

a. Kruskal–Wallis Test
b. Grouping Variable: GROUP

Ranks are very similar in the three groups, in respect of Symptom 1. The Chi Square value of 0.029 has an associated probability value of 0.986 – these results, then, can be attributed to sampling error – we conclude that there are no significant differences in symptom 1 among the three groups.

For symptom 2, the ranks are more dissimilar – the mean rank for group 3 is 12.00, whereas the mean rank for group 1 is 6.10. For this analysis, the value of Chi Square is 3.7 and the associated probability level is 0.157. This means that there is a 15.7% likelihood of the results being due to sampling error, assuming the null hypothesis is true. For this analysis as well, we conclude there are no significant differences between the groups.

Exercise 5: Friedman's

Ranks[a]

	Mean Rank
low	1.20
medium	2.00
high	2.80

Test Statistics

N	10
Chi-Square	12.800
df	2
Exact Sig.	.002

a. Friedman Test

The Friedman Test shows that the difference between ranks was significantly greater than would be expected by sampling error, assuming the null hypothesis to be true (chi-square = 12.8, $p = 0.002$).

Multiple choice questions

1. d, 2. d, 3. b, 4. d, 5. b, 6. a, 7. d, 8. a, 9. c, 10. b, 11. c, 12. c, 13. a, 14. a, 15. b, 16. a, 17. d, 18. c, 19. b, 20. d

Appendix 1

Table of z-scores and the proportion of the standard normal distribution falling above and below each score

z-score	Proportion below score	Proportion above score	z-score	Proportion below score	Proportion above score	z-score	Proportion below score	Proportion above score
0.00	0.5000	0.5000	1.01	0.8438	0.1562	2.01	0.9778	0.0222
0.01	0.5040	0.4960	1.02	0.8461	0.1539	2.02	0.9783	0.0217
0.02	0.5080	0.4920	1.03	0.8485	0.1515	2.03	0.9788	0.0212
0.03	0.5120	0.4880	1.04	0.8508	0.1492	2.04	0.9793	0.0207
0.04	0.5160	0.4840	1.05	0.8531	0.1469	2.05	0.9798	0.0202
0.05	0.5199	0.4801	1.06	0.8554	0.1446	2.06	0.9803	0.0197
0.06	0.5239	0.4761	1.07	0.8577	0.1423	2.07	0.9808	0.0192
0.07	0.5279	0.4721	1.08	0.8599	0.1401	2.08	0.9812	0.0188
0.08	0.5319	0.4681	1.09	0.8621	0.1379	2.09	0.9817	0.0183
0.09	0.5359	0.4641	1.10	0.8643	0.1357	2.10	0.9821	0.0179
0.10	0.5398	0.4602	1.11	0.8665	0.1335	2.11	0.9826	0.0174
0.11	0.5438	0.4562	1.12	0.8686	0.1314	2.12	0.9830	0.0170
0.12	0.5478	0.4522	1.13	0.8708	0.1292	2.13	0.9834	0.0166
0.13	0.5517	0.4483	1.14	0.8729	0.1271	2.14	0.9838	0.0162
0.14	0.5557	0.4443	1.15	0.8749	0.1251	2.15	0.9842	0.0158
0.15	0.5596	0.4404	1.16	0.8770	0.1230	2.16	0.9846	0.0154
0.16	0.5636	0.4364	1.17	0.8790	0.1210	2.17	0.9850	0.0150
0.17	0.5675	0.4325	1.18	0.8810	0.1190	2.18	0.9854	0.0146
0.18	0.5714	0.4286	1.19	0.8830	0.1170	2.19	0.9857	0.0143
0.19	0.5753	0.4247	1.20	0.8849	0.1151	2.20	0.9861	0.0139
0.20	0.5793	0.4207	1.21	0.8869	0.1131	2.21	0.9864	0.0136
0.21	0.5832	0.4168	1.22	0.8888	0.1112	2.22	0.9868	0.0132
0.22	0.5871	0.4129	1.23	0.8907	0.1093	2.23	0.9871	0.0129
0.23	0.5910	0.4090	1.24	0.8925	0.1075	2.24	0.9875	0.0125
0.24	0.5948	0.4052	1.25	0.8944	0.1056	2.25	0.9878	0.0122
0.25	0.5987	0.4013	1.26	0.8962	0.1038	2.26	0.9881	0.0119
0.26	0.6026	0.3974	1.27	0.8980	0.1020	2.27	0.9884	0.0116
0.27	0.6064	0.3936	1.28	0.8997	0.1003	2.28	0.9887	0.0113
0.28	0.6103	0.3897	1.29	0.9015	0.0985	2.29	0.9890	0.0110
0.29	0.6141	0.3859	1.30	0.9032	0.0968	2.30	0.9893	0.0107
0.30	0.6179	0.3821	1.31	0.9049	0.0951	2.31	0.9896	0.0104
0.31	0.6217	0.3783	1.32	0.9066	0.0934	2.32	0.9898	0.0102

▶

z-score	Proportion below score	Proportion above score	z-score	Proportion below score	Proportion above score	z-score	Proportion below score	Proportion above score
0.32	0.6255	0.3745	1.33	0.9082	0.0918	2.33	0.9901	0.0099
0.33	0.6293	0.3707	1.34	0.9099	0.0901	2.34	0.9904	0.0096
0.34	0.6331	0.3669	1.35	0.9115	0.0885	2.35	0.9906	0.0094
0.35	0.6368	0.3632	1.36	0.9131	0.0869	2.36	0.9909	0.0091
0.36	0.6406	0.3594	1.37	0.9147	0.0853	2.37	0.9911	0.0089
0.37	0.6443	0.3557	1.38	0.9162	0.0838	2.38	0.9913	0.0087
0.38	0.6480	0.3520	1.39	0.9177	0.0823	2.39	0.9916	0.0084
0.39	0.6517	0.3483	1.40	0.9192	0.0808	2.40	0.9918	0.0082
0.40	0.6554	0.3446	1.41	0.9207	0.0793	2.41	0.9920	0.0080
0.41	0.6591	0.3409	1.42	0.9222	0.0778	2.42	0.9922	0.0078
0.42	0.6628	0.3372	1.43	0.9236	0.0764	2.43	0.9925	0.0075
0.43	0.6664	0.3336	1.44	0.9251	0.0749	2.44	0.9927	0.0073
0.44	0.6700	0.3300	1.45	0.9265	0.0735	2.45	0.9929	0.0071
0.45	0.6736	0.3264	1.46	0.9279	0.0721	2.46	0.9931	0.0069
0.46	0.6772	0.3228	1.47	0.9292	0.0708	2.47	0.9932	0.0068
0.47	0.6808	0.3192	1.48	0.9306	0.0694	2.48	0.9934	0.0066
0.48	0.6844	0.3156	1.49	0.9319	0.0681	2.49	0.9936	0.0064
0.49	0.6879	0.3121	1.50	0.9332	0.0668	2.50	0.9938	0.0062
0.50	0.6915	0.3085	1.51	0.9345	0.0655	2.51	0.9940	0.0060
0.51	0.6950	0.3050	1.52	0.9357	0.0643	2.52	0.9941	0.0059
0.52	0.6985	0.3015	1.53	0.9370	0.0630	2.53	0.9943	0.0057
0.53	0.7019	0.2981	1.54	0.9382	0.0618	2.54	0.9945	0.0055
0.54	0.7054	0.2946	1.55	0.9394	0.0606	2.55	0.9946	0.0054
0.55	0.7088	0.2912	1.56	0.9406	0.0594	2.56	0.9948	0.0052
0.56	0.7123	0.2877	1.57	0.9418	0.0582	2.57	0.9949	0.0051
0.57	0.7157	0.2843	1.58	0.9429	0.0571	2.58	0.9951	0.0049
0.58	0.7190	0.2810	1.59	0.9441	0.0559	2.59	0.9952	0.0048
0.59	0.7224	0.2776	1.60	0.9452	0.0548	2.60	0.9953	0.0047
0.60	0.7257	0.2743	1.61	0.9463	0.0537	2.61	0.9955	0.0045
0.61	0.7291	0.2709	1.62	0.9474	0.0526	2.62	0.9956	0.0044
0.62	0.7324	0.2676	1.63	0.9484	0.0516	2.63	0.9957	0.0043
0.63	0.7357	0.2643	1.64	0.9495	0.0505	2.64	0.9959	0.0041
0.64	0.7389	0.2611	1.65	0.9505	0.0495	2.65	0.9960	0.0040
0.65	0.7422	0.2578	1.66	0.9515	0.0485	2.66	0.9961	0.0039
0.66	0.7454	0.2546	1.67	0.9525	0.0475	2.67	0.9962	0.0038
0.67	0.7486	0.2514	1.68	0.9535	0.0465	2.68	0.9963	0.0037
0.68	0.7517	0.2483	1.69	0.9545	0.0455	2.69	0.9964	0.0036
0.69	0.7549	0.2451	1.70	0.9554	0.0446	2.70	0.9965	0.0035
0.70	0.7580	0.2420	1.71	0.9564	0.0436	2.71	0.9966	0.0034
0.71	0.7611	0.2389	1.72	0.9573	0.0427	2.72	0.9967	0.0033
0.72	0.7642	0.2358	1.73	0.9582	0.0418	2.73	0.9968	0.0032
0.73	0.7673	0.2327	1.74	0.9591	0.0409	2.74	0.9969	0.0031
0.74	0.7704	0.2296	1.75	0.9599	0.0401	2.75	0.9970	0.0030
0.75	0.7734	0.2266	1.76	0.9608	0.0392	2.76	0.9971	0.0029
0.76	0.7764	0.2236	1.77	0.9616	0.0384	2.77	0.9972	0.0028
0.77	0.7794	0.2206	1.78	0.9625	0.0375	2.78	0.9973	0.0027
0.78	0.7823	0.2177	1.79	0.9633	0.0367	2.79	0.9974	0.0026
0.79	0.7852	0.2148	1.80	0.9641	0.0359	2.80	0.9974	0.0026
0.80	0.7881	0.2119	1.81	0.9649	0.0351	2.81	0.9975	0.0025
0.81	0.7910	0.2090	1.82	0.9656	0.0344	2.82	0.9976	0.0024

z-score	Proportion below score	Proportion above score	z-score	Proportion below score	Proportion above score	z-score	Proportion below score	Proportion above score
0.82	0.7939	0.2061	1.83	0.9664	0.0336	2.83	0.9977	0.0023
0.83	0.7967	0.2033	1.84	0.9671	0.0329	2.84	0.9977	0.0023
0.84	0.7995	0.2005	1.85	0.9678	0.0322	2.85	0.9978	0.0022
0.85	0.8023	0.1977	1.86	0.9686	0.0314	2.86	0.9979	0.0021
0.86	0.8051	0.1949	1.87	0.9693	0.0307	2.87	0.9979	0.0021
0.87	0.8078	0.1922	1.88	0.9699	0.0301	2.88	0.9980	0.0020
0.88	0.8106	0.1894	1.89	0.9706	0.0294	2.89	0.9981	0.0019
0.89	0.8133	0.1867	1.90	0.9713	0.0287	2.90	0.9981	0.0019
0.90	0.8159	0.1841	1.91	0.9719	0.0281	2.91	0.9982	0.0018
0.91	0.8186	0.1814	1.92	0.9726	0.0274	2.92	0.9982	0.0018
0.92	0.8212	0.1788	1.93	0.9732	0.0268	2.93	0.9983	0.0017
0.93	0.8238	0.1762	1.94	0.9738	0.0262	2.94	0.9984	0.0016
0.94	0.8264	0.1736	1.95	0.9744	0.0256	2.95	0.9984	0.0016
0.95	0.8289	0.1711	1.96	0.9750	0.0250	2.96	0.9985	0.0015
0.96	0.8315	0.1685	1.97	0.9756	0.0244	2.97	0.9985	0.0015
0.97	0.8340	0.1660	1.98	0.9761	0.0239	2.98	0.9986	0.0014
0.98	0.8365	0.1635	1.99	0.9767	0.0233	2.99	0.9986	0.0014
0.99	0.8389	0.1611	2.00	0.9772	0.0228	3.00	0.9987	0.0013
1.00	0.8413	0.1587						

Figures generated using Microsoft Excel 97.

Appendix 2

Table *r* to *zr*

r	zr	r	zr	r	zr	r	zr	r	zr
.0000	.000	.2000	.203	.4000	.424	.6000	.693	.8000	1.099
.0050	.005	.2050	.208	.4050	.430	.6050	.701	.8050	1.113
.0100	.010	.2100	.213	.4100	.436	.6100	.709	.8100	1.127
.0150	.015	.2150	.218	.4150	.442	.6150	.717	.8150	1.142
.0200	.020	.2200	.224	.4200	.448	.6200	.725	.8200	1.157
.0250	.025	.2250	.229	.4250	.454	.6250	.733	.8250	1.172
.0300	.030	.2300	.234	.4300	.460	.6300	.741	.8300	1.188
.0350	.035	.2350	.239	.4350	.466	.6350	.750	.8350	1.204
.0400	.040	.2400	.245	.4400	.472	.6400	.758	.8400	1.221
.0450	.045	.2450	.250	.4450	.478	.6450	.767	.8450	1.238
.0500	.050	.2500	.255	.4500	.485	.6500	.775	.8500	1.256
.0550	.055	.2550	.261	.4550	.491	.6550	.784	.8550	1.274
.0600	.060	.2600	.266	.4600	.497	.6600	.793	.8600	1.293
.0650	.065	.2650	.271	.4650	.504	.6650	.802	.8650	1.313
.0700	.070	.2700	.277	.4700	.510	.6700	.811	.8700	1.333
.0750	.075	.2750	.282	.4750	.517	.6750	.820	.8750	1.354
.0800	.080	.2800	.288	.4800	.523	.6800	.829	.8800	1.376
.0850	.085	.2850	.293	.4850	.530	.6850	.838	.8850	1.398
.0900	.090	.2900	.299	.4900	.536	.6900	.848	.8900	1.422
.0950	.095	.2950	.304	.4950	.537	.6950	.858	.8950	1.447
.1000	.100	.3000	.310	.5000	.549	.7000	.867	.9000	1.472
.1050	.105	.3050	.315	.5050	.556	.7050	.877	.9050	1.499
.1100	.110	.3100	.321	.5100	.563	.7100	.887	.9100	1.528
.1150	.116	.3150	.326	.5150	.570	.7150	.897	.9150	1.557
.1200	.121	.3200	.332	.5200	.576	.7200	.908	.9200	1.589
.1250	.126	.3250	.337	.5250	.583	.7250	.918	.9250	1.623
.1300	.131	.3300	.343	.5300	.590	.7300	.929	.9300	1.658
.1350	.136	.3350	.348	.5350	.597	.7350	.940	.9350	1.697
.1400	.141	.3400	.354	.5400	.604	.7400	.950	.9400	1.738
.1450	.146	.3450	.360	.5450	.611	.7450	.962	.9450	1.783
.1500	.151	.3500	.365	.5500	.618	.7500	.973	.9500	1.832
.1550	.156	.3550	.371	.5550	.626	.7550	.984	.9550	1.886
.1600	.161	.3600	.377	.5600	.633	.7600	.996	.9600	1.946
.1650	.167	.3650	.383	.5650	.640	.7650	1.008	.9650	2.014
.1700	.172	.3700	.388	.5700	.648	.7700	1.020	.9700	2.092
.1750	.177	.3750	.394	.5750	.655	.7750	1.033	.9750	2.185
.1800	.182	.3800	.400	.5800	.662	.7800	1.045	.9800	2.298
.1850	.187	.3850	.406	.5850	.670	.7850	1.058	.9850	2.443
.1900	.192	.3900	.412	.5900	.678	.7900	1.071	.9900	2.647
.1950	.198	.3950	.418	.5950	.685	.7950	1.085	.9950	2.994

Figures in this table were computed by the authors.

Index